MW01169959

The Essays of Michael De Montaigne

THE

ESSAYS

OF

MICHAEL DE MONTAIGNE,

TRANSLATED INTO ENGLISH,

WITH VERY CONSIDERABLE

AMENDMENTS AND IMPROVEMENTS

FROM

THE MOST ACCURATE FRENCH EDITION OF

PETER COSTE.

The Ninth Edition.

IN THREE VOLUMES.

VOL. II.

LONDON:

PRINTED FOR W. MILLER, ALBEMARLE STREET; WHITE AND COCHRANE, FLEET STREET; AND LACKINGTON, ALLEN, AND CO., FINSBURY SQUARE;

By C. Baldwin, New Bridge-street.

1811.

CONTENTS.

ESSAYS

OF

MICHAEL SEIGNEUR DE MONTAIGNE.

CHAPTER I.

Of Books.

I MAKE no doubt but I often happen to speak of things that are much better and more truly handled by those who are masters of the profession. This is purely an essay of my natural parts, and not of those which are acquired; and whoever shall catch me tripping in my ignorance, will do me no manner of harm; for I, who am not responsible to myself for my writings, nor pleased with them, should be loth to be answerable for them to another. He that seeks after knowledge, let him fish for it where it is to be found; there being nothing which I so little profess. These are fancies of my own, by which I do not aim to discover things, but myself. They will, perhaps, be known to me one day or other, or have formerly been so, according as my fortune brought me to the places where they were manifested; but now I have forgot them: and, though I am a man of some reading, yet I am a man of no retention; so that I can promise nothing certain, unless it be to discover at what degree the barometer of my knowledge now stands. Let not the subjects I write on be so much attended to, as my manner of treating them. Let it be observed whether, in what I borrow from others, I have chosen what tends to set off or support the invention, which is always my own: for I make others say for me what, either for want of language, or of sense, I cannot, myself, so well express. I do not count what I borrow, but I weigh it. And, if I had aimed to make a merit by the quantity, I should have borrowed twice as much as I have. They are all, or within a few, such celebrated ancient authors, as, I think, are too well known for me to mention them.*

Why Montaigne did not choose to name the authors from whom he quoted. In reasons, comparisons, and arguments, if I transplant any, from elsewhere, into my soil, and confound them with my own, I purposely conceal the author, to check the presumption of those hasty censures that are cast upon all kind of writings, particularly the juvenile, of men yet living, and composed in the vulgar tongue, which capacitates every man to speak of them, and seems to intimate, that there is nothing but what is vulgar, both as to design and conception, in those works. I am content that they give Plutarch a rap upon my knuckles, and that they burn their fingers by lashing Seneca through my sides. There was a necessity of screening my weakness by those great characters. I shall love the man that can strip me of my plumage, I mean, by the clearness of discernment, and by the strength and beauty of the arguments. For I, who, for want of memory, am, every now and then, at a loss to choose them by an exact knowledge of the places where they are to be found in the originals, am yet wise enough to know, by the measure of my own abilities, that my soil is incapable of producing any

---

* It was not till after Montaigne's death, that his editors undertook to name the authors whose words he had quoted. But I will presume to say, this was rather attempted than executed before this edition; which not only shows the places from whence Montaigne quoted those passages, but also many others, which he had only referred to in a very loose manner, though he had inserted the sense of them in his work.

of those rich flowers that I see planted there, and that they are worth more than all the fruits of my own growth. For this I hold myself responsible, though the confession makes against me, if there be any vanity and vice in my discourses, which I do not of myself perceive, or which I am not capable of perceiving when pointed out to me by another; for many faults escape our eye, but the infirmity of judgment consists in not being able to discern them when detected to us by another. We may possess knowledge and truth without judgment, and judgment without them; nay, the confession of ignorance is one of the fairest and surest testimonies of judgment that I know of. I have no herald to marshal my essays but chance. As fast as thoughts come into my head, which sometimes they do in whole bodies, and sometimes in single files, I pile them one upon another. I am content that every one should see my natural and ordinary pace, be it ever so much out of the way. I suffer myself to jog on in my old track: nor are these such subjects that a man shall be condemned for being ignorant of them, and for treating them casually and presumptuously. I could wish to have a more perfect knowledge of things, but I do not care to purchase it at so dear a rate. I would fain pass the remainder of my days easily and not laboriously. There is nothing that I choose to cudgel my brains about, no, not for science, how valuable soever.

All that I read books for, is to divert myself by an honest amusement; or, if I study, it is for no other science than what teaches me to know myself, and how to live and die well: *What is aimed to find in books.*

> Has meus ad metas sudet oportet equus.*
>
> —— This is the only course
> In which I think I ought to breathe my horse.

If any difficulties occur in reading, I do not bite

* Propert. lib. iv. eleg. 1.

my nails about them, but after an essay or two to
explain them, I give them over: were I to insist
upon them, I would lose both myself and my time,
for I have a genius that is extremely volatile; and
what I do not discern at the first essay, becomes the
more obscure to me the longer I pore on it. I do
nothing without gaiety: Perseverance, and a too
obstinate contention, · darken, stupify, and tire my
judgment. My sight is therein confounded and
dissipated.   I must withdraw it, and leave it to make
new discoveries, just as, in order to judge rightly of
the lustre of scarlet, we are ordered to pass it lightly
with the eye, and to run it over at several sudden
repeated views.   If one book does not please me, I
take another; but never meddle with any, except
at those times when I begin to be weary of doing
nothing.

Montaigne preferred the writings of the ancients to the moderns.   I do not much relish the writings of the moderns;
because I think the ancients fuller and more substan-
tial; neither am I fond of the Greek authors, my
knowledge in that language being too superficial to
read them with delight. Among the books that are
merely entertaining, I think those of the moderns,
viz. Boccace's Decameron, Rabelais,* and the Basia†
of Johannes Secundus (if these may be ranged under
that title) are worth reading. As to Amadis de
Gaul, and such kind of writings, they had not the
credit to take with me so much as in my childish
years.

* I must declare here, by the way, that no body better understood
the copiousness and energy of the French language, and so well
found his account in it, as Rabelais. This, which I take to be a
very important remark, I borrow from Rousseau, one of the best
poets of this age. It was also undoubtedly known to La Fontaine,
who has made a very good use of it.

† This is a collection of epigrams on the subject of kissing, by a
Dutch author, of which there have been several editions, particularly one at Lyons, by Seb. Gryphius, in 1539, now become very
scarce: which I do not mention to encourage another impression of
them, for I have no great relish for any Latin poetry composed by
the moderns, not even for the poetry of Buchanan, Grotius,
Heinsius, &c. I mean with regard to the versification.

Let me add, however rash the confession may ap- What he thought of Ovid, in the decline of his life.
pear, that this old dull fancy of mine is now no longer
tickled with Ariosto, nor even with honest Ovid : his
easy style, and his imaginations, with which I was
formerly charmed, are scarce of any entertainment
to me now. I speak my mind freely of all things,
nay, and of those that, perhaps, exceed my reach,
and which I do not consider as being at all within
my sphere : and the opinion I give of them is to
show the extent of my sight, and not the measure of
its objects. When I find myself disgusted with the
Axiochus of Plato,* as a performance which, with all
due respect to such an author, has no spirit, I am
not sure that my judgment is right. It is not so conceited of itself as to set up against the authority of
so many other famous judges of antiquity, whom it
esteems as its regents and masters, and with whom
it had rather be mistaken. In such a case it reproves and condemns itself, either for stopping at
the outward bark for want of power to penetrate to
the pith, or for considering the thing by some false
light. It is contented with securing itself only from
trouble and irregularity ; and, as to its own weakness, it is sensible of it, and frankly confesses it. It
thinks it gives a just interpretation by the appearances formed in its conception, but they are weak
and imperfect. Most of the fables of Æsop have several senses and meanings, of which the mythologists
choose some one that tallies with the fable, but, for
the most part, it is only what presents itself at the
first view, and is superficial, there being others more
lively, essential, and internal, into which they have
not been able to penetrate ; and the case is the very
same with me.

But, to proceed on my subject : I always thought, The Latin poets, whom he places in
that, in poetry, Virgil, Lucretius, Catullus, and Ho-
race excel the rest by many degrees ; and especially

---

* The best critics ascribe this dialogue not to Plato, but to
Æschines, a disciple of Socrates.

the first class,

Virgil, in his Georgics, which I esteem as the completest work in poetry, in comparison with which it is easy to discern some passages of the Æneid, to which the author would have given a little more of the file, had he had leisure. The fifth book of the Æneid seems to me to be the most perfect. I am also fond of Lucan, and often read him, not so much for the sake of the style, as for his own worth, and the truth of his opinions and judgments. As for Terence, I think the delicacy and elegance of his Latin so admirably adapted to represent our passions and manners to the life, that our actions make me have recourse to him every now and then; and, as often soever as I read him, I still discover some new grace and beauty.

Lucretius not to be compared to Virgil, and much less Ariosto.

Such as lived in the age near Virgil's were scandalised that any should compare Lucretius to him. I am, indeed, of opinion, that the comparison is very unequal; yet I can scarce settle myself in this belief, when I am captivated with some of those fine passages in Lucretius. But, if they were so piqued at this comparison, what would they have said of the brutish and barbarous stupidity of those who, at this hour, compare Ariosto to him; and what would Ariosto himself say of it?

*O seclum insipiens et inficetum !**
Oh silly senseless age!

Bad taste of those who compared Plautus to Terence.

I think the ancients had yet more reason to complain of those who matched Plautus with Terence (the latter being much more of the gentleman), than Lucretius with Virgil. It makes much for the honour and preference of Terence, that the father of the Roman eloquence has him so often in his mouth, the only one of his rank that he mentions, as does the sentence which the chief judge† of Roman poetry has passed upon the other.

* Catul. Epigram. xii. ver. 8.
† Horace, who says, in his Arte Poetica, ver. 270, &c.;

I have often observed, that those of our time, who
have taken upon them to write comedies (as the Italians, who are very happy in dramatic compositions),
take in three or four arguments of those of Terence
or Plautus to make one of theirs, and crowd five or
six of Boccace's tales into one single comedy. That
which makes them load themselves with so much
matter is the diffidence they have of being able to
support themselves by their own merit. They must
find out somebody to lean upon; and, having not matter enough of their own to amuse us with, they supply
the defect with some tale. But the case is quite
contrary with our author,* the beauty and perfections of whose style make us lose the appetite for
his plot. His elegance and delicacy captivate us
in every scene, and he is so pleasant throughout,

> *Liquidus, puroque simillimus amni,†*
> Smoothly running like a crystal stream,

and so possesses the soul with his graces of diction, that
we forget those of his fable. This very consideration draws me on farther: I perceive that the good
old poets avoided the affectation and pursuit not
only of fantastic Spanish and Petrarchist‡ flights, but
even of the softer and graver periods which have
adorned all the poetry of the succeeding ages. Yet
there is no good judge who will condemn this in
those ancients, and that does not incomparably more

> *At nostri proavi Plautinos et numeros, et*
> *Laudavere sales, nimium patienter utrosque,*
> *Non dicam stulte, mirati.*
>
> And yet our sires with joy could Plautus hear;
> Gay were his jests, his numbers charm'd their ear;
> Let me not say, too lavishly they prais'd,
> But sure their judgment was full cheaply pleas'd.

* Terence, who is in the same degree as inferior to the Greeks as
he is superior to the modern poets that Montaigne speaks of; for Terence has need sometimes of two Greek pieces to make up one Latin
one. See the prologue to his Eunuch.
† Hor. lib. ii. ep. 2, ver. 120.
‡ Passionate Rant of Lovers.

(margin note:) The comic poets of Montaigne's time wanted invention.

admire the equal smoothness, and that perpetual
sweetness and beauty which flourishes in the epigrams of Catullus, than all the stings with which
Martial has armed the tails of his. The reason is the
same as I gave just now, and as Martial said of himself, in preface, lib. viii. *Minus illi ingenio labor-
andum fuit, in cujus locum materia successerat :* " His
" subject was so fruitful, that he had the less need
" for the exercise of his wit." The epigrams of Catullus make themselves sufficiently felt without being
moved and disgusted; they have matter enough
throughout to create laughter ; they need not raise
the laugh themselves. Martial's epigrams have need
of foreign assistance ; as they have the less wit, they
must have the more bulk ; they mount on horseback
because they are not strong enough to stand on their
own legs. Just so, in our balls, those men of low
degree who teach to dance, because they cannot
represent the port and decency of our gentry, endeavour to recommend themselves by dangerous
leaps, and other odd motions practised by tumblers:
and the ladies come off better where there are several coupees and agitations of the body, than in some
other formal dances, wherein they are only to move
a natural pace, and to represent their ordinary grace
and gesture. And so I have seen excellent tumblers, dressed in the clothes which they wear every
day, and with their usual countenance, give us all
the pleasure that their art is capable of, while their
apprentices, not yet arrived to such a degree of
perfection, are fain to meal their faces, to disguise
themselves, and to use wild motions and grimaces to
make us laugh.

Compari-
son be-
tween the
Æneid and
the Orlan-
do Furioso
of Ariosto.
    This conception of mine is no where so demon-
strable as in the comparison of the Æneid and Orlando Furioso. The first we see with expanded
wings soaring aloft, and always stretching to its
point ; while the latter flutters and hops from tale to
tale, as from branch to branch, not venturing to
trust its wings but in very short flights, and perch-

ing at every turn, lest its breath and strength should fail it:

*Excursusque breves tentat.**

Those therefore, as to subjects of this kind, are the authors that please me best.

As to my other reading, which mixes a little more profit with pleasure, and from whence I learn how to regulate my opinions and humours; the books which I apply to, for this purpose, are Plutarch (since he is translated into French) and Seneca: they are both remarkably adapted to my temper, forasmuch as the knowledge which I there seek is communicated in loose pieces that are not very tedious to read, otherwise I should not have patience to look in them. Such are Plutarch's Opuscula, and the Epistles of Seneca, which are the most beautiful and profitable of all their writings. These I can take in hand, and lay aside at pleasure; for they have no connection with, or dependence upon, one another.

These authors generally concur in such opinions as are useful and true; and there is this farther parallel betwixt them, that they happened to be born much about the same time, that they were both the preceptors of two Roman emperors, that both came from foreign countries, and that both were rich, and both great men. Their lessons are the cream of philosophy, and delivered after a plain and pertinent manner. Plutarch is more uniform and constant. Seneca more irregular and various. The latter toils with all his might, to arm virtue against frailty, fear, and vicious appetites. The former seems not to think their power so great, and scorns to hasten his pace, and put himself upon his guard. Plutarch's opinions are Platonic, mild, and accommodated to civil society. The other's are Stoical and Epicurean, more remote from the common usage, but I think them more advantageous in particular, and more solid. It appears in Seneca, that he leans a little

Georg. lib. iv. ver. 194.

tó the tyranny of the emperors of his time, since I take it for granted, that he spoke against his judgment when he condemns the generous deed of those who assassinated Cæsar. Plutarch is frank everywhere. Seneca abounds with flights and sallies of expression. Plutarch with facts. Seneca warms and rouses you most; but Plutarch gives you the most satisfaction and profit. This leads us, the other pushes us.

Montaigne's opinion of the philosophical works of Cicero.As to Cicero, those works of his that can be of any use to me, are such as treat of philosophy, especially ethics or moral philosophy: but, not to mince the matter (for when a man has passed the barriers of impudence, he is not to be curbed), his way of writing seems to me tedious, as does every other composition of the like kind: for the greatest part of his work is taken up in prefaces, definitions, divisions, and etymologies: whatever there is of life and marrow is smothered by the long-winded apparatus to it. After I have spent an hour in reading him (which is a great deal for me), and call to mind what juice and substance I have extracted from him, I find nothing in him but wind for most part of the time; for he is not yet come to the arguments that serve for his purpose, and to the reasons that are proper for loosing the knot which I want to have untied. For my own part, who only desire to become more wise, not more learned or eloquent, these logical and Aristotelian rules are of no use to me; I am for an author that comes at once to the main point. I know so much of death and pleasure, that no man need be at the trouble of anatomising them to me. I look for good and solid reasons at the entrance, to instruct me how to stand the shock of them; to which purpose neither grammarian subtilties, nor the ingenious contexture of words and argumentations are of any use. I am for discourses that enter immediately into the heart of the doubt, whereas Cicero's creep about the bush: they are proper for the schools, for the bar, and the pulpit, where we have leisure to nod for a quarter of an hour, and to awake time enough to recover the thread of the discourse. It is necessary to talk after this manner to judges whom a man would gain over to his side, be it right or wrong; to children, and to the vulgar, to whom a man must say all he can, and wait for the event of it. I would not have an author make it his business to render me attentive, and call out fifty times to me, with an O yes, after the manner of our heralds. The Romans said, in their religion, *hoc age*, as we do in ours, *sursum corda;* but to me these are so many words lost; I come thither quite prepared for my lodging; I need no allurement nor sauce; I eat the meat quite raw; and instead of whetting my appetite by these prefaces and prologues, they overload and pall it.

Will the license of this age excuse my sacrilegious boldness to censure the Dialogues of Plato himself, as too long-winded, whilst his subject is much too stifled; and to complain of the time spent in so many tedious and needless preliminary interlocutions by a man who had so many better things to say? My ignorance of the Greek, to such a degree as not to perceive any beauty in his language, will be a better excuse for me: I am generally for books that make use of the sciences, not for those that set them off. Plutarch and Seneca, Pliny, and those of the same way of thinking, have no *hoc age;* they choose to have to do with men who are already instructed; or if they have a *hoc age*, it is a substantial one, and one that has a body by itself. *[And of Plato's Dialogues.]*

I am also in love with the Epistles to Atticus, not only because they contain a very ample account of the history and affairs of his own time, but much more because I therein discover the particular humours of the writer; for I have a singular curiosity, as I have said elsewhere, to know the souls and genuine opinions of my authors. Their abilities are to be judged of by the writings which they publish to the world, but not their manners nor their persons. *[A commendation of the Epistles to Atticus.]*

I have a thousand times lamented the loss of the treatise which Brutus wrote upon virtue, for it is good to learn the theory from those who understand the practice. But, forasmuch as there is a wide difference between the preacher and the sermon, I like as well to see Brutus in Plutarch, as in a book of his own writing. I would rather choose to be truly informed of the conference he had in his tent with some of his private friends the night before a battle, than the harangue he made to his army the next day: and of what he did in his closet and his chamber, rather than of his action in the forum and the senate.

Character of Cicero.

As for Cicero, I am of the common opinion, that, setting aside his learing, he had no extraordinary genius. He was a good citizen, and of an affable temper, as all fat men, and such merry souls as his was, generally are; but he loved his ease, and, to speak the real truth, had a very great share of vanity and ambition. Neither do I know how to

His poetry.

excuse him for thinking his poetry * good enough to be published. To make bad verses is no great imperfection, but it was an imperfection in him, that he did not judge how unworthy his verses were of

His eloquence.

his glorious character. As for his eloquence, it is beyond all comparison, and I believe it will never be equalled. The younger Cicero, who resembled his father in nothing but his name, whilst a commander in Asia, had several strangers one day at his table, and in particular Cestius, seated at the lower end, as the open tables of the great are generally

* Every body has not such a disadvantageous opinion of Cicero's poetry, there being, even at this day, very good judges who esteem it; and Plutarch says expressly, that Cicero was not only accounted the best orator, but also the best poet of the Romans, his cotemporaries. The glory of eloquence, adds he, and the honour of speaking well, has been ever ascribed to him to this very day, though there has since been a great alteration in the Latin tongue; but his fame and reputation for poetry have been quite lost by the appearance of others since his time, much more excellent than he was. Cicero's Life, chap. 1 of Amyot's translation.

crowded. Cicero asked one of his waiters, " Who
that man was," and he readily told him his name;
but Cicero, as one who had his thoughts intent upon
something else, and had forgot his name, asked him
the same question again two or three times: the
fellow, in order to be rid of the trouble of making
the same answer over and over again, and to imprint
the thing the more in his memory by some remarkable circumstance, " It is that very Cestius," said he,
" who, as you have been informed, makes no great
" account of your father's eloquence in comparison
" of his own." Cicero, being suddenly nettled at
this, ordered poor Cestius to be seized, and caused
him to be well whipped in his presence. A very
uncivil host!*

Yet even amongst those who, all things considered, have reckoned the eloquence of Cicero incomparable, there have been some who have not
scrupled to find faults in it. As, for example, his
friend, the great Brutus, who called his eloquence,
fractam et elumbem,† " shattered and feeble." The
orators also, in the next age to his, found fault with
him for his affectation of a certain long cadence at
the end of his sentences, and particularly took
notice of the words *esse videatur*,‡ which he therein so often makes use of. For my own part, I am
for a shorter cadence, formed in the iambic style;
yet sometimes he shuffles the members of his
sentence together very roughly, though it is very
seldom. One instance of this dwells upon my ears,
in the phrase, *Ego verò me minùs diù senem esse
mallem, quàm esse senem, antequàm essem :* § " For my

Censurers
of Cicero's
eloquence.

---

* M. Senec. in fine Suasoriarum.
† See the Dialogue De Oratoribus sive de Causis corruptæ Elo-
quentiæ, cap. 18.
‡ Ibid. cap 23.
§ I think this criticism of Montaigne's a little too severe; for,
without considering that words of the same found in the Latin are
agreeable, these are not to be blamed because there is nothing in
them that is quaint, or unsuitable to the style of Cicero's conversa-

" part, I had rather be old for a little time, than to
" be old before I am really so."

Why Mon-
taigne was
best pleas-
ed with
history. The historians are the authors I am most used to,
for they are pleasant and easy ; and the knowledge
of mankind in general, which is what I seek for, appears more clear and perfect in history than any
where else : there is to be seen the variety and reality of his internal qualities, in general, and in particular, with the diversity of methods contributing
to his composition, and the accidents that threaten
him. But they who write lives, by reason they take
more notice of counsels than events, more of what
proceeds from within doors than what happens without, are the fittest for my perusal, and therefore, of
all others, Plutarch is the man for me. I am very
sorry that we have not a dozen Laertiuses, or that
he was not more extensive, or better understood.
For I am equally curious to know the lives and fortunes of those great preceptors of the world, as to
know the diversity of their doctrines and opinions.
In the study of this kind of histories a man must
tumble over, without distinction, all sorts of authors,
both ancient and modern, in the barbarous as well
as the current languages, to learn the things of
which they variously treat.

A commen-
dation of
Cæsar's
Commenta
ries. But Cæsar, in my opinion, deserves particularly to
be studied, not for the knowledge of the history
only, but for his own sake, he has so much perfection and excellence above all the rest, not excepting
Sallust. In truth, I read this author with a little
more respect and reverence than I pay to human
compositions, considering him one while personally,
by his actions and his wonderful greatness ; and
another while by the purity and inimitable accuracy
of his language, wherein he has not only surpassed

tion throughout his work. Besides, if Montaigne was disgusted with
the sameness of sound in those three words that follow so close to
one another, *mallem, senem, essem,* he had nothing to do but to separate *ante* from *quam,* as it is in Gronovius's edition. Cicero de
Senectute, cap. 10.

all historians, as Cicero says, but, perhaps, even Cicero himself. For he speaks of his enemies with so much sincerity, that, setting aside the false colours with which he endeavours to palliate his bad cause, and the corruption of his pestilent ambition, I think the only thing for which he is to be blamed is his speaking too sparingly of himself; for so many great things could not have been performed under his conduct, if he had not had a greater share in them than he attributes to himself.

I love histories that are either very plain, or of distinguished excellency. The plain historians, who have nothing of their own to insert, and who only take the care and pains to collect every thing that comes to their notice, and to make a faithful register of all things, without choice or distinction, leave the discovery of the truth entirely to our own judgments. *Mere writers of facts, in what respect they are to be esteemed.*

Such, for example, among others, is honest Froissard, who has proceeded in his undertaking with such a frank plainness, that, when he has committed an error, he is never afraid to confess and correct it in the place where it is pointed out to him; and who even represents to us the variety of rumours that were then spread abroad, and the different reports that were brought to him. Thus the matter of his history is naked and unadorned, and every one may profit by it, according to his share of understanding. *Froissard ranked in this number, and commended.*

Excellent historians have the capacity of se'ecting what is fit to be known, and of two reports to single out that which is most likely to be true. From the condition of princes, and their tempers, they judge of their counsels, and attribute speeches to them that are therewith consistent; and such have a title for assuming the authority of regulating our belief by theirs, but certainly this is a privilege that belongs to very few. *Wherein consists the value of the best historians.*

The historians of the middle class (who are the most numerous) pervert us all. They aim to chew *What historians are to be despised.*

the morsels for us; they make it a law to themselves
to judge of, and consequently to bend the history to
their own fancy; for, while the judgment leans on
one side, the writer cannot avoid turning and wind-
ing his narrative according to that bias. They
undertake to choose things worthy to be known,
yet often conceal from us such an expression, or
such a private transaction, as would instruct us
better: they omit, as incredible, such things as they
do not understand, and some things, perhaps too,
because they know not how to express them in good
language. Let them vaunt their eloquence and
their reason with as much assurance as they please,
and let them judge as they fancy; but let them leave
us something to judge of after them, and neither
alter nor disguise any thing of the substance of the
matter by their abridgments and their own preference, but refer it to us pure and entire in all its
dimensions. In these latter ages especially, the
people who are most commonly appointed for this
task are culled out from the common people for no
other merit but their good style, as if we wanted
them to teach us grammar; and, as they are hired
for no other end, and vent nothing but tittle-tattle,
they are in the right to apply their thoughts chiefly
to this point. Thus, with a fine flourish of words,
they entertain us with a curious chain of reports,
which they pick up in the public places of the
towns.

What are
the only
good histo-
ries.
The only good histories are such as have been
written by the persons themselves who had the direction, or were sharers in the management, of the
affairs of which they write, or who happened, at least,
to have the conduct of others of the same kind.
Such are, in a manner, all the Greek and Roman
historians. For several eye-witnesses having wrote
of the same affair (as this happened at a time when
grandeur and literature commonly met in the same
person), if there happened to be an error, it must, of
necessity, be a very slight one, and about an event

very dubious. What can one expect from a physician who treats of war; or from a student, in his closet, that undertakes to lay open the secrets of the cabinets of princes?

If we would take notice how religious the Romans were in this point, there needs no more than this instance of it. Asinius Pollio * found, even in Cæsar's Commentaries, a mistake which he had fallen into, either from not having his eyes in all the parts of his army at once, and giving credit to particular persons, who had not given him a true account, or else from not having been exactly informed by his lieutenants, of what they had done in his absence. By this we may see how hard a matter it is to come at the truth, when one cannot depend for a right account of a battle upon the knowledge of the general who commanded in it, nor upon the very soldiers for what passed near them, unless, after the manner of examinations before a judge, the witnesses are confronted, and the objections admitted to the proof of the minutest circumstances of every event. In truth, the knowledge we have of our own affairs is very imperfect. But this has been sufficiently treated of by Bodin, and according to my own way of thinking. In order to give some little assistance to my treacherous memory, which is so extremely defective, that it has happened to me, more than once, to take books in my hand, as new and altogether unknown to me, which I had read carefully a few years ago, and scribbled my notes in them, I have made it a practice, for some time past, to add, at the end of every book (I mean of such as I desire never to use but once), the time that I finished the reading of it, and the judgment I had formed of it in gross; to the end that this may, at least, represent to me the general air and idea which I had conceived of

The mistakes that have been discovered in Cæsar's Commentaries.

. * In Suetonius's Life of Julius Cæsar, sect. 56, where the reader will find Pollio's criticism more severe than in Montaigne, who, however, must have taken it from Suetonius.

Montaigne's reflections upon Guicciardin.

I wrote what follows, about ten years ago, in my Guicciardin; for, in what language soever my books accost me, I speak to them in my own: " He is a " diligent historiographer, and one from whom, in " my opinion, we may know the truth of the affairs " of his time as exactly as from any other; for in " most of them he was himself an actor, and in an " honourable rank. There is no appearance that he " has disguised things out of hatred, favour, or va- " nity, of which we have ample testimony in the free " censures he has passed upon the great men, and es- " pecially those by whom he was advanced and em- " ployed in offices of trust, namely, Pope Clement VII. " in particular. As to that part for which he seems " to have valued himself most, viz. his digressions and " paraphrases; he has, indeed, some very good ones, " and enriched with beautiful expressions, but he is " too fond of them: for, because he would leave " nothing unsaid, as he had a subject so copious, and " a field so ample, and almost boundless, he becomes " flat, and has a little smack of the scholastic " prattle. I have also made this remark; that of so " many men and things, so many motives and coun- " sels on which he passes his judgment, he does " not so much as attribute a single motive to virtue, " religion, and conscience, as if they were all quite " extinct in the world; and he ascribes the cause of " all actions, how fair soever they appear in them- " selves, to some vicious occasion, or view of profit. " It is impossible to imagine but, among such an in- " finite number of actions, of which he gives his " judgment, there must be some one that was con- " ducted by reason. No corruption could have so " universally infected men, but some one must have " escaped the contagion; which makes me suspect " that his own taste was a little vitiated, and it might " happen that he judged of other men by himself."

Upon Philip de Comines.

In my Philip de Comines there is this written: " You will here find the language smooth and agree-

" ble, with an artless simplicity; the narration pure,
" and in which the author's regard to truth is fully
" displayed; free from vanity when he speaks of
" himself, and from affection and envy when he
" speaks of another: his reasonings and exhortations
" are accompanied with more zeal and truth than
" with any exquisite sufficiency, and with all that
" authority and gravity throughout the whole, which
" shows him to be a man of a good family, and that
" has had no ordinary education."

And this in my memoirs upon M. Du Bellay:* Upon the
" It is always pleasant to read things that are Du Bellay.
" written by those who have experienced how they
" ought to be carried on; but it cannot be denied,
" that in those two lords (William and Martin du
" Bellay) there is a great declension from that free
" and unconstrained manner of writing, which is so
" conspicuous in the ancients of their profession;
" such as M. de Jouinville, domestic to St. Lewis;
" Eginard, chancellor to Charlemagne; and as
" Philip de Comines of later date. This book is
" rather an apology for king Francis, against the
" emperor Charles V. than a history. I am not in-
" clined to think, that they have falsified any thing
" as to the fact in general; but they are dexterous
" at wresting the judgment of events to our advan-
" tage, though often contrary to reason; and of
" omitting whatever is of a ticklish nature in the
" life of their sovereign; witness the retreat of

* These Memoirs, published by Martin du Bellay, consist of ten
books, of which the first four, and last three, are Martin du Bellay's;
and the others, his brother William de Langey's, and were taken
from his fifth Ogdoade, from the year 1596 to 1540. They are entitled " Memoirs of Martin du Bellay, containing accounts of se-
" veral things that happened in France, from 1513 to the death of
" Francis I. in 1547." From all this it is obvious why Montaigne
speaks of two lords Du Bellay, after he had mentioned the memoirs
of M. Du. Bellay. I have made this remark, to save others from
the perplexity that I myself was involved in, at first, upon this occasion.

"Messieurs de Montmorency and Brion, who are
"here omitted; nay, the name of Madame de
"Estampes is not so much as once mentioned.
"Secret actions may be concealed by an historian;
"but to pass over in silence what is known to all
"the world, and things too that have produced
"effects of such consequence, is a defect not to be
"excused. In fine, whoever would have a perfect
"knowledge of king Francis, and the affairs of
"his time, must, if he will take my advice, look
"for it elsewhere. The only advantage he can
"reap from this work is, by the particular account
"of the battles and military achievements, in which
"those gentlemen were present; certain expressions
"and private actions of some princes of their time,
"and the practices and negotiations carried on by
"the lord de Langeay, wherein there are throughout
"things worthy to be known, and reasonings above
"the vulgar strain."

CHAPTER II.

Of Cruelty.

Virtue is superior to what is called goodness of nature.
VIRTUE seems to me to be quite another thing,
and more noble than the inclinations that are innate
in goodness. Those souls that are well tempered,
and as truly generous, pursue the same tract; and
their actions wear the same face as the virtuous. But
the word Virtue imports something, I know not
what, that is more great and active than a man's
suffering himself, with a happy constitution, to be
gently and quietly conducted by reason. The
person, who, from a mildness and sweetness in his
temper, despises injuries received, performs a thing
very amiable and commendable; but the man, who,
being provoked and enraged to the last degree by

some offence, arms himself with the weapons of reason against a furious thirst of revenge, and, after a great struggle, at last masters his own passion, undoubtedly performs much more. The first would do well, and the latter virtuously. One action might be called good-nature, the other virtue. For methinks the very name of Virtue presupposes difficulty and opposition, and cannot be exercised without something to contend with. It is for this reason, perhaps, that we call God by the attributes of good, mighty, bountiful, and just; but we do not give him that of virtuous, his works being all natural, and without any effort. The philosophers, not only the Stoics, but also the Epicureans (and this addition* I borrow from the vulgar opinion, which is false, notwithstanding the witty conceit of Arcesilaus, in answer to one, who, being reproached that many scholars went from his school to the Epicurean, but never any from thence to his school, said in answer, " I believe it indeed; numbers of capons being " made out of cocks, but never any cocks out of " capons†." For, in truth, the Epicurean sect is not at all inferior to the Stoic in steadiness, and the rigour of opinions and precepts. And a certain Stoic, discovering more honesty than those disputants, who, in order to quarrel with Epicurus, and to throw the game into their own hands, make

Virtue not to be practised without some difficulty.

---

* Montaigne stops here to make his excuse for thus naming the Epicureans with the Stoics, in conformity to the general opinion that the Epicureans were not so rigid in their morals as the Stoics, which is not true in the main, as he demonstrates at one view. This involved Montaigne in a tedious parenthesis, during which it is proper that the reader be attentive, that he may not entirely lose the thread of the argument. In some later editions of this author, it has been attempted to remedy this inconvenience, but without observing that Montaigne's argument is rendered more feeble and obscure by such vain repetitions: it is a licence that ought not to be taken, because he, who publishes the work of another, ought to give it as the other composed it. But, in Mr. Cotton's translation, he was so puzzled with this enormous parenthesis, that he has quite left it out.

† Diog. Laert. in the Life of Arcesilaus, lib. iv. sect. 43.

him say what he never thought, putting a wrong
construction upon his words, clothing his sentences,
by the strict rules of grammar, with another meaning, and a different opinion from that which they
knew he entertained in his mind, and in his morals,
the Stoic, I say, declared, that he abandoned the
Epicurean sect, upon this, among other considerations, that he thought their tract too lofty and inaccessible ; *Et ii qui φιλήδονοι vacantur sunt φιλόκαλοι
et φιλοδίκαιοι, omnesque virtutes et colunt et ratinent :*
" And those whom we call lovers of pleasure,
" being, in effect, lovers of honour and justice, cul-
" tivate and practise all the virtues ;" Cic. ep. 19.
lib. xv.) several, I say, of the Stoic and Epicurean
philosophers, thought that it was not enough to have
the soul in a good frame, well tempered, and well-
disposed to virtue ; that it was not enough to have
our resolutions and our reasonings fixed above all
the efforts of fortune ; but that it was ever necessary
to seek occasions to make trial of them : they were
for going in quest of pain, necessity, and contempt,
in order to combat them, and to keep the soul in
exercise. *Multum sibi adjicit virtus lacessita :* *
" Virtue by being attacked becomes the more cou-
" rageous." It is one of the reasons why Epaminondas, who was also of a third sect,† refused the
wealth which fortune put into his hand by very
fair means, because, said he, I may be able to fence
with poverty, in which extreme he always stood his
ground. Socrates methinks put himself to a severer
trial, keeping, for his exercise, a shrew of a wife ;
which was a trial with a vengeance. Metellus, the
only one of all the Roman senators, who attempted,
by the strength of his virtue, to support himself against
the violence of Saturninus, the tribune of the people
of Rome, who was resolved by all means to get an

* Senec. ep. 13.
† Of the Pythagorean sect. Epaminondas, the Theban, says
Cicero, was instructed by Lysis, a Pythagorean. De Offic. lib. i.
c. 44.

unjust law passed in favour of the commonalty, having, by such opposition, incurred the capital punishments which Saturninus had established for the recusants; this very Metellus said to the persons, who, in this extremity, were leading him to the place of execution: " That it was a very easy* and a base thing to " commit evil; and that to do good, where there " was no danger, was a common thing; but to do " good where there was danger, was the proper office " of a man of virtue." These words of Metellus clearly show what I would make out, that virtue refuses ease for its companion, and that the gentle ascent, that soft, smooth way, in which those take their steps who are regulated by a natural inclination to goodness, is not the path of true virtue. This requires a rugged thorny passage, and will have either difficulties from without to struggle with (like that of Metellus) by means whereof fortune delights to interrupt the speed of our career, or else internal difficulties that are introduced by the disorderly appetites and imperfections of our condition.

I am come thus far at my ease; but it just now falls into my imagination, that the soul of Socrates, the most perfect that ever has come to my knowledge, would, by this rule, have little to recommend it; for I cannot perceive, in this person, any effort of a vicious concupiscence. In the course of his virtue, I cannot imagine there was any difficulty or constraint. I know his reason had so much sway and authority over him, that it would never have suffered a vicious appetite so much as to rise in him. To a virtue so sublime as his I can set nothing in opposition. Methinks I see it stalk, with a victorious and triumphant pace, in pomp, and at ease, without molestation or disturbance. If virtue cannot shine but by struggling with contrary appetites, shall we therefore say, that she cannot subsist without the assistance of vice, and that it is from thence she derives her reputation

In noble souls, such as those of Socrates and Cato, virtue be- comes easy through ha- bit.

* Plutarch, in the Life of Marius, ch. 10 of Amyot's translation.

and honour? What would become also of that brave
and generous Epicurean pleasure, which pretends to
nourish and cherish virtue in its lap, giving it shame,
sickness, poverty, death, and hell for toys to play
with? If I presuppose that perfect virtue is known
by contending with, and patiently bearing, pain, and
even fits of the gout, without being moved in its
seat; if I give it roughness and difficulty for its necessary object, what will become of a virtue elevated
to such a degree, as not only to despise pain, but to
rejoice in it, and to be delighted with the racking
stitches of a violent colic, as is the quality of that
virtue which the Epicureans have established, and of
which many of them, by their actions, have left very
evident proofs? As have many others, who I find
have surpassed the very rules of their discipline:
witness the younger Cato; when I see him dying,
and tearing out his own bowels, I cannot be contented simply to believe that his soul was, at that
time, wholly exempt from trouble and fear; I cannot think, that he only supported himself in this step,
which was prescribed to him by the laws of the Stoic
sect, quite serenely, without emotion or passion:
there was, methinks, in that man's virtue too much
sprightliness and youth to stop there. I make no
doubt but he felt a pleasure and delight in so noble
an action, and that it was more agreeable to him
than any thing he ever did in his life. *Sic abiit è
vitâ ut causam moriendi nactum se esse gauderet:*
" He went out of life in such a manner, as if he was
" glad he had found a reason for dying."* And I
really question, whether he would have been glad to
have been deprived of the occasion of so brave an
exploit: and if that good-nature of his, which made
him espouse the public benefit rather than his own,
did not restrain me, I should be ready to believe,
that he thought himself obliged to fortune, for
having put his virtue to so severe a trial, and for

* Cic. Tusc. Quæst. lib. i. cap. 30.

having favoured the robber* in trampling the ancient liberty of his country under his feet. Methinks I read, in this action, I know not what exultation in his soul, and an extraordinary and manly emotion of pleasure, when he looked upon the nobleness and sublimity of his undertaking:

> *Deliberata morte ferocior.*†
>
> Grown fiercer now she is resolved to die.

Not stimulated by any hope of glory, as the vulgar and effeminate judgments of some men have concluded; for the consideration is too mean to touch a mind so generous, so aspiring, and so obstinate; but for the very beauty of the thing in itself, which he, who had the management of its springs, discerned more clearly, and in its perfection, than we are able to do. It gives me a pleasure to find it is the judgment of philosophy,‡ that so brave an action would have been indecent in any other life than Cato's, and that it only became his to have such a period. However, as reason required, he commanded his son, and the senators who accompanied him, to take another course. *Catoni, quum incredibilem natura tribuisset gravitatem, eamque ipse perpetuâ constantiâ roboravisset, xemperque in proposito consilio permansisset, moriendum potiùs quàm tyranni vultus aspiciendus erat :* " Cato having been endowed by nature with an incredible gravity, which he " had fortified by a perpetual constancy, without " ever departing from what he had once determined, " he must, of necessity, rather die than see the face

---

* Cæsar, who, notwithstanding the great qualities of his, which Montaigne set off with such lustre in the preceeding chapter, is here treated as he deserves for having committed the most heinous of all crimes.

† Hor. lib. i. od. 37, v. 29.

‡ This is what Cicero says, in his Offices, lib. i. cap. 31. Nonnunquam mortem sibi ipsi consciscere alius debet, alius in eadem causâ non debet. Nam enim aliâ in causâ M. Cato fuit, aliâ cæteri qui se in Africâ Cæsari tradiderunt? Atqui cæteris forsitan vitio datum esset si se interemisset, &c.

" of the tyrant." Every man's death must be suitable to his life : we do not become other men by dying. I always judge of the death by the life preceding ; and if any one tells me of a death that, in appearance, was accompanied with fortitude, after a
life that was feeble, I conclude the cause that produced it to be feeble, and suitable to the life before
it. The easiness therefore of this death, and the facility which he had acquired, in dying, by the vigour of his mind, shall we say that it ought to be
the least abatement of the lustre of his virtue ? Who,
that has his brain ever so little tinctured with true
philosophy, can imagine Socrates only free from fear
and passion under the circumstances of imprison-

The cheer-
fulness of
Socrates at
his death
rendered it
superior to
Cato's
death.

ment, fetters, and condemnation ? Who is there that
does not discover not only his stability and constancy
(which was his common quality), but, likewise, I know
not what fresh satisfaction and joyous alacrity in his
last words and actions ? By the pleasure he felt in
scratching his leg, after his irons were taken off, does
he not discover the like serenity and joy of soul, to
find himself disengaged from the past inconveniences, and on the point of entering into futurity ? Cato
may be pleased to pardon me, when I say his death
was more tragical and lingering, but yet that of Socrates was, I know not how, more desirable, insomuch that Aristippus, hearing some pitying the manner of his death, said, " May the gods grant me
" such a death."* We discern in the souls of these
two great men, and their imitators (for I very much
doubt whether they ever had their equals), so perfect a habit of virtue, that it was constitutional to
them. It is not that painful virtue, nor the law of
reason, to preserve which, the soul must be, as it
were, on the rack ; but it is the very essence of
their souls, their natural and common practise : they
have rendered it such by a long adherence to the
precepts of philosophy, imbibed by a rich genius,

* Diog. Laert. in the Life of Aristippus, lib. ii. sect. 76.

and a generous nature. The vicious passions, that are born in us, can find no entrance into their breasts: the fortitude and steadiness of their souls stifle and and extinguish carnal appetites as soon as they begin to be in motion.

Now, that it is not more noble by a sublime and divine resolution, to hinder the birth of temptations, and to be so formed to virtue, that the very seeds of the vices may be eradicated, than by mere force to hinder their growth, and, by giving way to the first motions of the passions, be obliged to arm and oppose their progress, and to conquer them; and that this second effect is not also much more noble than to be only furnished with an easy debonnair temper, disgusted of itself with debauchery and vice, I do not think can be doubted. As to this third and last sort of virtue, it seems, indeed, to render a man innocent, but not virtuous; free from doing ill, but not apt enough to do good. Besides, this is a condition so nearly approaching to imperfection and frailty, that I know not very well how to distinguish the limits. The very names of Goodness and Innocence are, for this reason, in some sort names of contempt. I perceive that several virtues, as chastity, sobriety, and temperance, may happen to us through bodily defects. Constancy in danger (if it must be so called), the contempt of death, patience under misfortunes may happen, and are often found in men, for want of well judging of such accidents, and conceiving of them as they really are. Dulness of apprehension and stupidity are therefore sometimes the counterfeit of virtuous deeds. As I have often seen it happen, that men have had praise for what deserved censure.

An Italian nobleman once made this remark, in my presence, to the disadvantage of his countrymen, viz. That the Italians were so subtle, and so quick of apprehension, that they forsaw dangers and accidents, which might happen to them, at so great a distance, that it is not to be thought strange, if they

often went to war to provide for their security, even
before they had discovered the danger: that we (the
French) and the Spaniards, who were not so cunning, were still more to be blamed, for that we must
both see and feel the danger before it could alarm
us, and that, even then, we were not resolute; but
that the Germans and the Swiss, being more heavy
and dull of apprehension, had not the sense to look
round them, even when the blows were dealt about
their ears. Perhaps he only talked at this rate by
way of banter; yet certain it is, that, in the trade of
war, those who have not yet learned it, often rush
into dangers with more temerity than they do after
they are well acquainted with it:

> ———— *Haud ignarus quantum nova gloria in armis*
> *Et prædulce decus primo certamine possit.*[*]
> Knowing how much the hope of glory warms
> The soldier in his first essay of arms.

For this reason, when we would judge of any particular action, we ought previously to consider the
several circumstances, and the character of the man
by whom it is performed.

In what
consisted
Mon-
taigne's
virtue. To say one word of myself, I have sometimes
known my friends commend that for prudence in me
which was mere fortune, and ascribe that to courage
and patience which was owing to judgment and
opinion, giving me one title for another, sometimes
to my advantage, at other times to my detriment:
as to the rest, I am so far from being arrived to this
first and more perfect degree of excellence, where
virtue is become a habit, that I have scarce made
any trial of the second. I have made no great
efforts to curb the desires by which I have been importuned. My virtue is virtue, or rather casual and
accidental innocence. If I had been born of a more
irregular constitution, I fear my case would have
been very lamentable; for I have scarce ever expe-

---

* Æneid. lib. xi. ver. 154, 155.

rienced a fortitude of mind to resist passions that
were ever so little vehement. I know not how to
nourish quarrels and debates in my own breast, so
that I owe no thanks to myself if I am exempt from
several vices:

——*Si vitiis mediocribus, ac mea paucis*
Mendosa est natura, alioqui recta (velut si
Egregio inspersos repréndas corpore navos).[*]
If trivial faults deform my upright soul,
Like a fair face when blemish'd with a mole.

I owe it more to my fortune than to my reason. I
happened to be descended from a race famous for
probity, and from a very good father. I know not
whether he has entailed any of his humours upon me,
or whether domestic examples, and the good instruction I received in my infancy, have insensibly contributed to it, or else whether I was born so:

Seu Libra, seu me Scorpius aspicit
Formidolosus, pars violentior
Natalis horæ, seu tyrannus
Hesperiæ Capricornus undæ.[†]
Whatever star did at my birth prevail,
Whether my fate was weigh'd in Libra's scale;
Or Scorpio reign'd, whose gloomy pow'r
Rules dreadful o'er the natal hour;
Or Capricorn with angry rays,
Those tyrants of the Western seas.

But so it is, that I have a natural abhorrence for most
of the vices. The answer which Antisthenes made
to one who asked him, " What was the best thing to
" learn ?" viz. " To unlearn evil,"[‡] seems very similar to this representation. I have them in abhorrence, I say, from an opinion so natural, and so much
my own, that the very instinct and impression of
them, which I brought with me from my nurse, I
still retain, no motive whatsoever having been effec-

* Horat. lib. i. sat. 6. ver. 65, &c.
† Hor. lib. ii. ode 17, ver. 17, &c.
‡ Diog. Laert. in the Life of Antisthenes, lib. vi. sect 7.

tual to make me alter it; nay, not my own discourses, which, by rambling, in some things, from
the common road, might easily license me to commit actions, which such natural inclination gives me
an aversion to.

Mon-
taigne's
opinions
not so regu-
lar as his
manners.

What I am going to say is monstrous, yet I will
say it. I find myself, in many things, more curbed
and regulated by my manners than my opinion, and
my concupiscence not so debauched as my reason.
Aristippus established such bold opinions in favour
of pleasure and riches, as made all the philosophers
declaim against him: but, as to his manners, Dionysius the Tyrant having presented three beautiful
wenches to him for his choice of one, he made answer, that he would have them all; and that Paris
was in the wrong, for preferring one before her other
two companions: but, when he carried them home
to his house, he sent them back untouched: his servant finding the money, which he carried after him,
too heavy a load for him,* he ordered him to pour
it out in the road, and there leave the quantity that
encumbered him. And Epicurus, whose doctrines
were so irreligious and effeminate, was, in his life,
very devout and laborious: he wrote to a friend of
his, that he lived upon nothing but biscuit and water,
and desired him to send him a little cheese, to reserve it till he had a mind to make a sumptuous feast.
Must it be true, that, in order to be perfect, we
must be so by an occult, natural, and universal property, without law, reason, or example? The irre-
gularities of which I have been guilty, are not, I
thank God, of the worst sort, and I have condemned
myself for them, in proportion to the guilt of them,
for they never infected my judgment. On the contrary, I accuse them more severely in myself than in
another; but that is all, for, as to the rest, I oppose
too little resistance, and too easily suffer myself to

* Diog. Laert. in the Life of Aristippus, lib. ii. sect. 67—77, and
Hor. lib. ii. sat. iii. ver. 100, &c.

incline to the other scale of the balance, only I moderate and prevent them from mixing with other vices, which are apt to intwine with, and hang to, one another, if a man does not take care. I have contracted and curtailed mine, to make them as simple and uncompounded as I could :

———*Nec ultra*
*Errorem foveo.**

Nor do I indulge my error farther.

For as to the opinion of the Stoics, who say, *The being addicted to* "That the wise man, when he works, operates by *one vice* "all the virtues together, though one be most appa- *does not render a* "rent, according to the nature of the action," (and, *man liable* as to this, the similitude of the human body might be *to all the* of some service to them, because choler cannot ope- *vices.* rate without the assistance of all the humours, though choler be predominant) if from thence they would likewise infer, that, when the wicked man acts wickedly, he acts by all the vices together, I do not believe it to be merely so, or else I do not understand them, for, indeed, I find the contrary. These are some of those acute but trifling subtleties which philosophy sometimes insists on. I am addicted to some vices, but I fly from others as much as a saint would do. The Peripatetics also disown this indissoluble connection and complication ; and Aristotle is of opinion, that a man may be prudent and just, and at the same time intemperate and incontinent. Socrates confessed to some who had discovered, in his physiognomy, an inclination to a certain vice, that he had, indeed, a natural propensity to it, but that he had, by discipline, corrected it :† and Stilpo, the philosopher's familiar friend, used to say, that he was born with an appetite both to wine and women, but that, by study, he had learned to abstain from both.‡

What I have in me that is good, I ascribe it, on *What Mon-* the contrary, to the lot of my birth, and am not be- *taigne's*

* Juv. sat. viii. ver. 194.   † Cic. Tusc. Quest. lib. iv. cap. 37.
‡ Cic. Lib. de Fato, cap. 5.

holden for it either to law, precept, or any other instruction: my innocence is perfectly simple, with little assurance, and less art. Among all the vices I mortally hate cruelty, both by nature and judg-. ment, as the very extreme of all vices: but, withal,. I am so tender-hearted, that it grieves me to see the throat of a fowl cut, nor can I bear to hear the cry of a hare in the teeth of my dogs, though hunting is my most favourite diversion. Such as have sensual pleasure to encounter with, willingly make use of this argument, to show that it is altogether vicious and unreasonable; that, when it is at the height, it masters us to such a degree, that reason can have no access to it; and they instance the commerce with the fair sex,

     —— *Cum jam præsagit gaudia corpus,*
     *Atque in eo est Venus, ut muliebria conserat arva.**

when they think that the pleasure transports us to such a degree, that our reason cannot perform its office while we are in such an extasy and rapture.

I know, however, that it may be otherwise; and that sometimes a man has it in his power, if he will, to turn his mind, even in the critical minute, to other thoughts; but then it must be bent to it deliberately, and of set purpose. I know that a man may triumph over the utmost effort of pleasure. I have experienced this myself, and have not found Venus so imperious a goddess, as many, and some more reformed than myself, declare her to be. I do not think it a miracle, as the queen of Navarre does, in one of the tales of her Heptameron (which is a very pretty book for her subject), nor a thing of extreme difficulty, to spend whole nights, where a man has all the conveniency and liberty he can desire, with a long wished-for mistress, and yet be true to the promise he may have made, to satisfy himself with kisses and gentle squeezes of the hand. I fancy,

       * Lucret. lib. iv. ver. 1099, &c.

that the diversion of hunting would be more proper
for the experiment, in which, though the pleasure
be less, yet the rapture and surprise are the greater,
when our reason, being astonished, has not such
leisure to prepare itself for the encounter, when,
after a long search, the beast starts up on a sudden,
and, perhaps, in a place where we least of all expected it. This shock, and the shouts of the hunters,
strike us to such a degree, that it would be difficult
for such as are fond of this kind of chase, to think
of any thing else at that very instant: also the poets
make Diana triumphant over the torch and arrows
of Cupid:

> *Quis non malorum, quas amor curas habet,*
> *Hæc inter obliviscitur ?**
>
> Amidst such happiness who will not forget
> The various cares of love's uneasy state ?

To return to my subject: I have a very tender
compassion for the afflictions of other persons, and
should readily cry, for company, if, upon any occasion whatsoever, I could cry at all. Nothing tempts
my tears but to see tears shed by others, whether
the passion which produces them be real, or only
feigned or counterfeit. I do not much lament the
dead, and should rather envy them; but I very much
lament those who are dying. The savages do not so
much offend me in roasting and eating the bodies of
the dead, as those who torment and persecute the
living. I do not like to be a spectator of executions, how just soever they are. A person having
undertaken to set forth the clemency of Julius Cæsar,
" He was," said he, " moderate in his revenge; for
" having forced the pirates to surrender to him,
" those very pirates who had before taken him pri-
" soner, and put him to ransom, and having sworn
" to hang them on a gibbet, he did, indeed, con-
" demn them to it, but it was after he had caused

*His tender-
heartedness.*

* Hor. Epod. od. ii. ver. 37, 38.

" them to be strangled : nor did he punish his secre-
" tary Philemon, who had attempted to poison him,
" with any greater severity than merely putting him
" to death." Without naming the Latin author,*
who durst allege, as a mark of clemency, the
killing of those by whom we have been offended,
it is easy to guess that he was struck with the horrid
and inhuman examples of cruelty practised by the
Roman tyrants.

The execu-
tions of jus-
tice ought
to be sim-
ple, and to
carry no
marks of
severity. My opinion is, that, even in the executions of
justice, whatever exceeds simple death, is mere
cruelty, especially in us, who ought to have so much
respect to the souls, as to dismiss them in a good
state, which cannot be when they are discomposed
and rendered desperate by intolerable torments.
Not long since a soldier, who was imprisoned for
some crime, perceiving from the tower wherein he
was confined, that the people were assembled at the
place of execution, and that the carpenters were
very busy, he thought that all their preparation was
for his execution, and therefore resolved to kill
himself, but could find nothing wherewith to do it
except an old rusty cart-nail which he chanced to
light upon : with this he first gave himself two great
wounds in his throat ; but, finding this was not sufficient, he soon after gave himself a third wound in
the belly, where he left the nail stuck up to the
head. The first of his keepers that came into his
room, found him thus mangled, and though still
alive, yet fallen on the floor, near expiring by his
wounds. They therefore made haste to pass sentence
on him before he should die, and thereby defeat the
law. When he heard his sentence, and that it was
only to be beheaded, he seemed to take fresh
courage, accepted of a glass of wine which he had

---

* This author was Suetonius, wherein I remember to have read
this passage, though Montaigne chose to conceal his name; and,
upon consulting it, was enabled to correct a small error I found in
all the editions of these Essays that I have seen, which write Philo-
mon for Philemon.

before refused, and thanked his judges for the unexpected mildness of their sentence, saying, " That he
" had taken a resolution to dispatch himself, for
" fear of being put to a kind of death more severe
" and insupportable, having entertained an opinion,
" from the preparations he had seen making in the
" place of execution, that he was to be put to some
" horrible torture." And the man seemed to be,
as it were, delivered from death by the change of it
from the manner in which he apprehended it. I
would advise that these examples of severity, which
are with a design to keep people in their duty, might
be exercised upon the dead bodies of the criminals;
for depriving them of burial, and quartering and
boiling them, would impress the vulgar almost as
much as the pains they see inflicted upon the living;
though, in effect, this is next to nothing, as is
said in the Scripture, " They kill the body, but after
" that have nothing more that they can do," Luke
xii. ver. 4. One day, while I was at Rome, I happened to be going by just as they were executing
Catena, a notorious robber. The spectators saw him
strangled with indifference; but when they proceeded
to quarter him, at every blow struck by the execu-
tioner, they gave a doleful groan, and made such
an outcry, as if every one had lent his sense of feeling to the miserable carcase. These inhuman excesses ought to be exercised upon the bark, and not
upon the pith. Thus, in a case much of the same
nature, Artaxerxes moderated the severity of the
ancient laws of Persia by an order, that the nobility
who debased themselves, instead of being lashed
as they used to be, should be stripped, and their
vestments whipped for them; and that, instead of
having the hair of their heads plucked off, as was
the practice, they should only take off their high-
crowned tiarae.* The Egyptians, who affected to be
so devout, thought they fully satisfied the justice of

* Plutarch, in his notable sayings of the ancient kings.

D 2

God by sacrificing swine to him in picture and
effigy.* A bold invention, to think to please the
divine Being, a substance so essential, with picture
and shadow!

Instances of extreme cruelty.

I live in times that abound with incredible instances of this vice, owing to the licentiousness of
our civil wars; and I may challenge the ransackers
of the ancient histories to produce any passage more
extraordinary than what we experience of it every
day; yet I am not at all reconciled to it. I could
scarce believe, till I had seen it, that there could be
such savage monsters, who could commit murder
purely for the delight they took in it, and that, from
that motive only, could hack and lop off the limbs
of their fellow-creatures, and rack their brains to
find out unusual torments and new deaths, without
enmity, without gain; and only to feast their eyes
and ears with the distressful gestures and motions,
and the lamentable cries and groans of a man in the
agonies of death. This is the utmost point to which
cruelty can attain; *Ut homo hominem non iratus, non
timens, tantùm spectaturus occidat :* i. e. "That one
"man should kill another without being pushed
"upon it by anger or fear, but only by a desire of
"seeing him die."

Montaigne's humanity with regard to beasts.

For my own part, it always gives me pain to see
a harmless beast, which is incapable of making any
resistance, and gives us no offence, pursued and wor-
ried to death: and, as it often happens, that the
stag, when hunted till it has lost its breath and
strength, finding no other remedy, falls on its back,
and surrenders itself to its pursuers, seeming, with
tears, to beg for mercy,

——*quæstuque cruentus.*
Atque imploranti similis.†

* Herodotus (lib. ii. p. 122.) says this was only done by the poorer
sort, who made swine in dough, which they baked, and then offered
in sacrifice.

† Æneid. lib. vii. ver. 501, 502.

I ever thought it a very unpleasant sight: I scarce take any beast alive, but I turn it abroad again: Pythagoras purchased fish and fowls alive for the same purpose:

> ———*Primoque a cæde ferarum*
> *Incaluisse puto maculatum sanguine ferrum.**
>
> With slaughter of wild beasts the sword began,
> Ere it was drawn to shed the blood of man.

They that thirst for the blood of beasts discover a natural inclination to cruelty. After they had accustomed themselves, at Rome, to spectacles of the slaughter of animals, they proceeded to that of men, and the combats of gladiators. Nature itself (I fear) has planted in man a kind of instinct to inhumanity: nobody is fond of seeing beasts play with and caress one another, nor should any body take a pleasure in seeing them dismember and worry one another. That I may not be jeered for my sympathising with them, we are enjoined to have some pity for them by religion itself: and, considering that one and the same master has lodged us in this world for his service, and that they are of his family as well as we, it had reason to command us to show some regard and affection for them.

Pythagoras borrowed the doctrine of the Metempsychosis from the Egyptians; but it was afterwards received by several nations, and particularly by our Druids: Pythagoras's doctrine of the transmigration of souls.

> *Morte carent animæ, semperque priore relictâ*
> *Sede, novis domibus vivunt, habitantque receptæ.†*
>
> Souls never die, but, having left one seat,
> Into new houses they admittance get,

The priests of our ancient Gauls maintained, that souls, being eternal, never ceased to remove and shift their stations from one body to another; mixing, moreover, with this fancy, some consideration

---

* Ovid. Metam. lib. xv. fab. 2, ver. 47, 48.
† Ovid. Metam. lib. xv. fab. 8, ver. 6, 7,

of the divine justice : for, according as the soul had
behaved whilst it had been in Alexander, they said
that God ordered it to inhabit another body, more or
less uneasy, and suitable to its condition :

> ————*Muta ferarum*
> *Cogit vincla pati, truculentos ingerit ursis.*
> *Prædonesque lupis, fallaces vulpibus addit :*
>
> *Atque ubi per varios annos, per mille figuras*
> *Egit, Lethæa purgatos flumine tandem*
> *Rursus ad humanæ revocat primordia formæ.*[*]

The yoke of speechless brutes he made them wear,
Blood-thirsty souls he did enclose in bears ;
Those that rapacious were, in wolves he shut ;
The sly and cunning he in foxes put ;
Where, after having, in a course of years,
In num'rous forms, quite finish'd their careers,
In Lethe's flood he purg'd them, and at last
In human bodies he the souls replac'd.

If the soul had been valorous, they lodged it in the
body of a lion ; if voluptuous, in that of a hog ; if
timorous, in that of a hart or hare ; if treacherous,
in that of a fox ; and so of the rest, till, purified by
this correction, it again entered into some human
body :

> *Ipse ego, nam memini, Trojani tempore belli,*
> *Panthoïdes Euphorbius eram.*[†]
>
> For I myself remember, in the days
> O'th' Trojan war, that I Euphorbus was.

As to the kindred between us and the beasts, I lay
no great stress on it, nor on the practice of several nations, and some, too, the most noted for antiquity and
dignity, said to have not only admitted brutes to their
society and company, but to have also preferred them
to a rank far above themselves ; some esteeming them
as familiars and favourites of their gods, and paying

* Claudian in Ruffin. lib. ii. ver. 482, 483, 484,—491, 492, 493.
† It is Pythagoras who speaks thus of himself, in Ovid. Metam. lib.
xv. fab. 3, ver. 8, 9.   Would you know by what means Pythagoras
could remember what he had been in the time of the Trojan war ;
see Diog. Laert. in the Life of Pythagoras, lib. viii. sect. 4, 5.

them respect and veneration more than human, while others acknowledged no god nor deity but them:

*Belluæ à Barbaris propter beneficium consecratæ.**

The Barbarians consecrated beasts for the benefit they received by them.

———— Crocodilon adorat
Pars hæc: illa pavet saturam serpentibus ibin ;
Effigies sacri nitet aurea cercopitheci :
———— hic piscem fluminis, illic
Oppida tota canem venerantur.†

One large domain the crocodile adores,
That strikes such terror on th'Egyptian shores ;
Another clime the long-bill'd ibis dreads,
Which pois'nous flesh of ugly serpents feeds ;
Advance yet farther, and your eyes behold
The statue of a monkey shine in gold :
A certain fish of Nile is worshipp'd here,
And there whole towns a snarling dog revere.

The very construction that Plutarch puts upon this error, which is very well fancied, is also to their honour: for he says, that it was not the cat, nor the ox (for example) that the Egyptians adored, but that, in those brutes, they reverenced some image of the divine faculties.‡ In the ox, patience and profit ; in the cat, vivacity, or like our neighbours, the Burgundians, with all the Germans, an impatience of confinement,§ by which they represented the liberty they loved and adored beyond every other faculty; and so of the others. But when, amongst the more moderate opinions, I meet with arguments to demonstrate the near resemblance between us and animals, and what a share they have in our greatest privileges, it really very much abates my presump-

---

* Cicer. de Nat. Deo. lib. i. cap. 36.
† Juv. sat. xv. ver. 2, 3, 4,—7, 8.
‡ In his treatise of Isis and Osyris, ch. 39 of Amyot's translation,
§ A passion natural to cats, which cannot endure to be pent up in a room.

tion, and I am ready to resign that imaginary roy-
alty which is ascribed to us over the other creatures.

We ought
to have
some re-
gard for
the brute
beasts.
Be all this as it will, there is, nevertheless, a certain kind of respect, and a general obligation of humanity, which attaches us, not only to the beasts
that have life and a sense of feeling, but also to trees
and plants. We owe justice to men, and favour and
good usage to other creatures that are susceptible of
it : there is a certain correspondence, and a mutual
obligation between them and us. I am not ashamed
to confess, that such is the tenderness of my nature,
that I cannot well refuse to play with my dog when
he caresses me, or desires it, though it be out of
season.

Remark-
able in-
stances of
this sort of
respect.
The Turks have alms-houses and hospitals for
beasts. The Romans made public provision for the
nourishment of geese, after the watchfulness of one
of them had saved their Capitol. The Athenians
made a decree, that the mules* which had been employed in the building of the temple, called Heca-
tompedon, should be free, and allowed to graze
any where without molestation. It was the common
practice of the Agrigentines† to give solemn interment to their favourite beasts, as horses of some rare
qualities, dogs, and birds, which they made a profit
of, and even such as had served for the diversion of
their children : and the magnificence which they
commonly displayed in all other things, appeared
particularly in the number of costly monuments
erected to this very purpose, which remained for a show
several ages after. The Egyptians‡ interred wolves,
bears, crocodiles, dogs, and cats in sacred places,
embalmed their bodies, and wore mourning at their
death. Cimon§ gave‖ an honourable burial to the
mares with which he had won three prizes at the

---

* Plutarch, in the Life of Cato the Censor, ch. 5.
† Diodorus of Sicily, lib. xiii. cap. 17.   ‡ Ibid.
§ Father of Miltiades, Herodot. lib. vi. p. 413.
‖ Herodot. lib. ii. p. 129.

Olympic races. Old Xanthippus * caused his dog
to be buried on a promontory near the sea side,
which has, ever since, retained its name. And
Plutarch‖ says, that he made conscience of selling
and sending to the shambles, for a small profit, an
ox that had served him a good while.

CHAPTER III.

An Apology for Raimond de Sebonde.

LEARNING is, in truth, a possession of very Learning,
great importance and utility, and they who despise ^{its useful-}
it, plainly discover their stupidity; yet I do not
prize it at that excessive rate as some men do, particularly Herillus the philosopher, who therein placed
the sovereign good, and maintained, that it was
alone sufficient to make us wise and happy; which I
do not believe, nor what has been said by others,
that learning is the mother of all virtue, and that all
vice is produced from ignorance. If this be true, it
is a point liable to a tedious discussion. My house
has been a long time open to men of learning, and
is very well known by them; for my father, who
was the master of it fifty years, and more, being
warmed with that zeal with which king Francis I.
had newly embraced literature, and brought it into
esteem, spared no pains nor expense to get an acquaintance with men of learning, treating them, at
his house, as persons sacred, who had divine wisdom
by some special inspiration, collecting their sentences
and sayings as so many oracles, and with the more
veneration and religion, as he was the less qualified
to judge of them; for he had no knowledge of letters any more than his predecessors. For my part,

* Plutarch's Cato the Censor. † Ibid.

I love them very well, but do not adore them.
Amongst others, Peter Bunel, a man of great reputation for learning, in his time, having, with others
of his class, spent some days at Montaigne with my
father, presented him, at his departure, with a book,
entitled, *Theologia Naturalis, sive Liber Creatu-*
rarum Magistri Raimondi de Sebonde : i. e. " Natural
" Theology, or a Treatise on the Animal Creation,
by Master Raimond de Sebonde." As both the
Italian and Spanish languages were familiar to my
father, and the book was written in Spanish, larded
with Latin terminations, M. Bunel hoped that, with
a very little assistance, my father would make it turn
out to his account ; and he recommended it to him
as a very useful book, and proper for the juncture of
time in which he gave it to him, which was when the
innovations of Luther began to be in vogue, and in
many places to stagger our ancient faith. Herein
he judged very right, forseeing plainly, by the dictates of reason, that, as the distemper appeared at
its breaking out, it would easily turn into execrable
atheism : for the vulgar, not being qualified to judge
of things as they are in themselves, but being governed by accidents and appearances, after they
have been once inspired with the boldness to contemn
and controul those opinions which they held before
in extreme reverence, particularly such as concern
their salvation, and, after any of the articles of their
religion are brought into question, are soon apt to
reject all the other articles of their belief, as equally
uncertain, and shake off the impressions they had
received from the authority of the laws, or the reverence of ancient custom, as a tyrannical yoke :

> *Nam cupidè conculcatur nimis antè metutum.* *
> For with most eagerness they spurn the law,
> By which they were before most kept in awe :

resolving to admit nothing, for the future, without

* Lucret. lib. v. ver. 1139.

[margin note:] The work of Rai- mond de Sebonde.

the interposition of their own decree and particular consent.

My father, a few days before his death, happening to meet with this book under a heap of other papers that were laid by, commanded me to translate it for him into French. It is good to translate such authors as this, wherein there is scarce any thing to represent, except the matter; but as for those books wherein the grace and elegancy of language are mainly affected, they are dangerous to undertake, for fear of translating them into a weaker idiom. It was an undertaking new, and quite strange to me; but happening, at that time, to have leisure, and not being able to resist the command of the best father that ever was, I did it as well as I could, and so much to his satisfaction, that he ordered it to be printed, which also, after his death, was performed.* I was charmed with the author's fine imagination, the regular contexture of his work, and the extraordinary piety of his design. Because many people take a pleasure in reading it, particularly the ladies, to whom we owe most service, I have often been ready to assist them, in defeating two main objections to this their favourite author. His design is bold; for he undertakes to establish and verify all the articles of the Christian religion, against the

Translated from the Spanish into French, by Montaigne.

* Montaigne, speaking of this first edition of it in the first edition of his Essays, at Bourdeaux, in 1580, and that of 1588, in quarto, says, it appears to have been carelessly printed, by reason of the infinite number of errors of the press, committed by the printer, who had the sole care of it. This translation was reprinted, and, no doubt, more correctly, because Montaigne has purged it of the printer's errors in the former. I have an edition printed at Paris in 1611, and said to be translated by Michael Seignour de Montaigne, knight of the king's orders, and a gentleman of his chamber in ordinary; the last edition revised and corrected. And, indeed, this is a very correct edition. There is such a perspicuity, spirit, and natural vivacity in this translation, that it has all the air of an original. Montaigne has added nothing of his own to it, but a short dedication of it to his father, wherein he owns, that he undertook this work by his order. The reader will find this dedication at the end of the third volume of this edition of the Essays.

atheists, from reasons that are human and natural;
wherein, to say the truth, he is so successful, that I
do not think it possible to do better upon the subject,
and believe that he has been equalled by none.*
This work seeming to me too sublime and too elegant
for an author whose name is so little known, and of
whom all that we learn, is that he was a Spaniard,
who professed physic at Thoulouse about two hundred years ago, I once asked Adrian Turnebus, a
man of universal knowledge, what he thought of this
treatise. The answer he made to me was, that he
believed it to be some extract from Thomas Aquinas;
for that, in truth, none but a genius like his, accompanied with infinite learning, and wonderful subtlety, was capable of such ideas. So it is, that, be
the author and inventor who he will (though without
greater reason than has yet appeared, it would not
be right to strip Sebonde of this title), he was a man
of great sufficiency, and of very fine parts.

The objec-
tion made
in the book,
and Mon-
taigne's an-
swer.
    The first fault they find with his work is his assert-
ing, " That Christians are in the wrong to endea-
" vour to make human reasoning the basis of their
" belief, since the object of it is only conceived by
" faith, and by a special inspiration of the divine
" grace." In this objection there seems to be a
pious zeal, and, for this reason, it is absolutely necessary that we should endeavour, with the greatest
mildness and respect, to satisfy those who have advanced it. This were a task more proper for a man
well versed in divinity, than for me who know nothing of it. Nevertheless, this is my judgment, that,
in a point of so divine and sublime a nature, and so
far transcending human understanding, as this truth,
with which it has pleased the divine goodness to
enlighten us, there is great need that he should also

* Grotius's treatise of the Truth of the Christian Religion was not
yet published, wherein that great man expressly says, that this subject had been before treated by Raimond de Sebonde, Philosophicâ
Subtilitate.

lend us the assistance, in the way of an extraordinary favour and privilege, to enable us to conceive and imprint it in our understandings, of which I do not think means merely human are, in any sort, capable of doing; for, if they were, so many men of rare and excellent talents, so abundantly furnished with natural abilities, in former ages, had not failed to attain to this knowledge by the light of reason. It is by faith alone that we have a lively and certain comprehension of the sublime mysteries of our religion; not but that it is a very laudable attempt to accommodate also the natural and human talents, which God has given us, to the service of our faith: it is not to be doubted, that this is the most noble use that we can put them to, and that there is no employment nor design more worthy of a Christian, than to aim, by all his studies and meditations, to illustrate, extend, and amplify the truth of his belief. We do not content ourselves by serving God with our hearts and understandings; we, moreover, owe and render him corporeal reverence; we apply our very limbs, and our external motions, &c. to do him honour; we must here do the same, and accompany our faith with all the reason we have, but always with this reserve, not to fancy that it depends upon us, nor that our efforts and arguments can attain to knowledge so supernatural and divine.

If it enter not into us by an extraordinary infusion, if we attain to it only by reason, and by human means, we do not comprehend it in its native dignity and splendour; and yet I really am afraid that we only possess it by this canal. If we laid hold upon God by the mediation of a lively faith, and not through our own merits; if we had a divine footing and foundation, human accidents would not have the power to shake us as they do; our fortress would not be the conquest of so weak a battery: the love of novelty, the constraint of princes, the success of a party, the rash and fortuitous change of our opinions, would not have power to stagger and alter our faith:

we should not then leave it to the mercy of some
new argument, and abandon it to the persuasion
even of all the rhetoric in the world: we should bear
up against those waves with a resolution inflexible
and immovable:

> *Illisos fluctus rupes ut vasta refundit,*
> *Et varias circum latrantes dissipat undas*
> *Mole suâ.**
>
> As a vast rock repels the rolling tides
> That dash and foam against its flinty sides
> By its own bulk.

A good life the mark of true Christianity. If this ray of divinity glanced upon any part of
us, it would illuminate the whole man; not only our
words, but our works also would shine with its
brightness and lustre; every thing that proceeded
from us, would be enlightened with this noble splendour. We ought to be ashamed, that in all
the human sects, there never was a man, notwithstanding the absurdity and novelty of the doctrine which he maintained, but conformed his
manner of life to Christianity in some measure; and
that so divine and heavenly an institution should only
distinguish Christians by the appellation. Would
you see a proof of this? Compare our manners with
those of a Mahometan or Pagan: you will after all
come short of them in that very point, where, in regard to the advantage of our religion, we ought to
outshine them beyond all comparison; and it must
be said, Are they so good, so just, so charitable? they
are therefore Christians. All other appearances are
common to all religions: hope, trust, events, ceremonies, penances, martyrdoms, &c. The peculiar

---

* These Latin verses are by a modern poet, who borrowed the
sentiment, and most of the words, from those fine lines of Virgil,
> *Ille, velut pelagi rupes immota, resistit:*
> *Ut pelagi rupes, magno veniente fragore,*
> *Quæ sese, multis circumlatrantibus undis,*
> *Mole tenet————　Æneid. lib. vii. ver. 587—591, &c.*

In some of Montaigne's editions we are referred to this place in
Virgil, as if Montaigne had really quoted him.

characteristic of our truth ought to be our virtue, as it is also the most celestial and difficult mark, and the best fruits of truth. However, when that king of the Tartars, on his embracing Christianity, designed to repair to Lyons to kiss the Pope's toe, and to be an eye-witness of the sanctity which he expected to find in our manners, our good St. Lewis* was in the right to divert him from it instantly, lest our licentious way of living should put him out of conceit with so holy a belief: yet the very reverse of this happened afterwards to another, who, going to Rome for the very same purpose, and observing the dissolute lives of the prelates and the laity of that time, was the more firmly established in our religion, by considering how great the power and divinity of it must be to maintain its dignity and splendour, in a sink of so much corruption, and in such vicious hands. " If we had but one single grain of faith, " we should be able to remove mountains from their " places," says sacred writ ; our actions, which would then be directed and accompanied by the divinity, would not be merely human, but would have something in them of the marvellous, as well as our belief. *Brevis est institutio vitæ honestæ beatæque, si credas :* " If thou believest, thou wilt soon learn the " duties of an honest and happy life." Some impose upon the world that they believe what they do not believe ; while others, more in number, make themselves believe that they have faith, not being able to penetrate what it is to believe.

We think it strange, if, in the civil war which at this time distresses our state, we see events float and vary, after the common and ordinary way ; and the reason is, because we bring nothing to it but our own. Justice, which is in one of the parties, is only there for ornament and a cloak : it is indeed well urged, but is neither received, settled, nor espoused by it. It is the same with that party, as words are

God gives
his assist-
ance to re-
ligion, not
to our pas-
sions.

* Jounville, ch. 19, p. 88, 89.

in the mouth of an advocate, not as in the heart and affection. God owes his extraordinary assistance to faith and religion, not to our passions.

Men make use of religion to satisfy their most unjust passions. In the latter, men are the guides, and therein they make use of religion, though it ought to be quite the contrary. Observe if it be not by our hands that we train it, like soft wax, to represent so many contrary figures from a rule so straight and firm. When was this more manifest than now-a-days in France? The heterodox, and the orthodox, they who call white black, and black white, employ it so much alike to serve their violent and ambitious undertakings, and proceed with such a conformity of riot and injustice, that their pretended difference in opinions, in an affair whereon depend the conduct and rule of our life, is thereby rendered doubtful, and hard of belief. Is it possible for a greater uniformity and sameness of manners to proceed from one and the same school and discipline? observe with what horrid impudence we pelt one another with divine arguments, and how irreligiously we have rejected and resumed them, just as fortune has shifted our station in these public storms. This so solemn a proposition, " Whether it is lawful for a subject to " rebel, and take arms against his prince for the de- " fence of religion?" do not you remember in whose mouths last year the affirmative of it was the prop of one party, and the negative the pillar of the other? and hearken now from * what quarter comes the votes and instruction both of the one and the other, and whether the guns roar less for this cause than for that. We condemn those to the flames, who say, that " Truth must be made to bear the " yoke of our necessity;" and yet does not France act worse than merely saying it? let us confess the real truth; whoever should make a draught from the army, which is raised by lawful authority, of those

* Here Montaigne (as Mr. Bayle says, in his Dictionary, at the article Hotman, Note 1,) gently lashes the Catholics.

who serve in it out of a pure zeal for religion, and of those also who have only in view the protection of the laws of their country, or the service of their prince, he would not be able, from both mustered together, to form one complete company of gens d'arms. Whence now does this proceed, that there are so few to be found who have maintained the same purpose, and the same progress in our public commotions, and that we see them one while jogging but a foot-pace, and another while riding full speed; and how comes it that we see the same men spoiling our affairs at one time by their violence and acrimony, at another time by their coldness, indolence, and dulness, but that they are swayed by partial and casual considerations, according to the variation of which they move.

I see plainly that we do not willingly afford devotion any other offices but such as flatter our passions. There is no warfare so excellent as that of the Christian. Our zeal performs wonders, when it seconds our inclination to hatred, cruelty, ambition, avarice, detraction, rebellion, &c. But if it be turned against the grain, towards good-nature, benignity, temperance, &c. unless, by a miracle, some uncommon disposition prompt us to it, it stirs neither hand nor foot. Our religion, which is framed for the extirpation of vices, screens, nourishes, and incites them. We must not mock God. If we believed in him, I do not say by faith, but with a simple belief, nay (to our great shame I speak it), if we believed and acknowledged him as we do any other history, or as any of our companions, we should love him above all other things, for the infinite goodness and beauty that shine in him; at least he would have the same rank in our affections, as riches, pleasures, glory, and our friends. The best of us all is not so much afraid of offending him, as offending a neighbour, a parent, or a master. Is there a man of so weak understanding, who, having any of our vicious pleasures in view on one side, and, on the other, as full a knowledge and persua-

The zeal of the Christians full of injustice and fury.

sion of a state of a glorious immortality, would be
willing to exchange the one for the other? and yet
we often renounce the latter, out of mere contempt;
for what lust tempts us to blaspheme, if not, perhaps, even the desire of offending? While the priest
was initiating Antisthenes the philosopher in the
mysteries of Orpheus, and telling him, that they
who devoted themselves to that religion, were to
receive eternal and perfect* happiness after their
death; the philosopher said* to him, "If thou be-
"lievest it, why dost not thou thyself die?" Diogenes,
more bluntly, according to his manner, though not
so much to our present purpose, said† to the priest,
who made the like speech to him, that he should
enter into his order, if he would be happy in the
other world? "Wouldst thou make me believe, that
"two such great men as Agesilaus and Epaminondas
"will be miserable; and that thyself, who art but a
"calf, and canst do no good, shalt be happy, be-
"cause thou art a priest?" If we received these
great promises of everlasting happiness, with the
same deference as we do a philosophical lecture, we
should not be so horribly afraid of death:

*Non jam se moriens dissolvi conquereretur,
Sed magis ire foras, vestemque relinquere ut anguis
Gauderet, prælonga senex aut cornu cervus.‡*

We should not on a death-bed grieve to be
Dissolv'd, but rather launch out cheerfully
From our old hut, and with the snake be glad
To cast off the corrupted slough we had;
Or with th' old stag rejoice to be now clear
From the large horns too pond'rous grown to bear.

"I am willing to be dissolved," we should say, "and
"to be with Jesus Christ."§ The force of Plato's
arguments for the immortality of the soul actually
made some of his disciples dispatch themselves, that

* Diog. Laert. in the Life of Antisthenes, lib. vi. sect. 4,
† Idem, in the Life of Diogenes the Cynic. lib. vi. sect. 39.
‡ Lucret. lib. iii. ver. 612, &c.
§ St. Paul's Ep. to the Philippians, chap. i. ver. 23.

they might the sooner enjoy the hopes he gave them.

All this very plainly demonstrates, that we only receive our religion after our own fashion, and by our own hands, and no otherwise than as other religions are received. Whether we happen to be in countries where it is in practice; whether we have a veneration for the antiquity of it, or for the authority of the professors of it; whether we fear the menaces which it fulminates against unbelievers, or are encouraged by its promises: these things ought to be considered only as auxiliaries to our faith, for they are obligations altogether human. Another country, other evidences, the like promises and threatenings, might, by the same rule, imprint a belief quite contrary. We are Christians by the same title as we are either Perigordins, or Germans : and what Plato says, that there are few men so obstinate in atheism, but a pressing danger will reduce them to an acknowledgment of the divine power, does not relate to a true Christian : it is for mortal and human religions to be received by human recommendation. What kind of faith must that be which is planted and established in us by pusillanimity and cowardice ? a pleasant faith, that only believes in its object, for want of the courage not to believe it! Can a vicious passion, such as inconstancy and astonishment, produce any thing regular in our minds ? The atheists, says Plato, are confident, upon the strength of their own judgment, that what is advanced about hell and future torments is a fiction ; but when an opportunity presents itself for their making the experiment, at the time that old age or sickness brings them to the confines of death, the terror of it possesses them with a new belief, from a horror of their future state. And, by reason they are terrified by such impressions, Plato, in his laws, forbids all such threatening doctrines, and all persuasive arguments, that any evil can come to man from the gods, unless it be for his great good when it happens to him, and

The foundation of the profession of the Christian religion.

for a medicinal effect. They say of Bion, that, being
infected with Theodorus's atheistical principles, he
had, for a long time, held religious men in derision,
but that, when death stared him in the face, he became superstitious to an extreme degree, as if the
gods[*] were to be managed just as Bion pleased.
From Plato, and these examples, we conclude that
we are reduced to the belief of a God, either by reason, or by force. Atheism being a proposition not
only unnatural and monstrous, but difficult, and
very hard to be digested by the mind of man, be he
ever so haughty and dissolute; there are instances
enough of men, who, out of the vanity and pride
of broaching uncommon opinions, and of being re-
formers of the world, outwardly affect the profession
of such opinions, who, if they are fools enough, have
not the power to plant them in their own consciences: nevertheless, if you plunge a dagger into
their breasts, they will not fail to lift up their hands
towards heaven; and when the fear, or the distemper, has abated and suppressed this licentious heat
of a fickle humour, they will immediately recover,
and suffer themselves, very discreetly, to be reconciled to the public creeds and forms. A doctrine
seriously digested is one thing, and these superficial
impressions another, which, springing from the depravity of an unsettled mind, float rashly and at
random in the fancy. Miserable, hair-brained
wretches, who would, if it was possible, fain be
worse than they are!

What thought to attach us firmly to God.   The errors of paganism, and the ignorance of our
sacred truths, led Plato, that great genius, but great
only with human grandeur, into another error, next
a-kin to it, that " Children and old people were
" most susceptible of religion;" as if it sprung and
derived its credit from our weakness: the knot that

[*] This reflection, which is so just and natural, is by Diogenes
Laertius himself, who having no great fund of his own, it would
have been cruel to rob him of this. See his Life of Bion, sect. 55.

ought to bind the judgment and the will; that ought
to restrain the soul, and fasten it to the creator,
must be a knot that derives its foldings and strength,
not from our considerations, our arguments and passions, but from a divine and supernatural constraint,
having but one form, one face, and one lustre,
which is the authority of God and his divine grace.
Now, the heart and soul being governed and commanded by faith, it is reasonable that it should draw
in the assistance of all our other faculties, as far as
they are able to contribute to its service.

Neither is it to be imagined, that this whole ma- The divine
chine has not some marks imprinted on it by the known by
hand of its almighty Architect; and that there is not, his visible
in the things of this world, some image that bears a works.
sort of resemblance to the workman who has built
and formed them. In these sublime works he has
left the stamp of his divinity, and it is only owing to our
weakness that we cannot discern it. It is what he himself tells us, that he manifests his invisible operations
to us by those that are visible. Sebonde applied himself to this worthy study, and demonstrates to us,
that there is not any 'piece in the world that dero-
gates from its Maker. It would be a wrong to the
divine goodness, if the universe did not concur in
our belief. The heavens, the earth, the elements,
our bodies, our souls, all things unite in this, if we
can but find out the way to make it of use to us:
they instruct us, if we are capable of learning: for
this world is a very sacred temple, into which man is
introduced to contemplate statues, not made with
mortal hands, but such as the divine purpose has
made the objects of sense, the sun, the stars, the
water, and the earth, to represent them to our understanding." " The invisible things of God," says St.
Paul, " from the creation of the world, are clearly
" seen, being understood by the things that are
" made, even his eternal power and godhead :" *

* Epistle to the Romans, chap. i. ver. 20.

Atque adeò faciem coeli non invidet orbi
Ipse Deus, vultusque suos, corpusque recludit
Semper volvendo : seque ipsum inculcat et offert,
Ut bene cognosci possit, doceatque videndo
Qualis eat, doceatque suas attendere leges. *

And God himself envies not men the grace
Of seeing and admiring heaven's face ;
But, rolling it about, he still anew
Presents its varied splendor to our view ;
And on our minds himself inculcates so,
That we th' almighty Mover well may know
Instructing us, by seeing him the cause
Of all, to reverence and obey his laws.

As to our human reason and arguments, they are
but as lumpish barren matter : the grace of God is
the form ; it is this which gives the fashion and value
to it.　As the virtuous deeds of Socrates and Cato
remain vain and fruitless, for not having had the love
and obedience due to the true Creator of all things for
their end and object, and for their not having known
God ; so is it with our imagination and reason : they
have a kind of body, but it is an inform mass, without fashion, and without light, if faith and God's grace
be not added to it.　Sebonde's arguments, being illu-
trated by faith, are thereby rendered firm and solid :
they are capable of serving as directions, and of being the principal guides to a learner, to put him into
the way of this knowledge : they, in some measure,
form him to, and render him capable of, the grace of
God, by means of which he afterwards completes
and perfects himself in our belief.　I know a person
of authority, bred up to letters, who confessed to
me, that he was reclaimed from the errors of infidelity by Sebonde's arguments : and should they be
stripped of this ornament, and of the assistance and
sanction of faith, and be looked upon as mere human
fancies, to contend with those who are precipitated
into the dreadful and horrible darkness of irreligion,

* Manil. lib. iv. at the latter end.

they would, even then, be found to be as solid and firm as any others of the same nature that could be brought against them; so that we shall be enabled to say to our opponents,

*Si melius quid habes, arcesse; vel imperium fer.**

If you have arguments more fit,
Produce them, or to these submit.

Let them either submit to the force of our proofs, or produce others, or on any other subject, that are better connected and more substantial. I am, unawares, already half way engaged in the answer which I proposed to make, in the vindication of Sebonde, against the second objection.

Some say, that "his arguments are weak, and unable to make good what he intends;" and they undertake, with great ease, to confute them. These objectors are to be handled a little more roughly, for they are more dangerous and more malicious than the former. Men are apt to wrest the sayings of another, to favour their own prejudiced opinions. To an atheist all writings lead to atheism: he infects innocent matter with his own venom: these have their judgments so prepossessed, that Sebonde's arguments appear insipid to them. As for the rest, they think we give them fair play, in allowing them the free use of weapons that are merely human, to combat our religion, which they durst not attack in its majesty, full of authority and command. The method which I take, and think to be the most proper for curing this frenzy, is to crush, and spurn under foot, this arrogance and pride of men; to make them sensible of their emptiness, vanity, and extreme nothingness; to wrest the wretched arms of their reason out of their hands; to make them bow down and bite the ground, under the authority and reverence of the divine majesty. It is that alone to which knowledge and wisdom appertain; that alone which can

Answer to the charge against Sebonde's book, that the arguments are weak.

* Hor. lib. i. ep. v. ver. 6.

form any estimate of itself, and from which we purloin whatever we value ourselves upon:

Οὐ γὰρ ἐᾶ φρονέειν ὁ Θεὸς μέγα ἄλλον ἢ ἑαυτόν.

God permits not any being, but himself, to be truly wise.

Let us demolish that presumption, the first foundation of the tyranny of the evil spirit: *Deus superbis
resistit, humilibus autem dat gratiam:*[*] " God re-
" sisteth the proud, but giveth grace to the hum-
" ble." Understanding is in all the gods, says
Plato, but in man there is little or none. However, it is very comforting to a Christian to see our
mortal and frail talents so fitly suited to our holy
and divine faith, that, when they are employed on
subjects which are in their own nature mortal and
frail, they are not more equally or more strongly
appropriated to them. Let us see then, if there are
stronger reasons than those of Sebonde in the power
of man; nay, if it be possible for him to arrive at
any certainty, by reason and argument. For St.
Augustine, pleading against these people, has good
cause to reproach their injustice for maintaining
those parts of our belief to be false, which our reason cannot comprehend. And, to demonstrate that
many things may be, and may have been, of which
our reason cannot discover the nature and causes,
he sets before them certain known and undoubted
experiments, into which man confesses he has no
insight. And this he does, as all other things, with
a curious and ingenious inquiry. We must do more
than this, and make them know, that, to evince the
weakness of their reason, there is no necessity of
calling out rare examples; and that it is so lame and
so blind, that there is no facility clear enough for it;
that what is difficult and easy are one and the same
to it; that all subjects equally, and nature in general, disclaim its jurisdiction and interposition. What

*1 Pet. ch. v. ver. 5.

does truth mean, when she preaches to us to beware
of worldly philosophy; * when it so often inculcates to
us, " that the wisdom of this world is foolishness with
" God ; † that of all vanities man is the vainest ; that
" the man who presumes upon his wisdom, does not
" so much as know what wisdom is ; and that man
" who is nothing, if he thinks himself any thing, is
" deceived ?" These sentences of the holy spirit
express in so clear and lively a manner what I am for
maintaining, that there needs no other proof to convince men, who would with all obedience submit to
such authority.

But these are willing to be scourged at their own The advan-
expense, and do not care that their reason should be above the
opposed by any thing but reason. Let us then, for other crea-
once, consider a man alone without foreign assistance, armed only with his own weapons, and destitute of the divine grace and wisdom, which is all
his honour, his strength, and the foundation of his
existence. Let him make me understand, by the
force of his reason, upon what foundation he has
built those great advantages which he thinks he has
above all other creatures : who has made him believe that this wonderful motion of the celestial arch,
the eternal light of those tapers that roll so majes-
tically over his head, the surprising motions of the
boundless ocean, should be established, and continue
for so many ages, purely for his convenience and
service ? can any thing be imagined so ridiculous as
that this miserable caitiff, who is not so much as master of himself, and exposed to be injured by all
things, should style himself master and emperor of
the world, of which it is not in his power to know
the least part, much less to command the whole ?
and this privilege, which he arrogates to himself, of
being the only creature, in this vast fabric, that has

* St. Paul to the Colossians, ch. ii. ver. 8.
† 1 Cor. ch. iii. ver. 19.

the capacity of distinguishing the beauty and the parts of it; the only one that can return his thanks to its architect, and keep an account of the revenues and disbursements of the world; who, I wonder, sealed that patent for him? let him show us his commission for this great and splendid employment. Was it granted in favour of the wise only? Few people are sharers in it. Are fools and knaves worthy of so extraordinary a favour, and, being the worst part of mankind, to be preferred before all the rest? Shall we believe the passage which says,[*] *Quorum igitur causâ quis dixerit effectum esse mundum? Eorum scilicet animantium, quæ ratione utuntur. Hi sunt Dii et homines, quibus profecto nihil est melius:* " For " whose sake, therefore, shall we conclude that this " world was made? For theirs who have the use of " reason. These are gods and men, than whom " certainly nothing is better.". We can never sufficiently decry the impudence of this conjunction. But, poor creature, what has he in himself worthy of such an advantage? To consider the incorruptible life of the celestial bodies, their beauty, magnitude, and continual motion, by so just a rule:

> *Cum suspicimus magni cœlestia mundi*
> *Templa super, stellisque micantibus æthera fixum,*
> *Et venit in mentem lunæ solisque viarum.*[†]

> When we the heavenly arch above behold,
> And the vast sky adorn'd with stars of gold,
> And mark the reg'lar courses that the sun
> And moon in their alternate progress run.

To consider the dominion and influence which those bodies have, not only over our lives and fortunes:

> *Facta et enim et vitas hominum suspendit ab astris;*[‡]

> Men's lives and actions on the stars depend;

---

[*] That is to say, Balbus the Stoic, who speaks thus in Cicero de de Natura Deorum, lib. ii. cap. 53.

[†] Lucret. lib. v. 1203.　　　[‡] Manil. lib. iii. ver. 58.

but over our very inclinations, our reason, our wills,
which are governed, animated, and agitated at the
mercy of their influences :

> —— *Speculataque longè*
> *Deprendit tacitis dominantia legibus astra,*
> *Et totum alternâ mundum ratione moveri,*
> *Fatorúmque vices certis discernere signis.* *

> Contemplating the stars, he finds that they
> Rule by a silent and a secret sway ;
> And that th' enamell'd spheres which roll above,
> Incessant by alternate causes move ;
> And, studying these, he also can foresee
> By certain signs the turns of destiny.

To observe, that no man, not even a king, is exempt,
but that monarchies, empires, and all this lower
world, are influenced by the motions of the least of
the celestial orbs :

> *Quantáque quam parvi faciant discrimina motus,*
> *Tantam est hoc regnum quod regibus imperat ipsis.* †

> How great a change a little motion brings,
> So great this kingdom is that governs kings!

If our virtues, our vices, our knowledge, and learning, and this same reasoning of ours upon the power
of the stars, and this comparison of them to us, proceed, as our reason judges, by their means, and
from their favour :

> —— *Furit alter amore,*
> *Et pontum tranare potest et vertere Trojan :*
> *Alterius sors est scribendis legibus apta :*
> *Ecce patrem nati perimunt, natósque parentes,*
> *Mutuáque armati coeunt in vulnera fratres.*
> *Non nostrum hoc bellum est : coguntur tante movere,*
> *Inque suas ferri pœnas, lacerandáque membra ;*

> *Hoc quoque fatale est, sic ipsum expendere fatum.* ‡

> One mad in love may cross the raging main,
> To level lofty Ilium with the plain ;

---

* Manil. lib. i. ver. 62, &c.
† Idem. lib. i. ver. 57, et lib. iv. ver. 93.
‡ Idem. lib. iv. ver. 79—85, 118.

Another's fate inclines him more by far,
To study laws and statutes for the bar.
Sons kill their fathers, fathers kill their sons,
And one arm'd brother 'gainst another runs.
This war's not their's, but Fate's that spurs them on
To shed the blood, which shed they must bemoan;
And I ascribe it to the will of Fate,
That on this theme I now expatiate.

If we hold this portion of reason which we have by
the bounty of Heaven, how is it possible that it
should make us equal to the donor? how can it subject his essence and qualities to our knowledge?
Whatever we see in those bodies astonishes us: *Quæ
molitio, quæ ferramenta, qui vectes, quæ machinæ, qui
ministri tanti operis fuerunt ?* * " What contrivance,
" what instruments, what levers, what machines, what
" operators were employed in so vast a work?" why do
we deprive them of soul, of life, and of reason? have
we, who have no correspondence with them, but in
obedience, discovered any immovable and insensible
stupidity in them? shall we say, that we have discovered the use of a reasonable soul in no other creature but man? and why? have we seen any thing
like the sun? does it cease to be, because we have
not seen any thing like to it? and do its motions
cease, because there are no other like to them? if
what we have not seen, is therefore not in being, our
knowledge is wonderfully contracted: *Quæ sunt
tantæ animi angustiæ!* † " How narrow are our un-
" standings!" Are they not dreams of human vanity
to make the moon a celestial world? to fancy, as
Anaxagoras did, that there are mountains and val-
lies in it? and there plant habitations and human
dwellings, and to raise colonies in it for our convenience, as Plato and Plutarch have done? and of
our earth, to make a bright shining star? *Inter
cætera mortalitatis incommoda, et hoc est, caligo men-
tium : nec tantum necessitas errandi, sed errorum
amor.* ‡ *Corruptibile corpus aggravat animam, et*

---

* Cic. de Nat. Deor. lib. i. cap. 8.   † Cic. de Nat. lib. i. cap. 31.
‡ In some editions of Montaigne, the passage that follows is

deprimit terrena inhabitatio sensum multa cogitantem ;
" Amongst other inconveniences of mortality, this
" is one, viz. the darkness of the understanding,
" which is not only under a necessity of erring, but
" takes delight in it." Senec. de Ira, lib. ii.
cap. 9.

Presumption is our natural and original infirmity : the most wretched and frail of all creatures is man, and yet, withal, the proudest : he sees and feels himself lodged here in the dirt and nastiness of the world, nailed and rivetted to the worst, the most stagnated, and most corrupted part of the universe, in the lowest story of it, and the farthest from the arch of heaven, on the same floor with animals of the worst condition of the three species ; * yet, in his imagination, he soars above the orb of the moon, and casts the sky under his feet.

By the vanity of this same imagination he makes himself equal with God, attributes to himself divine qualities, withdraws and separates himself from the croud of the other creatures, carves for the animals his brethren and companions, and distributes such a portion of faculty and force to them as he thinks fit. How does he know, by the strength of his understanding, the internal and secret motives of the animals ? From what comparison, between them and us, does he infer them to be so stupid as he thinks them ? When I play with my cat, who knows whether puss is not more diverted with me than I am with puss ? We divert each other with monkey tricks. If I have my time of beginning or leaving off, she

ascribed to Seneca, ep. 65, but it is not in that epistle ; and I fancy, by the style of it, it is not to be met with in any other of Seneca's discourses. However this be, it may be thus rendered into English: the corruptible body stupifies the soul of man, and this early habitation dulls the imagination, which is employed on a multitude of objects.—At length I met with this passage in St. Augustine de Civitate Dei, lib. xii. cap. 15.

* That is to say, with the animals of the terrestrial species, always creeping upon the earth, and therefore of a worse kind than the two other species that fly in the air, or swim in the water.

also has hers. Plato, in his picture of the Golden Age, under Saturn, reckons, among the principal advantages that a man then enjoyed, his communication with the beasts, of which, inquiring and informing himself, he knew their true qualities, and wherein they differed, by which he acquired a very perfect intelligence and prudence, and led his life more happily than we can do. Need we a fuller proof to judge of human impudence with regard to beasts? This great author was of opinion, that nature, in the greater part of the corporeal form which she had given them, had regard only to the use of the prognostications that were drawn from them in his time. The defect which hinders the communication between us and them, why is it not as bad for us as for them? It is yet to determine, where the fault is, that we do not understand one another; for we do not understand them any more than they do us: for this very reason they may reckon us beasts, as we do them. It is no great wonder if we do not understand them, any more than we do the Basques and the Troglodites: and yet some have boasted, that they understood them; as, for instance, Apollonius Thyaneus,* Melampus,† Tiresias, Thales, &c. And since, as cosmographers say,‡ there are nations that revere a dog for their king, they must, of necessity, put some construction upon his voice and motions.

The beasts communicate their thoughts to one another, as well ther, as well as men. We must take notice of the parity there is between us: we have a tolerable understanding of their sense, and the beasts have of our's much in the same degree: they threaten, caress, and entreat us, and so do we them: as for the rest, we plainly discover, that there is a full and entire communication between them, and that not only those of the same species, but even of different species, understand one another.

---

* Apollodorus, lib. i. cap. 9, sect. 11.   † Id. lib. iii. cap. 6, sect. 7.
‡ Plin. Nat. Hist. lib. vi. sect. 30. Ex Africæ parte Ptoembari, Proemphanæ qui canem pro rege habent, motu ejus imperia augurantes. ..

Et mutæ pecudes, et denique secla ferarum,
Dissimiles fuerunt voces variasque cluere,
Cùm metus aut dolor est, aut cùm jam gaudia gliscunt.[*]

The tamer herds, and wilder sort of brutes,
Though we, and rightly too, conclude them mutes;
Yet utter dissonant and various notes
From gentler lungs, and more distended throats;
As fear, or grief, or anger do them move,
Or as they near approach the joys of love.

The dog has a certain kind of barking, by which
the horse knows he is angry; and another manner
of barking, which excites no fear: even in the very
beasts that make no noise at all, we easily conclude,
from the social offices we observe amongst them,
that they have some other way of communication:
their very motions serve the same purpose as language:

Non aliâ longè ratione atque ipsa videtur
Protrahere ad gestum pueros infantia linguæ.[†]

As infants who, for want of words, devise
Expressive motions with their hands and eyes.

And why not, as well as our dumb folks, dispute,
argue, and tell stories by signs: I have seen some
so ready at this, that, really, they wanted nothing
of the perfection of making themselves understood:
lovers are angry, reconciled, entreat, thank, make
assignations, and, in short, speak every thing by their
eyes:

El silentio encor suole
Haver prieghi e parole.[‡]

Silence itself, in the fond lover,
His am'rous passion will discover.

Would you think it? With our very hands we require, promise, call, dismiss, threaten, supplicate,
deny, interrogate, admire, number, confess, repent,
fear, confound, doubt, instruct, command, incite,

[*] Lucret. lib. v. ver. 1058, &c.   [†] Ibid.
[‡] Aminto of Tasso, atto ii. nel choro, ver. 34, 35.

encourage, swear, testify, accuse, condemn, absolve, affront, despise, defy, provoke, flatter, applaud, bless, humble, mock, reconcile, recommend, exalt, entertain, rejoice, complain, repine, despair, wonder, exclaim, keep silence, and what not; and all this with a variation and multiplication, even to the emulation of speech: with the head we invite, dismiss, own, disown, give the lie, welcome, honour, reverence, disdain, demand, refuse, rejoice, lament, caress, rebuke, submit, huff, exhort, threaten, assure, and inquire? Would you think it, the same with the eye-brows? with the shoulders? There is not a motion that does not speak both a language intelligible, without discipline, and a public language; from whence it follows, that, considering the variety and distinguished use of the others, this ought rather to be judged the proper language of human nature. I omit what necessity particularly suggests, on a sudden, to those who are speechless; the alphabets on the fingers, grammars in gesture, and the sciences that are only by them exercised and expressed; nor do I mention the nations which, Pliny says,* have no language but *nutus motusque membrorum;* "the "nods and motion of the limbs." An ambassador from the city of Abdera, after a long speech he made to Agis, king of Sparta, demanded of him, "What "answer must I return to my fellow-citizens?" "Tell them," said he, "that I have given thee "leave to say what thou wouldst, and as much as "thou wouldst, without ever speaking a word."† Is not this a silent way of speaking, and very easy to be understood?

The incapacity which is observed in the beha-viour of the   As to the rest, what kind of sufficiency is there in us which we do not observe in the operations of the animals? Is there a police regulated with more order, diversified with more charges and offices, and

---

* Plin. Nat. Hist. lib. vi. cap. 30.
† Plutarch, in his notable sayings of the Lacedæmonians, at the ord Agis.

more inviolably maintained than that of the bees? Is it to be imagined, that so regular a disposition of actions and offices could be made without reason and prudence?

His quidam signis atque hæc exempla sequuti,
Esse apibus partem divinæ mentis, et haustus
Æthereos dixere.*

Some, from such instances as these, conclude
That bees, in part, with reason are endu'd.

The swallows, that we see, at the return of the spring, searching all the corners of our houses for the most commodious places wherein to build their nests, do they seek without judgment, and out of a thousand, choose the fittest for their purpose, without discernment? And, in that elegant and admirable architecture of theirs, can the birds prefer a square figure to one that is round, an obtuse angle to a right one, without knowing their qualities and effects? Do they first bring clay, and then water, without knowing that the moisture of the latter softens the hardness of the former? Do they line their palace with moss or feathers, without foreseeing that it would be more soft and easy for the tender limbs of their young? Do they covet shelter from the rainy winds, and place their lodgings towards the east, without knowing the different qualities of those winds, and considering that one is more comfortable to them than another? Why does the spider make its web thicker at one place than another, and why make one sort of noose now, and then another, if it has not deliberation, thought, and conclusion?

We sufficiently discover, in most of their works, how much animals excel us, and how unable our art is to imitate them. We see, nevertheless, that, to our more coarse performances, we apply all our faculties, and the utmost stretch of our minds: why do we

* Virg. Georg. lib. iv. ver. 219, &c.

this princi-
ple in fa-
vour of the
beasts, a-
gainst men.
not set as much value upon them? why should we
attribute to I know not what natural and servile inclination works which excel all that we can perform both
by nature and art? In this, before we are aware, we
give them a great advantage over us, in making nature, with the tenderness of a mother, accompany
and lead them, as it were, by the hand, to all the
actions and conveniences of their life, whilst she
abandons us to chance and fortune, and to fetch,
by art, the things that are necessary for our preservation: at the same time denying us the means of
being able, by any instruction or struggle of the understanding, to attain to the natural capacity of
beasts; so that their brutal stupidity, in all conveniences, surpasses whatever our divine intelligence
can do: really, at this rate, we should have good
reason to call her a very unjust step-mother; but it
is not so, our polity is not so irregular and deformed.

Nature has
been kind-
er to man
than is com-
monly ima-
gined.
Nature has shown a tenderness to all her creatures
universally, and there is not one which she has not
amply furnished with all the means necessary for the
preservation of its being: for, as to the vulgar complaints which I hear men make (the extravagance of
whose notions lifts them up one while to the clouds,
and then sinks them down to the antipodes), that we
are the only animal abandoned naked upon the bare
earth, tied and bound, not having wherewithal to
arm and clothe himself, but by robbing the other
animals; whereas all the other creatures are covered,
by nature, with shells, husks, bark, hair, wool,
prickles, leather, down, feathers, scales, fleece, and
bristles, according as is necessary for their existence;
armed with claws or talons, teeth and horns, for attack as well as defence; and nature itself has equipped them with what is necessary for their swimming, running, flying, singing; whereas man knows
neither how to walk, speak, eat, or do any thing
but weep, without serving a sort of apprenticeship
to it:

Tum porrò puer, ut sævis projectus ab undis,
Navita nudus humi jacet infans, indigus omni
Vitali auxilio, cùm primùm in luminis oras
Nexibus ex alvo matris natura profudit,
Vagituque locum lugubri complet, ut æquum est,
Cui tantum in vitâ restet transire malorum.
At variæ crescunt pecudes, armenta, feræque,
Nec crepitaculâ eis opus est, nec cuiquam adhibenda est
Almæ nutricis blanda atque infracta loquela :
Nec varias quærunt vestes pro tempore cœli :
Denique non armis opus est, non mœnibus altis,
Queis sua tutentur, quando omnibus omnia largè,
Tellus ipsa parit, naturaque dædala rerum.*

Like to the wretched mariner, when tost
By raging seas upon the desart coast,
The infant is cast naked on the earth,
Wanting life's necessaries at its birth :
When nature first presents it to the day,
Freed from the mother's womb in which it lay ;
Straight with most doleful cries it fills the room,
Too sure presages of its woeful doom :
But beasts, both wild and tame, greater and less,
Do of themselves in bulk and strength increase ;
They need no rattle, nor the broken chat,
By which the nurse coaxes her child to prate :
They look not out for diff'rent robes to wear,
According to the seasons of the year ;
Nor for their safety citadels prepare,
Nor forge the murd'rous instruments of war ;
Since earth uncultivated freely grants,
And nature's lavish hands supply their wants.

These complaints, I say, are false : there is in the policy of the world, a greater equality, and a more uniform relation. Our skins are as good a defence for us against bad weather, as theirs ; witness the several nations who have not yet known the use of clothes. Our ancient Gauls were but slenderly clad, as well as the Irish, our neighbours, in so cold a climate. But we may better judge of this by ourselves ; for all those parts of the body that we are pleased to expose to the air, are very able to bear it : if there be a tender part about us, which is most

* Lucret. lib. v. ver. 223—235.

likely to suffer by cold, it must be the stomach, in
which digestion is performed, yet our ancestors
always went open-breasted; and our ladies, as tender
and delicate as they are, go sometimes bare as low as
the navel. Neither is the binding and swathing of infants more necessary, for the Lacedæmonian mothers[*]
brought up their children by leaving their limbs to
all the freedom of motion, without any ligature at
all. Our infancy cries are common to most of the
other animals, there being scarce any but what are
observed to groan and bemoan themselves a long
time after their birth: it is a behaviour natural to
their weak condition.

As to the practice of eating, it is in us, as it is in
them, natural, and without instruction:

> *Sentit enim quisque suam quam possit abuti.*[†]

> For every one soon finds his nat'ral force,
> Which he, or better, may employ, or worse.

Who doubts but an infant, when able to feed itself,
may make a shift to get its living; and the earth
produces wherewithal to supply its necessity without
culture; but if not at all times, neither does it so
to the beasts; witness the provision we see the ants
and other creatures hoard up against the barren seasons of the year. Those nations, lately discovered,
with meat and natural drink, without care and without cookery, demonstrate to us, that bread is not
our only food; and that, even without tillage, we
should have been plentifully furnished with all that
is necessary for us; probably more so than at present:

> *Et tellus nitidas fruges vinetaque læta*
> *Sponte suâ primum mortalibus ipsa creavit:*
> *Ipsa dedit dulces fœtus, et patulâ læta,*
> *Quæ nunc vix nostro grandescunt aucta labore,*
> *Conterimusque boves, et vires agricolarum.*[‡]

> The earth did first spontaneously afford
> Choice fruits and wines to furnish out the board;

---

* Plutarch in the Life of Lycurgus, chap. 18.
† Lucret. lib. v. ver. 1032.   ‡ Lucret. lib. ii. ver. 1157, &c.

With herbs and flow'rs unsown in verdant fields,
But scarce by art so good a harvest yields ;
Though men and oxen mutually have strove,
With all their utmost force the soil t' improve :

the depravity of our appetites being too great for any
thing that we can invent to satisfy them.

In respect to arms, we have more, that are natural, than most of the other animals ; more various
motions of the limbs, and acquire more service from
them by nature, and without instruction. Those Man is fur-
who are trained up to fight naked, are sure to nished with
throw themselves into the like hazards that we do. weapons.
If any of the beasts surpass us in this advantage, we
surpass many others : and as to the industry of fortifying the body, and guarding it by acquired means,
we have it by the instinct and law of nature. So the
elephant grinds and whets the teeth he makes use of
in war (for he has particular teeth for that service,
which he spares, and never puts to any other use.)
When the bulls go to fight, they toss and throw
the dust all round them. The wild boars whet their
tusks ; and the ichneumon, when he is to engage
with the crocodile, fortifies his body, covers and
crusts it all over with a slimy sort of well-mixed mud,
which sticks to him like a cuirass ; and, may we not
say, it is as natural for us to arm with wood and iron ?

As to speech, it is certain, that, if it be not natural, it is not necessary ; yet it is my opinion, that, Whether
if an infant was to be brought up in a desert, remote speech is
from all society with mankind (which would be a man.
trial very hard to make), he would have some kind
of speech to express his meaning by : and it is not
to be supposed, that nature has denied us the means
which it has given to several other animals : for what The beasts
but speech is that faculty, which we discern in them, have a lan-
of complaining, rejoicing, calling to one another, for their own.
help, and the invitations of one another to love ; all
which they express by different sounds ? And why
should they not speak to one another ? They speak
to us, and we to them : in how many several tones

do we speak to our dogs, and they answer us? We
converse with them in another sort of style, and with
other appellations than we do with birds, swine,
oxen, horses; and alter the idiom according to the
species:

> Cosi per entro loro schiera bruna,
> S' ammusa l' una con l' altra formica,
> Forse aspiar lor via, et lor fortuna.*
>
> Thus from one swarm of ants some sally out,
> To spy another's stock, or mark its rout.

Lactantius, I think, attributes to beasts, not only
speech, but laughter: and the difference of language,
which is manifest amongst us, according to the variety of countries, is also observed in animals of one
and the same species. Aristotle, to this purpose, instances in the various calls of partridges, according
to the situations of the places:

> ———Variæque volucres
>
> Longe alias aliæ jaciunt in tempore voces,
>
> Et partim mutant cum tempestatibus und
> Raucisonos cantus.†
>
> And sev'ral birds do, from their warbling throats,
> At sev'ral times utter quite diff'rent notes;
> And some their hoarse ones with the seasons change.

But the thing to be known is, what language would
such a child speak, of which what is said by conjecture is not very probable?

Why those who are born deaf, do not speak. If, in opposition to this opinion, any man will tell
me, that they who are born deaf do not speak; I
answer, that this is the case, not so much because
they could not receive instruction to speak by the
ear, as because the faculty of hearing, which they
are deprived of, has a relation to that of speaking,
and they hold together by a natural connection, in
such a manner, that what we speak we must first

---

* Dante nel Purgatorio, cant. xxiv. ver. 34, &c.
† Lucret. lib. v. ver. 1077—1080, 1082, 1083.

speak to our own breasts, and make it sound in our ears, before we utter it to others.

All this I have said to prove the resemblance which there is in human things, and bring us back, and join us to the crowd. We are neither above nor below the rest. All that is under heaven (says the wise man) is subject to one law, and one fortune : *Men and the animals alike subject to the law of nature.*

> *Indupedita suis fatalibus omnia vinclis.**
> —————— All things remain
> Bound and entangled in one fatal chain.

There is some difference ; there are several ranks and degrees, but it is under the aspect of one and the same nature :

> —— *Res quæque suo ritu procedit, et omnes*
> *Fœdere naturæ certo discrimine servant.*†
> All things, arising from their proper cause,
> Remain distinct, and follow nature's laws.

Man must be confined and restrained within the barriers of this polity. The miserable creature is really not in a condition to put one leg over the fence : he is fettered and embarrassed, he is subject to the same obligation with the other creatures of his rank ; and his state is very mean, without any prerogative, or true and substantial pre-eminence. That which he ascribes to himself in his own fancy and opinion, has no reality. And if it be the real case, that he alone of all living creatures hath this privilege of imagination, and this irregularity of sentiments, representing to him that which is, that which is not, and the false and the true, as he pleases ; it is an advantage very dearly bought, and for which he has very little reason to value himself, since from hence arises the principal source of the evils that oppress him, sin, sickness, irresolution, affliction, and despair. I say, therefore (to return to my subject), that there is no appearance of reason to suppose that

* Lucr. lib. v. ver. 874.   † Lucr. lib. v. ver. 921, 922.

Animals
free agents
as well as
mankind.

the beasts should, by a natural and forced inclination, do the same things that we do by our choice and endeavour. We ought from like effects to conclude like faculties, and from richer effects richer faculties; and, by consequence, to confess, that this same reason, this same method, by which we operate, is common also to the animals, or some other that is better. Why should we imagine this natural constraint in them, while we experience no such effect from it in ourselves? Considering, moreover, that it is more honourable to be guided, and obliged to act regularly by a natural and inevitable disposition, and more approaching to that of the divine Being, than to act regularly by a fortuitous liberty; and more safe to trust the reins of our conduct to nature than to ourselves. The vanity of our presumption is the reason that we had rather ascribe our sufficiency to our own strength, than to the bounty of nature; and that we enrich the other animals with the bounties of nature, and renounce them in their favour, purely for the sake of honouring and ennobling ourselves with goods acquired; a humour which I take to be very silly, for I would as much value favours that were entirely my own by nature, as those that I acquire by education. We cannot enjoy greater happiness than to be the favourite of God and nature.

The fox's
faculty of
reasoning.

The Thracians, when they purpose to pass over any frozen river, turn out a fox before them, which, when he comes to the bank,* lays his ear down to the ice to listen if he can hear the noise of the current from a remote or nearer distance; and, according as he thereby finds the ice to be more or less thick, he draws back or goes forward. Now should we see a fox do thus, should we not have ground to conclude, that he reasoned just in the same manner as ourselves; and that it is a reasoning and consequence derived from natural sense, or a perception in the fox, that what makes a noise moves, that what

* Plutarch de Solertia Anim. &c. cap. 12 of Amyot's translation.

moves is not congealed, that what is not congealed
is liquid, and that what is liquid yields to weight?
For to ascribe this only to the quickness of the sense
of hearing without reasoning, and making an inference, is an argument that cannot be admitted. In
the same manner are we to judge of the many various
tricks and inventions, by which the beasts secure
themselves from the plots we form to surprise them.

If we think to make any advantage, even of this
argument, that it is in our power to seize them, to
employ them in our service, and to use them at our
pleasure; it is but still the same advantage that we
take one of another. We have our slaves upon this
condition. And were not the Climacidæ, women of
Syria that crouched to the ground on their hands and
feet to serve as a footstool,[*] or a step ladder, for the
ladies to get into their coaches, instances of this observation? The greatest part of free persons surrender their life and being to the power of another, for
very trivial advantages. The wives and concubines
of the Thracians contend who shall be chosen to be
slain[†] upon the tombs of their husbands. Have tyrants ever failed of finding men enough entirely at
their devotion and disposal? What armies have
bound themselves after this manner to their generals!
The form of the oath, in this severe school of fencers,
who were to fight it out to the last, was in these
terms: " We swear to suffer ourselves to be chained,
" burned, wounded, and killed with the sword, and
" to endure all that true gladiators suffer from their
" master, most religiously engaging both bodies and
" souls in his service :"

> *Ure meum, si vis, flammâ caput. et pete ferro*
> *Corpus, et intorto verbere terga seca.[‡]*
>
> Stab me, or lash me till my shoulders bleed,
> Or, with the red-hot iron, burn my head.

* Men slaves to other men, as well as the brutes are.

---

* Plutarch, chap. 3, in his discourse how to distinguish the flatterer from the friend.
† Herodot. lib. v. p. 331.　　‡ Tibullus, lib. i. eleg. x. ver. 21, 22.

Funeral obsequies of the Scythian kings. This was an obligation indeed, and yet there was one year in which 10,000 entered into it, and thereby lost their lives. When the Scythians interred their kings, they strangled upon his body the most favoured of his concubines, his cup-bearer, the master of his horse, his chamberlain, the gentleman-usher of his chamber, and cook.* And, upon his anniversary, they killed fifty horses, mounted by fifty pages, whom they impaled alive, and there left them, stuck by way of state, round his tomb.

What care men take of animals. The men who serve us come off cheaper, though they are not treated with all that nicety and favour, with which we treat our hawks, horses, and dogs. How anxious are we for their good? I do not think, that the lowest degree of slaves would willingly do that for their masters, which even princes think it an honour to do for their beasts. Diogenes, seeing his relations solicitous to redeem him from servitude, "They are fools," said he, "it is that which treats "and nourishes me, and that serves me."† And they who maintain beasts, may be said rather to serve them, than be served by them. And yet the beasts are in this respect the more generous, that never did a lion serve another lion, nor one horse submit to another for want of spirit. As we go to the chase of beasts, so do tigers and lions to the chase of men; and they do the same execution one upon the other, dogs upon hares, pikes upon tenches, swallows upon flies, and sparrow-hawks upon blackbirds and larks:

—————— Serpente ciconia pullos
Nutrit, et inventa per devia rura lacerta

Et leporem, aut capream, famulæ Jovis, et generosæ
In saltu venantur aves.‡

* Herodot. lib. iv. p. 280.
† Diogenes Laertius in the Life of Diogenes the Cynic, lib. v. sect. 75.
‡ Juv. sat. xiv. ver. 74, &c.

The stork her young ones nourishes with snakes
And lizards found in bye-ways and in lakes;
Jove's bird, and others of the nobler kind,
Hunt in the woods the hare and kid to find.

We divide the quarry, as well as the labour and
pains, with our hawks and hounds. And above
Amphipolis, in Thrace, the falconers divide the
booty between themselves and their wild hawks,
into two equal shares; just as along the Palus Mœ-
otis, if the fisherman does not leave an equal share of
what he catches to the wolves, they go immediately
and tear his nets to pieces.

As we have a sort of fishing which is managed Subtlety of
animals in
hunting.
more by cunning than force, namely, angling with
the hook and line, so the like is to be seen among
the animals. Aristotle says, that the cuttle-fish
casts a long gut from its neck like a line, which it
lets out and draws in at pleasure; and that, as soon
as it perceives any of the small fish approaching, it
gives it leave to nibble the end of this gut, while it
hides itself in the sand, or mud, and draws it to him
gently, till the little fish is so near, that, with one
spring, it can make a prey of it.

With respect to strength, there is not a creature in The
strength of
man infe-
rior to that
of animals.
the world exposed to so many injuries as man.
Not to mention a whale, an elephant, a crocodile,
and such sort of animals, of which one alone is
enough to put many men to flight: a swarm of lice
put an end to the dictatorship of Sylla, and the
heart and life of a great and triumphant emperor
was the breakfast of a little worm.

Why do we boast, that it is only for human know- Beasts di-
stinguish
what may
be of use
to them in
their mala-
dies.
ledge and learning to distinguish things useful to life,
and of service in sickness, from those that are not so,
and to know the virtue of rhubarb and the polypody?
When we see the goats of Candia, after being
wounded by an arrow, run and single out dittany,
among a million of herbs, fit for their cure: when
we see the tortoise, after eating a viper, search immediately for majoram to purge itself; when we see

see the dragon rub and clear its eyes with fennel;
the storks give themselves clysters with the water of
the sea, and elephants in battle not only pluck out
the javelin and dart that stick in the bodies of themselves and their companions, but those also of their
masters (witness king Porus, whom Alexander defeated), and that so dexterously, that we could not
do it ourselves, with so little pain to the wounded
person: when we see all this, I say, why do we not
confess in the same manner, that this is knowledge
and prudence? To argue, in order to disparage them,
that they know it only by instinct, is not robbing
them of their claim to knowledge and prudence, but
ascribing it to them with more reason than to us, to
the honour of so infallible a school-mistress.

Dogs ca- pable of reason. Chrysippus, though in all other things he had as
mean an opinion of the condition of the animals
as any other philosopher, observing the motions of a
dog (that had either lost his master, or was in pursuit of some prey) at a cross-way, where three roads
met, seeing him lay his nose in one road after another, and observing that, when he had no manner
of scent of what he was seeking in two of them, he
darted*. into the third road without any hesitation,
the philosopher was forced to confess, that the dog
must reason with himself in this manner, " I have
" traced my master to this cross-way, and one of
" these three roads he must needs be gone; but I
" do not perceive that he took this road or that;
" he must therefore infallibly be gone the other;"
and that, having made himself sure that he was in
the right by this inference and reasoning, he made
no further use of his sense in the third road, nor laid
his nose to it, but ran on in it, without any other
motive except the strength of his reason. This passage, which is the pure heart of reasoning, and this
stating of propositions divided and united together,
and the proper examination of the parts, is it not of

---

* Sextus Empiricus, Pyrrh. Hypot. lib. j. cap. 14, p. 15,

as much use to the dog to know it of himself, as if he was instructed in the knowledge of that figure in geometry, which they call a trapezium?

Nor are the animals incapable of being instructed *Animals capable of being instructed.* in our fashion. We teach blackbirds, ravens, magpies, parrots, &c. to talk; and the readiness with which we must acknowledge they give us their voice and breath, rendering both so supple and pliant as to be formed and restrained to a certain number of letters and syllables, shows us that they are endued with reason, which renders them so docile and willing to learn. Every one has seen enough, I should think, of the many monkey tricks that are played by dogs, which tumblers lead about the streets; their dancings, in which they keep exact measure with the sound of the music; their various motions and leaps, at the command of their leader; but I am more struck with admiration at the performance, which is nevertheless very common, of those dogs that lead the blind beggars in the fields, and in towns: I have taken notice how they stop at such doors where they have been used to receive charity, how they keep out of the way of coaches and carts, even when there has been room enough for themselves to pass: I have seen them, in walking along by a town-ditch, get out of the plain smooth path, and choose a worse, only to keep their master farther from the ditch. How could this dog be made to conceive that it was his business to be mindful only of the safety of his master, and to prefer his service to his own convenience? And how came he to know, that a way was wide enough for him, which was not so for a blind man? Could he comprehend all this without a faculty of reasoning?

We must not forget what Plutarch tells us* of a *A dog which feigned itself dead.* dog he saw at Rome, with the emperor Vespasian, the father, at the theatre of Marcellus. This dog belonged to a tumbler, who acted the farce of a pos-

* Plutarch de Solertia Animalium, cap. 18.

ture-master, and the dog also played a part.
Amongst other tricks, he was commanded to feign
himself dead for a space of time, by reason of eating
some poisonous drug. After he had swallowed a
piece of bread, which was pretended to be this drug,
he began soon to tremble and stagger, and at last,
stretching himself out on the ground, and appearing
stone-dead, he suffered himself to be dragged from
one place to another, as the business of the farce required; and, when he knew it was time for him to
come to life again, he began first to stir himself very
gently, as if he was just awakened out of a profound
slumber, and, lifting up his head, stared about him,
in such a manner as surprised all the spectators.

The oxen in the royal gardens of Susa.

The oxen that were employed in watering the
royal gardens at Susa, turned certain great wheels to
draw the water, to which buckets were hung (whereof there are many such in Languedoc) and they were
ordered to draw each a hundred turns a day. They
were so accustomed to this number,* that it was impossible, by any force, to make them draw one turn
more; but, when they had done their task, they
stopped quite short. We cannot count a hundred,
till we are a little advanced in years; and have lately discovered nations that have no knowledge at all
of numbers.

Nightin-gales teach their young to sing.

It requires a greater share of understanding to
give instruction than to receive it. But setting
aside what Democritus held and proved, that we
learn most of the arts we have from the other animals, as weaving and sewing from the spider, building from the swallow, music from the swan and the
nightingale, and the use of medicine from several of
the animals, by imitating them: Aristotle is of opinion, that the nightingales spend a great deal of
time and pains in teaching their young to sing; and
that to this it is owing, that those which we breed up in
cages, that have not had time to learn of their dams,

---

* Plutarch de Solertia Animalium, cap. 20.

want much of the grace of their singing. From
hence we may judge, that they improve by discipline and study : and, even amongst the wild ones,
every one is not alike, since each takes its learning
according to its capacity. And so jealous are they
one of another whilst learning, and they contend
so obstinately, that the vanquished drops down dead
for want of breath, rather than voice. The younger
nightingales ruminate, are pensive, and begin with
the imitation of some staves : the scholar listens to
his master's instruction, and follows it very carefully.
They are silent by turns : one may hear faults corrected, and observe some reproofs by the teacher.

I have formerly seen, says Arrius, an elephant Elephants
having a cymbal hung at each leg, and another at instructed
his head, at the sound of which all the others danced to dance to music.
round him, rising and falling at certain cadences,
according as they were guided by the instrument ;
and the harmony was delightful. At the spectacles
of Rome, it was common to see elephants trained
up to move and dance to vocal music, and such
dances too, wherein were such figurings in and out,
such crossings, and such a variety of steps, as were
very difficult to learn. Some have been known to
practise their lessons in private by themselves with
great care and study, that they might not be chid
and corrected by their keepers.*

But the story of a magpie, for which we have the A barber's
authority of Plutarch† himself, is very strange. This magpie that imita-
bird, which was in a barber's shop at Rome, imitated ted the
with her voice every thing that she heard to a degree sound of a trumpet.
that was miraculous. It happened one day that
some trumpets were sounded a good while before the
shop : after that, and all the next day, mag was very
pensive, quite mute, and melancholy ; which every
body wondered at, and believed that the sound of
the trumpets had totally stupified and stunned it,

* Pliny affirms the same thing, Nat. Hist. lib. viii. cap. 3.
† Plutarch de Solertia Animalium, cap. 18.

and that her voice and her hearing were both gone
together. But it appeared, at length, that it had
been in a profound meditation, and musing all the
while, within itself, how to exercise and prepare its
voice to imitate the sound of those trumpets, so that
the first essay it made was perfectly to imitate their
repetitions, stops, and changes; and this new lesson made it quit and despise all it had learned
before.

Though it be not quite in method, which I am
sensible I do not strictly pursue, nay, more in the
examples I bring, than in the rest of my discourses:
I will not omit to produce another instance, of a dog,
which, Plutarch says, he once saw aboard a ship:
this dog, being unable to come at some oil at the
bottom of a jar, which he could not reach with his
tongue, by reason of the narrow mouth of the
vessel, went and fetched stones, and let them fall
into the jar,* till the oil rose so high that he could
lap it. What is this, but the effect of great subtlety? It is said the ravens of Barbary do the same,
when the water they would drink is too low.†

This action bears a near resemblance to what is
reported of elephants by Juba, a king of their country, that when, by the craft of the hunters, one of
them is caught in the deep pits that are dug, and
covered over with bushes to intrap them, its com-
panions‡ hasten with stones and logs of wood to
enable him to get out. But this creature, in many
other performances, discovers such a degree of human capacity, that were I to give a detail of all the
facts, known by experience, I would easily gain assent to what I have commonly maintained, that there
is a wider difference between such and such men,
than there is between such a man and such a beast.
The keeper of an elephant, at a private house in
Syria, robbed him at every meal of one half of his

*The inven-
tion of a
dog to get
oil out of a
jar.*

*Of the sub-
tlety and
penetra-
tion of ele-
phants.*

---

* Plutarch de Solertia Animalium, cap. 12.   † Id. ibid. cap. 12.
‡ Id. ibid. cap. 16.

allowance. One day his master took in his head to feed the elephant himself, and poured into his manger the full measure of barley, which he had ordered for his meal. The elephant, giving his keeper an angry look, separated one half from the other with his trunk, and thrust it to one side,[*] thereby discovering the wrong that his keeper had done to him. And another, having a keeper who mixed stones with his provender, to swell the measure of it, went to the pot where he was boiling meat for his own dinner, and filled it with ashes.[†] These are facts of a private nature; but all the world has seen, and knows, that, in all the armies of the Eastern regions, their greatest strength consisted in elephants, with which they did greater execution beyond comparison, than we do now with our artillery, which is used in a pitched battle, as it were in the stead of elephants. This may easily be supposed by those who are acquainted with the ancient histories :

> —— Siquidem Tyrio servire solebant
> Annibali, et nostris ducibus, regique Molosso
> Horum majores, et dorso ferre cohortes
> Partem aliquam belli, et euntem in prœlia turrim.[‡]

The sires of these huge elephants did yield
To carry Hannibal into the field ;
Our gen'rals also did those beasts bestride,
And, mounted thus, Pyrrhus his foes defied.
Nay more, upon their backs they us'd to bear
Castles with armed cohorts to the war.

To be sure they placed a very great confidence in the fidelity and understanding of those beasts, when they posted them in the vanguard of the battle, where the least stop, by reason of the great bulk and weight of their bodies, the least fright that should have made them face about upon their own people, would have been enough to have ruined the whole army. There are but few examples where it has hap-

---

[*] Plutarch de Solertia Animalium, cap. 12.   [†] Id. ib.
[‡] Juv. sat. xii. cap. 107, &c.

pened, that they have fallen foul upon their own
troops; though we ourselves break into our own bat-
talions, and rout one another. They had the charge,
not of one simple motion only, but of a great variety, which they were to perform in the battle, as
the dogs of the Spaniards had when they first conquered the Indies,* to which they not only gave pay,
but a share in their spoil: and those animals showed
as much dexterity and judgment in pursuing the victory, and stopping the pursuit; in attacking or re-
treating, when occasion required; and in the distinguishing of friends from foes, as they did of ardour
and fury. We admire and value things that are
strange, more than those which are common. I had
not else amused myself with this long register. For
I fancy, whoever will strictly scrutinise into what we
commonly see in the animals which we have amongst
us, may there find as wonderful effects as those we
collect from different ages and countries. It is one
and the same nature that runs her course, and whoever shall sufficiently consider the present state of
things, may from thence certainly conclude both the
future and the past.

Men that came into France from foreign countries deemed savages.

I have formerly seen men brought hither by sea
from very distant countries, whose language being
quite unintelligible to us, and, moreover, their mien,
countenance, and clothes, being quite different from
ours, who of us did not think them savages and
brutes? Who did not impute it to stupidity, and
want of common sense, to see them mute, ignorant
of the French tongue, ignorant of our compliments
and cringes, our port and behaviour, which must for-
sooth be a model for all the human race. All that
seems strange to us, and that we do not understand,
we are sure to condemn; so it happens in the judgment we form of the beasts. They have several qualities similar to ours: from these we may by com-

---

* This is no more than what several nations had practised long
before. Pliny, lib. viii. cap. 40. Ælian. Var. Hist. lib. xiv. cap. 46.

parison draw some conjecture; but, from such as
are peculiar to themselves, what do we know of
them? Horses, dogs, the black cattle, sheep, birds,
and most of the animals that live with us, know our
voice, and suffer it to be their guide. So did Crassus and Lamprey,[*] which came to him at his call, as
the eels do in the lake Arethusa. And I have seen
many reservoirs, where the fish run to eat at a certain
call of their feeders:

> —— *Nomen habent, et ad magistri*
> *Vocem quisque sui venit citutus.*[†]
> They every one have names, and, one and all,
> Appear directly at their own master's call.

Of this we are capable to form a judgment. We
may also say, that the elephants have some share of
religion; since, after several ablutions and purifications, we see them lift up their trunks like arms, and,
with their eyes fixed towards the rising sun, continue
a long time, at certain hours of the day, in meditation and contemplation, of their own accord, without instruction or command. But, because we do
not see any thing like this in the other animals, we
are not from thence to conclude that they have no
religion at all, nor can we have any sort of comprehension of what is concealed from us.

Whether the elephants have any sentiments of religion.

Yet we discern something in this transaction taken
notice of by the philosopher Cleanthes, because it
somewhat resembles what we do ourselves. "He
"saw," he says,[§] "a swarm of ants going from
"their hill, with the dead body of an ant towards
"another hill, from which many other ants came
"forward to meet them, as if to confer with them;
"and, after having been some time together, the lat-
"ter returned to consult, you may suppose, with
"the community of their hill, and so made two or

Remarkable instance of a sort of conference between ants.

* Plutarch de Solertia Anim. cap. 24.
† Martial. lib. iv. ep. 30, ver. 6, 7.
‡ Plin. Nat. Hist. lib. viii, cap. 1.
§ Plutarch de Solertia Animal. cap. 12.

" three journies to finish their capitulation. In the
" conclusion, those that came last, brought to the
" first a worm out of their burrow, as it were for the
" ransom of the deceased ; which worm the first
" carried home on their backs, leaving the dead body
" with the others." That was the construction
which Cleanthes put upon this transaction, by which
he would give us to understand, that those animals
which have no voice have nevertheless mutual deal-
ings and communication, of which it is our own
fault that we do not participate, and for that reason
foolishly take upon us to give our opinion of it.

A little
fish that
can stop
a ship at
sea.

But they produce other effects far beyond our capacity, which it is so difficult for us to attain by imitation, that we can hardly conceive of it by imagination. Several are of opinion, that in that last great
sea-fight, wherein Antony was defeated by Augustus,
his admiral's galley was stopped, in the midst of her
course, by that small fish which the Latins called a
remora, which has the peculiar property of staying
all sorts of vessels to which it sticks. And the emperor Caligula,* sailing with a great navy on the
coast of Romania, his single galley was stopped on a
sudden by this same fish, which he caused to be
taken, stuck as it was to the keel of his ship, very
angry that so little an animal could resist the sea,
and the winds, and the force of all his oars, by being
only fastened by the beak (for it is a shell-fish) to
his galley ; and was moreover astonished, not without great reason, that, when it was brought to him
in the long-boat, it had lost that power.

A Hedge-
hog that
had fore-
knowledge
of what
wind
would
blow.

A citizen of Cyzicus formerly† acquired the reputation of a good mathematician, for having learned
the property of a hedge-hog. It has its burrow open
in divers places, and to several winds ; and, foreseeing the change of the wind, stops the hole on that
side ; which that citizen perceiving, gave the city

* Plin. Nat. Hist, lib. xxii. cap. 1.
† Plutarch de Solertia Animal. cap. 16, in fine.

certain predictions to what corner the wind would
shift next.

The camelion assumes a colour from * the place of
its situation; but the pourcontrel, or polypode fish,
gives itself what colour it will, according as it has
occasion to conceal itself from what it fears, or what
it designs to seize: in the camelion the change is
passive, but in the pourcontrel it is active. We have
some changes of colour, as in fear, anger, shame, and
other passions, which alter our complexions; but
the cause of this is suffering, as it is with the camelion. It is in the power of the jaundice, indeed, to
make us yellow, but it is not in the power of our
own will. Now these effects, which we discover in
other animals, greater than those which we ourselves
produce, imply some more excellent faculty in them,
which is hidden from us; as it is to be presumed,
that they have several other qualities and powers, of
which no appearances have yet come to us.

Of all the predictions of old time, the most ancient, and the most certain, were those taken from
the flight of birds. We have nothing like it, nor so
wonderful. Such was the rule and method of moving
their wings, from whence the consequences of future things were inferred, that the flight must necessarily be guided by some excellent means to so
noble an operation; for to attribute this great effect
to some natural direction, without understanding,
consent, and reason, in that which produces it, is an
opinion absolutely false. That it is so, appears from
the torpedo, or cramp-fish, which has this quality,
not only to benumb all the members that touch it,
but even, through the fishing-nets, to transmit a stiff-
ness to the hands of those that move and handle
them; nay, more, if water be poured on it, a
numbness† will ascend from it against the stream,

Change of colour in the camelion, and pourcon-trel, or polypode fish.

Predictions from the flight of birds.

* Plutarch de Solertia Animal. cap. 28.
† Montaigne would mislead us here, or, rather, is misled himself; for, because the cramp-fish benumbs the members of those who
touch it, and because the cranes, swallows, and the other birds of

and stupify the sense of feeling, through even the medium of water. This is a surprising power, but it is not useless to the cramp-fish: it knows it, and makes use of it; so that, in order to catch its prey, it lurks under the mud, that other fishes swimming over it, struck and benumbed with this cold quality of the cramp-fish, may fall into its power.

Birds of passage foresee the change of the seasons. The cranes, swallows, and other birds of passage, shifting their residence according to the seasons of the year, show plainly, that they have a knowledge of their own prescience, and put it in practice.

Bitches judge which is the best of their whelps. We are assured, by huntsmen, that the best way to choose out of a litter of whelps that which is fittest to be preserved, is to leave it to the choice of the dam, as thus: take them out of the kennel, a little way, and lay them down, when the first that she carries back will certainly be the best, as will that also be which she first runs to save, if you surround the kennel with fire, as if you intended to burn it. By this it appears, that they have a prog-

passage change their climate according to the seasons of the year, it by no means follows that the predictions, pretended to be derived from the flight of birds, are founded on certain faculties, which those birds have, of discovering things future to such as take the pains to watch their various motions. The vivacity of our author's genius has made him, in this place, confound things together that are very different. For the properties of the cramp-fish, cranes, and swallows, appear from sensible effects; but the predictions said to be derived from the flight of certain birds, by virtue of the rule and method of the motion of their wings, are only founded upon human imaginations, the reality whereof was never proved; which have varied according to times and places, and which, at length, have lost all credit with the very people that were most possessed with them: but I am of opinion, that Montaigne only makes use here of the divining faculty of the birds, to puzzle those dogmatists who decide so positively, that the animals have neither reason nor intellect; in this he has imitated Sextus Empiricus, in Pyrr. Hypot. lib. i. cap. 14, p. 16, who, attacking the dogmatist on this very article, says expressly, " That it cannot be denied, that the " birds have the use of speech, and more penetration than we " have; because, not only by their knowledge of the present, but " also of things future, they discover the latter, to such as are ca- " pable of understanding them, by their voice, and several other " means."

nosticating quality, which we have not; or that they
have some sense to judge of their whelps, which is
different from and quicker than ours.

The manner of coming into the world, of engen-
dering, nourishing, acting, moving, living, and
dying of beasts, so much resembling our manner,
whatever we retrench from their motives, and add
to our own condition above theirs, can by no means
proceed from the discussion of our reason. For the
regimen of our health, the physicians prescribe to
us the beasts' manner of living for our imitation; for
this is a common old saying:

> *Tenez chaults les pieds et la teste;*
> *Au demeurant, vivez en beste.*
>
> Keep hands and feet warm; for the rest,
> Thou must resolve to live a beast.

Viz. to eat and drink no more than will do thee good.

The chief of all natural actions is generation: we
have a certain disposition of members to that end,
which is the most proper for us; nevertheless,
we are ordered by Lucretius to conform to the
gesture and posture of the brutes as the most
effectual.

> ———————— *More ferarum,*
> *Quadrupedumque magis vitu, plerumque putantur*
> *Concipere uxores: quia sic loca sumere possunt,*
> *Pectoribus positis, sublatis semina lumbis.*[*]

And the same authority condemns, as hurtful, those
indiscreet and impudent motions, which the women
have added, of their own invention, to whom it proposes the more temperate and modest pattern and
practice of the beasts of their own sex:

> *Nam mulier prohibet se concipere atque repugnat,*
> *Clunibus ipsa viri Venerem si læta retractet,*
> *Atque exossato ciet omni pectore fluctus;*
> *Ejicit enim falci recta regione viaque*
> *Vomerem, atque locis avertit seminis ictum.*[†]

---

[*] Lucret. lib. iv. ver. 1258, &c.   [†] Idem. ib. ver. 1269, &c.

Proof of
the justice
and equity
of the
beasts.

If it be justice to render to every one their due, the beasts that serve, love, and defend their benefactors, and which pursue and fall upon strangers, and those who offend, do, in this, show a certain appearance of our justice, as also in observing a very just equality in the distribution of what they have to their young.

Their
friendship
more lively
and con-
stant than
that of the
men.

As to friendship, theirs is, without comparison, more lively and constant than that of human beings. When king Lysimachus died, his dog Hyrcanus lay upon his bed, obstinately refusing to eat or drink; and, on the day that his master's corpse was burnt, ran out of the house, and leaped into the fire, where he was also consumed.* The dog of one Pyrrhus did the like, which would not stir from off his master's bed from the time he died; and, when they carried him to be burnt, suffered itself to be carried along with him, and, finally, leaped upon the pile where they burnt the body of his master.† There are certain inclinations of affection that sometimes arise in us without the dictates of reason, which proceed from an accidental temerity, which some call sympathy: of this the beasts are also capable as well as we. We see horses contract such an acquaintance with one another, that we have much ado to make them eat or travel when separated. We observe them to be fond of a particular colour in those of their own kind, and, where they meet with it, run to it with great joy and tokens of goodwill, but have a dislike and hatred for some other colour.

The ani-
mals deli-
cate, whim-
sical, and
extrava-
gant in
their a-
mours, as
well as hu-
man beings.

The animals make choice in their amours as well as we, and cull out their females: they are not exempt from jealousies, and malice that is vehement and implacable, any more than we: their desires are either natural or necessary, as in eating or drinking; or natural and not necessary, as the coupling with the females; or they are neither natural nor neces-

* Plutarch de Solertia Animal. cap. 14.   † Id. ib.

sary, and of this last sort are, in a manner, all the
desires of human beings: they are all superfluous and
artificial; for one would wonder to think how little
will suffice nature, how little she has left us to desire:
the cookery of our kitchens is not of her ordering.
The stoics say, that a man might live upon an olive
a day. The delicate wines we have are not of nature's prescription, nor the over-charging the appetites of love;

> ————————————*Neque illa*
> *Magno prognatum deposcit consule cunnum.* *
> Nor, when it rages with its wild st fire,
> Does it a maid of quality require.

These roving desires, which the ignorance of good,
and a mistaken opinion, have infused into us, are so
many that they almost exclude all the natural ones,
just in the same manner as if there was so great a
number of strangers in a city, as to thrust out the
native inhabitants, and extinguish their ancient
power and authority, by usurping and engrossing it
entirely to themselves. The animals are much more
regular than we, and confine themselves, with greater
moderation, within the bounds which nature has prescribed; yet not so strictly but they bear some resemblance with our debauches: and, as there have
been instances of men that have been hurried by furious lust after beasts, so there have been the like of
beasts who have been smitten with the love of men,
and admitted the monstrous love of differing species:
witness the elephant,† who was rival to Aristophanes
the grammarian, when he courted a wench that used
to sell nosegays in the city of Alexandria, to whom
the elephant performed all the offices of the most
passionate suitor; for, going through the fruit-mar-
ket, he took some in his trunk, and carried it to her:
he kept her, as much as possible, in his sight, and

* Hor. lib. i. sat. 2. † Plutarch de Solert. Animal. cap. 16.

would sometimes run his trunk in her bosom, under her handkerchief, to feel her breasts. They tell also of a dragon that was in love with a maid; of a goose enamoured with an infant in the city of Asoph; and of a ram that was an humble servant of the minstrelless Glaucia: and we, every now and then, see baboons violently in love with women: we see also certain male animals that are fond of males of their own species: Oppianus and others give us some examples of the veneration* which beasts have to their kindred in their acts of copulation, though experience often shows us the contrary:

—— Nec habetur turpe juvencæ
Ferre patrem tergo: fit equo sua filia conjux :
Quasque creavit, init pecudes caper ; ipsaque cujus
Semine concepta est, ex illo concepit ales. †

The heifer thinks it not a shame to take
Her curled sire upon her willing back :
The horse his daughter leaps, goats scruple not
To use as freely those they have begot :
Birds, likewise, of all sorts in common live,
And by the seed they have conceiv'd, conceive.

The mischievous subtlety of a mule.

As for their mischievous subtlety, can there be a stronger instance of it than in the mule of the philosopher Thales; which happening to stumble as it was fording a rivulet with a load of salt on its back, so that the bags were all wet, and perceiving that the salt was thereby melted, and his burden rendered the lighter, never failed afterwards, when it came to any brook, to lie down in it with his load, till his master, discovering his trick, ordered him to be

* Of this there is a very remarkable instance, which I met in Varro de Re Rustica, lib. ii. cap. 7. As incredible as it may seem it ought to be remembered, that a stallion refusing absolutely to leap his mother, the groom thought fit to carry him to her with a cloth over his head, which blinded him, and by that means he forced him to cover her; but, taking off the veil as soon as he got off her, the stallion furiously rushed upon him, and bit him till he killed him.

† Ovid. Metam. lib. x. fab. 9. ver. 28, &c.

loaden with wool; after which the mule, finding that the same trick increased his burden instead of lightening it, he left it quite off.*

Several animals are the very pictures of our covetous people; for they take a vast deal of pains to catch all they can, and carefully to conceal it, though they make no use of it. ~ ~~ ʻʻ ·ʼ ‹ ʼ ⸲ *Animals that seem tainted with avarice.*

As to thrift, they surpass us not only in foresight, so far as to lay up and hoard for the time, but they have also many branches of knowledge necessary for that end. The ants bring out their corn and seeds, and spread them abroad in the sun, to air, refresh, and dry them, when they perceive they begin to stink and grow musty, lest they should corrupt and putrefy. But their precaution and prevention in nibbling the grains of wheat, surpass all imagination: because the wheat does not always continue sound and dry, but grows soft, dissolves, and looks as it were steeped in milk, whilst it hastens to sprout and shoot forth, for fear lest it should run to seed, and lose its nature, and the property of a magazine for their subsistence, they nibble off the end by which it usually sprouts. *Others that are very saving.*

In respect to war, which is the greatest and most pompous of human actions, I should be glad to know whether we choose it for an argument of some prerogative, or, on the contrary, for a testimony of our weakness and imperfection; as, in truth, the science of ruining and killing one another, and of destroying our own species, has nothing in it so tempting as to make it desirable by the beasts that have it not: *The passion for war, a proof of weakness in human beings, is in certain animals.*

———————— *Quando leoni*
Fortior eripuit vitam leo, quo nemore unquam
Exspiravit aper majoris dentibus apri ?†

---

* Plutarch de Solertia Animal. cap. 15, et Ælian de Animal. lib. vii. cap. 42.
† Juv. sat. xv. ver. 160, &c.

―― Who ever yet beheld
A weaker lion by a stronger kill'd ?
Or, in the forest, was it ever known
That a small boar dy'd by a mighty one ?

Yet they are not universally exempted ; witness the furious encounters of bees, and the enterprises of the princes of the two contrary parties :

――――――――――Sæpe duobus
Regibus incessit magno discordia motu,
Continuoque animis vulgi et trepidantia bello
Corda licet longe præsciscere.*

Between two kings strange animosities,
With great commotion, often do arise ;
When straight the vulgar sort are heard from far,
Sounding their little trumpets to the war.

I never read this divine description, but methinks I see a true picture of human folly and vanity : for, as to those warlike preparations that fill us with terror and astonishment, that rattle of drums, trumpets, and guns, and the noise of mighty shouts :

Fulgur ubi ad cœlum se tollit, totaque circum
Ære renidescit tellus, subterque virûm vi
Excitur pedibus sonitus, clamoreque montes
Icti rejectant voces ad sidera mundi.†

When burnish'd arms to heaven dart their rays,
And the earth glows with beams of shining brass,
And trampled is by horses and by men,
So that its centre even groans again ;
And that the rocks, struck by the thund'ring noise,
Reverberate the sound unto the skies.

this dreadful embattling of so many thousand men in arms, and such fury, ardour, and courage ; it is really pleasant to consider the many idle occasions by which war is kindled, and by what trifling causes it is extinguished :

* Virg. Georg. lib, iv. ver. 67, &c.   † Lucret. lib. ii, c. 327, &c.

———Paridis propter narratur amorem,
Græcia Barbariæ diro collisa duello.*
Of wanton Paris the illicit love
Did Greece and Troy to cruel warfare move.

All Asia was ruined and destroyed by war, on account of the lust of Paris. The envy of one single
man, a spite, a pleasure, a domestic jealousy, causes
which one would not think should set two oyster
wenches by the ears, is the spring and motive of all
this great disturbance. Will we believe the men
themselves, who are the principal authors and insti-
gators of such mischief? Let us then hear the
greatest, the most victorious, and most puissant
emperor † that ever was, with great merriment and
ingenuity, ridiculing the many battles risqued both
by sea and land; the blood and lives that were lost
of half a million of men that followed his fortune ;
and the power and wealth of half the world ex-
hausted for the expense of his expeditions:

‡ *Quod futuit Glaphyren Antonius, hanc mihi pœnam*
 Fulvia constituit, se quoque uti futuam :
Fulviam ego ut futuam ? quid si me Manius oret
 Pædicam, faciam ? non puto, si sapiam :
Aut futue, aut pugnemus ait ; Quid si mihi vitâ
 Charior est ipsâ mentula ? Signa canant.§

---

* Horat. lib. i. epist. 2. v. 6, 7. † Augustus.
‡ Martial, lib. x. epig. 21, ver. 3, &c.
§ This Epigram was composed by Augustus, but the luscious
Latin conveys such gross and licentious ideas, that there would be
no excuse for translating the lines without softening them ; and
therefore Peter Costa, who has enriched that edition of Montaigne
(which is here done into English) with his notes, has given this
French version of those lines by M. de Fontenelle, in one of his incomparable Dialogues of the Dead, which, though the language is
so very polite, lets us entirely into Augustus's meaning.

Parce qu'Antoine est charmé de Glaphire,
Fulvie a ses beaux yeux me veut assujettir.
Antoine est infidelle : He bien donc? Est ce adire
Que des fautes d'Antoine on me fera patir ?
 Qui-moy ? que je serve Fulvie ?
A ce compte on verroit se retirer vers moy
 Mille Epouses mal satisfaites.

(I use my Latin with the liberty of conscience you have been pleased to allow me.) Now, this great body has so many aspects and motions, as seem to threaten not only earth, but heaven :

Quam multi Libyco volvuntur marmore fluctus,
Sævus ubi Orion hybernis conditur undis,
Vel cum sole novo densæ torrentur aristæ,
Aut Hermi campo, aut Lyciæ flaventibus ervis,
Scuta sonant, pulsuque pedum tremit excita tellus.*

Thick as the waves on Lybia's coast that roar,
When Orion drives the billows to the shore ;
Or thick-set ears, matur'd by summer's rains,
Or Hermus' bank, or fruitful Lycia's plains ;
Are the bright shields that in the battles sound,
And troops of horse whose trampling shakes the ground.

This furious monster, with so many heads and hands, is still but feeble, calamitous, and miserable man. It is but a hillock of ants disturbed and proved by a spurn :

It nigrum campis agmen.*
The black army sallies out into the plain.

A puff of a contrary wind, the croaking of a flight of ravens, the stumble of a horse, the accidental passage of an eagle, a dream, a voice, a sign, a morning mist, are any one of them enough to overturn and lay him flat on the ground. Dart but a sun-beam in his face, he is melted and vanished. Blow but a little dust in his eyes, as our poet says of the bees, and all our ensigns and legions, with the great Pompey him-

Aime moi, *me dit elle,* ou combattons. *Mais quoy?*
Elle est bien laide? Allons, sonnez trompettes.

'Cause Anthony is fir'd with Glaphire's charms,
Fain would his Fulvia tempt me to her arms ;
If Anthony be false, what then? must I
Be slave to Fulvia's lustful tyranny?
Then would a thousand wanton, waspish wives
Swarm to my bed like bees into their hives.
Declare for LOVE, or WAR, she said, and frown'd :
No love I'll grant : to arms bid trumpets sound.

* Æneid, lib. vii. 718, &c. † Idem. lib. iv. ver. 404.

self at their head, are routed and crushed to pieces ;
for it was he, if I am not mistaken,* whom Sertorius defeated in Spain, with all those brave troops
which also served Eumenes against Antigónus, and
Surena against Crassus :

> *Hi motus animorum, atque hæc certamina tanta,*
> *Pulveris exigui jactu compressa quiescent.†*

> This mighty ferment, and these furious blows,
> A little dust dispers'd will soon compose.

Let us only slip our bees after them, and they
will have the power and courage to disperse them.
It is fresh in memory, how, when the city of Tamly,
in the territory of Xatina, was besieged by the Portuguese, the inhabitants, who had abundance of bee-
hives, put out a great number of them upon the wall,
and, setting fire to the hives, the bees sallied out so
furiously upon their enemies, that they gave over the
siege, not being able to stand their attacks, and endure their stings : thus their victory, and the liberty
of their city, was owing to this new kind of succours,
and with such good fortune too, that, at their return from the battle, *there was not a single bee miss-
ing.‡* The souls of emperors and coblers are cast in
the same mould. When we consider of what weight
and importance the actions of princes are, we imagine, that they are produced from some as weighty
and important causes : but we are mistaken, for they
are pushed on, and pulled back, in their motions, by
the same springs as we are in ours. The same reason that makes us wrangle with a neighbour, raises a

---

* Here Montaigne had reason to be a little distrustful of his memory ; for it was not against Pompey that Sertorius made use of this
stratagem, but against the Caracitanians, a people of Spain, who
lived in deep caves dug in a rock, where it was impossible to force
them. See Plutarch, in the Life of Sertorius, cap. 6.

† Virg. Georg. lib. iv. ver. 86, 87.

‡ Montaigne, to be sure does not mean, that this expression should
be taken in the literal sense ; for how could he be so exactly informed of the fate of all those bees ? Great wits naturally run into
hyperboles ; but, perhaps, I shall be told, that too severe critics
often mind trifles.

war between princes; and the same cause that makes
us horse-whip a foot-boy, falling into the breast of a
king, makes him ruin a province. They are as easily
moved as we are, but they can do more. The passion is the same in a maggot as an elephant.

As to fidelity, there is not an animal in the crea-
Dogs more faithful than men. tion to be compared with man for treachery. Our
histories inform us of the eager pursuits which have
been made, by dogs, after those who have murdered
their masters. King Pyrrhus, passing by a dog,
which he observed watched a dead man's body, and
hearing that he had done so for three days together,
ordered the corpse to be buried, and took the dog
along with him. One day, as he was at a general
muster of his army, the dog happened to spy the
very men that murdered his master, and, with
great barking and fury, attacked them; which
fierce accusation roused a revenge of this murder,
that was soon after taken by a course of justice.* The very same thing we read of the wise Hesiod's dog, which, in like manner, convicted the sons
of Ganister, of Naupacte, of having murdered his
master.† Another dog, that was set to guard a temple at Athens, perceiving sacrilege committed by a
thief, who carried away the richest jewels, barked at
him most furiously; which, however, not awaking
the church-wardens, he followed him, and, after day-
break, kept at a little more distance from him, but
without ever losing sight of him; though the thief
offered him something to eat, he would not take it,
but, to every passenger he met, he wagged his tail,
and took whatever they were pleased to give him:
mean time, wherever the thief laid down to sleep, he
likewise staid at the same place. The church-wardens having intelligence of this dog, they traced him,
by inquiring what colour he was of, and, at last,
found both the dog and the thief at the town of
Cromyon, from whence they brought back the latter
to Athens, where he was punished: and the judges,

* Plutarch de Solert. Animalium, cap. 12.   † Idem, ibid.

in acknowledgment of the dog's good office, ordered a certain measure of corn, out of the public granary, for his daily allowance, and that the priests should take care of it.[*] Plutarch relates this story as a certain fact, and as what happened in his time.

As for gratitude (for methinks we had needs bring this word into a little repute), this one example will suffice for it, which Appion[†] reports himself to have been an eye-witness of. " One day," says he, " as " they were entertaining the people at Rome with " the fighting of several wild beasts, and especially " lions of an unusual size ; there was one amongst " the rest, which, by its furious aspect, by the strength " and largeness of its limbs, and by its loud and " dreadful roaring, attracted the eyes of all that " were present. Among the other slaves, that were " brought to the theatre in this battle of the beasts, " was one Androdus of Dacia, who belonged to a " Roman nobleman of consular dignity. This lion, " perceiving him at a distance, first made a sudden " stop, as it were with a look of admiration, and " then softly advanced nearer in a gentle and peace- " able manner, as if it desired to be acquainted with " him. This done, and being now assured that he was " the man it wanted, the lion began to wag its tail " as dogs do when they fawn upon their masters, " and fell to kissing and licking the hands and legs " of the poor wretch, who was quite beside himself, " and half dead with fear ; but being, by this kind-

The noble
gratitude of
a lion.

---

* Plutarch de Solertia Animal. cap. 12, et in Ælian.

† Aulus Gellius (lib. v. c. 14.) has transmitted this story to us, on the credit of Appion : a learned man, says he, but whose great ostentation renders him, perhaps, too verbose in the narrative of things, which he says he had heard or read : as to this fact, Appion relates, that he was an eye-witness of it at Rome; and Seneca (lib. ii. cap. 19.) confirms it, in some measure, by these few words, Leonem in amphitheatro spectavimus qui unum e bestiariis agbitum, quum quondam ejus fuisset magister, protexit ab impetu bestiarum. " We saw " a lion in the amphitheatre, who, finding a man there condemned " to fight with the beasts, who had formerly been his master, pro- " tected him from the fury of the other beasts."

" ness of the lion, a little come to himself, and hav-
" ing taken so much heart as to look at the beast,
" and to make much of it, it was a singular pleasure
" to see the caresses of joy that passed between
" them. The people breaking into loud acclama-
" tions at this sight, the emperor caused the slave
" to be called to him, in order to know from him
" the cause of so strange an occurrence, and he
" gave him this strange and wonderful relation :
" My master, (said he), being a proconsul in
" Africa, I was constrained by his cruel usage of
" me, as he caused me to be beat every day, to steal
" from him and run away. And, in order to hide
" myself securely from a person of so great autho-
" rity in the province, I thought it my best way to
" fly to the sandy and solitary deserts of that coun-
" try, with a resolution, that, if I could get no-
" thing to support life, I would some way or other
" dispatch it. The sun being so burning hot at
" noon, that it was intolerable, I accidentally found
" a private and almost an inaccessible cave, into
" which I went. Soon after, this lion came to it
" with one paw wounded and bleeding; and the
" smart it endured made it complain and groan.
" Its approach terrified me very much ; but, no soon-
" er had he spied me lurking in a corner of its den,
" but it came to me very gently, holding up its
" wounded paw to my sight, as if it begged my as-
" sistance. I then drew out a great thorn from it,
" and, growing a little familiar with it, I squeezed
" the wound, pressed out the foul matter that was
" gathered in it, wiped it, and cleansed it in the
" best manner I could. The lion, finding its pain
" assuaged, and the cause of it removed, laid it-
" self down to rest, and slept all the time with his
" paw in my hands. From that time forwards, the
" lion and I lived together in this den three whole
" years upon one and the same diet; for, of the
" beasts which it killed in hunting, it brought me
" the best pieces, which I roasted in the sun for

" want of a fire, and then eat them. At length,
" being quite tired with this brutal savage life, as
" the lion was gone out, one day, as usual, in search
" of its prey, I set out from its den, and, on the
" third day after my departure, was seized by sol-
" diers, who brought me to this city from Africa,
" and delivered me up to my master, who presently
" condemned me to die, and to be exposed to the
" wild beasts. And, by what I saw, this lion was
" also taken soon after, which has now shown its in-
" clination to recompense me for the kindness and
" cure it received at my hands." This was the
story as related by Androdus to the emperor, and
which he also conveyed from hand to hand to the
people. Therefore, at the request of all the people,
he was set at liberty, and absolved from the sentence,
and the lion was, by their order, given to him as a
present. We afterwards saw (says Appion) Androdus leading this lion by nothing but a string, from
tavern to tavern, at Rome, and receiving the bounty
of the people, the lion being so gentle as to suffer
itself to be covered with the flowers that were thrown
upon it, while every one that met them cried, There
goes the lion that protected the man ; there goes the
man that cured the lion.

We often lament the loss of the beasts that we
love, and so do they the loss of us :

*Post bellator equus, positis insignibus, Æthon
It lachrymans, guttisque humectat grandibus ora.*

    —— The triumph more to grace,
Æthon, his horse of war, came next in place,
Which, of his trappings stript, show'd such regret,
That with large tears his hairy cheeks were wet.

As, in some nations of the world, wives are in common, and as, in some others, every man has his own
in particular, is not the same visible among the
beasts, and their marriages better kept than ours ?

* Virg. Æneid. lib. xi. v. 89, 90.

H 2

The society observable among the animals.

As to the society and agreement, which nations form amongst themselves to league together, and to give one another mutual assistance; we perceive that oxen, swine, and other animals, if any one of them that we offend cries out, all the herd or flock of the same kind run to its assistance, and rally to defend it.

Among the scare-fish.

When the scare-fish* has swallowed the fisherman's hook, its companions all crowd about it, and gnaw the line asunder; and if, by chance, one be got into the leap or weel, the others present their tails to it on the outside, which the scare holding fast with its beautiful teeth, is thereby disengaged and drawn out.

Among the fish called barbels.

Barbels, † when any one of their companions is hampered, throw the line over their backs, and with a fin, which they have there indented like a saw, they saw and cut it asunder.

Between the whale and a small fish.

As to the particular offices which we receive from one another for the service of life, there are many instances among them of the like kind. They say that the whale never moves, but a little fish like a sea-gudgeon‡ always goes before it, which is therefore called a guide. This the whale follows, suffering itself to be led and turned about by it, as easily as the ship is turned by its rudder: and in recompense, as it were, for this service, whereas every other thing, whether an animal or a vessel, which enters into the dreadful gulph of this monster's mouth, is instantly lost and swallowed up; this little fish retires into it with the greatest security, and there sleeps, during which the whale never stirs. But as soon as ever it goes out, the whale follows it, and if, by chance, it loses sight of its little guide, it wanders up and down in quest of it, and often rubs against the rocks like a ship that has lost her rudder. This Plutarch affirms he saw in the island of Anticyra.

---

* Plutarch de Solertia Animalium, c. 26.   † Idem, ibid.
‡ Idem, cap. 32.

There is the like communication between that lit- The wren and croco-dile.
tle bird they call a wren,* and the crocodile. The
wren keeps centry as it were over this great animal,
and if the ichneumon, its mortal enemy, approaches
to attack it, this little bird, for fear it should take the
crocodile napping, by singing, and pecking it with
its bill, awakes and warns it of its danger. The
bird feeds on the scraps left by this monster, which
admits it familiarly into its mouth, and suffers it to
peck in its jaws, and to pick and eat the bits of flesh
that stick between its teeth; and, when the crocodile has a mind to shut its mouth, it gives the bird
previous notice to go out of it, by closing it gra-
dually without bruising or hurting it.

The shell-fish, called the naker,† lives also upon The naker and shrimp.
the same good terms with the shrimp, a little animal
of the crab-fish kind, which serves it as a porter,
sitting at the opening of the shell which the naker
keeps continually open and gaping, till the shrimp
see some little fish go into the shell that is proper
for their prey; for then it likewise enters into the
shell, and, by pinching the naker to the quick,
forces it to shut the shell, where both together
devour the prey which is thus imprisoned in their
fort.

In the manner as the tunny-fish live, we observe The tunny-fish ac-quainted with the mathema-tics.
their singular knowledge of the three parts of the
mathematics. As to astrology, they teach it to
mankind; for at what place soever they are surprised by the winter's solstice,‡ there they stop, and
never stir from it till the next equinox; for which
reason, Aristotle himself readily attributes this
science to them. As to geometry and arithmetic,
they always form their body in the figure of a cube,
every-where square,§ and make up the body of a
solid, close battalion, with six sides exactly equal;

* Plutarch de Solertia Animal. cap. 32.
† Id. ibid. et Cic. de Nat. Deorum, lib. ii. cap. 48.
‡ Plutarch de Solertia Animal. cap. 29.
§ Idem, cap. 31,

and then they swim in this square disposition, as
broad behind as before; so that whoever sees and
counts one rank of them, may easily tell the number
of which the whole shoal consists, by reason that the
depth is equal to the breadth, and the breadth to the
length.

The magnanimity of an Indian dog. Respecting magnanimity, it is not easy to produce an instance that bears a greater appearance of
it, than this story of the great dog, that was sent
from the Indies to king Alexander. They first
brought a stag to fight it, next a wild boar, and then
a bear, all which he despised and disdained to stir
from its place; but when he saw a lion, he immediately rouzed* himself, evidently manifesting, that
he declared that beast alone to be worthy to enter
the lists with him.

Repentance of an elephant. As to repentance, and the acknowledgment of
faults, they tell of an elephant, which, having killed
its keeper in the violence of its rage, was so extremely sorry for it, that it would never eat afterwards, and starved itself to death.

The clemency of a tiger. Of clemency, we are told, that a certain tiger,
the most savage of all beasts, having a kid† delivered
up to him, suffered two days' hunger rather than he
would hurt it; and, on the third, broke open the
grate he was shut in to seek for some other pasture,
being unwilling to fall upon the kid, his familiar and
his inmate. And as to the laws of familiarity and
correspondence, formed by conversation, it is a common thing to see cats, dogs, and hares, brought up
tame together.

The wonderful qualities of the halcyons. But what they have experienced who have made
voyages, particularly in the sea of Sicily, as to the
quality of halcyons, surpasses all human thought.
What kind of animals has nature ever honoured so
much in their hatching,‡ birth, and production? the
poets say indeed, that one only island, viz. that of

* Plutarch de Solertia Animal. cap. 14.   † Idem, cap. 19.
‡ Idem, cap. 34.

Délos, which before was floating, was fixed for the
purpose of Latona's delivery; but God has been
pleased to order that the whole ocean should be
stayed, settled, and made smooth without waves,
without winds or rain, while the halcyon lays her
eggs, which is exactly at the winter's solstice, on
the shortest day of the year; so that by its privilege
we have seven days and seven nights in the very
depth of winter, wherein we may sail without any
danger. Their females never couple with any other
mate but their own, which they assist as long as they
live, without ever abandoning it: and, if it happens
to be weak and broken with age, they take it on their
shoulders, carry it from place to place, and serve it
till death.

But no one has yet been able to attain to the *The won-*
knowledge of that wonderful architecture, where- *derful fa-*
with the halcyon builds its nest for its young, nor to *bric of their nests.*
guess at the matter of its composition. Plutarch,
who saw and handled many of them, thinks they are
composed of the small bones of some fish, joined and
bound together, and interlaid, some lengthways, and
others across, with the addition of ribs and hoops in
such a manner, that she forms at last a round vessel
fit to be launched; and when she has quite finished
it, she carries it to the wash of the beach, where, the
sea beating gently against it, she is thereby enabled
to discover any part that is not well joined, and to
strengthen such parts as are leaky; and, on the contrary, what is well joined, is so closed and knit together, by the beating of the waves, that it is not to
be broke, or damaged, without very great difficulty,
by the strongest blows, either of stone or iron. But
what is most of all to be admired, is the proportion
and figure of the cavity within; for it is put together, and proportioned, in such a manner, that it
cannot possibly receive or admit any thing but the
bird which built it, it being to any thing else so im-

* Plutarch de Solertia Animal. cap. 34,

penetrably close and shut, that not even the water
of the sea can enter it. Thus you have had a very
clear description of this building, and from a good
authority ; and yet, methinks, it does not give a sufficient light into the difficulty of the architecture. Now
from what vanity can it proceed, that we should despise and put a disdainful construction upon facts
which we can neither imitate nor comprehend?

The faculty of imagina- tion com- mon to the beasts, as well as hu- man be- ings, and to horses, for example, and to dogs.
To pursue this equality and conformity between
us and the beasts a little farther, the privilege which
the soul of man so much boasts, of bringing every
thing it conceives to its own standard, of stripping
all things, that come before it, of their mortal and
corporeal qualities ; of ranging the things which it
deems worthy of its notice, of stripping and divest-
ing them of their corruptible qualities, and making
them lay aside thickness, length, depth, weight, colour, smell, roughness, smothness, hardness, softness,
and all sensible accidents, as so many mean and superfluous vestments, to accommodate them to her
own immortal and spiritual nature, so that, while I
think of Rome or Paris, I imagine and comprehend,
either without the ideas of greatness, situation, stone,
plaster, and timber : this very privilege, I say, seems
to be evident in beasts. For as a war-horse, accustomed to the sound of trumpets, the firing of mus-
kets, and the bustle of battles, will start and tremble
in his sleep, stretched out upon his litter, as if he was
engaged in fight ; it is certain, that it has some internal conception of the beat of a drum without
noise, and of an army without arms, and without
body :

*Quippe videbis equos fortes, cùm membra jacebant,
Insomnes, sudare tamen, spirareque sæpè,
Et quasi de palmâ summas contendere vires.**

You shall see running horses, in their sleep,
Sweat, snort, start, tremble, and a clutter keep,
Just as if striving with their utmost speed,
In the keen race to gain the victor's meed.

* Lucret. lib. iv. ver. 984.

The hare, which a grey-hound dreams of, and which
we see him pant after in his sleep, stretching out his
tail at the same time, shaking his legs, and perfectly
ly representing the motions of coursing, is a hare
without skin, and without bones:

Venantumque canes in molli sæpè quiete
Jactant crura tamen subito, vocèsque repentè
Mittunt, et crebras reducunt naribus auras,
Ut vestigia si teneant inventa ferarum :
Expergefactique, sequuntur inania sæpè
Corvorum simulacra, fugæ quasi dedita cernant ;
Donec discussis redeant erroribus ad se.[†]

And often hounds, when sleep has clos'd their eyes,
Will toss and tumble, and attempt to rise,
Snuff, and breathe quick and short, as if they went
In a full chase, upon a burning scent :
Nay, when awak'd, they fancy'd stags pursue,
As if they had them in their real view,
'Till, having shook themselves more broad awake,
They do, at last, discover the mistake.

We often observe the house-dogs snarling in their
dreams, then barking and starting up on a sudden, as
if they saw some stranger at the door; which stranger, all the while, is altogether spiritual and imper-
ceptible, without dimension, without complexion,
and without existence :

Consueta domi catulorum blanda propago
Degere, sæpè levem ex oculis volucremque soporem
Discutere, et corpus de terrâ corripere instant,
Proinde quasi ignotas facies atque ora tueantur.[†]

The fawning whelps of houshold curs will rise,
And, shaking the soft slumber from their eyes,
Oft bark and stare at ev'ry one within,
As upon faces they had never seen.

As to the beauty of the body, it is absolutely ne- ^{What con-}
cessary to know, in the first place, whether we are ^{stitutes}
agreed in the description of it. It is probable we ^{beauty.}
hardly know what beauty is in nature and in general,

---

* Lucret. lib. iv. ver. 988, &c,   † Idem, ibid. ver. 995, &c.

because to our own personal beauty we give so many
different forms, for which, were there any natural
prescription, we would acknowledge it in common,
as we do the heat of fire; but we fancy the forms
according to our own appetite :

Turpis Romano Belgicus ore color.[*]
A German hue ill suits a Roman face.

The Indians paint beauty black and tawny, with
great blubber lips, flat and broad noses, and load
the cartilage between the nostrils with great gold
rings, to make it hang down to the mouth, as also the
under lip with great hoops adorned with precious
stones that weigh it down to the chin, it being, with
them, a singular grace to show their teeth, even below the roots. In Peru, the longest ears being the
most beautiful, they stretch them out as much as
they can by art: and a man, now living, says that,
in an eastern nation, he saw this care of enlarging
the ears, and loading them with ponderous jewels, in
such high repute, that with great ease, he put his
arm, sleeve and all, through the hole of an ear.
There are nations, elsewhere, which take great care
to black their teeth, and hate to see them white,
whilst others paint them red. The women are reputed the more beautiful, not only in Biscay, but
elsewhere, and even in certain frozen countries, as
Pliny says,[†] for having their heads shaved. The
Mexicans reckon it a beauty to have a low forehead,
and, though they shave all other parts, they nourish
hair on their foreheads, and increase it by art ; and
they have great breasts in such esteem, that they affect to give their children suck over their shoulders:
this we should reckon a deformity. The Italians
like a woman that is fat and bulky : the Spaniards
one that is lean and slender ; and, with us, one is
for a fair complexion, another for a brown ; one for
soft and delicate limbs, another prefers a woman that,

[*] Propert. lib. ii. eleg. 18. ver. 26.   [†] Nat. Hist. lib. vi. cap. 18.

is strong and buxom ? one requires her to be fond
and gentle, another proud and stately : just so is the
preference in beauty, which Plato attributes to the
spherical figure, and the Epicureans to the pyramidal
or square, for they could not worship a god in the
form of a bowl.

But, be this as it will, nature has no more exempt- *Men are not privileged, in point of beauty, above the beasts.*
ed us from her common laws, in this respect, than
the rest : and if we think rightly of ourselves, we
shall find that, if there be some animals not so
much favoured in this quality as we are, there are
others, and in great number too, that are more so.
A multis animalibus decore vincimur ;[*] many animals
exceed us in comeliness, nay, even of the terrestrial
ones, our compatriots : for as to those of the sea (setting aside their shape, which cannot bear any manner
of resemblance, it is so much of another sort), we are
inferior to them in colour, cleanness, smoothness,
disposition ; and no less inferior, in all respects, to
those of the air. And as for the prerogative which
the poets cry up so much of our erect stature looking
towards heaven, our orignal :

> *Pronaque cum spectant animalia cætera terram,*
> *Os homini sublime dedit, cœlumque tueri*
> *Jussit, et erectos ad sydera tollere vultus.*[†]
>
> Whilst all the brutal creatures downward bend
> Their sight, and to their earthly mother tend,
> He set man's face aloft, that with his eyes
> Up-lifted, he might view the starry skies.

it is purely poetical ; for there are several little beasts
which have their sight absolutely turned towards
heaven, and I actually think the faces of camels and
ostriches much more raised and erect than ours.
What animals are there that have not their faces
above, and in front, and that do not look right against
them as well as we, and that do not in their true posture, see as much of heaven and earth as we do ? And

---

* Senec. ep. 124, towards the end.
† Ovid Met. lib. i. fab. 2, ver. 51, &c.

what qualities of our bodily constitution, described
by Plato and Cicero,* may not be as essential to
a thousand sorts of animals? The beasts that most
resemble us are the most deformed and despicable
of the whole class? those most like to us, in the outward appearance and make of the face, are monkeys:

> *Simia quam similis, turpissima bestia, nobis !*†
> How like to men, in visage and in shape,
> Is, of all beasts the most uncouth, an ape !

and, as for the intestines and vital parts, the hog.

Verily, when I entertain the idea of any of the
human species stark naked (even in that sex which
seems to have the greatest share of beauty), when
I consider of his defects, what he is naturally liable
to, and his imperfections, I think we have more
reason to be covered than any other animal, and are
to be excused for borrowing of those creatures, to
which nature has been kinder, in this respect, than
to us, in order to dress ourselves with their finery,
and to cover ourselves with their spoils of wool, feathers, hair, silk, &c. For the rest, it is observable,
that man is the only animal whose nakedness is offensive to his own companions, and the only creature
who steals from his own species to perform the offices of nature. Indeed, it is also a fact worthy of
consideration, that they, who are connoisseurs in the
mysteries of love, prescribe, as a remedy for the amorous passion, and to cool the heat of it, a free sight
of the beloved object:

Note in margin: Man has more reason to be covered than any other animal.

> *Ille quod obscœnas in aperto corpore partes*
> *Viderat, in cursu qui fuit hæsit amor.*‡
> The lover, when those nudities appear
> Open to view, flags in the hot career,

---

* By Plato in his Timæus, and by Cicero in his tract De Natura
Deorum, lib. ii. cap. 54, &c. But this is set in a better light by some
modern treatises of anatomy, where a comparison has been made
between the human body and those of several animals.
† Ennius apud Cic. de Nat. Deorum, lib. i. c. 35.
‡ Ovid. de Remed. Amor. lib. ii. v. 33, 34.

Although this receipt may, perhaps, proceed from a nice and cold humour, yet it is a strange sign of our imperfection, that habit and acquaintance should make us out of love with one another. It is not modesty, so much as art and prudence, that renders our ladies so circumspect as to refuse us admittance to their closets before they are painted and dressed for public view :

Nec Veneres nostras hoc fallit, quæ magis ipsæ
Omnia summopere hos vitæ postscœnia celant.
Quos retinere volunt adstrictoque esse in amore. *

Of this our ladies are full well aware,
Which makes them, with such privacy and care,
Behind the scene all those defects remove,
Likely to quench the flame of those they love.

Whereas, in many animals, there is nothing which we do not love, and which does not please our senses; even from their excrements and discharges we not only extract dainties for our table, but our richest ornaments and perfumes. This discourse only concerns our common class of women, and is not so sacrilegious as to comprehend those divine, supernatural, and extraordinary beauties that shine amongst us, like stars under a corporeal and terrestrial veil.

As to the rest, the very share of nature's favours that we allow to the animals, by our own confession, is very much to their advantage: we attribute to ourselves benefits that are imaginary and fantastical, such too as are future and absent, and for which it is not in the power of man to be answerable; or benefits that we falsely attribute to ourselves by the licentiousness of our opinion; such as reason, knowledge, and honour: and to the animals we leave, for their share, benefits that are substantial, agreeable, and manifest, such as peace, rest, safety, innocence, and health; I say, health, which is the fairest

Man lays claim to imaginary happiness, and leaves that which is real to the animals.

* Lucret. lib. iv. v. 1178, &c.

and richest present that is in the power of nature
to make to us, insomuch that the philosophers,* even
the stoic, are so bold as to say, that Heraclitus and
Pherecydas, if it had been possible for them to have
exchanged their wisdom for health, and thereby to
have delivered themselves, the one from the dropsy, the
other from the lousy disease, would have made a
good bargain.   By this they set the greater value
upon wisdom, comparing and putting it into the balance with health, than they do in the following proposition, which is also theirs.

Wherein
consists the
superior
excellence
of man to
the beasts.They say, that if Circe had given two draughts to
Ulysses, the one to make a fool wise, and the other
to make a wise man a fool, Ulysses ought rather to
have chose the last, than to have consented that
Circe should change his human figure into that of a
beast.   And they say, that wisdom itself would have
spoke to him after this manner : " Forsake me, let
" me alone, rather than lodge me under the figure
" and body of an ass."   What ! is this great and divine wisdom then abandoned by the philosophers for
this corporeal and terrestrial veil ?   At this rate it is
not by reason, conversation, and by a soul, that we
excel the beasts ; it is by our beauty, our fair complexion, and the curious disposition of our limbs, for
all which we must quite give up our understanding,
our wisdom, and all the rest.   Well, I approve this
natural and free confession ; certainly they knew
that those parts, with which we make such a parade,
are only mere fancy.   Though the beasts therefore
had all the virtue, knowledge, wisdom, and stoical
sufficiency, they would still be beasts, and would not be
comparable to man, wretched, wicked, and senseless
man : for, in fine, whatever is not as we are, is worth
nothing ; and a God, to procure himself esteem,
must condescend to the same, as we shall show anon.
By this it appears, that it is not by solid reason, but

---

* Plutarch, in his tract of the common conceptions, against the
Stoics, chap. 8 of Amyot's translation.

by a foolish and stubborn pride, that we prefer ourselves to the other animals, and separate ourselves
from their condition and society.

But, to return to my subject, we have, to our
share, inconstancy, irresolution, uncertainty, sorrow,
superstition, a solicitude for things to come, even
after our death, ambition, avarice, jealousy, envy,
irregular and ungovernable appetites, war, lying,
disloyalty, detraction, and curiosity; surely we have
strangely overpaid for this same fine reason, on
which we so much value ourselves, and for this capacity of judging and knowing, if we have bought it
at the price of that infinite number of passions to
which we are eternally subject; unless we shall think
fit, as Socrates indeed does, to throw into the other
scale this notable prerogative of man over the beasts,
that nature has prescribed to the latter certain seasons and limits for venereal pleasure, but* has given
the reins to the former at all hours and occasions.
† *Ut vinum ægrotis, quia prodest rarò, nocet sæ-
pissimè, melius est non adhibere omninò, quàm, spe
dubiæ salutis, in apertam perniciem incurrere: sic,
haud scio, an melius fuerit humano generi motum
istum celerem cogitationis, acumen, solertiam, quam
rationem vocamus, quoniam pestifera fuit multis,
admodum paucis salutaria, non dari omninò, quàm,
tam munificè et tam largè dari.* " As it is better
" to give no wine at all to the sick, because it
" often hurts them, and seldom does them good,
" than to expose them to manifest danger in hopes
" of an uncertain benefit; so I know it had been
" better for mankind, that this quickness and acute-
" ness of thought, which we call reason, had not
" been given to man at all, considering how de-
" structive it is to many, and how few there are
" to whom it is useful."

* Xenophontis Ἀπομνημονεύμ. lib. iv. cap. 4, sect. 12. Καὶ (Θεός)
τὰς τῶν ἀφροδισίων ἡδονὰς τοῖς μεν, ἄλλοις ζῶοις δέδωκε, περιγράψαντες τὸ
ἔτος χρόνον, ἡμῖν δὲ συνεχῶς μέχρι γήρως ταῦτα παρέχειν.
† Cic. de Nat. Deor. lib. iii. cap. 27, Edit. Gronov.

Know-
ledge does
not exempt
us from hu-
man incon-
veniences. Of what advantage can we suppose the knowledge
of so many things was to Varro and Aristotle? Did it
exempt them from human inconveniences? Were
they freed by it from the casualties that attend a
porter? Did they extract, from their logic, any consolation in the gout? Or, because they knew how
this humour is lodged in the joints, did they feel it
the less? Did they compound with death, because
they knew that some nations rejoice at its approach?
Or with cuckoldom, by knowing that there is a
country where the wives are in common? On the
contrary, though they were held in the highest reputation for their knowledge, the one amongst the
Romans, the other amongst the Greeks, and at a
time when learning flourished most, yet we have not
heard of any particular excellence in their lives;
nay, the Greek had enough to do to clear himself
from some remarkable blemishes in his. Have we
observed, that pleasure and health are best relished
by him who understands astrology and grammar?

> *Illiterati num minus nervi rigent ?**
>
> Is not th' illiterate as fit
> For Venus' pastime, as the wit ?†

And that shame and poverty are not so grievous to
him as others?

> *Silicet et morbis, et debilitate carebis,*
> *Et luctum et curam effugies, et tempora vitæ*
> *Longa tibi post hæc fato meliore dabuntur.‡*
>
> By this depend on't, that thou wilt remain
> Free from disease, infirmity, and pain,
> From care and sorrow, and thy life shall flow,
> Prolong'd, with ev'ry happiness below.

There are
more per- In my time I have seen a hundred artificers, and
a hundred labouring men, wiser and more happy

---

* Hor. Epod. lib. ode viii. ver. 17.
† Very far from it, if we will believe Fontaine, that faithful and
delicate copyist of simple nature, who says, " Au jeu d'amour le
" muletier fait rage."
‡ Juv. sat. xiv. ver. 156, &c.

than the heads of the university, and whom I would much rather resemble. I think learning stands in the same rank, among the necessaries of life, as glory, nobility, dignity, or at the most, as riches, and such other qualities as are, it is true, of service to life, but remotely, and more by fancy than by nature. We stand in very little need of more offices, rules, and laws for life, in our society, than are requisite for the cranes and emmets in theirs; and yet we see, that they behave very orderly, though without learning. If man were wise, he would value every thing, in proportion as it was useful and proper for life. Whoever will take a survey of us, according to our actions and behaviour, will find a greater number of excellent men among the ignorant than the learned; I mean, excellent in virtue of all kinds. Old Rome seems, to me, to have had more worthy men, both for peace and war, than that learned Rome which ruined itself: though, for the rest, they should be both equal, yet integrity and innocence would fall to the share of old Rome, for they best correspond with simplicity. But I leave this discourse, which would lead me farther than I am willing to follow; and have only this to add, that it is not only humility and submission that can make a complete good man: we must not leave it to every man to know his duty; it must be prescribed to him, and he must not be suffered to choose it by his understanding, otherwise we should, at last, forge to ourselves duties, according to the weakness and infinite diversity of our opinions, which would, as Epicurus says, put us upon eating one another.

The first law that God gave to man was a law of pure obedience: it was a naked, simple command, wherein man had nothing to inquire after, or dispute about; forasmuch as obedience is the proper duty of a rational soul, that acknowledges a heavenly superior and benefactor. From obedience and submission every other virtue springs, as every sin does from imagination. On the contrary, the very first temptation offered to human nature by the devil, his first poison, was infused into us by the promises he made to us of knowledge and wisdom. "Ye shall be as gods, knowing good and evil."[*] And the Syrens, in order to deceive Ulysses, in Homer, and to decoy him into their dangerous and destructive snare, offered him science for a present.

Ignorance recommended by our religion. The plague of mankind is the opinion of wisdom, which is the reason that ignorance is so much recommended to us, by our religion, as proper to faith and obedience: "Beware lest any man spoil "you through philosophy and vain deceit, after the "rudiments of the world."[†]

Presumption the quality only of human beings. The philosophers, of all sects, agree in this, that the sovereign good consists in the tranquillity of the soul and body: but where do we find it?

Ad summum, sapiens uno minor est Jove, dives,
Liber, honoratus, pulcher, rex denique regum :
Præcipuè sanus, nisi cum pituita molesta est. [‡]

In short, the wise man's only less than Jove,
Rich, free, and handsome, nay, a king above
All earthly kings, with health supremely blest,
Except when tickling phlegm disturbs his rest.

It seems to me, in truth, that nature has given us presumption only for the consolation of our wretched, forlorn state. It is, as Epictetus says, "that man has nothing properly his own, but the "use of his opinions." We have nothing but wind and smoke for our portion. The gods have health in essence, says philosophy, and sickness in intelligence; man, on the contrary, possesses his goods in fancy, and his ills in essence. We have had reason to extol the strength of our imagination, for all our happiness is only in dream. Hear the bravado of this poor calamitous animal. "There is nothing," says Cicero, "so charming as the knowledge of

* Gen. iii. 5.   † Coloss. ii. 8.   ‡ Hor. lib. i. epist. 1, ver. 106, &c.

" literature, of that branch of literature, I mean,
" which enables us to discover the infinity of
" things, the immensity of nature, the heavens, the
" earth, and the seas: this is that branch which
" has taught us religion, moderation, magnani-
" mity, and that has rescued our soul from obscu-
" rity, to make her see all things above and below,
" first and last, and between both; it is this that
" furnishes us wherewith to live well and happily,
" and guides us to pass our lives without displea-
" sure, and without offence."* Would not one think
he was describing the condition of the ever-living
and almighty God? But, in fact, there are a thousand poor women, in the country villages, whose
lives have been more regular, more agreeable and
uniform than his:

—— *Deus ille fuit Deus, inclyte Memmi,
Qui princeps vitæ rationem invenit eam, quæ
Nunc appellatur sapientia, quique per artem
Fluctibus è tantis vitam tantisque tenebris,
In tam tranquillâ et tam clarâ luce locavit.*†

He, noble Memmius, was a god, no doubt,
Who, prince of life, first found that reason out,
Now wisdom call'd; and by his art, who did
That life in tempests toss'd, and darkness hid,
Place in so great a calm, and clear a light.

These were fine pompous words; but a very slight
accident reduced the understanding of this man‡ to
a worse state than that of the meanest shepherd, notwithstanding this his preceptor God and his divine
wisdom. Of the same impudent stamp is that preface to Democritus's book, " I am going to treat of

* Cic. Tusc. Quæst. lib. i. cap. 26.   † Lucret. lib. v. ver. 8, &c.
‡ This was Lucretius, who, in the verses preceding this period,
speaks so pompously of Epicurus and his doctrine : for a love-po-
tion, that was given him either by his wife or his mistress, so
much disturbed his reason, that the violence of his disorder only af-
forded him a few lucid intervals, which he employed in composing
his book, and at last made him kill himself.   Eusebius's Chronicon.

" all things."[*] And that foolish title, which Aristotle gives us, " Of the mortal gods,"[†] and that opinion of Chrysippus, that Dion[‡] was as virtuous as God. And my Seneca says, that God gave him life, but that it was of himself to live well; which is of a piece with that other assertion,[§] *In virtute verè gloriamur, quod non contigeret, si id donum à deo, non à nobis haberemus :* " We truly glory in our " virtue, which would not be the case if it was " given us by God, and not of ourselves." This is also from Seneca,[||] that the wise man has fortitude equal with God, but attended with human frailty, wherein he surmounts him. There is nothing so common as to meet with passages of so much presumption. There is not one of us who would be so much offended at being placed on a par with God, as to find himself undervalued by being levelled to the rank of the other animals; so much more jealous are we of our own interest than of that of our Creator. But we must trample this foolish vanity under foot, and boldly shake the ridiculous foundations on which these false opinions are founded. So long as man shall be of opinion that he has any means or power of his own, he will never acknowledge what he owes to his maker. " He will reckon his chickens before they are " hatched," as the saying is; we must therefore strip him to his shirt.

Let us now see some noble effects of the Stoic philosophy. Possidonius, being tormented with a disease so painful, that it made him twist his arm

---

* " Qui ita sit ausus ordiri hæc loquor de universis nihil excipit de " quo non profitetur : quid enim esse potest extra universa ?" Cic. Acad. Quæst. lib. ii. cap. 23.

† Apud Ciceronem de Finibus Bon. et Mal. lib. ii. cap. 13. " Cy- " renaici philosophi non viderunt, ut ad cursum, equum; ad aran- " dum bovem; ad indagandum canem; sic hominem ad duas res, " ut ait Aristoteles, intelligendum et agendum, esse natum, quasi " mortalem deum."

‡ Plutarch, of the common conceptions of the Stoics, chap. 30.
§ Cic. de Nat. Deor. lib. iii. cap. 36. || Epist. 53, sub finem.

and gnash his teeth, made a jest of the pain by crying out against it, " Thou dost thy worst to a fine
" purpose : for I will not confess thou art an evil."*
He has the same sense of feeling as my footman, but
he vapours, because he restrains his tongue at least
within the laws of his sect.† *Re succumbere non
oportebat verbis gloriantem:* " As he talked so big,
" it did not become him to shrink." Carneades‡
visiting Arcesilaus, whom he found ill of the gout,
was going away very sorry to see him in that condition, when Arcesilaus called him back, and pointing
both to his feet and his breast, said to him, " There's
" nothing that affects these, touches this." This
was said with a little better grace than the other, for
he had a feeling of his distemper, and showed that
he would be glad to be rid of it. But, however, he
was heart-whole, and not cast down by it. The
other continued obstinate, but, I fear, rather in
words than in reality. And Dionysius Heracleotes,
being afflicted with a vehement pain in his eyes,
was obliged to recede from his Stoical resolutions.§

But though knowledge should have the effect, as The effects
they say, of blunting the point or abating the seve- of igno-
rity of the misfortunes which attend us, what does ferable to
it that ignorance cannot perform in a more simple those of
and clear manner? Pyrrho the philosopher, when in ledge.
danger of being shipwrecked in a great storm at sea,
proposed no other example for the imitation of those
that were with him, but a hog that was on board,
which discovered no fear at all in the storm. Philosophy, when it has said all it can, refers us to the
examples of a wrestler and a muleteer, in which
class of persons we commonly observe much less ap-

* Cic. Tusc. Quæst. lib. xi. cap. 25.   † Id. cap. 13.
‡ Cicero informs us, that Carneades was very intimate with Epicurus; and, by consequence, this cannot be he who founded the
New Academy; for Epicurus was dead about sixty years before
Carneades, the founder of the New Academy, was born. Cicero
de Finibus Bon. et Mal. lib. v. cap. 31.
§ Id. ibid. Cicero says elsewhere, that this philosopher, having a
disorder in his kidneys, exclaimed aloud, that the notion which he
had before conceived of pain was false.

prehension of death, pains, and other inconvenien^{ces,}
and more constancy than ever knowledge furnished
any person with, who was not born and prepared to
suffer them of himself, by natural habit. Whence
proceeds it that we make incisions, and cut the tender limbs of an infant, and those of a horse, with
less resistance than those of our own, but from ignorance? How many persons have been made sick
by the mere force of imagination? We commonly
see persons that bleed, purge, and take physic to
cure themselves of diseases, which only affect them
in opinion. When we are in want of real infirmities,
knowledge supplies us from its store. That colour,
that complexion, portend some defluxion or catarrh:
this hot season threatens us with a fever. That
crossing of the line of life, in the palm of your
left-hand, warns you of some remarkable indispo-
sition approaching: in short it makes a direct attack
upon life itself; that sprightliness and juvenile
vigour cannot last long: there must be some blood
taken away, and you must be brought low, lest
such a florid state of health turn to your prejudice.
Compare the life of a man who is a slave to such
imaginations to that of the labouring man, who is
governed by his natural appetite, measuring things
only as they appear to him at the present, without
knowledge and without prognostication; who feels
no pain or sickness but when he is really tormented
or diseased; whereas the other has often the stone
in his mind before he has it in his kidneys: as if it
were not time enough to suffer the evil when it
comes, he anticipates it in fancy and runs to meet
it.

A man's
acknow-
ledgement
of the
weakness
of his judg-
ment the
sovereign
good, ac-
cording to
some philo-
phers. What I say of medicine may be generally exem-
plified in all other sciences. From thence is derived that ancient opinion of the philosophers, who
placed the sovereign good in knowing the weakness
of our judgment. My ignorance affords me as much
room for hope as fear, and having no other regimen
for my health, but the examples of others, and of
events which I see elsewhere on the like occasions,

I find some of all sorts, and rely upon those which are by the comparison most favourable to me. I receive health with open arms, free, full, and entire; and enjoy it with a keener appetite, as it more seldom accompanies me now than formerly; so far am I from disturbing its repose and sweet relish by the bitterness of a new and constrained form of life.

The beasts show us plainly how much our diseases are owing to the perturbation of our minds. What we are told of the people in Brasil, that they die merely of old age, and that this is attributed to the serenity and tranquillity of the air they live in; I ascribe it rather to the serenity and tranquillity of their souls, free from all passion, thought, or employ-ment, that is laborious or unpleasant; as people that pass their lives in an admirable simplicity and igno-rance, without learning, without law, without king, or any manner of religion. And whence comes that which we know by experience, that the most stupid and unpolished boors are the strongest and the most desirable for amorous exploits, and that a muleteer is often better liked than a gentleman; if it be not that the agitation of the soul in the latter disturbs, breaks, and wearies his bodily strength, as it also generally tires and teases itself? What is it puts the soul besides itself, what more usually throws it into madness, but its own promptness, penetration, and activity, and, in short, its own power? From what is the most subtle folly derived but from the most subtle wisdom? As great enmities spring from great friendships, and mortal distempers from vigorous health; so do the most surprising and the wildest frenzies from the rare and lively agitations of our souls; and there is but a hair's-breadth between them.* In the actions of madmen, we perceive how exactly their folly tallies with the most vigorous ope-rations of our souls. Who does not know how indis-cernable the difference is between folly with the gay

Distempers both of the body and mind caused by the agita-tion of our souls.

* Great wits to madness, sure, are near allied,
  And thin partitions do their bounds divide.   Dryden.

elevations of a mind that is uncontrolled, and the effects of a supreme and extraordinary virtue? Plato says, that melancholy people are the most capable of discipline, and the most excellent: nor indeed have any of them so great a propensity to madness.

One of the most excellent of the Italian poets that lost the use of his reason some time before his death. Great wits are ruined by their own own strength and vivacity. One of the most judicious and ingenious Italian poets,* and who possessed more of the true genius of the ancients than any other Italian for a long time ; how is he fallen from that pleasant lively humour that his fancy was adorned with. Is he not to thank this vivacity of his for his destruction? Is it not that light of his which has blinded him? Is it not that exact and extended apprehension of reason that has put him besides his reason? Is it not his curious and laborious scrutiny into the sciences that has reduced him to stupidity? Is it not his uncommon aptitude to the exercises of the soul that has deprived him both of the exercise and the soul? I was even more piqued than sorry to see him at Ferrara in so pitiful a condition, out-living himself, forgetting both himself and his works, which, without his knowledge, though before his face, have been published incorrect and deformed.

Sensibility and stupidity are accompanied by vigour and health. Would you have a man healthy? would you have him regular and stable? muffle him up in the darkness of sloth and dulness. We must be made beasts in order to be made wise, and hood-winked for the sake of being led. And if any one shall tell me that the advantage of having a cold appetite blunted to a sense of pain and misfortunes draws this inconvenience after it, that it also renders us by consequence not so acute and delicate in the enjoyment of happiness and pleasure; this is very true; but

---

* The famous Torquato Tasso, author of the poem entit'ed Jerusalem Delivered. I cannot imagine how the translator of Montaigne's Essays came to put Ariosto in his place. Montaigne tells us, that he saw this famous poet at Ferrara, which he could not have said of Ariosto, who, being born in 1474, was 59 years old when Montaigne came into the world.

such is the wretchedness of our condition, that we
have not so much to enjoy as to avoid, and that extreme pleasure does not affect us so much as a light
grief. *Segnius homines bona quam mala sentiunt :*[*]
" We are not so sensible of perfect health as of the
" least sickness."

———————————— *Pungit*
In cute vix summi violatum plagula corpus,
Quando valere nihil quemquam movet.   Hoc juvat unum,
Quod me non torquet latus aut pes ;   cætera quisquam
Vix queat aut sanum sese aut sentire valentem.[†]

The body with a little sting is griev'd,
When the most perfect health is not perceiv'd.
This only pleases me that spleen nor gout
Either torment my side or wring my foot ;
Excepting these, scarce any one call tell,
Or e'er observes, when he's in health and well.

Our well-being is nothing but the privation of evil.
And, for this reason, that sect of philosophy which
has most cried up pleasure has also reduced it to
mere indolence. To be free from ill is the greatest
good that man can hope for; according to Ennius,

Nimium boni est, cui nihil est mali.[‡]

For that very titillation and pricking which we find
in certain pleasures, and that seem to raise us above
a mere state of health and insensibility; that active,
moving, or what shall I call it, itching, smarting
pleasure, even that only aims at insensibility as its
mark. The appetite which carries us away like a
torrent to the embraces of women, is merely to cure
the pain we suffer by that hot furious passion, and
only demands to be assuaged and composed by an
exemption from this fever. And so of the rest. I
say, therefore, that as simplicity puts us in the way
to be free from evil, so it leads us to a very happy
state according to our nature.

[*] Titus Livius, lib. xxx. cap. 21.
[†] Steph. Boetii Poemata, p. 115, lin. xi—xii. &c.
[‡] Ennius apud Cic. de Finibus Bon. et Mal. lib. xi. cap. 19.

Perfect in-
sensibility
neither pos-
sible nor
desirable.

And yet we are not to imagine a state so stupid as
to be altogether without sensation. For Crantor was
much in the right to controvert the insensibility of
Epicurus, if it was so deeply founded, that the very
approach and source of evils were not to be perceived. " I do not approve," says he, " of that
" boasted insensibility which is neither possible nor
" desirable. I do not wish to be sick ; but, if I am,
" I should be willing to know that I am ; and whe-
" ther caustics or incisions be made use of, I would
" feel them."* In truth, whoever would eradicate
the knowledge of evil, would in the same proportion
extirpate the knowledge of pleasure, and, in fact,
annihilate man himself. *Istud nihil dolere, non sine
magnâ mercede contingit immanitatis in animo, stu-
poris in corpore :*† " This insensibility is not to be ac-
" quired without making the mind become cruel,
" and the body stupid." Good and evil happen to
man in their turn. Neither has he trouble always to
avoid, nor pleasure always to pursue.

Know-
ledge re-
fers us to
ignorance
to screen
us from the
injuries of
fortune.

It is a very great advantage to the honour of ignorance, that knowledge itself throws us into its arms,
when it finds itself puzzled to support us under the
weight of evils ; for it is then constrained to come
to this composition to give us the reins, and permit
us to fly into the lap of the other, and to shelter ourselves by her favour from the strokes and injuries of
fortune. For what else does knowledge mean, when
it instructs us to take off our thoughts from the ills
that press upon us, and to entertain them with the
recollection of past pleasures. And to comfort ourselves under present afflictions with the remembrance
of former happiness, and to call to our assistance satisfaction that is vanished to oppose it to that which
presses us. *Levationes ægritudinum in avocatione à
cogitandâ molestiâ, et revocatione ad contemplandas
voluptates ponit.*‡ If it be not that where its strength

* Cic. Tusc. Quæst. lib. iii. cap. 6.   † Idem, ibid.
‡ Idem, ibid. cap. 15.

fails, it chooses to have recourse to policy, and to make use of a light pair of heels where the vigour of the body and arms is deficient? For not only to a philosopher, but to any sedate man, who has the thirst attending a burning fever upon him, what satisfaction is it to remember that he had the pleasure of drinking Greek wine? It would be rather making a bad bargain worse:

> *Che ricordarsi il ben doppia la noia.*
>
> Whoso remembers, all his gains
> Are that he doubles his own pains.

Of the same stamp is this other counsel which philosophy gives, only to remember the good fortune[*] past, and to forget the mortifications we have suffered; as if we had the science of oblivion in our power. A piece of advice this, for which we are not a straw the better.

A prescription of the same kind by philosophy to forget our past trouble.

> *Suavis est laborum præteritorum memoria.*[†]
>
> The recollection of past toils is sweet.

How? Is philosophy, that should put weapons into my hands to contend with fortune, and that should steel my courage to trample all human adversities under foot, become such a rank coward as to make me hide my head by such dastardly and ridiculous shifts? For the memory represents to us what it pleases, not what we choose: nay, there is nothing that so strongly imprints any thing in our remembrance as the desire to forget it. And to solicit the soul to lose any thing is a good way to make it retain it by rendering the impression of it the deeper. This is a false position. *Est situm in nobis ut et adversa quasi perpetua oblivione obruamus, et secunda jucundè et suaviter meminerimus.*[‡] " And it is in " our power to bury all adversity as it were in obli- " vion, and to call our prosperity to mind with

---

[*] Cic. Tusc. Quæst. lib. iii. cap. 16.
[†] Euripid. apud Cic. de Finibus Bon. et Mal. lib. ii. cap. 32.
[‡] Ibid. lib. i. cap. 17.

" pleasure and delight." And this is true. *Memini etiam quæ nolo : oblivisci non possum quæ volo.**
" I do also remember what I would not, but I can-
" not forget what I would." And whose counsel is
this ? *Hic qui se unus sapientem profiteri sit ausus.*
" Who only durst profess himself a wise man," viz.
Epicurus :

> *Qui genus humanum ingenio superavit, et omnes*
> *Præstrinxit stellas, exorsus uti æthereus sol.*†
>
> Who from mankind the prize of knowledge won,
> And put the stars out, like the rising sun.

To have the memory empty and unfurnished, is it
not the true and proper way to ignorance ?

> *Iners malorum remedium ignorantia est.*‡
> Ignorance is but a weak remedy for misfortunes.

We find several such precepts, by which we are allowed to borrow frivolous appearances from the
vulgar, where strong and vigorous reason is of no
avail, provided they give us comfort and contentment. Where they cannot heal the wound, they are
content to palliate and benumb it. I believe they
will not deny me this, that, if they could settle order
and constancy in a state of life, that could maintain
itself in pleasure and tranquillity by some defect and
disorder of judgment, they would approve of it, and
say with Horace :

> ——— *Potare et spargere flores*
> *Incipiam, patiarque vel inconsultus haberi.*§
> With garlands crown'd I'll take my hearty glass,
> Though for my frolic I be deem'd an ass.

There would be a great many philosophers of Lycas's
mind, who being in all other respects a man of very
good morals, living in peace and happiness in his
family, deficient in no obligation, either to his rela-

---

* Euripid. apud Cic. de Finibus Bon. et Mal. lib. ii. cap. 32.
† Lucret. lib. iii. ver. 1056. ‡ Senec. Œdip. act. iii. ver. 7.
§ Hor. lib. i. epist. v. ver. 14, 45.

tions or strangers, and very careful to guard himself
from any thing that might hurt him, was, nevertheless, by some disorder in his brain, strangely possessed with a conceit, that he was perpetually at the
theatre a spectator of the sports, pastimes, and the
best of comedies; and, being cured of his frenzy
by the physicians, he had a great mind to have entered an action against them, to compel them to
restore him to his pleasing imaginations :

————— *Pol me occidistis, amici,*
Non servastis ait, cui sic extorta voluptas,
Et demptus per vim mentis gratissimus error.[*]

By heav'n you've kill'd me now, my friends, outright,
And not preserv'd me, since my dear delight
And pleasing error, by my better sense
Unhappily return'd, is banish'd hence.

A madness of this sort possessed Thrasilaus, the son
of Polydorus,[†] who, conceiting that all the vessels
that sailed from or arrived at the port of Pyræum,
traded only for his profit, congratulated himself on
their happy voyages, and received them with the
greatest joy. His brother Crito having caused him
to be restored to his better understanding, he re-
gretted the loss of that sort of condition, in which
he had lived with so much glee and freedom from
anxiety. It is according to the old Greek verse,
that there is a great deal of convenience in not
being too wise :

Ἐν τῳ φρονεῖν γὰρ μηδὲν ἥδιςος βίος.[‡]

And the preacher, " In much wisdom is much grief;
" and he that increaseth knowledge increaseth
" sorrow."[§]

Another proof of the weakness of philosophy, is ^{Another}
that last receipt, to which philosophy in general ^{proof}
^{of the}

---

[*] Hor. lib. ii. epist. 2, ver. 138, &c.
[†] This entire passage is taken from Athenæus, lib. xii. near the
end. It is also in Ælian's Var. Hist. iv. cap. 25, where he is called
Thrasyllus.
[‡] Sophocles in Aj. ce Μαστιγοφόρῳ, ver. 551. [§] Ecclesiast. i. 18.

weakness of philosophy which in general permits the parting with that life which we cannot bear.

assents, and which it prescribes in all cases of necessity, viz. The putting an end to the life which we cannot support. *Placet? Pare: non placet? quacumque vis exi.*[*] *Pungit dolor? vel fodiat sanè; si nudus es, da jugulum: sin tectus armis Vulcaniis, id est, fortitudine, resiste.* " Does it please? Be obe-
" dient: Does it not please? Go out of it which
" way thou wilt. Does grief prick thee, or even
" pierce thy heart? If thou art naked, yield thy
" throat; but, if thou art covered with the arms of
" Vulcan, that is, fortitude, resist." And this
phrase, so much in use at the Greek festivals, *Aut*
" *bibat, aut abeat:*[†] " Let him drink or depart;"
which sounds not so well in the Ciceronian as in
the Gascoon[‡] language, wherein the B is changed
into a V.

> *Vivere si recte nescis, decede peritis.*
> *Lusisti satis, edisti satis atque bibisti:*
> *Tempus abire tibi, ne potum largius æquo*
> *Rideat, et pulset lasciva decentius ætas.*[§]

> If to live properly thou dost not know,
> Give peace, and leave thy room to those that do.
> Thou'st eat, and drank, and play'd, to thy content:
> 'Tis time to make thy parting compliment,
> Lest youth whose follies more become their age,
> Laugh thee to scorn, and push thee off the stage.

What is this[||] but a confession of its inability, and a

---

[*] These first words seem to be an imitation of Seneca's Ep. 70.
As to the remaining words, " Pungit dolor," &c. it is from Cicero's
Tusc. Quæst. lib. ii. cap. 14.

[†] It is an application from Cicero, whose words are these:
" Mihi quidem in vita servanda videtur illa lex quæ in Græcorum
" conviviis obtinetur," &c. Cic. Tus. Quæst. lib. v. cap. 41.

[‡] This remark upon the Gascoon pronunciation, which chooses
to alter B into V, is only to be applied to the word *bibat*, otherwise
it would not be very properly intended here; because, if the B in
the word *abeat* was changed into V, it would mar the construction
which Montaigne would put, according to Cicero, upon this phrase,
" Aut bibat aut abeat."

[§] Hor. lib. ii. epist. ii. ver. 213, &c.

[||] As this is a long period, and as the relation which this passage
stands in to that which goes before it, is very remote, it is here inserted in the last edition, " What is this," I say, " but the consent

recourse not only to ignorance for a shelter, but even
to stupidity, insensibility, and a non-entity:

> ——— *Democritum postquam matura vetustas*
> *Admonuit memorem, motus languescere mentis:*
> *Sponte suâ letho caput obvius obtulit ipse.*[*]

Democritus, perceiving age invade,
His body weaken'd and his mind decay'd,
Obey'd the summons, with a cheerful face,
Made haste to welcome death, and met him half the race.

It is what Antisthenes said,[†] " That a man must
" either be provided with sense to understand, or
" with a halter to hang himself." And what Chrysippus alleged to this purpose from the poet
Tyrtæus, viz.

> *De la vertu ou de mort approcher.*
> Or to arrive at valour or at death.

And Crates said,[‡] that love was to be cured by
hunger, if not by time ; or if neither of these remedies pleased, by a halter. That Sextius, of whom
both Seneca and Plutarch[§] speak with so high an en-
comium, having applied himself solely to the study
of philosophy, and finding the progress of his studies too slow and tedious, resolved to throw himself
into the sea. He ran to meet death, since he could
not overtake knowledge. The words of the law
upon this subject are these : " If, peradventure,
" some great inconvenience happen, for which there
" is no remedy, the haven is near, and a man may
" save himself by swimming out of the body as
" out of a leaky skiff ; for it is the fear of death, and

" if not confession of philosophy," &c. But this is incorporating the
commentary in the text ; a dangerous method, which has been used
by many critics in books of much more importance than Montaigne's
Essays.
* Lucret. lib. iii. ver. 1052, &c.
† Plutarch in the Contradictions of the Stoic Philosophers, cap. 24.
‡ Diog. Laert. in the Life of Crates, lib. vi. sect. 86.
§ Plutarch in his tract, How an amendment may be perceived in
the exercise of virtue, chap. 5.

" not the desire of life, that makes the fool so loth
" to part from the body."

The advantage of simplicity and ignorance. As life is rendered more pleasant by simplicity, it also becomes more innocent and better, as I was just now saying. The simple and the ignorant, says St. Paul, raise themselves up to heaven, and take possession of it; and we with all our knowledge plunge ourselves into the infernal abyss. I am neither swayed by Valentinian, the declared enemy of all science and learning, or by Licinius, both Roman emperors, who called them the poison and pest of every political state; nor by Mahomet, who (as I have heard interdicted learning to his followers: but the example and authority of the great Lycurgus ought surely to have great weight, as well as the reverence due to that divine Lacedæmonian policy so great, so admirable, and so long flourishing in virtue and happiness, without any institution or exercise of letters.

They live in the new world without magistrates or law more regularly than we do. Such as have been in the new world, which was discovered by the Spaniards in the time of our ancestors, can testify to us, how much more honestly and regularly those nations live without magistrates and without law, than ours do, where there are more officers, and more laws, than there are of other sorts of men and occupations :

> Di cittatoria piene e di libelli,
> D'esamina e di carte, di procure
> Hanno le mani e il seno, e gran fastelli
> Di chose, di consigli, e di letture,
> Per cui le facultà de poverelli
> Non sonò mai ne le città sicure,
> Hanno dietro e dinanzi e d' ambi i lati,
> Notai, procuratori, e advocati.*

Their bags were full of writs, and of citations,
    Of process, and of actions and arrests,
Of bills, of answers, and of replications,
    In courts of delegates, and of requests,

* The Orlando Furioso of Ariosto, cant. xiv. stanz. 84.

To grieve the simple sort with great vexations :
   They had resorting to them as their guests,
   Attending on their circuit, and their journeys,
   Scriv'ners, and clerks, and lawyers, and attorneys.

A Roman senator of the latter ages said, that their
ancestors' breath stunk of garlic, but their stomachs
were perfumed with a good conscience : and that,
on the contrary, those of his time were all fragant
without, but stunk within of all sorts of vices: that is
to say, as I take it, they abounded with learning, &c.
but were very deficient of moral honesty.   Incivility, ignorance, simplicity, and roughness, are the natural companions of innocence.   Curiosity, cunning,
and science, bring malice in their train.   Humility,
fear, obedience, and affability (which are the chief
props of human society) require no capacity, provided the mind is docile and free from presumption.

Christians have a particular reason to know what Fatal ef-
a natural and original evil curiosity is in man. The fects of cu-
thirst of increasing in wisdom and knowledge was riosity and pride.
the first ruin of man, and the means by which he
rushed headlong into eternal damnation.   Pride was
his destruction.   It is pride that throws man out of
the common track, that makes him embrace novel-
ties, and rather choose to be the head of a troop
wandering into the road to perdition, and rather the
regent and preceptor of error and lies, than to be a
disciple in the school of truth, and to suffer another
to lead and guide him in the right and beaten track.
This perhaps is the meaning of that old Greek saying, Ἡ δεισιδαιμονία καθάπερ πατρὶ τῷ τύφῳ πείθεται.
" That superstition follows pride, and obeys it as if
" it was its parent." Ah presumption ! how much
dost thou hinder us !

When Socrates was informed that the God of How So-
wisdom had attributed to him the title of a sage, he crates came to have the
was astonished at it, and carefully examining himself, appellati-
could not find any foundation for this divine sentence. on of Wise.
He knew others as just, temperate, valiant, and
learned as himself, and some that were more elo-

quent, more graceful, and more useful to their countrymen than he was. At last he concluded that he was distinguished from others, and pronounced to be a wise man, only because he did not think himself so; and that his god considered the opinion of knowledge and wisdom, as a stupidity in man; that his best doctrine was the doctrine of ignorance, and simplicity his best wisdom.[*] The sacred writ declares those of us miserable, who set a value upon themselves. " Dust and ashes," says he, " to " such, what hast thou to pride thyself in ?" And elsewhere, that " God has made man like to a " shadow," of which who can judge, when it is vanished by the disappearance of the light ? This concerns none but us.

Too curious an inquiry into the divine nature is to be condemned. We are so far from being able to comprehend the divine perfections, that, of the works of the Creator, those best bear the mark, and are more strictly his, which we the least understand. To meet with a thing which is incredible, is an occasion to Christians to believe; and the more it is opposite to human reason, the more reasonable is such faith. If it were according to reason, it would be no longer a miracle; and if there was a precedent for it, it would be no longer a singularity. St. Augustine. says, *Melius scitur Deus nesciendo.* " God is better " known by submitting not to know him." And says, Tacitus,[†] *Sanctius est et reverentius de actis deorum credere quàm scire.* " It is more holy and " reverent to believe the works of God, than to " know them." And Plato[‡] thinks it is somewhat impious to inquire too curiously into God, the world, and the first causes of things. *Atque illum quidem parentem hujus universitatis invenire difficile, at, quum jam inveneris indicare in vulgus, nefas* (says Cicero [§]): " It is a hard matter to find out the parent

* Plato's Apology for Socrates, p. 360, 361.
† De Moribus German. cap. 34.
‡ Ciceronis Timæus, or De Universo Fragmentum, cap. 2.
§ De Natura Deorum, lib. iii. cap. 15, without naming him.

" of the universe; and, when found out, it is not
" lawful to reveal him to the vulgar."

We pronounce indeed power, truth, justice, which _{What our notions of the divine Being amount to.}
are words that denote something great, but that very
thing we neither see nor conceive at all. We say
that God fears, that God is angry, that God
loves:

> *Immortalia mortali sermone notantes.* *
>
> Giving to things immortal, mortal names.

These are all agitations and emotions that cannot
be in God, according to our form; nor can we
imagine them according to his. It only belongs to
God to know himself, and to interpret his own
works; and he does it in our language improperly
to stoop and descend to us, who grovel upon the
earth. How can prudence,† which is the choice between good and evil, be properly attributed to him,
whom no evil can touch? How can the reason and
understanding which we make use of to arrive at
things apparent by those that are obscure, since
there is nothing obscure to God? And justice,
which distributes to every man what appertains to
him, a principle created for the society and inter-
course of men, how is that in God? How temperance, which is the moderation of corporeal pleasures, that have no place in the divinity? Fortitude
to support pain, labour, and danger as little appertains to him as the rest, these three things having
no access to him : for which reason, Aristotle‡ thinks
him equally exempt from virtue and vice. He is not
capable either of affection or indignation, because
they are both the effects of frailty: *Neque gratiâ
neque irâ teneri potest, quòd quæ talia essent imbe-
cilla essent omnia.*

The share we have in the knowledge of truth,

---

* Lucret. lib. v. ver. 122.

† Montaigne has here transcribed a long passage from Cicero,
De Natura Deorum, lib. iii. cap. 15.

‡ Cic. de Natura Deorum, lib. i. cap. 17.

From
whence
comes our
know-
ledge of
truth.
whatever it be, is not acquired by our own strength.
This is what God has plainly given us to understand
by the witnesses he has chosen out of the common
people, simple and ignorant men, to inform us of
his wonderful secrets.   Our faith is not of our own
acquiring, but purely the gift of another's bounty.
It is not by reasoning, or by virtue of our understanding, that we have acquired our religion, but by
foreign authority and command ; and the weakness
of our judgment is of more assistance to us in it,
than the strength of it ; and our blindness more
than the clearness of our sight.   It is more owing to
our ignorance, than to our knowledge, that we know
any thing of divine wisdom.   It is no wonder if our
natural and terrestrial faculties cannot conceive this
supernatural and celestial knowledge.   We can only
bring, on our part, obedience and submission :
" For it is written, I will destroy the wisdom of the
" wise, and will bring to nothing the understanding
" of the prudent. Where is the wise ? Where is the
" scribe ? Where is the disputer of this world ?
" Hath not God made foolish the wisdom of this
" world ? For, after that, in the wisdom of God,
" the world knew not God, it pleased God by the
" foolishness of preaching to save them that
" believe."*

Whether it
is in man's
power to
find out
truth.
Finally, were I to examine, whether it be in the
power of man to find out that which he seeks, and
if that search, wherein he has busied himself so
many ages, has enriched him with any new ability,
and any solid truth, I believe he will confess to me,
if he speaks from his conscience, that all he has got
by so long a disquisition, is only to have learned to
to know his own weakness. We have only by long
study confirmed and verified the ignorance we were
in by nature. The same has happened to men who
are truly wise, which befalls ears of corn : they shoot
up and raise their heads straight and lofty, whilst

* 1 Cor. i. 19, &c.

they are empty; but, when they are full, and
swelled with grain in maturity, begin to flag and
droop. So men, having tried and sounded all things,
and not having found, in that mass of knowledge
and provision of such variety, any thing solid and
firm, nor any thing but vanity, have quitted their
presumption, and acknowledged their state by nature. It is what Velleius reproaches Cotta and
Cicero* with, that they had, learned from Philo†
that they had learned nothing. Pherecides, one of
the seven wise men, writing on his death-bed to
Thales, said,‡ " I have ordered my people after
" my interment to carry my writings to thee. If
" they please thee, and the other sages, publish; if
" not, suppress them. They contain no certainty
" with which I myself am satisfied; neither do I
" pretend to know the truth, or to attain to it: I
" rather open than discover things." The wisest
man§ that ever was, being asked what he knew,
made answer, that he knew this, that he knew
nothing. By this he verified the assertion, that the
greatest part of what we know, is the least of what
we do not know; that is to say, that even that which
we think we know is but a portion, and a very small
portion, of our ignorance. We know things in
dreams, says Plato, and are ignorant of them in
reality. *Omnes pene veteres nihil cognosci, nihil per-
cipi, nihil sciri posse dixerunt : angustos sensus, imbe-
cilles animos, brevia curricula vitæ.*‖ " Almost all the
" ancients have declared, that there is nothing to be
" known, nothing to be perceived nor understood;
" that the senses are too limited, minds too weak, and
" the time of life too short." And of Cicero him-

* Cicero de Natura Deorum, lib. i, cap. 17.
† Cicero was one that attended the lectures of this Philo, who
was an academic philosopher.
‡ Diog. Laert. lib. i. at the end of the Life of the Pherecides,
sect. 122.
§ Socrates, Cic. Acad. Quæst. lib. i. cap. 4.
‖ Cic. Acad. Quæst, lib. i. cap. 12.

self, whose merit was all owing to his learning, Valerius says, that in his old age he began to despise
letters, and that, when he applied to study, it was
without dependance upon any one sect, following
what he thought probable, now in one sect, then in
another, evermore wavering under the doubts of the
Academy. *Dicendum est, sed ita ut nihil affirmem ;
quæram omnia, dubitans plerumque, et mihi diffidens.*
" Something I must say (as he told his brother), but
" without affirming any thing; I inquire ·into all
" things, but am generally doubting and diffident of
" myself." I should have too much of the best of
the argument, were I to consider man in his common way of living, and in the gross; and yet I
might do it by his own rule, who judges of truth,
not by the weight, but by the number of votes.
There we will leave the vulgar,

> ———— † *Qui vigilans stertit,*
> *Mortua cui vita est propè jam vivo atque videnti.*‡
> Half of his life by lazy sleep's possest,
> And when awake, his soul but nods at best :

who neither feel nor judge themselves, and let
most of their natural faculties lie idle.

Of the knowledge to which the greatest geniuses have attained by study and art.

I will take man in his sublimest state. Let us
view him in that small number of excellent and
select men, who, having been endowed with a curious and particular natural talent, have moreover
hardened and whetted it by care, study, and art,
and raised it to the highest pitch of wisdom to.which
it can possibly·arrive. They have adjusted their
souls to all senses and all biases, have propped and
supported them with all the foreign assistance proper
for them, and enriched and adorned them with all
that they could borrow for their advantage, both
from within and without. Those are they in whom

* Cic. de Div. lib. ii. cap. 3.
† Lucret. lib. iii. ver. 1061, ibid. ver. 1059.
‡ Montaigne has transposed these two verses of Lucretius to
adapt them the more nicely to his subject.

resides human nature, to the utmost degree of perfection. They have regulated the world with polity and laws. They have instructed it in the arts and sciences, and also by the example of their admirable manners. I shall bring to my account those men only, their testimony and experience. Let us see how far they have proceeded, and on what they depended. The maladies and defects, that we shall find amongst these men, the world may boldly declare to be purely their own.

Whoever enters upon the search of any thing, comes at last to this point:* he either says, that he has found it, or that it is not to be found, or that he is still in quest of it. The whole of philosophy is divided into these three kinds. Its design is to seek out truth, knowledge, and certainty. The Peripatetics, Epicuræns, Stoics, and others have thought they have found it. These established the sciences which we have, and have treated of them as of certainties. Clitomachus, Carneades, and the Academics despaired in their search, and were of opinion, that truth could not be conceived by our understandings. These place all to the account of human frailty and ignorance. This sect has had the most numerous and the most noble followers. *(All philosophy divided into three kinds.)*

Pyrrho, and other sceptics or doubters, whose doctrines were held by many of the ancients, as deduced from Homer, the seven wise men, Archilochus, Euripides, Zeno, Democritus, and Xenophon, say, that they are still in the search of truth. These judge that they, who think they have found it, are vastly deceived; and that it is also too daring a vanity in the second sort to affirm, that it is not in *(What was the profession of the Pyrrhonians.)*

* In this very style, does Sextus Empiricus, the famous Pyrrhonian, from whom Montaigne has taken many things, begin his treatise of the Pyrrhonian hypothesis; and infers, as Montaigne does, that there are three general methods of philosophising, the one dogmatic, the other academic, and the other sceptic. Some affirm they have found the truth, others declare it to be above our comprehension, and others are still in quest of it.

the power of man to attain to it. For this establishing the measure of our strength, to know and judge
of the difficulty of things, is a great and extreme
degree of knowledge, of which they doubt whether
man is capable :

> *Nil sciri quisquis putat, id quoque nescit,*
> *An sciri possit quo se nil scire fatetur.*[*]
>
> He that says nothing can be known, o'erthrows
> His own opinion, for he nothing knows,
> So knows not that.

The ignorance that knows itself, that judges and
condemns itself, is not total ignorance, which to be,
it must be ignorant of itself. So that the profession
of the Pyrrhonians is to waver, doubt, and inquire,
to be sure of nothing, and to be answerable for nothing. Of the three operations of the soul, the imagination, the appetite, and the consent, they admit
of the two first, but, as for the last, they support
and maintain it ambiguously, without inclination or
approbation either of one thing or another, it is so
trivial. Zeno described the state of his imagination,
according to this division of the faculties of the mind.
The hand, extended and open, indicated appearance ;
the hand half shut, and the fingers a little crooked,
showed consent ; the right fist clinched, comprehension ; and when with the left-hand he yet pressed the
fist closer, knowledge.[†]

The advan-
tage of
Pyrrho-
nism.
Now this upright and inflexible state of the opinion of the Pyrrhonians receiving all objects, without
application or consent, leads them to their ataraxy,
which is a peaceable state of life, composed and exempt from the agitations which we receive by the impression of that opinion and knowledge which we think
we have of things ; from whence arise fear, avarice,
envy, immoderate desires, ambition, pride, superstition, the love of novelty, rebellion, disobedience,
obstinacy, and most of the bodily evils. Nay, and
by that they exempt themselves from the jealousy

* Lucret. lib. iv. ver, 47 L.   † Cic. Acad. Quæst. lib. iv. cap. 47.

of their discipline. For they debate after a very
gentle manner, and in their disputes fear no revenge. When they say that weight presses downward, they would be sorry to be believed, and want
to be contradicted, for the sake of creating doubt
and suspense of judgment, which is their ultimate
end. They only advance their propositions to oppose
such as they imagine have gained our belief. If you
admit theirs, they are altogether as ready to maintain the contrary. It is all one to them. They have
no choice. If you maintain that snow is black, they
will argue, on the contrary, that it is white. If you say,
that it is neither the one nor the other, their business is to maintain, that it is both. If you adhere to the opinion that you know nothing of the
matter, they will maintain that you do : yea, and, if
by an affirmative axiom you assure them that you
doubt of a thing, they will argue that you do not
doubt of it, or that you cannot be sure that you do
doubt of it. And by this extremity of doubt, which
shocks itself, they separate and divide themselves
from many opinions, even of those who have, in
many forms, maintained doubt and ignorance. Why
shall it not be allowed to them, say they, as it is to
the dogmatists, one to say green, another yellow,
and even to doubt of these? Can any thing be proposed to us to acknowledge or deny, which is not
allowable for us to consider as ambiguous? And
where others are induced, either by the custom of
their country, or by the institution of parents, or by
accident, as by a tempest, without judgment, and
without choice, nay, most commonly before the age
of discretion, to such or such an opinion, to the sect
of the Stoics or Epicureans, and are thereto so enslaved and fast bound, as to a thing that they cannot
recede from; *Ad quamcumque disciplinam, velut
tempestate, delati, ad eam, tanquam ad saxum, adhæ-
rescunt :** " To whatsoever discipline they happen to

* Cic. Acad. Quæst. lib. ii. cap. 3.

" be introduced, to that sect they cleave, as they
" would to a rock, if drove to it by a storm ;" why
should not these be permitted, in like manner, to
maintain their liberty, and consider things without
obligation and servility ? *Hóc liberiores et solu-
tiores, quòd integra illis est judicandi potestas :*[*]
" Being, in this respect, the more free and uncon-
" strained, because they have the full power of
" judging." Is it not of some advantage to be disengaged from the necessity which curbs others ? Is it
not better for a man to continue in suspense, than
to entangle himself in so many errors as human fancy
has produced ? Is it not better for him to suspend his
opinion, than to meddle with those seditious and
wrangling divisions ? What shall I choose ? " What
" you please, provided you do but choose." As
silly as this answer is, yet it seems to be the language of all the dogmatists, by whom we. are not
permitted to be ignorant of what we are ignorant.
Take the most eminent side, it will never be so secure, but you will be under a necessity of attacking
a hundred and a hundred contrary opinions for the
defence of it. Is it not better to keep out of this
confusion ? You are permitted to embrace Aristotle's
opinion of the immortality of the soul, with as much
zeal as if your honour and life were at stake, and to
contradict and give the lie to Plato on that head ;
and shall they be forbid to doubt of it ? If it be lawful
for Panætius[†] to suspend his judgment concerning
augury, dreams, oracles, vaticinations, of which
things the Stoics make no manner of doubt, why
may not a wise man presume to do the same, in all
things, that this man dared to do in those things
which he learned from his master, established by the
school of which he is a disciple ? If it be a child that
judges, he knows nothing of the matter ; if a wise
man, he is prepossessed. They have reserved to
themselves a wonderful advantage in battle, having

---

[*] Cic. Acad. Quæst. lib. ii. cap. 3.　　　[†] Idem, lib. i. cap. ult.

eased themselves of the care of providing a fence.
They are not concerned at being struck, provided
they also strike; and they make every thing serve
their purpose. If they overcome, your argument
is lame; as theirs is, if you overcome: if they fall
short, they verify ignorance; as you do, if you
miss: if they prove that nothing is known, it goes
well; if they cannot prove it, it is altogether as
well. *Ut quum in eadem re paria in contrariis
partibus momenta inveniuntur, facilius ab utraque
parte assertio sustineatur :* " To the end that, as the
" reasons are equal *pro* and *con* upon the same sub-
" ject, the determination may easily be suspended on
" both sides;" and they make account to find out,
with much greater ease, why a thing is false, than
why it is true; and what is not, than that which is;
and what they do not believe, than what they do believe.

Their forms of speech are, " I establish nothing:
" it is no more so than so; or no more one than
" the other: I do not comprehend it: the appear-
" ances are, in all respects, equal: the rule of
" speaking, both *pro* and *con*, is alike: nothing
" seems true, that may not as well seem false."
Their sacramental word is ἐπέχω, that is to say, " I
" demur to it, I suspend my judgment." This is
their constant note, with other terms of the like
significancy, the effect of which is a pure, entire,
and absolute pause and suspension of the judgment.
They make use of their reason to inquire and dispute, but not to fix and determine. Whoever will
imagine a perpetual confession of ignorance, a
judgment without bias, and without inclination upon
any occasion whatsoever, conceives a true idea of
Pyrrhonism. I express this whimsicalness as well as
I can, by reason that many people can hardly conceive what it is, and authors themselves represent it
a little differently and obscurely.

As to the actions of life, they follow the common

The common style of the Pyrrhonians.

* Cic. Acad. Quæst. lib. i. cap. ult.

What is the behaviour of the Pyrrhonians in common life.

forms. They yield and give themselves up to the natural inclinations, to the impulse and power of the passions, to the constitutions of the laws and customs, and to the tradition of the arts ; *Non enim nos Deus ista scire, sed tantummodo uti voluit :*† " For God would not have us know, but only use " these things." They suffer their common actions to be guided by those things without any deliberation or judgment. For this reason I cannot well reconcile what is said of Pyrrho with this argument. They represent him stupid and immoveable, leading a savage and unsociable course of life, putting himself in the way of being jostled by carts, going upon precipices, and refusing to conform to the laws. This is to exaggerate his discipline. He would not be thought a stock or a stone. He would be represented as a man living, reasoning, and arguing, enjoying all natural conveniences and pleasures, employing and making use of all his corporeal and spiritual faculties in rule and reason. As to the fantastic, imaginary, and false privileges that man has usurped, of lording it, ordaining and establishing, he has, in good earnest, renounced and quitted them.

The wise man is determined in life by appearances.

Yet there is no sect‡ but is obliged to permit its wise man to follow several things not comprehended, nor perceived, nor consented to, if he means to live : and if he goes to sea, he pursues that design, not knowing whether it will be successful to him or no ; and is influenced only by the goodness of the ship, the experience of the pilot, the convenience of the season, and circumstances that are only probable. According to these, he is bound to go, and suffer himself to be governed by appearances, provided there be no express contrariety in them. He has a body, he has a soul, the senses push him, the mind

* Sextus Empiricus says this verbatim, Pyrrh. Hypot. lib. i. cap. 11, p. 6.

† Cic. de Div. lib. i. cap. 18.

‡ Montaigne only copies Cicero here. Acad. Quæst. lib. ii. cap. 32.

spurs him on. Although he do not find in himself this proper and peculiar token of judging, and though he perceives, he ought not to engage his consent, considering that there may be a false appearance, as well as a true, nevertheless he carries on the offices of his life with great liberty and convenience. How many arts are there, the profession of which consists in conjecture more than in knowledge? That decide not of truth or falshood, and only follow appearances? There is, they say, the right as well as the wrong, and we have, in us, wherewith to seek it, but not to stop it when we touch it. We are much the better for it, when we suffer ourselves to be governed by the world without inquiry. A soul free from prejudice is in a very fair way towards tranquillity; men that judge and control their judges, never duly submit to them.

How much more docile and easy to be reconciled ^{What} to religion, and the laws of civil policy, are simple ^{minds are best dis-} and incurious minds, than those over-curious wits ^{posed to} and pedagogues, that will still be prating of divine ^{submit to religion,} and human causes? There is nothing in human in-^{and the} vention that carries so much probability and profit. ^{rules of go-vernment.} This man is represented naked and empty, acknowledging his natural weakness, fit for receiving foreign strength from above, unfurnished with human science, and the more adapted for receiving divine knowledge, undervaluing his own judgment to make the more room for faith, neither disbelieving nor establishing any doctrine contrary to the laws and common observances; humble, obedient, docile, studious, a sworn enemy to heresy, and consequently free from the vain and irreligious opinions introduced by the false sects. He is as a charte blanche, prepared to receive such forms from the finger of God, as he shall please to engrave on it. The more we resign and commit ourselves to God, and the more we renounce ourselves, of the greater value we are. " Take in good part," says the preacher, " the things that present themselves to

" thee, as they seem and taste to thee from one day
" to another: the rest is out of thy knowledge."
*Dominus novit cogitationes hominum, quoniam vanæ
sunt:* " The Lord knoweth the thoughts of man,
that they are vanity."[*]

Thus we see, that of the three general sects of
philosophy, two make open profession of doubting
and ignorance; and in that of the Dogmatists, which
is the third, it is obvious, that the greatest part of
them have only assumed the face of assurance, to
give them the better air. They have not been so
solicitous to establish any certainty for us, as to
show us how far they proceeded in this pursuit of the
truth; *Quam docti fingunt magis quam norunt:* " How
" the learned rather feign than know."[†] Timæus,
being to inform Socrates of what he knew of the
Gods, the world, and men, proposes to speak of
them to him as one man does to another, and thinks
it sufficient if his reasons are as probable as another
man's, for the exact reasons were neither in his hand,
nor that of any mortal whatsoever; which one of his
followers has thus imitated; *Ut potero, explicabo:
nec tamen, ut Pythius Apollo, certa ut sint et fixa,
quæ dixero; sed ut homunculus, probabilia conjec-
turâ sequens:*[‡] " I will explain things in the best
" manner I can; yet not, as the oracle of Delphos,
" pronouncing them as fixed and certain, but like
" a mere man, who adheres to probabilities by con-
" jecture." And that other upon the natural and
popular topic of the contempt of death, as he has
elsewhere translated it from the very dissertation of
Plato; *Si fortè, de deorum naturâ ortúque mundi
disserentes, minus id quod habemus in animo conse-
quemur, haud erit mirum. Æquum est meminisse,
et me, qui disseram, hominum esse, et vos qui judice-
tis, ut si probabilia dicentur, nihil ultra requiratis:*[§]
" If, in discoursing of the nature of the Gods, and

---

[*] Psal. xciv. 11. 　　　　[†] Plato in Timæo, p. 526.
[‡] Cic. Tusc. Quæst. lib. i. cap. 9.
[§] Cicero's Timæus, seu de Universo Fragmentum, cap. 3.

" the origin of the world, we should happen not to
" express all that we conceive in our minds, it will
" be no wonder : for it is but just that we should re-
" member, that both I who argue, and you who
" are my judges, are but men: so that, if probable
" things are delivered, ye are to require nothing
" more." Aristotle commonly heaps up a great
number of the opinions and beliefs of other men,
for the sake of comparing them with his own, and to
show us how far he has gone beyond them, and how
much nearer he approaches to probability : for truth
is not to be judged by the authority and testimony
of others : and therefore Epicurus was very careful
not to quote them in his writings. Aristotle was the
prince of all dogmatists, and yet we are told by him,
that much knowledge administers occasion of doubting the more. In fact, we often find him wrapped
up in obscurity, so thick and impenetrable, that
we know not, by his opinion, what to choose. It
is, in effect, Pyrrhonism under the form of determination. Hear Cicero's protestation, who ex-
pounds another's fancy to us by his own: *Qui re-
quirunt, quid de quaque re ipsi sentiamus, curiosius,
id faciunt, quàm necesse est.—Hæc in philosophia ratio, contra omnia disserendi, nullamque rem apertè
judicandi, perfecta à Socrate, repetita ab Arcesilâ,
confirmata à Carneade, usque ad nostram viget
ætatem. Hi sumus, qui omnibus veris falsa quædam
adjuncta esse dicamus, tantâ similitudine, ut in iis
nulla insit certè judicandi et essentiendi nota :* * " They
" who desire to know what we think of every thing,
" are too inquisitive.—This rule in philosophy, of
" disputing against every thing, and of explicitly de-
" termining nothing, which was founded by So-
" crates, re-established by Arcesilaus, and con-
" firmed by Carneades, has continued in use even
" to our times. We are they who declare, that in
" every truth there is such a mixture of falshood,

* Cic. de Natura Deorum, lib. i. cap. 5.

" and that so resembling the truth, that there is no
" mark in them whereby to judge of, or assent to
" either with certainty." Why has not only Aristotle, but most of the philosophers, affected obscurity, but to enchance the value of the subject, and
to amuse the curiosity of our minds by furnishing
them with this bone to pick, on which there is no
flesh? Clitomachus * affirmed, that by the writings

---

* Montaigne has supposed this to be the meaning of Cicero,
whose words are these: " The opinion of which Calliphon Car-
" neades so studiously defended, that he even seemed to approve of
" it, although Clitomachus affirmed, that he never could understand
" what was approved by Carneades." Acad: Quæst. lib. x. cap.
45. But this is not saying, " That Clitomachus asserted, that by
" the writing of Carneades, he could never discover his opinion."
The dispute is not, what were the opinions of Carneades in the general, but what he used to say in defence of Calliphon's private opinion
concerning what constitutes man's chief good. Forasmuch as Carneades was an academician, he could not advance any thing positive
or clearly decisive upon this important question, which was the reason that Clitomachus never could understand what was the opinion
of Carneades in this matter. Calliphon made the chief good consist
in pleasure and virtue both together, which, says Cicero, Carneades
also was not willing to contradict, " not that he approved it, but
" that he might oppose the Stoics; not to decide the thing, but to
" embarrass the Stoics." Acad. Quæst. lib. iv. cap. 42. In this
same book Cicero explains to us several of Carneades's opinions;
and what is very remarkable is, that he only does it as they are set
forth by Clitomachus. " Having," says he, " explained all that
" Carneades says upon this subject, all those opinions of Antiochus
" (the Stoic) will fall to the ground. But, for fear lest I should be
" suspected of making him say what I think, I shall deliver nothing
" but what I collect from Clitomachus, who passed his life with Car-
" neades till he was an old man, and, being a Carthaginian, was a
" man of great penetration, very studious moreover, and very ex-
" act." Acad. Quæst. lib. iv. cap. 31. " I have," says Cicero,
" a little before explained to you from the words of Clitomachus,
" in what sense Carneades declared these matters." These very
things Cicero repeats afterwards, where he transcribes them from a
book which Clitomachus had composed and addressed to the poet
Lucilius. After this, how could Cicero make Clitomachus say, that
by the writings of Carneades in general, he could never discover
what were his sentiments? The truth is, that Clitomachus had not
read the writings of Carneades; for, except some letters that he
wrote to Anarathes, king of Cappadocia, which ran in his name,
the rest of his opinions, as Diogenes Laertius says expressly, were
preserved in the books of his disciples. In Vita Carneadis, lib. iv.

of Carneades he could never discover what opinion
he was of. Why did Epicurus affect to be abstruse,
and what else procured Heraclitus the surname of
σκοτεινὸς, or obscure ?

Obscurity is a coin which the learned make use of,
like jugglers, to conceal the vanity of their art,
and which the stupidity of mankind takes for current
pay :

> *Clarus ob obscuram linguam, magis inter inanes :*
> *Omnia enim stolidi magis admirantur amantque,*
> *Inversis quæ sub verbis latitantia cernunt.*[*]
>
> Bombast and riddle always puppies please,
> For fools admire and love such things as these ;
> And a dull quibble, ambiguously express'd,
> Seems to their empty minds a wond'rous jest.

Cicero reproves some of his friends for having
spent more time in astrology, law, logic, and geometry, than those arts deserved, saying, that the
study of these diverted them from the more useful
and honourable duties of life. The Cyrenaic philosophers equally despised natural philosophy and
logic. Zeno,[†] in the very beginning of the books
of the commonwealth, declared all the liberal arts
unprofitable. Chrysippus said, that what Plato and
Aristotle had wrote concerning logic, they only
composed for diversion, and by way of exercise ;
and he could not believe that they spoke of so vain
a thing in earnest. Plutarch says the same of me-
taphysics : Epicurus had also said as much of rhetoric, grammar, poetry, mathematics, and (natural
philosophy excepted) of all the other sciences : and
Socrates says the same of all, except ethics and the
science of life. Whatever instruction any man applied to him for, he always, in the first place, de-

The liberal arts despised by some of the sects of the philosophers.

---

sect. 65. The same historian tells us, that Clitomachus, who composed above 400 volumes, applied himself above all things, to illustrate the sentiments of Carneades, whom he succeeded. Diogenes
Laertius, in the Life of Clitomachus, lib. iv. sect. 67.

* Lucret. lib. i. ver. 640, &c.

† Diog. Laert. in the Life of Zeno, lib. vii. sect. 32.

sired him to give him an account of the conditions
of his life past and present, which he examined and
judged, esteeming all other learning as supernu-
merary. *Parum mihi placent eæ literæ quæ ad vir-
tutem doctoribus nihil profuerunt :* * " That learning
" is in small repute with me, which did not contri-
" bute to the virtue of the teachers as well as
" learners." Most of the arts have been disparaged
in like manner by the same knowledge. But they
did not consider that it was foreign to the purpose
to exercise their understanding on those very subjects, wherein there was no solid advantage.

What were Plato's real sentiments. As for the rest, some have reckoned Plato a
dogmatist; others a doubter: others in some things
the former, and in others the latter. Socrates, who
conducted his dialogues, is continually starting que-
ries and stirring up disputes, never determining,
never satisfying, and professes to have no other
science but that of opposition. Homer, their author,
has equally laid the foundations of all the sects of
philosophy, to show how indifferent it was to which
of them we inclined.

To how many sects Plato gave birth. It is said, that ten several sects sprung from Plato;
and, in my opinion, never did any instruction totter
and waver, if his does not.

Socrates compared himself to midwives. Socrates said, " that midwives, while they make
" it their business to assist others in bringing forth,
" lay aside the misery of their own generation: that,
" by the title of the sage, which the gods had con-
" ferred upon him, he was also disabled in his virile
" and mental love of the faculty of bringing forth,
" contenting himself to help and assist those that
" were pregnant, to open their nature, lubicrate
" their passages, facilitate the birth of the issue of
" their brains; to pass judgment on it; to baptize,
" nourish, fortify it; to swathe and circumcise it;
" exercising and employing his understanding in
" the perils and fortunes of others."

* Sallust, p. 94, Mattaire's edit. London, 1713.

The case is the same with the generality of the authors of this third class, as the ancients have observed of the writings of Anaxagoras, Democritus, Parmenides, Xenophon, and others. They have a manner of writing doubtful, both in substance and design, rather inquiring than teaching, though they intermix some dogmatical periods in their compositions. Is not this also visible in Seneca and Plutarch? How self-contradictory do they appear to such as pry narrowly into them? And the reconcilers of the lawyers ought first to reconcile them every one to themselves. Plato seems to me to have affected this form of philosophising by dialogues, to the end that he might with greater decency, from several mouths deliver the diversity and variety of his own fancies. To treat of matters variously is altogether as well as to treat of them conformably, and indeed better; that is to say, more copiously, and with greater profit. Let us only look at home; sentences or decrees are the utmost period of all dogmatical and determinative speaking: and yet those arrets which our parliaments make, those that are the most exemplary, and that are most proper to cultivate the reverence due from the people to that dignity chiefly, considering the ability of the persons vested with it, derive their beauty not so much from the conclusions, which are what they pass every day, and are common to every judge, as from the discussion and debating of the differing and contrary arguments which the matter of law admits of. And the largest field for the censures, which some philosophers pass upon others, is owing to the contradictions and variety of opinions, wherein every one of them finds himself entangled, either on purpose to show the wavering of man's understanding upon every subject, or else ignorantly compelled to it by the volubility and incomprehensibility of all matter: which is the very signification* of that maxim, so

The same thing may be said of many great philosophers and famous writers.

* To prove that this was exactly what Montaigne intended by

L 2

often repeated by Plutarch, Seneca, and many
other writers of their class, viz. " In a slippery track
" let us suspend our belief:" for, as Euripides says,

God's various works perplex the thoughts of men.[*]

Like that which Empedocles often makes use of in
his books, as if he was agitated By a divine fury, and
compelled by the force of truth. No, no, we feel
nothing, we see nothing, all things are concealed
from us ;[†] here is not one thing of which we can
positively determine what it is, according to the
divine saying, *Cogitationes mortalium timidæ, et
incertæ adinventiones nostræ et providentiæ :*[‡] " The
" thoughts of mortal men are miserable, and our
" devices are but uncertain."

The search
of truth a
very agree-
able occu-
pation.
It must not be thought strange if men, though
they despair of overtaking the prey, nevertheless
take a pleasure in the pursuit : study being of itself
a pleasant employment, so delightful, that, amongst
the other pleasures, the Stoics also forbid that which
proceeds from the exercise of the understanding, are
actually for curbing it, and think too much knowledge intemperance.

Democritus, having eaten figs[§] at his table which

those words, *Que signifie ce refrein*, &c. which Mr. Cotton has most
absurdly turned into an interrogation by this jargon. " What means
" this chink in the close ?" I need only point you to those that immediately preceded them in the quarto edition of 1588 ; where, after having spoken of those ancient philosophers " who had a form
" of writing dubious, both in substance and design, inquiring rather
" than instructing, though they intermix some dogmatical periods
" in their style," Montaigne says, in the same breath, " Where is
" this more visible than in our Plutarch ? How differently does he
" reason upon the same topic ? How often does he give us two or
" three contrary causes' for the same effect, and how many various
" arguments without preferring either to our choice?"

    [*] Plutarch' s Treatise of the Oracles that ceased, chap. 24.
    [†] Cic. Quæst. Acad. lib. iv. cap. 5.
    [‡] Wisdom, ix. 14.
    [§] Plutarch's Table Talk. Qu. 10, lib. i. This quotation, which I
found as soon as I had dipped into the last edition of Bayle's Critical Dictionary, at the article Democritus, note 1, is very just, as I
was fully convinced by consulting Plutarch himself ; but I have

tasted of honey, fell immediately to considering _{Democri-}
within himself from whence they derived that un- _{tus's pas-}
common sweetness; and, to be satisfied, was about _{quiries into}
to rise from the table, to see the place where the _{natural}
figs were gathered : the maid, being informed what _{phy.}
was the cause of the bustle, said to him, with a
smile, that he need give himself no trouble about
it, for she had put them into a vessel in which there
had been honey. He was vexed at the discovery,
because it had deprived him of the opportunity of
finding out the cause himself, and robbed his curiosity of matter to work upon. " Go thy way," said
he to her, " thou hast done me an injury; but,
" however, I will seek out the cause of it as if it
" was natural ;" and he would fain have found out
some true cause of an effect that was false and imaginary. This story of a famous and great philosopher does very clearly represent to us the studious
passion that amuses us in the pursuit of the things
which we despair of acquiring. Plutarch gives a
like example of one who would not be set right in
a matter of doubt, because he would not lose the
pleasure of seeking it ; and of another person who
would not suffer his physician to allay the thirst of
his fever, because he would not lose the pleasure of
quenching it by drinking. *Satius est supervacua
discere quam nihil :* " It is better to learn more than
" is necessary than nothing at all."

As many things which we eat are pleasant to the _{The consi-}
palate, though neither nourishing nor wholesome, in _{deration of} _{nature is}
like manner, what our understanding extracts from _{food for}
science, is nevertheless pleasant, though it is nei- _{the mind of} _{man.}
ther nutritive nor salutary. What they say is this:
" the consideration of nature is food proper for our
" minds; it elevates and puffs us up, makes us dis-
" dain low and terrestrial things, in comparison with

learnt from M. de la Monnoye, that, according to Plutarch, Democritus eat τὸν σίκυον, a cucumber, and not τὸ σῦκον, a fig, as Montaigne has translated it, copying after Amyot and Xylander.
* Senec. epist. 88.

" things that are sublime and celestial. The inqui-
" sition into great and occult things is very pleasant,
" even to him who acquires nothing by it but the
" reverence and awe of judging it." Those are the
terms of their profession. The vain image of this
sickly curiosity is yet more manifest by this other
example, which they are often fond of urging : Eudoxus* wished, and prayed to the gods, that he
might once see the sun near at hand, to comprehend
the form, magnitude, and beauty of it, though he
should be suddenly burnt by it. He was desirous,
at the peril of his life, to acquire a knowledge, of
which the use and possession would be taken from
him at the same instant ; and, for the sake of this
sudden and transitory knowledge, lose all the other
knowledge he had then, or might have acquired
hereafter.

The atoms of Epicurus, the ideas of Plato, the numbers of Pythagoras, to what end they were advanced.

I cannot easily persuade myself, that Epicurus,
Plato, and Pythagoras, have given us their atoms,
ideas, and numbers, for articles of our faith. They
were too wise to establish things so uncertain, and
so disputable, for their credenda. But, in the then
obscure and ignorant state of the world, each of
those great men endeavoured to strike out some
image of light, whatever it was, and racked their
brains for inventions, that had, at least, a pleasant
and subtle appearance, provided that, however false
they were, they might be able to stand their ground
against opposition ; *Unicuique ista pro ingenio fin-
guntur, non ex scientiæ vi :†* " Those are things
" which every one fancies, according to his genius,
" not by virtue of knowledge."

What is true philo-

One of the ancients, being reproached that he
professed philosophy, but nevertheless, in his own

* In Plutarch's Tract, " That it is impossible to live merrily ac-
" cording to the doctrine of Epicurus," chap. 3, you will find, in
Diogenes Laertius, lib. viii. sect. 86—91, the life of Eudoxus, that
celebrated Pythagorean philosopher, who was cotemporary with
Plato.

† M. Senec. Suasoriarum, lib. i, Suas. 4.

opinion, made no great account of it, made answer,
that this was the true way of philosophising: they
would consider all, and weigh every thing; and have
found this an employment suited to our natural curiosity. Something they have written for the use of
public society, as their religions; and for that consideration, as it was but reasonable, they were not
willing to sift the common notions too finely, that
they might not obstruct the common obedience to
the laws and customs of their country. Plato treats
this mystery with barefaced raillery; for, where he
writes according to his own method, he gives no
certain rule. When he personates the legislator, he
assumes a style that is magisterial and dogmatical;
and yet, therewith, boldly mixes the most fantastical
of his inventions, as fit to persuade the vulgar, as
they are too ridiculous to be believed by himself,
knowing very well how fit we are to receive all manner of impressions, especially the most violent and
immoderate. Yet, in his laws, he takes great care
that nothing be sung in public but poetry, of which
the fabulous fictions tend to some useful purpose:
it being so easy to imprint all phantasms in the human mind, that it were injustice not to feed it with
profitable lies, rather than with those that are unprofitable and prejudicial. He says, without any
scruple, in his republic, that it is very often necessary for men's good to deceive them. It is easy to
distinguish the sects that have most adhered to truth,
and those that have most view to profit, by which
the latter have gained credit. It often happens,
that the thing which appears to our imagination to
be the most true, seems not to be the most profitable
in life. The boldest sects, as the Epicurean, Pyrrhonian, and the new academic, are constrained,
after all is said and done, to submit to the civil law.
There are other subjects, which they have discussed,
some on the right, others on the left; and each sect
endeavours to give them some countenance, be it
right or wrong. For, finding nothing so abstruse

which they would not venture to treat of, they were
very often forced to forge weak and ridiculous conjectures; not that they themselves looked upon
them, as any foundation for establishing any certain
truth, but merely for the exercise of their study.
*Non tam id sensisse, quod dicerent, quam exercere in-
genia materiæ difficultates videntur voluisse :* " Not
" that they seem to have been persuaded of the truth
" of what they said, but rather that they were wil-
" ling to exercise their talents, by the difficulty of
" the subject." If this was not the case, how shall
we palliate so great inconstancy, variety, and vanity
of opinions, as we see have been produced by those
excellent and admirable souls? As, for instance,
what can be more vain, than to offer to define God
by our analogies and conjectures? To regulate him
and the world by our capacities and our laws? To
make use of that little scantling of knowledge,
which he has been pleased to allow to our state of
nature, to his detriment? And, because we cannot
extend our sight to his glorious throne, to bring him
down to a level with our corruption and our miseries?

The most probable of all human opinions touching religion. Of all human and ancient opinions concerning religion, that seems to me the most probable, and
the most excusable, which acknowledged God to
be an incomprehensible power, the original and
preserver of all things, all goodness, all perfection,
receiving and taking in good part the honour and
reverence, which man paid upon him, under what
appearance, name, or ceremonies soever :

> *S. Jupiter omnipotens rerum, regûmque deûmque,*
> *Progenitor genetrixque.**

" The almighty Jupiter, the author of all things, and the
" parent of kings and gods."

This zeal has been universally looked upon from

---

* Those which were the verses of Valerius Soranus, were preserved by Varro, from whom St. Augustine has inserted them in his
book de Civitate Dei, lib. vii. cap. 9, 11.

heaven with a gracious eye. All civilized nations have reaped fruit from their devotion. Impious men and actions have every-where had suitable events.

The pagan histories acknowledge dignity, order, justice, prodigies, and oracles, employed for their profit and instruction in their fabulous religions: God in his mercy vouchsafing, perhaps, by these temporal benefits, to cherish the tender principles of a kind of brutish knowledge, which they had of him, by the light of nature, through the false images of their dreams. And those which man has framed out of his own invention, are not only false, but impious and injurious. *(margin: The ideas which the Pagan histories give to God.)*

Of all the religions which St. Paul found in repute at Athens, that which they devoted to the secret and unknown God, seemed to him the most excusable. † *(margin: What St. Paul thought of the Athenians' unknown God.)*

Pythagoras shadowed the truth a little more closely, judging that the knowledge of this first cause, and being of beings, ought to be indefinite without prescription, without declaration: that it was nothing but the extreme effort of our imagination towards perfection, every man amplifying the idea of him, according to his capacity. But, if Numa attempted to conform the devotion of his people to this project, to unite them to a religion purely mental, without any present object and material mixture, he attempted a thing of no use. *(margin: What Pythagoras thought of the idea which man can form of God.)*

The mind of man cannot possibly maintain itself, floating in such an infinity of rude conceptions. There is a necessity of adapting them to a certain image proportioned to his capacity. The divine majesty has, therefore, in some measure, suffered himself, for our sakes, to be circumscribed in corporal limits. His supernatural and celestial mysteries have signs of our earthly state. His adoration is expressed by offices and words that are borrowed from the senses; for it is man that believes, and that prays. I omit the other arguments that are made use of upon this subject. But I can hardly be induced to *(margin: There must be a palpable religion for the people, according to Montaigne.)*

believe, that the sight of our crucifixes, that the
picture of our Saviour's passion, that the ornaments
and ceremonious motions in our churches, that the
voices accommodated to the devoutness of our
thoughts, and that this rousing of the senses, do not
warm the souls of the people with a religious passion of a very salutary effect.

The wor-
ship of the
sun the
most excu-
sable ado-
ration.

    Of the objects of worship, to which they have
given a body, according as necessity required in
this universal blindness, I should, I fancy, most incline to those who adored the sun:

> ———— *La lumiere commune,*
> *L'œil du monde: et si Dieu au chef porte des yeux,*
> *Les rayons du soleil sont ses yeux radieux,*
> *Qui donnent vie à tous, nous maintrennent et gardent,*
> *Et les faicts des hommes en ce monde regardent :*
> *Ce beau, ce grand soleil, qui nous faict les saisons,*
> *Selon qu'il entre, ou sort des ses douze maisons :*
> *Qui remplit l'univers de ses vertus cognuës,*
> *Qui d'un traict de ses yeux nous dissipre les nuës :*
> *L'esprit, l'ame du monde, ardent et flamboyant,*
> *En la course d'un jour tout le ciel tournoyant,*
> *Plein d'immense grandeur, rond, vagabond, et ferme :*
> *Lequel tient dessous luy tout le monde pour terme :*
> *En repos, sans repos, oysif et sans sejour,*
> *Fils aisne de nature, et le pere du jour.*

The common light that equal shines on all,
Diffus'd around the whole terrestrial ball ;
And, if th' almighty ruler of the skies
Has eyes, the sun-beams are his radiant eyes,
That life and safety give to young and old,
And all men's actions upon earth behold.
This great, this beautiful, and glorious sun,
Who makes their course the varied seasons run ;
That with his virtues fills the universe,
And with one glance can sullen clouds disperse;
Earth's life and soul, that, flaming in his sphere,
Surrounds the heavens in one day's career;
Immensely great, moving yet firm and round,
Who the whole world below has made his bound ;
At rest, without rest, idle without stay,
Nature's first son, and father of the day.

* Ronsard.

Forasmuch as, besides this his magnitude and beauty,
it is the piece of this machine which we discover at
the remotest distance from us, and therefore so little
known, that they were pardonable for entering into
the admiration and reverence of it.

Thales, who was the first that inquired* into things
of this nature, thought God to be a spirit, that made
all things of water. Anaximander, that the gods
were, at different and distant seasons, dying and entering into life,† and that there was an infinite number of worlds. Anaximenes, that the air was God,‡
that he was immense, infinite, and always in motion.
Anaxagoras§ was the first man who believed, that
the description and manner of all things, were conducted by the power and reason of an infinite spirit.
Alcmæon ‖ ascribed divinity to the sun, the moon,
the stars, and the soul. Pythagoras has made God¶
to be a spirit, diffused through the nature of all things,
from whence our souls are extracted. Parmenides,** a circle surrounding heaven, and supporting the world by its heat and light. Empedocles††
pronounced the four elements, of which all things
are composed, to be a god. Protagoras‡‡ had nothing to say, whether there were gods or not, or
what they were. Democritus§§ was one while of
opinion, that the images and their revolutions were
gods;‖‖ at another time he deified that nature,
which darts out those savages; and, at another time,
he pays this attribute to our knowledge and understanding. Plato¶¶ puts his opinion into various
lights. He says, in his Timæus, that the father of
the world cannot be named; and, in his book of
laws, that he thinks men ought not to inquire into
his being; and elsewhere, in the very same book,
he makes the world, the heaven, the stars, the earth,
and our souls, gods; admitting, moreover, those

---

* Cic. de Nat. Deor. lib. i. cap. 10.　† Id. ibid.　‡ Id. ibid.
§ Id. ibid. cap. 11.　‖ Id. ibid.　¶ Id. ibid.　** Id. ibid.
†† Id. ib. cap. 12.　‡‡ He was a sophist of Abdera, Id. ibid.
§§ Id. ibid.　‖‖ Id. ibid.　¶¶ Id. ibid.

which have been received by ancient institution in
every republic. Xenophon[*] reports a like perplexity
in the doctrine of Socrates; one while affirming that
men ought not to inquire in the form of God, and
presently making him maintain that the sun is God,
and the soul God : one while, he says, he maintains
there is but one God, and afterwards, that there are
many gods. Speusippus, Plato's nephew,[†] makes
God to be a certain power governing all things, and
that it is an animal. Aristotle[‡] one while says, it is
the soul, and another while the world; one while
he gives this world another master, and at another
time makes God the ardour of heaven. Xenocrates[§]
makes the gods to be eight in number, of whom
five were among the planets; the sixth consisted of
all the fixed stars, as so many of its members : the
seventh and eighth the sun and moon. Heraclides
Ponticus[||] is of a wavering opinion, and finally de-
prives God of sense, and makes him shift from one
form to another, and afterwards says, it is heaven
and earth. Theophrastus[¶] wanders in the same uncertainty amongst all his fancies, one while ascribing
the superintendency of the world to the understanding, at another time to heaven, and one while also
to the stars. Strato[**] will have it to be nature,
having the power of generation, augmentation, and
diminution, but without form and sentiment.
Zeno[††] makes it to be the law of nature, commanding good and forbidding evil, which law is an animal,
and takes away the accustomed gods, Jupiter, Juno,
Vesta, &c. Diogenes Apolloniates[‡‡] ascribes the

---

* Cic. de Natura Deorum, lib. i. cap. 12   † Idem, cap. 13.
‡ Id. ibid.   § Id. ibid. || Id. ibid.
¶ Id. ibid.   ** Id. ibid. cap, 14.   †† Id. ibid.
‡‡ I cannot imagine where Montaigne learned, that age was the
Deity acknowledged by Diogenes of Apollonia; *age* must surely
have been printed instead of *air*, in one of the first editions of his
Essays, from whence this error was continued in all the following
editions. It is certain, however, that Cicero says, expressly, that
air is the god of Diogenes Apolloniates, in his Natura Deorum, lib. i.
cap. 12, with whom agrees St. Austin, in his book de Civitate Dei,

11

deity to age. Xenophanes[*] makes God round, seeing and hearing, but not breathing, nor having any thing in common with the nature of man. Aristot[†] thinks the form of God to be incomprehensible, deprives him of sense, and knows not whether he be an animal or something else. Cleanthes[‡] one while supposes him to be reason, another while the world; sometimes the soul of nature, at other times the supreme heat, called æther, rolling about and encompassing all. Perseus,[§] the disciple of Zeno, was of opinion, that men who have been remarkably useful to society, are surnamed gods. Chrysippus[‖] made a confused collection of all the foregoing opinions, and reckons men also, who are immortalised amongst a thousand forms, which he makes of gods. Diagoras and Theodorus[¶] flatly deny that there were ever any gods at all. Epicurus[**] makes the gods shining, transparent, and perflable, lodged between the two worlds, as between two groves, secure from shocks, invested with a human figure, and the members that we have, but which are to them of no use :

lib. viii. cap. 2, from whom it also appears, that this philosopher ascribed sense to the air, and that he called it the matter out of which all things were formed, and that it was endowed with divine reason, without which nothing could be made. M. Bayle, in his dictionary, at the article of Diogenes of Apollonia, infers, that he made a whole, or a compound, of air and the divine virtue, in which, if air was the matter, the divine virtue was the soul and form ; and that, by consequence, the air, animated by the divine virtue, ought, according to that philosopher, to be styled God. As for the rest, this philosopher, by ascribing understanding to the air, differed from his master Anaximenes, who thought the air inanimate.

[*] Diog. Laert. in the Life of Xenophanes, lib. ix. sect. 19.
[†] Cic. de Nat. Deorum, lib. i. cap. 14.   [‡] Idem, ibid.
[§] Idem, ibid. cap. 15.
[‖] Id. ib. See a learned and judicious remark on this passage by the president Boulier, tom. i. of the translation, by the Abbé d'Olivet, p. 247.
[¶] Cic. de Nat. Deor. lib. i. cap. 23, and Sextus Empiric. adv. Mathem. lib. viii. p. 317.
[**] Cic. de Divinatione, lib. ii. cap. 17.

Ego Deúm genus esse semper duxi, et dicam cælitum,
Sed eos non curare opinor, quid agat humanum genus.

I ever thought that gods above there were,
But do not think they care what men do here.

Trust now, sirs, to your philosophy, and brag that
you have found out the very thing you wanted,
amidst this rattle of so many philosophical heads.
The perplexity of so many worldly forms have had
this effect upon me, that manners and opinions, differing from mine, do not so much disgust as instruct
me; and, upon a comparison, do not puff me up
so much as they humble me: and all other choice
than that, which comes expressly from the hand of
God, seems to me a choice of small prerogative. The
polities of the world are no less contrary upon this
subject than the schools, whereby we may learn that
fortune itself is not more variable and inconstant
than our reason, nor more blind and inconsiderate.

To make
gods of
men is the
utmost de-
gree of ex-
trava-
gance.

The things which are the most unknown, are the
most proper to be deified. Wherefore, to make gods
of ourselves, as the ancients did, is the most ridiculous and childish imagination possible. I would sooner adhere to those who worshipped the serpent, the
dog, and the ox; as their nature and existence are less
known to us, and we have more authority to imagine what we please of those beasts, and to ascribe
extraordinary faculties to them. But to have made
gods of those of our own condition, of whom we cannot but know the imperfection, and to have attributed
to them desire, anger, revenge, marriage, generation,
kindred, love and jealousy, our members and our
bones, our fevers and our pleasures, our deaths and
burials, must needs proceed from a marvellous intox-
ication of the human understanding:

Quæ procul'usque adeo divino ab numine distant,
Inque Deúm numero quæ sint indigna viderit.*

For these are so unlike the gods; the frame
So much unworthy of that glorious name.

* Lucret. lib. ver. 123, 124.

" The different forms of these Gods are known, to-
" gether with their ages, apparel, ornaments, gene-
" alogies, marriages, kindred; and they are exhi-
" bited, in respects, according to the similitude of
" human weakness; for they are represented to us
" with disturbed minds, and we read of the concu-
" piscence and anger of the gods."* It is equally
absurd to have ascribed divinity, not only to faith,
virtue, honour, concord, liberty, victory, piety, but
also to voluptuousness, fraud, death, envy, old age,
misery, fear, fever, ill-fortune, and other injuries of
our frail and transitory life :

> *Quid juvat hoc, templis nostros inducere mores ?*
> *O curvæ in terris animæ et cœlestium inanes ?* †
>
> O abject souls, stuck ever deep in clay !
> Souls unenlighten'd by celestial ray !
> Else, could we thus affront each sacred shrine,
> Could we to gods mere human dross assign ?

The Egyptians, with an impudent precaution, inter- *The impu-*
dicted, upon pain of hanging, that any one should *dent pre-*
caution of
say, that their gods, Serapis and Isis, had formerly *the Egyp-*
been men: yet no one was ignorant, that they had *tians about*
their gods.
been such. And their effigies, with the finger upon
the mouth, signified, says Varro, that mysterious decree to their priests, to conceal their mortal original,
as it must, by necessary consequence, cancel all the
veneration paid to them. Seeing that man so much
desired to equal himself to God, he had done better,
says Cicero, to have attracted the divine qualities to
himself, and drawn them down hither below, than to
send his corruption and misery upwards. But, to
take it right, he has several ways done both the one
and the other, with like vanity of opinion. When *Whether*
the philosophers search narrowly into the hierarchy *the philo-*
sophers
of their gods, and make a great bustle about distin- *were se-*
guishing their alliances, offices, and power ; I can- *rious in*
treating of
not believe they speak as they think. When Plato *the hier-*

---

* Cic. de Natura Deorum, lib. ii. cap. 23.
† Persius, sat. ii. v. 61.

archy of
their gods,
and of the
condition
of men in
another
life.
describes Pluto's verger to us, and the bodily conveniences or pain that attend us, after the ruin and
annihilation of our bodies, and accommodates them
to the sense we have of them in this life:

> *Secreti celant calles, et myrtea circùm*
> *Sylva tegit. Curæ non ipsâ in morte relinqunt.**
>
> In vales and myrtle groves they pensive lie;
> Nor do their cares forsake them when they die.

When Mahomet promises his followers a paradise
hung with tapestry, adorned with gold and precious
stones, furnished with wenches of excellent beauty,
rare wines, and delicate dishes: I plainly see that
they are in jest, when, to humour our sensuality,
they allure and attract us by hopes and opinions suitable to our mortal appetites: yet some, amongst
us, are fallen into the like error, promising to themselves, after the resurrection, a terrestrial and temporal life, accompanied with all sorts of worldly conveniences and pleasures. Can we believe, that Plato,
he who had such heavenly conceptions, and was so
well acquainted with the Divinity, as thence to
acquire the surname of the Divine Plato, ever
thought that the poor creature, man, had any thing
in him applicable to that incomprehensible power?
And that he believed, that the weak holds we are
able to take were capable, or the force of our understanding sufficient to participate of beatitude, or eternal pains? We should then tell him, from human reason, if the pleasures thou dost promise us, in the
other life, are of the same kind that I have enjoyed
here below, this has nothing in common with infinity: though all my five natural senses should be
even ravished with pleasure, and my soul full of all
the contentment it could hope or desire, we know
what all this amounts to, all this would be nothing:
if there be any thing of mine there, there is nothing
divine; if this be no more than what may belong to

---

* Æneid. lib. vi. ver. 443.

our present condition, it cannot be of any account:
all contentment of mortals is temporary; even the
knowledge of our parents, children, and friends, if
that can affect and delight us in the other world, if that
still continue a satisfaction to us there, we still remain in earthly and finite conveniences: we cannot,
as we ought, conceive the greatness of these high and
divine promises, if we could in any sort conceive
them. To have a worthy idea of them, we must imagine them to be incomprehensible, and absolutely
different from those of our wretched experience.
" Eye hath not seen," saith St. Paul,[*] " nor ear
" heard, neither have entered into the heart of man,
" the things that God hath prepared for them that
" love him." And if, to render us capable, our being
be reformed and changed (as thou sayest, Plato, by
thy purifications), it ought to be so extreme and total
a change, that, by natural philosophy, we shall be no
more ourselves:

What must be the change of our being, to qualify us for eternal happiness.

> *Hector erat tunc cum bello certabat, at ille*
> *Tractus ab Æmonio non erat Hector equo.*[†]

> He Hector was, whilst he did fight, but when
> Drawn by Achilles' steeds, no Hector then.

It must be something else that must receive these
rewards:

> —— *Quod mutatur, dissolvitur, interit ergo;*
> *Trajiciuntur enim partes atque ordine migrant.*[‡]

> Things, chang'd, dissolved are, and therefore die;
> Their parts are mix'd, and from their order fly.

For, in Pythagoras's metempsychosis, and the change
of habitation that he imagined souls underwent, can
we believe, that the lion, in whom the soul of Cæsar
is inclosed, does espouse Cæsar's passions, or that
the lion is he? For, if it was still Cæsar, they would
be in the right, who, controverting this opinion with
Plato, reproach him, that the son might be seen to

* 1 Cor. ii. 9.   † Ovid. Trist. lib. iii. el. 2, ver. 27.
‡ Lucret. lib. iii. ver. 756.

ride his mother transformed into a mule, and the
like absurdities; and can we believe, that, in the
transformations which are made of the bodies of animals into others of the same kind, that the new
comers are no other than their predecessors? From
the ashes of a phœnix,* they say a worm is engendered, and from that another phœnix; who can
imagine that this second phœnix is no other than the
first? We see our silk-worms, as it were, die and wither; and from this withered body a butterfly is produced, and from that another worm; how ridiculous
would it be to imagine, that this was still the first?
That which has once ceased to be, is no more:

> *Nec si materiam nostram collegerit ætas*
> *Post obitum, rursùmque redegerit, ut sita nunc est,*
> *Atque iterùm nobis fuerint data lumina vitæ,*
> *Pertineat quidquam tamen ad nos id quoque factum,*
> *Interrupta semel cùm sit repetentia nostra.†*

> Neither, though time should gather and restore
> Our ashes to the form they had before,
> And give again new life and light withal,
> Would that new figure us concern at all;
> Nor the same persons we e'ermore be seen,
> Our being having interrupted been.

And Plato, when thou sayest, in another place, that
it shall be the spiritual part of man, that will be concerned in the fruition of the rewards in another life,
thou tellest us a thing, wherein there is as little appearance of truth:

> *Scilicet avolsus radicibus, ut nequit ullam*
> *Dispicere ipse oculus rem, seorsum corpore toto.‡*

> As the eye stiffens, and becomes quite blind,
> When from its socket rent; so soul and mind
> Lose all their pow'rs, when from the limbs disjoin'd.

For, at this rate, it would no more be man, nor consequently us, who should be concerned in this enjoyment: for we are composed of two essential parts,

---

* Plin. Nat. Hist. lib. x. cap. 2.   † Lucret. lib. iii. ver. 859, &c.
‡ Id. ibid. ver. 562, &c.

the separation of which is the death and ruin of our being:

> *Inter enim jecta est vitaï pausa, vagïque*
> *Deerrarunt passim motus ab sensibus omnes.**
>
> When once that pause of life is come between,
> 'Tis just the same as we had never been.

We do not say that the man suffers, though the worms feed upon his members, and that the earth consumes them:

> *Et nihïl hoc ad nos, qui coïtu conjugioque*
> *Corporis atque animæ consistimus uniter apti.†*
>
> What's that to us? for we are only we,
> While soul and body in one frame agree.

Moreover, upon what principle of justice can the gods take notice of, or reward man, after his death, for his good and virtuous actions, which they themselves promoted and produced in him? And why should they be offended at, or punish him for wicked ones, since themselves have created him in so frail a condition, and when, with one glance of their will, they might prevent him from falling? Might not Epicurus, with great colour of human reason, object that to Plato? Did he not often save himself with this sentence, " that it is impossible to establish any " thing certain of the immortal nature by the mortal? " She does nothing but err throughout, but especially " when she meddles with divine things. Who does more evidently perceive this, than we do? for although we have given her certain and infallible principles, and though we have enlightened her steps with the sacred lamp of truth, which it has pleased God to communicate to us; we daily see, nevertheless, that if she swerve never so little from the ordinary path, and strays from, or wanders out of the way, set out and beaten by the church, how soon she

The foundation of rewards and punishments in another life.

---

* Lucret. lib. iii. ver. 872.   † Id. ibid. ver. 857.

M 2

loses, confounds, and fetters herself, tumbling and
floating in this vast, turbulent, and waving sea of
human opinions, without restraint, and without any
view; so soon as she loses this great and common
road, she is bewildered in a labyrinth of a thousand
several paths. Man cannot be any thing but what
he is, nor imagine beyond the reach of his capacity:
The ridi- "It is a greater presumption," says Plutarch, "in
culousness
of pretend- them who are but men, to attempt to speak and
ing to discourse of the gods and demi-gods, than it is in
know God
by compa- a man, ignorant of music, to judge of singers; or
ring him in a man, who never was in a camp, to dispute
with man. about arms and martial affairs, presuming, by
some light conjecture, to comprehend the effects
of an art he is totally a stranger to." Antiquity,
I believe, thought to pass a compliment upon the
Divinity, in assimilating it to man, investing it with
his faculties, and adorning it with his humours, and
more disparaging necessities; offering it our aliments
to eat, our dances, masquerades, and farces to divert it, our vestments to cover it, and our houses
to dwell in; caressing it with the odours of incense,
and the sounds of music, besides garlands and nosegays: and, to accommodate it to our vicious passions, soothing its justice with inhuman vengeance,
and supposing it delighted with the ruin and dissipa-
tion of things by itself created and preserved: as
Tiberius Sempronius, who caused the rich spoils and
arms he had gained from the enemy in Sardinia to
be burnt for a sacrifice to Vulcan: as did Paulus
Æmilius those of Macedonia to Mars and Minerva.
The gene- So Alexander, arriving in the Indian ocean, threw
ral practice
of appea- several great vessels of gold into the sea in favour of
sing the di- Thetis; and, moreover, loaded her altars with a
vinity, by
sacrificing slaughter, not of innocent beasts only, but of men
men to it. also; as several nations, and ours amongst the rest,
were ordinarily used to do: and I believe there is
no nation that has not tried the experiment:

—— Sulmone creatos
Quatuor hic juvenes; totidem quos educat Ufens,
Viventes rapit, inferias quos immolet umbris.*

He took of youths, at Sulmo born, four;
Of those at Ufens bred, as many more;
The whole alive, in most inhuman wise,
To offer to the god, in sacrifice.

The Getes[†] hold themselves to be immortal, and that their death is nothing but the beginning a journey towards their god Zamolxis. Once in five years they despatch one, from among them, to him, to entreat some necessaries of him ; which envoy is chosen by lot, and the form of despatching him, after having instructed him, by word of mouth, what he is to deliver, is, that three of the by-standers hold out so many javelins, against which the rest throw his body with all their force. If he happens to be wounded in a mortal part, and immediately dies, they think it a sure argument of the divine favour ; but if he escape, they think him wicked and accursed, and another is deputed, after the same manner, in his stead. Amestris,[‡] the mother of Xerxes, being grown old, caused, at once, fourteen young men, of the best families of Persia, to be buried alive, according to the religion of the country, to gratify some infernal deity: and yet, to this day, the idols of Themixtiran are cemented with the blood of little children, and they delight in no sacrifice but of these pure and infantine souls; a justice thirsty of the blood of innocents:

Zamolxis the god of the Getes.

Sacrifice of fourteen young men.

Tantum religio potuit suadere malorum.§

Such impious use was of religion made,
Such dev'lish acts religion could persuade.

The Carthaginians sacrificed their own children to

---

* Æneid. lib. x. ver. 517, &c.   † Herodot. lib. iv. p. 289.
‡ She was the wife of Xerxes, who was born of Atossa, daughter of Cyrus. Plutarch de Superstitione, cap. 13, et Herodotus, lib. vii. p. 477.
§ Luc. lib. i. ver. 102.

Carthagi-
nian chil-
dren sacri-
ficed to Sa-
turn.
The barba-
rity and
senseless-
ness of this
practice.
Saturn;. and they who had none of their own,
bought of others,* the father and mother being, in
the mean time, obliged to assist at the ceremony,
with a gay and contented countenance. It was a
strange fancy to gratify the divine bounty with our
affliction; like the Lacedæmonians, who regaled
their Diana with the tormenting of young boys,
whom they caused to be whipped,† for her sake,
very often to death. It was a savage humour to
think to gratify the architect by the subversion of his
building; to seek to take away the punishment due
to the guilty, by punishing the innocent; and to
imagine, that poor Iphigenia, at the port of Aulis,
should, by her death, and by being sacrificed, make
satisfaction to God for the crimes committed by the
army of the Greeks:

> *Et casta incestâ nubendi tempore in ipso*
> *Hostia concideret mactatu mœsta parentis.*‡
>
> That the chaste virgin, in her nuptial band,
> Should die by an unnat'ral father's hand.

And that the two noble and generous souls of the
two Decii, the father and the son, to incline the favour of the gods to be propitious to the affairs of
Rome, should throw themselves headlong into the
thickest of the enemy. *Quæ fuit tanta Deorum*
iniquitas, ut placari populo Romano non possent, nisi
tales viri occidissent?§ " How great was the resent-
" ment of the gods, that they could not be recon-
" ciled to the people of Rome, unless such men
" perished?" To which may be added, that it is
not in the criminal to cause himself to be scourged,
according to his own measure, nor at his own time,
but that it purely belongs to the judge; who considers nothing as chastisements, but what he appoints;
and cannot call that a punishment, which the suf-
ferer chooses. The divine vengeance presupposes

---

* Plutarch, ibid.
† Idem, in the Notable Sayings of the Lacedæmonians.
‡ Lucr. lib. i. ver. 99, 100.   § Cic. de Nat. Deor. lib. iii. cap. 6.

an absolute dissent in us, both from its justice, and
our punishments; and therefore it was a ridiculous
humour of Polycrates,* the tyrant of Samos; who,
to interrupt the continued course of his good fortune, and to balance it, went and threw the dearest
and most precious jewel he had into the sea; believing, that, by this misfortune of his own procur-
ing, he satisfied the revolution and vicissitude of fortune; and she, to ridicule his folly, ordered it so,
that the same jewel came again into his hands, being
found in the belly of a fish. And then to what end
are those tearings and dismemberings by the Cory-
baates, the Menades, and in our times by the Mahometans, who cut and slash their faces, bosoms, and
members, to gratify their prophet, forasmuch as the
offence lies in the will, not in the breast, eyes, genitals, beauty, the shoulders, or the throat? *Tantus
est perturbatæ mentis, et sedibus suis pulsæ, furor,
ut sic Dii placentur, quemadmodum ne homines quidem sæviunt :*† "So great is the fury of troubled
" minds, when once displaced from the seat of rea-
" son, as to think the gods should be appeased,
" with what even men are not so mad as to per-
" form." The use of this natural contexture has
not only respect to us, but also to the service of
God, and other men. And it is as unjust to hurt it
for our purpose, as to kill ourselves upon any pretence whatever. It seems to be great cowardice
and treachery to exercise cruelty upon, and to destroy the functions of, the body, that are stupid and
servile, in order to spare the soul the trouble of governing them according to reason. *Ubi iratos Deos
timent, qui sic propitios habere merentur? In regiæ
libidinis voluptatem castrati sunt quidam, sed nemo
sibi, ne vir esset, jubente domino, manus intulit:*
" How are they afraid of the anger of the gods, who
" think to merit their favour at that rate? Some, in-

* Herodot. lib. iii. p. 201, 202.
† Div. Aug. de Civitate Dei, lib. vi. cap. 10.

" deed, have been made eunuchs for the lust of princes ;
" but no man, at his master's command, has put
" his own hand to unman himself:" so did they fill
their religion with several ill effects :

——————— *Sæpiùs olim*
Religio peperit scelerosa, atque impia facta.[*]
Too true it is, that oft in elder times
Religious zeal produc'd notorious crimes.

The folly of judging of the power and perfections of God according to our conceptions. Now nothing of ours can in any sort be compared
or likened unto the divine nature, which will not
blemish it with much imperfection. How can that
infinite beauty, power, and bounty, admit of any
correspondence, or similitude, to such abject things
as we are, without extreme detriment and dishonour
to his divine greatness? *Infirmum Dei fortius est
hominibus; et stultum Dei sapientius est hominibus* :[+]
" For the foolishness of God is wiser than men, and
" the weakness of God is stronger than men."
Stilpo‡ the philosopher, being asked, whether the
gods were delighted with our adorations and sacrifices: you are indiscreet, answered he, let us withdraw apart, if you talk of such things. Nevertheless, we prescribe him bounds, we keep his power
besieged by our reasoning (I call our ravings and
dreams reason, with the dispensation of philosophy,
which says, both the fool and the knave run mad
by reason; but by a particular form of reason), we
endeavour to subject him to the vain and feeble appearances of our understandings; him, who has
made both us and our knowledge. Because that
nothing is made of nothing, God therefore could
not make the world without matter. What, has
God put into our hands the keys and most secret
springs of his power? Is he obliged not to exceed
the limits of our knowledge? Put the case, O man,
that thou hast been able here to mark some foot-

---

* Lucret. lib. i. ver. 83, 84.   + 1 Crr. i. 25.
‡ Diog. Laert. in the Life of Stilpo, lib. ii. sect. 117.

steps of his performance ; dost thou therefore think, that he has therein done all he could, and has crowded all his forms and ideas in this work? Thou seest nothing, but the order and government of this little vault, in which thou art lodged, if thou dost see so much: whereas his divinity has an infinite jurisdiction beyond: this part has nothing in comparison of the whole:

> —— *Omnia cum cœlo, terraque marique,*
> *Nil sunt ad summam summai totius omnem.*[*]

The earth, the sea, and skies, from pole to pole,
Are small, nay nothing to the mighty WHOLE.

It is a munieipal law that thou allegest, thou knowest not what is the universal. Tie thyself to that to which thou art subject, but not him; he is not of thy brotherhood, thy fellow-citizen, or companion; if he has in some sort communicated himself unto thee, it is not to debase himself to thy littleness, nor to make thee controller of his power. A human body cannot fly to the clouds: the sun runs every day his ordinary course without ever resting: the bounds of the sea and the earth cannot be confounded; the water is unstable, and without firmness: a wall, unless it has a breach in it, is impenetrable to a solid body: a man cannot preserve his life in the flames; he cannot be both in heaven and upon earth, and in a thousand places at once corporally. It is for thee, that he has made these regulations; it is thee, that they concern. He has manifested to Christians, that he has exceeded them all, whenever it pleased him. And, in truth, why, Almighty as he is, should he have limited his power within any certain measure? In whose favour should he have renounced his privilege? Thy reason has in no other thing more of probability and foundation, than where it persuades thee that there is a plurality of worlds:

* Lucret. lib. vi. ver. 678, &c.

Terrámque et solem, lunám, mare, cætera quæ sunt,
*Non esse unica sed numero magis innumerali.**

Earth, sun, moon, sea, whate'er's in space's bound.
Not single, but innumerable were found.

The plura-
lity of the
worlds no
new opi-
nion. The most eminent wits of the elder times believed
it; as do some of this age of ours, compelled by the
appearances of human reason: forasmuch as in this
fabric, that we behold, there is nothing single and
one:

—— *Cum in summâ res nulla sit una,*
Unica quæ gignatur: et unica solaque crescat.†

Since no production in this world below,
Without another, can beget, or grow.

And that all the kinds are multiplied in some number; by which it seems not to be likely, that God
should have made this work only without a companion, and that the matter of this form should have
been totally drained in this sole individual:

Quare etiam atque etiam tales fateare necesse est,
Esse alios alibi congressus materiai,
Qualis hic est avido complexu quem tenet æther.‡

'Tis necessary therefore to confess,
That there must elsewhere be the like congress
Of the like matter, which the airy space
Holds fast within its infinite embrace.

Especially if it be a living creature, which its motions render so credible, that Plato§ affirms it, and
that many of our people either confirm, or dare not
deny it. No more than that ancient opinion, that
the heavens, the stars, and other members of the
world, are creatures composed of body and soul:
mortal in respect of their composition, but immortal
by the determination of the creator. Now if there
be many worlds, as Democritus, Epicurus, and
almost all philosophy has believed, what do we

* Lucret. lib. ii. ver. 1084.   † Id. ibid. ver. 1076.
‡ Id. ibid. ver. 1063.   § In his Timæus, p. 527.

know, but that the principle and rules of this of ours may in like manner concern the rest? They may perhaps have another form, and another polity. Epicurus * supposes them either like or unlike.

We see in this world an infinite difference and variety according to the distance of places. Neither the corn, wine, nor any of our animals are to be seen in that new corner of the world discovered by our fathers; it is all there another thing. And, in times past, do but consider in how many parts of the world they had no knowledge either of Bacchus or Ceres. If Pliny or Herodotus are to be believed, there are in certain places a kind of men very little resembling us.† And there are mongrel and ambiguous forms, between the human and brutal natures. There are countries, where men are born without heads, having their mouth and eyes in their breast :‡ where they are all hermaphrodites; where they go on all four; where they have but one eye in their forehead, and a head more like a dog than one of us : § where they are half fish the lower part, and live in the water : where the women bear at five years old, and live but eight :‖ where the head and skin of the forehead are so hard, that a sword will not touch them, but rebounds again : where men have no beards : nations that know not the use of fire, and others that eject seed of a black colour.¶ What shall we say of those that naturally** change themselves

Extraordinary difference between the distant parts of the earth.

---

* Diog. Laert. in the Life of Epicurus, lib. x. sect. 85.

† Herod. lib. iv. p. 324, where are said to be some with heads like those of dogs.

‡ Plin. Nat. Hist. lib. viii. cap. 2. He took those for a sort of apes.

§ Herod. lib. iii. p. 234.

‖ Plin. Nat. Hist. lib. vi. cap. 30, et lib; vii. cap. 2.

¶ Herod. lib. iii. p. 229. A very able anatomist has assured me that this is false.

** Here Montaigne seems not to have rightly attended to his Pliny, who says, that a person who can be persuaded that men were ever metamorphosed into wolves, and afterwards into men again, will be ready to give his credit to all the fables that have been invented for so many ages past. Pliny, having there quoted some stories of such pretended metamorphoses, cries out, It is astonish-

into wolves, mares, and then into men again? and if it be true, as Plutarch* says, that, in some place of the Indies, there are men without mouths, who nourish themselves with the smell of certain odours, how many of our descriptions are false? man is no more risible, nor, perhaps, capable of reason and society. The disposition and cause of our internal structure would for the most part be to no purpose.

Many things in nature contrary to the rules we have prescribed to nature.   Moreover, how many things are there in our own knowledge, that oppose those fine rules we have cut out for, and prescribe to nature? Yet we undertake to reduce God himself to them! how many things do we call miraculous and contrary to nature? This is done by every nation, and by every man, in proportion to their share of ignorance. How many occult properties and quintessences do we discover? For our going according to nature is no more than going according to what we understand, as far as that is able to follow, and as far as we see into it: all beyond is monstrous and irregular. Now, by this account, all things will be monstrous to the wisest and most understanding men; since human reason has persuaded them, that it had no manner of ground or foundation, not so much as to be sure that snow is white: for Anaxagoras affirmed it to be black;† if there be any thing, or if there be nothing; whether we know, or do not know; which Metrodorus Chius denied that man was able to determine: or whether we live, as Euripides doubts, whether the life we live is life, or whether that be not life, which we call death:

ing, how far the Greeks have extended their credulity. There is no lie ever so impudent that wants a witness to prove it. Pliny, lib. viii. cap. 22.

* I cannot find the passage in Plutarch from whence Montaigne took this: but Pliny, in his Nat. Hist. lib. vii. cap 2, relates that at the extremity of the Indies, near the source of the Ganges, there is a nation of Astomes, i.e. a people without mouths, all whose bodies are covered with a shag hair, and dressed in the down of leaves, and who live only by the scents they draw in through their nostrils.

† Cic. Acad. Quæst. lib. iv. cap. 23. Sextus Empiricus also puts Metrodorus of Chios in the number of Sceptics. Εἰ ἔστι κρίλιχειν ἀληθείας, p. 146.

Τίς δ' οἶδεν εἰ ζῆν τὸθ ὃ κεκληται θανεῖν,
Τὸ ζῆν δὲ θνήσκειν ἐςι.*

Who knows if life been't that which we call death, ⟩
And death the state in which we draw our breath? ⟨

And not without some appearance. For why do we
from this instant derive the title of being, which is
but a flash of lightning in the infinite course of an
eternal night, and so short an interruption of our perpetual and natural condition? Death possessing all
that passed before, and all the future of this moment,
and also a good part of the moment itself.† Others
swear there is no motion at all, as the followers of
Melissus, and that nothing stirs. For, if there be Motion of
things be-
low denied.
but one, neither can that spherical motion be of any
use to him, nor the motion from one place to another, as Plato proves that there is neither generation nor corruption in nature. Protagoras‡ says, that
there is nothing in nature but doubt: that a man
may equally dispute of all things; and even of this,
whether a man may equally dispute of all things:
Mansiphanes,§ that, of things which seem to be, nothing is more than it is not: that there is nothing certain but uncertainty. Parmenides,‖ that of all which

* Plato in his Gorgias, p. 300, Diog. Laert. in the Life of Pyrrho,
lib. ix. sect. 73, and Sextus Empiricus, Pyrrh. Hypot. lib. iii. cap.
24, quote these verses differently from themselves, and what they
are here; and yet there is no real difference in the sense.
† Diog. Laert. in the Life of Melissus, lib. ix. sect. 24.
‡ Diog. Laert. in the Life of Protagoras, lib. ix. sect. 51. " Were
" I to believe Protagoras," says Seneca, " there is nothing in the
" nature of things but what is doubtful." Ep. 88.
§ This must certainly be a mistake of the press, for Nausiphanes,
who was a disciple and follower of Pyrrho, as such must maintain,
that there was nothing certain but uncertainty; and this is what
Montaigne would undoubtedly have us here understand, according
to the report of Seneca, who says expressly, " Were I to believe
" Nausiphanes, the only one thing certain is, that there is nothing
" certain." Ep. 88.
‖ " Unum esse omnia." This opinion which Cicero, in Quæst.
Acad. lib. iv. cap. 37, attributes to Xenophanes, was also that
of Parmenides, a disciple of Xenophanes, if we may believe Aristotle, who says, lib. i. Metaphys. cap. 5, that Parmenides really
believed there was but one single being, but that to serve appear-

seems, there is no one thing in general; that there is but one thing. Zeno,* that there is nothing. If there were one thing, it would either be in another, or in itself. If it be in another, they are two: if it be in itself, they are yet two; the comprehending and the comprehended. According to these doctrines, the nature of things is no other than a shadow, either false or vain.

The divine power ought not to be subject to the rules of our speech.

For a Christian to talk after this manner I always thought very indiscreet and irreverent, God cannot die; God cannot contradict himself; God cannot do this, or that. I do not like to have the Divine Power so limited by the rules of our speech. And the appearance which presents itself to us in these propositions, ought to be represented more religiously and reverently.

Human language very defective.

Our speech has its failing and defects, as well as all the rest. Grammar is that which creates most disturbance in the world. Our suits only spring from the interpretation of laws: and most wars proceed from the inability of ministers clearly to express the conventions and treaties of princes. How many quarrels, and of how great importance, has the doubt of the meaning of this syllable *hoc* created in the world? let us admit the conclusion that logic itself presents us with to be the clearest. If you say, it is fair weather, and that you say true, it is then fair weather. Is not this a very certain form of speaking? And yet it will deceive us: that it will do so, let us follow the example. If you say, you lie, and that

---

ances he admitted of two principles, heat and cold. I have this last quotation from the translator of Cic. de Natura Deorum, tom. iii. p. 276. Were I to believe Parmenides, says Seneca, ep. 88, there is nothing but one thing. And probably from hence it was that Montaigne took what he tells us here of Parmenides.

* This Zeno must be the Zeno of Eleus, the disciple of Parmenides. The Pyrrhonians reckoned him one of their sect. Diog. Laert. in the Life of Pyrrho, lib. ix. sect. 72. Montaigne here has also copied Seneca, ep. 88, where after these words, "Were I to "believe Parmenides, there is nothing besides one," he adds immediately, "If, Zeno, there is not so much as one."

you say true, then you do lie. The art, the reason, and the force of the conclusion of this, are like to the other, and yet we are gravelled.

The Pyrrhonian philosophers, I discern, cannot ex-press their general conception in any manner. For they absolutely require a new language on purpose. Ours is all formed of affirmative propositions, which are totally against them. Insomuch that when they say, I doubt, they are presently taken by the throat, to make them confess, that at least they know and are assured that they do doubt. By which means they have been compelled to shelter themselves under this medicinal comparison, without which their humour would be inexplicable. When they pronounce, I know not; or, I doubt; they say that this proposition carries off itself, with the rest, not more nor less than rhubarb,* that drives out the ill humours, and carries itself off with them. This fancy is better conceived by the interrogation: what do I know? (as I bear it in the emblem of a balance).† See what use they make of this irreverent way of speaking. In the present disputes about our religion,‡ if you press its adversaries too hard, they will roundly tell you, that it is not in the power of God to make it so, that his body should be in paradise, and upon earth, and in several places at once. And see what advantage the ancient scoffer made of this. However, says he, it is no little consolation to man to see that God cannot do all things: for he cannot kill himself, if he would: which is the greatest privilege we have in such a painful life: he cannot make mortals immortal, nor bring the dead again to life: nor make it so, that he who has lived, has not; nor that he, who has had honours, has not had

The margin notes to the right: The Pyrrhonians at a loss for words capable of representing their opinion.

---

* This is exactly the comparison which the Pyrrhonians were accustomed to make use of.

† This appears in Montaigne's picture, which is the frontispiece of the first volume of these Essays.

‡ This refers to what is said in the preceding page; that God cannot do this or that.

them, having no other right to the past, than that of
oblivion.* And that this comparison of a man to
God may also be made out by pleasant examples, he
cannot order it so, he says, that twice ten shall not
be twenty. This is what he says, and what a Christian ought to take heed of letting fall from his lips.
Whereas on the contrary, it seems as if some men
studied such impudent language, to reduce God to
their own measure:

———— *Cras vel atrâ*
Nube polum pater occupato,
Vel sole puro, non tamen irritum
Quodcumque retro est, efficiet : neque
Diffinget, infectumque reddet,
Quod fugiens semel hora vexit.†

To-morrow, let it shine or rain,
Yet cannot this the past make vain ;
Nor uncreate and render void,
That which was yesterday enjoy'd.‡

When we say, that the infinity of ages, as well past
as to come, are but one instant with God : that his
bounty, wisdom, and power are the same with his
essence : our mouths speak it, but our understandings apprehend it not : and yet such is our vain opinion of ourselves, that we must make the divinity
pass through our sieve ; from thence proceed all the
dreams and errors with which the world is possessed,
whilst we reduce and weigh in our balance a thing so
far above our poise. *Mirum quò procedat improbitas
cordis humani, parvulo aliquo invitata successu :§* " It
" is a wonder to what a length the pride of man's
" heart will proceed, if encouraged with the least
" success." How insolently is Epicurus reproved
by the Stoics for maintaining, that to be truly good
and happy appertained only to God, and that the
wise man had nothing but a shadow and resemblance

* Plin. Nat. Hist. lib. ii. cap. 7.
† Horat. Carm. lib. iii. od. 29, ver. 43, &c.
‡ Sir Richard Fanshaw.
§ Plin. Nat. Hist. lib. ii. cap. 23,

of it? How presumptuously have they bound God
by destiny (a thing, that, with my consent, none, *They deny*
that bears the name of a Christian, should ever do *it, and yet*
again); and Thales, Plato, and Pythagoras, have it. *actually do*
subjected him to necessity. This arrogance of attempting to discover God with our eyes, has been
the cause, that an eminent person, of our nation,
has attributed to the divinity a corporeal form; and
is the reason, of what happens among us every day,
of attributing to God important events, by a particular appointment: because they sway with us, they
conclude that they also sway with him, and that he
has a more entire and vigilant regard to them than
to others of less moment, or of ordinary course.
Magna Dii curant, parva negligunt : * " The gods
" are concerned in great matters, but slight the
" small." Observe his example, he will clear this
to you by his argument: *Nec in regnis quidem reges*
omnia curant : " Neither, indeed, do kings, in their
" administration, take notice of all the minute af-
" fairs." As if to that King of kings it were more
and less to subvert a kingdom, or to move the leaf
of a tree: or as if his Providence acted after another
manner in inclining the event of a battle, than in the
leap of a flea. The hand of his government is laid
upon every thing, after the same manner, with the
same tenor, power, and order: our interest does
nothing towards it; our inclinations and measures
sway nothing with him. *Deus ita artifex magnus in*
magnis, ut minor non sit in parvis :† " God is so great
" an artificer in great things, that he is no less in
" the least." Our arrogance sets this blasphemous
comparison ever before us: because our employments are a burden to us, Strato has presented the
gods with a freedom from all offices, as their priests
have. He makes nature produce and support all
things, and with her weights and motions constructs

---

* Cic. de Nat. Deor. lib. ii. cap. 66, et lib. iii. cap. 35.
† St. Augustine de Civitate Dei, lib. xi. cap. 22.

the several parts of the world, discharging human
nature from the awe of divine judgments, asserting,
*Quod beatum, æternumque sit, id nec habere negotii
quicquam, nec exibere alteri :** " That what is blessed
" and eternal, has neither any business itself, nor
" gives any to another." Nature wills, that in like
things there should be a like relation : the infinite
number of mortals, therefore, concludes a like
number of immortals ; the infinite things that kill
and destroy, presuppose as many that preserve and
profit. As the souls of the gods, without tongue, eyes,
or ears, do, every one of them, feel, amongst themselves, what the other feel, and judge our thoughts ;
so the souls of men, when at liberty, and loosed
from the body, either by sleep, or some ecstasy, divine, foretel, and see things, which, whilst joined
to the body, they could not. " Men," says St. Paul,
" professing them to be wise, they became fools,
" and changed the glory of the incorruptible God
" into an image made like to corruptible man."[†]
Do but take notice of the juggling in the ancient
deifications. After the great and stately pomp of
the funeral,[‡] so soon as the fire began to mount to
the top of the pyramid, and to catch hold of the
bier whereon the body lay, they, at the same time,
let fly an eagle, which, mounting upward, signified,
that the soul ascended into paradise. We have a
thousand medals, and particularly of that virtuous
Faustina, where this eagle is represented carrying
these deified souls, with their heels upwards, towards
heaven. It is pity that we should fool ourselves
with our own monkey tricks and inventions :

Quod finxere timent.[§]
They are afraid of their own inventions.

Like children who are frightened with the face of
their play-fellow, which they themselves have be-

---

* Cic. de Nat. Deor. lib. i. cap. 17.   † Rom. i. 22, 23.
‡ Herodian. lib. iv.   § Lucan. lib i. ver. 486.

smeared. *Quasi quicquam infelicius sit homine, cui sua figmenta dominantur.* " As if any thing could be " more unhappy than man, who is insulted by his own " fictions." It is very far from honouring him who made us, to honour him that we have made. Augustus had more temples than Jupiter, served with as much religion, and faith in miracles. The Thasians, in return of the benefits they had received from Age- silaus, coming to bring him word that they had canonised him : " Has your nation,"* said he to them, " that power to make gods of whom they " please ? Pray, first deify some one amongst your- " selves, and when I shall see what advantage he " has by it, I will thank you for your offer." Man is certainly stark mad; he cannot make a flea, and yet gods by dozens. Hear what Trismegistus says, in praise of our sufficiency : " Of all the wonderful " things, it surmounts all wonder, that man could " find out the divine nature, and make it." And take here the arguments of the school of philosophy itself :

> *Nosse cui Divos, et cœli numina, soli,*
> *Aut soli nescire datum.†*

> To whom to know the deities of heav'n,
> Or know he knows them not, alone 'tis giv'n.

" If there is a God, he is a living creature ; if he " be a living creature, he has sense ; and, if he has " sense, he is subject to corruption : if he be with- " out a body, he is without a soul, and conse- " quently without action ; and if he has a body, it " is perishable."‡ Is not here a triumph ? We are incapable of having made the world, there must then be some more excellent nature, that has put a hand to the work. It were a foolish arrogance to esteem ourselves the most perfect thing of this uni- verse. There must then be something that is better,

---

* Plutarch, in the Notable Sayings of the Lacedæmonians.
† Lucan. lib. i. ver. 452, &c.
‡ Cic. de Nat. Deor. lib. iii. cap. 13, 14.

and this is God.* When you see a stately and stu-
pendous edifice, though you do not know who is the
owner of it, you would yet conclude it was not
built for rats and weasels.† And this divine structure that we behold of the celestial palace, have we
not reason to believe that it is the residence of some
proprietor, who is much greater than we? Is not the
highest always the most worthy? And we are the
lowest. Nothing without a soul, and without
reason, can produce a living creature capable of
reason.‡ The world produces us; the world then
has soul and reason.§ Every part of us is less than
we. We are part of the world, the world therefore
is endued with wisdom and reason, and that more
abundantly than we.‖ It is a fine thing to have a
great government. The government of the world
then appertains to some happy nature. The stars
do us no harm, they are then bountiful. We have
need of nourishment, so have the gods also, and
feed upon the vapours of the earth.¶ Worldly goods
are not goods to God, therefore they are not goods
to us; offending and being offended, are equally testimonies of imbecility: it is therefore folly to fear
God. God is good by his nature, man by his industry, which is more. The divine and human wisdom have no other distinction, but that the first is
eternal. But duration is no accession to wisdom,
therefore we are companions. We have life, reason,
and liberty; we esteem bounty, charity, and justice; these qualities are in him. In fine, the building and destroying, and the conditions of the divinity, are forged by man, according as they relate
to himself. What a pattern, and what a model! let
us stretch, let us raise and swell human qualities as
much as we please: puff up thyself, vain man, yet
more, and more, and more:

Heaven
God's pa-
lace.

The go-
vernment
of the
world.

---

* Cic. de Nat. Deor. lib. ii. cap. 6.   † Idem, ibid.
‡ Idem, ibid. cap. 8.   § Idem, ibid. cap. 12.
‖ Idem, ibid. cap. 11.   ¶ Idem, ibid. cap. 16.

Nec si te ruperis, inquit.[*]
Swell even till thou burst, said he,
Thou shalt not match the deity.

*Profectò non Deum, quem cogitare non possunt,
sed semetipsos pro illo cogitantes ; non illum, sed
seipsos, non illi, sed sibi comparant.*[†] " Certainly
" they do not imagine God, of whom they can have
" no idea ; but, imagining themselves in his stead,
" they do not compare him, but themselves, not to
" him, but to themselves." In natural things the
effects do but half relate to their causes : how is this?
His condition is above the order of nature, too
sublime, too remote, and too mighty to permit himself to be bound and fettered by our conclusions.
It is not through ourselves that we arrive at that
place ; our ways lie too low : we are no nearer heaven on the top of mount Cenis, than in the bottom
of the sea ; take the distance with your astrolabe :
they debase God even to the carnal knowledge of
women, even to how many times, and how many
generations. Paulina, the wife of Saturninus, a ma-
tron of great reputation at Rome, thinking she lay
with the god Serapis[‡], found herself in the arms of
an amoroso of hers through the pandarism of the
priests of his temple. Varro, the most subtle and
most learned of all the Latin authors,[§] in his book
of Theology, writes, " That the sexton of Hercules's
" temple, throwing dice with one hand for himself,
" and with the other for Hercules, played with him
" for a supper and a whore : if he won, at the ex-
" pense of the offerings ; if he lost, at his own : the
" sexton lost, and paid the supper and the whore :
" her name was Laurentina, who saw, by night, this
" god in her arms ; by whom she was told, more-

[*] Hor. lib. ii. sat. 3.–ver. 319.
[†] St. Augustine de Civit. Dei, lib. xii. cap. 15.
[‡] Or Anubis, according to Josephus's Jewish Antiquities, lib. xviii. cap. 4, where this story is related at length.
[§] St. Augustine de Civit. Dei, lib. vi. cap. 7.

" over, that the first man she met, the next day,
" should give her a glorious reward: this was Taru-
" nicus,* a rich young man, who took her home
" to his house, and in time, left her his heiress.
" She, on the other hand, thinking to do a thing
" that would be pleasing to this god, left the peo-
" ple of Rome her heirs, and therefore had divine
" honours attributed to her." As if it had not been
sufficient that Plato was originally descended from
the gods, both by father and mother, and that he
had Neptune for the common father of his race.†
It was certainly believed at Athens, that " Aristo,
" having a mind to enjoy the fair Perictione, could
" not, and was warned by the god Apollo, in a
" dream, to leave her unpolluted and untouched till
" she was brought to bed."‡ These were the father
and mother of Plato. How many ridiculous stories
are there of like cuckoldings of poor mortals by the
gods? And of husbands injuriously disgraced in favour of their children? In the Mahometan religion
there are Merlins enough according to the belief of
the people, that is to say, children without fathers,
spiritual, divinely conceived in the wombs of vir-
gins; and they carry names that signify so much in
their language. We are to observe, that, to every
thing, nothing is more dear and estimable than its
being (the lion, the eagle, and the dolphin, prize
nothing above their own kind), and that each assimi-
lates the qualities of all other things to its own proper qualities, which we may, indeed, extend or
contract, but that is all; for beyond that relation
and principle our imagination cannot go, can guess

Nothing that both man and beast is fonder of than its species.

* Or Tarutius, according to St. Augustine: but according to Plutarch, who relates the same story in the life of Romulus, the first
man who met Larentia (as he calls her) was one Tarrutius, a very
old man, chap. 3 of Amyot's translation.
† Diogenes Laertius, in the Life of Plato, lib. iii. sect. 2.
‡ It is affirmed, for certain, that Apollo appeared, in a vision by
night, to Ariston, and forbade him to touch his wife for ten months.
Plutarch, in his Table-talk, lib. viii. qu. 1.

at nothing else, nor possibly go out thence, or
stretch beyond it. From hence spring these ancient ✗
conclusions: " Of all figures, the most beautiful is
" that of man; therefore God must be of that
" form: no one can be happy without virtue, nor
" can virtue be without reason, and reason cannot
" inhabit any where but in a human shape; God is
" therefore clothed in the human figure."* *Ita est
informatum, anticipatumque mentibus nostris, ut
homini, quum de Deo cogitet, forma occurrat hu-
mana:*† " It is so imprinted in our minds, and
" the fancy is so prepossessed with it, that when a
" man thinks of God, a human figure ever presents
" itself to the imagination." Therefore it was, that
Xenophanes pleasantly said, " That if beasts
" frame any gods to themselves, as it is likely they
" do, they certainly make them such as themselves
" are, and glorify themselves in it, as we do."‡ For
why may not a goose say thus, " All the parts of
" the universe I have an interest in; the earth serves
" me to walk upon, the sun to light me, the stars
" have their influence upon me: I have such advan-
" tage by the winds, and such conveniences by the
" waters: there is nothing that yonder heavenly
" roof looks upon so favourably as me: I am the
" darling of nature. Is it not a man that treats,
" lodges, and serves me? It is for me that he both
" sows and grinds: if he eats me, he does the same
" by his fellow-creature, and so do I the worms that
" kill and devour him." As much might be said
by a crane, and with greater confidence, upon the
account of the freedom of his flight, and the possession of that sublime and beautiful region. *Tam
blanda conciliatrix, et tam sui est lena ipsa natura.*§
" So flattering and wheedling a bawd is nature to
" herself." Now therefore, by the same consequence, Man ima-
the destinies are for us; for us is the world; it gines that
every thing

* Cic. de Nat. Deor. lib. i. cap. 18.   † Idem, ibid. cap. 27.
‡ Euseb. Evang. Prep. lib. xiii. cap. 13.   § Idem, ibid. cap. 27.

was made for him. shines, it thunders for us; and the creator and creatures are all for us.* The mark and point at which the universality of things aims is this. Look into the register that philosophy has kept, for two thousand years and more, of the affairs of heaven : the gods all that while have neither acted nor spoken but for man : she does not allow them any other consultation or vacation. But here we find them in war against us :

> —— Domitosque Herculea manu
> Telluris juvenes, unde periculum
> Fulgens contremuit domus
> Saturni veteris †——

> Earth's brawny offspring, conquer'd by the hand
> Of great Alcides on the Thracian strand,
> Where the rude shock did such a rattle make,
> As made old Saturn's shining palace shake.

The gods espousing the quarrels of mortals. And here we see them participate of our troubles, to make a return for our having so often shared in theirs :

> Neptunus muros magnóque emota tridenti
> Fundamenta quatit, totámque à sedibus urbem
> Eruit : Hic Juno Scæa sævissima portas
> Prima tenet.‡——

> Neptune his massy trident did employ,
> With which he shook the walls of mighty Troy,
> And the whole city from its platform threw ;
> Whilst to the Scæan gates the Græcians flew,
> Which Juno had set open to their view.

Strange gods banished. The Caunians, jealous of the authority of their own peculiar gods, arm themselves on the days of their devotion, and run all about their precincts, furiously brandishing their swords in the air, by that means to drive away all strange gods out of their Power of territory.§ Their powers are limited, according to

---

* I have known some divines, who laid down this principle for an article of faith, and ready to pronounce their anathemas against any who dared to question it.
† Hor. lib. ii. ode 12, ver. 6, &c.   ‡ Æn. lib. ii. ver. 610.
§ Herodot. lib. i. pag. 79.

our necessity. This cures horses, that cures men; one the gods li-
cures the plague, another the scurf; this the phthisic; mited to
one cures one sort of scurvy, another another; things.
Adeò minimis etiam rebus prava religio inserit Deos :[*]
" So fond is a false religion to create gods for the
" meanest uses : one makes the grapes to grow, ano-
" ther garlick." This has the presidence over lech-
ery, there is another over merchandise; for every
race of artizans there is a god : one has his province
in the east, another in the west :

Hic illius arma.————Hic currus fuit.[†]

Here lay her armour; here her chariot stood.

O sancte Apollo, qui umbilicum certum terrarum obtines.[‡]

O sacred Phœbus, who, with glorious ray,
From the earth's centre dost thy light display.

Pallada Cecropidæ, Minoia Creta Dianam,
Vulcanum tellus Hipsipylæa colit.
Junonem Sparte, Pelopeïadesque Mycenæ,
Pinigerum Fauni Mænalis ora caput,
Mars Latio venerandus.[§]——

Th' Athenians Pallas, Cynthia Crete adores,
Vulcan is worshipp'd on the Lemnian shores ;
Proud Juno's altars are by Spartans fed,
Th' Arcadians worship Faunus ; and 'tis said
To Mars by Italy is homage paid.

This has only one town, or one family in his possession : one lives alone, another lives in company, either voluntarily, or from necessity :

Junctaque sunt magno templa nepotis avo.[||]

Jove and his grandson in the same temple dwell.

There are some so wretched and mean (for the Sorry, val-
number amounts to six and thirty thousand), that they gar deities.
must pack five or six together, to produce one ear of
corn, and thence they take their several names. Three
to the door, viz. one to the plank, one to the hinge;
and one to the threshold. Four to an infant ; pro-

* Livy, lib. xxvii. cap. 23. † Æn. lib. i. ver. 20, 21.
‡ Cic. de Divin. lib. ii. cap. 56. § Ovid. Fast. lib. iii. ver. 81, &c.
|| Idem, ibid. lib. i. ver. 294.

tectors of its swathing-clouts, its pap, and the breasts
which it sucks. Some certain, some uncertain and
doubtful, and some that are not yet entered paradise:

Quos, quoniam cœli nondum dignamur honore,
*Quas dedimus certè terras habitare sinamus.**

Whom, since we yet not worthy think of heav'n,
We suffer to possess the earth we've giv'n.

There are amongst them physicians, poets, and civil
deities. Some middle ones, between the divine and
human nature, mediators between God and us, adored
with a diminutive sort of worship: infinite in titles
and offices: some good, and others ill; some old and
decrepid, and some that are mortal. For Chrysip-
pus† was of opinion, that, in the last conflagration of
the world, all the gods were to die but Jupiter: and
makes a thousand similitudes between God and him.
Is he not his countryman?

Jovis incunabula Creten.‡
Crete noted for Jupiter's cradle.

This is the excuse we have upon consideration of
this subject, from Scævola, a high-priest, and Varro,
a great divine, in their times: " That it is necessary
" for the people to be ignorant of many things that
" are true, and believe many things that are false,"
Quum veritatem, qua liberatur, inquirat: credatur ei
expedire, quod fallitur :§ " Seeing he inquires into
" the truth, by which he would be made free, it is
" fit he should be deceived." Human eyes cannot
perceive things, but by the forms they know of them.
And we do not remember what a fall poor Phaeton
had, for attempting to govern the reins of his father's
horses with a mortal hand. The mind of man falls
into as great a profundity, and is after the same
manner bruised and shattered by its own temerity.

* Ovid. Metam. lib. i. fab. 6, ver. 32, 33.
† Plutarch of Common Conceptions, chap. 27.
‡ Ovid. Met. lib. viii. fab. 1, ver. 91.
§ Aug. de Civit. Dei, lib. iv. cap. 31.

If you ask philosophy of what matter the sun is made? What answer will she return, if not that it is iron or stone, or some other matter that she makes use of? If a man require of Zeno, " what nature is?" " An artificial fire," says he, " proper for generation, " and regularly proceeding."[*] Archimedes, master of that science, which attributes to itself the precedency before all others, for truth and certainty, says, the sun is a god of red-hot iron. Was not this a fine imagination, extracted from the inevitable necessity of geometrical demonstration? Yet not so inevitable and profitable, but that Socrates thought it was enough to know so much of geometry only, as to measure the land a man bought or sold;[†] and that Polyænus, who had been a great and famous master in it, despised it, as full of falsity and manifest vanity,[‡] after he had once tasted the delicate gardens of Epicurus. Socrates, in Xenophon, speaking of Anaxagoras, reputed by antiquity learned above all others in celestial and divine matters, says, " That he had cracked his brain, as all other men " do, who too immoderately search into knowledge " of things which do not appertain to them."[§] When he made the sun to be a burning stone, he did not consider that a stone does not shine in the fire; and, which is worse, that it will there consume. And in making the sun and fire one, that fire[||] does not turn complexions black in shining upon them: that we are able to look steadily upon fire: and that fire kills herbs and plants. It is Socrates's opinion, and mine too, " That it is the best judgment con-

Geometry how far useful.

---

[*] Cic. de Nat. Deor. lib. ii. ver. 42.
[†] Xenophon. Mirabilium, lib. iv. sect. 7, cap. 2.
[‡] Cic. Acad. Quæst. lib. iv. cap. 33.   [§] Id. ibid. cap. 6, 7.
[||] Socrates was no great natural philosopher, if we may judge by what he says of fire, in opposition to the sun: for who does not know that fire will blacken the skin of any person, that should stay long very near it: that at a very small distance, one cannot look upon it fixedly; and that, at a proper distance, instead of killing herbs and plants, it nourishes them.

" cerning heaven, not to judge of it at all." Plato,
having occasion in his Timæus, to speak of dæmons : " This undertaking, says he, exceeds my
" ability. We are therefore to believe .those an-
" cients, who have pretended to have been be-
" gotten by them." It is against all reason to dis-
believe the children of the gods, though what they
say should not be proved by necessary or probable
reasons ; seeing they engage to speak of domestic
The sum of and familiar things. Let us see if we have a little
our know- more light in the knowledge of humah and natural
ledge of na-
turalthings. things. Is it not a ridiculous attempt for us to forge
for those things, to which, by our own confession,
our knowledge is not able to attain, another body,
and to lend a false form of our own invention ? as is
manifest in the motion of the planets ; to which, seeing our understanding cannot possibly attain, nor
conceive their natural conduct, we lend them material, heavy, and substantial springs of our own, by
which to move : *

> *Aureus axis erat, temo aureus, aurea summæ*
> *Curvatura rotæ, radiorum argenteus ordo.†*
>
> Gold was the axle, and the beam was gold ;
> The wheels with silver spokes on golden circles roll'd.

You would swear, that we had coach-makers,
wheel-wrights, and painters, that went aloft to erect
engines of various motions, and to range the car-
riages and intersections of the heavenly bodies of
different colours about the spindle of necessity, according to Plato :

* Montaigne will tell us presently, that the ancient philosophers
built a little too much upon authorities that are merely poetical :
and so far he is in the right ; but I cannot imagine why he pretends
to take an advantage against the natural philosophers, for some authorities of this kind, which have never been reputed but as arbitrary characters, invented to amuse the imagination, rather than to
inform the understanding.
† Ovid. Met. lib. ii. fab. 1. ver. 106.

Mundus domus est maxima rerum,
Quam quinque altitonæ fragmine zonæ
Cingunt, per quam limbus bis sex signis
Stellimicantibus, altus in obliquo æthere, lunæ
Bigas acceptat. *———

The world's a mansion that doth all things hold,
Which thund'ring zones, in number five infold,
Through which a border painted with twelve signs,
And that with sparkling constellations shines,
In th' oblique roof of heaven's lofty sphere,
Where Luna's course is mark'd with chaise and pair.

These are all dreams and fantastic follies. Will not
nature be pleased some day or other to lay open her
bosom to us, discover the means and conduct of
her movements, and prepare our eyes to see them?
Good God, what abuse, what mistakes would we
perceive in our poor science! I am mistaken, if it
holds any one thing, as it really is; and I shall depart hence more ignorant of every thing but my own
ignorance.

Have I not read in Plato this divine saying, that Philosophy
" Nature is nothing but an enigmatic poesy!"† As if is only poe-
a man might say, a shaded and obscure picture, break- ticated.
ing out here and there with an infinite variety of false
lights to exercise our conjectures. *Latent ista omnia*
crassis occultata et circumfusa tenebris, ut nulla acies
humani ingenii tanta sit quæ penetrare in cœlum, ter-
ram intrare possit : ‡ " All those things lie concealed
" and involved in so thick darkness, that no human
" wit can be so sharp as to penetrate either heaven

---

* Varro in Catal.
† Montaigne has here mistaken Plato's sense, whose words, in
Alcibiade II—p. 42. C, are these, Ἔτι τε φύσει ποιητική ἡ ξυμπᾶσα
αἰνιγματώδης: " All poetry is in its nature enigmatical." Plato says
this by reason of a verse in Homer's Margites, which he explains, and
which indeed has something in it that is enigmatical. Either Montaigne did not see this passage in Plato, or else he read it without
closely examining it. Nature is certainly a riddle with respect to us;
but it does not appear very plain in what sense it may be called
enigmatical poetry. Montaigne himself, to whom this term appears so divine, does not explain it to us very clearly
‡ Cic. in Acad. Quæst. lib. iv. cap. 39.

" or the earth." And certainly philosophy is no
other than a falsified poesy. From whence do the
ancient writers extract all their authorities, but from
the poets ? The first of them were poets themselves,
and wrote accordingly. Plato is but a poet uncon-
nected. All super-human sciences are set off in the
poetic style. Just as women make use of teeth of
ivory, where the natural are wanting, and, instead of
their true complexion, make one of some artificial
matter ; as they stuff themselves out with cotton, &c.
to appear plump, and, in the knowledge and sight of
every one, trick up themselves with false and borrowed beauty : so does science (and even our law itself has, they say, legitimate fictions, whereon it
founds the truth of its justice), she gives us in supposition, and, for a current pay, things which itself
informs us were invented : for by these epicycles, ex-
centrics, and concentrics, by which astrology is helped to carry on the motions of the stars, she gives us
for the best she could contrive upon that subject ; as
also, in all the rest, philosophy presents us, not that
which really is, or what she really believes, but what
she has contrived with the greatest plausibility.
Plato, discoursing of the state of human bodies, and
those of beasts, says, " I should know what I have
" said is truth, had I the confirmation of an oracle :
" but this is all I will affirm, that it is the most pro-
" bable of any thing I could say."

*The con-
fused idea
which man
has of him-
self.*
It is not to heaven only that philosophy sends her
ropes, engines, and wheels ; let us consider a little
what she says of ourselves and of our contexture.
There is not more retrogradation, trepidation, accession, recession, and rapture in the stars and celestial bodies, than they have feigned in this poor little human
body. In truth, they have good reason upon that very
account to call it a microcosm, or little world, so many
views and parts have they employed to erect and
build it. To assist the motions they see in man, and
the various functions and faculties that we find in
ourselves, into how many parts have they divided the

soul? In how many places lodged it? In how many ranks and stories have they stationed this poor crea-ture man, besides those that are natural, and percep-tible? And to how many offices and vocations have they assigned him? They make an imaginary of a public thing. It is a subject that they hold and han-dle: and they have full power granted to them, to rip, place, displace, patch, and stuff him, every one according to his own fancy, and yet they possess him not. They cannot, not in reality only, but even in dreams, so govern him, that there will not be some cadence or sound which will escape their architec-ture, as enormous as it is, and botched with a thou-sand false and fantastic patches. And there is no reason to excuse them; for though we pardon pain-ters when they paint heaven, earth, seas, mountains, and remote islands, and only give us some slight sketch of them, and, as of things unknown, we are content with a faint description; yet when they come to draw us, or any other creature which is known and familiar to us, according to the life, we then require of them a perfect and exact representa-tion of lineaments and colours, and despise them if they fail in it. I am very well pleased with the Mi-lesian wench,* who, observing the philosopher Thales always contemplating the celestial arch, and to have his eyes still gazing upward, laid something in his way that he might stumble at, to admonish him, " That it would be time enough to take up his " thoughts about things that are in the clouds, when " he had taken care of those that were under his " feet." Doubtless she advised him very well, " rather to look to himself than to gaze at heaven." For, as Democritus says, by the mouth of Cicero, *Quod est ante pedes, nemo spectat: cæli scrutantur*

---

* She was maid-servant to Thales according to Plato, from whom this story is taken; but he does not say that he stumbled at any thing laid in his way by his servant; but that as he was walking along, with his eyes lifted up to the stars, he fell into a well.

plagas : * " No man regards what is at his feet ; they
" are always prying towards heaven." But such is
our condition, that the knowledge of what we have
in hand is as remote from us, and as much above the
clouds, as that of the stars ; as Socrates says, in
Plato, " That whoevers tampers with philosophy,
" may be reproached as Thales was by the woman,
" that he sees nothing of that which is before him.†
" For every philosopher is ignorant of what his
" neighbour does : yea, and of what he does him-
" self, and is ignorant of what they both are, whe-
" ther beasts or men." As for these people who
think Sebonde's arguments too weak, who are ino-
rant of nothing, who govern the world, and know
every thing,

> *Quæ mare compescant causæ ; quid temperet annum ;*
> *Stellæ sponte sua, jussæve vagentur, et errent :*
> *Quid premat obscurum Lunæ, quid proferat orbem ;*
> *Quid velit, et possit rerum concordia discors.*‡

> What bounds the swelling tides, what rules the year ;
> Whether of force or will the planets err ;
> Why shadows darken the pale queen of night,
> Whence she renews her orb and spreads her light ;
> What means the jarring sympathy of things, &c.

Have they not sometimes in their writings sounded
the difficulties that occurred in the knowledge of
their own being ? We see very well that the finger
moves, and that the foot moves ; that some parts
move of themselves without our leave, and that
others stir by our direction ; that one sort of apprehension occasions blushing, another paleness ; such
an imagination works upon the spleen only, another
upon the brain, one occasions laughter, the other
tears, another stupifies and astonishes all our senses,
and stops the motion of our members ; at one object the stomach will rise, at another a member that

---

* Cic. de Divin. lib. ii. cap. 13.   † Plato in Theætato, p. 127.
‡ Horat. lib. i. epist. 12, cap. 16, &c.

lies something lower. But how a spiritual impression should make such a breach into a massy and solid subject, and the nature of the connection and contexture of these admirable springs and movements, never man yet knew : *Omnia incerta ratione, et in naturæ majestate abdita :* " All these things " are impenetrable by reason, and concealed in the " majesty of nature," says Pliny. And St. Augustine, *Modus quo corporibus adhærent spiritus, omnino mirus est, nec comprehendi ab homine potest : et hoc ipse homo est :*[†] " The manner whereby souls are united " to bodies, is altogether wonderful, and cannot be " conceived by man ; yet this union constitutes man " himself." Mean while it is not so much as doubted; for the opinions of men are received according as the ancients believed, by authority and upon trust, as if it were religion and law. The common notion of it is, it is received as gibberish ; but this truth, with all its pile of arguments and proofs, is admitted as a firm and solid body, that is no more to be shaken, no more to be judged of. On the contrary, every one, according to his talent, corroborates and fortifies this received belief with the utmost power of his reason, which is a supple tool, pliable, and easily accommodated to any figure. Thus the world comes to be filled with lies and fopperies.

The reason why men do not doubt of many things is, that they never examine common impressions : they do not dig to the root, where the faults and defects lie ; they only debate upon the branches : they do not examine whether such and such a thing be true, but if it has been so, and so understood. It is not inquired, whether Galen has said any thing to the purpose, but whether he has said so or so. In truth it was very reasonable, that this curb and constraint to the liberty of our judgments, and this tyranny over our opinions, should be extended to the

How it happens that men scarce doubt of things.

* Plin. lib. ii. cap. 37.   † St. Aug. de Spir. et Anim.

schools and arts. The god of scholastic knowledge
is Aristotle: it is irreligious to question any of his
decrees, as it was those of Lycurgus at Sparta: his
doctrine is an inviolable law to us, though perhaps
it is as false as another.

I do not know, why I should not as willingly embrace either the ideas of Plato, or the atoms of Epicurus, or the plenum or vacuum of Leucippus and
Democritus, or the water of Thales, or the infinity
of nature of Anaximander,* or the air of Diogenes,†
or the members and symmetry of Pythagoras, or
the infinity of Parmenides, or the one of Musæus,
or the water and fire of Apollodorus, or the similar
parts of Anagoras, or the discord and friendship of
Empedocles, or the fire of Heraclitus, or any other
opinion (in that infinite confusion of opinions and
sentiments, which this fine human reason produces
by its clear-sightedness in every thing it meddles
with), as I should the opinion of Aristotle upon this
subject of the principles of natural things: which
principles he builds of three pieces, matter, form,
and privation. And what can be more vain than to
make inanity itself the cause of the production of
things? Privation is a negative: of what humour
could he then make the cause and original of things
that are: and yet that were not to be controverted,
but for the exercise of logic. There is nothing disputed; the whole matter is to defend the author of
the school from foreign objections: his authority is
the *ne plus ultra*, beyond which it is not permitted
to inquire.

It is very easy upon approved foundations to build
whatever we please; for, according to the law, and
ordering of the beginning, the other parts of the
structure are easily carried on without any failure.

Difference of opinions concerning natural principles.

The receiving of principles without examination liable to all kind of mistakes.

* Sext. Empir. Pyrrh. lib. iii. cap. 4, p. 155.
† Of Diogenes Apolloniates, apud Sextum Empiricum in Pyrrh.
Hypot. This is a farther proof of a former note in this chaper, that
it was air, and not age, as Montaigne thought, must be the god of
this philosopher of Apollonia.

By this way we find our reason well-grounded, and have good warrant for what we say ; for our masters prepossess and gain before-hand as much room in our belief, as is necessary towards concluding afterwards what they please ; as geometricians do by their pos- tulata. The consent and approbation we allow them, giving them power to draw us to the right and left, and to whirl us about at their own pleasure. Whoever will have his presuppositions taken for grant- ed, is our master and god : he will lay the plan of his foundations so ample and easy, that by them he may mount us up to the clouds, if he pleases. In the practice of science, we have given entire credit to the saying of Pythagoras, " That every expert per- " son ought to be believed in his own art." The logician refers the signification of words to the gram- marian; the rhetorician borrows the state of argu- ments from the logician ; the poet his measure from the musician ; the geometrician his proportions from the arithmetician ; and the metaphysicians take the physical conjectures for their foundations. For every science has its principles presupposed, by which human judgment is every-where curbed. If you rush against this barrier, where the principal error lies, they have presently this sentence in their mouths, " That there is no disputing with persons, " who deny principles." Now men can have no principles, if not revealed to them by the divinity : of all the rest the beginning, the middle, and the end, is nothing but dream and vapour. As for those that contend upon presupposition, we must, in our turn, presuppose to them the same axiom upon which the dispute turns. For every human presup- position and declaration has as much authority one as another, if reason do not make the difference. Wherefore they are all to be put into the balance, and first the generals, and those that tyrannise over us. The persuasion of certainty is a certain testi- mony of folly and extreme uncertainty ; and there is not a more foolish sort of men, nor who have less

philosophy, than the Philodoxes of Plato.[*] We
must inquire whether fire be hot? whether snow be
white? if we know whether there be such things as
hard or soft?

Whether
philosophi-
cal uncer-
tainty is de-
terminable
by the ex-
perience
of the
senses.As to those answers of which they tell old stories,
as he that doubted if there was any such thing as
heat, whom they bid throw himself into the fire; and
he that denied the coldnes of ice, whom they bid put
a cake of ice into his bosom: they are pitiful things,
unworthy of the profession of philosophy. If they
had left us in our natural state, to receive the external appearances of things according as they present
themselves to us by our senses; and had permitted
us to follow our own natural appetites, and be governed by the condition of our birth; they might then
have reason to talk at that rate, but it is from them that
we have learned to make ourselves sit up for judges of
the world: it is from them that we derive this fancy,
" That human reason is controller-general of all that
" is above and below the firmament, that composes
" every thing, that can do every thing, and by the
" means of which every thing is known and under-
" stood." This answer would be good amongst canni-
bals, who enjoy the happiness of a long, quiet, and peaceable life, without Aristotle's Precepts, and without the
knowledge of the name of Physics. This answer
would perhaps be of more value and greater force
than all those which they borrow from their reason
and invention. Of this, all animals, and all, where
the power of the law of nature is yet pure and simple, would be as capable as we; but those they have
renounced. They need not tell us, it is true, for
you see and feel it so: they must tell me whether I
really feel what I think I do; and, if I do
feel it, then let them tell me why I feel it, and
how, and what: let them tell me the name,

---

* " Persons who are possessed with opinions of which they know
" not the grounds, whose heads are intoxicated with words, who
" see and affect only the appearances of things." This is taken
from Plato, who has characterised them very particularly at the end
of the fifth book of his Republic.

original, the bounds and borders of heat and cold, the qualities of the agent and patient; or let them give me up their profession, which is not to admit or approve of any thing, but by the way of reason; that is their touch-stone for essays of every sort.

But certainly it is a test full of falsity, error, weakness, and defect. Which way can we better prove it, than by itself? If we are not to believe it when speaking of itself, it can hardly be thought fit to judge of things foreign to it; if it knows any thing, it will at least be its own being and abode. It is in the soul, and either a part or an effect of it: for true and essential reason, from which we, by false colours, borrow the name, is lodged in the breast of the Almighty. There is its habitation and recess, and from thence that it proceeds, when God is pleased to impart any ray of it to mankind; Pallas issued from her father's head, to communicate herself to the world. *Whether our reason can judge of what immediately relates to itself.*

Now let us see what human reason tells us of itself, and of the soul: not of the soul in general, of which almost all philosophy makes the celestial and first bodies partake: nor of that which Thales* attributed to things, which are themselves reputed inanimate, being moved by the consideration of the loadstone: but of that which appertains to us, and which it concerns us most to know: *What reason tells us of the nature of the soul.*

Ignoratur enim quœ sit natura animaï,
Nata sit, an contrà nascentibus insinuetur,
Et simul intereat nobiscum morte dirempta,
An tenebras orci visat, vastásque lacunas,
An pecudes alias divinitùs insinuet se.†

For none the nature of the soul doth know,
Whether that it be born with us, or no;
Or be infus'd into us at our birth,
And dies with us when we return to earth;
Or then descends to the infernal shades,
Or, ceaseless, other animals pervades.

---

* Diog. Laert. in the life of Thales, lib. i. sect. 24.
† Lucret. lib. iv. 112, &c.

Crates and Dicæarchus* were induced to judge from
human reason, " That there was no soul at all;
" but that the body thus stirs by a natural motion :
" Plato,† that it was a substance moving of itself:
" Thales, a nature without repose:‡ Asclepiades, an
" exercising of the senses: Hesiod and Anaximan-
" der, a thing composed of earth and water: Par-
" menides, of earth and fire: Empedocles, of
" blood." §

> *Sanguineam vomit ille animam.*||
> His soul he vomited in streams of blood.

Possidonius, Cleanthes, and Galen, judged from
the same principle that it was heat, or a hot complexion :

> *Igneus est ollis vigor, et cœlestis origo.*¶
> From fire their vigour, and from heav'n their race.

" Hippocrates, that it was a spirit diffused all over
" the body: Varro, that it was an air received at the
" mouth, heated in the lungs, moistened in the
" heart, and diffused throughout the whole body.
" Zeno,** the quintessence of the four elements:

* Apud Sext. Empir. Pyrrh. Hypot. lib. ii. cap. 5, p. 57, et adv.
Mathem. περι αντεαων, p. 201. " Dicæarchus Phærecratem quendam
" Phthiotam senem—disserentem inducit nihil esse omninò ani-
" mum," &c. Cic. Tusc. Quæst. lib. i. cap. 10.
   † De Legibus, lib. x. p. 668.
   ‡ According to Plutarch de Placitis Philosophorum, lib. iv. cap. 2,
which moves of itself, αυτοκινητος.
   § " Empedocles animum esse censet, cordi suffusum sanguine,"
Cic. Tusc. Quæst. lib. i. cap. 9.
   || Virg. Æneid. lib. ix. ver. 349.
   ¶ Idem, ibid. lib. vi. ver. 730.
   ** I know not where Montaigne had this; for Cicero expressly
says, that this quintessence, or fifth nature, is a thought of Aristotle, who makes the soul to be composed of it; and that Zeno
thought the soul to be fire, Cic. Tusc. Quæst. lib. i. cap. 9 & 10.
After this, Cicero adds, " That Aristotle calls the mind, wh ch he
" derives from that fifth nature, Entelechia, a new-coined word,
" signifying a perpetual motion." Though Montaigne has cor ied
these last words, in what he proceeds to tell us of Aristotle, he
censures him for not having spoken of the origin and nature of the

" Heraclitus Ponticus, that it was the light: Xenocrates and the Egyptians, a moveable number: the
Chaldeans, a virtue without any determinate form:"

> *Habitum quandam vitalem corporis esse,*
> *Harmoniam Græci quam dicunt.**
>
> A certain vital habit in man's frame,
> Which harmony the Grecian sages name.

Let us not forget Aristotle, who held the soul to be
that which naturally causes the body to move; which
he called Entelechia, with a colder invention than
any of the rest; for he neither speaks of the essence,
the origin, nor the nature of the soul, and only
takes notice of the effect. Lactantius, Seneca, and
most of the dogmatists, have confessed, that it was
a thing they did not understand. After all this
enumeration of opinions: *Harum sententiarum quæ
vera sit, Deus aliquis viderit,*† says Cicero: " Of
" these opinions, which is the true, let some God de-
" termine." " I know by myself," says St. Bernard,
" how incomprehensible God is, seeing I cannot
" comprehend the parts of my own being." Heraclitus,‡ who was of opinion, that every place was
full of souls and demons, nevertheless maintained,
" That no one could advance so far towards the
" knowledge of his soul, as ever to arrive at it; of
" so profound a nature was its essence." Neither In what
is there less controversy and debate about the seat part of man
of it. Hippocrates and Hierophilus place it in the sides.

soul. But had he only cast his eye upon what Cicero had said a
little before, he would have been convinced, that Aristotle had taken care to explain himself concerning the origin of the soul, before he remarked the effect of it. If he has not thereby fully demonstrated what the nature of it is, Zeno has not given us much
better light into it, when he says, " The soul or mind seems to be
" fire :" and it would not to be difficult to show, that, in this article,
the other philosophers have not succeeded better than Zeno and
Aristotle.

* Lucret. lib. iii. ver. 100.
† Cic. in Tusc. Quæst. lib. i. cap. 11.
‡ Diog. Laert. in the Life of Heraclitus, lib. ix. sect. 7.

ventricle of the brain: [*] Democritus and Aristotle, throughout the whole body: [†]

> *Ut bona sæpe valetudo cum dicitur esse*
> *Corporis, et non est tamen hæc pars ulla valentis.*[‡]
>
> So health and strength are both said to belong
> To man, but are no parts of him that's strong.

Epicurus, in the stomach, or middle region of the breast; [§]

> *Hic exultat enim pavor, ac metus, hæc loca circùm*
> *Lætitiæ mulcent.*[§]
>
> For this the seat of horror is and fear,
> And joys alternate likewise triumph here.

The Stoics, about, and within, the heart: Erasistratus, close to the membrane of the epicranion: Empedocles, in the blood; as also Moses, which was the reason why he interdicted eating the blood of beasts, in which their soul is seated. Galen thought, that every part of the body had its soul: Strato [||] has placed it between the eye-brows; *Quâ facie quidem sit animus, aut ubi habitet, ne quærendum quidem est* [¶] "What figure the soul is of, or what part it " inhabits, is not to be inquired into," says Cicero. I very willingly deliver this author to you in his own words; for should I go about to alter the speech of eloquence itself? Besides, it were no great prize to steal the matter of his inventions. They are neither very frequent, nor very difficult, and they are pretty well known. But the reason why Chrysippus argues it to be about the heart, as the rest of that sect do, is not to be admitted. "It is," says he, [**] "because, " when we would affirm any thing, we lay our " hand upon our breasts: and when we are to pro-

[*] Plutarch de Placitis Philosophorum, lib. iv. cap. 5,
[†] Sextus Empiricus adv. Mathem. p. 201,
[‡] Lucret. lib. iii. ver. 103,   [§] Id. ibid. ver. 141,
[||] Plutarch de Placitis Philosoph. lib. iv. cap. 5.
[¶] Cic. Tusc. Quæst. lib. i. cap. 28.
[**] Apud Galenum, lib. ii. de Placitis Hippocratis et Platonis.

" nounce ἐγώ, which signifies I, we let the lower
" mandible sink towards the stomach." I cannot
omit here making a remark upon the vanity of so
great a man: for, besides that these considerations
are infinitely trivial in themselves, the last is only a
proof to the Greeks, that they have their souls lodged
in that part. No human judgment is so vigilant,
that it does not sometimes sleep. Why should we
be afraid to speak? We see the Stoics, who are the
fathers of human prudence, have found out, that the
soul of a man, crushed under a ruin,* long labours
and strives to get out, before it can disengage itself
from the burden, like a mouse caught in a trap. Some
hold, that the world was made to give bodies, by way
of punishment, to the angels that fell, by their own
fault, from the purity wherein they had been created:
the first creation having been no other than incorpo-
real; and that, according as they are more or less
depraved from their spirituality, so are they more or
less jocundly or dully incorporated. From thence
proceeds all the variety of so much created matter.
But the spirit that, for his punishment, was invested
with the body of the sun, must certainly have a very
rare and particular measure of thirst. All our in- The vanity
quiries terminate in a mist, as Plutarch† says of histo- of philoso-
ries, where, as it is in charts, all that is beyond the quiries.
coasts of known countries is represented as marshes,
impenetrable forests, deserts, and places uninhabita-
ble. And this is the reason why the most stupid
and childish reveries were mostly found in those authors, who treat of the sublimest subjects, and proceed the furthest in them: losing themselves in their
own curiosity and presumption. The beginning and
end of knowledge are equally reputed foolish. Observe
to what a height Plato soars in his poetic clouds: do
but take notice of his gibberish of the gods. But

* Senec. ep. 57.
† This reflection of Plutarch is in the preamble to his Life of
Theseus,

what did he dream of when he defined man to be a
two legged animal,* without feathers: giving those
who had mind to deride him, a pleasant occasion;
for, having plucked a capon alive, they called it
Plato's man. As for the Epicureans, how simple
were they to imagine, that their atoms, which they
said were bodies, having some weight, and a natural
motion downwards, had formed the world, until they
were put in mind by their adversaries, that according
to this description, it was impossible they could unite
with one another, their fall being so direct and per-
pendicular, and producing so many parallel lines
throughout? Wherefore, there was a necessity, that
they should afterwards add a fortuitous and lateral motion, and that they should, moreover, accoutre their
atoms with hooks and crooks, to adapt them for an
union and attachment to one another. Even then,
do not those that attack them upon this second consideration, put them hardly to it? If the atoms have,
by chance, formed so many sorts of figures, why did
it never fall out that they made a house or a shoe?
why, at the same rate, should we not as well believe
that an infinite number of Greek letters, strewed all
over a certain place, might possibly fall into the contexture of the Iliad? " Whatever is capable of reason,"
says Zeno, " is better than that which is not capable
" of it: there is nothing better than the world; the
" world is therefore capable of reason."† Cotta, by this
way of argument, makes the world a mathematician;
and it is also made a musician, and an organist, by
this other argument of Zeno: " The whole is more
" than a part; we are capable of wisdom, and are
" parts of the world; therefore the world is wise."‡
It would be endless to instance, not only in the arguments which are false in themselves, but likewise frivolous, which do not hold together, and accuse their

* Diog. Laert. in the Life of Diogenes the Cynic, lib. v. sect. 40.
† Cic. de Nat. Deor. lib. iii. cap. 9.
‡ Idem, lib. ii. cap. 12.

authors not so much of ignorance, as imprudence,
in the mutual reproaches of philosophers, upon their
dissensions in opinion. Whoever should bundle up
a faggot of the fooleries of human wisdom, would
produce wonders: I willingly muster up these few
for a pattern, by a certain bias, not less profitable
than the most moderate instructions. Let us judge
by these, what opinion we are to have of man,
of his sense and reason, when, in these great persons,
and such as have raised human knowledge so high,
there are so many gross and palpable errors. For *Whether*
my part, I am rather apt to believe, that they have *the ancient*
treated of knowledge casually, played with it, dallied *philoso-*
with reason, as a vain and frivolous instrument, like *phers treat-*
a shuttle-cock, and set on foot on all sorts of fancies *ed of know-*
ledge se-
riously.
and inventions, sometimes more nervous, and sometimes weaker. This same Plato, who defines man as if
he were a fowl, says elsewhere, after Socrates, " That
" he does not, in truth, know what man is, and that
" he is one of the members of the world the hardest
" to understand." By this variety and instability of
opinions, they tacitly lead us, as it were, by the hand,
to this certainty of their uncertainty : they profess
not always to deliver their opinions bare-faced and
apparent to us ; they have, one while, disguised them
in the fabulous shadows of poesy, and, another
while, in some other vizor : for our imperfection
carries this also along with it, that crude meats are
not always proper for our stomachs ; they must be
dried, altered, and mixed : the philosophers do the
same : they, now and then, conceal their real opinions and judgment, and falsify them to accommodate themselves to the public : they will not make
an open profession of ignorance, and of the imbecility of human reason, that they must not frighten
children ; but they sufficiently discover it to us by
the appearance of knowledge that is confused and
uncertain. I advised a person in Italy, who had a *Philoso-*
great mind to speak Italian, that, provided he only *phy full of*
had a desire to make himself understood, without *uncertain-*
ty and ex-

trava-
gance.

being ambitious to excel, he need but make use of
the first words that came to the tongue's end, whether Latin, French, Spanish, or Gascon ; and that by
adding the Italian terminations, he could not fail of
hitting upon some idiom of the country, either Tuscan, Roman, Venetian, Piedmontese, or Neapolitan,
and to apply himself to some one of those many
forms : I say the same of philosophy ; it has so many
faces, so much variety, and has said so many things,
that all our dreams and chimeras are therein to be
found. Human fancy can conceive nothing good or
bad that is not there : *Nihil tam absurdè dici potest,
quod non dicatur ab aliquo philosophorum :** " Nothing
" can be so absurdly said, that has not been said be-
" fore by some of the philosophers." And I am the
more willing to expose my whimsies to the public ;
forasmuch as, though they are spun out of myself,
and without any model, I know they will be found to
correspond with some ancient humour, and one or
another will be sure to say, " See whence he took
it." My manners are natural. I have not called in
the assistance of any discipline to form them : but,
weak as they are, when it came into my head to
publish them to the world, and when, in order to
expose them to the light in a little more decent garb,
I set out to corroborate them with reasons and examples, I wondered to find them accidentally con-
formable to so many philosophical discourses and examples. I never knew the regimen of my life, till
now that it is near worn out and spent. A new
figure ; an unpremeditated and accidental philoso-

The most
probable
hypothesis
concerning
the human
soul.

pher. But to return to the soul : as for Plato's having placed reason in the brain, anger in the heart,
and concupiscence in the liver : it was rather an interpretation of the movements of the soul, than that
he intended a division and separation of it, as of a
body, into several members : and the most likely of
their opinions is, that it is always a soul, which, by

* Cic. de Divin. lib. ii. cap. 58.

its faculty, reasons, remembers, comprehends, judges, desires, and exercises all its other operations by divers instruments of the body, as the pilot guides his ship according to his experience, one while straining or slacking the cordage, one while hoisting the mainyard, or moving the rudder, by one and the same power conducting several effects: that this soul is lodged in the brain, which appears in that the wounds and accidents, which touch that part, do immediately hurt the faculties of the soul; and it is not inconsistent, that it should thence diffuse itself into the other parts of the body:

> ———— Medium non deserit unquam
> Cæli Phœbus iter, radiis tamen omnia lustrat.[*]

> Phœbus ne'er deviates from the zodiac's way;
> Yet he enlightens all things with his ray.

As the sun sheds from heaven its light and influence, and therewith fills the world:

> Cætera pars animæ per totum dissita corpus
> Paret, et ad numen mentis, nomenque movetur.[†]

> The other part o' th' soul, which is confin'd
> To all the limbs, obeys the ruling mind,
> And moves as that directs.

Some have said, that there was a general soul, as it were a great body, from whence all particular souls were extracted, and thither return, always mixing itself again with universal matter: *Different opinions of the soul's origin.*

> ———— Deum namque ire per omnes
> Terrasque tractusque maris, cælumque profundum.
> Hinc pecudes, armenta, viros, genus omne ferarum,
> Quemque sibi tenues nascentem arcessere vitas.
> Scilicet huc reddi deinde, ac resoluta referri
> Omnia: nec morti esse locum.[‡]

> ———— For they suppose
> That God through earth, the sea, and heaven goes.
> Hence men, beasts, reptiles, insects, fishes, fowls,
> With breath are quicken'd, and attract their souls;

---

[*] Claud. in Paneg. de Consol. Hon. 411, 412.
[†] Lucret. lib. iii. ver 144, 145.   [‡] Virg. Georg. lib. iv. ver. 221, &c.

And into him at length resolve again,
No room is left for death.——

Others, that they only rejoined and re-united
themselves to it : others, that they were produced
from the divine substance : others, by the angels
from fire and air : others, that they were from all antiquity : some, that they were created at the very
point of time when the bodies wanted them : others
make them to descend from the orb of the moon,
and to return thither. The generality of the ancients believed, that they were engendered from father to son, after a like manner, and produced as all
other natural things, founding their argument on
the likeness of children to their parents :

> *Instillata patris virtus tibi,**
> *Fortes creantur fortibus et bonis.*†
>
> Thou hast thy father's virtues with his blood ;
> For still the brave spring from the brave and good.

And upon the observation, that not only bodily
marks, but moreover a resemblance of humours,
complexions, and inclinations of the soul, descend
from parents to their children :

> *Denique cur acrum violentia triste leonum*
> *Seminium sequitur, dolus vulpibus, et fuga cervis,*
> *A patribus datur, et patrius pavor incitat artus,*
> *Si non certa suo quia semine seminioque,*
> *Vis animi pariter crescit cum corpore toto ?*‡
>
> For why should rage from the fierce lion's seed,
> Or, from the subtle fox's, craft proceed,
> Or why the timorous and flying hart
> His fear and trembling to his race impart,
> But that a certain force of mind does grow,
> And still increases as the bodies do ?

They add, that this is a proof of the divine justice,
which hereby punishes, in the children, the faults of

---

* I am at a loss to know from whence Montaigne took this first
verse.
† Horat. lib. iv. ode 4, ver. 29.
‡ Lucret. lib. iii. ver. 741 to 743, 746, 747.

their fathers : forasmuch as the contagion of the parents' vices is in some sort imprinted in the soul of children, and that the irregularity of their will affects them.

Moreover, that if the souls had any other deriva- The opi-nion of the pre-exis-tence of the souls, be-fore their union to our bodies, confuted. tion than from a natural succession, and that they had pre-existed, they would retain some memory of their first being, considering the natural faculties that are proper to them of discoursing, reasoning, and remembering :

> —— *Si in corpus nascentibus insinuatur,*
> *Cur super anteactam ætalem meminisse nequimus,*
> *Nec vestigia gestarum rerum ulla tenemus ?*[*]
>
> For at our birth, if it infused be,
> Why do we then retain no memory
> Of our foregoing state, and why no more
> Remember any thing we did before ?

For, to make the condition of our souls such as we would have it to be, we must suppose them all knowing, even in their natural simplicity and purity. Of consequence they had been such, exempt from the prison of the body, as well before they entered into it, as we hope they will be after they are gone out of it. From which knowledge it must follow, that they would be sensible when in the body ; as Plato[†] said, " That what we learn is no other than a remem-" brance of what we knew before ;" a thing which every one by experience may maintain to be false. In the first place, as we do not justly remember any thing, but what we have been taught : and, if the memory perform its office aright, it would at least suggest to us something more than what we have learned. Secondly, what the soul knew, being in its purity, was true knowledge, knowing things as they are by its divine intelligence : whereas here we make it receive falshood and vice, when we instruct it wherein it cannot employ its remembrance, that image and conception having never been planted in it.

---

[*] Lucret. lib. iii. ver. 671.   [†] In Phædone, p. 382.

To say, that the corporeal prison does suffocate the soul's natural faculties, in such a manner, that they are thereby utterly extinct, is, first, contrary to this other belief of acknowledging its power to be so great, and the operations of it, which men sensibly perceive in this life, so admirable, as to have thereby concluded this divinity, and past eternity, and the immortality to come:

> *Nam si tantopere est animi mutata potestas,*
> *Omnis ut actarum exciderit retinentia rerum,*
> *Non (ut opinor) id ab letho jam longior errat.*[*]
>
> For if the mind be chang'd to that degree,
> As of past things to lose all memory;
> So great a change as that, I must confess,
> Appears to me than death but little less.

Besides, it is here, with us, and not elsewhere, that the force and effect of the soul ought to be considered: all the rest of its perfections are vain and useless to it; it is by its present condition, that all its immortality is to be rewarded and paid; and of the life of man only that it is to render an account: it had been injustice to have stripped it of its means and powers, to have disarmed it, from the time of its captivity and imprisonment, its weakness and infirmity, from the time when it was compelled to enter upon a course of action, which was to determine its misery to all eternity, and to insist upon the consideration of so short a time, perhaps but an hour or two, or, at the most, but an age (which have no more proportion with infinity, than an instant), for this momentary interval to ordain, and finally determine its whole existence. It were an unreasonable disproportion to infer an eternal recompence in consequence of so short a life. Plato, to defend himself from this inconvenience, will have " future " rewards limited to the term of a hundred years, " relatively to human duration:" and, of the moderns, there are enow who have given them tempo-

---

[*] Lucret. lib. iii. ver. 671.

ral limits. By this they judged, that " the generation of That the
" the soul followed the common condition of human soul is born, and
" things :" as also its life, according to the opinion grows
of Epicurus and Democritus, which has been the strong and weak with
most received, in consequence of these fine appear- the body.
ances, that they saw it born; and that, according as
the body grew more capable, they saw it increase in
vigour, as the other did; that its feebleness, in infancy, was very manifest; as was, in time, its vigour and maturity; after that, its declension and
old age; and, at last, its decrepitude:

> —— Gigni pariter cum corpore, et unā
> Crescere sentimus, pariterque senescere mentem.*

> As to the soul, this point we firmly hold,
> 'Tis with the body born, grows strong, and old.

They perceived it to be capable of diverse passions,
and agitated with several painful motions, from
whence it fell into a lassitude and uneasiness, capable of alteration and change, of cheerfulness, stupidity, and faintness, and subject to diseases and injuries, as well as the stomach, or the foot :

> —— Mentem sanari, corpus ut ægrum
> Cernimus, et flecti medicinā posse videmus.†

> Minds, as well as sickly bodies, feel
> The pow'r of medicines that kill or heal.

Intoxicated and disturbed with the fumes of wine,
jostled from her seat by the vapours of a burning
fever, dosed by the application of some medicaments, and roused by others :

> —— Corpoream naturam animi esse necesse est,
> Corporeis quoniam telis ictuque laborat.‡

> Hence the soul's union with the body's plain,
> Since by corporeal darts it suffers pain.

They perceived all its faculties overthrown by the
mere bite of a mad dog, and that it then had no

---

* Lucret. lib. iii. ver. 446.   † Idem, ibid. ver. 509.
‡ Idem, ibid. ver. 167, 177.

strength of reason, no sufficiency, no virtue, no philosophical resolution, no resistance that could exempt it from subjection to such accidents; the slaver of a mastiff cur, shed upon the hand of Socrates, was seen to shake his wisdom so much that there remained no trace of his former knowledge:

> ———— vis animaï
> Conturbatur——et divisa seorsum
> Disjectatur eodem illo distracta veneno.[*]

He's mad, because the parts of soul and mind
Are by the poison's violence disjoin'd,
Disturb'd, and toss'd.

This poison found no more resistance in his great soul, than in that of an infant of four years old: a poison sufficient, if philosophy were incarnate, to make it furious and mad; insomuch that Cato, who ever disdained death and fortune, could not endure the sight of a looking glass, or of water, confounded with horror and affright, at the thought of falling by the bite of a mad dog, into the disease, called, by physicians, hydrophobia;

> ——— Vis morbi distracta per artus
> Turbat agens animam, spumantes æquore salso
> Ventorum ut validis fervescunt viribus undæ.[†]

The venom, having through the body stole,
Makes such a strong commotion in the soul,
As boist'rous storms which o'er the ocean rave,
And raise white curls upon the foaming wave.

The soul of the wisest man liable to become the soul of a fool. Now, as to this particular, philosophy has sufficiently armed man to encounter all other accidents, either with patience, or, if the search of that costs too dear, by an infallible defeat, in totally depriving himself of all sensation: these are expedients of use to a soul that is capable of reason and deliberation; though of none, when the judgment is affected; a situation which many occasions may produce, as a too vehement agitation, or a wound in a certain

* Lucret. lib. iii. ver. 498.   † Idem, ibid. ver. 491, &c.

part of the body; or vapours in the stomach, that may dazzle the understanding, and turn the brain:

—— *Morbis in corporis avius errat*
Sæpè animus, dementit enim delirâque fatur,
Interdúmque gravi lethargo fertur in altum
Æternumque soporem, oculis nutúque cadenti.[*]

For when the body's sick, and ill at ease,
The mind not seldom shares in the disease,
Wanders, grows wild, and raves, and sometimes, by
A heavy and a fatal lethargy,
Is overcome, and cast into a deep,
An irresistible, eternal sleep.

The philosophers have touched but little on this subject, no more than on another of equal importance: they have this dilemma continually in their mouths, to comfort our mortal condition : " The soul " is either mortal, or immortal; it will suffer no " pain, if immortal; if mortal, it will change " for the better." They never touch the other branch; what if it change for the worse? and they leave to the poets the menaces of future torments; but thereby they give themselves a large scope. These are two omissions, that I often meet with in their discourses; I return to the first:[†] this soul loses the use of the sovereign stoical good, so constant and so firm. Our fine human wisdom must here yield, and lay down her arms. As to the rest, they also considered, by the vanity of human reason, that the mixture and association of two such contrary things, as mortal and immortal, was imaginable :

Quippe etenim mortale æterno jungere, et unâ
Consentire putare, et fungi mutua posse,
Desipere est: quid enim diversius esse putandum est,
Aut magis inter se disjunctum, discrepitánsque,
Quam mortale quod est, immortali atque perenni
Junctum in concilio, sævas tolerare procellas?[‡]

---

* Lucret. lib. iii. ver. 464, &c.
† That the soul lives, or may fare the worse.
‡ Lucret. lib. iii. ver. 801, &c.

The mortal and th' eternal, then, to blend,
And think they can pursue one common end,
Is madness : for what things more diff'rent are,
Distinct in nature, and dispos'd to jar ?
How can it then be thought, that these should bear,
When thus conjoin'd, of harms an equal share ?

Moreover, they perceived that the soul declined, as well as the body :

———— Simul ævo fessa fatiscit.*
Fatigu'd together with the weight of age.

Which, according to Zeno, the image of sleep sufficiently demonstrates to us : for he looks upon it as a fainting and fall of the soul, as well as of the body. *Contrahi animum, et quasi labi putat, atque decidere :†* " He thinks the mind is convulsed, and that it " slips and falls :" and what they perceived in some, that the soul maintained its force and valour to the last gasp of life, they attributed to the variety of diseases, as it is observable in men at the last extremity, that some retain one sense, and some another, one the hearing, and another the smell, without any manner of alteration ; and that there is not so universal a decay, that some parts do not remain vigorous and entire :

*Non alio pacto quàm si pes cum dolet ægri,
In nullo caput intered si fortè dolore.‡*

So, often of the gout a man complains,
Whose head is, at the same time, free from pains.

The soul's immortality weakly maintained by the holdest dogmatists. Truth is as impenetrable by the sight of our judgment, as the sun by the eyes of the owl, says Aristotle. By what can we better convince him, than by so gross blindness in so apparent a light ? For the contrary opinion of the immortality of the soul, which, Cicero says, was first introduced (by the testimony of authors at least §) by Pherecides Syrius, in the time of king Tullus (though others attribute

* Lucret. lib. iii. ver. 459.   † Cic. de Divinat. lib. ii. cap. 58.
‡ Lucret. lib. iii. ver. 111, 112.   § Tusc. Quæst. lib. i. cap. 16.

it to Thales, and some to others), is the part of human science, which is treated of with the most
doubt and reservation. The most positive dogmatists
are forced, in this point, principally to take shelter
under the Academy. No one knows what Aristotle
has established upon this subject, no more than all
the ancients in general, who handle it with a wavering belief: *Rem gratissimam promittentium magis
quam probantium :*[*] " He conceals himself in a cloud
" of words of difficult and unintelligible sense, and
" has left his sectaries as much divided about his
" judgment as his subject." Two things render The found-
this opinion plausible to them : one, " that without ation of the
" the immortality of souls, there would be nothing the soul's
" whereon to ground the vain hopes of glory," immortali-
which is a consideration of wonderful repute in the
world: The other, " that it is a very useful impres- Vice pu-
" sion, as Plato says, that vices, when they escape the divine
" the discovery and cognizance of human justice, justice af-
" are still within the reach of the divine, which will ter death.
" pursue them even after the death of the guilty."
Man is excessively solicitous to prolong his being,
and has, to the utmost of his power, provided for it :
he lays his body in the earth to preserve it, and aims
at glory to perpetuate his name : he has employed
all his thoughts to the rebuilding of himself (uneasy
at his fortune), and to prop himself by his inventions.
The soul, by reason of its anxiety and feebleness,
being unable to stand by itself, wanders up and
down to seek out comfort, hope, and foundations,
and alien circumstances, to which it adheres and
fixes : and, how light or fantastic soever they
are, relies more willingly, and with greater assurance upon them, than itself. But it is wonderful to
observe, how short the most obstinate maintainers

* These words are taken from Seneca's epistle 102, where he says
to his friend, that he took delight in his inquiry into the eternity of
souls ; nay, that he believed it by an easy acquiescence in the opinions of the great men, who gave greater promises than proofs of
a thing so very acceptable.

of this so just and clear persuasion of the immortality of the soul do fall, and how weak their arguments are, when they go about to prove it by human reason. *Somnia sunt non docentis sed optantis,*[*] says one of the ancients.[†] By this testimony man may know, that he owes the truth he himself finds out, to fortune and accident; since that even then, when it is fallen into his hand, he has not wherewith to grasp and maintain it, and his reason has not force to avail himself of it. All things produced by reason and sufficiency, whether true or false, are subject to uncertainty and controversy. It was for the chastisement of our pride, and to convince us of our misery and incapacity, that God caused the perplexity and confusion at the tower of Babel. Whatever we undertake without his assistance, whatever we see without the lamp of his grace, is but vanity and folly. We corrupt and debase the very essence of truth, which is uniform and constant, by our weakness, when fortune puts it into our possession. What course soever man takes of himself, God still permits it to end in the same confusion, the image whereof he so lively represents to us in the just chastisement wherewith he crushed Nimrod's presumption, and frustrated the vain attempt of his pyramid. *Perdam sapientiam sapientum, et prudentiam prudentium reprobo*:[‡] " I will destroy the wisdom of the wise, " and will bring to nothing the understanding of the " prudent." The diversity of idioms and languages with which he disturbed this work, what is it else but the infinite and perpetual altercation and discordance of opinions and reasons, which accompanies and confounds the vain building of human wis-

---

* Cic. Acad. lib. iv. cap. 38.
† " They are the dreams of a man, who wishes that things were " true, which he takes no pains to prove." Cicero, in this passage, has his aim only at Democritus, who, by supposing a vacuum and atoms of different kinds, ridiculously pretended to account for the formation of all things.
‡ 1 Cor. i. 19.

dom? And it is to very good effect, that it does so.
For what would hold us if we had but one grain of
knowledge? This saint has very much pleased me
by saying, *Ipsa veritatis occultatio, aut humilitatis
exercitatio est, aut elationis attritio :* "The very
" concealment of the truth tends either to exercise
" man to humility, or to mortify his pride." To
what a pitch of presumption and insolence do we
carry our blindness and folly?

But to return to my subject; it was truly very good *It is by re-*
reason, that we should be beholden to God only, and *velation we*
to the favour of his grace, for the truth of so noble a *of the soul's*
belief, since from his sole bounty we receive the *immortali-*
fruit of immortality, which consists in the enjoyment of eternal beatitude. Let us ingenuously confess, that God alone has dictated it to us, and that
faith is its basis. For it is no lesson of nature and
our own reason. And whoever will make fresh trial
of his own being and power, both within and without, without this divine privilege; whoever shall
consider man without flattery, will see nothing in him
of efficacy, nor faculty, that relishes of any thing but
death and earth. The more we give and owe and
render to God, we are the greater Christians. That
which this stoic philosopher says, he held from the
fortuitous consent of the popular voice; had it not
been better, that he had held it from God? *Cum de
animorum æternitate disserimus, non leve momentum
apud nos habet consensus hominum, aut timentium in-
feros, aut colentium. Utor hac publica persuasione.†*
" When we discourse of the soul's immortality, the
" consent of men, that either fear or adore the in-
" fernal power, is of no small moment to us. I
" make use of this public persuasion."

Now the weakness of human reasoning, upon this *What con-*
subject, is particularly manifest by the fabulous argu- *stitutes the*
ments they have superadded to this opinion, in or- *mortality,*

---

* Augustin. de Civit. Dei, lib. xi. cap. 22.
† Senec. epist. 117.

der to find out of what condition this immortality
of ours is. Let us omit the Stoics, who give to
souls a life after this, but finite. *Usuram nobis lar-
giuntur, tanquam cornicibus; diù mansuros aiunt animos: semper negant:*[*] " They give us a long life,
" as also they do to crows; they say the soul will
" continue long; but that it will exist always, they
" deny." The most universal and received fancy,
and which continues down to our times (in Persia) is
that of which they make Pythagoras the author; not
that he was the original inventor, but because it received a great deal of weight and repute by the authority of his approbation, viz. " That souls, at their
" departure out of us, did nothing but shift from one
" body to another, from a lion to a horse, from a
" horse to a king, continually travelling, at this rate,
" from one habitation to another." And he himself said, " That he remembered he had been Atha-
" lides,[†] then Euphorbus, and afterwards Hermoti-
" mus; and finally, from Pyrrhus, was passed into Py-
" thagoras, having remembered himself two hundred
" and six years." And some have added, that the
very same souls sometimes remount to heaven, and
come down again :

*O pater, anne aliquas ad cœlum hinc ire putandum est
Sublimes animas iterúmque ad tarda reverti
Corpora? Quæ lucis miseris tàm dira cupido?*[‡]

O father, is it then to be conceiv'd,
That any of these spirits, so sublime,
Should hence to the celestial regions climb,
And thence return to earth to re-assume
Their sluggish bodies rotting in a tomb?
For wretched life, whence does such fondness come?

Origen makes them eternally go and come, from a
good to a worse estate. The opinion mentioned by
Varro is, that after four hundred and forty years re-

---

[*] Cic. Tusc. lib. i. cap. 31.
[†] Diogenes Laertius, in the Life of Pythagoras, lib. viii. cap. 4, 5.
[‡] Virg. Æneid. lib. vi. ver. 719, &c.

volution, they are re-united to their first bodies. Chrysippus held, that this would happen after a certain space of time not known or limited. Plato* (who professes to have embraced this opinion from Pindar, and the ancient poets) thinking " It is to " undergo infinite vicissitudes of mutation, for which " the soul is prepared, having neither punishment " nor reward in the other world, but what is tempo- " ral, as its life in this is but temporal, concludes " that it has a singular knowledge of the affairs of " heaven, of hell, and of the world, through all " which it has passed, repassed, and made stay in its " several voyages ; matters enough for its memory." Observe its progress elsewhere : " The soul that has " lived well is re-united to the star to which he is " assigned : that which has lived ill, removes into a " woman ; and, if it do not then reform, is again " metamorphosed into a beast of a condition suita- " ble to its vicious manners, and shall see no end of " his punishments, till it be returned to its native " constitution, and has by the force of reason purged " itself from those gross, stupid, and elementary " qualities it was possessed with." But I will not omit the objection the Epicureans make against this transmigration from one body to another, and a pleasant one it is. They ask, " What should be done, " if the number of the dying should chance to be " greater than that of those who are coming into the " world ? for the souls, turned out of their old habi- " tation would tread on one another, striving first to " get possession of the new lodging." And they farther demand, " How they shall pass away their " time, whilst waiting till the new quarters were " made ready for them ? Or, on the contrary, if " more animals should be born than die, the body, " they say, would be but in an ill condition, whilst in " expectation of a soul to be infused into it ; and it

* In Menone, p. 16, 17.

" would fall out, that some bodies would die, before
" they had been alive :"

> *Denique connubia adveneris, partúsque ferarum,*
> *Esse animas præsto deridiculum esse videtur,*
> *Et spectare immortales mortalia membra*
> *Innumero numero, certareque præproperanter*
> *Inter se, quæ prima potissimaque insinuetur.**
>
> 'Tis fond to think that whilst wild beasts beget,
> Or bear their young, a thousand souls do wait,
> Expect the falling body, fight and strive
> Which first shall enter in and make it live.

Others have stopped the soul in the body of the
deceased, with it to animate serpents, worms, and
other vermin, which are said to be bred out of the corruption of our members, and even out of our ashes ;
others divide the soul into two parts, the one mortal,
the other immortal. Others make it corporeal, and
nevertheless immortal. Some make it immortal
without science or knowledge. There are even some
of us who have believed, that devils were formed of
the souls of the damned ; and Plutarch thinks
that gods were made of those that were saved. For
there are few things which that author is so positive in, as he is in this ; maintaining elsewhere a
doubtful and ambiguous way of expression. " We
" are to hold," says he, " and stedfastly to believe,
" that the souls of virtuous men, both according to na-
" ture and the divine justice, become saints ; and from
" saints, demi-gods ; and from demi-gods, after they
" are perfectly, as in sacrifices of purgation, clean-
" sed and purified, being delivered from all passibi-
" lity, and all mortality, they become, not by any
" civil decree, but in real truth, and according to
" all probability of reason, entire and perfect gods,
" in receiving a most happy and glorious end." But
whoever desires to see him, the man, I say, who is
yet the most sober and moderate of the whole tribe of

* Lucret. lib. iii. ver. 757, &c.

philosophers, lay about him with greater boldness, and relate his miracles upon this subject, I refer him to his Treatise of the Moon, and his Dæmon of Socrates, where he may, more evidently than in any other place whatever, satisfy himself, that the mysteries of philosophy have many strange things in common with those of poesy; the human understanding losing itself, in attempting to sound and search all things to the bottom: even as we, tired and worn out with a long course of life, relapse into infancy. Thus much for the fine and certain instructions, which we extract from human science concerning the soul. Neither is there less temerity in what it teaches us touching our corporeal parts. Let us single out one or two examples; for otherwise we should lose ourselves in this vast and troubled ocean of errors. We would first know, whether at least they agree about the matter, whereof men produce one another. For, as to their first production, it is no wonder, if, in a thing so sublime, and so long since past, human understanding finds itself puzzled and distracted. Archelaus the naturalist, whose disciple and favourite Socrates was, according to Aristoxenus, said, "That both men and beasts were "made of a lacteous slime, produced by the heat "of earth."* Pythagoras says, "That our seed is "the froth or cream of our better blood."† Plato, "That it is the distillation of the marrow of the "back-bone;"‡ and he raises his arguments from this; "That that part is first sensible of lassitude in "the·act." Alcmeon, "That it is part of the sub- "stance of the brain; and that it is so," says he, "appears from the weakness of eyes, in those who "are overmuch addicted to that exercise."§ De- mocritus, "That it is a substance extracted from "the whole mass of the body."‖ Epicurus, "That "it is extracted from soul and body."¶ Aristotle,

Variety of opinions as to the matter that produces the human body.

---

* Diogenes Laertius, in the Life of Archelaus, lib. ii. sect. 17.
† Plutarch de Placitis Philosophorum, lib. v. cap. 3.
‡ Idem, ibid.   § Idem, ibid.   ‖ Idem, ibid.   ¶ Idem, ibid.

" That it is an excrement drawn from the aliment of
" the last blood, which is diffused in our members."*
Others, " That it consists of the blood concocted
" and digested by the heat of the genitals ;" which
they judge to be so, by reason that, in excessive efforts, a man voids pure florid blood; wherein there
seems to be the more likelihood, could any likelihood be deduced from so infinite a confusion.

By what means the seed be- comes pro- lifie.

Now, to bring this seed to operate, how many
contrary opinions do they set on foot? Aristotle and
Democritus† are of opinion, " That women have
" no sperm." Galen, on the contrary, and his followers, believe, " That, without the concurrence of
" seeds, there can be no generation."

Time of women's pregnancy undeter- mined.

Here are the physicians, the philosophers, the
lawyers, and divines, together by the ears, with
our wives, about the dispute, upon what terms women bear their fruit: and I, for my part, by what I
know myself, join those who maintain that a woman
goes eleven months with child. The world is built
upon this experience; there is not so despicable a
wife that cannot give her judgment in all these
controversies, and yet we cannot agree. This is
enough to prove, that man is no better instructed in
the knowledge of himself, in his corporeal, than in
his spiritual part. We have proposed himself to himself, and his reason to his reason, to see what it
would say; and, I think, I have sufficiently demonstrated how little it understands of itself. In earnest, Protagoras told us a pretty flam, in making
man the measure of all things, who never knew so
much as his own :§ If it be not he, his dignity will
not permit, that any other creature should have this
advantage : now, he being so inconsistent in him-

---

* Plutarch de Placitis Philosophorum, lib. v. cap. 3.

‡ Plutarch adds Zeno to Aristotle, and says expressly, that Democritus believed that the females shed their seed. De Placitis
Philosophorum, lib. v. cap. 5.

§ Apud Sext. Empiric. advers. Mathem. p. 148.

self, and one judgment so incessantly subverting another, this favourable proposition was but a mockery,
which induced us necessarily to conclude the nothingness of the measure and the measurer. When
Thales reputes the knowledge of man very difficult for
man to attain to, he gives him to understand, that it
was impossible for him to know any thing else. You,
for whom I have taken the pains, contrary to my custom, to write so long a discourse, will not refuse to
maintain your Sebonde, by the ordinary forms of arguing, wherewith you are every day instructed, and in
this will exercise both your wit and study: for this
last rule, in fencing, is never to be made use of, but
as an extreme remedy. It is a desperate thrust,
wherein you are to quit your own arms, to make
your adversary abandon his; and a secret slight,
which must be very rarely and cautiously put in
practice. It is great temerity to ruin yourself, that
you may destroy another; you must not venture
your life, to be revenged, as Gobrias did: for, being
in close combat with a lord of Persia, Darius coming
in with his sword in his hand, and fearing to strike
lest he should wound Gobrias; he called out to him
boldly to fall on, though he should run them both
through at once. I have known the arms and desperate conditions of single combat, wherein he, that
offered them, put himself and his adversary upon
terms of inevitable death to them both, censured
for unjust. The Portuguese, in the Indian sea, took
certain Turks prisoners, who, impatient of their captivity, resolved to blow up the ship, with themselves
and company; which they did accordingly, by
striking the nails of the ship one against another,
and making a spark fall into the barrels of powder
that were set in the place, where they were guarded.
We have here touched the utmost limits of the
sciences, wherein the extremity is vicious: as in
virtue keep yourselves in the common road; it is
not good to be so subtle and cunning: remember
the Tuscan proverb:

Chi troppo s'assottiglia, si scavezza.*
He that spins his thread too fine, will break it.

I advise you, in all your opinions and discourses,
as well as in your manners, and all other things, to
keep yourself in moderation and temperance, and to
avoid novelty. I am an enemy to all extravagant
ways : you, who by the authority you derive from
your grandeur, and yet more by the advantages
which those qualities give you that are most your
own, can, with a nod, command whom you please,
ought to have given this caution to some professor
of letters, who might have proved and illustrated
these things to you in quite another manner: but
here is as much as you will stand in need of.

The neces-
sity of laws
to keep
men in or-
der.

Epicurus said of the laws, " that the worst were
" so necessary for us, that, without them, men
" would devour one another." And Plato proves,
" that, without laws, we should live like beasts."
Our wit is a rambling, dangerous, and rash tool : it
is hard to affix any rule or measure to it : as for the
men of my time, we see that almost all who are endued with any rare excellence above others, and
any extraordinary vivacity, launch out into a licentiousness of opinions and manners ; and it is a miracle to find one that is sober and sociable. It is right
to confine human wit within the strictest limits possible. 'In study, as in other things, its inquiry
ought to be confined within certain bounds. It is
curbed and fettered by religions, laws, and customs,
by science, precepts, punishments and rewards,
mortal and immortal; and yet we see, that by its
volubility and dissoluteness, it escapes from all these
restraints. It is a thin body, which has nothing to
hold or handle it by ; a various and shapeless body,
incapable of being either tied or touched. In truth,
there are few souls so regular, firm, and well bred,
as to be trusted with their own conduct, and that

* Proverb.

can, with moderation, and without temerity, sail
in the liberty of their own judgments, beyond the
common opinions. It is more expedient to put
them under guardianship: wit is a dangerous weapon, even to the possessor, if he knows not how to
use it discreetly; and there is not a beast for which
a head board is more necessary to hinder him from
wandering, here and there, out of the tracks which
custom and the laws have made for him. Therefore it will much better become you to keep yourself
in the beaten path, let it be what it will, than to
take a flight with such unbridled licence. But if
any of these new doctors will pretend to be ingenious in your presence, at the expense both of your
soul and his own; in order to be safe from this dangerous plague, which spreads daily in your way, this
preservative, in extreme necessity, will prevent the
poison from hurting either you or your company.

The liberty, therefore, and gaiety of the ancient
wits, produced in philosophy, and the human
sciences, several sects of different opinions, every
one undertaking to judge and make choice of his
party. But now that men go all one way: *Qui
certis quibusdam destinatisque sententiis addicti et
consecrati sunt, ut etiam, quæ non probant, cogan-
tur defendere :** " Who are so devoted to certain de-
" termined articles of belief, that they are bound to
" defend even those they do not approve." And
now that we receive the arts by civil authority and
decree, insomuch that the schools have but one
pattern, and a like circumscribed institution and
discipline, we no more take notice what the coin
weighs, and is worth, but every one, in his turn,
receives it according to the value that the common
approbation and currency puts upon it: the alloy is
not disputed, but how much it goes for; and, in
like manner, all things are at par. The tricks of

The sciences are now esta-blished by the civil au-thority.

---

* Cic. Tusc. Quæst. lib. ii. cap. 2.

11

hocus pocus, enchantments, correspondence with the souls of the dead, prognostications, and even the ridiculous pursuit of the philosopher's stone, all pass current, without scruple. We need to know no more, than that Mars's house is in the middle of the triangle of the hand, that of Venus in the thumb, and that of Mercury in the little finger; that, when Sign of cruelty. the table line cuts the tubercle or ball of the fore-finger, it is a sign of cruelty; that when it falls short of the middle finger, and the natural median line makes an angle with the line of life, in the same Of a miserable death. side, it is a sign of a miserable death; that if, in a woman, the natural line be open, and does not Of unchastity. close the angle with the vital, it denotes that she will not be very chaste. I leave you to judge, whether a man thus qualified, may not pass, with reputation and favour, in all companies.

The extent of human knowledge. Theophrastus said, " That human knowledge, " guided by the senses, might judge of the causes " of things to a certain degree; but that, when " they arrived to the first and extreme causes, it " must stop short, by reason either of its own infir-" mity, or the difficulty of investigation." It is a moderate and gentle opinion, that our own understandings may conduct us to the knowledge of some things, and that it has certain bounds, beyond which it is rashness to employ it. This opinion is plausible; but it is hard to limit our wit; it is curious and inquisitive, and will no more stop at a thousand, than at fifty paces: having myself experimentally found, that on the thing wherein one has failed, another has hit; that what was unknown to one age, the age following has explained; and that the arts and sciences are not cast in a mould, but formed and perfected by degrees, by often handling and polishing, as bears leisurely lick their cubs into shape: what I have not strength to discover, I do not yet desist to sound and try it, but by handling and kneading this new matter over again, and by turning

and heating it, I pave the way for him that should
succeed me, to enjoy it more at his ease, and render
it more manageable and supple for him :

> —————— *Ut Hymettia sole*
> *Cera remollescit, tractatàque pollice multas*
> *Vertitur in facies, ipsoque fit utilis usu.*[*]
>
> As wax more fluid in the sun becomes,
> And temper'd 'tween the fingers and the thumbs,
> Will various forms, and sev'ral shapes admit,
> Till for the present use 'tis render'd fit.

As much will the second do to the third, which is
the cause that the difficulty ought not to make me
despair, and my own imbecility as little; for it is
nobody's but my own. Man is capable of all things, The human understanding incapable of attaining to the evident knowledge of things.
as well as of some : " And if he confesses," as Theo-
phrastus says, " the ignorance of first causes and
" and principles, let him surrender to me all the
" rest of his knowledge :" if he is defective in foundation, his reason is on the ground : disputation and
inquisition have no other aim nor stay but principles ; if this do not stop his career, he wavers *ad in-
finitum*. *Non potest aliud alio magis minúsve comprehendi, quonium omniam rerum una est definitio
comprehendi :*[†] " One thing is equally comprehen-
" sible with another, because the rule of compre-
" hending all things is one and the same." Now
it is very likely, that, if the soul knew any thing, it
would, in the first place, know itself; and, if it knew
any thing out of itself, it would be its own body
and case before any thing else. If we see the gods
of physic, to this very day, debating about our anatomy,

> —— *Mulciber in Trojam, pro Troja stabat Apollo.*[‡]
> Vulcan against, for Troy Apollo stood.

When are we to expect, that they will be agreed?

* Ovid. Metam. lib. x. fab. 8, ver. 42.
† Cic. Acad. Quæst. lib. iv. cap. 41.
‡ Ovid. Trist. lib. i. el. 2, ver. 5.

We are nearer neighbours to ourselves than the whiteness of snow, or the weight of stone, are to us. If man does not know himself, how should he know his forces and functions? No question we have some true knowledge in us, but it is by chance; and as errors are received into our soul the same way, after the same manner, and by the same conduct, it has not wherewithal to distinguish them, nor to choose the truth from falsehood. The Academics admitted a certain inclination of judgment, and thought it too crude to say, that it was not more likely, that snow was white than black; and that we were not more assured of the motion of a stone, thrown by the hand, than that of the eighth sphere. To avoid this difficulty, which cannot, in truth, easily lodge in our imagination, though they concluded, that we were not capable of knowledge, and the truth is ingulphed in so profound an abyss, that it is not to be penetrated by human sight; yet they acknowledged some things to be more likely than others, and admitted that they had a power to incline to one appearance more than another: they allowed it this propensity, but excluded all resolution. The Pyrrhonists' opinion is more solid, and also more probable: for this Academic inclination, and this propensity to one proposition rather than another, what is it but an acknowledgment of some more apparent truth in this, than in that? If our understanding be capable of discovering the form, lineaments, and face of truth, it might as well see it entire, as by halves, in its birth and imperfection. This appearance of probability, which makes them rather incline to the left than to the right, augments it: multiply this ounce of verisimilitude, that turns the scales to a hundred, to a thousand ounces, it will happen, in the end, that the balance will, itself, end the controversy, and determine one choice, and one entire truth. But how do they suffer themselves to incline to verisimilitude, if they know not the truth? How should they know the probability of that, whereof they do not know

The opinion of the Academics not so easy to be defended as that of the Pyrrhonists.

the essence: either we can absolutely judge, or absolutely we cannot. If our intellectual and sensible faculties are without footing or foundation; if they only waver and totter, it is to no purpose that we suffer our judgment to be carried away with any thing of their operation, what appearance soever it may seem to present us: and the surest and most happy seat of our understanding would be that, where it kept itself serene, upright, and inflexible, without tottering, and without agitation. *Inter visa, vera, aut falsa, ad animi assensum, nihil inter- est :* " Amongst things that are seen, whether true " or false, it signifies nothing to the assent of " the mind." That things do not lodge in us in their form and essence, and do not there make their entry by their own force and authority, we plainly see: because, if it were so, we should receive them after the same manner: wine would have the same relish with the sick, as with the healthy: he who has his finger chopped or benumbed, would find the same hardness in wood or iron, which he handles, that another does. Strange subjects then surrender themselves to our mercy, and are seated in us as we please: now if, on our part, we received any thing without alteration, if human grasp were capable and strong enough to seize on truth by our own means, these means being common to all men, this truth would be conveyed from hand to hand, from one to another; and, at least, there would be some one thing to be found in the world, amongst so many as there are, that would be believed, by men, with an universal consent. But, as there is no one proposi- tion, that is not debated and controverted amongst us, or that may not be, this makes it very manifest, that our natural judgment does not, very clearly, discern what it embraces: for my judgment cannot make my companion approve of what it approves;

* Cic. Acad. lib. iv. cap. 28.
Q 2

which is a sign that I seized it by some other means, than by a natural power that is in me, and in all other men. Let us lay aside this infinite confusion of opinions, which we see even amongst the philosophers themselves, and this perpetual and universal dispute about the knowledge of things; for it is admitted, that men, I mean the most knowing, the best bred, and of the best parts, are not agreed about any one thing; not that heaven is over our heads; for they who doubt of every thing, also doubt of that; and they who deny that we able to comprehend any thing, say, that we have not comprehended that the heaven is over our heads; and these two opinions are, without comparison, the strongest in number. Besides, this infinite diversity and division, through the trouble which our judgment gives ourselves, and the uncertainty that every one finds in himself, it is easy to perceive that its seat is very unstable. How variously do we judge of things? How often do we alter our opinions? What I hold and believe to-day, I hold and believe with my whole belief: all my instruments and engines take fast hold of this opinion, and become responsible to me for it, as much as in them lies; I could not embrace nor preserve any truth with greater assurance, than I do this. I am wholly and entirely possessed with it: but has it not befallen me not only once, but a hundred, nay a thousand times, and every day to have embraced some other notion with all the same instruments, and in the same condition, which I have afterwards judged to be false? A man must, at least, become wise at his own expense. If I have often found myself betrayed under this colour; if my touch prove ordinarily false, and my balance unequal and unjust, what assurance can I now have, more than at others? Is it not stupidity and madness to suffer myself to be so often deceived by my guide? nevertheless, let fortune remove us five hundred times from place to place; let her do nothing but incessantly empty and fill into our belief, as into a vessel, various other opi-

The uncertainty which every one may perceive in his own judgment.

nions, yet still the present and ·the last is the certain
and infallible ; for this we must abandon goods, honour, life, health, and all :

———— *Posterior res ille reperta*
*Perdit, et immutat sensus ad pristina quæque.**

The last things we find out are always best,
And give us a disrelish of the rest.

·Whatever is preached to us, and· whatever we learn,
we should still remember, that it is man that gives,
and man that receives ; it is a mortal hand that presents it to us, it is a mortal hand that accepts it. The
·things that come to us from heaven, have the sole
right ·and authority of persuasion, they only have
the stamp of truth ; which also we do not see with
our own eyes, nor receive by our own means : this
great and sacred image could not abide in so wretch-
.ed a habitation, if God, for this end, did not prepare
it, if God did not, by his particular and supernatural grace and favour, reform and fortify it ; at least
our frail condition ought to make us comport ourselves with more reservedness and moderation in our
changes. We ought to remember, that, whatever
·we receive into the understanding, we often receive
things that are false, and that it is by the same instruments that so often give themselves the lie, and
are often deceived. Now, it is no wonder they ^{The judg-}
should contradict themselves, being so easy to be ^{ment de-}
turned and swayed by very light occurrences. It is ^{much on the}
certain, that our apprehensions, our judgment, and ^{alterations}
the faculties of the soul in general, suffer according ^{of the body.}
to the movements and alterations of the body, which
alterations are continual : are not our wits more
sprightly, our memories quicker, and our discourses
more lively in health, than in sickness ? Do not joy
and gaiety make us receive subjects that present
themselves to our souls, in quite another light, than
care and melancholy ? Do you believe, that Catul-

* Lucret. lib. v. ver. 1413.

lus's verses, or those of Sappho, please an old doting
miser, as they do a youth that is vigorous and amorous ? Cleomenes, the son of Anaxandridas, being
sick, his friends reproached him, that he had humours and whimsies which were new and unaccus-
tomed : " I believe it,"* said he, " neither am I
" the same man now, as when I am in health : be-
" ing now another creature, my opinions and fancies
" are also different from what they were before."
In our courts of justice, this word is much in use,
which is spoken of criminals, when they find the
judges in a good humour, gentle, and mild; *Gaudeat
de bona fortuna :* " Let him rejoice in his good for-
" tune :" for it is certain, that men's judgments are
sometimes more prone to condemn, more crabbed
and severe, and at others more easy, and inclined to
excuse. He that carries with him from his house the
pain of the gout, jealousy, or theft by his man, having his whole soul possessed with grief and anger, it is
not to be doubted but that his judgment will lean that
way. That venerable senate of the Areopagites was
want to hold their courts by night, lest the sight of
the parties might corrupt their justice. The very
air itself and the serenity of the sky, cause some
change in us, according to these Greek verses in Cicero :

> *Tales sunt homimum mentes, quales pater ipse*
> *Jupiter, auctiferâ lustravit lampade terras.†*
> Men's minds are influenc'd by th' external air,
> Dark or serene, as days are foul or fair.

Not only fevers, debauches, and great accidents
overthrow our judgment; the least things in the
world whirl it about : we may be sure, though we
are not sensible of it, that, if a continued fever
can overwhelm the soul, a tertain will in some degree alter it. If an apoplexy stupifies and totally
extinguishes our understanding, a great cold will un-

---

* Plutarch, in his Notable Sayings of the Lacedæmonians.
† Cicero's Fragmenta Poematum.

doubtedly affect it : consequently, there is hardly
one single hour in a man's whole life, wherein our
judgment is in its due state, our bodies being subject to so many continual mutations, that I believe
the physicians when they say, that there is always
some one or other out of order.

As to what remains, this malady does not very *The weak-*
easily discover itself, unless it be extreme and past *ness of our*
remedy; because reason goes always lame and hob- *not easy to*
bling, as well with falsehood, as with truth, and there- *be disco-*
fore it is hard to discover its deviations and mistakes.
I always call that appearance of mediation, which
every one forges in himself, reason : this reason, of
which there may be a hundred different sentiments
on the same subject, is an instrument extremely
ductile, and pliable, to all biasses and measures; so
that nothing is wanted but the art how to turn and
wind it. Let a judge mean ever so well, if he be
not very circumspect, his inclination to friendship,
to relation, to beauty, or revenge, and not only things
of such weight, but even the fortuitous instinct that
makes us favour one thing more than another, and
which, without reason's leave, affects our choice ; or
some shadow, of like vanity, may insensibly insinuate
into his judgment, the recommendation or disfavour
of a cause, and make the balance dip. I, that watch
myself as narrowly as I can, and that have my eyes
continually bent upon myself, like one that has no
great business elsewhere to do,

——— *Quis sub arcto*
Rex gelidæ metuatur oræ,
Quid Tyridatem terreat, unicè
Securus——— .*

I care not who the northern climes reveres.
Or what's the king whom Tyridates fears.

dare hardly tell the vanity and weakness I find in
myself. My footing is so unstable and slippery, I
find myself so apt to totter and reel, and my sight

* Her. lib. i. ode 26, ver. 3, &c.

so disordered, that fasting, I am quite another man,
than when full : if health and a fair day smile upon
me, I am a good-natured man; if a corn trouble my
toe, I am sullen, out of humour, and not to be seen.
The same pace of a horse seems to be one while hard,
and another easy; and the same road one while
shorter, and another longer; and the same form
one while more, and another less taking: I am one
while for doing every thing, and another for doing nothing at all; and what pleases me now, would be a trouble to me at another time. I am subject to a thousand senseless and casual humours within myself:
either I am possessed by melancholy, or swayed by
choler; now by its own private authority, sadness
predominates in me, and by and by I am as merry as
a cricket. When I take a book in hand, I have then
discovered admirable graces in some particular passages, and such as have struck my soul; at another
time, I may turn and toss, tumble and rattle the
leaves over and over, and not see any sense or beauty
in it. Even in my own writings, I do not always
find the air of my first fancy: I know not what I
would have said, but am often put to it to correct
and find out a new sense, because I have lost the
first that was better. I am ever in motion: my
judgment does not always advance, but floats and
roams :

———— *Velut minuta mogno*
Deprensa navis in mari vesaniente vento.[*]
Like a small bark that's toss'd upon the main,
When winds tempestuous heave the liquid plain.

Very often (as I am apt to do) having, for the sake
of exercise and argument, undertaken to maintain
an opinion contrary to my own, my mind, bending
and applying itself that way, attaches me to it so
thoroughly, that I no more discern the reason of my
former belief, and forsake it: I am, as it were,
drawn in by the side to which I incline, be it what it

* Catull. ep. 23, ver. 12, 13.

will, and carried away by my own weight. Every person, I believe, would acknowledge the same weakness, if he considered himself, as I do.

Preachers very well know, that the emotions which steal upon them in speaking, animate them towards belief; and that, in passion, we are more obstinate in the defence of our proposition, are more deeply impressed by it, and embrace it with greater vehemence and approbation, than we do in our cooler and calmer state. You only give your council a simple breviate of your cause, he returns you a dubious and uncertain answer, by which you find him indifferent, which side he takes: have you fee'd him well, that he may relish it the better; does he begin to be really concerned, and do you find him zealous for you? His reason and learning will, by the same degrees, grow hot in your cause; behold an apparent and undoubted truth presents itself to his understanding; he discovers a new light in your business, and does in good earnest believe and persuade himself that it is so: nay, I do not know, whether the ardour that springs from spite and obstinacy against the power and violence of the magistrate and danger, or the interest of reputation, may not have made a man, even at the stake, maintain the opinion, for which, at liberty, and amongst friends, he would not have burned his finger. The shocks and jostles that the soul receives from the corporeal passions, can do much in it, but its own can do a great deal more; to which it is so subjected, that perhaps it has no other pace and motion, but from the blowing of those winds, without the agitation of which, it would be becalmed, like a ship in the middle of the sea, to which the winds have denied their assistance: and whoever should maintain this, siding with the Peripatetics, would do us no great wrong, because it is very well known, that the greatest part of the most noble actions of the soul proceed from, and stand in need of, this impulse of the passions. Valour, they say, cannot be perfect without the assistance of anger :

*Semper Ajax fortis, fortissimus tamen in furore.**
Ajax was always brave, but most when mad.

Neither do we encounter the wicked and the enemy vigorously enough, if we be not angry ; nay, the advocate is to inspire the judges with indignation, to obtain justice.

Irregular passions animate and accompany the most shining virtues. Strong desires animated Themistocles and Demosthenes ; they put the philosophers upon watching, fasting, and pilgrimages ; and they lead us to honour, learning, and health, which are all very useful ends. And this meanness of soul, while it suffers vexation and trouble, serves to breed penitency and repentance in the conscience, and to make us sensible of the scourge of God, and of political correction for the chastisement of our offences. Compassion is a spur to clemency and prudence; the prudence of preserving and governing ourselves is roused by our fear ; and how many brave actions by ambition ? How many by presumption ? In short, there is no eminent and sprightly virtue, without some irregular agitation.

Why the Epicureans discharged the divinity from all kind of care. Was it not one of the reasons which moved the Epicureans to discharge God from all care and solicitude of our affairs, that even the effects of his goodness could not be exercised in our behalf, without disturbing his repose, by the means of the passions, which are so may incentives, like spurs, to prick on the soul to virtuous actions ? Or, did they think otherwise, and take them for tempests, that shamefully hurry the soul from her tranquillity ? *Ut maris tranquillitas intelligitur, nulla, ne minima quidem, aurâ fluctus commovente : sic animi quietus et placatus status cernitur, quùm perturbatio nulla est quà moveri queat :†* " As it is understood to be a " calm sea, when there is not the least breath of

* Cic. Tusc. lib. iv. ver. 23.   † Idem, lib. v. cap. 6.

" air stirring; so the state of the soul is quiet
" and placid, when there is no perturbation to
" move it."

What variety of sentiments and reason, what contrariety of imagination does the diversity of our passions inspire us with ? What assurance then can we
take of a thing so mobile and unstable, subject, by
its condition, to the dominion of trouble, and never
going other than a forced and borrowed pace ? If
our judgment be in the power even of sickness and
perturbation; if it be from folly and temerity, that
it is held to receive the impression of things; what
security can we expect from it ?

Is it not a great boldness in philosophy to judge,
that men perform the greatest actions, and such as
nearest approach the divinity, when they are furious,
mad, and beside themselves ? The two natural ways
to enter into the cabinet of the gods, and there to
foresee the course of destiny, are fury and sleep.
This is pleasant to consider. By the dislocation that
the passions cause in our reason, we became virtuous: by its extirpation, occasioned by madness,
or by sleep, the image of death, we become diviners
and prophets. I was never so willing to believe philosophy in any thing, as this. It is a pure enthu-
siasm, wherewith sacred truth has inspired the spirit
of philosophy, which makes it confess, contrary to
its own proposition, that the calm, composed, and
most healthful state of the soul, that philosophy can
seat it in, is not its best condition: our waking is
more a sleep than sleep itself; our wisdom not so
wise as folly; our dreams are worth more than our
meditations; and the worst place we can take is in
ourselves. But does not philosophy think, we are
wise enough to consider, that the voice which the
spirit utters, when dismissed from man, so clear-
sighted, so great, and so perfect, and, whilst it is in
man, so terrestrial, ignorant, and dark, is a voice
proceeding from the spirit of a dark, terrestrial, and

12

ignorant man, and, for this reason, a voice not to
be trusted and believed ?

What an
ascendant
the passion
of love has
over the
human
mind. I have no great experience of these vehement agitations (being of a soft and heavy complexion), the
most of which surprise the soul, on a sudden, without giving it leisure to recollect itself : but the passion, that is said to be produced by idleness, in the
hearts of young men, though it proceed leisurely,
and with a moderate progress, evidently manifests,
to those who have tried to oppose its power, the violence our judgment suffers in this alteration and con-
version.   I have formerly attempted to withstand
and repel it : for I am so far from being one of those
who invite vices, that I do not so much as follow
them, if they do not drag me along : I perceived it
to spring, grow, and increase in spite of my resistance ; and, at last, though my eyes were open, it
wholly seized and possessed me ; so that, as if newly
roused from drunkenness, the images of things began to appear to me quite other than they were
wont to be : I evidently saw the person I desired
grow and increase in beauty, and expand and blow
fairer by the influence of my imagination ; and, as
the difficulties of my attempt grew more easy and
smooth, both my reason and conscience drew back ;
but, this fire being evaporated in an instant, as a
flash of lightning, my soul resumed another state,
and another judgment. The difficulties of my retreat appeared great and invincible, and the same
things had quite another taste and aspect, than
those which the heat and desire had represented to
me ; than which Pyrrho himself knows nothing more
truly : we are never without sickness ; agues have
their hot and cold fits ; from the effects of an ardent
passion, we fall again to those of a shivering one : as
much as I had advanced, so much I retired :

Qualis ubi alterno procurrens gurgite pontus,
Nunc ruit ad terras scopulisque superjacit undam,
Spumeus, extremamque sinu perfundit arenam :

Nunc rapidus retro, atque æstu revoluta resorbens
Saxa fugit, littusque vado labente relinquit.*

So swelling surges, with a thund'ring roar,
Driv'n on each other's backs, insult the shore;
Bound o'er the rocks, incroach upon the land,
And from the bottom throw up shoals of sand;
Then backward, rapidly, they take their way,
Rolling the rattling pebbles to the sea.

Now from the knowledge of this volubility of mine, *Why Montaigne did not easily embrace novel opinions.*
I have accidentally begot, in myself, a certain con-
stancy of opinions, and have not much altered those
that were first and natural in me: for, what appearance soever there may be in novelty, I do not easily
change, for fear of losing by the bargain; and, besides, I am not capable of choosing; I take other
men's choice, and continue in the station wherein
God has placed me; I could not otherwise keep
myself from perpetual rolling. Thus have I, by
the grace of God, preserved myself entire, in the
ancient tenets of our religion, without disturbance
of mind, or trouble of conscience, amidst so many
sects and divisions as our age has produced. The
writings of the ancients, the best authors I mean,
being full and solid, tempt, and carry me, which
way almost they will: he, that I am reading, seems
always to have the most force, and I find that every
one, in turn, has reason, though they contradict
one another. The facility that good wits have of
rendering every thing probable which they would
recommend; and there being nothing so strange,
to which they do not understand to give colour
enough to deceive such a simplicity as mine; this
evidently shows the weakness of their testimony.
The heaven and the stars have been three thousand
years in motion, and all the world were of that belief, till Cleanthes the Samian,† or (according to

* Æneid, lib. xi. ver. 624, &c.
† Plutarch, in his Treatise of the face that appears in the Moon's
Orb, cap. 4, where he says, that Aristarchus was of opinion, that the
Grecians ought to have brought Cleanthes, of Samos, to justice, and

Theophrastus) Nicetas, of Syracuse, affirmed, that it
was the earth which moved about its axis through
the oblique circle of the zodiac. And Copernicus
has, in our time, so demonstrated this doctrine, that
he very regularly makes use of it in accounting for
all astrological consequences. What can we infer
from it, but that we ought not much to care which
is the true opinion? And who knows but that a
third, a thousand years hence, may rise, and overthrow the two former?

> *Sic volvenda ætas commutat tempora rerum,*
> *Quod fuit in pretio, fit nullo denique honore,*
> *Porro aliud succedit, et è contemptibus exit,*
> *Inquè dies magis appetitur, floretque repertum*
> *Laudibus, et miro est mortales inter honore.**

> Thus ev'ry thing is chang'd in course of time,
> What now is valu'd, passes soon its prime;
> To which some other thing, despis'd before,
> Succeeds, and grows in vogue still more and more;
> And once receiv'd, too faint all praises seem,
> So highly it is rais'd in men's esteem.

Why new opinions are to be distrusted. So that, when any new doctrine presents itself to
us, we have no great reason to mistrust it; and to
consider, that, before that was set on foot, the contrary had been generally received; and that, as that
has been overthrown by this, a third invention may
start up in time to come, and damn the second.
Aristotle's principles in vogue. Before the principles that Aristotle introduced, were
in reputation, other principles contented human
reason, as these satisfy us now. What patent have

to have condemned him for blasphemy against the gods, for giving
out, that the heavens remained immoveable, and that it was the
earth which moved through the oblique circle of the zodiac turning
round its own axis. But, as it appears elsewhere, that Aristarchus,
of Samos, did believe the earth's motion, there must be some mistake in this place, as is the opinion of Menage, who, by a little variation only of Plutarch's text, makes him say, not that Aristarchus
meant to accuse Cleanthes of impiety, for having maintained the
earth's motion, but that, on the contrary, Cleanthes would have imputed it to Aristarchus, as a crime. See Menage, in his Commentary upon Diogenes, lib. viii. sect. 85, p. 388, 389.
  * Lucret. lib. v. ver. 1275, &c.

these opinions, what particular privilege, that the career of our invention must be stopped by them, and that to them should appertain the sole possession of our future belief? They are no more exempt from being thrust out of doors than their predecessors were. When any one presses me with a new argument, I ought to believe, that what I cannot answer, another can; for to believe all likelihoods, that a man cannot confute, is great simplicity: it would, by that means, come to pass, that all the vulgar (and we are all of the vulgar) would have their belief as changeable as a weathercock: for the soul being so easily imposed upon, and so non-resisting, must incessantly receive impressions, the last still effacing all traces of that which went before. He that finds himself weak, ought to answer according to modern practice, that he will speak with his counsel, or refer himself to the sages, from whom he received his instruction. How long is it that physic has been practised in the world? It is said, that a new comer, called Paracelsus, changes and overthrows the whole order of ancient rules, and maintains, that, till now, it has been of no other use, but to kill men. I do believe, that he will easily make this good; but I do not think it were great wisdom to venture my life in making trial of his new experience. " We " are not to believe every one (says the precept) " because every one can say all things." A man of this stamp, who was much given to novelty and physical reformation, not long since, told me, " That all the ancients were notoriously mistaken in " the nature and motions of the winds, which he " would evidently demonstrate to me, if I would " give him the hearing." After I had, with some patience, heard his arguments, which were all full of probability: " What then," said I, " did those " that sailed according to the rules of Theophrastus, " make way westward, when they had the prow to- " wards the east? Did they go sideward or back- " ward?" " That is as it happened," answered he;

" but so it is, that they are mistaken." I then replied, " That I had rather be governed by facts than " reason." Now, these are things that often clash, and I have been told, that, in geometry (which, of all sciences, pretends to the highest point of certainty), there are demonstrations which subvert the truth of all experience. As Jaques Pelletier told me, at my own house, that " He had found out two " lines, stretching one towards the other to meet, " which nevertheless he affirmed, though extended " to all infinity, would never touch one another." The Pyrrhonians make no other use of their arguments and their reason, than to contradict experience ; and it is a wonder how far the suppleness of our reason has followed them in this design of controverting the evidence of facts : for they affirm, " That we do not move, that we do not speak, and " that there is neither weight nor heat," with the same force of argument, with which we prove the most probable things. Ptolemy, who was a great man, had established the bounds of this world of ours ; and all the ancient philosophers thought they had the measure of it, excepting some straggling islands, that might escape their knowledge. It had been Pyrrhonism, a thousand years ago, to doubt of the science of cosmography, and of the opinions that every one had thence received : it was heresy to believe there were antipodes ; and, behold, in this age, there is an infinite extent of firm land discovered, not an island, or a particular country, but a part almost as great as that we knew before. The geographers of our time stick not to assure us, that now all is found, and all is seen :

Nam quod adest præsto, placet, et pollere videtur.*
What present pleases, and appears the best.

But I would fain know, whether, if Ptolemy was deceived, upon the foundation of his reason, it were

* Lucret. lib. v. ver. 1411.

not folly in me to trust now to what these people
say: and whether it is not more likely, that this
great body, which we call the world, is quite another thing, than what we imagine.

Plato says, " That it changes countenance in all Several
" respects: that the heavens, the stars, and the sun, opinions concerning
" have all of them sometimes motions retrograde to the world.
" what we see, changing east into west." The
Egyptian priests told Herodotus, " That, from the
" time of their first king, which was eleven thou-
" sand and odd years (and they shewed him the
" effigies of all their kings, in statues taken from
" the life), the sun had four times altered his
" course :* that the sea and the earth alternately
" changed into one another; and that the beginning
" of the world is undetermined, which is also
" said by Aristotle and Cicero." And some
amongst us are of opinion, " That it has been from all
" eternity, is temporary, and renewed again by se-
" veral vicissitudes;" calling Solomon and Isaiah to
witness, in order to evade the objections, that God
was once a creator without a creature, that he had
then nothing to do; that, to counteract such va-
cancy, he put his hand to this work; and that, consequently, he is subject to change. In the most
famous of the Greek schools, the world is taken for
a god, made by another god, who is greater, and
composed of a body, and of a soul, fixed in its
centre, and dilating itself, by musical numbers, to
its circumference; divine, most happy, most great,
most wise, and eternal. In him are other gods, the
sea, the earth, the stars, who entertain one another
with harmonious and perpetual agitation and divine
dance; sometimes meeting, sometimes retiring from
one another; concealing and discovering themselves,
changing their order, one while before, and another
behind. Heraclitus† was positive, " That the world

---

* Herodot. lib. ii. page 163, 164.
† Diog. Laert. in the Life of Heraclitus, lib. ix. sect. 8.

" was composed of fire, and, by the order of the des-
" tinies, was one day to be inflamed and con-
" sumed in fire, and to be again renewed." And
Apuleius‡ says of men: *Sigillatim mortales, cunctim
perpetui:* " That they are mortal in particular, and
" immortal in general." Alexander sent his mother
the narrative of an Egyptian priest, drawn from
their monuments, testifying the antiquity of that nation to be infinite, and containing the true birth
and progress of other countries. Cicero and Diodorus say, " That in their time, the Chaldees kept a
" register of four hundred thousand and odd years."
Aristotle, Pliny,† and others, " That Zoroaster
" flourished six thousand years before Plato's time."
Plato‡ says, " That the city of Sais has records in
" writing of eight thousand years; and that the city
" of Athens was built a thousand years before the
" said city of Sais." Epicurus, " That at the same
" time things are here in the posture we see, they
" are alike, and in the same manner in several other
" worlds :" which he would have delivered with
greater assurance, had he seen the similitude and
concordance of the new-discovered world of the
West-Indies, with ours, present and past, in such
strange instances. In reality, considering what is
arrived at our knowledge of the course of this terrestrial polity, I have often wondered to see, in so
vast a distance of places and times, such a concurrence of so great a number of popular and wild opinions, and of savage manners and articles of faith;
which, by no means, seem to proceed from our natural reason. The human mind is a great worker
of miracles. But this relation has, moreover, I
know not what of extraordinary in it, even in names,
and a thousand other things: for they found nations
there (that, for aught we know, never heard of us),

Circumci-
sion.
where circumcision was in use; where there were

---

* Apuleius, in his tract de Deo Socratis.
† Plin. Nat. Hist. lib. xxx. cap. 1.   ‡ In his Timæus, p. 524.

11

states and civil governments maintained by women only, without men; where our fasts and lent were represented, to which was added the abstinence from women; where our crosses were, several ways, in repute; where they were made use of to honour their sepultures; where they were erected, and, namely, that of St. Andrew, to protect themselves *St. Andrew's cross.* from nocturnal visions, and to lay upon the cradles of infants against enchantments: in some places there was found one of wood, of a very great height, which was adored for the God of rain; and this was *A cross adored for the god of rain.* a great way up in the main land, where there were seen a very clear image of our shriving priests, with the use of mitres, the celibacy of priests, the art of divination by the entrails of sacrificed animals, abstinence from all sorts of flesh and fish in their diet, the form for priests officiating in a particular, and not the vulgar, language: and this fancy, that the first god was expelled by a second, his younger brother; that they were created with all sorts of ac- *The creation of the world.* commodations, which have since been taken from them for their sins, their territory changed, and their natural condition made worse: that they were, of old, drowned by an inundation of water from heaven; that but few families escaped, who retired into caves of high mountains, the mouths of which they stopped, so that the waters could not get in, having shut up, together with themselves, several sorts of animals; that, when they perceived the rain to cease, they sent out dogs, which returning clean and wet, they judged that the water was not yet much abated; but afterwards sending out others, and seeing them return dirty, they issued out to re-people the world, which they found only full of serpents. In one place it appeared, they were per- *The day of judgment.* suaded of a day of judgment; insomuch that they were greatly displeased at the Spaniards for discomposing the bones of the dead, in rifling the graves for riches; saying, that those bones, so scattered, could not easily be rejoined. They traffic by ex-

change, and no other way, in fairs and in markets :
Dwarfs at the tables of princes. dwarfs and deformed people are retained for the ornament of the tables of their princes : they use falconry, according to the nature of their birds ; tyrannical subsidies, fine gardens, dances, tumbling tricks, and juggling instruments of music, armories, **Divers sorts of games.** tennis-playing, dice, and lotteries, wherein they are sometimes so eager, as to stake themselves, and their liberty : physic, no otherwise than by charms ; the way of writing in hieroglyphics ; the belief of only one first man, the father of all nations ; the **Adoration of one God made man.** adoration of one God, who formerly lived a man in perfect virginity, fasting, and penance, preaching the law of nature, and the ceremonies of religion, and who vanished from the world without a natural death ; the opinion of giants ; the custom of making themselves drunk with their beverages, and drinking as long as they could stand ; religious ornaments painted with bones and dead men's sculls ; surplices ; holy water sprinkled ; wives and servants, who strive to be burned and interred with the dead husband or master ; a law by which the eldest succeeds to all the estate, no other provision being made for the younger, but obedience ; the custom, that, upon promotion to a certain office of great authority, the person promoted is to take upon him a new name, and to leave that which he had before ; another, to strew lime upon the knee of the newborn child, with these words, " from dust thou " camest, and to dust thou must return ;" as also the art of argury : these poor shadows of our religion, which are observable in some of these examples, are testimonies of its dignity and divinity. It is not only, in some sort, implanted in all the infidel nations on this side of the world, but in the before-named barbarians also, as by a common and supernatural inspiration ; for we also find there the belief **A new sort of purgatory.** of purgatory, but of a new form ; that which we give to the fire, they give to the cold, and imagine that the souls are purged and punished by the rigour

of excessive cold. This example puts me in mind of
another pleasant diversity: for, as there were, in
that place, some people who chose to strip and un-
muffle the glans of their penis, and clipped off the
prepuce, after the Mahometan and Jewish manner;
there were others, who made so great conscience of
laying it bare, that they carefully pursed it up with
little strings, to keep the end from the air. And I
remember this other diversity, that whereas we, in
honour of kings and festivals, put on the best clothes
we have, in some regions, to express their disparity
and submission to their king, his subjects present
themselves before him in their vilest habits, and, entering his palace, throw some old tattered garment
over their better apparel, to the end that all the
lustre and ornament may solely remain in him.

But, to proceed: if nature inclose, within the
bounds of her ordinary progress, the beliefs, judgments, and opinions of men, as well as all other
things; if they have their revolution, their season,
their birth and death, like cabbage plants; if the
heavens agitate and rule them at their pleasure, what
magisterial and permanent authority do we attribute
to them? If we experimentally see, that the form
of our existence depends upon the air, the climate,
and the soil where we are born; and not only the
colour, the stature, the complexion, and the countenance, but the faculties of the soul itself: *Et
plaga cœli non solum ad robur corporum, sed etiam
animorum facit:*[*] "The climate contributes not
"only to the strength of bodies, but to that of the
"mind also," says Vegetius: and that the goddess,
who founded the city of Athens, chose, for its situation, a temperate air, fit to make the men prudent, as
the Egyptian priests told Solon: *Athenis tenue cœlum: ex quo etiam acutiores putantur Attici: cras-
sum Thebis; itaque pingues Thebani, et valentes* †

***

[*] Veget. lib. i. cap. 2.   † Cic. de Fato, cap. 4.

" The air of Athens is thin, from whence also the
" Athenians are reputed to be more acute: and at
" Thebes it is thick, wherefore the Thebans are
" looked upon as fat and strong." In such sort
that, as the fruits and animals differ, the men are
also more or less warlike, just, temperate, and docile; here given to wine, elsewhere to theft or un-
cleanness; here inclined to superstition, elsewhere
to infidelity; in one place to liberty, in another to
servitude; capable of a science or an art, dull or
witty, obedient or mutinous, good or bad, according
as the place, where they are seated, inclines them;
and assume a new constitution, if removed, like
trees; which was the reason why Cyrus would not
grant the Persians leave to quit their rough and
craggy country, to remove to another that was pleasant and plain; saying, " That fat and tender soils
" made men effeminate; and fertile soils produced
" barren minds." If we see one art and one belief
flourish one while, and another while another, by
some celestial influence; if we see such an age produce such natures, and incline mankind to such or
such a bias; the spirits of men one while gay, and
another gloomy, like our fields; what becomes of
all those fine prerogatives we so sooth ourselves
withal? Seeing that a wise man, a hundred men, or
many nations, may be mistaken, nay, that human
nature itself, as we believe, is many ages wide in
one thing or another, what assurances have we
that she sometimes is not mistaken, or not in this
very age?

The incon-   Methinks, that, amongst other testimonies of our
stancy of   imbecility, this ought not to be forgotten, that man
man's de-
sires a good cannot, by his own desire, find out what is necessary
proof of his for him; that, neither in fruition, nor in imagination
weakness.   and wish, can we agree about what we want to content us. If we leave it to our own thought, to cut
out, and make up as it please, it cannot so much as
desire what is proper for it, and satisfy itself:

———— *Quid enim ratione timemus*
Aut cupimus ? Quid tàm dextro pede concipis, ut te
Conatûs non pœniteat, votique peracti ?*

How void of reason are our hopes and fears !
What in the progress of our life appears
So well design'd, so dext'rously begun,
But, when we have our wish, we wish undone ?

For this reason it was, that Socrates begged nothing Socrates's prayers. of the gods, but what they knew to be best for him : and the prayers of the Lacedæmonians, both private and public, were only to obtain such things as were good, referring the choice of them to the discretion of the supreme power ;

Conjugium petimus, partûmque uxoris, at illis
Nolum qui pueri, qualisque futura sit uxor.†

We pray for wives and children, they above
Know only, when we have them, what they'll prove.

And Christians pray to God, " that his will may be " done ;" that they may not fall into the inconve- nience the poet feigns of king Midas. " He prayed " to the gods, that all he touched might be turned " into gold : his prayer was heard ; his wine was " gold, his bread was gold, and the feathers of his " bed, his shirt, and clothes were turned into gold;" so that he found himself ruined with the fruition of his desire, and, being enriched with an intolerable wealth, was fain to unpray his prayers :

Attonitus novitate mali, divesque, miserque,
Effugere optat opes, et quæ modò voverat, odit.‡

Astonish'd at the strangeness of the ill,
To be so rich, yet miserable still ;
He wishes now he could his wealth evade,
And hates the thing for which before he pray'd.

To instance in myself; being young, I desired of The order of St. Mi- chael of high esteem in France. fortune, above all things, the order of St. Michael, which was then the highest distinction of honour

---

* Juv. sat. x. ver. 4, &c.   † Idem, ibid. ver. 352, 353.
† Ovid, Metam. lib, xi. fab. 3, ver. 43, &c.

among the French noblesse, and very rare. She pleasantly gratified my longing: instead of raising me, and lifting me up from my own place to attain to it, she was much kinder to me, for she brought it so low, and made it so cheap, that it stooped down to my shoulders, and lower. Cleobis and Biton,[*] Trophonius and Agamedes,[†] having requested, the two first of their goddess, the two last of their god, " a " recompence worthy of their piety," had death for a reward: so different from ours are the heavenly opinions concerning what is fit for us. God might grant us riches, honours, life, and even health, sometimes, to our own hurt; for every thing that is pleasing to us, is not always wholesome for us: if he sends us death, or an increase of sickness, instead of a cure, *Virga tua, et baculus tuus, ipsa me consolata sunt:*[‡] " Thy rod and thy staff have comforted me:" he does it by the rule of his providence, which knows better what is proper for us, than we can do; and we ought to take it in good part, as coming from a most wise and most gracious hand:

> ———— *Si consilium vis,*
> *Permittes ipsis expendere numinibus quid*
> *Conveniat nobis, rebusque sit utile nostris:*
> *Charior est illis homo, quàm sibi.*[§]
>
> If thou'lt be rul'd, leave to the gods, in pray'rs,
> To weigh what's fit for us in our affairs:
> Still best to them man's happiness is known,
> And in their sight far dearer than his own.

To pray for honours and commissions is to pray that he may throw you into a battle, set you upon a cast at dice, or something of the like nature, whereof the issue is to you unknown, and the consequence doubtful. There is no dispute so sharp and violent amongst the philosophers, as about the question of the " sovereign good of man;" which, by

---

[*] Herodot. lib. ii. and xiii.
[†] Plutarch's consolation to Apollonius on the death of his son.
[‡] Psal. xxiii. 4.   [§] Juv. sat. x. ver. 312, &c.

the calculation of Varro, gave birth to two hundred
and fourscore sects. *Qui autem de summo bono dis-
sen t, de totâ philosophiæ ratione disputat :*[*] " For
" whoever enters into controversy concerning the
" supreme good, disputes upon the whole system of
" philosophy."

> *Tres mihi convivæ prope dissentire videntur,*
> *Poscentes vario multum diversa palato,*
> *Quid dem? Quid non dem? Renuis tu quod jubet alter;*
> *Quod petis, id sanè est invisum, acidumque duobus.*[†]
>
> Methinks I've three invited to a feast,
> A diff'ring palate too has ev'ry guest,
> Requiring each to gratify his taste ;
> To please them all what dishes shall I choose ?
> What not ? What he prefers, you two refuse ;
> What you yourself approve, offends their sight,
> Will mar their meal, and pall their appetite.

Such must naturally be the answer to their contests
and debates. Some say that our well-being consists
in virtue, others in pleasure, others in submitting to
nature; one in knowledge, another in being exempt
from pain, another in not suffering ourselves to be
carried away by appearances; and this fancy seems
to have some relation to that of the ancient Pytha-
goreans :

> *Nil admirari prope res est una, Numici,*
> *Solaque quæ possit facere, et servare beatum.*[‡]
>
> Not to admire, believe me, is the best,
> If not the only means to make us blest.

Which is the drift of the Pyrrhonian sect. Aristotle
attributes the admiring of nothing to magnanimity :
and Arcesilaus said, " that constancy, and an in-
" flexible state of judgment, were a real good ; but
" consent and conformity, vices and evils."[§] It is
true, that, in thus establishing it by a certain axiom,
he quitted Pyrrhonism.[||]

---

[*] Cic. de Fin. lib. v. cap. 5.   [†] Hor. lib. ii. epist. 2, ver. 61, &c.
[‡] Idem, lib. i. epist. 6, ver. 1, 2.
[§] Sext. Empir. Pyrr. Hypot. lib. i. cap. 33, p. 48.   [||] Idem, ibid.

The ataraxy of the Pyrrhonists.

The Pyrrhonians, when they say that the ataraxy, which is the immobility of judgment, is the sovereign good, mean it not affirmatively; but that the same motion of the soul, which makes them avoid precipices, and take shelter from the air, presents them with this fancy, and makes them refuse another.

Character of Justus Lipsius.

How much do I wish, that, whilst I live, either some other, or Justus Lipsius, the most learned man of the present age, of a most polite and judicious understanding, and truly resembling my Turnebus, had the will, health, and leisure sufficient, to collect into

Plan of a treatise of the different sects of philosophers.

a register, according to their divisions and classes, as many as are to be found of the opinions of the ancient philosophers, about the subject of our being and manners, their controversies, the succession and reputation of the sects, with the application of the lives of the authors, and their disciples, to their own precepts, in memorable accidents, and upon exemplary occasions. What a beautiful and useful work that would be!

The confusion into which men run, about the regularity of their manners.

For if it be from ourselves that we are to extract the rules of our manners, into what a confusion do we throw ourselves? For that which our reason advises us to, as the most probable, is generally for every one to obey the laws of his country, as it was the advice of Socrates, inspired, as he pretends himself, by a divine counsel. And what does this mean, but that our duty has no other rule but what is accidental? Truth ought to have a like and universal visage; if man could know equity and justice, that it had a body, and a true being, he would not fetter it to the conditions of this country, or that: it would not be from the whimsies of the Persians or Indians, that virtue would receive its form.

Laws subject to continual changes.

There is nothing more subject to perpetual fluctuation than the laws. In my own time, I have known those of the English, our neighbours, three or four times changed, not only in matters of civil government, which is the only thing wherein constancy is dispensed with, but in the most important

subject that can be; namely, religion : at which I am
vexed and ashamed, because it is a nation, with
whom those of my province have formerly had so
great familiarity, that there yet remain, in my family,
some foot-steps of our ancient kindred.   And here,
with us at home, I have known a thing that was capital to become lawful ; and we that hold others, are
likewise, according to the chance of war, in a possibility of being found, one day, guilty of high-trea-
son, both against God and man, should the justice
of our arms fall into the power of injustice, and, after a few years' possession, take a quite contrary being.   How could that ancient god* more clearly accuse the ignorance of human knowledge concerning
the divine Being, and give men to understand, that
their religion was but a thing of their own contrivance, useful as a bond to their society, than by
declaring, as he did to those who came to his tripod
for instruction, " That every one's true worship was
" that which he found in use in the place where he
" chanced to be ?" O God, what infinite obligation
have we to the bounty of our Sovereign Creator, for
having purged our belief from those wandering and
arbitrary devotions, and for having placed it upon
the eternal foundation of his holy word! But what
will then philosophy say to us in this necessity, that we must follow the laws of our country ? that is to say, the floating sea of the opinions
of a republic, or a prince, that will paint out justice for me in as many colours, and reform it as
many ways, as there are changes of passions in themselves.   I cannot suffer my judgment to be so flexible : where is the goodness of a thing, which I saw
yesterday in repute, and to-morrow in none, and
which, on the crossing of a river, shall become a
crime ? What truth is it that these mountains inclose,
but is a lie to the world beyond them ?

* Apollo.

Natural
laws, whe-
ther con-
stant and
immutable.

But they are pleasant, when, to give some certainty to the laws, they say, " that there are some firm, per- " petual, and unchangeable," which they call na- tural, " that are imprinted in human kind by the " condition of their own essence;" and those some reckon three, some four, some more, some less; a sign that it is a mark as doubtful as the rest. Now, they are so unfortunate (for what can I call it else but misfortune, when, of such an infinite number of laws, there should not be found one, at least, that fortune, and the temerity of chance, has suffered to be universally received by the consent of all nations ?) they are, I say, so miserable, that, of these three or four select laws, there is not one that is not contradicted and disowned, not only by one nation, but by many. Now the only likely sign by which they can prove any laws to be natural, is the universality of appro- bation ; for we would, without doubt, all agree to fol- low that which nature had truly ordained us ; and not only every nation, but every particular man, would resent the force and violence that any one should do him, who would put him upon any thing contrary to this law. Let them produce me but one of this kind.

The found-
ation of the
justice of
laws.

Protagoras and Aristo gave no other essence to the justice of laws, than " The authority and opinion " of the legislator, and that, these laid aside, the " things honest and good would lose their qualities, " and remain empty names of things indifferent." Thrasymachus, in Plato, is of opinion, that " There " is no other right but the convenience of the supe- " rior." There is not any thing wherein the world is so various, as in laws and customs ; such a thing is abominable here, which is elsewhere in esteem, as in Lacedæmonia, the dexterity of stealing : marriages within the degrees of consanguinity are capitally interdicted among us ; they are elsewhere in honour ;

————— *Gentes esse feruntur,*

In quibus et nato genitrix, et nata parenti
*Jungitur, et pietas geminato crescit amore.**

There are some nations in the world, 'tis said,
Where fathers daughters, sons their mothers wed ;
And their affections thereby higher rise,
More firm and constant by these double ties.

The murder of infants, murder of fathers, communication of wives, robberies, license in all sorts of voluptuousness : in short, there is nothing that is not
permitted by the custom of some nation or other.

It is probable, from our observations on other Those of na-
creatures, that there are natural laws, but in us they ture lost a-
mong men.
are lost : this fine human reason, every-where so in-
sinuating itself to govern and command, as to confound the face of things, according to its own vanity
and inconstancy. *Nihil itaque amplius nostrum est ;*
quod nostrum dico, artis est : " Therefore nothing is
" any more truly ours; what we call ours is the effect
" of art." Subjects appear in a great variety of different
lights ; and from thence the diversity of opinions principally proceeds: one nation considers a subject in one
aspect, and stops there ; another takes it in another view.

Nothing can be imagined so horrible, as for a The bodies
man to eat his father : yet the people of old, whose of their de-
custom it was so to do, looked upon it as a testimony ceased fa-
thers eaten
of piety and affection, meaning thereby to give their by some
progenitors the most worthy and honourable sepul- people, and
why.
ture ;† lodging in themselves, and, as it were, in
their own marrow, the bodies and relics of their
fathers ; and, in some sort, vivifying and regenerat-
ing them, by transmutation, into their living flesh,
by means of digestion and nourishment. It is easy
to consider, what a cruelty and abomination it must
have appeared to men possessed and tinctured with
this superstition, to throw their parents' remains to
corrupt in the earth, and become the nourishment of
beasts and worms.

* Ovid. Met. lib. x. fab. 9, ver. 34.
† Sext. Empir. Pyrr. Hypot. lib. iii. cap. 24, p. 157.

Theft allowed by Lycurgus, and why.

Lycurgus considered, in theft, the vivacity, diligence, boldness, and dexterity of purloining any thing from our neighbours, and the utility that redounded to the public, that every one might look more narrowly to the preservation of what was his own; and believed, that, from this double institution of assaulting and defending, an advantage accrued to military discipline (which was the principal science and virtue to which he aimed to inure the Lacedæmonians), of greater consideration than the disorder and injustice of taking another man's goods.

A perfumed robe refused by Plato, and accepted by Aristippus.

Dionysius, the tyrant, offered Plato a robe of the Persian fashion, long, damasked, and perfumed. Plato refused it, saying, "That, being born a man, "he would not willingly dress himself in woman's "clothes;"* but Aristippus accepted it, with this answer, "That no garment could impair a man's "fortitude." His friends reproaching him with meanness of spirit, for laying it no more to heart, that Dionysius had spit in his face: "Fishermen," said he, "suffer themselves to be dashed with the "waves of the sea, from head to foot, to catch a "gudgeon."† Diogenes was washing cabbages, and, seeing him pass by, "If thou couldst live on cab- bage," said he, "thou wouldst not fawn upon a ty- "rant."‡ To whom Aristippus replied, "And if "thou knewest how to live amongst men, thou "wouldst not be washing cabbages." Thus rea- son finds a colour for diverse effects: it is a pot with two ears, that a man may take by the right or left:

> ——— Bellum, ô terra hospita, portas;
> Bello armantur equi; bellum hæc armenta minantur:
> Sed tamen iidem olim curru succedere sueti .

---

* Diog. Laert. in the Life of Aristippus, lib. ii. sect. 78.
† Idem. ibid. sect. 67.
‡ Idem. ibid. sect. 68, and Hor. lib. i. ep. 17, ver. 13, &c.

Quadrupedes, et fræna jugo concordia ferre ;
Spes est pacis.*

A war this foreign land seems to declare,
Horses are arm'd, for herds do threaten war ;
And yet these brutes having with patience bore
The yoke, and yielded to the reins before,
There's hopes of peace.

Solon being importuned, by his frends, not to ˢᵒˡᵒⁿ'ˢ shed unprofitable tears for the death of his son : " It ᵗᵉᵃʳˢ ᶠᵒʳ ᵗʰᵉ ᵈᵉᵃᵗʰ " is for that very reason that I shed them," said he, ᵒᶠ ʰⁱˢ ˢᵒⁿ. " because they are unavailing and unprofitable."† Socrates's wife exasperated her grief by this circum- stance, " Oh, how unjustly do these wicked judges ᵀʰᵉ ᵐᵒᵘʳⁿ- " put him to death !" " Why," replied he, " hadst ⁱⁿᵍ ᵒᶠ ˢᵒ- ᶜʳᵃᵗᵉˢ'ˢ " thou rather they should justly execute me ?"‡ We ʷⁱᶠᵉ. have our ears bored ; the Greeks looked upon that as a mark of slavery : § we retire in private to en- joy our wives ; the Indians do it in public :‖ the Scythians sacrificed strangers in their temples ; ¶ else- where temples are a refuge :

Inde furor vulgi, quòd numina vicinorum,
Odit quisque locus, cùm solos credat habendos
Esse Deos, quos ipse colit.**

This 'tis that spite and vulgar spleen creates,
That all their neighbours' gods each city hates ;
Each calls the other's god a senseless stock ;
Its own divine, though carv'd from the same block.††

I have heard of a judge, that where he read a sharp

---

* Æneid, lib. iii. ver. 539, &c.
† Diog. Laert. in the Life of Solon, lib. i. sect. 63.
‡ Idem, in the Life of Socrates, lib. ii. sect. 35.
§ Sext. Empir. Pyrrh. Hypot. lib. iii. cap. 24, p. 152.
‖ Idem, lib. i. cap. 14, p. 30.   ¶ Idem, ibid.
** Juv. sat. xv. ver. 37.

†† Juvenal speaks here of Egypt, where, he says, the people were enraged against one another, to the last degree, because some wor- shipped deities, whom others abhorred, &c. And do we not see, that the Christians, though they worship but one and the same only God, the Creator of the heavens, and the earth, are no less en- raged one against another, because some of them believe in certain things, which others of them cannot.

conflict between Bartolus and Baldus, and some
point greatly controverted, he wrote in the margin
of his book, " a question for a friend:" that is to
say, that truth was there so perplexed and disputed,
that, in such a cause, he might favour which of the
parties he thought fit: it was only for want of wit
and capacity, that he did not write, " a question for
a friend," throughout. The advocates and judges
of our times find bias enough, in all causes, to accommodate them to what they themselves think fit:
in so infinite a science, depending upon the authority of so many opinions, and so arbitrary a subject,
it cannot be but that an extreme confusion of judgments must arise. There is also hardly any suit so
clear, wherein opinions do not differ: what one
court has determined, another determines quite contrary, and itself contrary to that at another time: of
which we see very frequent examples, by this license, which is a great blemish to our justice, of
not acquiescing in decisions, but running from judge
to judge, to decide one and the same cause. As to
the liberty of philosophical opinions concerning vice
and virtue, it is a subject not necessary to be expa-
tiated upon, and wherein are found many opinions,
that are better concealed, than published to weak
minds: Arcesilaus* said, " That, in fornication, it
" was no matter where, or with whom, it was com-
" mitted."† *Et obscænas voluptates, si natura re-
quirit, non genere, aut loco, aut ordine, sed formâ,
ætate, figura metiendas Epicurus putat.—Ne amores
quidem sanctos à sapiente alienos esse arbitrantur.—
Quæramus ad quam usque ætatem juvenes amandi
sint :* " And obscene pleasures, if nature requires,
" Epicurus thinks, are not to be measured, either
" by race, place, or rank, but by age, shape, and
" beauty.—Neither are sacred amours thought to be

---

* Plutarch's dialogue of the rules and maxims of health, cap. 5.
† Cic. Tusc. Quæst. lib. v. cap. 33.

" foreign to wise men ;—we are to inquire till what
" age young men are to be loved."* These two
last stoical quotations, and the reproach that Di-
cæarchus† threw in the teeth of Plato himself, upon
this account, show how much the soundest philosophy indulges licences that are excessive, and very
remote from common usage. Laws derive their au- Laws authority from possession and usage ; it is dangerous thorised by
to trace them backward to their beginning ; they customs.
grow great, like our rivers, by running ; but follow
them upward to their source, it is but a little spring,
scarce discernible, that thus swells and fortifies itself by growing old. Do but consult the ancient
considerations, that gave the first motion to this famous torrent, so full of dignity, honour, and reverence, you will find them so slight and delicate, that
it is no wonder if these people, who weigh and reduce every thing to reason, and who admit nothing
by authority, have their judgments very remote from
those of the public. It is no wonder if people, who
take their pattern from the first image of nature,
should, in most of their opinions, swerve from the
common path : as for example, few amongst them
approved of the strict conditions of our marriages,
and most of them were for having wives in common :
they refused our ceremonies. Chrysippus said,
" That a certain philosopher would have made a
" dozen antic skips, and turned up his bare breech,
" for a dozen of olives." That philosopher would
hardly have advised Callisthenes to have refused
Hippoclides the fair Agarista, his daughter,‡ for
having seen him stand on his head upon a table.

* Cic. de Fin. Bon. et Mal. lib. iii. cap. 2. Senec. epist. 123.
† In all the editions of Montaigne, as well as in Mr. Cotton's translation, it is printed Diogarchus, instead of Dicæarchus, which, undoubtedly, is the right name, as appears from the passage of Cicero,
Tusc. Quæst. lib. iv. cap. 33 and 34, where he says, that the philosophers, and particularly Plato, were justly blamed, by Dicæarchus,
for approving of amours with boys.
‡ Herodot. lib. vi. p. 428, 429, 430.

Metrocles let a f——t, a little indiscreetly, in disputation, in the presence of his scholars, and kept himself hid in his own house for shame, till Crates came
to visit him,* who, adding to his consolations and
reasons his own example, fell to f——t with him, bet-
ting who should let most; by which means he cured
him of that scruple, and also drew him to his own
Stoical sect, from that more polite one of the Peripatetics, of which he had been till then. That
which we call decency, to be afraid to do that·in
public, which it is decent enough to do in private,
the Stoics call folly; and to be so modest as to conceal and disown what nature, custom, and our desires publish and proclaim of our actions, they reputed a vice. The other thought it was undervaluing the mysteries of Venus, to draw them out of
her private oratory, to expose them to the view of
the people; and that to bring her sports out from
behind the curtain, was to spoil them: modesty is a
thing of weight: secrecy, reservation, and circum-
scription are qualities to be esteemed; and pleasure
acted very ingeniously, when, under the visor of
virtue, she sued not to be prostituted in the open
streets, trodden under foot, and exposed to the
public view, being destitute of the dignity and convenience of her private cabinets. Hence some say,
that to suppress public stews is the way to render
fornication more general, by the difficulty of gratify-
ing lascivious desires:

> *Mœchus es Aufidiæ qui vir, Cervine, fuisti;*
> *Rivalis fuerat qui tuus, ille vir est :*
> *Cur aliena placet tibi, quæ tua non placet uxor ?*
> *Nunquid securus non potes arrigere?* †

This experience is diversified in a thousand examples:

> *Nullus in urbe totâ, qui tangere vellet*
> *Uxorem gratis, Cæciliane, tuam,*

* See the Life of Metrocles, in Diog. Laert. lib. vi. sect. 94.
† Mart. lib. iii. epig. 70.

Dum licuit : sed nunc positis custodibus, ingens
Turba fututorum est. Ingeniosus homo es.[*]

A philosopher, being taken in the very act, and
asked what he was doing, coldly replied, " I am
" planting man ;" no more blushing to be so caught,
than if they had found him planting garlic.

It is, I suppose, out of a tender and respectful
opinion, that a great and religious author[†] thinks,
" This act is so necessarily confined to privacy, that
" he cannot persuade himself there could be any ab-
" solute performance in those licentious embraces
" of the Cynics, but that they only made it their
" business to represent lascivious gestures, to main-
" tain the professed impudence of their schools ;
" and that, to eject what shame had with-held and
" confined, it was afterwards necessary for them to
" withdraw into the shade." But he had not seen
far enough into their debauches ; for Diogenes, de-
filing himself in public, wished, in the hearing of all
that saw him, " That he could satiate himself by
" that exercise."[‡] To those who asked him, " Why
" he did not find out a more commodious place to
" eat in, than the open street ;" he made answer,
" Because I am hungry in the open street."[§] The
women philosophers, who mixed with their sect,
mixed also with their persons, in all places, without
reserve : and Hipparchia[||] was not received into
Crates's society, but upon condition that she should,
in all things, conform to the usages and customs of
his sect. These philosophers set a great price upon
virtue, and renounce all other discipline but mora-
lity ; yet, in all actions, they held their sage to
be above the authority of the laws ; admitting no
other restraint upon voluptuousness, but moderation
only, and a regard to the liberty of others.

The impu-
dence of the
Cynic.

* Mart. lib. i. epig. 74.
† St. Augustine, de Civit. Dei, lib. xiv. cap. 20.
‡ Diogenes the Cynic, in his Life, by Diog. Laert. lib. vi. sect. 69.
§ Idem, ibid. sect. 58.
|| Diog. Laert. in her Life, lib. vi. sect. 96, 97.

s 2

Philoso-
phers who
held, that
one and the
same sub-
ject had
contrary
appear-
ances.
Heraclitus and Protagoras (observing that wine seemed bitter to the sick, and pleasant to the sound; the rudder crooked in the water, and straight when out ; and such-like contrary appearances as are found in subjects) argued from thence, " That all " subjects had, in themselves, the causes of these " appearances; and that there was some bitterness " in the wine, which had some sympathy with the " sick man's taste; and the rudder some bending " quality, sympathising with him that looks upon " it in the water.:" and so of all the rest, which is to say, " That all is in all things, and consequently " nothing in any one; for, where all is, there is " nothing."

This opinion puts me in mind of the experience we have, that there is no sense, or aspect of any thing, whether bitter or sweet, straight or crooked, that human wit does not find out in the writings he The purest
way of
speaking,
capable of
various in-
terpreta-
tions. undertakes to tumble over. Into the cleanest, purest, and most perfect discourse that can possibly be, how many lies and falsehoods are there suggested? What heresy has not there found ground and testimony sufficient to make it be embraced and defended? It is for this, that the authors of such errors will never depart from proof of the testimony of the The philosopher's'
stone ap-
proved. interpretation of words. A person of dignity, who would prove to me, by authority, the search of the philosophers' stone, wherein he was over head and ears engaged, quoted to me, lately, five or six passages in the Bible, upon which he said he first founded his attempt, for the discharge of his conscience (for he is, by profession, a divine); and, in truth, the invention was not only pleasant, but, likewise, very well accommodated to the defence of this fine science.

Obscure
writings
easily find
interpret-
ers who do
them ho-
nour.
By this way the reputation of divining fables is acquired : there is no fortune teller, if he have this authority, but, if a man will take the pains to search him, and narrowly pry into all the folds and glosses of his words, he may make him, like the Sibyls, say

what he will. There are so many ways of interpretation, that it will be hard but that, either obliquely, or in a direct line, an ingenious wit will find out, in every subject, some air that will serve for his purpose. On this account, an obscure and ambiguous style has been so much used. Let the author but make himself master of this, he may attract and employ posterity about his predictions; which not only his own parts, but the accidental favour of the matter itself, may as much or more assist him to obtain. Let him, as to the rest, express himself after a foolish or a subtle manner, whether obscurely or contradictorily, it is no matter; a number of wits, shaking and sifting him, will squeeze out of it a great many forms, either corresponding to his meaning, or even contrary to it, which will all redound to his honour: he will see himself enriched by the means of his disciples, like the regents of colleges, by their pupils and yearly presents. This it is which has given reputation to many things of no real worth; that has brought several writings in vogue, and given them all sorts of matter that can be desired; one and the same thing receiving a thousand and a thousand images, and various considerations, nay, even as many as we please.

Is it possible, that Homer could mean to say all that we make him; and that he designed so many and so various figures, as that the divines, law-givers, philosophers, and all sorts of men who treat of sciences, how variously and oppositely soever, should quote him, and support their arguments by his authority, as the master-general of all offices, works, and artisans, and counsellor-general of all enterprises? Whoever has had occasion for oracles and predictions, has there found sufficient to serve his turn. It is a wonder how many, and how admirable occurrences, a learned friend of mine has there found out in favour of our religion, who cannot easily be put out of the conceit, that it was Homer's design (yet he is as well acquainted with

How Homer came to be reckoned the leader of all generals.

this author, as any man of his time) ; and what he has
found in favour of ours, very many, anciently, have
found in favour of theirs. Only observe, how Plato
is tumbled and tossed, every one thinking it an
honour to apply him to himself, and to set him on
what side they please : they draw him in, and in-
graft him in all the new opinions the world receives ;
and, according to the different course of things, set
him in opposition to himself: every one makes him
disavow, according to his own sense, the manners
and customs which were lawful in his age, because
they are unlawful in ours ; and all this with an appearance of probability, in proportion to the force
and sprightliness of the wit of the interpreter. From
the same foundation that Heraclitus and this sentence of his had, " That all things had in them those
" forms which we discerned,"* Democritus drew a
quite contrary conclusion ; namely, " That subjects
" had nothing at all in them of what we find in
" them ; and, because honey is sweet to one, and
" bitter to another," he argued, " that it was nei-
" ther sweet nor bitter." The Pyrrhonians would
say,† " That they knew not whether it is sweet or
" bitter, or neither the one, or the other, or both,"
for these always aspire to the high point of dubita-
tion. The Cyrenaics held,‡ that " Nothing was per-
" ceptible from without, and that only was percepti-
" ble, which internally touched us, as grief and
" pleasure ; acknowledging neither sound, nor co-
" lour, but certain affections only that we receive
" from them, and that man's judgment had no other
" seat." Protagoras believed,§ " That what seemed
" so to every one, was true to every one." The
Epicureans lodged, " All judgment in the senses,
" and in the knowledge of things, and in pleasure."
Plato would have " The judgment of truth, and

* In Sext. Empir. Pyrrh. Hypot. lib. i. cap. 23.
† Idem, advers. Mathem. p. 163.
‡ Cic. Acad. Quæst. lib. iv. cap. 7.   § Idem, ibid. cap. 46.

" truth itself, derived from opinions and the senses,
" to appertain to the mind and thought."

This discourse has put me upon the consideration Our know-
of the senses, in which lies the greatest foundation ledge com-
and proof of our ignorance; whatsoever is known, terminates
is, doubtless, known by the faculty of the knower; in the
for, seeing the judgment proceeds from the opera- senses.
tion of him that judges, it is an argument, that this
operation performs it by his own means and will, not
by the constraint of another; as it would happen, if
we knew things by the power, and according to the
law of their essence; now all knowledge makes its
way in us by the senses, they are our masters:

—————— Via qua minuta fidei
*Proxima fert humanum in pectus, templaque mentis.**

The nearest path that certainty can find,
By which to occupy the human mind.

Science begins by them, and is resolved into them:
after all, we should know no more than a stone, did
we not know that there is sound, smell, light, taste,
measure, weight, softness, hardness, sharpness, colour, smooothness, breadth, and depth: these are
the platforms and principles of the whole structure of
our knowledge: and, according to some, science is
nothing else but sense: he that could make me contradict the senses, would have me by the throat, he
could not make me go farther back: the senses are
the beginning and the end of human knowledge:

Invenies primis ab sensibus esse creatam
Notitiam veri, neque sensus posse refelli:
Quid majore fide porrò quam sensus haberi
Debet ?†

Of truth, whate'er discoveries are made,
Are by the senses to us first convey'd;
Nor will one sense be baffled; for on what
Can we rely more safely than on that?

* Lucret. lib. v. ver. 103.
† Idem, lib. iv. ver. 480, 481,—484, 485.

Let us attribute to them the least we can, we must, however, of necessity, grant them this, that it is by their means and mediation that all our instruction makes its way. Cicero says,[*] "That "Chrysippus, having attempted to extenuate the "force and virtue of the senses, represented to him- "self arguments, and so vehement oppositions to "the contrary, that he could not be satisfied in him- "self therein:" whereupon Carneades, who main- tained the contrary side, boasted, "That he "would make use of the same words and arguments "that Chrysippus had done, to controvert and con- "fute him;" and therefore thus cried out against him, "O wretch! thy own force has destroyed "thee."[†] There can be nothing absurd to a greater degree, than to maintain, that fire does not warm, that light does not shine, and that there is no weight nor solidity in iron, which are ideas con- veyed to us by the senses; neither is there belief nor knowledge in man, that can be compared to that for certainty.

Doubt whe- The first consideration I have upon the subject of
ther man
have all the the senses is, that I make a doubt, whether, or no,
senses. man be furnished with all the natural senses. I see several animals, who live, some without sight, others without hearing: who knows, whether to us also, one, two, three, or many other senses may not be wanting? For, if any one be wanting, our reason cannot discover the want thereof: it is the privilege of the senses to be the utmost limit of our percep- tion: there is nothing beyond them that can assist us in discovering them; nor can any one sense dis- cover the extent of another:

> *An poterunt oculos aures reprehendere, an aures*
> *Tactus, an hunc porro tactum sapor arguet oris,*
> *An confutabunt nares, oculive revincent?*[‡]

[*] Cic. Acad. Quæst. lib. iv. cap. 27.
[†] Plutarch, in the Contradictions of the Stoic Philosophers, chap. 9.
[‡] Lucret. lib. iv.

Can ears the eyes, the touch the ears correct ﹐
Or is that touch by tasting to be check'd :
Or th' other senses, shall the nose, or eyes,
Confute in their peculiar faculties ?

They are the limits which circumscribe our ability.

——— *Seorsum cuique potestas*
Divisa est, sua vis cuique est.*

Each has its power distinctly, and alone,
And every sense's power is its own.

It is impossible to make a man, born blind, conceive
that he does not see ; impossible to make him desire sight, or to lament the want of it ; for which
reason, we ought not to derive any assurance from
the soul's being contented and satisfied with those
we have ; considering, that it cannot be sensible
herein of its infirmity and imperfection, if there be
any such thing ; it is impossible to say any thing to
this blind man, either by reason, argument, or similitude, that can possess his imagination with any notion of light, colour, and sight : there nothing remains behind, that can produce the sense to evidence. Those that are born blind, who say they
wish they could see, it is not that they understand
what they desire : they have learned from us, that
they want something ; that there is something to be
desired, that we have, which they name indeed, together with its effects and consequences, but yet
they know not what it is, nor have any idea of it. I
have seen a gentleman, of a good family, who was
born blind, or, at least, blind from such an age,
that he knows not what sight is ; who is so little sensible of his defect, that he makes use, as we do, of
words proper to seeing, and applies them after a
manner wholly particular, and his own. They
brought him a child, to which he was god-father,
which having taken into his arms : " Good God,"
said he, " what a fine child is this, what a pretty

* Lucret. lib. iv.

" face it has!" He will say, like one of us, " This
" room has a very fine prospect; it is clear weather;
" the sun shines bright." And, moreover, as
hunting, tennis, and shooting at butts are our exercises, and he has heard so; he has taken a fancy
to them, makes them his exercise, believes he has
as good a share of the sport as we have, and will
express himself angry or pleased, as we do, and yet
knows nothing of it but by the ear. One cries out
to him, " here's a hare," when he is upon some
even plain, where he may gallop; and, afterwards,
when they tell him, " the hare is killed," he will be
as overjoyed, and proud of it, as he hears others
are. He will take a tennis-ball in his left-hand, and
strike it away with the racket; he will shoot with a
musket at random, and is contented with what his
people tell him, that he is over or wide of the mark.
Who knows whether mankind commits not the like
absurdity for want of some sense, and that, through
this defect, the greatest part of the face of things is
concealed from us? What do we know, but that the
difficulties, which we find in several works of nature,
are owing to this; and that diverse effects of animals, which exceed our capacity, are produced by
the power of some sense, that we are defective in?
And whether some of them have not, by this means,
a life more full and entire than ours? We seize an
apple, as it were, with all our senses : we find red-
ness,* smoothness, smell, and sweetness in it; but
it may have other qualities besides these, as drying
up or binding, which no sense of ours can reach to.
Is it not likely, that there are sensitive faculties in
nature, that are fit to judge of and to discern those,
which we call the occult properties in several things,
as for the loadstone to attract iron; and that the
want of such faculties is the cause that we are ignorant of the true essence of such things? it is, per-

* All this is taken from Sextus Empiricus's Pyrrhon. Hypotypos.
lib. i. cap. 14, p. 20.

haps, some particular sense, that gives cocks to understand what hour it is of morning, or of midnight,
and makes them to crow accordingly; that teaches
chickens, before they have any experience of what
they are, to fear a sparrow-hawk, and not a goose,
or a peacock, though birds of a much larger size:
that warns them of the hostile quality a cat has
against them, and makes them not to fear a dog; to
arm themselves against the mewing (a kind of flattering voice) of the one, and not against the barking
(a shrill and angry note) of the other: that teaches
wasps, ants, and rats to fall upon the best pear, and
the best cheese, before they have tasted them; and
inspires the stag, elephant, and serpent, with the
knowledge of a certain herb proper for their cure.
There is no sense that has not a great dominion,
and that does not produce an infinite number of discoveries. If we were defective in the intelligence of
sounds, of music, and of the voice, it would cause
an inconceivable confusion in all the rest of our
science: for, besides what is annexed to the proper
effect of every sense, how many arguments, consequences, and conclusions do we draw to other things,
by comparing one sense with another? Let an understanding man imagine human nature originally
produced without the sense of seeing, and consider
what ignorance and trouble such a defect would
bring upon him, what a darkness and blindness in
the soul; he will then see, by that, of how great
importance to the knowledge of truth the privation
of such another sense, or of two or three, should we
be so deprived, would be: we have formed a truth
by the consultation and concurrence of our five
senses; but, perhaps, we should have the consent
and contribution of eight or ten, to make a certain
discovery of it, and of its essence.

The sects that controvert the knowledge of man, Human
do it principally by the uncertainty and weakness of knowledge
our senses: for since all knowledge is, by their controvert.
means and mediation, conveyed unto us, if they weakness and uncer-

fail in their report, if they corrupt or alter what
they bring us from without, if the light which, by
them, creeps into the soul, be obscure in the passage, we have nothing else to hold by. From this
extreme difficulty all these fancies proceed, that
every subject has, in itself, all we there find: that it
has nothing in it of what we think to find there;
and the Epicureans' notion, that the sun is no bigger
than it is judged, by our sight, to be:

> Quicquid * id est, nihilo fertur majore figurâ,
> Quam nostris oculis quam cernimus esse videtur.†
>
> But, be it what it will in our esteem,
> It is no bigger than to us doth seem.

That the appearances, which represent a body great
to him that is near, and less to him that is far from
it, are both true:

> Nec tamen hic oculis falli concedimus hilem;
> Proinde animi vitium hoc oculis adfingere noli.‡
>
> Yet that the eye's deceived, we deny;
> Charge not the mind's fault therefore on the eye.

And, positively, that there is no deceit in the senses;
that we are to lie at their mercy, and seek elsewhere
reasons to account for the difference and contradictions we therein find, even to the inventing of lies,
and other flams (for it is come to that), rather than
accuse the senses. Timagoras swore, " That, by
" pressing or turning his eye,§ he could never per-
" ceive the light of the candle to double, and that
" the seeming so proceeded from the mistake of opi-
" nion, and not from the eye." The most absurd
of all absurdities, in the judgment of the Epicureans, is, in " Denying the force and effect of the
" senses."

---

* Lucret. lib. v. ver. 677.
† What Lucretius says here of the moon, Montaigne applies to
the sun, of which, according to Epicurus's principles, the same
thing may be affirmed.
‡ Lucret. lib. iv. ver. 380,—386.
§ Cic. Acad. Quæst. lib. iv. cap. 25.

Proinde quod in quoque est his visum tempore, verum est,
Et si non potuit ratio dissolvere causam,
Cur ea quæ fuerint juxtim quadrata, procul sint
Visa rotunda : tamen præstat rationis egentem
Reddere mendos? causas utriusque figuræ,
Quàm manibus manifesta suis emittere quoquam,
Et violare fidem primam, et convellere tota
Fundamenta, quibus nixatur vita salusque :
Non modò, enim ratio ruat omnis, vita quoque ipsa
Concidat extemplo, nisi credere sensibus ausis,
Præcipitesque locos vitare, et cætera quæ sint
In genere hoc fugienda.

That what we see exists, I will maintain,
And if our feeble reason can't explain
Why things seem square when they are very near,
And at a greater distance round appear ;
'Tis better yet, for him that's at a pause,
T' assign to either figure a false cause,
Than shock his faith, and the foundations rend,
On which our safety and our life depend :
For reason not alone, but life and all,
Together will with sudden ruin fall ;
Unless we trust our senses, nor despise,
To shun the various dangers that arise.

This so desperate and unphilosophical advice expresses only this, " That human knowledge cannot " support itself but by reason, that is unreasonable, " foolish, and mad ; but that it is yet better, that " man, to give himself a credit, make use of this, " and any other remedy, how fantastic soever, than " to confess his necessary ignorance ; a truth so " disadvantageous to him." He cannot avoid owning, that the senses are the sovereign masters of his knowledge ; but they are uncertain, and deceitful. It is there that he is to fight it out to the last, and if just forces fail him, as they do, he must supply that defect with obstinacy, temerity, and impudence. In case that what the Epicureans say be true, viz. " That we have no knowledge, if what the senses " make appear be false;" and if that also be true, which the Stoics say, " That what appears from the

* Lucret. lib. iv. ver. 502—513.
12

" senses is so false that they can furnish us with no
" manner of knowledge;" we shall conclude, to the
great disadvantage of these two dogmatical sects,
" That there is no knowledge at all."

As to the error and uncertainty of the operation
of the senses, one may furnish himself with as many
examples as he pleases; so common are the frauds
and tricks they put upon us.   In the echo of a
valley, the sound of the trumpet seems to meet us,
which comes from a place behind :

> *Extantesque procul medio de gurgite montes*
> *Classibus inter quos liber patet exitus, iidem*
> *Apparent et longè divolsi licet, ingens*
> *Insula conjunctis tamen ex his una videtur.*
> *Et fugere ad puppim colles, campique videntur*
> *Quos agimus præter navim.**

> And rocks in seas, that proudly raise their head,
> Though far disjoin'd, though royal navies spread
> Their sails between; yet, if from distance shown,
> They seem an island all combin'd in one:
> Thus ships, though driven by a prosp'rous gale,
> Seem fix'd to sailors, those seem under sail
> That ride at anchor safe ; and all admire,
> As they row by, to see the rocks retire.

> —— *Ubi in medio nobis equus acer obhæsit*
> *Flumine, equi corpus transversum ferre videtur*
> *Vis, et in adversum flumen contrudere raptim.†*

> Thus, when in rapid streams my horse hath stood,
> And I look'd downward on the rolling flood ;
> Though he stood still, I thought he did divide
> The headlong streams, and strive against the tide,
> And all things seem'd to move on ev'ry side.‡

Like a musket bullet, under the fore-finger, the
middle-finger being lapped over it, which feels so
like two, that a man will have much ado to persuade
himself there is but one ; the end of the two fingers
feeling, each of them, one at the same time.

---

* Lucret. lib. iv. ver. 398, &c.   † Idem, ibid. ver. 422.
‡ Mr. Creech.

That the senses are, very often, masters of our reason, and constrain it to receive impressions which it judges and knows to be false, is frequently seen. I set aside the sense of feeling, which has its functions nearer, more lively and substantial; that so often, by the effect of the pains it brings to the body, overthrows all those fine stoical resolutions, and compels him to cry out of his belly, who has resolutely established this doctrine in his soul, that the cholic, as well as all other pains and diseases, are indifferent things, not having the power to abate any thing of the sovereign felicity, wherein the wise man is seated by his virtue. There is no heart so effeminate, that the rattle and sound of our drums and tabors will not inflame with courage; nor so sullen, that the harmony of our music will not rouse and cheer; nor so stubborn, that will not feel itself struck with some reverence, in viewing the vast gloominess of our churches, the variety of ornaments, and the order of our ceremonies, and to hear the solemn music of our organs, and the composed and devout harmony of our voices: even those that come with contempt, feel a certain shivering in their hearts, and something of dread, that makes them doubt of their own opinion. For my part, I do not think myself hardy enough to hear an ode of Horace, or Catullus, sung by a pretty young mouth without emotion: and Zeno had reason to say, " That the voice was the flower of beauty."[*] A certain person would once make me believe, that a man, whom all we Frenchmen know, had imposed upon me, in repeating some verses which he had made; that they were not the same upon the paper that they were in the tune, and that my eyes would form a contrary judgment to my ears: so great a power has pronunciation to give fashion and value to works that are left to the modulation of the voice. Therefore Philoxenus was not so much to blame for breaking a person's furniture, whom he

That the senses sometimes impose upon our reason.

The voice the flower of beauty.

---

* Diog. Laert. in the Life of Zeno, lib. vii. sect. 23.

heard give an ill accent to some composition of his,[*] saying, " I break what is yours, because you spoil what " is mine." To what end did those men, who, with a positive resolution, destroyed themselves, turn away their faces rather than see the blow they gave themselves? And why is it, that those, who, for their health, desire and command incisions and caustics, cannot endure the sight of the prepara- tions, instruments, and operations of the surgeon: considering that the sight is not, any way, to parti- cipate in the pain? are not these proper examples, to confirm the authority which the senses have over reason? It is to much purpose to know these tresses were borrowed from a page, or a lacquey; that this vermillion came from Spain, and this ceruse from the ocean: our sight will nevertheless, compel us to con- fess the subject of it more agreeable, and more lovely, against all reason: for, in this, there is no- thing of its own:

> *Auferimur cultu : gemmis, auroque teguntur*
>   *Crimina : pars minima est ipsa puella sui :*
> *Sæpe ubi sit quod ames inter tam multa requiras,*
>   *Decipit hac oculos, Ægide, dives amor.*[†]

> By dress we're won: gold, gems, and rich brocades
> Make up the pageant that your heart invades;
> In all that glitt'ring figure which you see,
> The far least part of her own self is she :
> In vain for her you love, amidst such cost,
> You search, the mistress in such dress is lost.

<small>Narcissus in love with his own per- son.</small>

What a strange power do the poets attribute to the senses, who feign Narcissus so desperately in love with his own shadow!

> *Cunctaque miratur, quibus est mirabilis ipse,*
> *Se cupit imprudens, et qui probat, ipse probatur.*
> *Dumque petit, petitur : pariterque accendit et ardet.*[‡]

> Admireth all, for which to be admir'd;
> And, inconsiderately, himself desir'd

* Diog. Laert. in the Life of Arcesilaus, lib. iv. sect. 26.
† Ovid. de Rem. Amor. lib. i. ver. 343.
‡ Ovid. Met. lib. iii. fab. 5 et 6, ver. 85, &c.

The praises which he gives, his beauty claim'd;
Who seeks, is sought, th' inflamer is inflam'd.

And Pygmalion's judgment so disturbed by the im- *And Pygmalion with his statue.* pression of the sight of his ivory statue, that he loves and adores it, as if it were a living woman:

Oscula dat, reddique putat, sequiturque tenetque,
Et credit tactis digitos insidere membris,
Et metuit pressos veniat ne livor in artus.*

He kisses, and believes he's kiss'd again,
Seizes, and 'tween his arms his love doth strain,
And thinks the polish'd ivory, thus held,
Does to his fingers am'rous pressure yield,
And has a tender fear, lest black and blue
Should in the parts with ardour press'd ensue.

Let a philosopher be put into a cage of small *How we are deceived by the sight, the ear, &c.* thin set bars of iron, and hang him on the top of the high tower of Nostre Dame at Paris; he will see, by manifest reason, that he cannot possibly fall, and yet he will find (unless he have been used to the tilers' trade) that the excessive height will unavoidably frighten and astonish him: for we hardly think ourselves safe in the galleries of our steeples, if they are railed with an open balluster, although of stone; and some there are that cannot endure so much as to think of it. Let there be a beam thrown over between the two towers, of breadth sufficient to walk upon, there is no philosophical wisdom so firm, that can give us the courage to walk over it, as we would do if it was upon the ground. I have often tried this upon our mountains; and though I am one who am not extremely fearful, yet I was not able to look down that vast depth without horror, and a trembling of my hams and legs, though I stood above my length from the edge of the precipice, and could not have fallen down unless I chose it. Here I also observed, that what height soever the precipice were, provided there was some tree, or some jutting out of a rock, a little to support and

* Ovid. Met. lib. x. fab. 8, ver. 14, &c.

divide the sight, it somewhat eases our fears, and gives some courage, as if these things might break our fall: but that we are not able to look down steep smooth precipices without being giddy: *Ut despici vertigine simul oculorum animique non possit:* "Which " is a manifest imposition of the sight." And therefore it was, that the famous philosopher put out his own eyes,* to free his soul from being corrupted by them, and that he might philosophise at greater liberty. But, by the same rule, he should have dammed up his ears, which, Theophrastus says, are the most dangerous organs about us, for receiving violent impressions to alter and disturb us; and, finally, should have deprived himself of all the other senses, that is to say, of his life and being; for they have all the power to command our soul and reason: *Fit etiam sæpe specie quadam, sæpe vocum gravitate et cantibus, ut pellantur animi vehementiùs; sæpe etiam curâ et timore:*† "For it often happens, that " minds are more vehemently struck by some as-" pect, by the quality and sound of the voice, or " by singing; and oft times also by grief and fear." Physicians hold, "That there are certain constitu-" tions which are agitated by some sounds and in-" struments, even to fury." I have seen some, who could not bear to hear a bone gnawed under the table; and there is scarce a man, who is not disturbed at the sharp and harsh noise that the file makes in grating upon iron. Also to hear chewing near them, or to hear any one speak, who has an impediment in the throat or nose, will move some people even to anger and hatred. Of what use was that piping prompter of Gracchus, who softened, raised, or modelled his master's voice as he pleased, whilst he declaimed at Rome, if the motion and quality of the sound had not the power to move and

---

* Democritus in Cic. de Finibus, lib. v. cap. 29. But Cicero only spoke of it as of a thing uncertain; and Plutarch says positively that it is a falsehood. See his Discourse of Curiosity, cap. xi.
† Cic. de Divin. lib. i. cap. 37.

alter the judgments of the auditory? In truth, there
is wonderful reason to keep such a clutter about the
firmness of this fine piece, that suffers itself to be
turned and twined by the breath and accidents of
so light a wind.

The same cheat that the senses put upon our un- *The senses
derstanding, they receive in their turn. The soul *altered and corrupted
also, sometimes, has its revenge; they lie and con- *by the passions of the
tend which should most deceive one another: what *soul.
we see and hear when we are transported with passion, we neither see nor hear as it is:

Et solem geminum, et duplices se ostendere Thebas. *

Thebes seems two cities, and the sun two suns.

The object that we love, appears to us more beautiful than it really is;

Multimodis igitur pravas, turpesque videmus,
Esse in deliciis, summoque in honore vigere.†

Hence 'tis that ugly things, in fancy'd dress,
Seem gay, look fair to lover's eyes, and please.

As does that we hate, more ugly. To a discon-
tented and afflicted man, the light of the day seems
dark and gloomy : our senses are not only depraved,
but often totally stupified by the passions of the
soul: how many things do we see, that we do not
take notice of, if the mind be taken up with other
thoughts ?

——— In rebus quoque apertis noscere possis,
Si non advertas animum, proinde esse, quasi omni
Tempore semotæ fuerint, longeque remotæ.‡

Nay, even in plainest things, unless the mind
Take heed, unless she sets herself to find,
The thing no more is seen, no more belov'd,
Than if the most obscure, and most remov'd.

It appears that the soul retires within, and amuses
the powers of the senses; and so both the inside,

---

* Æneid. lib. iv. ver. 470.   † Lucret. lib. iv. ver. 1148, &c.
‡ Idem, ibid. ver. 809, &c.

and the outside of man, is full of infirmity and deceit.

The life of
man com-
pared to a
dream.
They who have compared life to a dream, were perhaps more in the right than they were aware of; when we dream, the soul lives, operates, and exercises all its faculties, neither more nor less than when awake, but more gently and obscurely; yet not with so much difference, as there is between night and noon-day, between night and shade; there she sleeps, here she slumbers; but whether more or less, it is still dark, and Cimmerian darkness: we wake sleeping, and sleep waking. I do not see so clearly in my slumber; but, as to my being awake, I never found it clear enough, and free from clouds. Moreover, sleep, when it is profound, sometimes rocks even dreams themselves asleep; but our awaking is never so sprightly, as thoroughly to purge and dissipate those whimsies, which are the dreams of persons awake, and worse than dreams. Our souls receiving those fancies and opinions that arise in dreams, and authorising the actions of our dreams, with the like approbation that they do those of the day; wherefore do we doubt, whether our thought and action is not another sort of dreaming, and our waking a kind of sleep?

If the senses be our chief judges, it is not ours alone that we are to consult; for, in this faculty the animals have as great or greater right than we: it is certain that some of them have the sense of hearing more quick than man; others that of seeing; others that of feeling; others that of touch and taste. Democritus said,* "That the gods and brutes had "the sensitive faculties much more perfect than "man."

But, between the effects of their senses and ours, the difference is extreme: our spittle cleanses and dries up our wounds; it kills the serpent:

* Plutarch de Placitis Philosophorum, lib. iv. cap. 10.

Tantaque in his rebus distantia, differitasque est,
Ut quod aliis cibus est, aliis fuat acre venenum :
Sæpe etenim serpens, hominis contacta salivâ,
Disperit, ac sese mandendo conficit ipsa.[*]

And in those things the diff'rence is so great,
That what's one's poison, is another's meat ;
For serpents often have been seen, 'tis said,
When touch'd with human spittle, to go mad,
And bite themselves to death.

What quality do we attribute to our spittle, either
in respect to ourselves, or to the serpent? By which
of the two senses shall we prove its true essence that
we seek for? Pliny says,[†] "That there are certain
"sea-hares in the Indies, that are poison to us, and
"we to them; insomuch that, with the least touch,
"we kill them." Which is truly the poison, the
man, or the fish? Which shall we believe, whether
the fish poisons the man, or the man the fish? one
quality of the air infects a man, that does the
ox no harm; some other infects the ox, but hurts
not the man: which of the two has in truth and
nature the pestilent quality? To them who have
the jaundice, all things seem yellow and paler than
to us:

Lurida præterea fiunt quæcunque tuentur
Arquati.[‡]———
Besides, whatever jaundic'd persons view,
Looks pale as well as those, and yellow too.

They who are troubled with the disease the physicians call hyposphagma,[§] which is a suffusion of
blood under the skin, see all things red and bloody :
what do we know but that these humours, which
thus alter the operations of our sight, predominate over
beasts, and are usual with them? For we find some
whose eyes are yellow, like our people who have the

[*] Lucret. lib. iv. ver. 640, &c.
[†] Nat. Hist. lib. xxii. cap. 1.
[‡] Lucret. lib. iv. ver. 333, &c.
[§] Sext. Empyr. Pyrrh. Hypot. lib. i. cap. 14, p. 29.

jaundice, and others of a bloody red. It is likely
that the colour of objects seems other to them than
to us; of which of the two shall we make a right
judgment? For it is not said that the essence of
things has relation to man only: hardness, whiteness, depth, and sharpness, have reference to the
service and knowledge of animals, as well as to us;
and nature has equally designed them for their use.
When we press down the eye, we perceive the
body, that we look upon, to be longer and more extended; many beasts have their eyes so pressed
down: this length, therefore, is perhaps the true
form of that body, and not that which our eyes give
it in their usual state: if we press the eye under-
neath, things appear double to us:

Bina lucernarum florentia lumina flammis,
Et duplices hominum facies, et corpora bina. [*]
One lamp seems double, and the men appear
Each on two bodies double heads to bear.

If our ears be clogged, or the passage of hearing stopped up, we receive sound quite otherwise
than we usually do; the animals likewise, who have
either the ears hairy, or but a very little hole instead
of an ear, do not, consequently, hear as we do,
but another kind of sound. We see at festivals and
theatres, that by opposing a painted glass of a certain colour, to the light of the flambeaux, all things
in the room appear to us green, yellow, or violet:

Et volgo faciunt id lutea, russaque vela,
Et ferrugina, cum magnis intenta theatris,
Per malos volgata trabesque trementia flutant:
Namque ibi consessum caveai subter, et omnem
Scenai speciem, patrum matrumque deorumque
Inficiunt, coguntque suo fluitare colore. [†]

Thus when pale curtains, or the deeper red,
O'er all the spacious theatre are spread,

* Lucret. lib. iv. ver. 78,—452,—454, &c.
† Idem, ibid. ver. 73, &c.

Which mighty masts, and sturdy pillars bear,
And the loose curtains wanton in the air ;
Whole streams of colours from the summit flow,
The rays divide them in their passage through,
And stain the scenes, and men, and gods below.

It is likely, that the eyes of animals, which we see of divers colours, produce to them the appearance of bodies the same with their eyes.

We should, therefore, to make a judgment of the operations of the senses, be first agreed with the animals, and secondly amongst ourselves, which we by no means are, but enter, at every turn, into dispute concerning what one hears, sees, or tastes, something otherwise than another does ; and we dispute as much as upon any other thing, about the diversity of the images, which the senses represent to us. A child, by the ordinary rule of nature, hears, sees, and tastes otherwise than a man of thirty years old, and he than one of threescore. The senses are, in the one, more obscure and dull, and more open and acute in the others ; and we are impressed by things variously, according to the condition in which we happen to be, and as they appear to us. Now our perception being so uncertain, and so controverted, it is no more a wonder, if we are told, that we may declare that snow appears white to us ; but that to establish that it is, in its own essence, really so, is more than we are able to maintain : and this foundation being shaken, all the knowledge in the world must, of necessity, come to nothing. What ! do our senses themselves embarrass one another ?* A picture seems embossed to the sight, which in the handling seems flat : musk, which delights the smell and is offensive to the taste, shall we call it agreeable, or no? There are herbs and unguents, proper for one part of the body, that are hurtful to another : honey is pleasant to the taste, but offensive to the sight. They who, to assist

margin note: How uncertain is our judgment of the operation of the senses.

* Sext. Empir. Pyrr. Hypot. lib. i. cap. 14, p. 19.

their lust, were wont, in ancient times, to make use
of magnifying glasses, to represent the members
they were to employ bigger, by that ocular tumi-
dity, to please themselves the more; to which of the
two senses did they give the prize, whether to the
sight that represented the members large and great
as they would desire? or to their feeling, which represented them little and contemptible? Are they
our senses that supply the subject with these different
conditions, and yet the subjects themselves have, nevertheless, but one? As we see in the bread we eat,
it is nothing but bread; but, by being eaten, it becomes bones, blood, flesh, hair, and nails:

> *Ut cibus in membra atque artus cum diditur omnes*
> *Desperit, atque aliam naturam sufficit ex se.**
>
> As meats, diffus'd through all the members, lose
> Their former state, and diff'rent things compose.

The humidity, sucked up by the root of a tree,
becomes trunk, leaf, and fruit;† and the air, though
but one, is modulated, in a trumpet, to a thousand
sorts of sounds. Are they our senses, I say, that
in like manner form these subjects with so many
diverse qualities, or have they them really such in
themselves? And, upon this doubt, what can we
determine of their true essence? Moreover, since
the accidents of diseases, of delirium, or sleep,
make things appear otherwise to us than they do to
the healthy, the wise, and those that are awake; is
it not likely that our right state, and our natural
humours, have also wherewith to give a being to
things that have relation to their own condition, and
to accommodate them to themselves as well as when
the humours are disordered; and is not our health as
capable of giving them an aspect as sickness? Why
has not the temperate a certain form of objects relative to it as well as the intemperate;‡ and why may

* Lucret. lib. iii. ver. 705, &c.
† Sext. Empir. Pyrrh. Hypot. lib. i. cap. 14, p. 12.
‡ Idem, ibid. p. 21.

it not as well stamp them with its own character?
He whose taste is vitiated says the wine is flat; the
healthy man commends its flavour, and the thirsty its
briskness. Now our condition always accommodating things to itself, and transforming them accordingly, we cannot know what things truly are in
themselves; because that nothing comes to us but
what is altered by our senses. Where the compass,
the square, and the rule are awry, all proportions
drawn from thence, and all building erected by those
guides, must, of necessity, be also crazy and defective. The uncertainty of our senses renders every
thing uncertain that they produce:

> *Denique ut in fabricâ, si prava est regula prima,*
> *Normaque si fallax rectis regionibus exit,*
> *Et libella aliquâ si ex parte claudicat hilum,*
> *Omnia mendosè fieri, atque obstipa necessum est,*
> *Prava, cubantia, prona, supina, atque absona tecta,*
> *Jam ruere ut quædam videantur velle ruantque*
> *Prodita judiciis fallacibus omnia primis:*
> *Hic igitur ratio tibi rerum prava necesse est,*
> *Falsaque sit falsis quæcunque à sensibus orta est.**

But lastly, as in building, if the line
Be not exact and straight, the rule decline,
Or level false, how vain is the design!
Uneven, an ill-shap'd, and tott'ring wall
Must rise, this part must sink, that part must fall,
Because the rules are false that fashion'd all:
Thus reason's rules are false, if all commence,
And rise from failing, and from erring sense.

As to what remains, who can be fit to judge of these
differences? As we say in controversies of religion,
that we must have a judge, neither inclining to the
one side nor the other, free from all prejudice and
affection, which cannot be amongst Christians: just
so it falls out in this; for if he be old, he cannot
judge from the sense of old age, being himself a
party in this case; if young, there is the same ex-
ception; if healthy, sick, asleep, or awake, he is

* Lucret. lib. iv. ver. 516, &c.

still the same incompetent judge: we must have some one exempt from all these qualities, to the end that, without prejudice or prepossession, he may judge of these, and of things indifferent to him; and, by this rule, we must have such a judge as never existed.

It is impossible to judge definitively of a subject, by the appearances we receive of it from the senses. To judge of the appearances that we receive of subjects, we ought to have a deciding instrument; to prove this instrument, we must have demonstration; to verify the demonstration, an instrument; and here is our *ne plus ultra*. Seeing the senses cannot determine our dispute, being full of uncertainty themselves, it must then be reason that must do it; but every reason must have another to support it, and so we run back to infinity: our fancy does not apply itself to things that are strange, but is conceived by the mediation of the senses; and the senses do not comprehend the foreign subject, but only their own passions, by which means fancy and appearance are no part of the subject, but only of the passion and suffering of the sense, which passion and subject are different things; wherefore, whosoever judges by appearances, judges by another thing than the subject; and if we say, that the passions of the senses convey to the soul the quality of strange subjects by resemblance; how can the soul and understanding be assured of this resemblance, having, of itself, no commerce with the foreign subjects? As they who never knew Socrates, cannot, when they see his picture, say it is like him.

Now whoever would, notwithstanding, judge by appearances, if it be by all, it is impossible; because they oppose one another by their contrarieties and and differences, as we see by experience; shall some select appearances govern the rest? You must verify this select by another select, the second by the third, and, consequently, there will never be any end of it. Finally, there is no constant existence, neither of the objects being, nor our own: both we and our judgments, and all mortal things, are incessantly

running and rolling, and, consequently, nothing certain can be established from the one to the other,
both the judging and the judged being in a continual motion.

We have no communication with Being; by reason that all human nature is always in the midst,
between being born and dying, giving but an obscure appearance and shadow, a weak and uncertain
opinion of itself; and if, perhaps, you fix your
thoughts to comprehend your being, it would be
but like grasping water, for the more you clinch
your hand, to squeese and hold what is, in its own
nature, flowing, so much more you lose of what
you would grasp and hold: therefore, seeing that all
things are subject to pass from one change to another, reason, that looks for what really subsists, finds
itself deceived, not being able to comprehend any
thing that is permanent, because that every thing is
either entering into being, and is not yet wholly arrived at it, or begins to die before it is born. Plato
said,* " That bodies had never any existence, but
" only birth : conceiving that Homer had made
" the Ocean and Thetis father and mother of the
" gods, to show us, that all things are in a perpetual
" fluctuation, motion, and variation ; the opinion of
" all the philosophers," as he says, " before his time,
" Parmenides only excepted, who would not allow
" any thing to have motion ;" of the power whereof
he makes a great account. Pythagoras was of opinion, " That all matter was flowing and unstable :"
the Stoics, " That there is no time present, and that
" what we call so, is nothing but the juncture and
" meeting of the future and past." Heraclitus,†
" That never any man entered twice into the same
" river :" Epicharmus, " That he who borrowed
" money an hour ago, does not owe it now ; and

marginal note: Nothing that exists, except God, is really and constantly sub-sisting.

* In Theæteto, p. 190.
† Seneca, ep. 58, and Plutarch, in his tract, entitled, The signification of the word, lib. i. cap. 12.

" that he who was invited over-night to come the
" next day to dinner, comes that day uninvited,
" considering, that they are no more the same men,
" but are become others;" and that * " there could
" not a mortal substance be found twice in the same
" condition; for, by the suddenness and levity of
" the change, it one while disperses, and another
" while re-assembles; it comes and then goes, after
" such a manner, that what begins to be born never
" arrives to the perfection of being; forasmuch as
" that birth is never finished and never stays, as
" being at an end, but, from the seed, is evermore
" changing and shifting from one to another; as,
" from the human seed, first in the mother's womb
" is made a formless embryo; after being delivered
" thence, a sucking infant; afterwards it becomes a
" boy, then a youth, then a full-grown man, then
" a man in years, and, at last, a decrepid old man:
" so that age, and subsequent generation, is always
" destroying and spoiling that which went before :

> *Mutat enim mundi naturam totius ætas,*
> *Ex alioque alius status excipere omnia debet,*
> *Nec manet illa sui similis res, omnia migrant,*
> *Omnia commutat natura, et vertere cogit.*†
>
> For time the nature of the world translates,
> And from preceding gives all things new states;
> Nought like itself remains, but all do range,
> And nature forces ev'ry thing to change.

" And yet we foolishly fear one kind of death,
" whereas we have already passed, and do daily pass
" so many other." " For not only," as Heraclitus
said, " the death of fire is the generation of air,
" and the death of air the generation of water."
" But, moreover, we may more clearly discern it
" in ourselves: the prime of life dies, and passes
" away when old age comes on: and youth is ter-

---

* The following lines, marked " are a verbal quotation from the
last mentioned tract of Plutarch, except the verses of Lucretius.
† Lucret. lib. v. ver. 826, &c.

" minated in the prime of life; infancy in youth,
" and the first age dies in infancy : yesterday died
" in to-day, and to-day will die in to-morrow; and
" there is nothing that remains in the same state, or
" that is always the same thing. For, that it is so,
" let this be the proof: if we are always one and
" the same, how comes it to pass that we are now
" pleased with one thing, and by and by with ano-
" ther? How is it that we love or hate, praise or
" condemn, contrary things? How comes it to pass
" that we have different affections, and no more re-
" tain the same sentiment in the same thought? for
" it is not likely, that, without mutation, we should
" assume other passions ; and that which suffers
" mutation does not remain the same; and if it be
" not the same, it is not therefore existing ; but the
" same that the being is, does, like it, change its
" being, becoming evermore another from another
" thing; and, consequently, the natural senses abuse
" and deceive themselves, taking that which seems,
" for that which is, for want of well knowing what
" that which is, is. But what is it then that truly
" is? That which is eternal ; that is to say, that
" never had beginning, nor never shall have ending,
" and to which time never brings any mutation :
" for time is a moving thing, and that appears as in Time a
" a shadow, with a matter evermore flowing and moving thing, with-
" running, without ever remaining stable and per- out perma-
" manent ; and to which those words appertain be- nency.
" fore, and after, has been, or shall be ; which, at
" the first sight, evidently show, that it is not a
" thing that is ; for it were a great folly, and an ap-
" parent falsity, to say that that is, which is not yet
" in being, or that has already ceased to be; and
" as to these words, Present, Instant, and Now,
" by which it seems that we principally support
" and found the intelligence of time, reason disco-
" vering it, does presently destroy it ; for it imme-
" immediately divides and splits it into the future
" and past ; being, of necessity, to consider it di-
" vided in two. The same happens to nature that

" is measured, as to time that measures it ; for she
" has nothing that is subsisting and permanent, but
" all things are either born, bearing, or dying. By
" which means it were sinful to say of God, who is
" he who only is, that he was, or that he shall be ;
" for those are terms of declension, passage, or vi-
" cissitude, of what cannot continue, or remain in
" being. Wherefore we are to conclude, that God
" only is, not according to any measure of time,
" but according to an immutable and an immove-
" able eternity, not measured by time, nor subject
" to any declension ; before whom nothing was,
" and after whom nothing shall be, either more new
" or more recent ; but a real being, that with one
" sole Now fills the For ever, and that there is no-
" thing that truly is, but he alone ; without being
" able to say, he has been or shall be, without be-
" ginning, and without end."
To this religious conclusion of a pagan I should
only add this testimony of one of the same condition,* for the close of this long and tedious discourse, which would furnish me with endless matter.
" What a vile and abject thing," says he, " is man,
" if he do not raise himself above humanity ?" It
is a fine sentence, and a profitable desire, but equally
absurd ; for to make a handful bigger than the hand,
and the cubit longer than the arm, and to hope to
stride further than the legs can reach, is both impossible and monstrous, or that man should rise above
himself and humanity, for he cannot see but with
his eyes, nor seize but with his power. He shall be
exalted, if God will lend him his extraordinary hand;
he shall exalt himself, by abandoning and renounc-
ing his own proper means, and by suffering himself
to be raised and elevated by means purely celestial :
it belongs to our Christian faith, and not to Seneca's
stoical virtues, to pretend to this divine and miraculous metamorphosis.

* Seneca, in his Natural Question, lib. i. in the preface.

CHAPTER IV.

Of judging of the Death of another.

WHEN we judge of another's courage in death, which, without doubt, is the most remarkable action of human life, we are to take notice of one thing, which is, that men very hardly believe themselves to be arrived to that period. Few men die with an assurance that it is their last hour, and there is nothing wherein the flattery of hope more deludes us. It never ceases to whisper in our ears, " Others have No very re-
" been much sicker without dying; my condition solute as-
" is not so desperate as it is thought, and, at the the article
" worst, God has wrought other miracles." This of death. happens, by reason that we set too much value upon ourselves. It seems, to us, as if the universality of things were, in some measure, to suffer by our annihilation, and that it commiserated our condition; because our depraved sight represents things to itself after the same manner, and that we are of opinion, they stand in as much need of us, as we do of them; like people at sea, to whom mountains, fields, cities, heaven, and earth, are tossed at the same rate as they are :

> *Provehimur portu, terræque urbesque recedunt.*[*]
> Out of the port, with a brisk gale we speed,
> Advancing, while the shores and towns recede.

Who ever saw an old man that did not applaud the past and condemn the present time, laying the fault of his misery and discontent upon the world, and the manners of men ?

> *Jamque caput quassans grandis suspirat arator,*
> *Et cum tempora, temporibus præsentia confert*
> *Præteritis, laudat fortunas sæpe parentis,*
> *Et crepat antiquum genus ut pietate repletum.*[†]

[*] Æneid, lib. iii. ver. 72.   [†] Lucret. lib. ii. ver. 1164.

Now the old ploughman sighs, and shakes his head,
And present times comparing with those fled,
His predecessors' happiness does praise,
And the great piety of that old race.

The impor-
tant conse-
quences
men are apt
to ascribe
to their
death.
We draw all things along with us; whence it follows, that we consider our death as a very great
thing, and that does not so easily pass, nor without
the solemn consultation of the stars: *Tot circa unum
caput tumultuantes Deos;* as if there was a rout
among so many of the gods about the life of one
man; and the more we value ourselves, the more we
think so. " What! shall so much knowledge be
" lost, with so much damage to the world, without
" a particular concern of the Destinies? Does so
" rare and exemplary a soul cost no more the kill-
" ing than one that is vulgar, and of no use to the
" public? This life that protects so many others,
" upon which so many other lives depend, that em-
" ploys so vast a number of men in his service, and
" that fills so many places; shall it drop off like one
" that hangs but by its own single thread?" None
of us lays it enough to heart that we are but one.
Thence proceeded these words of Cæsar to his pilot,
more tumid than the sea that threatened him :

——— *Italiam si cœlo authore recusas,*
Me pete: sola tibi causa hæc est justa timoris,
Vectorem non nosse tuum, perrumpe procellas
Tutelâ secure mei———.[*]
If thou to sail for Italy decline
Under the gods' protection, trust to mine ;
The only just cause that thou hast to fear,
Is that thou dost not know thy passenger ;
But I being now aboard, though Neptune raves,
Fear not to cut through the tempestuous waves.

And these :

——— *Credit jam digna pericula Cæsar*
Fatis esse suis: tantusque evertere (dixit)
Me super labor est, parvâ quem puppe sedentem,
Tam magno patiere mari.———[†]

[*] Lucan. lib. v. ver. 579.   [†] Idem, ibid, ver. 653, &c.

> These dangers, worthy of his destiny,
> Cæsar did now believe, and then did cry,
> What, is it for the gods a task so great
> To overthrow me, that, to do the feat,
> In a poor little bark they must be fain
> Here to surprise me on the swelling main?

And that idle fancy of the public, that the sun *The sun's mourning for the death of Cæsar.* mourned for his death a whole year:

> *Ille etiam extincto miseratus Cæsare Romam,*
> *Cùm caput obscurâ nitidum ferrugine texit.**
>
> The sun, when Cæsar fell, was touch'd for Rome
> With tender pity, and bewail'd its doom.

and a thousand of the like kind, wherewith the world suffers itself to be so easily imposed upon, believing that our interests alter the heavens, and that they are concerned at our minute actions. *Non tanta cælo societas nobiscum est, ut nostro fato mortalis sit illi quoque siderum fulgor :*† " There is no such con- " nection between us and heaven, that the bright- " ness of the stars should decay by our death."

Now to judge of the constancy and resolution of *What we ought to judge of the fortitude of ma-ny who have put themselves to death.* a man, that does not yet believe himself to be cer- tainly in danger, though he really is, is no reason ; and it is not enough that he dies in this proceeding, unless he purposely put himself upon it for this end. It commonly falls out, in most men, that they set a good face upon the matter, and speak big, to acquire a reputation, which they hope also, whilst living, to enjoy. Of all that I have seen die, fortune has dis- posed their countenances and not their design ; and even of those who, in ancient times, have dispatched themselves, it is much to be noticed, whether it were a sudden or a lingering death. That cruel Roman emperor would say of his prisoners, " That he would " make them feel death ;" and if any one killed himself in prison, " That fellow," said he, " has

---

* Virg. Georg. lib. i. ver. 460, &c.
† Plin. Nat. Hist. lib. ii. cap. 8.

" escaped from me." He was for prolonging death,
and making it felt by torments :

Vidimus et toto quamvis in corpore cæso,
Nil animæ leihale datum moremque nefandæ
Durum sævitiæ, pereuntis parcere morti.[*]

And in tormented bodies we have seen,
Amongst those wounds, none that have mortal been ;
Inhuman method of dire cruelty,
That means to kill, yet will not let men die !

In plain truth, it is no such great matter for a
man in health, and in a settled frame of mind, to
resolve to kill himself; it is very easy to boast before
one comes to the push : insomuch that Heliogabalus,
the most effeminate man in the world, amongst his
most sensual pleasures, contrived to make himself
die delicately, when he should be forced to it : and,
" That his death might not give the lie to the rest
" of his life,[†] had purposely built a sumptuous
" tower, the front and base whereof was covered
" and laid with planks enriched with gold and
" precious stones, thence to precipitate himself;
" and also caused cords, twisted with gold and
" crimson silk to be made, wherewith to strangle
" himself; and a sword, with the blade of gold, to
" be hammered out to fall upon ; and kept poison
" in vessels of emerald and topaz, wherewith to
" poison himself, according as he should like to
" choose either of these ways of dying :"

Impiger, et fortis virtute coacta.[‡]
By a forc'd valour resolute and brave.

Yet, as for this person, the effeminacy of his preparations makes it more likely, that his heart would
have failed him, had he been put to the test.　But
in those who, with great resolution, have determined
to dispatch themselves, we must examine, whether

[*] Lucan. lib. ii. ver. 171, &c.
[†] Æl. Lamprid. p. 112, 113. Hist. August.
[‡] Lucan. lib. iv. ver. 798, Edit. Grov. in octavo.

it were with one blow which took away the leisure
of feeling the effect; for it is not to be questioned,
whether perceiving life, by little and little, to steal
away, the sentiment of the body mixing itself with
that of the soul, and the means of repenting being
offered, whether, I say, constancy and obstinacy, in
so dangerous a will, is to be found.

In the civil wars of Cæsar,[*] Lucius Domitius, The cow-
being taken in Abruzzo, and thereupon poisoning ardice of Domitius
himself, afterwards repented of it. It has happened and others
in our time, that a certain person being resolved to who seemed resolved
dispatch himself, and not having gone deep enough to put
themselves
at the first thrust, the sensibility of the flesh repuls- to death.
ing his arm, he gave himself three or four wounds
more, but could never prevail upon himself to thrust
home. Whilst Plantius Sylvanus was upon his trial,[†]
Virgulantia, his grandmother, sent him a poniard,
with which, not being able to kill himself, he made
his servants to cut his veins. Albucilla,[‡] in Tiberius's time, having, to kill himself, struck with too
much tenderness, gave his adversaries opportunity
to imprison and put him to death their own way.
That great leader Demosthenes, after his rout in
Sicily, did the same; and C. Pembria,[§] having
struck himself too weakly, intreated his servants to
kill him outright. On the contrary, Ostorius,[‖] who
could not make use of his own arm, disdained to
employ that of his servants to any other use, but
only to hold the poniard straight and firm, whilst he
run his neck full drive against it, so that it pierced
through his throat. It is, in truth, a morsel that is
to be swallowed without chewing, and requires the
palate of an ostrich; and yet Adrian, the emperor,
made his physician mark and encircle in his pap the
very place wherein the man he had ordered to kill

* Plutarch in the Life of Julius Cæsar, cap. 10.
† Tacit. Annal. lib. iv.   ‡ Idem, lib. vi.
§ Plutarch in the Life of Nicias, cap. 10.
‖ Tacit. Annal. lib. xvi.

him 'was to give the stab. For this reason it was,
that Cæsar, being asked, " What death he thought
" to be most desirable?" made answer, " The
" least premeditated, and the shortest."* If Cæsar
dared to say it, it is no cowardice in me to believe
it. " A short death," says Pliny,† " is the sove-
" reign happiness of human life." They do not
much care to own it: no one can say, that he is resolved for death who boggles at it, and cannot undergo it with his eyes open. They that we see, in
exemplary punishments, run to their death, hasten
and press their execution, do it not out of resolution, but they will not give themselves leisure to
consider it ; it does not trouble them to be dead, but
to die :

> Emori ‡ nolo, sed me esse mortuum nihili æstimo.§
> To be dead is nothing to me ; but I fear to die.

It is a degree of constancy to which I know, by experience, that he could arrive, like those who
plunge themselves into dangers, as into the sea, with
their eyes shut.

The con-
stant and
resolute
death of
Socrates.
There is nothing, in my opinion, more illustrious
in the life of Socrates, than that he had thirty whole
days wherein to ruminate upon the sentence of his
death; to have digested it all that time with a
most assured hope, without emotion, and without
alteration, and with words and actions rather careless and indifferent than any way stirred or discomposed by the weight of such a thought. That Pomponius Atticus, to whom Cicero writes so oft, being
sick, caused Agrippa, his son-in-law, and two or
three more of his friends, to be called to him, and
told them, " That having found all means practised

The death
of Pompo-
nius Atticus
by fasting.

---

* Suet. in Cæsare, sect. 87.
† Nat. Hist. lib. vii. cap. 53.
‡ Epicharmus, the Greek philosopher, was the author of the
verse here translated by Cicero into Latin prose.
§ Cic. Tusc. lib. i. cap. 8.

" upon him, for his recovery, to be in vain, and
" that all he did to prolong his life did also prolong
" and augment his pain ; he was determined to put an
" end both to one and the other, desiring them to
" approve of his resolution, or, at least, not to lose
" their labour in endeavouring to dissuade him."*—
Now, having chosen to detroy himself by abstinence,
his disease was accidentally cured, and the remedy
he made use of to kill himself restored him to health.
His physicians and friends, rejoicing at so happy an
event, and coming to congratulate him, were, nevertheless, very much deceived, it being impossible for
them to make him alter his purpose ; he telling
them, " That be it as it would, he must one day die ;
" and that, being now so far on his way, he would
" save himself the labour of beginning again ano-
" ther time." This man, having surveyed death at
leisure, was not only not discouraged at meeting it,
but fully bent on it ; for being satisfied that he had
engaged in the combat, he thought he was obliged
in honour to see the end of it. It is far beyond not
fearing death to desire to taste and relish it.

The story of the philosopher Cleanthes is very Cleanthes's
like this : " He having his gums swelled and rot- resolution
to die.
" ten, his physicians advised him to great absti-
" nence : having fasted two days, he was so much
" better that they pronounced him cured, and per-
" mitted him to return to his ordinary course of
" diet ; he, on the contrary, would not be persuaded
" to go back, but resolved to proceed, and to finish
" the course he had so far advanced in."†

Tullius Marcellinus,‡ a young man of Rome, The reso-
lute death
of a young
Roman.
having a mind to anticipate the hour of his destiny,
in order to be rid of a disease that was more trouble
to him than he was willing to endure ; though his
physicians assured him of a certain though not sud-

* Corn. Nepos, in the Life of Atticus.
† Diog. Laert. in the Life of Cleanthes, lib. viii. sect. 176.
‡ Senec. ep. 77.

den cure, called a council of his friends, to consult
about it : " Some," says Seneca, " gave him the
" counsel which, from pusillanimity, they would
" have taken themselves; others, out of flattery,
" prescribed what they thought he would best like ;"
but a Stoic said thus to him : " Do not tease thy-
" self, Marcellinus, as if thou didst deliberate of
" a thing of importance; it is no great matter to
" live; thy servants and beasts live; but it is a
" great thing to die handsomely, wisely, and with
" fortitude; do but think how long thou hast done
" the same thing; eat, drink, and sleep; drink,
" sleep, and eat. We are incessantly wheeled round
" in one and the same circle; not only ill and in-
" supportable accidents, but even the satiety of
" living inclines a man to desire to die."* Marcellinus did not stand in need of a man to advise, but
of a man to assist him; his servants were afraid to
meddle in the business; but this philosopher gave
them to understand, " That domestics are suspected
" even when it is in doubt whether the death of the
" master were voluntary or no; otherwise, that it
" would be of as ill example to hinder him as to
" kill him ;" forasmuch as,

> *Invitum qui servat, idem facit occidenti.*†
> Who makes a person live against his will,
> As cruel is, as if he did him kill.

The Stoic afterwards told Marcellinus, " That it
" would not be indecent, as what is left on our
" tables when we have dined is given to the waiters,
" so, life being ended, to distribute something to
" those who have been our servants." Now Marcellinus was of a free and liberal spirit; he therefore
divided a certain sum of money among his attendants and made them easy : as to the rest, he had no
need of steel nor of blood; he was resolved to go

---

* Senec. ep. 77.
† Horat. in Art. Poet. ver. 467.

out of this life, and not to run out of it; not to escape from death, but to try it: and, to give himself
leisure to parley with it, having forsaken all manner
of nourishment, the third day following, when he
had caused himself to be sprinkled with warm water,
he fainted by degrees, and not without some kind
of pleasure, as he himself declared. In earnest, such
as have been acquainted with these faintings, proceeding from weakness, do say, that they are therein
sensible of no manner of pain, but rather feel a kind
of delight, as in a passage to sleep and rest: these
are deaths studied and digested.

But, to the end that Cato only may furnish out _Death
the whole example of virtue, it seems as if his good _bravely
destiny had put his ill one into his hand, with which _confronted
he gave himself the blow; seeing he had the leisure _by Cato._
to confront and struggle with death, reinforcing his
courage in the highest danger, instead of slackening
it. And had I been to represent him to the greatest
advantage, I would have done it in the posture of
one tearing out his bloody bowels, rather than with
his sword in his hand, as did the statuaries of his
time: for this second murder would have been much
more furious than the first.

CHAPTER V.

How the Mind hampers itself.

IT is a pleasant imagination, to fancy a mind ex- _How the
actly balanced between two equal desires: for, _mind is de-
doubtless, it can never pitch upon either, as the _its choice
choice and application would manifest an inequality _between
of value; and were we set between the bottle and _indifferent._
the ham, with an equal appetite to drink and to
eat, there would be no remedy, but to die for thirst

and hunger. To provide against this inconvenience, the Stoics, when they are asked, " Whence proceeds " this election in the soul of two indifferent things " (so as, out of a great number of crowns, rather " to take one than another, there being no reason " to incline us to such a preference);" make an- swer, " That this movement of the soul is extraor- " dinary and irregular; that it enters into us by a " strange, accidental, and fortuitous impulse." It might rather, methinks, be said, that nothing pre- sents itself to us wherein there is not some difference, how little soever; and that, either by the sight or touch, there is always some choice, which, though it be imperceptibly, tempts and attracts us. Who- ever likewise shall suppose a packthread equally strong throughout, it is utterly impossible it should break; for, where will you have the fracture to be- gin? And that it should break altogether is not in nature. Whoever also would hereunto join the geo- metrical propositions, that, by the certainty of their demonstrations, conclude the contained to be greater than the containing, the centre to be as great as the circumference, and that should find out two lines incessantly approaching each other, with no possi- bility of their ever meeting; and the philosopher's stone, and the quadrature of the circle, where rea- son and the effect are so opposite, might, peradven- ture, draw some argument to prove it, to support this bold saying of Pliny :* *Solum certum nihil est certi, et homine nihil miserius aut superbius:* " That " it is only certain there is nothing certain, and " that nothing is more miserable or proud than " man."

* Plin. lib. ii. cap. 7.

CHAPTER VI.

That our Desires are augmented by the Difficulty of obtaining them.

THERE is no reason that has not its contrary, say the wisest of philosophers. I sometimes ruminate on the excellent saying urged by one of the ancients for the contempt of life; " No good can " bring pleasure, unless it be that for the loss of " which we are prepared :" *In æquo est dolor amissæ rei, et timor amittendæ :* " The grief of having " lost a thing, and the fear of losing it, are equal." Meaning, by that, that the fruition of life cannot be truly pleasant to us, if we are in fear of losing it.

It might, however, be said on the contrary, that we grasp and embrace this good the more closely and affectionately, the less assured we are of holding it, and the more we fear to have it taken from us; for it is evident, that as the fire burns with greater fury when cold mixes with it, so our wills are more sharpened by being opposed:

> *Si nunquam Danaen habuisset ahenea turris,*
> *Non esset Danae de Jove facta parens.†*
>
> A brazen tow'r if Danae had not had,
> She ne'er by Jove had been a mother made.

And that there is nothing, in nature, so contrary to our taste as the satiety which proceeds from facility; nor any thing that so much whets it, as rarity and difficulty. *Omnium rerum voluptas ipso quo debet fugare periculo crescit :‡* " The pleasure of " every thing increases by the very danger that " should deter us from it."

> *Galla nega, satiatur amor nisi gaudia torquent.§*

---

* Senec. ep. 98. † Ovid. Am. lib. ii. el. 19, ver. 27.
‡ Sen. de Ben. lib. vii. cap. 9. § Mart. lib. iv. epig. 38.

> Galla deny, be not too eas'ly gain'd,
> For love will glut with joys too soon obtain'd.

To keep love in breath, Lycurgus made a decree, that the married people of Lacedæmonia should never enjoy one another, but by stealth; and that it should be as great a shame for them to be taken in bed together, as with others. The difficulty of assignations, the danger of surprise, and the shame of the next day:

> *Et languor, et silentium,*
> *Et latere petitus imo spiritus.**
> The languor, silence, and the far-fetch'd sighs.

These are what give the *haut-gout* to the sauce: how many very wantonly pleasant sports arise from the cleanly and modest way of speaking of the works of love? The pleasure itself seeks to be heightened with pain: it is much sweeter when it smarts and excoriates. The courtezan Flora said, " She " never lay with Pompey, † but that she made him " carry off the prints of her teeth."

> *Quod petiere, premunt arctè, faciuntque dolorem*
> *Corporis, et dentes inlidunt sæpe labellis :*
> *Et stimulis subsunt, qui instigant lædere id ipsum*
> *Quodcunque est, rabies unde illæ germina surgunt.‡*
> What they desir'd, they hurt, and, 'midst the bliss,
> Raise pain; and often, with a furious kiss,
> They wound the balmy —————
> But still some sting remains, some fierce desire,
> To hurt whatever 'twas that rais'd the fire.

And so it is in every thing: difficulty gives all things their value. The people of the marquisate of Ancona, most cheerfully make their vows to St. James de Compostella, and those of Galicia to our lady of Loretto; they make wonderful boasts, at Liege, of the baths of Lucca, and in Tuscany of

* Hor. Epod. ode xi. ver. 13.
† Plutarch, in the Life of Pompey, cap. 1.
‡ Lucret. lib. iv. ver. 1072, &c.

those of the Spa: there are few Romans seen in the fencing-school at Rome, which is full of French: the great Cato also, like us, was out of conceit with his wife while she lived with him, and longed for her when in the possession of another. I turned out an old stallion into the paddock, because he was not to be governed when he smelt a mare; the facility presently sated him, with regard to his own, but on the sight of strange mares, and of the first that passed by his pasture, he would again fall to his importunate neighings, and his furious heats, as before. Our appetite contemns and passes by what it has in possession, to run after what it has not;

*Transvolat in medio posita, et fugientia captat.**

Thou scorn'st that lass thou may'st with ease enjoy,
And court'st those that are difficult and coy:
So (sings the rake) my passion can despise
An easy prey, but follows when it flies.†

To forbid us any thing, is to make us eager for it:

—————— *Nisi tu servare puellam*
Incipis, incipiet desinere esse mea.‡

If thou no better guard that girl of thine,
She'll soon begin to be no longer mine.

To give it wholly up to us, is to beget a contempt of it in us: want and abundance are attended with the same inconvenience;

Tibi quod super est, mihi quod desit, dolet.§

Thy superfluities do trouble thee,
And what I want, and pant for, troubles me.

Desire and fruition equally afflict us: the coyness of mistresses is disagreeable, but facility, to say truth, is more so; as discontent and anger spring from the esteem we have of the thing desired; love warms and

---

* Horat. lib. i. sat. 2, ver. 108.   † Mr. Francis.
‡ Ovid. Amor. lib. ii. el. 19, ver. 47.
§ Terent. Phormio, act. i. sc. 3, ver. 9,

stimulates, but satiety begets disgust; it is a blunt, dull, stupid, and sleepy passion:

> *Si qua volet regnare diu, contemnat amantem :*
> *———— Contemnite, amantes,*
> *Sic hodie veniet, si qua negavit heri.**
>
> She that would keep a youth in love's soft chain,
> If she be wise, will sometimes give him pain :
> And the same policy with men will do,
> If they sometimes do slight their misses too;
> By which means she that yesterday said nay,
> Will come and offer up herself to-day.†

Why did Poppea invent the use of a mask to hide her beautiful face, but to enhance it to her lovers? Why have they veiled, even below the heels, those beauties that every one desires to show, and every one desires to see? Why do they cover, with so many hindrances, one over another, the parts where our desires, and their own, have their principal seat? And to what end are those great hooped bastions, with which our ladies fortify their haunches, but to allure our appetite, and to draw us the nearer to them, by removing us the farther from them:

> *Et fugit ad salices, et se cupit ante videri.‡*
> And to the willows flies to be conceal'd,
> Yet still desires to have her flight reveal'd.
>
> *Interdum tunica duxit operta moram.§*
> Things, being laid too open to the sight,
> Instead of raising, lessen the delight.

To what use serves the artifice of this virgin modesty, this grave, this severe countenance, this profession to be ignorant of things that they know better than we who instruct them, but to increase in us the desire to overcome, control, and take our

---

* Ovid. Amor. lib. ii. el. 19, ver. 33.
† Propert. lib. ii. eleg. 14, ver. 19, 20.
‡ Virg. eclog. 3, ver. 65.
§ Propert. lib. ii. eleg. 15, ver. 6.

will, in spite of all this ceremony, and all these ob-
stacles? for it is not only a pleasure, but a glory, to
conquer and debauch that soft sweetness, and that
childish modesty, and to reduce a cold and matron-
like gravity to the mercy of our ardent desires: " It
" is a glory," said they, " to triumph over mo-
" desty, chastity, and temperance;" and whoever
dissuades ladies from those qualities, betrays both
them and himself. It must be believed that their
hearts tremble with fear; that the very sound of our
words offend their chaste ears; that they hate us for
talking so, and only yield to our importunity by a
compulsion. Beauty, powerful as it is, has not
wherewith to make itself relished, without the inter-
vention of these little arts. Look into Italy, where
there is the most and the finest beauty to be sold,
how it is under a necessity to have recourse to other
means, and other artifices, to render itself charming; and yet, in truth, whatever it does, being ve-
nial and public, it remains feeble and languishing
in itself: even as in virtue, of two like effects, we,
notwithstanding, look upon that as the best, and
most worthy, wherein the most hindrance and
hazard is proposed.

It is an effect of the divine Providence to suffer Why God
his holy church to be afflicted, as we see it, with so suffers his church to
many storms and trouble, by this opposition to rouse be harassed.
pious souls, and to awake them from that lazy lethargy, into which, by so long tranquillity, they had
been immerged: were we to put the loss we have
sustained, by the number of those who have gone
astray, in the balance against the benefit we have
had, by being again put in breath, and by having
our zeal and forces exercised by reason of this opposition, I know not whether the utility would not
surmount the damage.

We have thought to tie the nuptial knot more fast Whether
and firm, by taking away all means of dissolving it; the mar-riage tie is
but the knot of the will and affection is so much the rendered
more slackened, by how much that constraint is the firmer by taking

away the
means of
dissolving
it.

drawn closer together. On the contrary that which
kept the marriages at Rome so long in honour, and
inviolate, was the liberty every one, that would,
had to break them. They kept their wives the better, because they might part with them if they
would; and in the full liberty of divorces they lived
fifty years, and more, before any one made use of
it:

> *Quod licet, ingratum est, quod non licet, acrius urit.*[*]
> What's free we are disgusted at, and slight;
> What is forbidden whets the appetite.

We might here introduce the opinion of one of the
ancients, upon this occasion, "That executions ra-
"ther whet than dull the edge of vices: that they
"do not beget the care of doing well, that being
"the work of reason and discipline, but only a care
"not to be taken in doing ill."

> *Latiùs excisæ pestis contagia serpunt.*[†]
> The plague-sore being lanc'd, th' infection spreads.

I do not know that this is true; but I experimentally know that civil government never was, by that
means, reformed: the order and regulation of manners depend upon some other expedient.

People
who have
lived con-
tentedly
and secure-
ly without
offensive
arms.

The Greek histories make mention of the Agrip-
pians,[‡] neighbours to Scythia, who live either without rod or stick to offend, that not only no one attempts to attack them, but whoever can fly thither
is safe, by reason of their virtue and sanctity of life,
and no one is so bold as there to lay hands upon
them; and they have applications made to them, to
determine the controversies that arise between men
of other countries. There is a certain nation, where
the inclosures of gardens and fields, which they
would preserve, is made only of a string of cotton-
yarn; and, so fenced, is more firm and secure than

---

* Ovid. Amor. lib. i. el. 19, ver. 3.
† Rutilius in Itinerario, lib. i. ver. 397.
‡ Herodot. lib. iv. p. 263.

our hedges and ditches. *Furem signata solicitant : aperta effractarius præterit :*[*] " Things sealed up, " invite a thief; house-breakers pass by open " doors."

Perhaps the facility of entering my house, amongst other things, has been a means to preserve it from the violence of our civil wars: defence allures an attempt, and defiance provokes an attack. I enervated the soldiers' design, by depriving the exploit of all danger, and all matter of military glory, which is wont to serve them for pretence and excuse. Whatever is done courageously, is ever done honourably, at a time when the laws are silent. I render the conquest of my house cowardly and base to them; it is never shut to any one that knocks. My gate has no other guard than a porter, by ancient custom and ceremony, who does not so much serve to defend it, as to offer it with more decency, and the better grace. I have no other guard or centinel than the stars. A gentleman would be in the wrong to make a show of defence, if he be not really in a condition to defend himself. He that lies open on one side, is every where so. Our ancestors did not think of building frontier garrisons. The methods of assaulting, I mean, without battery and army, and of surprising our houses, increase every day above the means to guard them. Men's wits are generally sharp set that way : invasion every one is concerned in, none but the rich in defence. Mine was strong for the time when it was built; I have added nothing to it of that kind, and should fear lest its strength would turn against himself; besides which, we are to consider that a peaceable time would require it to be dismantled. There is danger never to be able to regain it, and it would be very hard to secure it: for, in intestine commotions, your man may be of the party you fear: and where religion is the pretext, even a man's nearest

Montaigne safe, in a defenceless house, during the civil wars.

---

* Senec. ep. 68.

relation becomes faithless with a colour of justice. The public exchequer will not maintain our domestic garrisons; they would exhaust it: we ourselves have not wherewith to do it without our ruin, or, which is more inconvenient and injurious, without ruining the people: as to the rest you thereby lose all, and even your friends will be ready to accuse your want of vigilance, and your improvidence, than to pity you, as well as to blame your ignorance or lukewarmness in the duties of your profession. That so many garrisoned houses have been lost, while this of mine remains, makes me apt to believe, that they were only lost by being guarded. This gives an enemy both a strong inclination and colour of reason: all watching and warding shows a face of war. Let who will come to me, in God's name, but I shall not invite them: it is the retirement I have chosen for my repose from war: I endeavour to sequester this corner from the public tempest, as I also do another corner in my soul. Our war may put on what forms it will, multiply and diversity itself into new parties; for my own part I shall not budge. Amongst so many garrisoned houses, I am the only person, of my condition, that I know of, who have purely intrusted mine to the protection of heaven, without removing either plate, deeds, or hangings. I will neither fear nor save myself by halves. If a full acknowledgment can acquire the divine favour, it will continue with me to the end: if not, I have staid long enough to render my continuance remarkable, and fit to be recorded: How? Why, I have lived there thirty years.

CHAPTER VII.

Of Glory.

THERE is the name and the thing; the name is a word which denotes and signifies the thing; the name is no part of the thing, or of the substance; it is a foreign piece joined to the thing, and yet without it.

God, who is all fulness in himself, and the height How the of all perfection, cannot augment or add any thing name of to himself intrinsically; but his name may be aug- God may be increased. mented and increased by the blessing and praise we attribute to his exterior works: which praise, seeing we cannot incorporate it in him, as he can have no accession of good, we attribute to his name; which is the part out of him that is nearest to us. Thus is it, that to God alone glory and honour appertain; and there is nothing so remote from reason, as that we should go in quest of it for ourselves; for being indigent and necessitous within, our essence being imperfect, and having continual need of melioration, it is for that we ought to labour: we are all hollow and empty; it is not with wind and voice that we are to fill ourselves; we want a more solid substance to repair us. A man, starved with hunger, would be very simple to look out rather a gay garment, than a good meal: we are to look after that whereof we have most need: as we have it in our ordinary prayers, *Gloria in excelsis Deo, et in terrâ pax hominibus:*[*] " Glory be to God " on high, and in earth peace, &c." We are in great want of beauty, health, wisdom, virtue, and such like essential qualities: exterior ornaments should be looked after, when we have made provision for necessary things. Theology treats amply,

---

[*] St. Luke, chap. ii. ver. 14.

and more pertinently of this subject; but I am not
much versed in it.

Philoso-
phers who
preached
up the con-
tempt of
glory. Chrysippus and Diogenes* were the first and the
stoutest champions for the contempt of glory; and
maintained, " That, of all pleasures, there was
" none more dangerous, nor more to be avoided,
" than that which proceeds from the approbation of
" others." And, in truth, experience make. us
sensible of its very hurtful treachery. There is
nothing that so much poisons princes, as flattery,
nor any thing whereby wicked men more easily obtain credit with them : nor is there any pandarism
so proper, and so often made use of, to corrupt the
chastity of women, as to wheedle and entertain them
with their own praises. The first charm the
Syrens made use of to inveigle Ulysses, is of this
nature :

> Deca vers nous, deca ò tres louable Ulysse,†
> Et le plus grand honneur dont la Grece fleurisse.‡
>
> Noble Ulysses, turn thee to this side,
> Thou Greece's greatest ornament and pride.

Those philosophers said, " That all the glory of the
" world was not worth an understanding man's
" holding out his finger to obtain it."

> Gloria quantalibet quid erit, si gloria tantum est ? §
> What more than glory is the greatest fame ?

Glory to be
courted for
the advan-
tages it
brings. I say, that alone : for it often brings several commo-
dities along with it, for which it may be desired : it
acquires us good-will, and renders us less subject
and exposed to the injuries of others, and the like.
It was also one of the principal doctrines of Epicurus ; for this precept of his sect, live obscurely, that
forbids men to encumber themselves with offices and
public negotiations, does also, necessarily, presuppose a contempt of glory, which is the world's ap-

---

* Cic. de Finibus, lib. iii. cap. 17.   † Petrarch.
‡ Homer. Odyss. lib. xii. ver. 184.   § Juv. sat. vii. ver. 81.

probation of those actions we produce to light. He that bids us conceal ourselves, and to have no other concern but for ourselves, and that will not have us known to others, would much less have us honoured and glorified. He advises Idomeneus also, " Not, in any sort, to regulate his actions by the " common reputation or opinion, except it be to " avoid the other accidental inconveniences, which " the contempt of men might bring upon him."

Those discourses are, in my opinion, very just and rational; but we are, I know not how, of a twofold nature, which is the cause, that what we believe, we do not believe, and cannot disengage ourselves from what we condemn. Let us see the last dying words of Epicurus; they are great, and worthy of such a philosopher, and yet they carry some marks of the recommendation of his name, and of that humour he had decried by his precepts. Here is a letter that he dictated a little before his last gasp :*

Proof that Epicurus courted glory.

Epicurus *to* Hermachus, *Greeting.*

" WHILST I was passing over the happy and " the last day of my life, I wrote this ; but, at the " same time, was afflicted with such a pain in my " bladder and bowels, that nothing can be greater : " but it was recompensed with the pleasure, which " the remembrance of my inventions and doctrines " suggested to my soul. Now, as the affection thou " hast ever had, from thy infancy, for me, and " philosophy does require ; take upon thee the pro- " tection of Metrodorus's children."

So much for his letter. And that which makes me interpret, that the pleasure he says he felt in his soul, concerning his inventions, has some reference to the reputation he hoped for after his

* Cic. de Fin. lib. ii. cap. 30.

death, is the disposition of his will. In which he
gives order, "That Aminomachus* and Timocrates,
"his heirs, should every January defray the ex-
"pense for the celebration of his nativity, which
"Hermachus should appoint; and also the expense
"that would be incurred, the twentieth day of
"every moon, in entertaining the philosophers, his
"friends, who should assemble in honour of the
"memory of him and Metrodorus."

Glory desirable for itself.

Carneades was head of the contrary opinion; and
maintained, "That glory was to be desired for it-
"self, even as we embrace our posthumous issue for
"themselves, without any knowledge or enjoyment
"of them."† This opinion was more universally
followed, as those readily are, that are most suitable
to our inclinations. Aristotle gives it the first place
amongst external goods; and avoids, as two vicious
extremes, the immoderate pursuit of it, or running
from it.

The mistake of those who thought that virtue was only desirable for the glory that accompanied it. Cicero very desirous of glory.

I believe, that had we the books which Cicero
wrote upon this subject, we would there read fine
stories of it; for he was so possessed with this passion, that, if he had dared, I think he would willingly have fallen into the excess that others did,
viz. "That virtue itself was only to be coveted on
"account of the honour that always attends it:"

> *Paulum sepultæ distat inertiæ*
> *Celata virtus* ————‡
>
> Inactive virtue is the same as none.

Which is an opinion so false, that I am surprised it
could ever enter into the understanding of a man
who was honoured with the name of a philosopher.
If this was true, men need not be virtuous but in
public, nor be any farther concerned to keep the
operations of the soul, which is the true seat of vir-

* Cic. de Fin. lib. ii. cap. 31.
† Idem, lib. iii. cap. 17.   Here Montaigne is guilty of a mistake,
for Cicero did not charge Carneades with this opinion, but other
philosophers of Zeno's sect.
‡ Hor. lib. iv. od. 9, ver. 29.

9

tue, regular, and in order, than as they are to arrive
at the knowledge of others. Is there no more in it
than doing an ill thing slily? " If thou knowest,"
says Carneades, " of a serpent lurking in a place,
" where, without suspicion, a person is going to sit
" down, by whose death thou expectest an advan-
" tage, thou dost ill if thou dost not give him cau-
" tion of his danger; and so much the more, be-
". cause the action is to be known by none but
" thyself."* If we do not ourselves maintain a rule
of well-doing; if impunity passes with us for justice;
to how many sorts of wickedness shall we, every day,
abandon ourselves? I do not find what Sext. Pedu-
ceus did, in faithfully restoring the treasure that C.
Plotius had committed to his sole confidence (a thing
that I have often done myself), so commendable, as
I should think it execrable, had he done otherwise:
and think it of good use, in our days, to call to
mind the example of P. Sextilius Rufus,† whom Cicero accuses of " having entered upon an inheri-
" tance contrary to his conscience, not only not
" against law, but even by the determination of the
" laws themselves." And M. Crassus and Q. Hor-
tensius, who, from their authority and power, having
been called in, by a stranger, to share in a succession, by virtue of a forged will, that so he might secure his own part, satisfied themselves with having
no hand in the forgery, and refused not to make
their advantage of it; thinking themselves safe
enough, if they could shroud themselves from accu-
sations, witnesses, and the cognizance of the laws.
*Meminerint Deum se habere testem, id est (ut ego
orbitror) mentem suam :‡* " Let them consider, they
" have God to witness, that is, (as I interpret it)
" their own consciences."

Virtue is a very vain and frivolous thing, if it de- Virtue
rives its recommendation from glory: and it is to would be a
                                                    frivolous

---

* Cic. de Fin. lib. ii. cap. 18.   † Idem, ibid. cap. 17.
‡ Cic. de Offic. lib. iii. cap. 10.

thing, if it derived its recommendation from glory. no purpose, that we endeavour to give it a station by itself, and separate it from fortune ; for what is more accidental than reputation ? *Profecto Fortuna in omni re dominatur : ea res cunctas ex libidine, magis quàm ex vero celebrat, obscuratque :*[*] " For-" tune rules in all things, and advances and de-" presses them more from caprice than from right " and justice." So to order it, that actions may be known and seen, is purely the work of fortune ; it is a chance that helps us to glory, according to its own temerity. I have often seen her go before merit, and very much outstrip it. He that first likened glory to a shadow, did better than he was aware of : they are both of them things egregiously vain : glory also, like a shadow, goes sometimes before the body, and sometimes in length very much exceeds it. They that instruct gentlemen only to employ their valour for the obtaining of honour : *Quasi non sit honestum, quod nobilitatum non sit :*[†] " As though " it were not honourable, unless ennobled ;" what do they intend by that, but to instruct them never to hazard themselves, if they are not seen ; and to take great care, that there be witnesses present, who may spread the news of their valour : whereas a thousand occasions of well-doing present themselves, when we cannot be taken notice of ? How many brave actions are buried in the crowd of a battle ? Whoever takes upon him to censure another, in such a confusion, has scarce any hand in it ; and the testimony he gives of his companion's behaviour, is evidence against himself. *Vera et sapiens animi magnitudo honestum illud quod maxime naturam sequitur, in factis positum, non in gloria judicat :*[‡] " True magnanimity " judges, that the bravery which most follows na-" ture consists in the action, not in the glory." All the glory that I pretend to in my life, is that I have lived in quiet ; in a tranquillity, not according to

* Sallust. in Catalin. p. 5. Mattaire.
† Cic. de Offic. lib. i. cap. 4.   ‡ Idem, lib. i. cap. 19.

Metrodorus, Arcesilaus, or Aristippus, but according to myself; for, seeing philosophy has not been able to find out any way to tranquillity, that is good in common, let every one seek it in particular. To what do Cæsar and Alexander owe the infinite grandeur of their renown, but to Fortune? How many men has she extinguished in the beginning of their progress, of whom we have no knowledge; who brought as much courage to the work as they, if their evil destiny had not stopped them short at their first setting out? Amongst so many and so great dangers, I do not remember I have any where read, that Cæsar was ever wounded; a thousand have fallen in less dangers, than the least of those he went through. A great many brave actions must have perished without witness, and before one turns to account. A man is not always on the top of a breach, or at the head of an army, in the sight of his general, as upon a scaffold. A man is oft surprised between the hedge and the ditch; he must run the hazard of his life against a hen-roost; he must dislodge four rascally musketeers out of a barn; he must single out himself from his party, and make some attempts alone, according as necessity requires: and whoever will observe, will, I believe, find it experimentally true, that actions of the least lustre are the most dangerous; and that, in the wars of our own times, there have more brave men been lost on slight occasions, and in the dispute about some paltry fort, than in places of note and dignity.

He who thinks his death unworthy of him, unless he fall on some signal occasion, instead of rendering his death celebrated, wilfully obscures his life, suffering, in the mean time, many proper opportunities of hazarding himself, to slip out of his hands: and every just one is illustrious enough; every man's conscience being a sufficient trumpeter to him. *Gloria nostra est, testimonium conscientiæ nostræ :*

Virtue must be courted for its own sake, independent of popular approbation.

* 2 Cor. chap. i. ver. 12.

" For our rejoicing is this, the testimony of our con-
" science." He who is a good man only that men
may know it, and that he may be the better esteemed
for it, when it is known; he who will not do well,
but upon condition that his virtue may be known
to men, is one from whom much service is not to
be expected :

> *Credo ch' el resto di quel verno cose*
> *Facesse degne di tenerne conto :*
> *Ma fur fin a quel tempo si nascose,*
> *Che non e colpa mia s'hor'non le conte,*
> *Perche Orlando a far' opre virtuose*
> *Piu ch'a narrar le poi sempre era pronto ;*
> *Ne mai fu alcun' de suoi fatti espresso,*
> *Se non quand' hebbe i testimoni appresso.* *

The rest o' th'winter, I presume, was spent
 In actions worthy of eternal fame ;
Which hitherto are in such darkness pent,
 That, if I name them not, I'm not to blame :
Orlando's noble mind was still more bent
 To do great acts, than boast him of the same :
So that no deeds of his were ever known,
But those that luckily had lookers on.

A man must go to the war to discharge his duty,
and wait for the recompence that never fails to attend all brave actions, how concealed soever, nor so
much as virtuous thoughts; it is the satisfaction that
a well-disposed conscience receives in itself, to do
well : a man must be valiant for himself, and for the
advantage it is to him, to have his courage in a firm
and secure situation, against the assaults of fortune :

> *Virtus repulsæ nescia sordidæ,*
> *Intaminatis fulget honoribus :*
> *Nec sumit, aut ponit secures*
> *Arbitrio popularis auræ.† *

Virtue, that ne'er repulse admits,
In taintless honour glorious sits ;
Nor grandeur seeks, nor from it flies,
As the mere noise of vulgar cries.

* Orlando's Ariosto, cant. xi. stanz. 81.
† Hor. lib. iii. ode 2, ver. 17, &c.

It is not to make a parade, that the soul is to play its part, but for ourselves within, where no eyes can pierce, but our own; there she defends us from the fear of death, of pains, and shame itself: she there arms us against the loss of our children, friends, and fortunes: and, when opportunity presents itself, she leads us on to the hazards of war. *Non emolumento aliquo, sed ipsius honestatis decore:* "Not for any "emolument, but for the honour of virtue." This Honour, is a much greater advantage, and more worthy to be what it is. coveted and hoped for than honour and glory; which is no other than a favourable judgment formed of us.

A dozen men must be culled out of a whole na- How con- tion, to judge of an acre of land; and the judgment temptible is the judg- of our inclinations and actions, the most important ment of the of all things, we refer to the *vox populi*, too often multitude. the mother of ignorance, injustice, and inconstancy. Is it reasonable, that the life of a wise man should depend upon the judgment of fools? *An quidquam stultius, quam quos singulos contemnas, eos aliquid putare esse universos?*[*] "Can any thing be more "foolish than to think, that those you despise sin- "gle, are estimable in the bulk?" He that makes it his business to please them, will never succeed; it is a mark that never is to be reached or hit. *Nil tam inestimabile est, quam animi multitudinis:* "No- "thing is to be so little esteemed, as the judgment "of the multitude." Demetrius pleasantly said of the voice of the people, "That he made no more of "that which came from above, than of that which "fumed from below." Cicero[†] says more, *Ego hoc judico, si quando turpe non sit, tamen non esse non turpe, quam id à multitudine laudetur:* "I am of opinion, that though a thing be not "foul in itself, yet it cannot but become so when "commended by the multitude." No art, no dexterity could conduct our steps, in following so wandering and so irregular a guide. In this windy

* Cic. Tusc. Quæst. lib. v. ver. 36.
† Cic. de. Fin. lib. ii. cap. 15.

confusion of the noise of vulgar reports and opinions, that drive us on, no good path can be chosen. Let us not propose to ourselves an end so floating and wavering; let us follow constantly after reason; let the public approbation follow us in that road, if it will; and as it wholly depends upon fortune, we have no rule sooner to expect it by any other way than that. Though I would not follow the right way, because it is right, I should, however, follow it, for having experimentally found, that, at the end of the reckoning, it is commonly the most happy, and of the greatest utility. *Dedit hoc providentia hominibus munus, ut honesta magis juvarent:* " This " gift Providence has given to man, that honest " things should be most delightful." The mariner said thus to Neptune, in a great storm, " O God, " thou mayest save me if thou wilt, and, if thou wilt, " thou mayest destroy me; but I will steer my rud-" der true." I have seen, in my time, a thousand men of supple mongrel natures, and who no one doubted but they were more worldly wise than I, ruin themselves where I have saved myself:

> *Risi successus posse carere dolos.**
> I laugh'd to see their unsuccessful wiles.

Paulus Æmilius, going upon the glorious expedition of Macedonia, above all things charged the people of Rome, " not to speak of his actions during " his absence." What a disturbance is the licence of judgments to great affairs! every one has not the constancy of Fabius, to oppose common, adverse, and injurious tongues, who rather suffered his authority to be dissected by the vain fancies of man, than to fail in his duty, with a favourable reputation, and popular applause.

Praise and reputation set at too high a price.

There is I know not what natural sweetness in hearing a man's self commended; but we are a great deal too fond of it:

> *Laudari haud metuam, neque enim mihi cornea fibra est,*

---

* Ovid. Ep. Penelopes ad Ulyssem.

Sed recti finemque extremumque esse recuso
Euge tuum, et belle. —————*

I fear not to be prais'd, I must confess,
My heart is not of horn ; but, ne'ertheless,
I must deny the only end and aim
Of doing well is to hear man exclaim,
O·noble act ! eternal be thy fame !

I care not so much what I am in the opinion of
others, as what I am in my own : I would be rich
of myself, and not by borrowing. Strangers see nothing but events and outward appearances ; every
body can set a good face on the matter, when they
have trembling and terror within. They do not see
my heart, they only see my countenance. It is with
good reason that men decry the hypocrisy that is in
war ; for what is more easy to an old soldier, than
to step aside from dangers, and to bluster, when he
has no more heart than a chicken? There are so
many ways to avoid hazarding a man's own person,
that men have deceived the world a thousand times,
before they are engaged in a real danger ; and, even
then, finding themselves at a nonplus, they can
make shift, for that time, to conceal their apprehensions, by setting a good face on the business, though
the heart beats within ; and whoever had the use of
the Platonic ring, which renders those invisible that
wear it, if turned inward towards the palm of the
hand, a great many would, very often, hide themselves when they ought most so appear ; and would
repent being placed in so honourable a post, where,
of necessity, they must be bold :

Falsus honor juvat, et mendax infamia terret,
Quem nisi mendosum, et mendacem ?†

False honour pleases, false rumours do disgrace
And frighten : whom ? Dunces, and liars base.

Thus we see how uncertain and doubtful are all the
judgments that are founded upon external appearances, and that there is not so sure a testimony as

* Persius, sat. i. ver. 47. † Hor. lib. i. epist. 16, ver. 39, 40.

every man is to himself: in those others, how many
powder-monkeys have we companions of our glory?
He that stands firm in an open trench, what does he,
in that, more than what fifty poor pioneers, who
open the way for him, and cover it with their own
bodies, for five pence a day, have done before him?

> —— Non quicquid turbida Roma
> Elevet, accedas, examenque improbum in illa
> Castiges trutinâ, nec te quæsiveris extra.*
> —— Whatever muddy-headed Rome
> Extols or censures, trust not to its doom;
> Stand not to th'award of an ill-judging town,
> Nor by its falset scale adjust your own;
> No, no, for other judgments ask no more,
> To know thyself, thyself alone explore.

The extending and scattering our names into
many mouths, we call aggrandising them; we would
have them there well received, and that this increase
turn to their advantage, which is all that can be excusable in this design; but the excess of this disease
proceeds so far, that many covet to have a name, be
it what it will. Trogus Pompeius says of Herostra-
tus, and Titus Livius of Manlius Capitolinus,† "That
"they were more ambitious of a great reputation,
"than a good one." This vice is very common:
we are more sollicitous that men speak of us, than
how they speak; and it is enough, for us, that our
names are often mentioned, be it after what manner
it will. It should seem, that to be known, is, in
some sort, to have a man's life, and its duration, in
another's keeping. I, for my part, hold, that I am
not but in myself; and of that other life of mine,
which lies in the knowledge of my friends, to consider it naked and simply in itself, I know very well,
that I am sensible of no fruit nor enjoyment of it,
but by the vanity of a fantastic opinion; and, when
I shall be dead, I shall be much less sensible of it;
and if I shall, withal, absolutely lose the use of those

---

* Persius, sat. i. ver. 5, &c.   † Tit. Liv. lib. vi. cap. 11.

real advantages, that, sometimes, accidentally follow
it, I shall have no more handle whereby to take
hold of, or to reach to me: for, to expect that my
name should be advanced by it, in the first place, I
have no name that is enough my own; of two that I
have, one is common to all my race, and even to others
also: there is one family at Paris and Montpelier,
whose surname is Montaigne; another in Brittany,
and another Montaigne in Xaintonge. The trans-
position of one syllable only will so confound our
affairs, that I shall, perhaps, share in their glory,
and they in my shame; and, moreover, my ancestors have, formerly, been surnamed Eyquem, 'a
a name that borders on that of a family well known
in England: as to my other name, every one may
take it that will: and so, perhaps, I may honour a
porter in my own stead. Besides, though I had a
particular distinction by myself, what can it distinguish when I am no more? Can it point out and favour annihilation:

> —— *Nunc levior cippus non imprimit ossa,*
> *Laudat posteritas, nunc non è manibus illis,*
> *Nunc non è tumulo fortunataque favilla*
> *Nascuntur violæ ?* * ————

> Will, after this, thy monumental stones
> Press with less weight upon thy rotted bones?
> Posterity commends thee: happy thou!
> Will not thy manes such a gift bestow,
> As to make violets from thy ashes grow?

But of this I have spoken elsewhere. As to what
remains, in a great battle, where ten thousand men
are maimed or killed, there are not fifteen that are
taken notice of: it must be some very eminent greatness, or some circumstance of great importance, which
fortune has tacked to it, that must signalise a private action, not of a musketeer only, but of a great
captain; for to kill a man, or two, or ten, to expose
a man's self bravely to death, is indeed something
to every one of us, because we all run the hazard;

* Pers. sat. i. ver. 37.

but as for the world in the general, they are things
so common, so many of them are every day seen,
and there must, of necessity, be so many of the same
kind, to produce any notable effect, that we cannot
expect any particular renown from them:

—— *Casus multis hic cognitus, ac jam*
*Tritus, et è medio fortunæ ductus acervo.**

Many have known this case, which now, worn old,
With common acts of fortune is enroll'd.

Of so many thousands of valiant men that have
died, within these fifteen hundred years, in France,
with their swords in their hands, not a hundred have
come to our knowledge: the memory, not of the
commanders only, but of the battles and victories, is
buried. The fortunes of above half of the world,
for want of a record, stir not from their place, and
vanish without duration. If I had unknown events
in my possession, I should think, with great ease, to
out-do those that are recorded in examples of every
kind. Is it not strange, that, even of the Greeks and
Romans, amongst so many writers and witnesses,
and so many rare and noble exploits, so few are arrived at our knowledge?

Ad nos vix tenuis famæ perlabitur aura.†

Which fame to these our times has scarce brought down.

The Muses It will be much if, a hundred years hence, it be re-
sacrificed
unto by the membered, in gross, that, in our times, there were
Lacedæ- civil wars in France. The Lacedæmonians entering
monians,
and why. into battle, sacrificed to the Muses, to the end that
their actions might be well and worthily written;
looking upon it as a divine and no ordinary favour,
that brave acts should find witnesses that could give
them life and remembrance. Do we expect, that,
at every musket-shot we receive, and at every hazard
we run, there must be a register ready to record
them? Besides, a hundred registers may enrol them,

* Juv. sat. xiii. ver. 9, 10.   † Æneid. lib. vii. ver. 646.

whose commentaries will not last above three days, and never come to the sight of any reader. We have not the thousandth part of the ancient writings; it is Fortune that gives them a shorter or longer life, according to her favour; and we may well doubt, whether those we have be not the worst, having not seen the rest. Men do not write histories of things of so little moment: a man must have been general in the conquest of an empire, or a kingdom; he must have won two and fifty set battles, and always the weakest in number of men, as Cæsar did. Ten thousand brave fellows, and several great captains lost their lives, gallantly and courageously, in his service, whose names lasted no longer than their wives and children lived:

Quos fama obsura recondit. *

Whom time has not deliver'd o'er to fame.

Even of those we see behave the best; three months, or three years after they have been knocked on the head, they are no more spoken of than if they had never been.

Whoever will justly consider, what kind of men, and what sort of actions are recorded, with honour, in history, will find, that there are few actions, and very few persons, of our times, who can there pretend any right. How many worthy men have we seen survive their own reputation, who have seen the honour and glory, most justly acquired in their youth, extinguished in their own presence? And for three years of this fantastic and imaginary existence, are we to go and throw away our true essential life, and engage ourselves to a perpetual death? The sages propose to themselves a nobler and more just end to so important an enterprise. *Recte facti, fecisse merces est : officii fructus, ipsum officium est* :† " The reward of a thing well done is to have done " it : the fruit of a good office is the office itself."

What sort of glory that is, the remembrance of which is preserved in books.

* Æneid. lib. v. ver. 302.   † Senec. ep. 81.

It were, perhaps, excusable in a painter, or any other
artisan, or even in a rhetorician, or a grammarian, to
endeavour to raise themselves a name by their works;
but the actions of virtue are too noble in themselves
to seek any other reward than from their own value,
and especially to seek it in the vanity of human judgment.

Why the public ap-probation ought to be courted.   If this false opinion, nevertheless, be of that use
to the public, as to keep men in their duty; if the
people are thereby stirred up to virtue; if princes
are touched to see the world bless the memory of
Trajan, and abominate that of Nero; if it moves
them to see the name of that great beast, once so
terrible and dreaded, so freely cursed and reviled by
every school boy, let it, in the name of God, increase, and be, as much as possible, cherished among
us.   And Plato, bending his whole endeavour to
make his citizens virtuous, also advises them, not to
despise the good esteem of the people; and says,
" That it falls out, by a certain divine inspiration,
" that even the wicked themselves, oft-times, as well
" by word as opinion, can rightly distinguish the
" virtuous from the wicked." This person, and his
tutor, are marvellous bold artificers, to add divine
operations and revelations wherever human force is
wanting: and, perhaps, for this reason it was, that
Timon, railing at him, called him, " The great forger
" of miracles." *Ut tragici poetæ confugiunt ad
deum, cum explicare argumenti exitum non possunt :*
" As tragic poets fly to some god, when they are
" at a loss to wind up their piece." Seeing that
men, by their insufficiency, cannot pay themselves
well enough with current money, let the counterfeit
be superadded: it is a way that has been practised by
all the legislators; and there is no government that
has not some mixture, either of ceremonial vanity,
or of false opinion, which serves for a curb to keep
people in their duty: it is for this that most of them

* Cic. de Nat. Deor. lib. i. cap. 20.

have their fabulous originals and beginnings, and so enriched with supernatural mysteries: it is this that has given credit to false religions, and caused them to be countenanced by men of understanding; and for this that Numa and Sertorius, to possess their men with a better opinion of them, pretended, one, that the nymph Egeria, the other, that his white hind, brought them all their resolutions from the gods. The authority that Numa gave to his laws, under the sanction of this goddess's patronage, Zoroaster, legislator of the Bactrians and Persians, gave to his, under the name of the god Oromazis; Trismegistus, legislator of the Egyptians, under that of Mercury; Zambooxis, legislator of the Scythians, under that of Vesta; Charondas, legislator of the Chalcedonians, under that of Saturn; Minos, legislator of the Cretans, under that of Jupiter; Lycurgus, legislator of the Lacedæmonians, under that of Apollo; and Draco and Solon, legislators of the Athenians, under that of Minerva. And every government has a god at the head of it; others falsely, that truly which Moses set over the Jews at their departure out of Egypt. The religion of the Bedoins, as the Sieur de Joinville reports,* amongst other things, enjoined a belief " That the soul of him, amongst " them, who died for his prince, went into another " more happy body, more beautiful and more ro- " bust than the former;" by which means they much more willingly ventured their lives:

In ferrum mens prona viris, animæque capaces
Mortis, et ignavum est reditura parcere vitæ.†
Eager for wounds, with thirst of death they burn,
Lavish of life that happier will return.

This is a very comfortable belief, however erroneous it is. Every nation has many such examples of its own: but this subject would require a treatise by itself.

* In his Memoirs, chap. 57, p. 357, 358. † Lucan. lib. i. ver. 461.
VOL. II.   Y

The differ-
ence be-
tween that
which the
ladies term
honour,
and their
duty.

To add one word more to my former discourse, I would advise the ladies no more to call that honour, which is but their duty, *Ut enim consuetudo loquitur, id solum dicitur honestum, quod est populari fama gloriósum :*[*] " According to the vulgar style, that " only is honourable, which has the public ap- " plause :" their duty is the grape, their honour but the outward husk. Neither would I advise them to give that excuse as payment for their denial : for I suppose, that their intentions, their desire, and will, which are things wherein their honour is not at all concerned, as nothing of it appears externally, are much better regulated than the effects :

> *Quæ quia non liceat, non facit, illa facit.*[*]
> She, who sins not, because 'tis against law,
> Is chaste no farther than she's kept in awe.

The offence both towards God, and in the con- science, would be as great to desire, as to do it : and, besides, they are actions so secret of themselves, as would be very easily kept from the knowledge of others, wherein the honour consists ; if they had no other respect to their duty, and to the affection they bear to chastity for its own sake : every woman of honour rather chooses to wound her honour, than her conscience.

CHAPTER VIII.

Of Presumption.

THERE is another sort of glory, which is the hav- ing too good an opinion of our own merit. It is an inconsiderate affection, with which we flatter our- selves, and that represents us to ourselves other than

[*] Cic. de Fin. lib. ii. cap. 15.   † Ovid. Amor. lib. iii. el. 4, ver. 4,

what we truly are: like the passion of love, that lends beauties and graces to the object of it; and makes those who are caught with it, by a depraved and corrupt judgment, consider the thing they love other and more perfect than it is.

I would not, nevertheless, that a man, for fear of failing in this point, should mistake himself, or think himself less than he is; the judgment ought, in all things, to keep its prerogative: it is all the reason in the world he should discern, in himself, as well as in others, what truth sets before him; if he be Cæsar, let him boldly think himself the greatest captain in the world. We are nothing but ceremony; ceremony carries us away, and we leave the substance of things; we hold by the branches, and quit the trunk. We have taught the ladies to blush, when they hear but that named, which they are not at all afraid to do: we dare not call our members by their right names, and yet are not afraid to employ them in all sorts of debauchery. Ceremony forbids us to express, by words, things that are lawful and natural, and we obey it: reason forbids us to do things unlawful and ill, and nobody obeys it. I find myself here fettered by the laws of ceremony; for it neither permits a man to speak well of himself, nor ill. We will leave her there for this time. They whom fortune (call it good or ill) has made to pass their lives in some eminent degree, may, by their public actions, manifest what they are: but they whom she has only employed in the crowd, and of whom nobody will speak, if they do not speak for themselves, are to be excused, if they take courage to talk of themselves, to such who are concerned to know them, by the example of Lucilius:

The fear of being guilty of presumption ought not to give us too mean an opinion of ourselves, nor to hinder us from making ourselves known.

Ille velut fidis arcana sodalibus olim
Credebat libris, neque si malè cesserat, usquam
Decurrens: alio neque si bene: quo fit ut omnis
Votiva pateat veluti descripta tabella
*Vita senis.** ———

* Hor. lib. ii. sat. 1, ver. 30, &c.

Y 2

His secrets to his books he did commend,
As free as to his dearest bosom friend :
Whether he wrote with, or against the grain,
The old man's life his verses do explain.

He committed to paper his actions and thoughts,
and there pourtrayed himself such as he found himself to be. *Nec id Rutilio, et Scauro citra fidem, aut
obtrectationi fuit :* " Nor were Rutilius or Scaurus
" misbelieved or condemned for so doing."

Montaigne's particular gesture a plain token of his silly pride. I remember then, that, from my infancy, there
was observed in me I know not what kind of carriage and gesture that seemed to relish of foolish
pride. I will say this, in the first place, that it is
not unlikely, that there are qualities and propensities so deeply implanted in us, that we have not the
means to feel and know them : and of such natural
inclinations the body is apt to retain a certain bent,
without our knowledge or consent. It was affectation that made Alexander carry his head on one side,
and Alcibiades to lisp ; Julius Cæsar† scratched his
head with one finger, which is the mark of a man
possessed with uneasy thoughts ; and Cicero, as I
remember, was wont to turn up his nose, a sign of
a man given to scoffing : such motions as these may,
imperceptibly, happen in us. There are other artificial ones, which I meddle not with ; as salutations
and congees, by which men, for the most part, unjustly acquire the reputation of being humble and
courteous ; or, perhaps, humble out of pride. I
am prodigal enough of my hat, especially in summer, and never am so saluted, but I pay it again,
from persons of what quality soever, unless they be
in my pay. I should be glad that some princes,
whom I know, would be more sparing of that ceremony, and bestow that courtesy where it is more
due ; for, being so indiscreetly profuse of it, it is
thrown away to no purpose, if it be without respect-

* Tacit. in Vita Agricolæ, cap. 1.
† Plutarch, in the Life of Cæsar, cap. 1.
12

of persons : amongst irregular countenances, let us not forget that severe one of the emperor Constantius,* who always, in public, held his head upright and straight, without bending or turning it on either side, not so much as to look upon those who saluted him on one side, planting his body in a stiff immoveable posture, without suffering it to yield to the motion of his coach ; not daring so much as to spit, blow his nose, or wipe his face before people. I know not whether the gestures that were observed in me, were of this first quality, and whether I had really any secret propensity to this vice, as it might well be ; and I cannot be responsible for the swing of the body.

But as to the motions of the soul, I must here confess what I am sensible of. This vanity consists of two parts ; the setting too great a value upon ourselves, and too little a value upon others. *Presumption divided into two parts.*

As to the one, methinks these considerations ought, in the first place, to be of some weight. I feel myself importuned by an error of the soul, that displeases me, both as it is unjust, and the more, as it is troublesome : I attempt to correct it, but I cannot root it out ; which is that I lessen the just value of things that I possess, and over-value others, because they are foreign, absent, and none of mine. This humour spreads very far : as the prerogative of the authority makes husbands look upon their own wives with a vicious disdain, and many fathers their children, so do I : and, between two equal merits, I should always be swayed against my own : not so much that the jealousy of my preferment, and the bettering of my affairs troubles my judgment, and hinders me from satisfying myself, as because dominion, of itself, begets a contempt of what is our own, and over which we have an absolute command. Foreign governments, manners, and languages insinuate themselves into my esteem ; and I am very *Montaigne apt to undervalue his person and possessions.*

‡ Ammian. Marcell. lib. xxi. cap. 14.

sensible, that Latin allures me, by its dignity, to value it above its due, as happens to children, and the common sort of people. The economy, house, and horse of my neighbour, though no better than my own, I prize above my own, because they are not mine: besides that, I am very ignorant in my own affairs; I admire the assurance that every one has of himself: whereas there is not, almost, any thing that I am sure I know, or that I dare be responsible to myself that I can do: I have not my means of doing any thing stated and ready, and am only instructed after the effect, being as doubtful of my own force, as I am of another's; whence it comes to pass, that, if I happen to do any thing commendable, I attribute it more to my fortune than industry; forasmuch as I design every thing by chance, and in fear. I have this also in general, that, of all the opinions antiquity has held of men in gross, I most willingly embrace, and most adhere to those that most contemn, vilify, and annihilate us. Methinks philosophy has never so fair a game to play, as when it falls upon our vanity and presumption; when it discovers man's irresolution, weakness, and ignorance. I look upon the too good opinion, that man has of himself, to be the nursing mother of the falsest opinions, both public and private. Those people who ride astride upon the epicycle of Mercury, who see so far into the heavens, are worse to me than pickpockets: for, in my study, the subject of which is man, finding so great a variety of judgments, so profound a labyrinth of difficulties one upon another; so great a diversity and uncertainty, even in the school of wisdom itself; you may judge, seeing those people could not be certain of the knowledge of themselves, and their own condition, which is continually before their eyes, and within them; seeing they do not know how that moves which they themselves move, nor how to give us a description of the springs they themselves govern and make use of; how can I be-

lieve them about the ebbing and flowing of the
Nile? " The curiosity of knowing things has been
" given to man for a scourge," says the holy scripture. But, to return to what concerns myself, I
think it very hard, that any other should have a
meaner opinion of himself; nay, that any other
should have a meaner opinion of me, than I have of
myself. I look upon myself as one of the common
sort, saving in what I am obliged for to myself;
guilty of the meanest and most popular defects, but
not disowned or excused ; and do not value myself
upon any other account, than because I know my
own value.

If I have any vanity, it is superficially infused into Montaigne
me by the treachery of my constitution, and has no always dis-
body that my judgment can discern. I am sprin- with his
kled, but not died : for, in truth, as to the produc- own writ-
tions of the mind, no part of them, be it what it especially
will, ever satisfied me, and the approbation of others cal essays.
is no coin for me; my judgment is tender and nice,
especially in my own concern; I feel myself float
and waver by reason of my weakness. I have nothing of my own that satisfies my judgment : my
sight is clear and regular enough, but, in opening it,
it is apt to dazzle, as I most manifestly find in
poesy : I love it infinitely, and am able to give a tolerable judgment of other men's works : but, in
good earnest, when I apply myself to it, it is so
puerile, that I cannot endure myself. A man
may play the fool in every thing else, but not in
poetry :

  —— *Mediocribus esse poetis*
Non homines, non dii, non concessere columnæ.[*]

Nor men, nor gods, nor pillars ever deem
Indifferent poets worthy of esteem.

I would to God this sentence was writ over the
doors of all our printers, to forbid the entrance of
so many rhymers :

  * Horat. de Art. Poet. ver. 372, 373.

—— *Verum*
*Nihil securius est malo poeta.**
—— But the truth is, and all the critics show it,
None's more conceited than a sorry poet.

The public notice which the people took of Dionysius's poetry, he who was the tyrant of Sicily.

Have not we such people? Dionysius, the father, valued himself so much upon nothing as his poetry. At the Olympic games, with chariots surpassing all others in magnificence, he sent also poets and musicians to present his verses, with tents and pavilions royally gilt, and hung with tapestry. When his verses came to be recited, the grace and excellency of the pronunciation, at first, attracted the attention of the people; but when they, afterwards, came to reflect on the meanness of the composition, they disdained it, and their judgments, being more and more nettled, presently proceeded to fury, and ran to pull down, and tear all his pavilions to pieces. And forasmuch as his chariots never performed any thing to purpose in the race,† and as the ship, which brought back his people, failed of making Sicily, and was, by the tempest, driven and wrecked upon the coast of Tarentum, they did certainly believe the gods were incensed, as they themselves were, against that paltry poem: and even the mariners, who escaped from the wreck, seconded this opinion of the people; to which the oracle that foretold his death, also seemed, in some measure, to subscribe; which was, "That Dionysius‡ " should be near his end, when he should have " overcome those who were better than himself." This he interpreted of the Carthaginians, who surpassed him in power; and, having war with them, often declined and moderated victory, lest he should incur the sense of this prediction: but he misunderstood it; for the god pointed at the time of the advantage, that, by favour and injustice, he obtained

* Mart. lib. xii. epig. 64.
† Diodorus of Sicily, lib. xiv. cap. 28.
‡ Id. ibid. lib. xv. cap. 29.

at Athens, over the tragic poets, better than himself, having caused his own play, called the Leneians,
to be acted in emulation; presently after this victory
he died, and partly of the excessive joy he conceived
at the success of it. What I find tolerable of mine,
is not so really, and in itself; but in comparison of
other worse things, that, I see, are well enough received : I envy the happiness of those that can
please and hug themselves in what they do, for it
is a very easy thing to be so pleased, because a man
extracts that pleasure from himself, especially if he
be constant in his self-conceit. I know a poet,
against whom both the intelligent in poetry, and the
ignorant, abroad and at home, both heaven and
earth, exclaim, that he has no notion of it; and
yet, for all that, he has never a whit the worse opinion of himself, but is always falling upon some new
piece, always contriving some new invention, and
still persists, with so much the more obstinacy, as it
only concerns himself to stand up in his own defence.

My works are so far from pleasing me, that as oft
as I review them, they disgust me :

*What na-
tion Mon-
taigne had
of his own
works.*

> *Cum relego, scripsisse pudet, quia plurima cerno,*
> *Me quoque qui feci, judice digna lini.**
> When I peruse, I blush at what I've writ,
> And think 'tis only for the fire fit.

I have always an idea, in my mind, of a better form
than that I have made use of, but I cannot catch it,
nor fit it to my purpose; yet even that idea is but of
the middle class; by which I conclude that the pro-
ductions of those rich and great geniuses, of former
times, are very much beyond the utmost strength
of my imagination, or my wish. Their writings not
only satisfy, but astonish and ravish me with admiration : I judge of their beauty, I see it, if not to perfection, yet so far, at least, as it is possible for me

* Ovid. de Ponto, lib. i. eleg. 6, ver. 15, 16.

to aspire to. Whatever I undertake, I owe a sacrifice to the Graces, as Plutarch says of some one, to cultivate their favour :

> ———————— *Si quid enim placet,*
> *Si quid dulce hominum sensibus infuit,*
> *Debentur lepidis omnia Gratiis.*
>
> If aught can ever please that I indite,
> If to men's minds it ministers delight,
> All's to the lovely Graces due.

Montaigne's style.They abandon me throughout: all I write is rude, and wants polishing and beauty : I cannot set things off to the best advantage, my handling adds nothing to the matter ; for which reason I must have a subject forcible, very copious, and that has a lustre of its own. If I pitch upon subjects that are popular and gay, it is to follow my own inclination, who do not affect a grave and ceremonious wisdom, as the world does ; and to make myself, not my style, more sprightly, which requires them rather grave and severe, at least, if I may call that a style which is rough and irregular phraseology, a vulgar jargon, and a proceeding without definition, division, or conclusion, and perplexed, like that of Amafanius and Rabirius.[*] I can neither please nor delight, much less ravish : the best story in the world is tarnished by my handling. I cannot speak but in earnest, and am totally unprovided of that facility, which I observe in many of my acquaintance, of entertaining the first comers, and keeping a whole company in breath, or amusing the ears of a prince, with all sorts of discourse, without being weary ; they never wanting matter, by reason of the faculty and grace they have in taking hold of the first thing that is started, and accommodating it to the humour and capacity of those with whom they have to do. Princes do not much affect solid discourses, nor I to tell stories. The first and easiest reasons, which are

---

[*] Cic. Acad. Quæst. lib. i. cap. 2.

commonly the most liked, I know not how to employ: I am a bad orator to the common sort: I am
apt, of every thing, to say the utmost that I know.
Cicero is of opinion, " That,* in treatises of philo-
" sophy, the exordium is the hardest part ;" which,
if it be true, I am wise in sticking to the conclusion :
and yet we are to know how to wind the string to
all notes, and the sharpest is that which is the most
seldom touched ; there is, at least, as much perfection in elevating an empty, as in supporting a
weighty thing: a man must sometimes superficially
handle things, and sometimes sift them to the bottom : I know, very well, that most men keep themselves in this lower form, for not conceiving otherwise than by this surface ; but I likewise know, that
the greatest masters, and Xenophon and Plato, often
condescend to this low and popular manner of speaking and treating of things, and yet maintaining them
with graces, which are never wanting to them.

As to the rest, my language has nothing in it that
is easy and fluent ; it is rough, free, and irregular ;
and therefore best pleases my inclination, if not my
judgment : but I very well perceive, that I sometimes give myself too much rein ; and that, by endeavouring to avoid art and affectation, I fall into
it from another quarter :

———— *Brevis esse laboro,*
Obscurus fio.†————
Striving to be concise, I prove obscure.

Plato says, " That neither the long nor the short
" are properties that ever take away or give worth
" to language." Should I attempt to follow the
other more even, smooth, and regulated style, I

---

* Montaigne only quotes this sentiment to ridicule Cicero, whom
he treats rather as a fine orator than an acute philosopher, in which
he was not much in the wrong ; for whoever nicely examines Cicero's philosophical works, will easily see, that they are only the
sentiments of Plato, Aristotle, Epicurus, Zeno, &c. elegantly and
politely translated into Latin.

† Horat. Art. Poet. ver. 25, 26.

should never attain to it; and, though the short round periods and cadences of Sallust best suit with my humour, yet I find Cæsar greater and harder to imitate; and though my inclination would rather prompt me to imitate Seneca's way of writing, yet I nevertheless more esteem that of Plutarch. Both in silence and speaking, I simply follow my own natural way; from whence, perhaps, it falls out that I am better at speaking than writing. Motion and action animate words, especially in those who lay about them briskly, as I do, and grow hot. The comportment, the countenance, the voice, the robe, and the tribunal, may set off some things that of themselves would appear no better than prating.—Messala complains, in Tacitus,* of the " Straight- " ness of some garments in his time, and of the " form of the rostra where the orators were to de- " claim, which weakened their eloquence."

His French spoiled by the dialect of his native country.

My French tongue is corrupted, both in pronunciation and language, by the barbarism of my country; I never saw a man who was a native of any of the provinces on this side of the kingdom, who had not the brogue of his place of birth, and which was not offensive to ears that were purely French; yet it is not that I am so perfect in my Perigordin; for I am no more conversant in it than High Dutch, nor do I much care.

The language of that country.

It is a language, like the rest about me on every side, those of Poitou, Xaintonge, Angoulesme, Limosin, and Auvergne, a mixed, drawling, dirty language.

The Gascon language.

There is, indeed, above us, towards the mountains, a sort of Gascon spoke that I am mightily taken with, which is dry, concise, significant, and, in truth, a more manly and military language than any other I am acquainted with; as nervous, potent, and pertinent, as the French is graceful, delicate, and copious.

---

* In his dialogue, " De Causis corruptæ Eloquentia," sub finem.

As to the Latin, which was given me for my mo- With what
ther-tongue, I have, by disuse, lost the faculty of ease he learned the
speaking it, and indeed of writing it too, wherein I Latin.
formerly excelled; by which you may see how in-
considerable I am on that side.

Beauty is a thing of great esteem in the corre- The advan-
spondence amongst men; it is the principal means tage of the beauty of
of acquiring the favour and good-liking of one ano- the body.
ther, and no man is so barbarous and morose that
does not perceive himself, in some sort, struck
with its comeliness. The body has a great share in
our being, has an eminent place there, and therefore its structure and composition are of very just
consideration. They who go about to disunite and
separate our two principal parts from one another,
are to blame; we must, on the contrary, unite and
rejoin them. We must command the soul not to
withdraw to entertain itself apart, not to despise
and abandon the body (neither can she do it, but by
some ridiculous counterfeit); but to unite herself
close to it, to embrace, cherish, assist, govern, and
advise it, and to bring it back, and set it into the
true way when it wanders; in sum, to espouse and
be a husband to it, forasmuch as their effects do not
appear to be diverse and contrary, but uniform and
concurring. Christians have a particular instruction
concerning this connection, for they know, that the
divine justice embraces this society and conjunction
of body and soul, even to the making the body capable of eternal rewards, and that God has an eye
to every man's ways, and will have him to receive
entire the chastisement or reward of his actions.—
The sect of the Peripatetics, of all others the most
sociable, attributes to wisdom this sole care, equally
to provide for and procure the good of these two
associate parts; and the other sects, in not sufficiently applying themselves to the consideration of
this union, show themselves to be partial, one for
the body and the other for the soul, with equal er-

for; and to have lost their subject, which is Man; and their guide, which they generally confess to be Nature. The first distinction that ever was amongst men, and the first consideration that gave some pre-eminence over others, it is likely, was the advantage of beauty:

> ———— *Agros diviscre, atque dedere*
> *Pro facie cujusque, et viribus, ingenioque :*
> *Nam facies multum valúat, viresque vigebant.**

> ———— Then steady bounds
> Mark'd out to ev'ry man his private grounds ;
> Each had his proper share, each one was fit,
> According to his beauty, strength, or wit ;
> For beauty then and strength had most command.

Montaigne's stature, &c. Now I am something lower than the middle stature; a defect that is not only disagreeable, but inconve-nient, especially to those who are in office and com-mand, for want of the authority derived from a graceful presence and a majestic stature. C. Marius did not, willingly, list any soldiers under six feet high. The courtier has, indeed, reason to desire a common stature in the person he is to make, rather than any other, and to reject all strangeness that should make him be pointed at ; but, in choosing, if it be necessary, in this mediocrity, to have him ra-ther below than above the common standard, I would not have a soldier to be so. " Little men," says Aristotle, " are very pretty, but not handsome; " the greatness of soul is discovered in a great " body, as beauty is in a large tall one. The Ethi-" opians and Indians," says he, " in choosing their " kings and magistrates, had a special regard to the " beauty and stature of their persons." They had reason, for it creates respect in those that follow them ; and to see a leader of a brave and godly sta-ture march at the head of a battalion strikes a terror into the enemy:

* Lucret. lib. v. ver. 1109.

Ipse inter primos præstanti corpore Turnus,
Vertitur, arma tenens, et toto vertice suprà est.[*]
The graceful Turnus, tallest by the head,
Shaking his arms, himself the warriors led.

Our holy and heavenly King, of whom every circumstance is most carefully, and with the greatest
religion and reverence, to be observed, has not himself refused bodily recommendation, *Speciosus forma*
præ filiis hominum: " He is fairer than the children
" of men."[†] And Plato, with temperance and fortitude, requires beauty in the conservators of his Republic. It would vex you, that a man should apply
himself to you, amongst your servants, to inquire
where Monsieur is, and that you should only have
the remainder of the compliment of the hat that is
made to your barber or your secretary; as it happened to poor Philopœmen, who arriving the first of
all his company at an inn where he was expected,
the hostess, who knew him not, and saw him a
mean-looking man,[‡] employed him to help her maids
to draw a little water, or make a fire against Philopœmen's coming: the gentlemen of his train arriving presently after, and surprised to see him busy
in this fine employment (for he failed not to do as
he had been bid) asked him, " What he was doing
" there?" " I am," said he, " paying the penalty of
" my ugliness." The other beauties belong to the
women, but the beauty of stature is the only beauty
of the men. Where there is a lowness of stature,
neither the largeness and roundness of the forehead,
nor fair lovely eyes, nor the moderate size of the
nose, nor the littleness of the ears and mouth, nor
the evenness and whiteness of the teeth, nor the
thickness of a well-set brown beard, shining like the
husk of a chesnut, nor curled hair, nor the just proportion of the head, nor a fresh complexion, nor a

---

[*] Virg. Æneid, lib. vii. ver. 783, &c.
[†] Psal. xlv. ver. 2.
[‡] In the Life of Philopœmen, by Plutarch, chap. 1.

pleasing air of the face, nor a body without any offensive scent, nor the just proportion of limbs, can make a handsome man.

I am, as to the rest, strong and well knit; my face is not puffed, but full; my complexion between jovial and melancholic, moderately sanguine and hot:

> *Unde rigent setis mihi crura, et pectora villis.* *
> Whence 'tis my thighs so rough and bristled are,
> And that my breast is so thick-set with hair.

My health vigorous and sprightly, even to a well advanced age, and rarely troubled with sickness.— Such I was, I say, for I do not make any reckoning of myself now that I am engaged in the avenues of old age, being already past forty:

> —— *Minutatim vires, et robur adultum*
> *Frangit, et in partem pejorem liquitur ætas.†*
> Thence, by degrees, our strength melts all away,
> And treach'rous age creeps on, and things decay.

What I shall be from this time forward will be but a half being, and no more me; I every day escape and steal away from myself:

> *Singula de nobis anni prædantur euntes.‡*
> Every year steals something from us.

Agility and address I never had, and yet am the son of a very active and sprightly father, who continued to be so to an extreme old age; I have seldom known any man of his condition his equal in all bodily exercises; as I have seldom met with any who have not excelled me, except in running, at which I was pretty good. In music or singing, for which I have a very unfit voice, or to play on any sort of instrument, they could never teach me any thing. In dancing, tennis, or wrestling, I could never arrive to more than an ordinary pitch; in

---

* Mart. lib. ii. ep. 36, ver. 5.   † Lucret. lib. ii. ver. 1130.
‡ Hor. lib. ii. ep. 2, ver. 55.

swimming, fencing, vaulting, and leaping, to none
at all. My hands are so benumbed that I can only
write so as to read it myself; so that I had rather
mend what I have scribbled, than to take the trouble
to write it over fair; and I do not read much better
than I write. I cannot handsomely fold up a letter,
nor could ever make a pen, or carve at table, nor
saddle a horse, nor carry a hawk and fly her, nor
call the dogs, nor speak to birds, nor horses. In
fine, my bodily qualities are very well suited to those
of my soul; there is nothing sprightly, only a full
and firm vigour: I am patient enough of labour
and pains, provided I go voluntarily to the work,
and only so long as my own desire prompts me
to it:

> *Molliter austerum studio fallente laborem.**
> Whilst the delight makes you ne'er mind the pain.

Otherwise, if I am not allured with some pleasure,
or have any other guide than my own pure and free
inclination, I am therein good for nothing; for I
am of a humour that, life and health excepted,
there is nothing for which I will beat my brains,
and that I will purchase at the price of vexation and
constraint:

> ———— *Tanti mihi non sit opaci*
> *Omnis arena Tagi, quodque in mare volvitur aurum.†*
> Rich Tagus' sands so dear I would not buy,
> Nor all the riches in the sea that lie.

Being extremely idle, and quite unrestrained both
by nature and art, I would as willingly lend a man
my blood as my pains. I have a soul free and entirely its own, and accustomed to guide itself after
its own fashion; and having hitherto never had
either master or governor set over me, I have walked
as far as I would, and the pace that best pleased

---

* Hor. lib. ii. sat. 2, ver. 12.   † Juv. sat. iii. ver. 54, 55.

myself; this is it that has rendered me effeminate, and of no use to any but myself.

He was contented with his condition. And, for my part, there was no need of forcing my heavy and lazy disposition; for being born to such a fortune as I had reason to be contented with (a reason, nevertheless, which a thousand others of my acquaintance would have rather made use of for a plank upon which to pass over to a higher fortune, to tumult and disquiet), I sought for no more, and also got no more:

> Non agimur tumidis ventis, Aquilone secundo,
> Non tamen adversis ætatem ducimus Austris :
> Viribus, ingenio, specie, virtute, loco, re,
> Extremi primorum, extremis usque priores.*
>
> I am not wafted by the swelling gales
> Of winds propitious, with expanded sails;
> Nor yet expos'd to tempest bearing strife,
> Adrift to struggle through the ways of life;
> For health, wit, virtue, honour, wealth, I'm cast
> Behind the foremost, but before the last.

I wanted but a competency to content me; which, nevertheless, is a government of soul, to take it right, equally difficult in all sorts of conditions, and which, by custom, we see more easily found in want than abundance; forasmuch, perhaps, as, according to the course of our other passions, the desire of riches is more sharpened by the use we make of them, than by the need we have of them, and the virtue of moderation more rare than that of patience. I never had any thing to desire, but quietly to enjoy the estate that God, by his bounty, had put into my hands; I have never known any work that was troublesome, and have had little to manage besides my own affairs; or, if I have, it has been upon condition to manage them at my own leisure, and after my own method, they having been committed to my trust by such as had a confidence in me, that did

* Hor. lib. ii. ep. 2, ver. 201.

not importune me, and that knew me well; for
men of experience will get service out of a resty
and broken-winded horse.

I was trained up from a child after a gentle and
free manner, and, even then, exempt from any rigorous subjection; all this has helped me to a complexion delicate and careless, even to such a degree
that I love to have my losses, and the disorders
wherein I am concerned, concealed from me; in
the account of my expenses I put down what my
negligence costs me to feed and maintain it:

> ———— *Hæc nempe supersunt,*
> *Quæ dominum fallunt, quæ profint furibus.*[*]

> ———— Where no superfluous wealth unknown
> To its rich lord,[†] that thieves may make their own.

I do not care to know what I have, that I may be
less sensible of my loss; I intreat those that live
with me, where affection and good deeds are wanting, to deceive me, and put me off with something
that may look tolerably well. For want of resolution
enough to support the shock of the adverse accidents to which we are subject; and seriously applying myself to the management of my affairs, I indulge this opinion as much as I can, wholly leaving
it all to fortune; to take all things at the worst, and
to resolve to bear that worst with meekness and patience; that is the only thing I aim at, and to which
I apply my whole meditation; in danger, I do not
so much consider how I shall escape it, as of how
little importance it is whether I escape it or no;
should I be left dead upon the place, what matter?
Not being to govern events I govern myself, and
apply myself to them, if they do not apply themselves to me. I have no great art to turn off, escape
from, or to force, fortune, and wisely to guide and

[*] Hor. lib. i. ep. 6, ver. 45.
[†] Here Montaigne diverts Horace's words from their true sense,
to adapt them to his own thought.

z 2

incline things to my own bias; I have yet less patience to undergo the troublesome and painful care
therein required; and the most uneasy condition
for me is to be kept in suspense on urgent occasions,
and to be agitated between hope and fear.

He was an
enemy to
delibera-
tion. Deliberation, even in things of lightest moment,
is very troublesome to me; and I find my mind
more put to it, to undergo the various tumbling and
tossing of doubt and consultation, than to set up
its rest, and to acquiesce in whatever shall happen
after the die is thrown. Few passions break my
sleep; but, of deliberations, the least disturbs me.
As, in the roads, I willingly avoid those that are
sloping and slippery, and put myself into the beaten
track, how dirty or deep soever, where I can fall
no lower, and there seek my safety; so I love misfortunes that are purely so, such as do not torment
and teaze me with the uncertainty of their growing
better; but, at the first push, plunge me directly
into the worst that can be expected:

*Dubia plus torquent mala.**
Doubtful ills do plague us worst.

In events, I carry myself like a man, in the conduct
of them like a child; the fear of the fall more
shakes me than the fall itself; it will not quit cost.
The covetous man fares worse with his passion than
the poor man, and the jealous man than the cuckold; and a person oft-times loses more by defending
his vineyard than if he gave it up. The lowest
walk is the safest, it is the seat of constancy; you
have there need of no one but yourself, it is there
founded, and wholly stands upon its own basis.—
Has not this example, of a gentleman very well
known, some air of philosophy in it? He married,
being well advanced in years, having spent his youth
in good-fellowship, a great talker, and a free joker;
and calling to mind how much the subject of cuck-

* Senec. Agamemnon; act iii. sc. 1, ver. 29.

oldom had given him occasion to talk of and banter
others, in order to prevent them from paying him in
his own coin, he married a wife from a place where
any man may have flesh for his money : " Good-
" morrow whore ; good-morrow cuckold ;" and
there was not any thing wherewith he more commonly and openly entertained those that came to see
him, than with this design of his, by which he stopped the private muttering of mockers, and blunted
the edge of this reproach.

As to ambition, which is neighbour, or rather *Disgusted*
daughter, to presumption, fortune, to advance me, *at ambi-*
must have come and taken me by the hand ; for to *cause of its*
trouble myself for an uncertain hope, and to have *uncertain-*
submitted myself to all the difficulties that accom- *ty.*
pany those who endeavour to bring themselves into
credit, in the beginning of their progress, is what I
never could have done :

—————— *Spem pretio non emo.**

I will not purchase hope with money.

I apply myself to what I see, and to what I have in
my hand, and scarce stir out of my harbour :

Alter remus aquas, alter tibi radat arenas.†

Into the sea I plunge one oar,
And with the other rake the shore.

Besides a man rarely arrives to these advancements,
but in first hazarding what he has of his own ; and
I am of opinion, that if a man have sufficient to
maintain him in the condition wherein he was born
and bred, it is a great folly to hazard that upon the
uncertainty of augmenting it. He to whom fortune
has denied whereon to set his foot, and a quiet and
composed establishment, is to be excused if he ven-
tures what he has ; because, happen what will, necessity puts him upon shifting for himself :

* Terent. Adelph. act ii. sc. 2, ver. 11.
† Prop. lib. iii. el. 3, ver. 23.

*Capienda rebus in malis præceps via est.**
A desperate case must have a desperate course.

I rather excuse a younger brother to expose what his friends have left him to the courtesy of fortune, than him with whom the honour of his family is entrusted, who cannot be necessitous but by his own fault. I found a much shorter and more easy way, by the advice of the good friends I had in my younger days, to free myself from any such ambition, and to sit still:

Cui fit conditio dulcis, sine pulvere palmæ.†
Too happy in his country seat,
To gain the palm with dust and sweat.

Judging also rightly enough of my own abilities, that they were not capable of any great matters, and calling to mind the saying of the late chancellor Olivier, " That the French were like monkies, that " climb up a tree from branch to branch, and never " stop till they come to the highest, and there show " their breech."

Turpe est quod nequeas capiti committere pondus,
Et pressum inflexo mox dare terga genu.‡
It is a shame to load the shoulders so,
That they the burden cannot undergo;
And, the knees bending with the weight, to quit
The pond'rous load, and turn the back to it.

The age in which Montaigne was born not at all agreeable to his humour.

I should find the best qualities I have useless in these times; my easy behaviour would have been called weakness and negligence; my faith and conscience, scrupulosity and superstition; my liberty and freedom would have been reputed troublesome, inconsiderate, and rash: " Ill luck is good for " something." It is good to be born in a very depraved age; for so, in comparison of others, you

* Senec. Agamem. act ii. ver. 47.
† Horat. lib. i. epist. 1, ver. 51.
‡ Propert. lib. iii. el. 9, ver. 5, 6.

shall be reputed virtuous very cheap. He that, in
our days, is a parricide and a sacrilegious person, is
an honest man, and a man of honour:

Nunc si depositum non inficiatur amicus,
Si reddat veterem cum tota ærugine follem,
Prodigiosa fides, et Tuscis digna libellis,
Quæque coronata lustrari debeat agna. *

Now if a friend infringes not his trust,
But the old purse restores with all its rust ;
'Tis a prodigious faith, that ought, in gold,
Amongst the Tuscan annals be enroll'd ;
And a crown'd lamb should on the altar bleed,
In honour of the meritorious deed.

Never was there a time or place wherein princes
might expect more certain or greater rewards for
their virtue and justice. The first that shall make it
his business to get himself into favour and esteem
by those ways, I am much deceived if he do not
fairly get the start of his companions. Force and
violence can do some things, but not all; we see
merchants, country justices, and artisans, go cheek
by jowl with the best gentry in valour and military
knowledge ; they perform honourable actions, both
public and private ; they fight duels, and defend
towns in our present wars. A prince stifles his renown in this crowd; let him shine bright in humanity, truth, loyalty, temperance, and especially in
justice ; characters rare and almost unknown ; it is
by the sole good-will of the people that he can do
his business, and no other qualities can attract their
good-will like those, as being of greatest utility to
them. *Nil est tam populare quam bonitas.*† " No-
" thing is so popular as goodness." By this proportion I had been great and rare, as I find myself now
a pigmy, and vulgar in proportion to some past
ages ; wherein, if other better qualities did not concur, it was common to see a man moderate in his

* Juv. sat. xiii. ver. 60, &c.
† Cicero pro Ligario, cap. 12.

revenges, gentle in resenting injuries, true to his
word, neither double nor supple, nor accommodating his faith to the will of others, and the turns of
times : I would rather see all affairs go to wreck and
ruin than falsify my faith to secure them.

Dissimula-
tion an
odious
vice, which
Montaigne
held in the
utmost ab-
horrence.

For as to this virtue of hypocrisy and dissimulation, which is now in so great request, I mortally
hate it ; and of all vices find none that show such
baseness and meanness of spirit ; it is a cowardly
and servile humour for a man to hide and disguise
himself under a vizor, and not dare to show himself
what he is. By this our followers are trained up to
treachery ; being brought up to speak what is not
true, they make no conscience of a lie ; a generous
heart ought not to give the lie to its own thoughts,
but will make itself seen within, where all is good,
or, at least, humane. Aristotle reputes it " The
" office of magnanimity openly and professedly to
" love and hate, to judge and speak with all free-
" dom ; and not to value the approbation or dislike
" of others, at the expense of truth." Apollonius said, " It was for slaves to lie, and for freemen
" to speak truth." It is the chief and fundamental
part of virtue ; we must love it for its own sake ; he
that speaks the truth, because he is otherwise obliged
so to do, and because he serves, and that is not
afraid to lie, when it signifies nothing to any body,

Lying con-
demned.

is not sufficiently true. My soul naturally abomi-
nates lying, and hates the very thought of it ; I
have an inward bashfulness, and a smart remorse, if
ever a lie escapes me, as sometimes it does, being
surprised and hurried by occasions that allow me no
premeditation. A man must not always tell all, for
that were folly ; but what a man says should be
what he thinks, otherwise it is knavery ; I do not
know what advantage men pretend to by eternally
counterfeiting and dissembling, if not never to be
believed, even when they speak the truth. This
may, once or twice, pass upon men ; but to profess
concealing their thoughts, and to boast, as some of

9

our princes have done, " That they would burn
" their shirts if they knew their true intentions ;"
which was a saying of the ancient Metellus of Macedon ; and, " That he who knows not how to dis-
" semble knows not how to rule." This is giving
warning to all who have any thing to do with them,
that all they say is nothing but lying and deceit.—
*Quo quis versutior, et callidior est, hoc invisior et
suspectior, detracta opinione probitatis :*[*] " The more
" subtle and cunning any one is, the more is he
" hated and suspected, the opinion of his integrity
" being lost and gone." It were a great simplicity
to any one to lay any stress either on the countenance or word of a man that has put on a resolution
to be always another thing without than he is within,
as Tiberius did ; and I cannot conceive what interest such can have in the conversation with men,
seeing they produce nothing that is admitted for
truth ; whoever is disloyal to truth is the same to
falsehood also.

Those of our time who have considered, in the
establishment of the duty of a prince, the welfare of
his affairs only, and have preferred that to the care
of his faith and conscience, might say something to
a prince, whose affairs fortune had put into such a
posture, that he might for ever establish them by
only once breaking his word ; but it will not go so,
they often come again to the same market, they
make more than one peace, and enter into more
than one treaty in their lives. Gain tempts them
to the first breach of faith, and almost always presents itself, as to all other ill acts ; sacrileges, murders, rebellions, treasons, are undertaken for some
kind of advantage ; but this first gain has infinite
mischievous consequences, as it throws the prince out
of all correspondence and negotiation, by the example of infidelity. Solyman, of the Ottoman race,
a race not very solicitous of keeping their promises

Of what importance it is to princes to avoid knavery.

---

[*] *Cic. de Offic. lib. ii. cap. 9.*

or articles, when, in my infancy, he made a descent
with his army at Otranto, being informed that Mer-
curino de Gratinare and the inhabitants of Castro
were detained prisoners, after having surrendered
the place, contrary to the articles of their capitulation with his forces, he sent an order to have them
set at liberty, saying, " That, having other great
" enterprises in hand in those parts, this breach of
" faith, though it carried a show of present utility,
" would, for the future, bring on him a disrepute
" and diffidence of infinite prejudice."

Montaigne
naturally
open and
free with
great men.

Now, for my part, I had rather be troublesome
and indiscreet, than a flatterer and a dissembler : I
confess, that there may be some mixture of pride
and obstinacy, in keeping myself so resolute and
open as I do, without any regard to others ; and,
methinks, I am a little too free, where I ought least
to be so ; and that I grow hot, if I meet not with
respect : it may be also, that I suffer myself to follow the propensity of my own nature for want of
art ; when I bring the same liberty of speech and
countenance to great persons, that I use at my own
house, I am sensible how much it declines towards
incivility and indiscretion : but, besides that I am
so bred, I have not a wit supple enough to shift off
from a sudden question, and to escape by some
crafty avoidance ; nor to feign a truth, nor memory
enough to retain it, so feigned ; nor, truly, assurance enough to maintain it ; and yet, weak as I
am, I stand on terms : therefore it is that I resign
myself to pure nature, always to speak as I think,
both by complexion and design, leaving the event
to fortune. Aristippus* was wont to say, " That
" the principal benefit he had extracted from philo-
" sophy, was, that he spoke freely and openly to
" all."

Memory is a faculty of wonderful use, and without which the judgment very hardly performs its

* Laertius, in the Life of Aristippus, lib. ii. sect. 68.

office; for my part, I have none at all: what any
one will propose to me, he must do it by parcels,
for, to answer a speech consisting of several heads,
I am not able. I could not receive a commission,
without entering it into a book; and when I have
a speech of consequence to make, if it be long, I am
reduced to the vile and miserable necessity of get-
ting, word for word, what I am to say, by heart; I
should, otherwise, have neither method nor assurance, being in fear that my memory would play me
a slippery trick: but this way is no less difficult to
me than the other: I must have three hours to learn
three verses: And, besides, in a work of man's own,
the liberty and authority of altering the order, of
changing a word, incessantly varying the matter,
makes it harder to retain in the author's memory.
The more I mistrust it, the more confused it is; it
serves me best by chance; I must negligently solicit
it, for, if I strive for it, it is confounded: and, after
it once begins to stagger, the more I sound it, the
more it is perplexed and embarrassed; it serves me
at its own hour, not at mine.

Memory very useful to the judgment, but Montaigne's was very treacherous.

The same defect I find in my memory I perceive
also in several other parts. I cannot endure command, obligation, and constraint: that which I can
otherwise naturally and easily do, if I impose it
upon myself by an express and strict injunction, I
cannot do it: even the members of my body, over
which a man has a more particular freedom and jurisdiction, sometimes refuse to obey me, if I enjoin
them a necessary service at a certain hour: this
compulsive and tyrannical appointment baffles them;
they shrink up either through fear or spite, and are
benumbed.

He was an enemy to all obligation and constraint.

Being once in a place, where it is looked upon as
the greatest rudeness imaginable not to pledge those
that drink to you; though I had there all the freedom allowed me, I tried to play the good-fellow, out
of respect to the ladies that were there, according
to the custom of the country; but there was sport

enough; for this threatening and preparation, that I
was to force upon myself, contrary to my custom
and inclination, did so stop my throat, that I could
not swallow one drop, and was deprived of drinking
so much as at my meal: I found myself gorged, and
my thirst quenched by so much drink as I had swallowed in imagination. This effect is most manifest
in such as have the most vehement and powerful
imagination: but it is natural notwithstanding, and
there is no one that does not, in some measure, find
it. An offer was made to an excellent archer, condemned to die, to save his life, if he would show
some notable proof of his art; but he refused to try,
fearing lest the too great contention of his will
should make him shoot wide, and that, instead of
saving his life, he should also lose the reputation
he had got of being a good marksman. A man that
thinks of something else, will not fail to take, over
and over again, the same number and measure of
steps, even to an inch, in the place where he walks:
but, if he makes it his business to measure and count
them, he will find, that what he did by nature and
accident, he cannot so exactly do by design.

How de-
fective
M in-
taigne's
memory
was.

My library, which is of the best sort of country
libraries, is situated in a corner of my house; if
any thing comes into my head, that I have a mind
to look for, or to write out, lest I should forget it,
in but going across the court, I am forced to commit it to the memory of some other. If I venture,
in speaking, to digress never so little from my subject, I am infallibly lost; which is the reason, that,
in discourse, I keep strictly close to my text. I am
forced to call the men, that serve me, either by the
names of their offices, or their country; for their
own names are very hard for me to remember: I
can tell, indeed, that a name has three syllables,
that it has a harsh sound, and that it begins or ends
with such a letter; but that's all; and, if I should
live long, I do not think but I should forget my
own name, as some others have done. Messala Cor-

vinus was two years without any trace of memory,* which is also said of Georgius Trapezuntius. For my own interest, I often think what a kind of life theirs was, and whether, without this faculty, I should have enough left to support me with any manner of ease; and prying narrowly into it, I fear that this privation, if absolute, destroys all the other functions of the soul:

Plenus rimarum sum, hac atque illac perfluo.†
I'm as a leaky vessel, that runs out every way.

It has befallen me, more than once, to forget the word I had, three hours before, given or received, and the place where I had hid my purse, whatever Cicero is pleased to say to the contrary. I am mighty apt to lose what I have a particular care to lock safe up: *Memoria certe non modo philosophiam, sed omnis vitæ usum, omnesque artes, una maxime continet:‡* "The memory is the receptacle and "sheath of all science;" and therefore mine being so treacherous, if I know little, I cannot much complain: I know, in general, the names of the arts, and of what they treat, but nothing more: I turn over books, I do not study them; what I retain of them I do not know to be another's: it is this only of which my judgment has made its advantage, the discourses and imaginations with which it has been possessed. The author, place, words, and other circumstances, I immediately forget, and am so excellent at forgetting, that I no less forget my own writings and compositions than the rest. At every turn I quote myself, and am not aware of it; and whoever should ask me, where I had the verses and examples that I have here huddled together, would puzzle me to tell him, and yet I have not begged

The author's memory.

---

* Plin. Nat. Hist. lib. vii. cap. 4.
† Terent. Eunuch. act. i. sc. 2. ver. 25.
‡ Cic. de Senect. cap. 7.

them but from famous and well-known authors; not satisfying myself that they were rich, if I, moreover, had them not from hands both rich and honourable, where authority and reason concurred together: it is no great wonder, if my book meets with the same fortune that other books do, and if my memory lose what I have writ as well as what I have read, and what I give as well as what I receive.

The character of Montaigne's genius. Besides the defect of memory, I have others which very much contribute to my ignorance; I have a slow and heavy wit, the least cloud stops its progress, so that, for example, I never proposed a riddle to it, though ever so easy, that it could find out: there is not the least idle subtlety, that will not gravel me: in games where cunning is required, as cards, chess, draughts, and the like, I understand only the common tricks and movements: I have a slow and perplexed apprehension, but what it once catches, it embraces, and holds thoroughly well, for His sight. the time it retains it. My sight is perfectly clear, and discovers at a very great distance, but is soon weary; which makes me that I cannot read long, but am forced to have one to read to me. The younger Pliny* can inform such as have not tried it, what a considerable impediment this is to those who addict themselves to books: there is not so wretched a brute, who has not some particular shining faculty; no soul so buried in sloth and ignorance, but it will sally at one time or another: and how it comes to pass, that a man, blind and asleep to every

---

* Montaigne seems here to have had in view the fifth epistle of Pliny, lib. iii. wherein giving an account to a friend of his, how old Pliny, his uncle, spent his time in study; he observes, that, one day as his uncle was reading a book to his friend, and the latter stopping him, to desire him to repeat certain words, which he had mispronounced, his uncle said to him, "What! did not you understand " the meaning?" "Undoubtedly," said his friend. "And why " then," said he, "did you stop the reader? We have lost above " ten lines by your interruption." So great a husband was he of his time.

thing else, shall be found sprightly, clear, and excellent in some one particular purpose, we are to inquire of our masters.

But the choice spirits are they that are universal, His igno-
open, and ready for all things; if not instructed, at the most
least capable of being so: this I say to accuse my common
own; for, whether it be through infirmity or negligence (and to neglect that which lies at our feet,
which we have in our hands, and what most nearly
concerns the use of life, is far from my doctrine),
there is not a soul in the world so awkward and ignorant as mine, of several vulgar things, and things or
which it is even a shame to be ignorant.

I must give some examples of this: I was born
and bred in the country, and amongst husbandmen;
I have had business and husbandry in my own hands,
ever since my predecessors, who were lords of the
estate I now enjoy, left me to succeed them; and
yet I cannot cast up a sum, either by pen or coun-
ters: I do not know most of our coins, nor the difference between one grain and another, either growing, or in the barn, if it be not too apparent; and
scarcely can distinguish the cabbage and lettuce in
my garden: I do not so much as understand the
names of the chief instruments of husbandry, nor
the most ordinary elements of agriculture, which
the very children know; much less the mechanic
arts, traffic, merchandise, the variety and nature of
fruits, wines, and meats; nor how to make a hawk
fly, nor to physic a horse, or a dog. And since I
must publish my whole shame, it is not above a
month ago, that I was trapped in my ignorance of the
use of leaven to make bread, or to what end it was to
keep wine in the vat. They conjectured, of old,
at Athens,* that a man, whom they saw dexterously

* If Montaigne quoted this from his memory, as is highly probable, he was mistaken in fixing the fact at Athens; for, according to
Diogenes Laertius, lib. ix. sect. 53, it was Protagoras, of Abdera,
who being observed by Democritus to be very ingenious at making
faggots, he thought him capable of attaining to the sublimest

make a faggot of brush-wood, had a genius for the
mathematics. In earnest, they would draw a quite
contrary conclusion from me; for to give me all the
necessaries of a kitchen, I would starve. By these
features of my confession, men may imagine others
to my prejudice; but whatever I deliver myself to
be, provided it be such as I really am, I have my
end; neither will I make any excuse for committing
such mean and frivolous things as these to paper:
the meanness of the subject compels me to it. They
may, if they please, accuse my project, but not my
progress. So it is, that, without any-body's telling
me, I plainly see of how little weight and value all
this is, and the folly of my design. It is enough
that my judgment does not contradict itself, in these
my Essays:

> *Nasutus sis usque licet, sis denique nasus,*
> *Quantum noluerit ferre rogatus Atlas;*
> *Et possis ipsum tu deridere Latinum,*
> *Non potes in nugas dicere plura meas,*
> *Ipse ego quam dixi: quid dentem dente juvabit*
> *Rodere? Carne opus est, si satur esse velis:*
> *Ne perdas operam, qui se mirantur, in illos*
> *Virus habe, nos hæc novimus esse nihil.**

> Be nos'd, be all nose, till thy nose appear
> So great, that Atlas it refuse to bear;
> Though ev'n against Latinus thou inveigh,
> Against my trifles thou no more canst say
> Than I have said myself: then to what end
> Should we to render tooth for tooth contend?
> You must have flesh, if you'll be full, my friend,
> Lose not thy labour; but on those that do
> Admire themselves thy utmost venom throw;
> That these things nothing are, full well we know.

I am not obliged to utter absurdities, provided I
am not deceived in them, and know them to be

---

sciences, and took care therein to instruct him. From hence it
is very likely, that this was not at Athens, but at Abdera, which
was the country both of Protagoras and Democritus; and Aulus
Gellius expressly says so, lib. v. cap. 3.
  * Mart. lib. xiii. epig. 2.

such; and to trip knowingly is so ordinary with me, that I seldom do it otherwise, and rarely trip by chance: it is no great matter to add ridiculous actions to the temerity of my humour, since I cannot ordinarily help supplying it with those that are vicious. ^{His fickleness.}

I was one day at Barleduc, when king Francis the second, for a memorial of Rene, king of Sicily, was presented with a picture he had drawn of himself. Why is it not, in like manner, lawful for every one to draw himself with a pen, as he did with a crayon? I will not therefore omit this blemish, though very unfit to be published, which is irresolution; a defect very detrimental in the negotiations of the affairs of the world: in doubtful enterprises, I know not what to resolve on: ^{The picture of Rene, king of Sicily, drawn by himself.}

Ne si, ne no, nel cor mi suona intero.

I can't, from my heart, pronounce yes, or no.

I can maintain an opinion, but I cannot choose one, by reason that, in human things, to what party soever a man inclines, many appearances present themselves, that confirm us in it; and the philosopher Chrysippus said,[*] " That he would only learn " the doctrines of Zeno and Cleanthes, his masters; " for as to proofs and reasons, he would find enough " of his own:" which way soever I turn, I still furnish myself with cause, and probability, enough to fix me there; which makes me detain doubt, and the liberty of choosing, till occasion presses me; and then, to confess the truth, I, for the most part, throw the feather into the wind, as the saying is, and commit myself to the mercy of fortune; a very light inclination and circumstance carries me along with it:

Dum in dubio est animus, paulo momento huc atque illus impellitur.[†]

[*] Diog. Laert. in the Life of Chrysippus, lib. vii. sect. 179.
[†] Terent. Andr. act. i. sc. 6. ver. 32.

> While he is divided in his mind, a little matter will turn him
> one way, or the other.

The uncertainty of my judgment is so equally balanced in most occurrences, that I could willingly
refer it to be decided by lot, or the turn of a die:
and I observe, with great consideration of our human infirmity, the examples that the divine history
itself has left us of this custom of referring the determination of elections, in doubtful things, to fortune and chance: *Sors cecidit super Mutthiam :* [*]
" The lot fell upon Matthias." Human reason is
a two-edged and a dangerous sword: observe, in
the hand of Socrates, its most intimate and familiar
friend, how many several points it has. I am also
good for nothing but to follow, and suffer myself to
be easily carried away with the crowd: I have not
confidence enough in my own strength to take upon
me to command and lead: I am very glad to find
the way beaten before me by others: if I must run
the hazard of an uncertain choice, I am rather willing to have it under such a one as is more confident
in his opinions than I am in mine, whose ground
and foundation I find to be very slippery.

Not given
to change,
with regard
to state af-
fairs.

Yet I do not easily change, by reason that I discern the same weakness in contrary opinions. *Ipsa
consuetudo assentiendi periculosa esse videtur, et lu-
brica :*[†] " The very custom of assenting seems to be
" dangerous and slippery." Especially in political
affairs, there is a large field open for wavering and
dispute :

> *Justa pari premitur veluti cùm pondere libra,*
> *Prona nec hac plus parte sedet, nec surgit ab illa.*[‡]
>
> Like a just balance press'd with equal weight,
> Nor dips, nor rises, but the beam is straight.

Machiavel's writings, for example, were solid enough
for the subject, yet they were easy enough to be

* Acts, chap. i. ver. 26.   † Cic. Acad. lib. iv. cap. 21.
‡ Tibullus, lib. iv. Panegyr. ad Messalam, ver. 41, 42.

controverted; and they who have taken up the cud-
gels against him, have left it as easy to controvert
theirs. There were never wanting, in that kind of
argument, replies upon replies, *rejoindres sur rejoindres*, and that infinite contexture of debates,
which our wrangling pettifoggers have spun out in
favour of law-suits:

Cædimur, et totidem plagis consumimus hostem.[*]
By turns the foe beats us, and we the foe,
Dealing to each, alternate, blow for blow.

Reasons having little other foundation therein than
experience, and the variety of human events presenting us with infinite examples of all sorts of forms.
An understanding person, of our times, says, " That
" whoever would, in contradiction to our almanacks,
" write cold where they say hot, and wet where
" they say dry, and always put the contrary to what
" they foretel; if he were to lay a wager on the
" events, he would not care which side he took, ex-
" cepting things wherein no uncertainty could fall
" out; as to promise excessive heats at Christmas,
" or extremity of cold at Midsummer, which can-
" not possibly be." I have the same opinion of
these political controversies; be on which side you
will, you have as fair a game to play as your adversary, provided you do not proceed so far as
to jostle principles that are too manifest to be
disputed: yet, in my opinion, in public affairs
there is no management so ill, provided it be ancient, and has been constant, that is not better
than change and motion. Our manners are extremely corrupted, and wonderfully incline to the
worse: of our laws and customs, there are many
that are barbarous and monstrous: nevertheless, by
reason of the difficulty of reformation, and the danger of stirring things, if I could put a peg to the

* Hor. lib. ii. epist. 2, ver. 97.
2 A 2

wheel, and keep it where it is, I would do it withall my heart:

> —— *Nunquam adeo fœdis adeoque pudendis*
> *Utimur exemplis, ut non pejora supersint.**
>
> Bad as the instances we give, 'tis plain,
> Others might be produc'd of fouler stain.

The worst thing I find in our state, is the instability of it; and that our laws, no more than our old clothes, cannot settle in any certain form. It is very easy to accuse a government of imperfection, for all mortal things are full of it: it is very easy to beget in a people a contempt of ancient observances; never any man undertook it, but he did it; but to establish a better regimen in the stead of that which a man has overthrown, many who have attempted it, have been baffled. I very little consult my prudence in my conduct; I am willing to be guided by the public rule: happy people, who do what they are commanded better than they who command, without tormenting themselves with the causes; who suffer themselves gently to roll with the celestial revolution; obedience is never pure nor calm in him who argues and disputes.

Upon what Montaigne's esteem of himself is founded. In fine, to return to myself, the only thing by which I esteem myself to be something, is that wherein never any man thought himself to be defective; my recommendation is vulgar and common, for who ever supposed he wanted sense? It would be a proposition that would imply a contradiction in itself; it is a disease that never is where it is discerned; it is tenacious and strong, but a disease, nevertheless, which the first ray of the patient's sight pierces through, and disperses, as the beams of the sun do thick mists. To accuse one's self would be to excuse, in this case; and to condemn, to absolve. There never was a porter, or the silliest wench, that

---

* Juv. sat. viii. ver. 183.

did not think they had sense enough to do their business. We readily enough confess an advantage of
courage, strength, experience, good-nature, and
beauty in others; but an advantage in judgment we
yield to none, and the reasons that simply proceed
from the natural sense of others, we think, if we had
but turned our thoughts that way, we should ourselves have found them out. As for knowledge,
style, and such parts as we see in others' works, we
are soon sensible if they excel our own; but, for the
mere products of the understanding, every one thinks
he could have found out the like, and is hardly sensible of the weight and difficulty, if not (and then
with much ado) in an extreme and incomparable distance: and whoever could be able clearly to discern
the height of another's judgment, would be also able
to raise his own to the same pitch; so that it is a
sort of exercise, from which a man is to expect very
little praise, and a kind of composition of small repute: besides, for whom do you write? The learned, Whether a
to whom the authority appertains of judging books, person is to
know nothing valuable but learning, and allow of no self for his
other progress in our minds but that of erudition and writings.
art. If you have mistaken one of the Scipios for
another, what is all the rest you have to say worth?
Whoever is ignorant of Aristotle, according to their
rule, is, in the same measure, ignorant of himself:
heavy and vulgar souls cannot discern the grace of
refined reasoning: now, these two classes constitute
the bulk of mankind. The third sort, into whose
hands you fall, of souls that are regular and strong
of themselves, is so rare, that it justly has neither
name nor place amongst us; and it is so much time
lost to aspire to it, or endeavour to please it.

It is commonly said, that the justest dividend na- What
ture has given us of her favours, is that of sense, for Montaigne
there is no one that is not contented with his share: had for
is it not for this reason? Whoever could discern be- his opi-
yond that, would see beyond his sight. I think my nions right.
opinions are good and sound; but who does not

think the same of his? One of the best proofs I have
that mine are so, is the small esteem I have of myself; for, had they not been very well settled, they
would easily have suffered themselves to have been
deceived by the peculiar affection I bear to myself,
as one that reduces it almost wholly to myself,
and does not let scarce any run by. All that others
distribute of it amongst an infinite number of friends
and acquaintance, to their glory and grandeur, I dedicate wholly to the repose of my own mind, and to
myself. That which escapes of it from me, is not
properly by the rule of my reason :

> *Mihi nempe valere, et vivere doctus.* *
> To love myself I very well can tell,
> So as to live content, and to be well.

Now I find my opinions very bold and constant, in
condemning my own imperfection; and, to say the
truth, it is a subject upon which I exercise my judgment, as much as upon any other. The world looks
always opposite; I turn my sight inwards, there fix
and employ it : every one looks before him, I look
into myself; I have no other business but myself; I
am eternally meditating upon myself, control and
taste myself: other men's thoughts are ever wandering abroad; if they set themselves to serious thinking, they are always looking before them :

> *Nemo in sese tentat descendere.* †
> No man attempts to dive into himself.

For my part, I wheel myself in my own sphere : and
this capacity of trying the truth, whatever it be, in
me, and this free humour of not easily subjecting my
belief, I owe principally to myself; for the strongest
and most general imaginations I have, are those
that, as a man may say, were born with me ; they are
natural, and entirely my own : I produced them
crude and simple, in a strong and bold manner, but
a little confused and imperfect ; I have since esta-

* Lucret. lib. v. ver. 958.   † Pers. sat. iv. ver. 23.

blished and fortified them with the authority of others, and by the sound examples of the ancients, whom I have found of the same judgment: they have given me faster hold, and a clearer enjoyment and possession of it; the reputation that every one courts of vivacity and readiness of wit, I aim at from regularity; the glory they pretend to from a brave and signal action, of some particular ability, I claim from order, correspondence, and tranquillity, of opinions and manners. *Omnino si quidquam est decorum, nihil est profecto magis quàm æquabilitas universæ vitæ, tum singularum actionum: quam conservare non possis, si aliorum naturam imitans, omittas tuam :* [*] " If " any thing be entirely decent, nothing certainly " can be more, than an uniformity of the whole life, " and in every particular action of it; which thou " canst not possibly preserve, if, in imitating other " men's, thou neglectest to cultivate thy own genius." Here then you see to what degree I find myself guilty of this, which I said was the first part of the vice of Presumption.

As to the second, which consists in not having a sufficient esteem for others, I know not whether I can so well excuse myself; but, whatever comes of it, I am resolved to speak the truth: and whether perhaps, it be, that the continual acquaintance I have had with the humours of the ancients, and the idea of those great souls of past ages, disgusted me, both with others and myself; or that, in truth, the age we live in produces but very indifferent things; yet so it is, that I see nothing worthy of any great admiration; neither, indeed, have I such an intimacy with many men, as is requisite to form a judgment of them; and those with whom my condition makes me the most frequent, are for the most part, men that take little care of the culture of the mind, but look upon honour as the sum of all blessings, and valour as the height of all perfection.

Montaigne not much prepossessed in favour of his own times.

* Cic. Offic. lib. i. cap. 31.

He loved
to com-
mend me-
rit, whe-
ther in his
friends or
enemies.

What I see that is handsome in others, I very readily commend and esteem; nay, I often say more in their commendation, than, I think, they really deserve, and give myself so far leave to lie; for I cannot invent a false subject. My testimony is never wanting to my friends, in what I conceive deserves praise; and where a foot is due to them, in point of merit, I am willing to give them a foot and half; but to attribute to them qualities that they have not, I cannot do it, nor openly defend their imperfections: nay, I frankly give my very enemies their due testimony of honour: my affection alters, my judgment does not; I never confound my controversy with other circumstances that are foreign to it; and am so jealous of the liberty of my judgment, that I can very hardly part with it for any passion whatever: I do myself a greater injury in lying, than I do him

Enemies
honoured
by the Per-
sians for
their vir-
tue.

of whom I tell a lie. This commendable and generous custom is observed of the Persian nation, " That they spoke of their mortal enemies, and those " with whom they were at deadly wars, as honour- " ably and justly as their virtues deserved." I know men enough that have several fine parts; one wit, another courage, another address, another conscience, another language, one one science, another another; but a man generally great, and that has all these accomplishments united, or any one of them to such a degree of excellence, that we should admire him, or compare him with those we honour of times past, my fortune never brought me acquainted with one; the greatest I ever knew, I mean for natural parts, and the best-natured man living, was

Praise of
Stephen
Boetius.

Stephen Boetius; his was a capacious soul indeed, and had every way a beautiful aspect; a soul of the old stamp, and that would have produced great deeds, had fortune been so pleased, as he had added much to those great natural parts by learning and study.

But how comes it to pass I know not, and yet it is certainly so, there is as much vanity and weakness

of judgment in those who profess the greatest abili- From
ties, who take upon them learned callings, and book- whence it
ish employments, as in any sort of men whatever ; pass that
either because more is required and expected from men of let-
them, and that common defects are inexcusable in vain, and
them ; or, truly, because the opinion they have of of weak
their own learning makes them more bold to expose standing.
and lay themselves too open, by which they lose and
betray themselves. As an artificer more betrays his
want of skill in a rich work that he has in his hand,
if he disgrace it by ill handling, and working contrary
to the rules required, than in a mean subject ; and
men are more displeased at a fault in a statue of
gold than in one of alabaster ; so do these, when they
exhibit things that, in themselves, and in their place,
would be good : for they make use of them without
discretion, honouring their memories at the expense
of their understanding, and making themselves ridiculous, to honour Cicero, Galen, Ulpian, and St.
Jerome.

I willingly fall again into the discourse of the folly
of our education ; the end of which has not been to
render us good and wise, but learned, and it has obtained it : it has not taught us to follow and embrace
virtue and prudence, but has imprinted in us the de-
rivation and etymology of those words: we know how
to decline virtue, yet we know not how to love it :
if we do not know what prudence is in effect, and
by experience, we have it, however, by jargon and
by heart. We are not content to know the extrac-
tion, kindred, and alliances of our neighbours; we
desire, moreover, to have them our friends, and to
establish a correspondence and intelligence with
them : this education of ours has taught us definitions, divisions, and partitions of virtue, as so many
surnames and branches of a genealogy, without any
farther care of establishing any familiarity or intimacy
between it and us. Our education has culled out,
for our initiary instruction, not such books as contain the soundest and truest opinions, but those that

speak the best Greek and Latin; and by their florid
words have instilled in our fancy the vainest humour
of antiquity.

A good education alters the judgment and manners; as it happened to Polemon, a young debauched Greek, who going, by chance, to hear one of
Xenocrates's lectures, not only observed the eloquence and learning of the reader, and not only
brought home the knowledge of some fine matter;
but he gained more manifest and solid profit, which
was the sudden change and reformation of his former life.   Who ever found such an effect of our discipline.?

> ———— Faciásne quod olim
> Mutatus Polemon, ponas insignia morbi,
> Fasciolas, cubital, focalia, potus ut ille
> Dicitur ex collo furtim carpuisse coronas,
> Postquam est impransi correptus voce Magistri ?*

> Canst thou, like Polemon reclaim'd, remove
> Thy foppish dress, those symptoms of thy love;
> As he when drunk, with garlands round his head,
> Chanc'd once to hear the sober Stoic read;
> Asham'd, he took his garlands off, began
> Another course, and grew a sober man ?

The manners of the meaner sort of people more regular than those of the philosophers. That seems to me to be the least contemptible condition of men, which, by its simplicity, is seated in
the lowest degree, and invites us to a more regular
conduct. I find the manners and language of the
country people commonly better suited to the prescription of true philosophy, than those of our philosophers themselves. *Plus sapit vulgus, quia tantum,
quantum opus est, sapit :†* " The vulgar are so much
" the wiser, because they only know what is needful
" for them to know."

The greatest warriors in Montaigne's time. The most remarkable men, as I have judged by
outward appearances (for, to judge of them accord-
ing to my own method, I must penetrate into them
a great deal deeper), for war and military conduct,

---

* Hor. lib. ii. sat. 3, ver. 253, &c.   † Lactant. Institut. lib. iv.

were the duke of Guise, who died at Orleans and the
late marshal Strozzy.

For gownsmen of great ability, and no common ^{For the}
virtue, Olivier and De l'Hospital, chancellors of ^{greatest}_{ability and}
France. _{worth.}

Poesy too, is my opinion, has flourished in this ^{Several}
age. We have abundance of very good artists in ^{good Latin}_{poets.}
this class, Aurat, Beze, Buchanan, l'Hospital, Mont-
dore, and Turnebus.

As to the French poets, I believe they have ^{Excellency}
raised it to the highest pitch to which it will ever ar- ^{of the}_{French}
rive; and, in those parts of it wherein Ronsard and _{poets.}
Du Bellay excel, I find them little inferior to the
ancient perfection.

Adrian Turnebus knew more, and what he did know, ^{Character}
better than any man of his time, or long before him. _{of Turne-}_{bus.}

The lives of the last duke of Alva, and of our con- ^{Of the}
stable De Montmorency, were both of them noble, ^{duke of}_{Alva and}
and had many rare resemblances of fortune; but the _{the consta-}
beauty and the glory of the death of the last, in the _{ble de}_{Montmo-}
sight of Paris, and of his king, in their service, _{rency.}
against his nearest relation, at the head of an army,
through his conduct, victorious, and with sword in
hand, at so extreme an old age, merits, methinks, to
be recorded amongst the most remarkable events of
our times: as also the constant goodness, sweetness
of behaviour, and conscientious facility of monsieur _{And of M.}
De la Noue, in so great an injustice of armed parties _{De la Noue.}
(the true school of treason, inhumanity, and robbery),
wherein he always kept up the reputation of a great
and experienced captain.

I have taken a delight to publish, in several places, _{And of}
the hopes I have of Mary de Gournay le Jars, my _{Mary de}_{Gournay.}
adopted daughter,* and certainly beloved by me

* As to the meaning of these words, Adopted Daughter, see the
article GOURNAY in Bayle's Dictionary; where you will find, that
this young lady's opinion of the first Essays of Montaigne gave the
occasion for this adoption, long before she ever saw Montaigne.
But here I cannot help transcribing a part of a passage, which Mr.
Bayle quoted from M. Pasquier, in the note A, which contains some

9

with more than a paternal love, and involved in my
solitude and retirement, as one of the best parts of
my own being.   I have no regard to any thing in
this world but her; and, if a man may presage from
her youth, her soul will, one day, be capable of
the noblest things; and, amongst others, of the perfection of sacred friendship, to which we do not
read that any of her sex could ever yet arrive: the
sincerity and solidity of her manners are already sufficient for it; her affection towards me is more than
superabundant, and such, in short, as that there is
nothing more to be wished, if not that the apprehension she has of my end, being now five and fifty
years old, might not so cruelly afflict her.   The
judgment she made of my first Essays, being a woman
so young, and in this age, and alone in her own
country, and the famous vehemency wherewith she
loved, and desired me upon the sole esteem she had
of me, before she ever saw me, is an accident very
worthy of consideration.

Valour is
become
popular in
France.   Other virtues have had little or no credit in this
age, but valour is become popular by our civil wars;
and in this respect we have souls brave, even to perfection, and in so great number, that the choice is
impossible to be made.   This is all of extraordinary,
and not common, that has hitherto arrived at my
knowledge.

remarkable particulars of this sort of Adoption. " Montaigne,"
says Pasquier, " having, in 1588, made a long stay at Paris, Made-
" moiselle de Jars came thither, on purpose to see his person; and
" she and her mother carried him to their house at Gournay, where
" he spent two months in two or three journeys, and met with as
" hearty a welcome as he could desire; and, finally, that this vir-
" tuous lady, being informed of Montaigne's death, crossed almost
" through the whole kingdom of France, with passports, as well
" from her own motive, as by invitation from Montaigne's widow
" and daughter, to mix her tears with theirs, whose sorrows were
" boundless."

CHAPTER IX.

Of giving the Lie.

WELL, but some one will say to me, " This de- ^{Why Mon-}
" sign of making a man's self the subject of his wri- ^{taigne so}
" ting were excusable in rare and famous men, who, ^{often of}
" by their reputation, had given others a curiosity ^{himself in}
" to be fully informed of them." It is most true, I
confess it, and know very well, that artificers will
scarce lift their eyes from their work to look at an
ordinary man, when they will forsake their work-
houses and shops to stare at an eminent person,
when he comes to town : it misbecomes any person
to give his own character, except he has qualities
worthy of imitation, and whose life and opinions
may serve for a model. The great actions of Cæsar
and Xenophon were a just and solid basis on which
to fix and found their narratives : and it were also to
be wished, that we had the Journals of Alexander
the Great, and the Commentaries that Augustus,
Cato, Sylla, Brutus, and others have left of their actions. We love and contemplate the very statues of
such personages, both in copper and marble. This
remonstrance is very true, but it very little concerns
me :

Non recito cuiquam, nisi amicis, idque rogatus ; [*]
Non ubivis, coramve quibuslibet : in medio qui
Scripta foro recitant, sunt multi, quique lavantes. [†]

I seldom e'er rehearse, and when I do
'Tis to my friends, and with reluctance too,
Not before every one, and every where ;
We have too many that rehearsers are,
In baths, the forum, and the public square.

---

[*] Instead of *coactus*, as Horace has it in the first verse, Montaigne
has substituted *rogatus*, which more exactly expresses his thought.
[†] Hor. lib. i. sat. 4, ver. 73, &c.

I do not here form a statue to erect in the centre of a city, in the church, or any public quadrangle:

Non equidem hoc studeo, bullatis ut mihi nugis
Pagina turgescat :
Secreti loquimur.*

With pompous trash to swell the frothy line
Is not, indeed, my friend, what I design :
Whatever be the secrets I indite,
To you I trust, to you alone I write.

It is for some corner of a library, or to entertain a neighbour, a kinsman, or a friend, that has a mind to renew his acquaintance and familiarity with me in this my picture. Others have been encouraged to speak of themselves, because they found the subject worthy and rich; I, on the contrary, am the bolder, by reason my subject is so poor and sterile, that I cannot be suspected of ostentation. I judge freely of the actions of others; I give little of my own to judge of, because of their nothingness: I am not so conscious of any good in myself, as to tell it without blushing. What contentment would it be to me to hear any thus relate to me the manners, faces, countenances, the ordinary words and fortunes of my ancestors? How attentively should I listen to it! In truth, it would be ill-nature to despise even the pictures of our friends and predecessors, the fashion of their clothes, and of their arms. I preserve my father's writings, his seal, and one particular sword of his, and have not thrown the long staves he used to carry in his hand, out of my closet. *Paterna vestis, et annulus, tanto charior est posteris, quanto erga parentes major affectus :*† " A " father's robe and ring are so much the dearer to " his posterity, in proportion to the affection they " retain for him." If my posterity, nevertheless, shall be of another mind, I shall be even with them; for they cannot care less for me, than I shall then do for them. All the traffic that I have, in this, with

* Pers. sat. v. ver. 19.   † Aug. de Civitate Dei, lib. i. cap. 13.

the public, is, that I borrow their writing tackle, as
it is more easy, and at hand; and, in recompense,
shall, perhaps, keep a dish of butter from melting in
the market.

Ne toga cordyllis, ne penula desit olivis, *
Et laxas scombris sæpe dabo tunicas. †

I'll furnish plaice and olives with a coat,
And cover mack'rel when the sun shines hot.

And though no body should read me, have I lost Montaigne talks so much of himself, that he might the better know himself, and give his own true character.
my time in entertaining myself so many idle hours,
in thoughts so pleasing and useful? In moulding
this figure upon myself, I have been so oft constrained to curry and turn myself, as it were, inside out,
that the copy is truly taken, and has, in some sort,
formed itself. But, as I paint for others, I represent
myself in more exquisite colouring than in my own
natural complexion. I am as much formed by my
book, as my book is by me: it is a book consubstan-
tial with the author; of a peculiar tenor; a member
of my life, and whose business is not designed for
others, as that of all other books is. In giving so
continual and so curious an account of myself,
have I lost any time? for he who sometimes cursorily
surveys himself only, doth not so strictly examine
himself, nor penetrate so deep, as he who makes it
his business, his study, and his whole employment;
who intends to give a lasting record, with all his fidelity, and with all his force. The most delicious pleasures, however digested internally, avoid leaving any
trace of themselves, and shun the sight not only of
the people, but of any other man. How oft has
this affair diverted me from uneasy thoughts? And
all that are frivolous should be reputed so. Nature
has presented us with a large faculty of entertaining
ourselves apart; and oft call us to it, to teach us,
that we owe ourselves, in part, to society, but chiefly
to ourselves. In order to habituate my fancy, even
to meditate in some method, and to some end, and

* Mart. lib. xiii. ep. 1, ver. 1.   † Catullus, ep. 92, ver. 8.

to keep it from losing itself, and roving at random,
it is but to give it a body, and to register all the
pretty thoughts that present themselves to it. I
give ear to my whimsies, because I am to record
them. How oft has it fallen out, that, being displeased at some action which civility and reason did
not permit me openly to reprove, I have here dis-
gorged myself of them, not without design of public
instruction : and yet these poetical lashes, (

> *Zon des sur l' œil, zon sur le groin,*
> *Zon sur le dos du Sagoin.**
>
> A jerk over the eye, over the snout,
> Let Sagoin be jerk'd throughout.

imprint themselves better upon paper, than upon the
most sensible flesh. What if I listen to books a little more attentively than ordinary, since I watch if I
can purloin any thing that may adorn or support my
own ? I have not at all studied to make a book ; but
I have, in some sort, studied because I had made it,
if it be studying, to scratch and pinch, now one
author, and then another, either by the head or foot;
not with any design to steal opinions from them, but
to assist, second, and to fortify those I had before
embraced.

The little
regard
paid to
truth, an
odious
vice.

But who shall we believe in the report he makes
of himself, in so corrupt an age ? Considering there
are so few, if any at all, whom we can believe when
speaking of others, where there is less interest to lie.
The first step to the corruption of manners is banish-
ing of truth; for, as Pindar says, " To be sincerely
" true is the beginning of a great virtue," and the
first article that Plato requires in the government of
his republic. The truth of these days is not that
which really is such, but what every man persuades
himself or another to believe; as we generally give
the name of money, not only to lawful coin, but to
the counterfeit also, if it be current. Our nation has

* Marot contre Sagoin.

long been reproached with this vice; for Salvianus Massiliensis, who lived in the time of the emperor Valentinian, says, " That lying and perjury is not a " vice with the French, but a way of speaking." He that would improve upon this testimony, might say, " That it is now a virtue with them." Men form and fashion themselves to it, as to an exercise of honour; for dissimulation is one of the most notable qualities of this age.

I have often considered, whence comes this cus-*Whence* tom, that we so religiously observe, of being more *it comes* highly offended with the reproach of a vice so fami-*that men are so stung* liar to us than with any other, and that it should be *with the reproach of* the highest injury that can, in words, be done us, to *being li-* reproach us with a lie: upon examination, I find, *ars.* that it is natural to disclaim those faults most, with which we are most tainted: it seems as if, by resenting and being moved at the accusation, we, in some sort, acquitted ourselves of the fault; if we are guilty of it in fact, we condemn it, at least in appearance: may it also not be that this reproach seems to imply cowardice, and meanness of spirit? of which can there be a more manifest sign, than for a man to eat his own words? What, to lie against a man's own knowledge: lying is a base vice; a vice that one *Lying an* of the ancients paints in the most odious colours, *argument of the con-* when he says, " That it is too manifest a contempt *tempt of* " of God, and a fear of man." It is not possible *God.* more copiously to represent the horror, baseness, and irregularity of it; for what can be imagined more vile, than a man, who is a coward towards man, so courageous as to defy his Maker? Our intelligence being by no other canal to be conveyed to one another but by words, he, who falsifies them, betrays public society: it is the only tube through which we communicate our thoughts and wills to one another; it is the interpreter of the soul, and, if it fails us, we no longer know, nor have any farther tie upon another: if that deceive us, it breaks all our corres. pondence, and dissolves all the bands of our govern.

ment. Certain nations of the new-discovered Indies
(no matter for naming them, since they are no more;
for, by wonderful and unheard of example, the de-
solation of that conquest extended to the utter abo-
lition of names, and the ancient knowledge of places)
offered to their Gods human blood, " But only such
" as was drawn from the tongue and ears, to atone
" for the sin of lying, as well heard as pronounced."
The good fellow of Greece* was wont to say, " That
" children were amused with rattles, and men with
" words."

The Greeks and Romans not so delicate in the article of lying, as we are. As to the various usages of our giving the lie, and
the laws of honour in that case, and the alterations
they have received, I shall defer saying what I know
of them to another time, and shall learn, if I can,
in the mean while, at what time the custom took
beginning, of so exactly weighing and measuring
words, and of engaging our honour to them; for it
is easy to judge, that it was anciently amongst the
Greeks and Romans; and I have often thought it
strange to see them rail at, and give one another
the lie, without any farther quarrel. The laws of
their duty steered some other course than ours.
Cæsar is sometimes called thief, and sometimes
drunkard, to his teeth. We see the liberty of in-
vectives, which they practised upon one another, I
mean the greatest chiefs of war of both nations,
where words were only revenged with words, without any other consequence.

* Lysander, in Plutarch's Life of him, chap. 4.

CHAPTER X.

Of Liberty of Conscience.

IT is usual to see good intentions, if pursued without moderation, push men on to very vicious effects. In the dispute, which has now engaged France in a civil war, the best and the soundest cause, no doubt, is that which maintains the ancient religion and government of the kingdom. Nevertheless, amongst the good men of that party (for I do not speak of those that make a pretence of it, either to execute their own particular revenge, or to gratify their avarice, or to court the favour of princes; but of those who engage in the quarrel out of true zeal to religion, and a regard to the peace and government of their country), of these, I say, we see many whom passion transports beyond the bounds of reason, and sometimes inspires with counsels that are unjust and violent, and also rash. *Religion zeal often extravagant and consequently unjust.*

It is true, that in those primitive times, when our religion began to gain authority with the laws, zeal armed many against all sorts of Pagan books, by which the learned suffered an exceeding great loss; which, I conceive, did more prejudice to letters than all the flames kindled by the barbarians. Of this Cornelius Tacitus is a very good witness; for though the emperor Tacitus, his kinsman, had, by express order, furnished all the libraries in the world with his book, nevertheless, one entire copy could not escape the curious search of those who desired to abolish it, for only five or six idle clauses in it, that were contrary to our belief. *This zeal induced the Christians, when they became masters, to destroy Pagan books.*

They were also very ready to lend undue praises to all the emperors who did any thing for us, and universally to condemn all the actions of those who were our adversaries, as is manifest in the emperor Julian, surnamed the Apostate; who was, in truth, *And to praise bad emperors, who favoured Christianity, and to* blame Julian, and others, who opposed it. The character of the emperor Julian the Apostate. His chastity.

a very great and rare man, a man in whose soul that philosophy was imprinted in lively characters, by which he professed to govern all his actions ; and, in truth, there is no sort of virtue, of which he has not left behind him very notable examples. In chastity (of which the whole course of his life has given manifest proof) we read the like of him, as was said of Alexander and Scipio,* that, being in the flower of his age (for he was slain by the Parthians at one and thirty), of a great many very beautiful captives, he would not touch, nor so much as look upon one. As to his justice,† he took himself the pains to hear the parties, and although he would, out of curiosity, inquire what religion they were of; nevertheless the hatred he had to ours, never turned the balance. He made several good laws, and cut off a great part of the subsidies and taxes levied by his predecessors.‡

Julian blamed by two historians, eye-witnesses of his actions.

We have two good historians, who were eye-witnesses of his actions ; one of whom, Marcellinus, in several places of his history, sharply reproves an edict of his, whereby " He interdicted all Christian " rhetoricians and grammarians from keeping school, " or teaching," and says, " he could wish that act " of his had been buried in silence."§ It is very likely, that, had he done any more severe things against us, the historian, who was so affectionate to our party, would not have passed it over in silence.

His moderation, by the report of a Christian author.

He was, indeed, sharp against us, but yet no cruel enemy : for our own people tell us this story of him, " That, one day, walking about the city " of Chalcedon, Maris, bishop of that place, called " out to him, and told him, that he was an atheist, " and an apostate :" to which he only answered, " Go, wretch, and lament the loss of thy eyes :" to this the bishop replied again, " I thank Jesus

---

* Ammian. Marcell. lib. xxiv. chap. 8.
† Idem, lib. xxi. cap. 10.
‡ Idem, lib. xxv. cap. 5, 6.   § Idem, lib. xxii. cap. 10.

" Christ for taking away my sight, that I might not
" see thy impudent face."* So it is, that this action
of his savours nothing of the cruelty that he is said
to have exercised towards us ; though they say, that
his answer to the bishop was but an affectation of
philosophic patience. " He was (says Eutropius,[†]
my other witness) an enemy to Christianity, but
" without shedding blood."   And, to return to his His justice.
justice, there is nothing in that whereof he can be
accused, but the severity he practised in the beginning of his reign, against those who had followed the
party of Constantius, his predecessor.[‡]

As to his sobriety, he lived always a soldier kind His sobrie-
of life ; and kept a table, in times of the most pro- ty.
found peace, like one that prepared and inured himself to the rigours of war.§

His vigilance was such, that he divided the night His vigi-
into three or four parts, of which always the least lance.
was dedicated to sleep ; the rest was spent either in
visiting his army and guards, or in study; for,
amongst other rare qualities, he was excellent in all
sorts of literature. It is said of Alexander the
Great, " That, when he was in bed, lest sleep
" should divert him from his thoughts and studies,
" he had always a bason set by his bed-side, and
" held one of his hands out with a bullet of copper
" in it, to the end that, if he fell asleep, and his
" fingers left their hold, the bullet, by falling into
" the bason, might awake him."|| But this Julian
was so bent upon what he had a mind to do, and so
little disturbed with fumes, by reason of his singular
abstinence, that he had no need of any such invention.

As to his military experience, he was admirable His milita
in all the qualities of a great captain, as it was ry experi ence.

* Sozomen's Ecclesiastical History, lib. v. cap. 4.
† Eutrop. lib. x. cap. 8.
‡ Ammian. Marcell. lib. xxii. cap. 2.
§ Idem, lib. xvi. cap. 2, et xxvi. cap. 5.
|| Idem, lib. xvi. cap. 2.

likely he should, having been, almost all his life, in a continual exercise of war, and most of that time with us in France, against the Germans and Franconians : we hardly read of any man that ever encountered more dangers, or that gave more frequent proofs of his personal valour.

His death.   His death has something in it like that of Epaminondas ; for he was wounded with an arrow, which he tried to pull out, and would have done it, but that, being two-edged, it cut the sinews of his hand. He called out forthwith, " That they would carry " him, in this condition, into the midst of the bat- " tle to encourage his soldiers," who very bravely disputed the battle without him, till night parted the armies.* He was obliged to his philosophy for the singular contempt he had for his life, and all human things ; and he had a firm belief of the immortality of the soul.

He was addicted to the worship of false gods.   In matters of religion, he was vicious throughout, and was surnamed the Apostate, for having relinquished ours : though, methinks, it is more likely, that he had never thoroughly embraced it, but had dissembled, out of obedience to the laws, till he came to the empire.

Excessively superstitious.   He was, in his own, so superstitious, that he was laughed at for it, by those of the same opinion of his own time, who said, " That, had he got the " victory over the Parthians, he would have de- " stroyed the breed of oxen in the world to supply " his sacrifices."† He was, moreover, a bigot to the art of divination, and gave authority to all sorts of predictions. He said, amongst other things, at his death,‡ " That he was obliged to the gods, and " thanked them, in that they had not been pleased " to cut him off by surprise, having, long before, ad- " vertised him of the place and hour of his death ; " nor by a mean and unmanly death, more becom-

---

* Ammian. Marcell. lib. xxv. cap. 3.
† Idem, ibid. cap. 6,   ‡ Idem, ibid. cap. 4.

" ing lazy and delicate people; nor by a death that
" was languishing, and painful; and that they had
" thought him worthy to die after that noble man-
" ner, in the career of his victories, and in the
" height of his glory." He had a vision like that
of Marcus Brutus, that first threatened him in Gaul,[*]
and afterwards appeared to him in Persia, just before his death.[†] These words, that some make him
say, when he felt himself wounded, " Thou hast
" overcome, Nazarene;"[‡] or, as others, " Content
" thyself, Nazarene," would hardly have been
omitted, had they been believed by my witnesses;
who, being present in the army, have set down even
the least motions and words of his latter end, no
more than certain other strange things that are recorded of him.

To return to my subject, " He long nourished,"[A]
says Marcellinus, " Paganism in his heart; but, all
" his army being Christians, he durst not own it :[§]
" but, in the end, seeing himself strong enough to
" dare to discover himself, he caused the temples
" of the gods to be thrown open, and did his ut-
" most to set on foot an idolatry.[||] The better to
" effect this, having at Constantinople, found the
" people disunited, and also the prelates of the
" church divided amongst themselves, and having
" convened them all before him, he gravely and
" earnestly admonished them to calm those civil
" dissentions; and that every one might freely, and
" without fear, follow his own religion : this he did
" the more sedulously solicit, in hopes that this li-
" cence would augment the schisms and faction of
" their division, and hinder the people from reunit-
" ing, and consequently fortifying themselves
" against him by their unanimous intelligence and
" concord; having experienced, by the cruelty of

He aimed to re-esta-blish Paga-nism, and to destroy the Chris-tians, by keeping up their divi-sions by a general to-leration.

---

* Ammian. Marcell. lib. xx. cap. 5. † Idem, lib. xxv. cap. 3.
‡ Vicisti, Galilæe. Theodoret. Hist. Eccles. lib. iii. cap. 20.
§ Idem, lib. xxi. cap. 2. || Ammian. Marcell. lib. xxii. cap. 5.

" some Christians, that there is no beast in the
" world so much to be feared by man, as man."

These are very near his words, wherein this is
worthy of consideration, that the emperor Julian
made use of the same receipt of liberty of conscience, to inflame the civil dissensions, that our
kings have now done to extinguish them: so that it
may be said, on one side, " That to give the people the reins to entertain every man his own opinion is to scatter and sow division, and, as it
were, to lend a hand to augment it, there being
no barrier nor correction of law to stop and hinder its career;" but, on the other side, a man
may also say, " That to give people the reins to entertain every man his own opinion, is to mollify
and appease them by facility and toleration, and
dulls the point which is whetted and made sharper
by singularity, novelty, and difficulty." And, I
think, it is more for the honour of the devotion of
our kings, that, not having been able to do what
they would, they have made a show of being willing
to do what they could.

CHAPTER XI.

That we taste nothing Pure.

SO weak is our condition, that things cannot fall
into our use in their natural simplicity and purity;
the elements that we enjoy are changed, even metals themselves; and gold must be debased, by some
alloy, to fit it for our service. Neither has virtue,
so simple as that which Aristo, Pyrrho, and also the
Stoics have made the principal end of life: nor the
Cyrenaic and Aristippic pleasure been useful to it
without a mixture. Of the pleasure and goods that

we enjoy, there is not one exempt from some mixture of evil and inconvenience:

> —— *Medio de fonte leporum,*
> *Surgit amari aliquid, quod in ipsis floribus angat.*[*]
> Something that's bitter will arise,
> Even amidst our jollities.

Our greatest pleasure has some air of groaning and complaining in it; would you not say, that it is dying of anguish? Nay, when we forge the image of it, in its excellency, we paint it with sickly and painful epithets, languor, softness, feebleness, faintness, morbidezza, a great testimony of their consanguinity and consubstantiality. Excessive joy has more of severity than gaiety in it; the fullest contentment, more of the sedate than of the merry. *Ipsa felicitas, se nisi temperat, premit:*[†] " Even felicity, unless it moderates itself, oppresseth." Pleasure preys upon us, according to the old Greek verse,[‡] which says, " That the gods sell us all the " good they give us;" that is to say, that they give us nothing pure and perfect, and which we do not purchase but at the price of some evil.

Labour and pleasure, very unlike in nature, associate, nevertheless, by I know not what natural conjunction. Socrates says, " That some god tried to " mix in one mass, and to confound pain and plea- " sure, but not being able to do it, he bethought " him at least to couple them by the tail."[||]   Metrodorus said, " That in sorrow there is some mix- " ture of pleasure."[§]   I know not whether he intended any thing else by that saying; but, for my part, I am of opinion, that there is design, consent,

Side note: Pain and pleasure joined at one end, as appears from melancholy.

---

* Lucret. lib. iv. ver. 1126.   † Senec. ep. 74.
† —— τῶν πόνων
   Πωλῦσιν ἡμῖν πάντα τἀγαθὰ Θεοί.
   Epicharmus apud Xenophon. lib. xi. ἀπομνημονευμ.
|| In Plato's dialogue, entitled Phædon, p. 376.
§ Metrodorus, Senec. ep. 99.

and complacency in giving a man's self up to melancholy; I say, that, besides ambition, which may also have a stroke in the business, there is some shadow of delight and delicacy, which smiles upon, and flatters us, even in the very lap of melancholy. Are there not some complexions that feed upon it?

> ———— *Est quædam flere voluptas.* *
> A certain kind of pleasure 'tis to weep.

And one Attalus, in Seneca, says, " That the me-
" mory of our deceased friends is as graceful to us
" as the bitterness in the wine, very old, is to the
" palate,†

> *Minister vetulis puer Falerni*
> *Ingere mi calices amariores.‡*
> Thou boy that fill'st the old Falernian wine,
> The bitt'rest pour into the bowl that's mine.

" and as apples that have a sweet tartness." Nature discovers this confusion to us. Painters hold, " That the same motions and screwings of the face " that serve for weeping, serve for laughter too ;" and indeed, before the one or the other be finished, do but observe the painters' conduct, and you will be in doubt to which of the two the design does tend ; and the extremity of laughter is mixed with tears : *Nullum sine auctoramento malum est :‖* " No " evil is without its compensation."

Constant and universal pleasure not to be borne by man. When I imagine man surrounded with all the conveniences that are to be desired, let us put the case, that all his members were always seized with a pleasure like that of generation in its most excessive height; I fancy him melting under the weight of his delight, and see him utterly unable to support so pure, so continual, and so universal a pleasure ; indeed he is running away whilst he is there, and na-

---

* Ovid. Trist. el. 3, ver. 37.   † Senec. epist. 63.
‡ Catul. epist. 25, ver: 1, 2.   ‖ Senec. epist. 69.

turally makes haste to escape, as from a place where
he cannot stand firm, and where he is afraid of sinking.

When I religiously confess myself, I find that the Moral good
best good quality I have has in it some tincture of and evil confound-
vice; and am afraid that Plato, in his purest virtue ed in man.
(I, who am as sincere and perfect a lover of him,
and of the virtues of that stamp, as any other whatever), if he laid his ear close to himself (and he did
so), he would have heard some jarring sound of human mixture, but so obscure as only to be perceived
by himself; man is wholly and throughout but a
patched and motley composition.

Even the laws of justice themselves cannot sub- The justest
sist without some mixture of injustice; insomuch laws have some mix-
that Plato says, " They undertake to cut off the ture of in-
" Hydra's head, who pretend to purge the laws of justice.
" all inconvenience." *Omne magnum exemplum
habet aliquid ex iniquo, quod contra singulos utilitate
publicá rependitur :* " Every great example of jus-
" tice has in it some mixture of injustice, which re-
" compenses the wrong done to particular men, by
" its public utility," says Tacitus.

It is likewise true, that for the business of life, Common
and the service of public commerce, there may be understanding
some excesses in the purity and perspicacity of our more pro-
mind; that penetrating light has too much of sub- per for affairs than
tlety and curiosity; it must be a little stupified and what is
most re-
blunted, to be rendered more obedient to example fined.
and practice; and a little veiled and obscured, to
bear the better proportion to this dark and terrestrial life; and yet common and less speculative
souls are found to be more proper, and more successful in the management of affairs; and the elevated and exquisite opinions of philosophy are unfit
for business; this acute vivacity of the mind, and
the supple and restless volubility of it, disturb our

* Tacit. Annal. lib. xiv.

negotiations; we are to manage human enterprises more superficially and roughly, and leave a great part to the determination of fortune. It is not necessary to examine affairs with so much subtlety, and so deeply; a man loses himself in the consideration of so many lustres, and various forms. *Voluntantibus res inter se pugnantes, obtorpuerant animi* :* " Whilst they considered of things so inconsistent in themselves, they were astonished." It is what the ancients say of Simonides,† " That by " reason his imagination suggested to him, upon " the question king Hiero had put to him (to an" swer which he had many days to consider it) seve" ral witty and subtle arguments, whilst he doubted " which was the most likely, he totally despaired " of the truth." He that dives into, and in his inquisition comprehends all circumstances and consequences, hinders his choice; a little engine, well handled, is sufficient for executions of less or greater weight and moment; the best managers are those who are least able to tell us why they are so; and the greatest talkers, for the most part, do nothing to the purpose. I know one of this sort of men, and a most excellent manager in theory, who has miserably let an hundred thousand livres yearly revenue slip through his hands. I know another who says, that he is able to give better advice than any of his council; and there is not, in the world, a fairer show of a soul, and of a good understanding, than he has; nevertheless, when he comes to the test, his servants find him quite another thing; not to bring his misfortune into the account.

* Livy, lib. xxxii. cap. 20.
† King Hiero had desired him to define what God was. Cic. de Nat. Deor. lib. i. cap. 22.

CHAPTER XII.

Against Sloth.

THE emperor Vespasian, being sick of the disease *In what* whereof he died, did not, for all that, neglect to in- *posture a* quire after the state of the empire, and, even in *prince* bed, continually dispatched affairs of great conse- *die.* quence ; for which being reproved by his physician, as a thing prejudicial to his health, " An emperor," said he, " must die standing."* A fine saying, in my opinion, and worthy of a great prince. The emperor Adrian afterwards made use of one to the same purpose ;† and should be often put in mind of it, to make them know that the great office confer- red upon them of the command of so many men is not an idle employment ; and that there is nothing can so justly disgust a subject, and make him un- willing to expose himself to labour and danger for the service of his prince, than to see him in the mean time devoted to his ease, and to vain and un- manly amusements ; nor will the subject be solicitous of his prince's preservation who so much neglects that of his people.

Whoever offers to maintain that it is better for a *He ought* prince to carry on his wars by others than in his own *to com-* person, fortune will furnish him with examples *mand his armies in* enough of those whose lieutenants have brought *person.* great enterprises to a happy issue, and of those also whose presence has done more hurt than good. But no virtuous and valiant prince can bear to be tutored with such scandalous lessons ; under colour of saving his head, like the statue of a saint, for the happiness of his kingdom, they degrade him from, and make

---

* Suetonius in Vespasian. sect. xxiv.
† Æl. Spartiani Ælius Verus, sect. xvi. Hist. August.

him incapable of, his office, which is military
throughout. I know one who had much rather be
beaten than sleep whilst another fights for him, and
who never, without envy, heard of any brave thing
done even by his own officers in his absence; and
Selima the first said, with very good reason in my
opinion, " That victories obtained without the so-
" vereigns were never complete." Much more readily would he have said, that that sovereign ought to
blush for shame to pretend to any share in it, when
he had contributed nothing to it but his voice and
thought; nor even so much as those, considering,
that in such works the direction and command that
deserve honour are only such as are given upon the
place, and in the heat of the business. No pilot
performs his office by standing still. The princes of
the Ottoman family, the chief in the world of military fortune, have warmly embraced this opinion;
and Bajazet the second, with his son that swerved
from it, spending their time in the sciences, and
other employments within doors, gave great blows
to their empire; and Amurath the third, now
reigning, following their example, begins to do the
same. Was it not Edward the third, king of England, who said this of our king Charles the fifth?
" There never was king so seldom put on his arms,
" and yet never king who cut me out so much
" work." He might well think it strange, as an
effect of change more than of reason; and let those
seek out some other advocate for them than me,
who will reckon the kings of Castile and Portugal
amongst the warlike and magnanimous conquerors,
because, at the distance of twelve hundred leagues
from their lazy residence, by the conduct of their
agents, they made themselves masters of both Indies; which it is a question if they had but the courage to go and enjoy them.

The acti-
vity and ro-
busty re-   The emperor Julian said yet farther, " That a
philosopher and a brave man ought not so much

" as to breathe ;" this is to say, not to allow any ^{quisite in}
more to bodily necessities than what we cannot re- ^{princes.}
fuse, " Keeping the soul and body still intent and
" busy about things honourable, great, and vir-
" tuous ;" he was ashamed if any one in public saw
him spit or sweat (which is said by some also of the
Lacedæmonian young men, and which Xenophon
says of the Persian), because he conceived, that exercise, continual labour, and sobriety, ought to have
dried up all those superfluities. What Seneca says
will not be unfit for this place, which is, " That
" the ancient Romans kept their youth always
" standing, and taught them nothing that they were
" to learn, sitting." *

It is a generous desire to wish to die usefully, and ^{The desire}
like a man ; but the effect lies not so much in our ^{of making}
resolution as in our good fortune. A thousand have ^{exit is}
proposed to themselves in battle either to conquer ^{though the}
or die, who have failed both in the one and the ^{thing be}
other ; wounds and imprisonment crossing their de- ^{not in our}
sign, and compelling them to live against their wills. ^{power.}
There are diseases that obliterate even our desires
and our knowledge. Fortune was not obliged to second the vanity of the Roman legions, who bound
themselves, by oath, " either to overcome or die."
*Victor, Marce Fabi, revertar ex acie ; si fallo,
Jovem patrem gradivumque Martem, aliosque iratos
invoco deos :*† " I will return (Marcus Fabius) a con-
" queror from the army ; and, if I fail, I wish the
" indignation of Jove, Mars, and the other offended
" gods, may light upon me." The Portuguese
say, " That in a certain place of their conquest of
" the Indies, they met with soldiers who had damned
" themselves, with horrible execrations, to enter
" into no composition, but either to kill or be kill-
" ed ; and had their heads and beards shaved in
" token of this vow." It is to much purpose to
hazard ourselves, and to be obstinate ; it seems as

* Senec. ep. 88.   † Tit. Liv. lib. ii. cap. 45.

if blows avoid those that present themselves too
briskly to danger; and do not readily fall upon those
who too willingly seek them, and so defeat their design. There was one, who had tried all ways, and
could not obtain dying by the hand of the enemy,
was constrained, in order to make good his resolution of bringing home victory, or of losing his life, to
kill himself, even in the heat of battle. Among
other examples, this is one : " Philistus, general of
" the naval army of Dionysius the younger, against
" the Syracusans, presented them battle, which was
" sharply disputed, their forces being equal. In
" which engagement he had the better at first,
" through his valour : but the Syracusans surround-
" ed his galley, after he had, with great feats of
" arms,* tried to disengage himself, and hoping for
" no relief, with his own hand he took away that
" life he had so liberally, but in vain, exposed to the
" enemy."

" Muley Moluck, king of Fez, who, anno 1578,
" won the battle against Sebastian, king of Portugal,
" so famous for the death of three kings, and the
" translation of that great kingdom to the crown of
" Castile, was extremely sick when the Portuguese
" entered, in a hostile manner, into his dominions :
" and, from that day forward, grew worse and
" worse, still drawing nearer to, and forseeing, his
" end : yet never did man employ himself more vi-
" gorously and bravely, than he did upon this occa-
" sion. He found himself too weak to undergo the
" pomp and ceremony of entering into his camp,
" which, after their manner, is very magnificent,
" and full of bustle; and therefore resigned that
" honour to his brother: but the office of a general
" was all that he resigned; all the rest of utility and
" necessity, he most exactly and gloriously perform-
" ed : his body lying upon a couch, but his judg-
" ment and courage upright and firm to his last

---

* Plutarch, in the Life of Bion, cap. 8.

" gasp, and, in some sort, beyond it : he might have
" wasted his enemy, who was indiscreetly advanced
" into his dominions, without striking a blow ; and
" it was very grievous to his heart, that, for want of
" a little life, or somebody to substitute in the con-
" duct of this war,* and of the affairs of a troubled
" state, he found himself compelled to seek a doubt-
" ful and bloody victory, when he had another, bet-
" ter and surer, already in his power : yet he won-
" derfully managed the continuance of his sickness,
" in wasting the enemy, and in drawing them from
" the naval army, and the sea-ports in the coast of
" Africa, even till the last day of his life, which he
" designedly reserved for this great battle. He
" formed the main battle in a circle, environing the
" Portugal army on every side; which circle, com-
" ing to draw up close together, did not only hinder
" them in the conflict (which was very sharp,
" through the valour of the young invading king), con-
" sidering they were every way to make a front ; but
" also prevented their flight, after the defeat ; so that,
" finding all passages possessed and shut up, they were
" constrained to close up together again ; *coacervan-*
" *turque non solem cæde, sed etiam fuga ;* and there
" they who stood, and they who fled, were slain in
" heaps upon one another, leaving to the conqueror
" a very bloody and entire victory. As he was dy-
" ing, he caused himself to be carried and hur-
" ried from place to place, where most need was ;
" and, passing through the files, encouraged the cap-
" tains and soldiers one after another. But, a cor-
" ner of his main battle being broke, he was not to
" be restrained from mounting on horseback, sword
" in hand. He did his utmost to break from those
" about him, and to rush into the thickest of the
" battle, they all the while stopping him, some by
" the bridle, some by his robe, and others by his
" stirrups. This last effort totally deprived him of

---

* Thuanus, Hist. lib. lxv. p. 248, the Geneva edition, in 1720.

" the little life he had left; they again laid him upon his
" couch, but, coming to himself again, he started, as it
" were, out of his swoon, all other faculties failing, to
" give his people notice, that they were to conceal his
" death (the most necessary command he had then to
" give, that his soldiers might not be discouraged with
" the news), he expired with his finger upon his
" mouth, the ordinary signal for keeping silence."[*]
Who ever lived so long and so far in death? Who
ever died more like a man? The most natural degree of entertaining death, is to look upon it, not
only without astonishment, but without care, con-
tinuing the wonted course of life even into it; as
Cato did, who entertained himself in study, and went
to sleep, having a violent and bloody design upon
himself in his heart, and the weapon in his hand to
execute it.

CHAPTER XIII.

Of Posts.

I HAVE been none of the least able in this exercise, which is proper for men of my pitch, well set
and short; but I give it over, it shakes us too much
to continue long. I was just now reading, " That
king Cyrus, the better to have news brought him
from all parts of the empire, which was of a vast
" extent, caused it to be tried, how far a horse could
" go in a day, before he baited; and at that distance
" appointed men whose business it was to have
" horses always in readiness to accommodate those
" who were dispatched away to him."[†] And some
say, that this swift way of travelling is equal to the
flight of cranes.

Post horses first set up by Cyrus.

[*] Thuanus, lib. v., p. 248, observes, that it was said Charles of
Bourbon gave the same signal when he was expiring at the foot of
the walls of Rome, which his troops took by storm, just after his
death.

[†] Xenophon's Cyropædia, lib. viii, cap. 6, sect. 9.

Cæsar says, " That Lucius Vibulus Rufus,[*] being
" in great haste to carry intelligence to Pompey,
" rid day and night, often taking fresh horses for the
" greater speed ;" and " Himself,"[†] as Suetonius reports, " travelled a hundred miles a day in a hired
" coach ; but he was a furious courier, for, where
" rivers stopped his way, he always passed them by
" swimming, without turning out of his way to look
" for either bridge or ford." Tiberius Nero, going
to see his brother Drusus,[‡] who was sick in Germany,
travelled two hundred miles in four and twenty hours,
having three coaches. In the war of the Romans against
king Antiochus, T. Sempronius Gracchus, says Livy,
*Per dispositos equos propè incredibilii celeritato ab
Amphissà tertio die Pellam pervenit :*[§] " By horses
" purposely laid on the road, he rode with almost in-
" credible speed, in three days, from Amphissa to
" Pella." And it appears there, that they were established posts, and not just ordered for this occasion.

Cecinna's invention, to send back news to his family, was performed with much more speed, for " He
" took swallows along with him from home, and
" turned them out towards their nests, when he
" would send back any news ; setting a mark of
" some colour upon them to signify his meaning,
" according to what he and his people had before
" agreed upon."[‖] At the theatre at Rome, masters
of families carried pigeons in their bosoms, to which
they tied letters, when they had a mind to send any
orders to their people at home ; and the pigeons
were trained up to bring back an answer. D. Brutus[¶] made use of the same device, when besieged in
Multina ; and others elsewhere have done the same.

In Peru, they rode post upon men's shoulders, who
took them up in a kind of litter, and ran with full

---

* De Bello Civili, lib. iii. cap. 4. † In Cæsare, sect. 57.
‡ Plin. Nat. Hist. lib. vii. cap. 20. § Tit. Liv. lib. xxxvii. cap. 7.
‖ Plin. Nat. Hist. lib. x. cap. 24. ¶ Idem, ibid. cap. 37.

speed, the first bearers throwing their load to the second, without making any stop; and so on.

I understand, that the Walachians, who are the grand seignior's couriers, perform wonderful journies, by reason they have liberty to dismount the first horseman they meet on the road, giving him their own tired horse: to keep themselves alert, they gird themselves tight about the middle with a broad belt, as many others do; but I could never find any advantge by it.

CHAPTER XIV.

Of ill Means employed to a good End.

Political states subject to the same accident as the human body.

THERE is a wonderful relation and correspondence in this universal system of the works of nature, which makes it plainly appear, that it is neither accidental, nor carried on by diverse masters. The diseases and conditions of our bodies are also manifest in states, and governments of the world: kingdoms and republics rise, flourish, and decay with age, as we do. We are subject to a repletion of humours that are useless and dangerous, either of those that are good, for even those the physicians are afraid of: and since we have nothing in us that is stable, they say, "That a true brisk and vigorous perfection "of health must be lowered and abated by art, lest, "as our nature cannot rest in any certain situation, "and has not whither to rise to mend itself, it should "make too sudden and too disorderly a retreat;" and therefore they prescribe to wrestlers to purge and bleed, to take down that superabundant health; "Or "else a repletion of evil humours, which is the or- "dinary cause of maladies." States are very often

* Plin. Nat. Hist. cap. 37.

tick of the like repletion, and therefore diverse sorts of purgations have commonly been used. Sometimes a great multitude of families are turned out to clear the country, who seek out new abodes elsewhere, or live upon others. After this manner our ancient Francs came from the heart of Germany, seized upon Gaul, and drove thence the first inhabitants; so was that infinite deluge of men formed, that came into Italy under the conduct of Brennus, and others: so the Goths and Vandals, also the people who now possess Greece, left their native country, to go and settle abroad, where they might have more room; and there are scarce two or three little corners of the world, that have not felt the effect of such removals. The Romans, by this means, erected their colonies; for, perceiving the city to increase beyond measure, they eased it of the most unnecessary people, and sent them to inhabit and cultivate the land which they had conquered.

Sometimes also they purposely fomented wars with some of their enemies, not only to keep their men in action, lest idleness, the mother of corruption, should bring some worse inconvenience upon them, ^{Why t Romans chose to make wars.}

> Et patimur longæ pacis mala, sævior armis
> Luxuria incubuit, victumque ulciscitur orbem.*
>
> For luxury has introduc'd such harms,
> As take revenge for our victorious arms.

but also to serve for a blood-letting to their republic, and a little to exhale the too vehement heat of their youth, to prune and clear the branches from the too luxuriant trunk; and to this end it was, that they formerly maintained so long a war with Carthage.

In the treaty with Brittany, Edward the third, king of England, would not, in the general peace he then made with our king, comprehend the controversy about the duchy of Brittany,† that he might have a place wherein to discharge himself of his sol- ^{Politics of Edward III. king of England.}

---

* Juv. sat. vi. ver. 192.   † Froissart, vol. i. cap. 213.

diers; and that the vast number of English he had
brought over to serve him in that expedition, might
not return back into England. And this was also
one reason why our king Philip consented to send
his son John on the expedition beyond sea, that he
might take along with him a great number of hot-⎱
brained young fellows, that were then in his troops. ⎰

The utility
of a fo-
reign war. In our times, there are many who talk at this rate,
wishing that this hot commotion now amongst us,
might discharge itself in some neighbouring war, lest
the peccant humours which now reign in the politic
body, if not diffused farther, should keep the fever
still raging, and end in our total ruin; and, in truth, a
foreign is much more supportable than a civil war;
but I do not believe, that God will favour so unjust
a design, as to offend and quarrel with others for our
own advantage;

> *Nil mihi tam valde placeat, Rhamnusia virgo,*
> *Quod temerè invitis suspiciatur heris.*[*]
>
> In unjust war, against another's right,
> For sake of plunder, may I ne'er delight.

Men forced
to use bad
means for
obtaining a
good end. Yet the weakness of our condition often puts us
under the necessity of making use of ill means to a
good end. Lycurgus, the most virtuous and perfect
legislator that ever was, invented this unjust practice of making " The Helotes, who were their slaves,
" drunk by force, and so doing to teach his people
" temperance, and an aversion to drunkenness."[†]
Yet they were more to blame, who, of old, gave leave
that criminals,[‡] to what sort of death soever they
were condemned, should be dissected alive by the
physicians, that they might view our inward parts
before death, and thereby build their art upon greater certainty. For, if we must run into excesses, it is

---

* Catul. Carm. 66, ver. 78.
† Plutarch, in the Life of Lycurgus, chap. 21 of Amyot's transla-
tion.
‡ This is reported by Celsus, who does not disapprove it. A.
Corn. Celsi Medicina in Præfat. p. 7, edit, Th, I. ab Almeloven,
Amst. 1713.

more excusable to do it for the health of the soul,
than that of the body; as the Romans trained up the
people to valour, and the contempt of dangers and
death, by those furious spectacles of gladiators and
fencers, who fought it out till the last, cut, and killed
one another in their presence:

Quid vesani aliud sibi vult ars impia ludi,
Quid mortes juvenum, quid sanguine pasta voluptas ?ᵃ

Of such inhuman sports what farther use ?
What pleasure can the blood of men produce?

And this custom continued till the emperor Theodo-
sius's time:

Arripe dilatam tua, dux, in tempora famam,
Quodque patris superest successor laudis habeto ;
Nullus in urbe cadat, cujus sit pœna voluptas,
Jam solis contenta feris infamis arena,
Nulla cruentatis homicidia laudat in armis.†

Prince, take the honours destin'd for thy reign,
Inherit of thy father what remain,
Henceforth let none at Rome for sport be slain,
Let none but beasts' blood stain the theatre,
And no more homicides be acted there.

It was, in truth, a wonderful example, and of very
great advantage for the instruction of the people, to
see every day before their eyes a hundred, two hundred, nay, a thousand couples of men armed against
one another, cut one another to pieces with such intrepidity, that they were never heard to utter so
much as one syllable of weakness or commisera-
tion; never seen to turn back, nor so much as to
make one cowardly motion to evade a blow, but rather exposed their necks to the adversaries' sword,
and presented themselves to receive the stroke. And
many of them, when mortally wounded, have sent to
ask the spectators, " If they were satisfied with their
" behaviour ?" and then lay down to give up the
ghost upon the place. It was not enough for them
to fight and die bravely, but cheerfully too; inso-

---

* Prudent. lib. ult. ver. 649.   † Idem, ibid.

much that they were hissed and cursed, if they made
any dispute about receiving their death. The very
maids themselves egged them on:

—— *Consurgit ad ictus :*
Et quoties victor ferrum jugulo inserit, illa
Delicias ait esse suas, pectusque jacentis
Virgo modesta jubet conservo pollice rumpi.*

The modest virgin is delighted so
With the fell sport, that she applauds the blow ;
And when the victor bathes his bloody hand
In's fellow's throat, and lays him on the sand ;
Then she's most pleas'd, and shows, by sign, she'd fain
Have him rip up the bosom of the slain.

The ancient Romans employed criminals in this lesson; but they afterwards employed innocent slaves
in the work, and even freemen too, who sold themselves to this effect; nay, moreover, senators and
knights of Rome ; and also women :

Nunc caput in mortem vendunt, et funus arenæ,
Atque hostem sibi quisque parat cum bella quiescunt.†

They sell themselves to death, and, since the wars
Are ceas'd, each for himself a foe prepares.

Hos inter fremitus, novosque lusus
Stat sexus rudis, insciusque ferri,
Et pugnas capit improbus viriles.‡

Amidst these tumults and alarms,
The tender sex, unskill'd in arms,
Challeng'd each other to engage,
And fought, as men, with equal rage.

Which I would think strange and incredible, were
we not accustomed every day to see, in our own wars,§
many thousands of men, of other nations, staking
their blood and their lives for money, often in quarrels wherein they have no manner of concern.

* Prudent. lib. ult. ver. 617.   † Manil. Astron. lib. iv. v. 225, 226.
‡ Statius, Syl. 6, lib. i. ver. 52, 53, 54.
§ Witness the Swiss, who, though of the same country, and perhaps of the same family, serve one against another for pay, in the armies of France, Holland, &c.

CHAPTER XV.

Of the Roman Grandeur.

I WILL only say a word or two of this extensive subject, to show the simplicity of those who compare the pitiful grandeur of these times to that of Rome. In the seventh book of Cicero's Familiar Epistles (but let the grammarians expunge the surname of Familiar, if they please, for, in truth, it is not very proper; and they who, instead of Familiar, have substituted *ad familiares*, may gather something to justify them for so doing, out of what Suetonius says, in the life of Cæsar, "That he had a volume "of letters of his, *ad familiares*"), there is one directed to Cæsar, being then in Gaul, wherein Cicero repeats these words, which were in the end of another letter that Cæsar had wrote to him : "As for " Marcus Furius, whom you have recommended to " me, I will make him king of Gaul; and, if you " would have me advance any other friend of yours, " send him to me."* It was no new thing for a mere citizen of Rome, as Cæsar then was, to dispose of kingdoms; for he took away that of king Deiotarus from him, to give it to a gentleman of the city of Pergamus, called Mithridates.† They who wrote his life, record several cities sold by him; and Suetonius says, "That he had, at once, from king "Ptolemy, near six thousand talents, or three mil- " lions and six hundred thousand crowns," which was almost the same as selling him his own kingdom :

Tot Galatæ, tot Pontus, tot Lydia nummis.‡
Such sums of money did he raise, as these,
From Pontus, Lydia, and the Galates.

---

* Lib. vii. ep. 5. Ciceronis Cæsari imper,
† Cic. de Divinat. lib. ii. cap. 37.
‡ Claud. in Eutrop. lib. i. cap. 203.

A great king deprived of his conquests, by a letter from the Roman senate, Mark Anthony said, "That the grandeur of the "people of Rome was not so much seen in what "they took, as in what they gave."* Yet, many years before Anthony, they had dethroned one amongst the rest with so wonderful authority, that, in all the Roman history, I have not observed any thing that more denotes the height of their power. Antiochus possessed all Egypt, and was, moreover, ready to conquer Cyprus, and other appendices of that empire; when, being upon the progress of his victories, C. Popilius came to him from the Senate, and, at their first meeting, refused to take him by the hand, till he had read his letters, which after the king had perused, and told him, he would consider of them, Popilius made a circle about him with the stick he had in his hand, saying, "Return me "an answer, that I may carry it back to the senate, "before thou stirrest out of this circle."† Antiochus, astonished at the roughness of so urgent a command, after a little pause, replied, "I will obey "the senate's command;" and then it was that Popilius saluted him as a friend to the people of Rome. After having quitted claim to so great a monarchy, and in such a torrent of successful fortune, upon three words in writing; in earnest he had reason, as he did, to send the senate word, by his ambassadors, "That he had received their order with the same "respect, as if it had arrived from the immortal "gods.‡

Why the Romans restored their conquered kingdoms to their owners. All the kingdoms that Augustus gained by the right of conquest, he either restored to those who had lost them, or presented them to strangers. And Tacitus, in reference to this, speaking of Cogidunus, king of England, gives us a wonderful instance of that infinite power: "The Romans," says he, "were, from all antiquity, accustomed to leave the "kings they had subdued, in possession of their

---

* Plutarch, in the Life of Anthony, cap. 8.
† Tit. Liv. lib. xiv. cap, 12.   ‡ Idem, ibid. cap. 23.

" kingdom under their authority, that they might
" have even kings to be their slaves :" *Ut haberent
instrumenta servitutis et reges.* It is likely, that
Solyman, whom we have seen make a gift of Hungary, and other principalities, had therein more respect to this consideration, than to that he was wont to
allege, viz. " That he was glutted and overcharged
" with so many monarchies, and so much dominion,
" as his own valour, or that of his ancestors, had
" acquired."

CHAPTER XVI.

Not to counterfeit Sickness.

THERE is a choice epigram in Martial, for he has
of all sorts, where he pleasantly tells the story of
Cælius, who, to avoid making his court to some
great men of Rome, to go to their levee, and to attend them abroad, pretended to have the gout ; and
the better to colour it, anointed his legs, had them
swathed up, and perfectly counterfeited both the
gesture and countenance of a gouty person ; till, in
the end, fortune did him the kindness to give him
the gout in earnest :

<small>Gout coun-
terfeit be-
came a real
gout.</small>

> *Tantum cura potest et ars doloris,*
> *Desiit fingere Cælius podagram.†*
> So much has counterfeiting brought about,
> Cælius has ceas'd to counterfeit the gout.

I think I have read, somewhere in Appian, a
story like this, of one who, to escape the proscrip-
tions of the triumviri of Rome, and the better to be
concealed from the discovery of those who pursued

<small>Instance of
a man, who
became
really blind
in one eye,
after he had</small>

---

* Tit. Liv. in Vità Julii Agricolæ.
† Mart. epig. 38, lib. vii. ver. 8, 9.

counter-
felted it.

him, having masked himself in a disguise, did also
add this invention, " To counterfeit having but one
" eye ; but, when he came to have a little more li-
" berty, and went to take off the plaster he had a
" great while worn over his eye, he found he had
" totally lost the sight of it." It is possible, that
the action of sight was dulled, for having been so
long without exercise, and that the optic power was
wholly retired into the other eye : for we evidently
perceive, that the eye we keep shut, sends some
part of its virtue to its fellow, which thereby swells
and grows bigger ; moreover, the sitting still, with
the heat of the ligatures and plasters, might very
well have brought some gouty humour upon this
dissembler in Martial.

Ridiculous
vow of some
young Eng-
lish gal-
lants.

Reading, in Froissard,* the vow of a company of
young English gallants, " To carry their left eyes
" bound up till they were arrived in France, and
" had performed some notable exploit against
" us :" I have often been tickled with the conceit
of its befalling them as it did the before-named Roman, and that they found they had but one eye
a-piece when they returned to their mistresses, for
whose sakes they had entered into this ridiculous
vow.

It is pro-
per to hin-
der chil-
dren from
counter-
feiting per-
sonal de-
fects.

Mothers have reason to rebuke their children,
when they counterfeit having but one eye, squint-
ing, lameness, or other such personal defects ; for,
besides that their bodies, being then so tender, may
be subject to take an ill bent, fortune, I know not
how, sometimes seems to delight to take us at our
word ; and I have heard several instances of people
who have become really sick, by only feigning to be
so. I have always used, whether on horseback, or
on foot, to carry a stick in my hand, and so as to
affect doing it with a grace. Many have threatened
me, that this affected hobbling would, one day, be

* Vol. i. chap. 29.

turned into necessity, that is, " That I should be
" the first of my family to have the gout."

But let us lengthen this chapter, and eke it out *Instance of*
with another piece, concerning blindness. Pliny *a man who*
was depriv-
reports of one, " That dreaming he was blind, found *ed of sight*
in his sleep.
" himself so next day, without any preceding ma-
" lady."* The force of imagination might assist in
this case, as I have said elsewhere, and Pliny seems
to be of the same opinion ; but it is more likely, that
the motions the body felt within (whereof the physicians, if they please, may find out the cause), which
took away his sight, were the occasion of his
dream.

Let us add another story, of much the same na- *A foolish*
woman,
ture, which Seneca relates, in one of his epistles.† *who fell*
blind,
" You know," says he, writing to Lucillius, " that *blind,*
" Harpaste, my wife's fool, is thrown upon my fa- *found fault*
with the
" mily as an hereditary charge, for I have naturally *house she*
lived in,
" an aversion to those monsters ; and, if I have a *that it was*
" mind to laugh at a fool, I need not seek him far, *too dark ;*
" I can laugh at myself. This fool has suddenly *a resem-*
blance of
" lost her sight : I can tell you a strange, but a very *most men's*
folly.
" true thing ; she is not sensible that she is blind,
" but eternally importunes her keeper to take her
" abroad, because she says my house is dark : but,
" believe me, that what we laugh at in her,
" happens to every one of us : no one knows him-
" self to be avaricious. Besides the blind call for
" a guide, but we wander of our own accord. I am
" not ambitious, we say, but a man cannot live
" otherwise at Rome : I am not wasteful, but the
" city requires a great expense : it is not my fault if
" I am choleric ; and, if I have not yet established
" any certain course of life, it is the fault of youth.
" Let us not look abroad for our disease, it is in us,
" and planted in our intestines : and our not per-
" ceiving ourselves to be sick even renders us more
" hard to be cured : if we do not betimes begin to

* Nat. Hist. lib. vii. cap. 50.   † Ep. 50.
11

" dress ourselves, when shall we have done with so
" many wounds and evils that afflict us? And yet
" we have a most pleasant medicine in philosophy;
" of all others, we are not sensible of the pleasure
" till after the cure; this pleases and heals at the
" same time." This is what Seneca says, who has
carried me from my subject; but it is a digression
not unprofitable.

CHAPTER XVII

Of Thumbs.

A custom of screwing the thumbs, wounding them, and sucking the blood. TACITUS* reports, that, amongst certain bar-
barian kings, their manner was, when they would
make a firm obligation, to join their right hands
close together, and twist each other's thumbs; and
when, by force of pressure, the blood appeared in
the ends, they lightly pricked them with some sharp
instrument, and mutually sucked them.

Etymology of the Latin word pollex, for thumb. Physicians say, " That the thumb is the master-
" finger of each hand, and that the Latin etymology
" is derived from *pollere*."† The Greeks called it
ἀντιχειρ, as who should say, another hand. And it
seems, that the Latins also sometimes take it, in this
sense, for the whole hand:

> *Sed nec vocibus excitata blandis,*
> *Molli pollice nec rogata surgit.*‡

When the thumbs denoted favour, and when disgust. It was, at Rome, a signification of favour; to turn
down and clap in the thumbs:

> *Fautor utroque tuum laudabit pollice ludum.*§

---

* Annal. lib. xii.
† This seems to be taken from Macrobius's Saturn. lib. vii. cap. 13,
who took it, in his turn, from Atticus Capito.
‡ Mart. lib. xii. epig. 99, ver. 8, 9.
§ Horat. lib. i. ep. 18, ver. 66.

Thy patron, when thou mak'st thy sport,
Will with both thumbs applaud thee for't.

And of disfavour to lift them up, and thrust them outward:

—— *Converso pollice vulgi*
*Quemlibet occidunt populariter.**

The vulgar, with up lifted thumbs,
Kill each one that before them comes.†

The Romans exempted from war all such as were maimed in the thumbs, as persons not able to bear arms. Augustus confiscated the estate of a Roman knight, " Who had maliciously cut off the thumbs " of two young children he had, to excuse them " from going into the armies;"‡ and, before him, the senate, in the time of the Italian war, condemned Caius Valienus to perpetual imprisonment, and confiscated all his goods, " For having purposely " cut off the thumb of his left hand, to exempt him- " self from that expedition."§

[margin: Those who cut off their thumbs, why punished by the Romans.]

Some one, I have forgot who, having won a naval battle, " Cut off the thumbs of all his vanquished " enemies, to render them incapable of fighting, " and of handling the oar." The Athenians also caused the thumbs of those of Ægina to be cut off, " To deprive them of the preference in the art of " navigation."‖ And, in Lacedæmonia, pedagogues chastised their scholars by biting their thumbs.

[margin: Thumbs of the vanquished enemy cut off.]

* Juv. sat. iii. ver. 36.
† This was a metaphorical manner of speech, taken from the arena. When a gladiator was thrown in fighting, the people asked his life, by turning down their thumbs, or his death by lifting them up.
‡ Suet. in Cæsar. Augusto, sect. 24.
§ Val. Max. lib. v. cap. 3, sect. 3.
‖ Idem, lib. ix. in Externis, sect. 8.

CHAPTER XVIII.

Cowardice the Mother of Cruelty.

Cruelty the common effect of cowardice. I HAVE often heard it said, " That cowardice is the mother of cruelty:" yet I have found, by experience, that that malicious and inhumane animosity and fierceness is usually accompanied with a feminine faintness. I have seen the most cruel people, and upon frivolous occasions, very apt to cry. Alexander, the tyrant of Pheres, durst not be a spectator of tragedies on the theatre, lest his subjects should see him weep at the misfortunes of Hecuba and Andromache :* " Though he himself caused so " many people every day to be cruelly murdered." Is it not meanness of spirit, that renders them so pliable to all extremities? Valour (whose effect is only to be exercised against resistance,

Nec nisi bellantis gaudet cervice juvenci.†

——— Neither, unless it fight,
In conquering a bull does he delight.)

stops when it sees the enemy at its mercy; but pusillanimity, to say that it was also in the action, not having courage to meddle in the first act, rushes into the second, of blood and massacre. The murders in victories are commonly performed by the rascality, and officers of the baggage; and that which causes so many unheard of cruelties, in domestic wars, is, " That the dregs of the people are " flushed in being up to the elbows in blood, and " ripping up bodies that lie prostrate at their feet, " having no sense of any other valour."

---

* Plutarch, in the Life of Pelopidas, ch. xv.
† Claud. ad Hadrianum, ver. 30.

Et lupus, et turpes instant morientibus ursi,
*Et quæcunque minor nobilitate fera est.**

None but the wolves, the filthy bears, and all
Th' ignoble beasts, will on the dying fall.

Like cowardly curs, that, in the house, worry and
tear in pieces the skins of wild beasts, which they
durst not attack in the field. What is it, in these
times, that causes our mortal quarrels? And how
comes it that, where our ancestors had some degree
of revenge, we now begin with the last degree, and
that, at the first meeting, nothing is to be said, but
kill? What is this but cowardice?

Every one is sensible, that there is more bravery Revenge
and disdain in subduing an enemy, than in cutting is rendered of no effect
his throat; and in making him yield, than in putting by killing
him to the sword: besides that, the appetite of re- an enemy.
venge is better assuaged and gratified, because its
only aim is to make itself felt: and this is the reason
why we do not fall upon a block or a stone when
they hurt us, because they are not capable of feeling
our revenge; and to kill a man is to shelter
him from the hurt we intend him. And as
Bias cried out to a wicked fellow, " I know
" that, sooner or later, thou wilt have thy reward,
" but I am afraid I shall not see it." And as the
Orchomenians complained, " That the penitence of
" Lyciscus, for the treason committed against them,
" came at a time when there was no one remaining
" alive of those who had been concerned in it, and
" whom the pleasure of this penitency must have af-
" fected;" so revenge is to be repented of, when the
person on whom it is executed loses the means of
suffering it: for as the avenger desires to see and
enjoy the pleasure of his revenge, so the person on
whom he takes revenge, should be a spectator too,
to be mortified by it, and brought to repentance.
He shall repent it, we say, and, because we have
given him a pistol-shot through the head, do we

‡ Ovid. Trist. lib. iii. eleg. 5, ver. 35.

imagine he will repent? On the contrary, if we but
observe, we shall find, that he makes a mouth at us
in falling; and is so far from repenting, that he does
not so much as repine at us: and we do him the
kindest office of life, which is to make him die speedily and insensibly: we are afterwards to hide ourselves, and to shift and fly from the officers of justice, who pursue us; and all the while he is at rest.
Killing is good to frustrate a future injury, not to
revenge one that is already past; and it is more an
act of fear than bravery, of precaution than courage,
and of defence than of offence; it is manifest that
by it we abandon both the true end of revenge, and
the care of our reputation; we are afraid, if he lives,
he will do us such another injury. It is not out of
animosity to him, but care of thyself, that thou rid-
dest him out of the way.

Duels com-
mon, and
authorised
in the king-
dom of
Narsingua.

In the kingdom of Narsingua, this expedient
would be useless to us: there not only soldiers, but
tradesmen also end their differences by the sword.
" The king never denies the field to any one that
" will fight; and, when they are persons of quality,
" he looks on, rewarding the victor with a chain of
" gold; for which any one that will, may fight with
" him who wears it: thus, by coming off from one
" combat, he is engaged in many." If we thought, by
valour, to be always masters of our enemies, and to
triumph over them at pleasure, we would be sorry
they should escape from us as they do, by dying;
but we have a mind to conquer more with safety
than honour, and, in our quarrel, pursue more the
end than the glory.

Pollio's li-
bel against
Plancus.

Asinius Pollio, who, for being a worthy man, was
less to be excused, committed a like error, who, having wrote a libel against Plancus, " Deferred to pub-
" lish it, till he was long dead:"* which is to make
mouths at a blind man, to rail at one that is deaf,
and to wound a man that has no feeling, rather than

* Pliny's Preface to Vespasian.

to run the hazard of his resentment. And Plancus is made to say, in his own behalf, " That it was only " for ghosts to struggle with the dead." He that stays to see the author die, whose writings he intends to quarrel with, what does he but declare, that he would bite, but has not teeth? It was told Aristotle, " That some one had spoken ill of him." " Let him do more," said he, " let him whip me " too, provided I am not there."

Our fathers contented themselves to revenge an injury with the lie, the lie with a box on the ear, and so forth; they were valiant enough not to fear their adversary, both living and provoked: we tremble for fear, so long as we see them on foot. And, that this is so, is it not our noble practice of these days equally to prosecute to death both him that has offended us, and him whom we have offended?

The lie re-
venged
with a box
on the ear.

It is also a kind of cowardice, that has introduced the custom of seconds, thirds, and fourths in our duels: they were formerly duels, they are now skir-mishes and battles. The first inventors of this prac-tice feared to be alone: *Quum in se cuique minimum fiduciæ esset ;* " They had little confidence in them-" selves." For, naturally, any company whatever is comfortable and assisting in danger. Third per-sons were formerly called in to prevent disorder and foul play only, and to be witnesses of the success of the combat. But since they have brought it to this pass, that they themselves engage, whoever is in-vited cannot handsomely stand by as an idle spec-tator, for fear of being suspected either of want of af-fection or courage. Besides the injustice and un-worthiness of such an action, the engaging other force and valour, in the protection of your honour, than your own; I conceive it a disadvantage to a brave man, and who wholly relies upon himself, to shuffle his fortune with that of a second, since every one runs hazard enough for himself, without running it for another, and has enough to do to depend on his own valour for the defence of his life, without in-trusting a thing so dear in a third man's hand: for,

Seconds in-
troduced,
in duels,
by coward-
ice.

2 D 2

:if it be not expressly agreed on before to the contrary, it is a combined party of all four, and, if your
second be killed, you have two to deal withal with
good reason. And to say, that it is foul play; it is
so indeed, as it is for one, well-armed, to attack a
man that has but the hilts of a broken sword in his
hand, or for a man clear, and in a whole skin, to
fall on a man that is already desperately wounded;
but, if these be advantages you have got by fighting,
you may make use of them without reproach: all
that is weighed and considered is the disparity and
inequality of the condition of the combatants when
they begun; as to the rest, you charge it upon fortune: and though you had alone three enemies upon
you at once, your two companions being killed, you
have no more wrong done you, than I should do,
in a battle, by running a man through, whom I
should see engaged with one of our men, at the like
advantage. The nature of society requires, that
where there is troop against troop (as where our
duke of Orleans* challenged Henry king of England, a hundred against a hundred; where the Ar-
gives challenged three hundred against as many of
the Lacedæmonians,† and three to three, as the
Horatii against the Curatii), the multitude on either
side is considered but as one single man. Wherever
there is company, the hazard is confused and
mixed.

A story of
a duel br-
tween some
French
gentlemen,
in which a
brother of
Montaigne
was engag-
ed. I have a domestic interest in this discourse; for
my brother the Sieur de Matecoulom, was at Rome
entreated by a gentleman, with whom he had no
great acquaintance, and who was defendant, and
challenged by another, to be his second; in this
duel he found himself matched with a gentleman,
his neighbour, much better known to him, where,
after having dispatched his man, seeing the two
principals still on foot, and sound, he ran in to disengage his friend. What could he do less? Should

* Monstrelet's Chronicle, vol. i. chap. 9.
† Herodot. lib. i. p. 37.

he have stood still, and, if chance had ordered it so,
have seen him he was come thither to defend killed
before his face? What he had hitherto done signified
nothing to the business, the quarrel was yet unde-
cided: the courtesy that you may, and certainly
ought, to show to your enemy, when you have reduced him to an ill condition, and have a great advantage over him, I do not see how you can show it,
where the interest of another is in the case, where
you are only called in as an assistant, and where the
quarrel is none of yours; he could neither be just
nor courteous at the hazard of him he had agreed to
second, and he was also enlarged from the prisons of
Italy, at the speedy and solemn request of our king.
Indiscreet nation! we are not content to make our
vices and follies known to the world by report only
but we must go into foreign countries, there to show
them what fools we are. Put three Frenchmen into
the deserts of Lybia, they will not live a month together without quarrelling and fighting; so that you
would say, that this peregrination were a thing purposely designed to give strangers the pleasure of
our tragedies, and often to such as rejoice and laugh
at our miseries. We go into Italy to learn to fence,
and fall to practice at the expense of our lives before we have learned it; and yet, according to the
rule of discipline, the theory should precede the
practice. We discover ourselves to be but learners:

> *Primitiæ juvenum miseræ, bellique futuri*
> *Dura rudimenta.*[*]———
>
> To youth the first instructions irksome prove,
> Nor soon the rules of future war they love.

I know fencing is an art very useful to its end, and Fencing
have experimentally found that skill in it hath in- hath no-
spired some with courage above their natural ta- in it.
lent;[†] but this is not properly valour, because it

---

[*] Æneid. lib. xi. ver. 156.
[†] In a duel between two princes, cousin-german, in Spain, the
elder (says Pliny) by his craft and dexterity in arms, easily surmounted the awkward strength of the younger, lib. xxviii. cap. 21.

supports itself by skill, and is founded upon something besides itself; the honour of combat consists in the emulation of courage, and not of skill; and therefore I have known a friend of mine, famed for a great master of this exercise, make choice of such arms in his quarrels as might deprive him of the means of this advantage, and wholly depended upon fortune and assurance, to the end that they might not attribute his victory rather to his skill in fencing than his valour. When I was young, gentlemen avoided the reputation of good fencers, as injurious to them; and learned to fence with all imaginable privacy, as a trade of subtlety, derogating from true and native virtue:

> *Non schivar, non parar, non ritirarsi,*
> *Voglion costor, ne qui destrezza ha parte,*
> *Non danno i colpi finti hor pieni, hor scarsi,*
> *Toglie l'ira e il furor l'uso de l'arte.*
> *O di le spade horribilmente utarsi*
> *Amenzo il ferro, il pie d'orma non parte :*
> *Sempre è il pie fermo, è la man sempre in moto ;*
> *Ne scende taglio in van ne punta à voto.*

> They neither shrank, nor vantage sought of ground,
>   They travers'd not, nor skipp'd from part to part;
> Their blows were neither false nor feigned found,
>   Their wrath, their rage, would let them use no art.
> Their swords together clash with dreadful sound,
>   Their feet stand fast, and neither stir nor start;
> They move their hands, stedfast their feet remain,
> Nor blow nor foin they struck, or thrust in vain.†

Butts, tilts, and tournaments, the images of warlike fights, were the exercises of our forefathers.

An indecent art, because it induces us to break the laws.

This other exercise is so much the less noble, as it only respects a private end; as it teaches us to ruin one another, against law and justice, and as it always produces mischievous effects. It is much more worthy and becoming to exercise ourselves in things that strengthen than that weaken our governments, and that tend to the public safety and common glory. Publius Rutilius Consus was the first

* Tasso's Her. cant. 12, stanz. 55.   † Mr. Fairfax.

that taught soldiers " To handle their arms with
" skill, and joined art to valour ; not for the use of
" private quarrel, but for war, and the quarrels of
" the people of Rome :"* a popular and civil art of
fencing. And, besides the example of Cæsar, " Who
" commanded his men to shoot chiefly at the faces
" of Pompey's gens-d'armes, in the battle of Phar-
" salia," a thousand other commanders have also
bethought them to invent new forms of weapons,
and new ways of striking and defending, according
as occasion should require.

But as Philopæmen " Condemned wrestling, *It is useless
" wherein he excelled, because the preparatives and detri-
" that were therein employed were different from military
" those that appertain to military discipline, to combat.
" which alone he conceived men of honour ought
" to apply themselves ;" so it seems to me, that
this address, to which we form our limbs, those
writhings and motions young men are taught in this
new school, are not only of no use, but rather contrary and hurtful to the manner of fight in battle ;
our people also commonly make use of particular
weapons, peculiarly designed for duel. And I have
known, when it has been disapproved, that a gentleman, challenged to fight with rapier and poniard,
should appear in the equipage of a man at arms ;
or that another should go thither with his cloak instead of a poniard. It is worthy of consideration,
that Lachez, in Plato, speaking of learning to fence
after our manner, says, " That he never knew any
" great soldier come out of that school, especially
" the masters of it :"† and indeed, as to them, our
own experience tells us as much. As to the rest,
we may at least conclude, that they are abilities of
no relation nor correspondence ; and, in the education of the children of his government, Plato ‡ pro-

* Valer. Max. lib. ii. cap. 3. sect. 2.
† Plato's dialogue, entitled Lachez, p. 247.
‡ De Legibus, lib. vii. p. 630.

The art of boxing prohibited by Plato. hibits the art of boxing, introduced by Amicus and Epeius, and that of wrestling by Antus and Cecyo,* because " They have another end than to " render youth fit for the service of the war, and " contribute nothing to it." But I see I am too far strayed from my theme.

The emperor Maurice, being advertised by dreams and several prognostics, that one Phocas, an obscure soldier, would kill him, questioned his son-in-law Philip, " Who this Phocas was, and what was his " nature, qualities, and manners;" and as soon as Philip, amongst other things, had told him, " That Cruel and bloody men naturally cowards, " he was cowardly and timorous," the emperor immediately thence concluded, " That he was a mur-" derer and cruel." What is it that makes tyrants so bloody? It is only the solicitude for their own safety, and that their faint hearts can furnish them with no other means of securing themselves, than in exterminating those that may hurt them, even so much as the women, for fear of a scratch :

Cuncta ferit, dum cuncta timet.†

He strikes at all, who every one does fear.

One act of cruelty necessarily produces others. The first cruelties are exercised for themselves; from thence springs the fear of a just revenge, which afterwards produces a series of new cruelties, to obliterate one by the other. Philip, king of Macedon, who had so much upon his hands with the people of Rome, agitated with the horror of so many murders committed by his appointment, and doubting of being able to regain his credit with so many families, whom he had at diverse times offended, " Resolved to seize all the children of those " he had caused to be slain, to dispatch them daily " one after another, and thereby establish his own " repose." Good subjects become any place; and

---

* Or rather Cercyo, Κερκύων, Plato de Legib. lib. vii. p. 630.
† Claud. in Eutrop. lib. i. ver. 182.

therefore I, who more consider the weight and utility
of what I deliver than its order and connexion,
need not fear in this place to bring in a fine story,
though it be a little by the by ; for when such subjects are rich in their own native beauty, and are
able to justify themselves, the least end of a hair
will serve to draw them into my discourse.

" Amongst others condemned by Philip, Hero- A remark-
" dicus, Prince of Thessaly, had been one.* He able story
" had, moreover, after him, caused his two sons-in-ject.
" law to be put to death, who each left a son very
" young behind him. Theoxena and Archo were
" the two widows. Theoxena, though warmly
" courted to it, could not be persuaded to marry
" again ; Archo was married to Poris, the greatest
" man of the Ænians, and by him had a great
" many children, which she, dying, left all minors.
" Theoxena, moved with a maternal charity towards
" her nephews, that she might have them under her
" own conduct and protection, married Poris ;
" when presently comes a proclamation of the
" king's edict. This bold spirited mother, suspect-
" ing the cruelty of Philip, and afraid of the inso-
" lence of the soldiers towards these lovely young
" children, was so bold as to declare, that she would
" rather kill them with her own hands than deliver
" them up. Poris, startled at this protestation, pro-
" mised her to steal them away, and to transport
" them to Athens, and there commit them to the
" custody of some trusty friends of his. They took
" therefore the opportunity of an annual feast,
" which was celebrated at Ænia, in honour of
" Æneas, and thither they went. Having appeared
" by day at the public ceremonies and banquet,
" they stole, the night following, into a vessel laid
" ready for that purpose, to make their escape by
" sea. The wind proved contrary, and finding
" themselves, in the morning, within sight of the

---

* The entire story is taken from Titus Livy, lib. xi. cap. 4.

" land, from whence they had launched over night,
" were pursued by the guards of the port; which
" Poris perceiving, he laboured all he could to has-
" ten the mariners to put off. But Theoxena, fran-
" tic with affection and revenge, in pursuance of
" her former resolution, prepared both arms and poi-
" son, and exposing them before them; ' Go to, my
" children,' said she, ' death is now the only means
" of your defence and liberty, and 'will administer
" occasion to the gods to exercise their sacred jus-
" tice; these drawn swords, these full cups, will
" open to you the way to it; be of good courage;
" and thou my son, who art the eldest, take this
" steel into thy hand, that thou mayest the more
" bravely die.' The children having, on one side,
" so hearty a counsellor, and the enemy at their
" throats on the other, ran all of them eagerly to
" dispatch themselves with what was next to hand;
" and, when half dead, were thrown into the sea.
" Theoxena, proud of having so gloriously pro-
" vided for the safety of her children, clasping her
" arms with great affection about her husband's
" neck; ' Let us, my dear,' said she, ' follow these
" boys, and enjoy the same sepulchre they do;'
" and thus embraced, they threw themselves head-
" long overboard into the sea; so that the ship was
" carried back without its owners into the har-
" bour."

Tyrants, at once both to kill and to make their anger felt, have racked their wit to invent the most lingering deaths: they will have their enemies dispatched, but not so fast that they may not have leisure to taste their vengeance: and herein they are mightily perplexed; for, if the torments they inflict are violent, they are short; if long, they are not then so painful as they desire; and thus torment themselves, in contriving how to torment others. Of this we have a thousand examples in antiquity, and I know not whether we, unawares, do not retain some traces of this barbarity.

Tyrants contrive to lengthen the torments of those they put to death.

All that exceeds a simple death, appears to me *Executions* mere cruelty; neither can our justice expect that *of justice beyond* he, whom the fear of death, by being beheaded or *merely* hanged, will not restrain, should be any more awed *putting to* by the imagination of a slow fire, burning pincers, *lute cruel-* or the wheel. I know not whether we do not even *ty.* drive them into despair by that means; for in what condition can the soul of a man be who expects death four and twenty hours together, whether he is broke upon a wheel, or after the old way nailed to a cross? Josephus relates, " That in the time of the " war which the Romans made in Judea, happening " to pass by where they had, three days before, " crucified certain Jews, he knew three of his " own friends amongst them, and obtained the fa- " vour of having them taken down. Two of " them," he says, " died, the third, lived a great " while after."

Chacondilas, a writer of good credit, in the re- *Barbarous* cords he has left behind him of things that happened *punish-* in his time, and near him, tells us; as one of the *flicted by* most excessive torments, of what the emperor *ror Mech.* Mechmed often practised, viz. " Cutting off men *med.* " in the middle by the diaphragma, with one blow " of a scimitar; by which it followed that they " died, as it were, two deaths at once, and both the " one part," says he, " and the other were seen to " stir a great while after with the torment." I do not think there was any great suffering in this mo- tion; the torments that are most dreadful to look on are not always the greatest to endure; and I think those that other historians relate to have been practised upon the Epirot lords to be more cruel, who were " Condemned to be flayed alive by piece- " meal, in so malicious a manner that they conti- " nued in this misery a fortnight;" as also these other two that follow.

" Crœsus, having caused a gentleman, the favou- *Two more* " rite of his brother Pantaleon, to be seized on, *of exces-*

sive cruel-
ty.

" carried him into a fuller's shop, where he caused
" him to be scratched and carded with cards and
" combs belonging to that craft, till he died.*—
" George Sechel, chief commander of the peasants
" of Poland, who committed so many mischiefs un-
" der the title of the Crusado, being defeated in
" battle, and taken by the vayvod of Transylvania,
" was three days bound naked upon the rack, ex-
" posed to all sorts of torments that any one
" could inflict upon him ; during which time many
" other prisoners were kept fasting.   At last,
" while he was living and looking on, they made
" his beloved brother Lucat, for whose safety alone
" he entreated, by taking upon himself the blame
" of all their evil actions, to drink his blood, and
" caused twenty of his most favoured captains to
" feed upon him, tearing his flesh in pieces with
" their teeth, and swallowing the morsels ; the re-
" mainder of his body and bowels, as soon as he
" was dead, were boiled, and others of his followers
" compelled to eat them."

CHAPTER XIX.

All Things have their Season.

SUCH as compare Cato the censor with the
younger Cato that killed himself, compare two
beautiful natures and forms much resembling one
another.   The first acquired his reputation several
ways, and excelled in " military exploits, and the
The virtue " utility of his public vocations ;" but the virtue
of Cato of
Utica pre. of the younger, besides that it were blasphemy to

* Herodot. lib. i. p. 44.

compare any to him in vigour, was much more pure; *ferable to for who can acquit the censor of envy and ambition, that of Cato the after " He had dared to offend the honour of Scipio, censor.* " a man in goodness and all excellent qualities in-" finitely beyond him, or any other of his time?"

That which they report of him, amongst other *Cato the censor took to learn Greek too late in life.* things, " That in his extreme old age he set him-" self to learn the Greek tongue with so greedy an " appetite, as if he was to quench a long thirst," does not seem to make for his honour; it being pro-perly what we call being twice a child.

" All things have their season," good and bad, and a man may say his Pater-noster out of time; as they accused T. Quintus Flaminius, " That, being " general of an army, he was seen praying apart in " the time of a battle that he won."*

Imponet † finem sapiens, et rebus honestis.‡
The wise man limits even decent things.

Eudemonidas, seeing Xenocrates, when very old, still very intent upon his school lectures, " When " will this man be wise," said he, " if he yet " learn ?"§ and Philopæmen, to those who cried up king Ptolemy, for inuring his person every day to the exercise of arms : " It is not," said he, " com-" mendable in a king of his age to exercise himself " in those things, he ought now really to employ " them. The young are to make their preparations, " the old to enjoy them, say the sages;" and the greatest vice they observe in us is, " That our de-" sires incessantly grow young again; we are always " beginning again to live."

Our studies and desires should sometimes be sen- *Our desires ought to be mortified with old age.* sible of old age; we have one foot in the grave, and yet our appetites and pursuits spring up every day:

---

* See Plutarch's Comparison of him to Philopæmen, sect. 2.
† Juv. sat. vi. ver. 344.
‡ The words which Montaigne here applies to his own design, have another meaning in the original.
§ Plutarch's Notable Sayings of the Lacedæmonians.

Tu secanda marmora
Locas sub ipsum funus, et sepulcri
*Immemor, struis domos.**

When death, perhaps, is near at hand,
Thou fairest marbles dost command
But cut for use, large poles to rear,
Unmindful of thy sepulchre.

The longest of my designs is not above a year's extent; I think of nothing now but my end; abandon all new hopes and enterprises; take my last leave of every place I depart from, and every day dispossess myself of what I have. *Olim jam nec perit quicquam mihi, nec acquiritur; plus superest viatici, quam viæ :*† " I now shall neither lose nor " get; I have more wherewith to defray my jour- " ney than I have way to go :"

Vixi, et quem dederat cursum fortuna peregi.‡

I've liv'd, and finish'd the career
Which fortune had prescrib'd me here.

To conclude; it is the only comfort I find in my old age, that it mortifies in me several cares and desires, wherewith life is disturbed; the care how the world goes; the care of riches, of grandeur, of knowledge, of health, and myself. There are some who are learning to speak, at a time when they should learn to be silent for ever. A man may always study, but he must not always go to school. What a contemptible thing is an old man learning his A, B, C!

Diversos diversa juvant, non omnibus annis,
Omnia conveniunt.

For several things do several men delight,
And all things are not for all ages right.

---

* Hor. lib. ii. ode 18, ver. 17, &c.
† Sen. epist. 77.
‡ Æneid. lib. iv. ver. 653.

If we must study, let us follow that study which is suitable to our present condition, that we may be able to answer as he did; who, being asked, " To " what end he studied in his decrepid age ?" " That " I may go the better off the stage," said he, " and " at greater ease." Such a study was that of the younger Cato, at feeling his end approach, when he was reading Plato's discourse of the " Immortality " of the soul :" not, as we are to believe, that he was not long before furnished with all sorts of provision for such a departure; for, of assurance, an established will and instruction he had, more than Plato had in all his writings ; his knowledge and courage were, in this respect, above philosophy. He employed himself thus, not for the service of his death, but as a man whose sleep is not once disturbed in the importance of such a deliberation; he also, without choice and change, continued his studies with the other customary actions of his life. The night that he was denied the prætorship he spent in play : that wherein he was to die he spent in reading : the loss either of life, or of office, was all one to him.

What study suits best with old age.

CHAPTER XX.

Of Virtue.

I FIND, by experience, that there is a vast difference between the starts and sallies of the mind, and a resolute and constant habit ; and very well perceive, there is nothing we may not do, nay, even to the surpassing the divinity itself, says a certain person, forasmuch as it is more for a man to render himself impassible or dispassionate, than to be such by his original condition ; and even to be able to conjoin to

Man seldom attains to a capacity of acting steadily and regularly, according to the principles of solid virtue.

man's imbecility and frailty a godly resolution and
assurance. But this is by fits and starts; and, in
the lives of those heroes of times past, there are sometimes miraculous sallies, and such as seem infinitely
to exceed our natural strength; but they are indeed
sallies; and it is hard to believe, that these so elevated qualities can be so thoroughly imprinted on the
mind, that they should become common, and, as it
were, natural to it; it accidentally happens, even to
us, who are the most imperfect of men, that sometimes our mind gives a spring, when roused by the
discourses or examples of others, much beyond
its ordinary stretch; but it is a kind of passion,
which pushes and pricks it on, and, in some sort, ra-
vishes it from itself: but, this whirlwind once blown
over, we see, that it insensibly flags and slackens itself, if not to the lowest degree, at least so as to be
no more the same; insomuch as that, upon every
trivial occasion, the losing of a bird, or the breaking
of a glass, we suffer ourselves to be moved little less
than one of the common people. I am of opinion,
that, order, moderation, and constancy excepted, all
things are to be done by a man that is, in general,
very deficient. " Therefore," say the sages, " in
" order to make a right judgment of a man, you are
" chiefly to pry into his common actions, and sur-
" prise him in his every-day habit."

Pyrrho
tried, in
vain, to
conform
his life to
his doc-
trine.

Pyrrho, he who erected so pleasant a system of
knowledge upon ignorance, endeavoured, as all the
rest, who were really philosophers, did, to make his life
correspond with his doctrine : and because he maintained the imbecility of human judgment to be so
extreme, as to be incapable of any choice or inclination, and would have it perpetually wavering and
suspending, considering and receiving all things as
indifferent, it is said, " That he always comported
" himself after the same manner and countenance :[*]

* Diog. Laert. in Pyrrho's Life, lib. ix. sect. 63.

" if he had begun a discourse, he would always end
" what he had to say,* though the person he was
" speaking to was gone away : and, if he walked, he
" never turned out of his way for any impediment,
" being preserved from precipices, the jostle of carts,
" and other like accidents, by the care of his friends ;
" for to fear, or to avoid any thing, had been to con-
" tradict his own propositions, which deprived the
" senses themselves of all certainty and choice :
" sometimes he suffered incisions and cauteries with
" so great constancy, as never to be seen so much
" as to wink his eyes." It is something to bring the
soul to these imaginations ; more to join the effects
to it, and yet not impossible ; but to conjoin them
with such perseverance and constancy as to make
them habitual, is certainly, in attempts so remote
from the common usance, almost incredible to be
done. Therefore it was, " That being, one day,
" found at his house terribly scolding at his sister,
" and being reproached that he therein transgressed
" his own rules of indifference : ' What,' said he,
" must this foolish woman also serve for a testimony
" to my rules ?' Another time, being to defend
" himself against a dog : ' It is ' said he, ' very hard
" totally to put off man ; and we must endeavour
" and force ourselves to encounter things, first by
" effects, but at the worst by reason and argument."

About seven or eight years since, a countryman, Extraordi-
yet living at a village but two leagues from my house, tions pro-
having been long tormented with his wife's jealousy, duced by a
coming, one day, home from his work, and she wel- solution.
coming him with her accustomed railing, he entered
into so great a fury, " That, with a sickle he had
" yet in his hand, he totally cut off all those parts
" that she was jealous of, and threw them in her
" face." And, it is said, " That a young gentle-

---

* Yet Montaigne says, in the 3d chapter of this volume, that
they who represent Pyrrho in this light, extend his doctrine beyond
what it really was ; and that, like a rational man, he made use of
all his corporeal and spiritual faculties as rule and reason.

" man of our nation, brisk and amorous, having, by
" his perseverance, at last mollified the heart of a fair
" mistress, enraged, that, upon the point of fruition,
" he found himself unable to perform, and that,

—————— *Non viriliter*
Iners senile penis extulit caput,*

" so soon as ever he came home he deprived himself
" of it, and sent it to his mistress ; a cruel and
" bloody victim for the expiation of his offence." If
this had been done upon a mature consideration, and
upon the account of religion, as the priests of Cy-
bele did, what should we have said of so choleric
an action ?

A woman   " A few days since, at Bergerac, within five leagues
that drown- " of my house, up the river Dordogne, a woman
ed herself ,
for being   " having, over-night, been abused and beaten by her
beat by her " husband, a peevish ill-natured fellow, resolved to
husband,
              " escape from his ill usage at the hazard of her life ;
" and going, so soon as she was up the next morning,
" to visit her neighbours, as she was wont to do, she
" dropped a hint of the recommendation of her affairs,
" she took a sister of her's by the hand, led her to a
" bridge, and after having taken leave of her, as it
" were in jest, without any manner of alteration or
" change in her countenance, she threw herself head-
" long into the river, and was there drowned.   That
" which is the most remarkable, is, that this resolu-
" tion was a whole night forming in her head."

Voluntary   But it is quite another thing with the Indian wo-
death of   men ; for it being the custom there for the men to
the Indian
wives.   have many wives, and for the best beloved of them to
kill herself at her husband's decease, every one of
them makes it the business of her whole life to obtain this privilege, and gain this advantage over her
companions ; and the good offices they do their husbands, aim at no other recompence, " but to be pre-
" ferred in accompanying them in death."

* Tib. lib. iv. eleg. Pen. ad Priapum in veterum Poet. Cata-
lectis.

Ubi mortifero jacta est fax ultima lecto,
Uxorum fusis stat pia turba comis:
Et certamen habent lethi, quæ viva sequatur
Conjugium, pudor est non licuisse mori,
Ardent victrices, et flammæ pectora præbent,
*Imponuntque suis ora perusta viris.**

When to the pile they throw the kindling brand,
The pious wives with hair dishevell'd stand,
Striving which living shall in death attend
Her spouse, and gain an honourable end ;
Those thus preferr'd, their breasts to flame expose,
And their scorch'd lips to their dead husband's close.

A certain author, of our times, reports, that he
has seen this custom in those oriental nations, that
not only the wives bury themselves with their husbands, but even the slaves he has enjoyed also ; which
is done after this manner : " The husband being
" dead, the widow may, if she will (but few do it),
" demand two or three months to order her affairs.
" The day being come, she mounts on horseback,
" dressed as fine as at her wedding, and, with a
" cheerful countenance, says she is going to sleep
" with her spouse, holding a looking-glass in her
" left-hand, and an arrow in the other. Being thus
" conducted in pomp, accompanied with her kin-
" dred and friends, and a great concourse of people,
" with great joy, she is at last brought to the pub-
" lic place appointed for such spectacles : this is a
" spacious place, in the midst of which is a pit full of
" wood, and, adjoining to it, a mount raised four or
" five steps, to which she is led, and served with a
" magnificent repast ; which being done, she falls
" to dancing and singing, and gives order when she
" thinks fit, to kindle the fire ; which being per-
" formed, she descends, and, taking the nearest of
" her husband's relations by the hand, they walk
" together to the river close by, where she strips
" herself stark naked, and, having distributed her
" clothes and jewels to her friends, plunges herself

* Propert. lib. iii. eleg. 13, ver. 17, &c.
2 E 2

" into the water, as if to cleanse herself from her
" sins : coming out thence, she wraps herself in a
" yellow linen robe, five and twenty ells long, and
" again giving her hand to her said husband's rela-
" tions, they return back to the mount, where she
" makes a speech to the people, and recommends
" her children to them, if she have any. Between
" the pit and the mount, there is commonly a cur-
" tain drawn, to skreen the burning furnace from
" their sight ; which some of them, to manifest the
" greater courage, forbid. Having ended what she
" has to say, a woman presents her with a vessel of oil,
" wherewith to anoint her head, and her whole body ;
" which having done with, she throws it into the fire,
" and, in an instant, leaps in after it : immediately
" the people throw a great many logs upon her, that
" she may not be long in dying, and convert all their
" joy into sorrow and mourning. If they are per-
" sons of mean condition, the body of the deceased
" is carried to the place of sepulture, and there
" placed sitting, the widow kneeling before him,
" and embracing him, while a wall is built round
" them, which so soon as it is raised to the height
" of the woman's shoulders, some of her relations
" come behind her, and, taking hold of her head,
" twist her neck, and, so soon as she is dead, the
" wall is presently raised up, and closed, where they
" remain entombed."

*The resolu-
tion of the
Gymnoso-
phists, who
voluntarily
burn them-
selves.*

There was, in this same country, something like it
in their Gymnosophists ; for, not by constraint of
others, nor by the impetuosity of a sudden humour,
but by the express profession of their order, their
custom was, " So soon as they arrived at a cer-
" tain age,* or saw themselves threatened by any
" disease, to cause a funeral pile to be erected for
" themselves, and on the top a neat bed, where af-
" ter having joyfully feasted their friends and ac-
" quaintance, they laid them down with such reso-

a Strabo, lib. xv. p. 1043, tome ii. Amsterdam, 1707.

" lution, that, when the fire was applied to it,
" they were never seen to stir hand or foot; and
" after this manner one of them, Calanus by name,
" expired in the presence of the whole army of Alex-
" ander the Great;" and he was neither reputed
holy, nor happy amongst them, that did not thus destroy himself; dismissing his soul, purged and purified by the fire, after having consumed all that was
earthly and mortal. This constant premeditation of
the whole life is that which makes the wonder.

Amongst our other controversies, that about fate Doctrine
is crept in, and to tie things to come, and even our which esta-
blishes the
own wills, to a certain and inevitable necessity, we necessity
are yet upon this argument of time past; "Since of things to
come.
" God foresees, that all things shall so fall out, as
" doubtless he does, it will then necessarily follow,
" that they must so fall out :" to which our masters
reply, " That the seeing any thing come to pass,
" as we do, and as God himself also does (for,
" all things being present with him, he rather sees
" than foresees), is not to compel it to happen; nay,
" we see because things do fall out because we see.:
" the events cause the knowledge, but the know-
" ledge does not cause the events: that which we
" see happen does happen; but it might have hap-
" pened otherwise: and God, in the register of the Causes of
" causes of events, which he has in his prescience, events in
the pre-
" has also those which we call accidental and volun- science of
" tary, which depend upon the liberty he has given almighty
God.
" to our determination, and knows that we shall do Fortuitous
" amiss, because we would do so." and volun
tary causes.
I have seen a great many commanders encourage
their soldiers with this fatal necessity; for, if our life
be limited to a certain hour, neither the enemies'
shot, nor our own boldness, nor our flight and cowardice, can either shorten or prolong it. This is
easily said, but see who will put it in practice; and,
if it be so that a strong and lively faith draws along
with it actions of a correspondent nature, certainly this
faith we so much brag of is very light in the present

age, unless the contempt it has of works, makes it disdain their company. So it is, that to this very purpose the Sieur de Joinville,* as credible a witness as any other whatever, tells us of the Bedoins, a nation against the Saracens, with whom the king Saint Lewis had to do in the Holy Land. " That they, in " their religion, did so firmly believe the number of " every man's days to be, from all eternity, prefixed, " and set down by an inevitable predestination, that " they went naked to the wars, excepting a Turkish " sword, and their bodies only covered with a white " linen cloth : and for the greatest curse they could " invent, when they were angry, this was always in " their mouths, Cursed be thou, as he that always arms " himself for fear of death." This is a testimony of

To what proof two friars of Florence were for submitting their different opinions. faith very much beyond our's. And of this sort is that also which two friars of Florence gave in our fathers' days.† Being engaged in some controversy of learning, they agreed each to undergo a fiery trial, for the verification of his argument, in presence of all the people, and in the public square ; and all things were already prepared, and just upon the point of execution, when it was interrupted by an unexpected accident.

A young Turk, that had a hare to teach him courage. A young Turkish lord, having performed a notable exploit, in his own person, in the sight of both armies, that of Amurath, and that of Hunniades, ready to join battle, being asked by Amurath, " Who it was that, in so tender and unexperienced " years (for it was his first sally into arms), had in- " spired him with so noble a courage," replied, " That his chief tutor, for valour, was a hare : for " being," said he, " one day a-hunting, I found a " hare sitting, and though I had a brace of excellent " greyhounds with me, yet methought it would be " best, for sureness, to make use of my bow, for " she sat very fair. I then let fly my arrows, and

* Joinville's Memoirs, vol. i. cap. 30, p. 190.
† Memoirs of Philip de Comines, lib. viii. cap. 19.

" shot forty that I had in my quiver, not only
" without hurting, but without starting her from her
" form : at last I slipped my dogs after her, but to
" no more purpose than I had shot : by which I un-
" derstood, that she had been secured by her des-
" tiny ; and that neither darts nor swords can wound
" without the permission of fate, which we can nei-
" ther hasten, nor put back." This story may
serve, by the way, to let us see how flexible our reason is to all sorts of images.

A personage advanced in years, name, dignity,
and learning, boasted to me, that he had been induced to a certain very important change in his
faith, by a strange whimsical incitation, and also so
very absurd, that I thought it much stronger, being
taken the contrary way : he called it a miracle, I
look upon it quite otherwise.

The Turkish historians say, " That the persua-
" sion, rooted in those of their nation, of the fatal
" and unalterable prescription of their days, does
" manifestly conduce to the giving them great assur-
" ance in dangers ;" and I know a great prince, who
makes very successful use of it ; whether it be, that
he does really believe it, or that he makes it his excuse for so wonderfully hazarding himself ; provided fortune be not too soon weary of her favour
to him.

The comment on the fatal foundation of the Turks.

There has not happened, in our memory, a more
admirable effect of resolution, than in those two who
conspired the death of the prince of Orange.* It is
to be wondered how the second, that executed it,
could ever be animated to an attempt, wherein his
companion, who had done his utmost, had proved
so unsuccessful ; and, after the same method, and
with the same arms, to go and attack a nobleman,
armed with so fresh a handle for distrust, powerful
in followers, and of bodily strength, in his own hall,
amidst his guards, and in a city wholly at his devo-

Assassination of the prince of Orange.

* The founder of the republic of Holland.

tion. He, doubtless, employed a very resolute
arm, and courage inflamed with a furious passion: a
dagger is surer for striking home, but by reason that
more motion, and a stronger arm is required, than
with a pistol, the blow is more subject to be put by,
or hindered. That this man ran upon certain death,
I make no great doubt; for the hopes any one could
flatter him with, could not find place in any calm
mind, and the conduct of his exploit sufficiently manifests, that he had no want of that, any more than
of courage. The motives of so powerful a persuasion may be diverse, for our fancy does what it will
both with itself and us.

The duke of Guise. The execution near Orleans was nothing like
this; there was in that more of chance than vigour,
the wound was not mortal, if fortune had not made
it so. To attempt to shoot on horseback, and at a
great distance, and at one whose body was in motion
by the moving of his horse, was the attempt of a
man who had rather miss his blow, than fail of saving himself, as was apparent by what followed after;
for he was so astonished and stupified with the
thought of so desperate an execution, that he totally lost his judgment, both to find his way to escape,
and how to govern his tongue in his answers. What
needed he to have done more than to fly back to his
friends cross a river? It is what I have done in less
dangers, and what I think of very little hazard, how
broad soever the river may be, provided your horse
have good going in, and that you see, on the other
side, good landing. The other (viz. the prince of
Orange's assassin), when they pronounced his dreadful sentence: "I was prepared for this," said he,
"beforehand, and I will make you wonder at my
"patience."

A people who believe assassination the surest path to paradise. The Assassins, a nation dependant upon Phœ-
nicia, are reputed, amongst the Mahometans, a peo-
ple of great devotion, and purity of manners. They
hold, "That the nearest way to gain paradise, is to
"kill some one of a contrary religion;" which is

the reason they have often been seen, being but one
or two, without arms, run madly against powerful
enemies, at the price of certain death, and without
any consideration of their own danger. So was our
count Raimond of Tripoli, assassinated (which word
is derived from their name) in the heart of his city,
during our enterprises of the holy war; and likewise Conrade, marquis of Montferrat, the murderers
going to their execution with great pride and glory,
that they had performed so brave an exploit.

CHAPTER XXI.

Of a monstrous Child.

I SHALL tell the story simply, and leave it to the
physicians to reason upon it. Two days ago, I saw
a child, which two men and a nurse, who called
themselves the father, the uncle, and the aunt of it,
carried about to get money by showing it, because
it was so strange a creature. It was, as to all the
rest, of a common form, and could stand upon its
feet, walk and gabble much like other children of
the same age: it had never, as yet, taken any other
nourishment but from the nurse's breasts; and what,
in my presence, they tried to put into its mouth, it
only chewed a little, and spit out again without
swallowing; the cry of it seemed, indeed, a little
odd and particular, and it was just fourteen months
old. Under the breast it was joined to another
child, that had no head, and that had the spine of
the back stopped up, the rest entire; it had one
arm shorter than the other, because it had been broken, by accident, at their birth; they were joined
breast to breast, as if a lesser child was to clasp its
arms about the neck of one somewhat bigger. The

part where they were joined together, was not above
four fingers broad, or thereabouts, so that if you
turned up the imperfect child, you might see the
navel of the other below it, and the joining was between the paps and the navel. The navel of the imperfect child could not be seen, but all the rest of the
belly; so that all the rest that was not joined of the
imperfect one, as arms, buttocks, thighs, and legs,
hung dangling upon the other, and might reach to
the mid-leg. The nurse, moreover, told us, that it
urined at both bodies, and also that the members of
the other were nourished, sensible, and in the same
plight with that she gave suck to, excepting that
they were shorter, and less. This double body, and
the several limbs relating to one head, might be interpreted as a favourable prognostic to the king, of
maintaining those various parts of our state under
the union of his laws; but lest the event should
prove otherwise, it is better to let it alone, for in
things already past, there is no divination : *Ut quum
facta sunt, tum ad conjecturam aliqua interpreta-
tione revocantur :* * " So as when they are come to
" pass, they should then, by some interpretation,
" be recalled to conjecture." As it is said of Epi-
menides, " That he always prophesied of things

A man who
had no ge-
nitals.

" past."† I have lately seen a herdsman, in Me-
doc, of about thirty years of age, who has no sign
of any genital parts ; he has three holes by which he
incessantly voids his water ; he is bearded, has desire, and loves to stroke the women.

Whether
there are
monsters
properly so
called.

Those that we call monsters, are not so to God,
who sees, in the immensity of his work, the infinite
forms that he has therein comprehended : and it is to
be believed, that this figure, which astonishes us,
has relation to some other of the same kind, unknown to man. From a God of all wisdom nothing
but what is good and regular proceeds ; but we do

* Cic. de Divin. lib. ii. cap. 31.
† Aristotle's Rhetoric, lib. iii. cap. 12.

not discern the disposition and relation of things: *Quod crebro videt, non miratur, etiamsi, cur fiat, nescit: quod ante non videt, id, si evenerit ostentum esse censet:*[*] " What man often sees, he does not ad-" mire, though he be ignorant how it comes to " pass; but, when a thing happens he never saw " before, that he looks upon as a prodigy." What falls out contrary to custom, we say is contrary to nature; but nothing, whatever it be, is contrary to her. Let, therefore, this universal and natural reason expel from us the error and astonishment which novelty brings along with it.

CHAPTER XXII.

Of Anger.

PLUTARCH is admirable throughout, but espe-cially where he judges of human actions: what fine things does he say in the comparison of Lycurgus and Numa, upon the subject of our great folly in abandoning children to the care and government of their fathers! " The most of our civil governments," as Aristotle says, " leave, to every one, after the " manner of the Cyclops, the ordering of their " wives and children, according to their own foolish " and indiscreet fancy; and the Lacedæmonian and " Cretensian are almost the only governments that " have committed the discipline of children to the " laws." Who does not see, that, in a state, all depends upon their nurture and education? And yet they are indiscreetly left to the mercy of the parents, let them be as foolish and ill-natured as they will.

[*] Cic. de Divin. lib. ii. cap. 22.

Of the in-
discretion
of parents,
who punish
their chil-
dren in the
madness of
passion.

Amongst other things, how often have I, as I have
passed along the streets, had a good mind to write a
farce, to revenge the poor boys, whom I have seen
flayed, knocked down, and almost murdered, by
some father or mother, when in their fury, and mad
with rage? You see them come out with fire and fury
sparkling in their eyes:

> —— *Rabie jecur incendente feruntur*
> *Præcipites, ut saxa jugis abrupta, quibus mons*
> *Subtrahitur, clivoque latus pendente recedit.*[*]

> With rapid fury they are headlong borne,
> As when huge stones are from the mountains torn.

(And, according to Hippocrates, " The most dan-
" gerous maladies are they that disfigure the countenance") with a sharp and roaring voice, very often
against those that are but newly come from nurse,
and there they are lamed and stunned with blows,
whilst our justice takes no cognizance of it; as if
these were not the maims and dislocations of the
members of our commonwealth :

> *Gratum est quòd patriæ civem, populoque dedisti,*
> *Si facies ut patriæ sit idoneus, utilis agris,*
> *Utilis et bellorum et pacis rebus agendis.*[†]

> It is a gift most acceptable, when
> Thou to thy country giv'st a citizen,
> If thou take care to teach him with applause,
> In war or peace how to maintain her cause.

There is no passion that so much perverts men's true
judgment, as anger. No one would demur upon
punishing a judge with death, who would condemn
a criminal from a motive of anger; why then should
fathers and school-masters be any more allowed to
whip and chastise children in their anger? This is
not correction, but revenge. Chastisement is instead of physic to children; and should we bear with
a physician, that was animated against and enraged
at his patient?

---

[*] Juvenal. sat. vi. ver. 548.   [†] Idem, sat. xiv. ver. 60, &c.

If we would do well, we should never lay a hand The faults upon our servants whilst our anger lasts; whilst the of the per- son whom pulse beats high, and we feel an emotion in ourselves, we punish let us defer the business; for it is passion that com- in anger, seem to us mands, and passion that speaks then, not we: but different from what faults seen through passion, appear much greater to they are in us than they really are, as bodies when seen through reality. a mist. He that is hungry uses meat, but he that will make use of correction should have no appetite to it, neither of hunger or thirst. Besides, chastise- ments that are inflicted with weight and discretion, are much better received, and with greater benefit by him who suffers them. Otherwise he will not think himself justly condemned by a man transported with anger and fury, and will allege his master's ex- cessive passion, his inflamed countenance, his un- usual oaths, his turbulence, and rashness, for his own justification:

Ora tument irâ, nigrescunt sanguine venæ,
*Lumina Gorgonio sævius igne micant.**

Rage swells the lips, with black blood fills the veins,
And in their eyes fire worse than Gorgon's reigns.

Suetonius† reports, " That, Caius Rabirius having " been condemned by Cæsar, the thing that most " prevailed upon the people (to whom he had ap- " pealed) to determine the cause in his favour, was, " the animosity and vehemency that Cæsar had ma- " nifested in that sentence."

Saying is one thing, and doing is another; we are A digres- to consider the sermon and the preacher apart. sion on Plu- tarch's good Those men thought themselves much in the right, nature and who in our times have attempted to shake the truth equity. of our church by the vices of her ministers; but she extracts her evidence from another source, for that is a foolish way of arguing, and would throw all

* Ovid. de Art. lib. iii. ver. 503, 504.
† Sueton. in Jul. Cæs. sect. 12.

12

things into confusion. A man whose morals are
good may hold false opinions, and a wicked man
may preach truth, nay, though he believe it not
himself. It is doubtless a fine harmony when doing
and saying go together ; and I will not deny but that
saying, when actions follow it, is of greater authority and efficacy, as Eudamidas said, hearing a philosopher talk of military affairs, " These things are
" finely said,* but he that speaks them is not to be
" believed, for his ears have not been used to the
" sound of the trumpet." And Cleomenes, hearing
an orator declaiming upon valour, burst out into
laughter, at which the other being angry, " I
" would," said he to him, " do the same if it were
" a swallow that spoke of this subject ; but if it were
" an eagle, I would willingly hear him." I perceive, methinks, in the writings of the ancients, that
he who speaks what he thinks, strikes more home
than he that only dissembles. Hear Cicero speak of
the love of liberty; hear Brutus speak of it ; you
may judge by his style that he was a man who

Cenure of would purchase it at the price of his life. Let
Cicero and Cicero, the father of eloquence, treat of the con-
Seneca. tempt of death, and let Seneca do the same ; the
first languishingly drawls it out, so that you perceive he would make you resolve upon a thing on
which he is not resolved himself. He inspires you
not with courage, for he himself has none ; the other
animates and inflames you.

I never read an author, even of those who treat of
virtue and of actions, that I do not curiously examine what kind of a man he was himself. For the
Ephori at Sparta, " Seeing a dissolute fellow propose
" wholesome advice to the people,† commanded him
" to hold his peace, and entreated a virtuous man
" to attribute the invention to himself, and to pro-

---

* Plutarch, in the Notable Sayings of the Lacedæmonians.
† Aul. Gell. lib. xviii. cap. 3.

" pose it." Plutarch's writings, if well understood,
sufficiently speak their author; and I think I know
his very soul; yet I could wish that we had some
better account of his life. I have thus far wandered
from my subject, upon the account of the obligation
I have to Aulus Gellius, for having left us in writing this story of his manners,* that brings me back
to my subject of anger : " A slave of his, a vicious *Plutarch
" ill-natured fellow, but who had the precepts of *reproached*
" philosophy sometimes rung in his ears, having, *by a slave*
" for some offence, been stripped, by Plutarch's *of his.*
" command, whilst he was whipping, muttered at
" first that it was without cause, and that he had
" done nothing to deserve it; but at last falling in
" good earnest to exclaim against, and to rail at
" his master, he reproached him, that he did not
" act as became a philosopher; that he had often
" heard him say it was indecent to be angry, nay,
" had wrote a book to that purpose; and, that caus-
" ing him to be so cruelly beaten, in the height of his
" rage, totally gave the lie to his writings." To
which Plutarch calmly and coldly answered, " How,
" ruffian," said he, " by what dost thou judge that
" I am now angry? Does either my face, my co-
" lour, my voice, or my speech give any manifesta-
" tion of my being moved? I do not think my eyes
" look fierce, that my countenance is disturbed, or
" that my voice is dreadful: Do I redden? Do I
" foam? Does any word escape my lips of which I
" ought to repent? Do I start? Do I tremble with
" wrath? For these, I tell thee, are the true signs
" of anger." And so, turning to the fellow that
was whipping him, " Lay on," said he, " whilst this
" gentleman and I dispute." This is the story.
Archytas Tarentinus, returning from a war wherein
he had been captain-general, found all things in his
house in very great disorder, and his lands uncultivated, through the bad husbandry of his receiver,

* Noct. Attic. lib. i. cap. 26.

That cor-
rection ne-
ver ought
to be given
in anger. whom having sent for, " Go,"* said he, " if I were
" not in wrath I would soundly drub you." Plato,
likewise, being highly offended with one of his
slaves, " Gave Speusippus order to chastise him,† ex-
" cusing himself from doing it, because he was in
" anger." And Carillus a Lacedæmonian, to a
Helot who carried himself insolently and audaciously
towards him, " By the gods,"‡ said he, " if I was
" not angry, I would immediately cause thee to be
" put to death."

Anger sub-
ject to self-
flattery. It is a passion that is pleased with and flatters itself. How oft, when we have been wrongfully misled, have we, on the making a good defence or excuse, been in a passion at truth and innocence itself?
In proof of which I remember an extraordinary instance in ancient history of antiquity: " Piso,§
" otherwise a man of very eminent virtue, being
" moved against a soldier of his, for that, returning
" alone from forage, he could give him no account
" where he had left his comrade, took it for granted
" that he had killed him, and presently condemned
" him to death. He was no sooner mounted upon
" the gibbet but behold his strayed companion ar-
" rives, at which all the army were exceeding glad;
" and, after many caresses and embraces of the
" two comrades, the hangman carried both into
" Piso's presence, all the spectators believing it
" would be a great pleasure even to him himself;
" but it proved quite contrary; for, through shame
" and spite, his fury, which was not yet cool, re-
" doubled; and, by a subtlety which his passion
" suddenly suggested to him, he made three crimi-
" nal for having found one innocent, and caused

---

* See Tusc. Quæst. lib. iv. cap. 36.
† Senec. de Irà, lib. iii. cap. 12.
‡ Plutarch, in his Notable Sayings of the ancient kings, &c.
§ Montaigne, for what reason I know not, gives him a better
character than Seneca, who, de Irà, lib. i. cap. 15, says, though
he was free from many vices, that he was ill-tempered and extremely
rigorous.

" them all to be dispatched; the first soldier, be-
" cause sentence had passed upon him; the second,
" who had lost his way, because he was the cause
" of his companion's death; and the hangman, for
" not having obeyed his order."

Such as have had to do with testy women may see into what a rage it puts them to see their anger treated with silence and coldness, and that a man disdains to nourish it. The orator Celius was wonderfully choleric by nature, insomuch that when a certain man supped in his company, of a gentle and sweet conversation, and who, that he might not move him, was resolved to approve and consent to all he said; he, impatient that his ill-humour should thus spend itself without aliment, " For God's sake," said he, " contradict me in " something, that we may be two."* Women, in like manner, are only angry that others may be angry with them again, in imitation of the laws of love. Phocion, to one that interrupted his speaking by sharp abuse, made no other return than silence, and gave him full scope to vent his spleen; and then, without any mention of this interruption, he proceeded in his discourse where he had left off before. No answer can nettle a man like such a contempt.

Of the most choleric man I know in France (anger being always an imperfection, but more excusable in a soldier, for in that profession it cannot sometimes be avoided) I often say, that he is the most patient in bridling his passion, it agitates him with so great violence and fury:

> —— *Magno veluti cùm flamma sonore*
> *Virgea suggeritur costis undantis aheni,*
> *Exultantque æstu latices; furit intus aquæ vis,*
> *Fumidus, atque altè spumis exuberat amnis:*
> *Nec jam se capit unda, volat vapor ater ad auras.*†
>
> So when unto the boiling caldron's side
> A crackling flame of brush-wood is apply'd,

* Senec. de Irâ, lib. iii. cap. 8.   † Æneid. lib. vii. ver. 462, &c.

The bubbling liquors there like springs are seen
To swell, and foam to higher tides within;
Above the brims they force their fiery way,
Black vapours climb aloft, and cloud the day.

That he must of necessity cruelly constrain himself
to moderate it; and, for my part, I know no passion which I could with so much violence to myself
attempt to cover and support. I would not set wisdom at so high a price; and do not so much consider what he does, as how much it costs him not to
do worse. Another boasted to me of his good-nature and behaviour, which is in truth very singular;
to whom I replied, " That it was indeed something,
" especially in persons of so eminent quality as
" himself, upon whom every-one had their eyes, to
" appear always well-tempered to the world; but
" that the principal thing was to make provision for
" within, and for himself; and that it was not, in
" my opinion, very well to order his business in-
" wardly to fret himself, which I was afraid he did,
" for the sake of maintaining this mask and modera-
" tion in outward appearance." A man incorpo-
rates anger by concealing it, as Diogenes told Demosthenes, who, for fear of being seen in a tavern,
withdrew himself the farther into it, " The more
" you recede, the farther you enter in."[*] I would
rather advise that a man should give his servant a
box on the ear a little unseasonably, than torture his
mind by putting on such a sedate countenance; and
had rather discover my passions than brood over
them at my own expense; they grow less by being
vented and expressed; and it is much better their
point should operate outwardly than be turned towards ourselves: *Omnia vitia in aperto leviora sunt :
et tunc perniciosissima, quum simulatâ sanitate sub-
sidunt :*[†] " All vices are less dangerous when open

* Diog. Laert. in the Life of Diogenes the Cynic, lib. vi. sect.
34.

† Senec. epist. 56.

" to be seen, and then most pernicious when they
" lurk under a dissembled temper."

Rules to be
observed in
the discove-
ry of angr r
against do-
mestics.

I admonish all who have authority to be angry in
my family, in the first place, to be sparing of their
anger, and not to lavish it upon every occasion ; for
that both lessens the weight and hinders the effect
of it. Loud exclamation is so customary that every
one despises it ; and, that your clamour at a servant
for a theft is not minded, because it is no more than
what he has seen you make a hundred times, against
him, for having ill washed a glass, or misplaced a
stool. Secondly, that they do not spend their
breath in vain, but make sure that their reproof
reach the person in fault ; for ordinarily they are apt
to bawl before he comes into their presence, and
continue scolding an age after he is gone :

*Et secum petulans amentia certat.**

And peevish madness with itself contends.

They quarrel with their own shadows, and push the
storm in a place where no one is either chastised or
interested, but in the clamour of their voice, which
is unavoidable. I likewise, in quarrels, condemn
those who huff and vapour without an adversary ;
such rodomontades are to be reserved to discharge
upon the offending party :

*Mugitus veluti cum prima in prælia taurus
Terrificos ciet, atque irasci in cornua tentat,
Arboris obnixus trunco ; ventosque lacessit
Ictibus, et sparsa ad pugnam proludit arena.†*

Like angry bulls that make the valleys ring,
Press'd to the fight, with dreadful bellowing ;
Which whet their horns against the sturdy oak,
And, kicking back their heels, the winds provoke ;
And, tossing up the earth, a dust to raise,
As furious preludes to ensuing frays.

* Claudian. in Eutrop. lib. i. ver. 237.
† Æneid. lib. xii. ver. 103, &c.

2 F 2

The au-
thor's an-
ger on great
and little
occasions. When I am angry, my anger is very sharp, but withal very short, and as private as possible; I am indeed hasty and violent, but never am beside myself, so that I throw out all manner of injurious words at random, and without choice, and never consider properly to dart my raillery where I think it will give the deepest wound; for I commonly make use of no other weapon in my anger than my tongue. My servants have a better bargain of me in great occasions than in little ones; the latter surprise me; and the mischief of it is, that, when you are once upon the precipice, it is no matter who gives you the push, for you are sure to go to the bottom; the fall urges, moves, and makes haste of itself. In great occasions this satisfies me, that they are so just every-one expects a warrantable indignation in me, and then I am proud of deceiving their expectation; against these I gird and prepare myself; they disturb my head, and threaten to crack my brain, should I give way to them. I can easily contain myself from entering into one of these passions, and am strong enough, when I expect them, to repel their violence, be the cause ever so great; but if a passion once prepossess and seize me, it carries me away, be the cause ever so small; which makes me thus indent with those who may contend with me, viz. when they see me first moved, let me alone, right or wrong, I will do the same for them. The storm is only begot by the concurrence of resentments, which easily spring from one another, and are not born together. Let every one have his own way, and we shall be always at peace: a profitable advice, but hard to practise. Sometimes also it falls out, that I put on a seeming anger, for the better governing of my family, without any real emotion. As age renders my humours more sharp, I study to oppose them; and will, if I can, order it so, that for the future I may be so much the less peevish and hard to please, the more excuse and inclination I have to be so, although I have heretofore been

12

reckoned amongst those that have the greatest patience.

A word to conclude this chapter; Aristotle says, "That anger sometimes serves to arm virtue and valour." It is likely it may be so; nevertheless they who contradict him pleasantly answer, "That it is a weapon of novel use; for we move other arms, this moves us; our hands guide it not, it is it that guides our hands; it holds us; we hold not it." *Whether wrath is proper to animate virtue and valour.*

CHAPTER XXIII.

Defence of Seneca and Plutarch.

THE familiarity I have had with these two authors, and the assistance they have lent to my age and to my book, which is wholly compiled of what I have borrowed from them, obliges me to stand up for their honour.

As to Seneca, amongst a million of pamphlets that those of the pretended reformed religion disperse abroad for the defence of their cause (and which sometimes proceed from a pen so good, that it is pity it is not employed in a better subject), I formerly saw one, which, in order to draw a complete parallel between the government of our late poor king Charles the ninth and that of Nero, compares the late cardinal of Lorrain with Seneca, in their fortunes (as they were both of them prime ministers to their princes), in their manners, conditions, and departments, as having been very near alike. Herein I think he does the said lord cardinal a great honour; for though I am one of those who have a great esteem for his wit, eloquence, and zeal for religion, and for the service of his king, and *Comparison between Seneca and the cardinal of Lorrain.*

reckon it was his happiness to be born in an age wherein it was a thing so new, so rare, and also so necessary for the public weal, to have an ecclesiastical person of so high birth and dignity, and so sufficient and capable for his place ; yet, to confess the truth, I do not think his capacity by many degrees equal to Seneca's, nor his virtue either so pure, entire, or steady.

The malicious and unfair character which Dion gives of Seneca, quite contrary to what is reported of him by Tacitus.

Now this book whereof I am speaking, to bring about its design, gives a very injurious description of Seneca, by reproaches borrowed from Dion the historian, whose testimony I do not at all believe ; for setting aside the inconsistency of this writer, who, after having called Seneca in one place very wise, and in another a mortal enemy to Nero's vices, makes him elsewhere avaricious, an usurer, ambitious, effeminate, voluptuous, and a false pretender to philosophy. Seneca's virtue appears so lively and vigorous in his writings, and his vindication is so clear against any of these imputations, and particularly as to his riches and extraordinary expenses, that I cannot believe any testimony to the contrary. Besides, it is much more reasonable to believe the Roman historians in such things than the Greeks and foreigners. Now Tacitus and the others speak very honourably both of his life and death, and represent him to us as a very excellent and virtuous personage in all things. I will allege no other reproach against Dion's report but this, which I cannot avoid, namely, that he has so crazy a judgment in the Roman affairs, that he dares to maintain Julius Cæsar's cause against Pompey, and that of Anthony against Cicero.

Bodinus, a good author, vilifies Plutarch, whom Montaigne vindicates.

Let us now come to Plutarch : John Bodinus is a good author of our time, and of much greater judgment than his cotemporary class of scribblers, so that he deserves to be carefully read and considered. I find him though a little bold in that passage of his Method of History, where he accuses Plutarch not only of ignorance (wherein I would

have let him alone, this not being a subject for me
to speak to), but " That he oft writes things incre-
" dible and absolutely fabulous," which are his own
words : if he had simply said, " That he writes
" things otherwise than they really are," it had been
no great reproach ; for what we have not seen we
receive from other hands, and take upon trust ; and
I see that sometimes he purposely relates the same
story in a different manner ; as the judgment of the
three best captains that ever were formed by Hannibal, which is given otherwise in the life of Flaminius, and another way in that of Pyrrhus ; but to
charge him with having believed things incredible
and impossible, is to accuse the most judicious author in the world of want of discernment. And
this is his example : " As," says he, " when he re- The bowels
" lates that a Lacedæmonian boy suffered his bowels of a Lace-
dæmonian
" to be torn out by a fox-cub which he had stolen, boy torn
" and kept it concealed under his coat, till he fell out by a
fox-cub.
" down dead, rather than he would discover his Whether it
" theft."* In the first place, I find this example ill be an ab-
surd and
chosen, forasmuch as it is very hard to limit the ef- incredible
forts of the faculties of the soul, whereas we have story ?
better authority to limit and know the strength of
the body ; and therefore, had I been in his place, I
should rather have chosen an example of this second sort ; and there are some that are incredible ;
amongst others, that which he relates of Pyrrhus,
" That all over wounded as he was, he struck one
" of his enemies, who was armed from head to foot,
" so great a blow with his sword, that he clave him
" down from his crown to his seat, whereby the
" body was divided into two parts."† In this example I find no great miracle ; nor do I admit of
the excuse he makes for Plutarch, by his having
added the words " as it is said," by way of caution
to suspend our belief ; for, unless it be in things re-

---

* In the Life of Lycurgus, chap. 14 of Amyot's translation.
† In the Life of Pyrrhus, cap. 12.

ceived by authority, and from a reverence to antiquity or religion, he would never have himself admitted, nor proposed to us to believe, things incredible in themselves; and that the words " as it is
" said," are not put by him in this place to that effect, is easy to be seen, because he elsewhere mentions the patience of the Lacedæmonian children,
examples happening in his time, more unlikely to
prevail upon our faith; as what Cicero has testified *

The pati- before him, who, he says, was upon the spot, " That
ence of the " even to their times, there were children found,
Lacedæ- " who, in the trial of patience which they were put
children. " to before the altar of Diana, suffered themselves
" to be there whipped till the blood ran down their
" bodies, not only without crying out, but without
" so much as a groan; and some till they there vo-
" luntarily lost their lives:"† and that which Plutarch also, amongst an hundred other witnesses, re-
ates, viz. " That, at a sacrifice, a burning coal be-
" ing fallen into the sleeve of a Lacedæmonian boy,
" as he was censing, he suffered his whole arm to
" be burned, till the smell of the broiling flesh was

Thievery " perceived by the assistants." There was nothing,
odious to according to their custom, wherein their reputation
the Spar- was more concerned, nor which would expose them
tans: to more blame and disgrace, than the being taken
in theft. I am so fully satisfied of the magnanimity
of those people, that Plutarch's account, far from
appearing to me, as it has to Bodinus, incredible, I
do not think it so much as rare and strange. The
Spartan history is full of a thousand more cruel
and rare examples, and is indeed all miracles in
this view. Marcellinus reports, concerning theft,

Thievery " That, in his time, there were no sort of torments
very much " which could compel the Egyptians, when taken
practised

---

* Tusc. Quæst. lib. ii. cap. 14.

† We have, says Cicero, seen numbers of their lads fighting
with incredible fury, with their fists, heels, nails, and teeth, till
they died, before they would own they were conquered. Life of
Pyrrhus, lib. v. cap. 27.

" in this misdemeanor, though a people very much by the Egyptians.
" addicted to it, so much as to tell their name."*

A Spanish peasant, being put to the rack about Fortitude of a Spanish peasant put to the torture.
the accomplices of the murder of the prætor Lucius
Piso, cried out in the height of the torment, " That
" his friends should not leave him, but look on
" without any sort of fear; forasmuch as no pain
" had power to force one word of confession from
" him:"† this was all they could get from him the
first day. The next day, as they were leading him
a second time to the torture, rushing with violence
out of the hands of his guards, he furiously ran his
head against a wall, and beat out his brains.

Epicharis, having tired and glutted the cruelty of Death of Epicharis on the rack.
Nero's guards, and undergone their burnings, their
bastinadoes, and their engines, a whole day together, without one syllable of confession of her conspiracy; being the next day brought again to the
rack, with her limbs all bruised, so that she could
not stand, she put the lace of her robe, with a running noose, over one of the arms of her chair, and,
suddenly slipping her head into it, with the weight
of her own body, hanged herself.‡ As she had the
courage to die after that manner, is it not to be presumed that she purposely lent her life to the trial of
her fortitude the day before, purely to mock the tyrant, and encourage others to the like attempt?—
Whoever will inquire of our light-horsemen what
experience they have had in these our civil wars,
will find examples of suffering and obstinacy in this
miserable age, and amongst the soft and effeminate
crew, worthy to be compared with those we have
now related of the Spartan virtue.

I know there have been simple persons amongst Wonderful constancy of certain peasants,
us, who have endured the soles of their feet to be
broiled upon a gridiron, their fingers' ends smashed

* Amm. Marcell. lib. xxii. cap. 16.
† Tacit. Annal. lib. iv. cap. 45.
‡ Idem, lib. xv. cap. 57.

during the civil wars in Montaigne's time. to pieces with the cock of a pistol, and their bloody eyes squeezed out of their heads, by force of a cord twisted about their brows, before they would so much as consent to ransom. I saw one left stark naked for dead in a ditch, his neck black and swelled, with a halter yet about it, with which they had dragged him all night at a horse's tail; his body pinked in a hundred places with stabs of daggers which had been inflicted, not to kill him, but to put him to pain, and to terrify him. Having endured all this, and even to being speechless and insensible, he resolved, as he himself told me, rather to die a thousand deaths (one of which indeed, as to matter of suffering, he had already suffered) before he would promise any thing; and yet he was one of the richest husbandmen of all the country. How many have been seen patiently suffer themselves to be burned and roasted, for opinions taken upon trust from others, and by them not at all understood.!

Women obstinate. I have known a hundred and a hundred women (for Gascony, they say, has a certain prerogative for obstinacy) whom you might sooner have made to eat fire than quit an opinion they had conceived in anger. They are more exasperated by blows and constraint; and he, that forged the story of the woman who, in defiance of all correction, threats, and bastinadoes, ceased not to call her husband lousy knave; and when she was plunged over head and ears in water, and durst not open her mouth for fear of being choked, could yet lift her hands above her head, and make a sign of cracking lice.; feigned a tale, of which in truth we every day see a manifest image in the obstinacy of women; and obstinacy is the sister of constancy, at least in vigour and stability.

The false measure of possibility and impossibility. We are not to judge what is possible and what is not, according to what is credible and incredible to our apprehension, as I have said elsewhere; and it is a great fault, yet a fault most men are guilty of (which nevertheless I do not mention in regard to Bodinus), to make a difficulty of believing that in another, which they could not or would not do themselves. Every one thinks that the sovereign stamp of human nature is imprinted in him, and that from him all others must take their rule; and that all proceedings, which are not like his, are feigned and false. Is any thing of another's actions or faculties proposed to him? The first thing he calls to the consultation of his judgment is his own example; and as matters go with him so they must of necessity do with all the world besides. O dangerous and intolerable folly! For my part I consider some men as very far beyond me, especially among the ancients; and yet, though I clearly discern my inability to come near them by a mile, I do not forbear to keep them in sight, and to judge of what so much elevates them, of which I also perceive some seeds in myself; as I also do of the extreme meanness of some other minds, which I neither am astonished at, nor yet do misbelieve. I very well perceive the turns those great souls take to raise themselves, and I admire their grandeur; and those flights that I think the bravest I am glad to imitate, where, though I want wing, yet my judgment goes along with them.

The other example he introduces of things incredible, and wholly fabulous, delivered by Plutarch, is, " That Agesilaus* was fined by the Ephori for having " too far engrossed the hearts and affections of the " citizens to himself alone." And herein I do not see what sign of falsity is to be found; but so it is, that Plutarch there speaks of things that must needs be better known to him than to us: and it was no new thing in Greece to see men punished and exiled only for being too acceptable to the people: witness the ostracism and petalism.

There is yet in this place another accusation laid against Plutarch, which I cannot well digest; where he says, " That he has faithfully matched Romans with

Side note: Agesilaus mulcted by the Ephori for ingratiating himself into the hearts of the people.

Side note: Whether Plutarch, in his parallel of the

* In the Life of Agesilaus, cap. 1.

Greeks and Romans, was unjust in giving preference to the latter. " Romans, and Greeks with Greeks; but not the Ro-
" mans with the Greeks: witness, says he, Demos-
" thenes and Cicero, Cato and Aristides, Sylla and
" Lysander, Marcellus and Pelopidas, and Pompey
" and Agesilaus." Supposing that he has favoured
the Greeks in giving them companions so unequal,
which is really to attack what in Plutarch is most excellent, and most to be commended; for in his pa-
rallels (which is the most admirable piece of all his
works, and with which, in my opinion, he was himself the most pleased) the fidelity and sincerity of
his judgments equal their depth and weight. He is
a philosopher that teaches us virtue: let us see whether we cannot defend him from this reproach of
prevarication and falsity. All that I can imagine
could give occasion to this censure, is the great and
shining lustre of the Roman names, with which we
are captivated: it does not seem likely to us that
Demosthenes could rival the glory of a consul, proconsul, and questor of that great republic; but, if a
man consider the truth of the fact, and the men in
themselves, which is Plutarch's chiefest aim, and more
to balance their manners, their natures, and parts,
than their fortunes, I think, contrary to Bodinus, that
Cicero and the elder Cato come short of the men
with whom they are compared. I would sooner, for
his purpose, have chosen the example of the younger
Cato compared with Phocion, for in this couple
there would have been a more likely disparity to the
Roman's advantage. As to Marcellus, Sylla, and
Pompey, I very well discern that their exploits of
war are greater and more full of pomp and glory than
those of the Greeks whom Plutarch compares with
them; but the bravest and most virtuous actions, no
more in war than elsewhere, are not always the most
renowned: I often see the names of captains obscured by the splendor of other names of less merit,
witness Labienus, Ventidius, Telesinus, and several
others; and, to take it that way, were I to complain
on the behalf of the Greeks, might I not say that

Camillus was much less comparable to Themistocles, the Gracchi to Agis, and Cleomenes and Numa to Lycurgus? But it is folly to judge of things that have so many aspects at one view.

When Plutarch compares them, he does not for all that make them equal. Who could more elegantly and sincerely have marked their distinction? Does he insinuate that the victories, martial achievements, the power of the armies conducted by Pompey, and his triumphs, were equal to those of Agesilaus? " I do not believe,"* says he, " that Xeno- " phon himself, if he were now living, though he " was allowed to write whatever pleased him, to the " advantage of Agesilaus, would dare to bring them " into comparison." Where he speaks of comparing Lysander to Sylla, " There is,†" says he, " no " comparison, either in the number of victories, or " in the hazard of battles; for Lysander only won " two naval victories, &c." This is not to derogate from the Romans; for, having only simply named them with the Greeks, he can have done them no injury, what disparity soever there may be between them: and Plutarch does not weigh them entirely one against another; there is no preference in the main; he only compares the pieces and circumstances one after another, and judges of every one separately; wherefore, if any one would convince him of partiality, he ought to pick out some one of those particular judgments, or say, in general, that he was mistaken in comparing such a Greek to such a Roman, when there were others more fit for a parellel.

(marginal note:) Plutarch did not mean an equality between those whom he compared together.

---

* In the Comparison of Pompey with Agesilaus.
† In his Comparison of Sylla and Lysander.

CHAPTER XXIV.

The Story of Spurina.

PHILOSOPHY thinks she has not ill employed her talent, when she has given the sovereignty of the soul, and the authority of checking our appetites, to reason. Of these, they who judge that there are none more violent than those which love breeds, are of the opinion, " That they seize both body and " soul, and possess the whole man ;" so that health itself depends upon them, and is the medicine some-times constrained to pimp for them : but it might be said, on the contrary, that the mixture of the body brings an abatement to them, for such desires are subject to satiety, and capable of material remedies.

Whether the amor-ous appe-tites are the most violent.

Many, being determined to rid their souls from the continual alarms of this appetite, have made use of inci-sion and amputation of the restless and unruly mem-bers : others have subdued their force and ardour, by the frequent application of cold things, as snow and vinegar : the sackcloths of our ancestors were used to this purpose, which was a cloth woven of horse-hair, whereof some made shirts, and others girdles to tor-ture their reins. A prince, not long ago, told me, " That, in his youth, upon a solemn festival in the " court of king Francis I. where every-body was " finely dressed, he would needs put on his father's " hair-shirt, which was still kept in the house ;" but, how great soever his devotion was, he had not pa-tience to wear it till night, and was sick a long time after ; adding withal, " That he did not think " there could be any youthful heat so fierce, that " the use of this receipt would not mortify ;" yet, perhaps, he never tried the most violent ; for expe-rience shows us, that such emotions often happen under coarse beggarly clothes, and that a hair-shirt does not always render those innocent that wear it.

Means used to mortify them.

Xenocrates proceeded with greater severity in this affair; for his disciples, to make trial of his continency, having slipped Lais, that beautiful and famous courtezan, into his bed, quite naked, Xenocrates finding, without the charms of her beauty, and her alluring philtres, that, in spite of his reason, and philosophical rules, there was a war rising in his flesh, he caused those members of his to be burned, that he found consenting to this rebellion:* whereas the passions, which wholly reside in the soul, as ambition, avarice, and the rest, find the reason much more to do, because it cannot there be relieved but by its own means; neither are those appetites capable of satiety, but grow sharper and increase by fruition.

The sole example of Julius Cæsar may suffice to demonstrate to us the disparity of those appetites; for never was man more addicted to amorous delight; of which one proof is, the delicate care he took of his person, to such a degree as to use the most lascivious means to that end, which were then practised, viz. to have the hairs of his body twiched off by pincers, and to be daubed all over with delicate perfumes; and he was a beautiful person in himself, of a fair complexion, tall and sprightly, full-faced, with brisk hazle eyes, if we may believe Suetonius;† for the statues that we see at Rome, do not, in all points, answer this description. Besides his wives, which he four times changed, without reckoning the amours of his childhood with Nicomedes, king of Bithynia, he had the maidenhead of the renowned Cleopatra, Queen of Egypt: witness the little Cæsario that he had by her.‡ He also made love to Eunoe, queen of Mauritania; and, at Rome, to Posthumia, the wife of Servius Sulpitius; to Lollia, the wife of Gabinius: to Tortulla, the wife of Crassus; and even to Mutia, wife to the great Pompey; which

Note (margin): How Xenocrates preserved his continency.

Note (margin): Cæsar's example a proof that ambition is harder to be tamed than love.

* Diog. Laert. in the Life of Xenocrates, lib. iv. sect. 7.
† In the Life of Julius Cæsar, sect. 45.
‡ Plutarch, in the Life of Cæsar, cap. 13, sect. 50.

was the reason, the Roman historians say, that she
was repudiated by her husband, which Plutarch owns
he did not know: and the Curios, both father and
son, afterwards reproached Pompey, when he married Cæsar's daughter, " That he had made himself
" son-in-law to a man who had made him a cuckold,
" and one that he himself was wont to call Ægys-
" tus."*   Besides all these, he kept Servilia, Cato's
sister, and mother to Marcus Brutus, from whence
every one believes the great affection he had to Brutus proceeded.   So that I have reason, methinks, to
take him for a man extremely given to this debauch,
and of a very amorous constitution : but the other
passion of ambition, with which he was also exceedingly infected, arising in him to contend with the
former, soon compelled it to give way.

The exam-
ple of Ma-
homet ano-
ther proof. And here calling to mind Mahomet, who subdued
Constantinople, and totally exterminated the Grecian name, I do not know where these two passions
are so evenly balanced, being equally an indefatiga-
ble lecher and soldier : but where they both meet in
his life, and jostle one another, the quarrelsome passion always gets the better of the amorous : and this,
though it was out of its natural season, did not regain an absolute sovereignty over the other, till he
came to be very old indeed, and unable to undergo
the fatigues of war.

A notable
example
proving
love to be
stronger
than ambi-
tion. What is related, for a contrary example, of Ladi-
slaus, king of Naples, is very remarkable ; that being
a great captain, valiant and ambitious, he proposed
to himself, for the principal end of his ambition, the
execution of his pleasure, and the enjoyment of some
rare beauty which he obtained, and thereby his
death ; for having, by a close and tedious siege, reduced the city of Florence to so great distress, that
the inhabitants were glad to capitulate ; he was content to set them free, provided they would deliver
up to him a most beautiful virgin, whom he had

* Suetonius, in Cæsar's Life, sect. 250.

heard of in their city. They were forced to yield her to
him, and by a private injury to avert the public ruin.
She was the daughter of a physician of eminence in
his time, who, finding himself involved in so foul a
necessity, resolved upon a high attempt; for as every
one was setting a hand to trick up his daughter, and
to adorn her with ornaments and jewels, to render
her agreeable to this new lover; he also gave her a
handkerchief, most richly wrought, and of an exquisite
perfume (an implement they never go without in those
parts), which she was to make use of in their first approaches. This handkerchief, which he had the art
to poison, coming to be rubbed between the chafed
flesh and open pores, both of the one and the other,
so suddenly infused its poison, that their warm sweat
soon turned into a cold sweat, and they expired in
one another's arms.

But I return to Cæsar: his pleasures never made The plea-sures of love never hindered Cæsar's views of aggrandiz-ing him-self.
him steal one minute, nor turn one step aside from
occasions that offered for his aggrandisement. That
passion was so sovereign in him over all the rest,
and with such absolute authority possessed his soul,
that it guided him at pleasure. In earnest, it troubles me, when (as to every thing else) I consider the
greatness of this man, and the wonderful parts wherewith he was endued, learned to such a degree, in all
sorts of knowledge, that there is hardly any one
science of which he has not written: he was so great
an orator, that many have preferred his eloquence
to that of Cicero: and he, I conceive, did not think
himself inferior to him in that particular; for his two
Anti-Catos were chiefly written to counter-balance the
eloquence that Cicero had expended in his Cato. As
to the rest, was ever soul so vigilant, so active, and
so patient of labour as his? And, doubtless, it was
embellished with many rare seeds of virtue, I mean,
innate, and not assumed.

He was singularly sober, and so far from being His singu-lar sobri-ety.
delicate in his diet, Oppius relates, "That, having
" one day at table physical instead of common oil,"

" in some sauce set before him, he eat heartily of it,
" that he might not put his entertainer out of coun-
" tenance."* Another time he caused his baker to
be whipped, for serving him with a finer sort of
bread than common. Cato himself was wont to.say
of him, " That he was the first sober man that took
" a course to ruin his country." And as to the same
Cato's calling him, one day, drunkard, it fell out
thus: being both of them in the senate, at a time
when Cataline's conspiracy was in question, of which
Cæsar was suspected, one came and brought him a
letter sealed up : Cato,† believing it was some intelligence from the conspirators, " Called to him to de-
" liver it into his hand," which Cæsar was constrained to do to avoid farther suspicion. This proved to
be a love-letter, that Servilia, Cato's sister, had writ-

Cæsar call- ten to him ; which Cato having read, he threw it
ed drunk- back to him, saying, " There, drunkard, take it."
ard by
Cato, in the This, I say, was rather a word of disdain and anger,
senate. than an express reproach of this vice, as we often
rate those that anger us, with the first injurious words
that come into our mouths, though by no means applicable to those we are offended at. To which may
be added, that the vice which Cato cast in his dish,
is wonderfully near akin to that wherein he had
Venus ac- caught Cæsar; for Bacchus and Venus, according to
companies
Bacchus. the proverb, " Agree like hand in glove ;" but, with
me, Venus is most sprightly when I am most sober.

Cæsar's The examples of his mildness and clemency to
clemency
towards his those by whom he had been offended, are infinite; I
enemies. mean, besides those he gave during the time of the
civil wars, which, as plainly enough appears by his
writings, he practised to cajole his enemies, and to
make them less afraid of his future dominion and victory. But I must also say, that if these examples are
not sufficient proofs of his natural good temper, they,
at least, manifest a marvellous confidence and mag-

---

* Cæsar's Life by Suetonius.
† Plutarch in the Life of Cato of Utica, cap. 7,

hanimity in this personage. He had often sent back
whole armies, after having overcome them, to his
enemies, without ransom, or deigning so much as to
bind them by oath, if not to favour him, at least no
more to bear arms against him. He has three or four
times taken some of Pompey's captains prisoners,
and as oft set them at liberty.* Pompey declared
all those to be his enemies, who did not follow him
to the war; and he proclaimed all those to be
his friends, who sat still, and did not actually
take arms against him. To such captains of his, as
ran away from him to alter their condition, he sent,
moreover, their arms, horses, and equipage. The
cities he had taken by force, he left at full liberty to
take which side they pleased, imposing no other garrison upon them, but the memory of his mildness and
clemency. He gave strict charge, on the day of his
great battle of Pharsalia, that, without the utmost
necessity, no one should lay a hand upon the citizens
of Rome. These, in my opinion, were very hazardous proceedings; and it is no wonder if those, in
our civil war, who, like him, fight against the ancient
state of their country, do not follow his example;
they are extraordinary means, such as only Cæsar's
fortune and his admirable foresight could happily
conduct. When I consider his incomparable magnanimity, I excuse victory, that it could not disengage
itself from him, even in that most unjust and wicked
cause. To return to his clemency; we have many
strong examples of it in the time of his government,
when all things being reduced to his power, he had
no more need to dissemble. Caius Memmius had
wrote very severe orations against him, which he as
sharply answered; yet he soon after used his interest
to make him consul. Caius Calvus, who had composed several injurious epigrams against him, having
employed his friends to mediate a reconciliation
with him, Cæsar, of his own accord, wrote first to

* Cæsar's Life by Suetonius, sect. 75.

him. And our good Catullus, who had so ruffled him under the name of Mamurra, coming to make his excuses to him, he made him, the same day, sup with him at his table. Having intelligence of some who spoke ill of him, he did no more but, in a public oration, declare that he had notice of it. He also less feared his enemies than he hated them. Some conspiracies and cabals, that were made against his life, being discovered to him, he satisfied himself in publishing, by proclamation, " That they were " known to him," without farther prosecuting the conspirators.

As to the respect he had to his friends; Caius Op-pius being with him upon a journey, and finding himself ill, " He left him the only lodging he had " for himself, and lay all night upon the hard " ground in the open air." As tó his justice : " He " put a beloved servant of his to death for lying with " a noble Roman's wife, though there was no com-" plaint made." Never had man more moderation in his victory, nor more resolution in his adverse fortune.

Boundless ambition the only ruin of Cæsar's actions, and the bane of his memory with all good men. But all these good inclinations were stifled and spoiled by his furious ambition, by which he suffered himself to be so far transported, a man may easily maintain, that this passion was the rudder whereby all his actions were steered : of a liberal man, it made him a public robber, to supply his bounty and profusion, and made him utter this vile and most unjust saying, " That, if the most wicked and pro-" fligate persons in the world had been faithful in " serving him towards his advancement, he would " cherish and prefer them to the utmost of his power, " as much as the best of men :" it intoxicated him with such excessive vanity, that he dared to boast, in the presence of his fellow-citizens, " That he had " made the great commonwealth of Rome a name " without body, and without form;" and to say, " That his answers, for the future, should stand for " laws ;" and also to receive the body of the senate,

coming towards him, sitting; to suffer himself to be
adored, and to have divine honours paid to him in
his own presence. To conclude: this sole vice, in
my opinion, spoiled, in him, the richest fund of
good-nature that ever was, and has rendered his
name abominable to all good men, for aiming to
erect his glory upon the ruins of his country, and
the subversion of the greatest and most flourishing
republic the world shall ever see. There might, on the
contrary, many examples be produced of great men;
whom pleasures have made neglect the conduct of
their affairs, as Mark Antony, and others; but where
love and ambition should be in equal balance, and
come to jostle with equal forces, I make no doubt
but the last would have the turn of the scale.

But to return to my subject: it is a very great
point to bridle our appetites by the dictates of reason, or, by violence, to constrain our members
within their duty: but to lash ourselves for our
neighbour's interest, and not only to divest ourselves
of the charming passion that tickles us, and of the
pleasure we feel in being agreeable to others, and
courted and beloved of every one; but also to conceive a hatred and aversion to the charms which produce that effect, and to condemn our beauty because
it inflames another, is what, I confess, I have met
with few examples of. This, indeed, is one: Spu-
rina, a young man of Tuscany,

An extraordinary instance of a young man, of very fine features, who scarcely fled his face all over, to suppress the passion with which such beauty might be apt to fire those that are the most continent.

> *Qualis gemma micat fulvum quæ dividit aurum;*
> *Aut collo decus, aut capiti, vel quale per artem*
> *Inclusum buxo, aut Oricia Terebintho,*
> *Lucet ebur.* ——

> As shines a gem in yellow gold enchac'd,
> On neck or head for decoration plac'd;
> Or as the iv'ry is improv'd by foil,
> Amidst the sable jet's contrasting soil.

" being endowed with singular beauty, and so ex-
" cessive, that the chastest eyes could not chastely

---

* Æneid. lib. x. ver. 134, &c.

" behold its lustre; displeased with himself for leav-
" ing so much flame and fever as he everywhere
" kindled, without relief, entered into a furious spite
" against himself, and those rich endowments nature
" had so liberally conferred upon him; as if a man
" were responsible to himself for the faults of others:
" and purposely flashed and disfigured, with many
" wounds and scars, the perfect symmetry and pro-
" portion that nature had so curiously imprinted in
" his face."* To give my free opinion, I more admire than honour such actions: such excesses are
enemies to my rules.

Wherein the action was blameable. The design was conscientious and good, but, I
think, a little defective in prudence. What if his de-
formity served afterwards to make others guilty of
the sin of hatred, or contempt, or of envy, at the glory
of so commendable an action; or of calumny, inter-
preting this humour a mad ambition? Is there any
form from whence vice cannot, if it will, extract occasion to exercise itself one way or another? It had
been more just, and also more noble, to have made of
these gifts of God a subject of exemplary virtue and
regularity.

They who secrete themselves from the common offices of society have the best bargain. They who secrete themselves from the common
offices, from that infinite number of crabbed and dou-
ble-minded rules that fetter a man of strict honesty
in civil life, are, in my opinion, very discreet, what
peculiar severity soever they impose upon themselves
in so doing. It is, in some sort, a kind of dying to
avoid the pain of living well. They may have other
reward, but the reward of the difficulty I never could
think they had, nor that in uneasiness there can be
any thing beyond keeping himself upright in the
waves of the busy world, truly and exactly perform-
ing and answering all parts of his duty. It is perhaps more easy for a man to live clear from the whole
sex, than to maintain himself exactly in all points
in the company of his wife; and a man may more

* Val. Max. in Externis, lib. iv. sect. 1.

incuriously slip into want than abundance, duly dispensed. Custom, carried on according to reason,
has in it more of sharpness than abstinence has : moderation is a virtue that has more work than sufferance. The well-living of Scipio has a thousand
fashions, that of Diogenes but one. This as much
excels the ordinary lives in innocence, as the most
exquisite and accomplished excel that in utility and
force.

CHAPTER XXV.

*Observations on Julius Cæsar's Methods of making
War.*

I T is said of many great leaders, " That they have
" had certain books in particular esteem, as Alexander
" the Great, Homer ; Scipio Africanus, Xenophon ;
" Marcus Brutus, Polybius ; Charles V. Philip de
" Comines ; and it is said, that in our times, Ma-
" chiaval is elsewhere in repute ;" but the late marshal Strossy, who took Cæsar for his man, doubtless
made the best choice ; for in truth this book ought
to be the breviary of every great soldier, as being
the true and sovereign pattern of the military art.
And, moreover, God knows with what grace and
beauty he has embellished that rich subject, with
such pure, delicate, and perfect expression, that,
in my opinion, there are no writings in the world
comparable to his in this respect. I will here record
some rare and peculiar passages of his wars that remain in my memory.

His army being in some consternation upon the
rumour that was spread of the great forces which
king Juba was leading against him, instead of abating the apprehension which his soldiers had conceived at the news, and of lessening the strength of

[marginal notes:] Cæsar's Commentaries a problem for every lesson for every general.

How Cæsar encouraged his troops when alarmed by the superior numbers of the enemy.

the enemy, having called them all together to re-
animate and encourage them, he took a quite contrary method to what are used to do; for he told
them, "That they should trouble themselves no
"more with inquiring after the enemy's strength,
"for that he was certainly informed of it:"* and
then he mentioned a number much surpassing both
the truth and the report that was rumoured in his
army. In this he followed the advice of Cyrus in
Xenophon; forasmuch as the imposition is not of so
great importance to find an enemy weaker than we
expected, as it is to find him really very strong,
after having been made to believe that he was
weak.

The ready
obedience
of Cæsar's
soldiers.

It was his way to accustom his soldiers simply to
obey, without taking upon them to control, or so
much as to speak of their captain's designs; which
he never communicated to them but upon the point
of execution; and he took a delight, if they discovered any thing of what he intended, immediately
to change his orders to deceive them; to which purpose, when he had assigned his quarters in a particular place, he often passed forward and lengthened
his march, especially if it was foul weather.

How he
amused the
enemy, in
order the
better to
surprise
them.

The Swiss, in the beginning of his wars in Gaul,
having sent to him to demand a free passage through
the Roman territories, though he resolved to hinder
them by force, he, nevertheless, spoke kindly to the
messengers, and took some days to return an answer, in order to make use of that respite for assem-
bling his army. These silly people did not know
how good a husband he was of his time; for he often repeats it, "That it is the excellency of a cap-
"tain to seize the critical juncture;" and his diligence in his exploits is, in truth, unparalleled and
incredible.

The virtue
he required

As he was not very conscientious in taking advantage of an enemy under colour of a treaty of

* Suetonius, in his Life of Julius Cæsar, cap. 66.

agreement, he was as little in this, that he required ^{In his sol-} no other virtue in a soldier but valour,* and seldom ^{diers.} punished any other faults but mutiny and disobedience.

After his victories, he often gave them all manner The licence of liberty, dispensing them, for some time, from in which he the rules of military discipline, saying, " That he had them. " soldiers so well trained up, that, though powdered " and perfumed, they would run furiously to bat- " tle."

In truth, he loved to have them richly armed, He loved and their furniture to be engraved, gilt, and silvered that they over, to the end that the care of saving their arms richly arm- might engage them to a more obstinate defence. ed.

When he harangued them, he called them by the The title he name of fellow-soldiers, as we do to this day; which honoured his successor Augustus reformed, supposing he had them with. done it upon necessity, and to cajole those who only followed him as volunteers:

——— *Rheni mihi Cæsar in undis,*
Dux erat, hic socius, facinus quos inquinat, æquat.†

Great Cæsar, who my gen'ral did appear
Upon the banks of Rhine, 's my fellow here ;
For wickedness, where once it hold does take,
All men whom it defiles does equal make.

But that this carriage was too low for the dignity of an emperor and general of an army ; and therefore he brought up the custom of calling them soldiers only.

With this courtesy Cæsar mixed great severity, to His severity keep them in awe. The ninth legion having muti- to his sol- nied near to Placentia, he ignominiously cashiered diers. them, though Pompey was yet on foot, and did not receive them into favour till after many supplications : he quieted them more by authority and boldness than by gentle ways. Where he speaks of his passage over the Rhine towards Germany, he says,

* Suetonius, in the Life of Julius Cæsar, cap. 67.
† Lucan, lib. v. ver. 289.

11

" That, thinking it unworthy of the honour of Ro-
" man people to waft over his army in vessels, he
" built a bridge, that they might pass over dry
" foot."* There it was that he built that wonderful bridge, of which he gives so particular a description ; for he is no where so fond of displaying his
own actions, as in representing to us the subtlety of
his invention in such mechanical performances.

Exhorta-
tions to sol-
diers be-
fore a bat-
tle of great
import-
ance. I have also observed this, that he was fond of giving exhortations to the soldiers before a battle ; for
where he would show, that he was either surprised,
or reduced to a necessity of fighting, he always
brings in this, " That he had not so much as leisure
" to harangue his army." Before that great battle
with those of Tournay, " Cæsar"† says he, " having
" given order for every thing else, presently ran
" where fortune carried him to encourage his men,
" and meeting the tenth legion, had no more time
" to say any thing to them but this, that they
" should remember their wonted valour, and not be
" astonished, but bravely sustain the enemy's
" shock:" and, as the enemy already approached
within a dart's cast, he gave the signal of battle ; and,
going suddenly thence elsewhere to encourage
others, he found that they were already engaged.
By his own account, his tongue indeed did him notable service upon several occasions ; and his military
eloquence was in his own time so highly reputed,
that many of his army collected his harangues, by
which means there were volumes of them preserved
a long time after him. He had so peculiar a grace
in speaking, that they who were particularly acquainted with him, and Augustus amongst others,
hearing those orations read, could distinguish even
the phrases and words that were none of his.

The rapidi-
ty of Cæ-
sar's pro- The first time that he went out of Rome with any
public command, he arrived in eight days at the

* De Bello Gallico, lib. iv. cap. 2.
† Idem, lib. ii. cap. 3.

river Rhone,* having with him in his coach a secre- ^{gress in his}
tary or two before him, who were continually writ- ^{military ex-}
ing; and one that carried his sword behind him. ^{peditions.}
Yet, as if he had nothing to do but to drive on, hav-
ing been every-where victorious in Gaul, he speedily
left it, and, following Pompey to Brundusium, in
eighteen days time he subdued all Italy, returned
from Brundusium to Rome; from Rome he marched
into the very heart of Spain, where he surmounted
extreme difficulties in the war against Afranius and
Petreius, and in the long siege of Marseilles; from
thence he proceeded to Macedonia, beat the Roman
army at Pharsalia, passed from thence, in pursuit of Pompey, into Egypt, which he also subdued;
from Egypt he went into Syria and the territories of
Pontus, where he fought Pharnaces; from thence
into Africa, where he defeated Scipio and Juba;
and again brushed through Italy into Spain, where
he defeated Pompey's sons:

> *Ocyor et cœli flammis, et tigride fœtâ.†*
> *Ac veluti montis saxam de vertice præceps ‡*
> *Cum ruit avulsum vento, seu turbidus imber*
> *Proluit, aut annis solvit sublapsa vetustas,*
> *Fertur in abruptum magno mons improbus actu,*
> *Exultatque solo, silvas, armenta, virosque,*
> *Involvens secum.*

> Swifter than lightning, or the furious course
> Of the fell tigress when she is a nurse.
> As when a fragment from a mountain torn
> By raging tempests, or a torrent borne;
> Or sapp'd by time, or loosen'd from the roots,
> Prone through the void the rocky ruin shoots;
> Rolling from crag to crag, from steep to steep,
> Down sink at once the shepherds and the sheep;
> Involv'd alike, they rush to nether ground,
> Stunn'd with the shock they fall, and, stunn'd, from earth
>   rebound.

Speaking of the siege of Avaricum, he says, ^{He would}
" That it was his custom to be night and day with ^{see every}

---

* Plutarch, in Cæsar's Life, chap. 5.
† Lucan. lib. v. ver. 405.
‡ Virg. Æn. lib. xi. ver. 684.

thing him-
self. "the pioneers."* In all enterprises of consequence he reconnoitred in person, and never brought
his army to a place which he had not first viewed.
And, if we may believe Suetonius,† when he invaded
England, "He was the first man that sounded the
"passage."

He liked to   He was wont to say, "That he more valued a vic-
conquer by "tory obtained by stratagem than force." And in
wisdom ra-
ther than the war against Petreius and Afranius, fortune pre-
strength. senting him with a very manifest occasion of advantage, he declined it, saying, "That he hoped with
"a little more time, and less hazard, to overthrow
"his enemies." He there also performed a notable
part, in commanding his whole army to pass the
river by swimming, without any manner of necessity:

> ——— Rapuitque ruens in prœlia miles
> Quod fugiens timuisset iter ; mox uda receptis
> Membra fovent armis, gelidosque à gurgite, cursu
> Restituunt artus.‡

> The soldiers rush through a pass to fight,
> Which would have terrify'd them in a flight ;
> Then with their arms their wet limbs cover o'er,
> And their numb'd joints by a swift race restore.

Was more   I find him a little more wary and considerate in
circum-
spect in his his enterprises than Alexander, for the latter seems
enterprises to seek and run headlong upon dangers like an im-
than Alex-
ander. petuous torrent, which rushes against and attacks
every thing it meets, without choice and discretion :

> Sic tauri-formis volvitur Aufidus,
> Qui regna Dauni perfluit Appuli,
> Dum sævit horrendamque cultis
> Diluviem meditatur agris.§

> So the biforked Aufidus amain
> Roars loud and foams along th' Apulian plain,

---

* De Bell. Gall. lib. vii. cap. 3.   † In Jul. Cæs. sect. 58.
‡ Lucan. lib. iv. ver. 151, &c.
§ Hor. lib. iv. ode 14, ver. 25, &c.

When it with rage and swelling floods abounds,
Threat'ning a deluge to the tilled grounds.

And indeed he was a general in the flower and
first vigour of life, whereas Cæsar took to the wars
at a ripe and well-advanced age. Moreover, Alexander was of a more sanguine, hot, and choleric
constitution, which he also inflamed with wine, from
which Cæsar was very abstinent; yet, where neces- *But, when
sity required, never did any man venture his person *necessity required,
more than he: and, for my part, methinks I read in *he boldly
many of his exploits a certain resolution to throw *faced dan-
himself away, to avoid the shame of being overcome. *ger.
In his great battle with those of Tournay, he charged
up to the head of the enemies without his shield,
when he saw the van of his army begin to give
ground; which he did also at several other times.
Hearing that his men were surrounded, he passed
through the enemy's army in disguise, to encourage
them with his presence.* Having crossed over to
Dyrrachium with a very slender force, and seeing
the remainder of his army, which he left to Anthony's conduct, slow in following him, he attempted
alone to repass the sea in a very great storm; and
stole away to reassemble the rest of his forces, the
ports on the other side being seized by Pompey, who
was master of all that sea. As to what he performed
by main force, there are very many exploits too
hazardous for the rational part of war; for with how
weak a force did he undertake to subdue the kingdom of Egypt, and afterwards to attack the forces
of Scipio and Juba, ten times greater in number
than his! those people had I know not what more
than human confidence in their fortune; and he was
wont to say, " That men must execute, and not de-
" liberate upon, great enterprises." After the battle of Pharsalia, when he had sent his army away before him into Asia, and was passing the strait of
the Hellespont in one single vessel, he met Lucius

* Sueton. in Jul. Cæs. sect. 58.

Cassius at sea, with ten stout men of war, where he
had the courage not only to lay by for them, but to
bear up to them, and, summoning Cassius to
yield, made him surrender.

His cou-
rage and
confidence
at the siege
of Alexia.

Having undertaken that furious siege of Alexia,
where there were fourscore thousand men in garrison, and all Gaul was in arms to raise the siege, having set an army on foot of a hundred and nine thousand horse,* and of two hundred and forty thousand foot, what a boldness and mad confidence was
it in him, that he would not give over his attempt,
but resolved to oppose two so great difficulties at
once, which nevertheless he sustained! And, after
having won that great battle against those without,
he soon reduced those within to his mercy. The
same happened to Lucullus, at the siege of Tigrano-
certa, against king Tigranes; but the hazard was
not the same, considering the effeminacy of those
with whom Lucullus had to deal.

I will here set down two rare and extraordinary
events concerning this siege of Alexia; one, that
the Gauls, having drawn their powers together to
encounter Cæsar, after they had made a general
muster of all their forces, resolved, in their council
of war, to dismiss a good part of this great multitude, that they might not fall into confusion : this
example of fearing to be numerous is new; but, to
take it right, it stands to reason that the body of an
army should be of a moderate number, and restrained to certain bounds, both in regard to the
difficulty of providing for them, and the difficulty of

Monstrous
armies of
a great ef-
fect.

governing and keeping them in order; at least it is
very easy to make it appear, by example, that
armies so monstrous in number have seldom done
any thing to the purpose. According to the saying
of Cyrus in Xenophon, " It is not the number of
" men, but the number of good men, that gives the

* Cæsar de Bello Gallico, lib. vii. cap. 12. where only 8000 horse
are mentioned.

" advantage :" the remainder serving rather to em-
barrass than assist. And Bajazet principally grounded ^{That great}
his resolution of giving Tamerlane battle, contrary ^{numbers of}
to the opinion of all his captains, upon this, that his ^{confusion.}
enemy's vast number of men gave him assured hopes
of their being in confusion. Scanderbeg, a very
good and expert judge in these matters, was wont to
say, " That ten or twelve thousand faithful fighting
" men were sufficient for a good leader, to secure
" his reputation on all military occasions." The
other thing, which seems to be contrary both to the
custom and rationale of war, is, that Vercingetorix,
who was made general of all the revolted parts of
Gaul, should go shut himself up in Alexia; for he
who has the command of a whole country ought
never to confine himself, but in such an extremity
when the only hopes he had left was in the defence
of that city ; otherwise he ought to keep himself always at liberty, that he may have means to provide
in general for all parts of his government.

To return to Cæsar : he grew in time more slow, ^{Cæsar be-}
and more considerate, as his friend Oppius testifies ; ^{came in time more}
conceiving that he ought not easily to hazard the ^{cautious.}
glory of so many victories, which one misfortune
might deprive him of. The Italians, when they
would reproach the rashness and fool-hardiness of
young people, call them *bisognosi d'honore*, " Neces-
" sitous of honour ;" and they say, that being in
so great a want and dearth of reputation, they have
reason to seek it at what price soever ; which they
ought not to do, who have acquired enough already. There may be some just moderation in this
thirst of glory, and some satiety in this appetite, as
well as in other things ; and there are enough who
practise it. He was far from the religious scruple
of the ancient Romans, who would never prevail
in their wars, but by mere valour ; and yet he was
more conscientious than we should be in these days,
and did not approve of all sorts of means to obtain
a victory. In the war against Ariovistus, whilst he

was parleying with him, there happened a tumult between the two armies, which was occasioned by the fault of Ariovistus's cavalry, wherein, though Cæsar saw he had a very great advantage over his enemy, he would not lay hold on it, lest he should be reproached with a treacherous action. He was always wont to wear a rich garment, and of a shining colour in battle, that he might be the more remarkable. He always carried a stricter hand over his soldiers, and kept them closer together when near an enemy.

Cæsar was a skilful and successful swimmer.

When the ancient Greeks would accuse any one of extreme insufficiency, they would say, in a common proverb, "That he could neither read nor " swim:" Cæsar also was of this opinion, that swimming was of great use in war, and himself found it so, when being to use diligence, he commonly swam over the rivers in his way; for he loved to march on foot, as also did Alexander the Great. Being in Egypt forced, for safety, to go into a little boat, and so many people leaping in with him,* that it was in danger of sinking, though he was of an advanced age, he chose rather to commit himself to the sea, and swam to his fleet, which lay two hundred paces off, holding, in his left-hand, his pocketbook above-water, lest it should be wet, and drawing his coat-armour in his teeth, that it might not fall into the enemy's hand.

No general better beloved by his soldiers.

Never had any general so much credit with his soldiers: in the beginning of the civil wars, his centurions offered to find, every one, a man at arms at his own charge, and the foot-soldiers to serve him at their own expense; those who were best able, moreover, undertaking to defray the most necessitous. The late admiral Chastillion furnished us the like case in our civil wars, for the French of his army expended money out of their own purses to pay the foreigners that were with them. It is but rare that

---

* Suet. in Jul. Cæs. sect. 64.

we meet with examples of so ardent and ready an affection amongst the soldiers of old times, who kept strictly to the ancient police. Passion has a more absolute command over us than reason; and yet it happened, in the war against Hannibal, that, after the generous example of the people of Rome in the city, the soldiers and captains refused their pay in the army; and, in Marcellus's camp, those who would receive any, were branded with the name of Mercenaries. Having been worsted near Dyrrachium, his soldiers came and offered themselves to be chastised and punished, so that he was more inclined to comfort than reprove them.

One single cohort of his withstood four of Pompey's legions above four hours together, till it was almost demolished with arrows, of which there were a hundred and thirty thousand found in the trenches.* A soldier, called Scæva, who commanded at one of the avenues, invincibly maintained his ground, having lost an eye, besides being wounded in one shoulder, and one thigh, and his shield shot in two hundred and thirty places. It happened that many of his soldiers, being taken prisoners, rather chose to die than promise to take the contrary side. When Granius Petronius was taken by Scipio, in Africa, Scipio, having put his companions to death, sent him word, " That he gave him his life, for he " was a man of quality and a questor;" Petronius returned for answer, " That Cæsar's soldiers were " wont to give life to others,† and not to receive " it;" and immediately, with his own hand, killed himself.

Of their fidelity there are infinite examples; amongst which, that of those who were besieged in Salona, a city that stood for Cæsar against Pompey, is not to be forgotten, on account of an extraordi-

Instances of their intrepidity.

Fidelity of the garrison of Salona.

* Sueton. in Jul. Cæs. sect. 58, Cæsar makes the number but thirty thousand.
† Plutarch, in the Life of Cæsar, chap. 5.

nary accident that there happened. Marcus Octavius kept them close besieged; they within being
reduced to an extreme necessity, so that, to supply
the want of men, most of them being either slain or
wounded,* they had set all their slaves at liberty,
and had been constrained to cut off all the women's
hair, to twist instead of cordage, besides a wonderful dearth of victuals, yet they continued resolute
never to yield: after having drawn the siege to a
great length, by which Octavius was grown more
negligent, and less attentive to his enterprise, they
made choice of one day about noon, and, having
first placed the women and children upon the walls
to make a show, they sallied upon the besiegers with
such fury, that, having routed the first, second, and
third corps, and afterwards the fourth, and then the
rest, and beaten them all out of their trenches, they
pursued them even to their ships; and Octavius
himself was forced to fly to Dyrrachium, where
Pompey lay. I do not at present remember, that
I have met with any other example, where the besieged ever gave the besiegers a total defeat, and
won the field; nor that a sally ever was attended
with a pure and entire victory.

CHAPTER XXVI.

Of three good Women.

True proof THEY do not run thirteen to a dozen as every one
of a good knows, and especially in the duties of marriage; for
marriage. that is a bargain full of so many nice circumstances,
that it is hard for a woman's will to keep to it long:

* Cæsar de Bell. Civil. lib. i. cap. 3.

12

men, though their condition be something better
under that tie, have yet enough to do: the true
touchstone and test of a happy marriage respects the
time of their cohabitation only, whether it has been
constant, mild, loyal, and commodious.

In our age, women commonly reserve the publica- Mon-
tion of their good offices, and their vehement affec- taigne's opinion of
tion for their husbands, till they have lost them; or, the women,
at least, then it is that they deign to give proofs of who never declare
their good-will: a too slow testimony, and that comes their love
too late; by which they rather manifest, that they husbands
never loved them till dead. Their life is full of till they are dead.
combustion, their death full of love and courtesy;
as fathers conceal their affections from their children, women likewise conceal theirs from their husbands, to maintain a modest respect. This is a
mystery I do not relish; it is to much purpose that
they scratch themselves and tear their hair. I whisper in a waiting-woman's or a secretary's ear, "How
"were they? How did they live together?" I always have that saying in my head, *Janctantius mœ-
rent quæ minus dolent*: " They make the most ado
" who are least concerned." Their whimpering is
offensive to the living, and vain to the dead; we
would willingly give them leave to laugh after we
are dead, provided they will smile upon us whilst we
are alive. Is it not enough to make a man revive
in spite, that she who spit in my face whilst I was in
being, shall come to kiss my feet when I am no
more? If there be any honour in lamenting a husband, it only appertains to those who smiled upon
them whilst they had them; let those who wept
during their lives laugh at their deaths, as well outwardly as inwardly. Besides, never regard those
blubbered eyes and that pitiful voice; but consider
her deportment, her complexion, and the plump-
ness of her cheeks, under all those formal veils; it
is there the discovery is to be made. There are
few who do not mend upon it, and health is a quality that cannot lie; that starched and ceremonious

countenance looks not so much back as forward,
and is rather intended to get a new husband, than
to lament the old. When I was a boy, a very beautiful and virtuous lady, who is yet living, and the
widow of a prince, had, I know not what, more ornament in her dress than our laws of widowhood
will well allow; which being reproached with, as a
great indecency, she made answer, " That it was
" because she was not cultivating more friendships,
" and would never marry again."

I have here, not at all dissenting from our custom, made choice of three women, who have also
expressed the utmost of their goodness and affection
about their husbands' death ; yet are they examples
of another kind than are now in use, and so severe,
as will hardly be drawn into imitation.

The younger Pliny * had, near a house of his in
Italy, a neighbour who was exceedingly tormented
with certain ulcers in his private parts; his wife,
finding him languish so long, entreated that he
would give her leave to see, and at leisure to consider of the state of his disease, adding, that she
would freely tell him what she thought of it : this
permission being obtained, she curiously examined
the business, found it impossible he could ever be
cured, and that all he was to expect was to linger
out a painful and miserable life for a great while ;
therefore, as the most sure and sovereign remedy,
she resolutely advised him to kill himself ; but finding him a little tender and backward in so rude an
attempt, " Do not think, my dear," said she, " that
" I have not an equal feeling of the torments which
" I see thou endurest, and that, to deliver myself
" from them, I will not myself make use of the
" same remedy I have prescribed to thee: I will
" accompany thee in the cure, as I have done in
" the disease ; fear nothing, but believe that we
" shall have pleasure in this passage that is to free

* Ep. 24. lib. vi.

" us from so many miseries, and go off happily to-
" gether." Having said this, and roused up her
husband's courage, she resolved that they should
throw themselves headlong into the sea, out of a
window that leaned over it; and that she might
maintain to the last the loyal and vehement affection
wherewith she had embraced him during his life, she
would yet have him die in her arms; but for fear
they should fail, and lest they should leave their
hold in the fall, and through fear, she tied herself
fast to him by the waist, and so gave up her own
life to procure her husband's repose. This was a
woman of a mean family, and even amongst that
condition of people it is no very new thing to see
some examples of uncommon good-nature:

———— *Extrema per illos*
Justitia excedens terris vestigia fecit.[*]
From hence Astræa took her flight, and here
The prints of her departing steps appear.

The other two are noble and rich, where examples of virtue are rarely lodged. Arria, the wife of
Cecina Pætus, a consular person, was the mother
of another Arria, the wife of Thrasea Pætus, whose
virtue was so renowned in the time of Nero, and,
by means of this son-in-law, the grand-mother of
Fannia; for the resemblance of the names of these
men and women, and their fortunes, had led many
into a mistake. This first Arria (her husband Ce- The Story
cina Pætus having been made prisoner by some of of the
the emperor Claudius's people, after Scribonianus's Arria, the
defeat, whose party he had embraced in the war) wife of
" Begged of those who were carrying him prisoner Pætus.
" to Rome, that they would take her into their
" ship, where she should be of much less charge
" and trouble to them than a great many persons
" they must otherwise have to attend her husband,
" and that she alone would undertake to serve him

* Virg. Georg. lib. ii. ver 473.

" in his chamber, his kitchen, and all other of-
" fices.*" But they refused her, wherefore she put
herself into a fishing-boat she hired on a sudden,
and in that manner followed him from Sclavo-
nia. Being come to Rome, Junia, the widow of
Scribonianus, one day, considering the resemblance
of their fortunes, and accosting her in the emperor's
presence, in a familiar way, she rudely repulsed her
with these words, " Shall I," said she, " speak to
" thee, or give ear to any thing thou sayest; to
" thee in whose lap Scribonianus was slain, and
" thou yet alive ?" These words, with several other
signs, gave her friends to understand that she would
undoubtedly dispatch herself, impatient of supporting her husband's fortune ; and Thrasea, her son-in-
law, beseeching her not to throw away herself, and
saying to her, " What! if I should run the same
" fortune that Cecina had done, would you that
" your daughter, my wife, should do the same ?"—
" Would I ?" replied she, " yes, yes, I would, if
" she had lived as long, and in as good agreement
" with thee as I have done with my husband."—
These answers made them more careful of her, and
to have a more watchful eye on her deportment.
One day, having said to those that looked to her,
" It is to much purpose that you take all this pains
" to prevent me; you may indeed make me die an
" ill death, but to keep me from dying is not in
" your power ;" and suddenly rushing from a
chair wherein she sat, she ran her head madly, with
all her force, against the next wall, by which blow
being laid flat in a swoon, and very much wounded,
after they had with much ado brought her to herself,
" I told you," said she, " that, if you refused me
" some easy way of dying, I should find out ano-
" ther, how painful soever." The conclusion of so
admirable a virtue was thus; her husband Pætus,
not having resolution enough of his own to dispatch

* Plin. ep. 16. lib. iii.

himself, as he was by the emperor's cruelty enjoined,
one day, amongst others, having first employed all
the reasons and exhortations which she thought
most prevalent, to persuade him to it, she snatched
the poniard he wore from his side, and holding it
ready in her hand, to make short of her admoni-
tions, "Do thus, Pætus," said she; and in the same
instant gave herself a mortal stab in her breast, and
then, drawing it out of the wound, presented it to
him, ending her life with this noble, generous, and
immortal saying, *Pæte, non dolet:* "Pætus, it hurts
"me not;" having only strength to pronounce
those never to be forgotten words:

> *Casta suo gladium cum traderet Arria Pæto,*
>   *Quem de visceribus traxerat ipsa suis:*
> *Si qua fides, vulnus quod feci, non dolet, inquit;*
>   *Sed quod tu facies, id mihi, Pæte, dolet.*[*]

> When the chaste Arria gave the reeking sword,
>   That had new gor'd her heart, to her dear lord;
> Pætus, the wound I've made hurts not, quoth she;
>   The wound which thou wilt make 'tis that hurts me.

The action was much more noble in itself, and of a
richer dye than the poet could express; for she was
so far from being deterred by her husband's wound
and death, and her own, that she had been the pro-
motress and adviser of both; but having performed
this high and courageous enterprise only for her
husband's convenience, she had, even in the last
gasp of her life, no other concern but for him, and
for dispossessing him of the fear of dying with her.
Pætus presently struck himself to the heart with the
same weapon, ashamed, I believe, to have stood in
need of so dear and precious an example.

Pompeia Paulina, a young and very noble Roman Seneca's
lady, had married Seneca in his extreme old age.— wife.
Nero, his hopeful pupil, sent his guards to denounce
the sentence of death to him, which was performed
after this manner: when the Roman emperors of

* Mart. lib. i. ep. 14.

those times had condemned any man of quality,
they sent to him, by their officers, to choose what
death he would, and to make that election within
such or such a time, which was limited, according
to their indignation, to a shorter or longer period,
that they might therein have leisure to dispose of
their affairs; and sometimes depriving them of the
means of doing it by the shortness of the time. If
the condemned seemed unwilling to submit' to the
order, they had people ready at hand to execute it,
either by cutting the veins of his arms and legs, or
by compelling them to swallow a draught of poison;
but persons of honour would not stay this necessity,
and made use of their own physicians and surgeons
for this purpose. Seneca,* with a calm and steady
countenance, heard the charge, and then called for
paper to write his will, which being denied by the
captain, he turned himself towards his friends, saying to them, " Since I cannot leave you any other
" acknowledgment of the obligation I have to you,
" I leave you, at least, the best thing I have,
" namely, the image of my life and manners, which
" I entreat you to keep in memory of me; that, so
" doing, you may acquire the glory of sincere and
" real friends." One while appeasing the sorrows
he saw them in with gentle words, and then raising
his voice to reprove them: " What," said he, " is
" become of all our fine precepts of philosophy?
" What is become of all the provisions we have so
" many years laid in against the accidents of for-
" tune? Was Nero's cruelty unknown to us? What
" could we expect from him who had murdered his
" mother and his brother, but that he should put
" his governor to death, who had bred him up and
" educated him?" After speaking these words, he
turned himself towards his wife, and embracing her
fast in his arms, as, her heart and strength failing
her, she was ready to sink down with grief, he beg-

* Tacit. Annal. lib. xv. cap. 61, 62.

ged of her, " For his sake to bear this accident
" with a little more patience, telling her that now
" the hour was come wherein he was to show, not
" by any more argument and reason, but by effect,
" the fruit he had reaped from his studies; and
" that he really embraced his death, not only without
" grief, but with joy : wherefore, my dearest," said
he, " do not dishonour it with thy tears, that it
" may not seem as if thou lovest thyself more than my
" reputation. Moderate thy grief, and comfort
" thyself in the knowledge thou hast had of me
" and of my actions, leading the remainder of thy
" life in the same virtuous manner thou hast hitherto
" done." To this Paulina, having a little recovered
her spirits, and warmed her great soul with a most
generous affection, replied, " No, Seneca," said
she, " I am not a woman to suffer you to go with-
" out my company in such a necessity ; I will not
" have you to think that the virtuous examples of
" your life have not yet taught me how to die well ;
" and when can I ever better or more decently do
" it, or more to my own desire, than with you ?
" Therefore assure yourself I will go along with
" you." Seneca, taking this so amiable and glorious resolution of his wife exceeding kindly at her
hands, and being also willing to free himself from
the fear of leaving her exposed to the mercy and
cruelty of his enemies after his death ; " I have,
" Paulina," said he, " sufficiently instructed thee
" what would serve thee to live happily ; but thou
" more covetest I see the honour of dying; in
" truth I will not grudge it thee ; the constancy
" and resolution in our common end may be the
" same, but the beauty and glory of thy part is
" greater."* This said, the surgeons at the same
time cut the veins of both their arms, but, because
those of Seneca being more shrunk up, as well with

* Tacit. Annal. lib. xv. cap. 63.

age as abstinence, made his blood flow too slowly, he commanded them likewise to open the veins of his thighs; and lest the torments he endured from it might pierce his wife's heart, and also to free himself from the affliction of seeing her in so bad a condition, after having taken a very affectionate leave of her, "He entreated she would suffer them "to carry her into the next room," which they accordingly did; but all these incisions being not enough to make him die, he commanded Statius Anneus,[*] his physician, to give him a draught of poison, which had not much better effect; for, by reason of the weakness and coldness of his limbs, it could not reach to his heart, wherefore they were forced to superadd a very hot bath; and then, feeling his end approach, whilst he had breath, he continued excellent discourses upon the subject of his present condition, which his secretaries wrote down, as long as they could hear his voice; and his last words were long after in high honour and esteem amongst men, and it is a great loss to us that they were not preserved down to our times; then, feeling the last pangs of death, with the bloody water of the bath he bathed his head, saying, "This water I "dedicate to Jupiter the deliverer." Nero, being presently advertised of all this, fearing lest the death of Paulina, who was one of the best descended ladies of Rome, and against whom he had no particular enmity, should turn to his reproach, he sent orders,[†] in all haste, to bind up her wounds, which her attendants, without his knowledge, had done before; she being already half dead, and without any manner of sense. Thus, though she lived, contrary to her own design, it was very honourably, and consistent with her own virtue; her pale complexion ever after manifesting how much of her vital spirit was run out of her wounds.

* Tacit. Annal. lib. xv. cap. 64.   † Idem, ibid.

These are my three very true stories, which, I think, I find as diverting, and as tragic, as any of those we make of our own heads wherewith to entertain the common people; and I wonder they who are addicted to such relations do not rather cull out ten thousand very fine stories, which are to be found in very good authors, that would save them the trouble of invention, and be more useful and entertaining. Whoever would compose a whole play from them would need to add nothing of his own but the connection only, as it were the solder of metal; and might, by this means, compile a great many true events of all sorts, disposing and diversifying them according as the beauty of the work should require, after the same manner almost as Ovid has patched up his Metamorphosis of that infinite number of various fables.

In this last couple it is moreover worthy of consideration, "That Paulina voluntarily offered to lose "her life for the love of her husband, and that her "husband had formerly also forbore dying for the "love of her." There is no mighty counterpoise in this exchange as to us; but, according to his Stoical humour, I presume he thought he had done as much for her, in prolonging his life upon her account, as if he had died for her. In one of his letters to Lucilius,* after he has given him to understand, that, being seized with an ague in Rome, he presently took coach to go to a house he had in the country, contrary to his wife's opinion, who would by all means persuade him to stay; and that he told her, "That the ague he was seized with was not a fever "of the body, but of the place:" it follows thus; "She let me go," says he, "with giving me a strict "charge of my health: now I, who know that her "life is involved in mine, begin to make much of "myself, that I may preserve her; and I lose the "privilege my age has given me, of being more

The writer, of tragedy must have recourse to history for the subject of their plays.

Seneca's great affection to his wife.

* Epist. civ.

" constant and resolute in many things, when I call
" to mind, that there is a young lady who is inter-
" ested in this old man's health; and, since I cannot
" persuade her to love me more courageously, she
" makes me more solicitously to love myself; for
" we must allow something to honest affections;
" and sometimes, though occasions importune us to
" the contrary, we must call back life, even though
" it be with torment; we must hold the soul within
" our teeth, since the rule of living amongst good
" men is not so long as they please, but as long as
" they ought: he that loves not his wife and his
" friend so well as to prolong his life for them, but
" will obstinately die, is too delicate and too effemi-
" nate: the soul must impose this upon itself, when
" the utility of our friends does so require: we must
" sometimes lend ourselves to our friends, and,
" when we would die for ourselves, must break that
" resolution for their sakes: it is a testimony of a
" noble courage to return to life for the sake of ano-
" ther's, as many excellent persons have done: and
" it is a mark of singular good-nature to preserve old
" age (of which the greatest convenience is an in-
" difference for its duration, and a more stout and
" disdainful use of life) when a man perceives that
" this office is pleasing, agreeable, and useful to
" some person whom we are very fond of; and a
" man reaps a very pleasing reward from it; for
" what can be more delightful than to be so dear to
" one's wife, as, upon her account, to become dear
" to one's self? Thus has my Paulina imputed to
" me not only her fears, but my own; it has not
" been sufficient for me to consider how resolutely I
" could die, but I have also considered how unable
" she would be to bear it: I am enforced to live,
" and sometimes to live is magnanimity." These
are his own excellent words; according to his usual
manner.

CHAPTER XXVII.

Of three most excellent Men.

IF I should be asked who I prefer, of all the men Homer pre-
that have come to my knowledge, I would answer, ferred to
"That I think three more excellent than all the rest:" geniuses.
one of them Homer; not but Aristotle and Varro,
for example, were perhaps as learned as he; and
possibly Virgil might compare with him, even in his
own art; I leave this to be determined by such as
know them both; I, who, for my part, understand
but one of them, can only say this, according to my
poor talent, "That I do not believe the Muses
"themselves ever surpassed the Roman."

> *Tale facit carmen doctâ testudine, quale*
> *Cynthius impositis temperat articulis.*[*]
>
> As rapt'rous joys his lute and verse inspire,
> As when we hear Apollo's voice and lyre.

And yet in this judgment we are not to forget, that
it is chiefly from Homer that Virgil derives his excellence; that he is his guide and teacher; and that the
Iliad only has supplied him with body and matter,
out of which to compose his great and divine Æneis.
I do not reckon upon that alone, but take in several
other circumstances that render this poet admirable
to me, even as it were above human condition: and,
in truth, I often wonder, that he who has erected,
and by his authority given so many deities reputation in the world, was not deified himself, being both
blind and poor, and so well acquainted with the
sciences, before they were reduced into rule and certain observations, that all those who have since taken
upon them to establish governments, to carry on
wars, and to write either of philosophy or religion, of
what sect soever, or of the arts, have made use of

* Propert. lib. ii. eleg. ult. ver. 79, 80.

him, as of a most perfect instructor, in the knowledge of all things; and of his books as a nursery of all sorts of learning:

Qui quid sit pulchrum, quid turpe, quid utile, quid non,
Plenius ac melius Chrysippo ac Crantore dixit.[*]

Who hath what's brave, what's base, what's hurtful, and
    what's good,
Clearer than Crantor or Chrysippus show'd.

and as this other says,

——— *A quo ceu fonte perenni*
Vatum Pieriis labra rigantur aquis.[†]

At that clear spring the poets take their swill,
Which ever flows from the Pierian hill.

and another,

Ad Heliconiadum comites, quorum unus Homerus
Astra potitus.[‡]

Of all the poets, Homer is alone
Judg'd the most worthy of the Muses' throne.

and another,

——— *Cujusque ex ore profuso*
Omnis posteritas latices in carmina duxit,
Amnemque in tenues ausa est deducere rivos,
Unius fœcunda bonis.[§]

——— From whose abundant spring
Succeeding poets draw the songs they sing ;
From him they take, from him adorn their themes,
And into little channels cut his streams :
Rich in his store. ———

It is contrary to the order of nature that he has made the most excellent production that can possibly be ; for the ordinary birth of things is imperfect; they thrive and gather strength by growing : whereas he has rendered even the infancy of poesy, and of several other sciences, mature, perfect, and complete.

* Hor. lib. i. epist. 2, ver. 3.
† Ovid. Amor. lib. iii. eleg. 9, ver. 25.
‡ Lucret. lib. iii. ver. 1050.
§ Manil. Astron. lib. ii. ver. 8, &c.

For this reason he may be called the first and the last
of the poets, according to the fair testimony antiquity
has left us of him, " That, as there was none before
" him whom he could imitate, so there has been
" none since that could imitate him."* His
words, according to Aristotle,† are the only words
that have motion and action, and are the only substantial words. Alexander the Great, having found
a rich little coffer amongst Darius's spoils,‡ gave order " It should be reserved for him to keep his
" Homer in ;" saying, " That he was the best and
" most faithful counsellor he had in his military af-
" fairs."§ For the same reason it was that Cleomenes, the son of Anaxandridas, said, " That he was
" the Lacedæmonian poet, because he was the best
" master for the discipline of war."‖ This singular
and particular commendation is also left of him in
the judgment of Plutarch, " That he is the only
" author in the world that never glutted nor dis-
" gusted his readers, presenting himself always in
" in different lights, and always flourishing in some
" new grace."¶ · That merry droll Alcibiades, having asked one who pretended to learning for a book
of Homer, gave him a box on the ear because he
had none, which he thought as scandalous as we
should for one of our priests to be without a Breviary.** Xenophanes complained one day to Hiero,††
the tyrant of Syracuse, " That he was so poor he
" had not wherewithal to maintain two servants :"
the tyrant replied, " Homer, who was much poorer
· " than you are, keeps above ten thousand now he is

* Velleii Paterculi Hist. lib. i. cap. 5.
† Arist. de Politica, cap. 24.
‡ Plin. Nat. Hist. lib. vii, cap. 29.
§ Plutarch, in the Life of Alexander, cap. 2.
‖ In the Notable Sayings of the Lacedæmonians.
¶ Plutarch, in his Treatise of Loquacity, chap. 5.
** Idem, in the Life of Alcibiades, chap. 8.
†† Idem, in the Notable Sayings of the ancient Kings, &c. at the
word Hiero.

" dead." What did Panætius [*] leave unsaid when he
called Plato the Homer of philosophers? Besides,
what glory can be compared to his? Nothing is so
frequent in men's mouths as his name and works;
nothing so known and received as Troy, Helen, and
the war about her, when perhaps there was never
any such thing. Our children are still called by
names that he feigned above three thousand years ago.
Who is ignorant of the story of Hector and Achilles?
Not only some particular families, but most nations
seek their original in his inventions. Mahomet, the
second of that name, emperor of the Turks, writing
to our Pope Pius the second; " I am astonished,"
says he, " that the Italians should appear against
" me, considering that we have our common descent
" from the Trojans; and that it concerns me, as
" well as it does them, to revenge the blood of Hec-
" tor upon the Greeks, whom they countenance
" against me." Is it not a noble farce wherein
kings, republics, and emperors have so many ages
played their parts, and to which all this vast universe
serves for a theatre? Seven Grecian cities contended
for his birth, so much honour did he derive even
from his obscurity.

Smyrna, Rhodus, Colophon, Salamis, Chios, Argos, Athens.[†]

Alexander the Great, the second of these excellent personages.

The second of my three personages is Alexander
the Great: for whoever will consider the age at
which he began his enterprises; the small means by
which he effected so glorious a design; the authority he obtained, at so slender an age, with the greatest and most experienced captains of the world, by
whom he was followed; and the extraordinary favour wherewith fortune embraced him, and rendered
him successful in so many hazardous, I had almost
said rash designs of his!

[*] Cic. Tusc. Quæst. lib. i. cap. 32.
[†] Aul. Gell. lib. iii. cap. 11.

—— *Impellens quicquid sibi summa petenti,*
Obstaret, gaudensque viam fecisse ruinâ.[*]
Whose high designs no hostile force could stay,
And who by ruin lov'd to clear his way.

That grandeur, to have, at the age of thirty-three
years, passed victorious through the whole habitable
earth, and in half a life to have attained to the utmost effort of human nature: so that you cannot
imagine its duration, nor the continuance of his increase in virtue and fortune, to a due maturity of
age, but that you must withal imagine something
more than man: to have made so many royal
branches spring from his soldiers; leaving the world,
at his death, divided amongst four successors, who
were no better than captains of his army, whose
posterity have so long continued, and maintained
that vast possession; so many excellent virtues as he
was possessed of, justice, temperance, liberality, truth
in his word, love towards his own people, and humanity towards those he overcame; for his manners, in
general, seem, in truth, incapable of any just reproach, though some particular and extraordinary
action of his may, perhaps, fall under censure. But
it is impossible to carry on so great things, as he did,
with the strict rules of justice; such as he, are willing to be judged in gross, by the governing motive
of their actions. The ruin of Thebes; the murder
of Menander;[†] and of Ephestion's physician;[‡] the
massacre of so many Persian prisoners at once; of a
troop of Indian soldiers,[§] not without prejudice to
his word; and of the Cosseyans,[||] so much as to the
  r y children; are sallies that are not well to be excused: for, as to Clytus, the fault was more than
recompensed in his repentance, and that very ac-

* Lucan. lib. i. ver. 149, 150.
† Plutarch, in the Life of Alexander, cap. 18.
‡ Idem, ibid. cap. 22, Q. Curtius, lib. ii. sect. 4.
§ Plutarch, cap. 18.
|| Idem, ibid. cap. 22.

tion, as much as any other whatever, manifests the gentleness of his nature; a nature excellently formed to goodness; and it was ingeniously said of him, " That he had his virtues from nature, and his vices " from fortune."[*]   As to his being a little given to boasting, and a little too impatient of hearing himself ill spoken of; and as to those mangers, arms, and bits he caused to be strewed in the Indies; all those little vanities, methinks, may very well be allowed to his youth, and the prodigious prosperity of his fortune: and who will consider, withal, his many military virtues, his diligence, foresight, patience, discipline, subtlety, magnanimity, resolution, and good fortune, wherein (though we had not had the authority of Hannibal to assure us) he was the chief of men: the uncommon beauty of his person, even to a miracle, and his majestic port, with a face so young, so ruddy, and so radiant:

> *Qualis ubi oceani perfusus Lucifer undâ*
> *Quem Venus ante alios astrorum diligit ignes,*
> *Extulit os sacrum cœlo, tenebrasque resolvit.*[†]

> So does the day-star from the ocean rise,
> Above all lights, grateful to Venus' eyes;
> When he from heaven darts his sacred light,
> And dissipates the sullen shades of night.

Whoëver, likewise, considers the excellency of his knowledge and capacity, the duration and grandeur of his glory, pure, clear, without spot or envy; and that, even long after his death, it was a religious belief, that his very medals brought good fortune to all that carried them; and that more kings and princes have written of his acts, than other historians have written the acts of any other king or prince whatever;. and that, to this very day, the Mahometans, who despise all other histories, admit of, and honour his alone, by a special privilege: whoever, I say, will seriously consider all these particulars, will confess, that I had reason to prefer him

---

* Q. Curtius, lib. x. sect. 5.   † Æneid. lib. viii, ver. 589, &c.

12

before Cæsar himself, who alone could make me
doubtful in my choice : and it cannot be denied,
but that there was more of his own conduct in his
exploits, and more of fortune in those of Alexander.
They were, in many things, equal, and, perhaps,
Cæsar had the advantage in some particular qualities. They were two fires, or two torrents, to ravage
the world by several ways :

> *Et velut immissi diversis partibus ignes*
> *Arentem in sylvam, et virgulta sonantia lauro :*
> *Aut ubi decursu rapido de montibus altis*
> *Dant sonitum spumosi amnes, et in æquora currunt,*
> *Quisque suum populatus iter.*[*]
>
> And like to fires in sev'ral parts apply'd
> To a dry grove of crackling laurel's side ;
> Or like the cataracts of foaming rills,
> To tumble headlong from the lofty hills,
> To hasten to the ocean ; even so
> They bear all down before them where they go.

But though Cæsar's ambition was, in itself, more
moderate, it was so mischievous, having the ruin of
his country, and the universal devastation of the
world for its abominable object, that, all things collected together, and put into the balance, I cannot
but incline to Alexander's side.

The third great man, and, in my opinion, the Epaminon-
most excellent of all, is Epaminondas : of glory he das, the
has not near so much as the other two (which also is the most
but a part of the substance of the thing) : of valour excellent.
and resolution, not of that sort which is pushed on by
ambition, but of that which wisdom and reason plants
in a regular soul, he had all that could be imagined.
Of this virtue he has, in my opinion, given as ample
proof as Alexander himself, or Cæsar : for, although
his military exploits were neither so frequent, nor so
renowned, they were yet, if duly considered in all
their circumstances, as important, as vigorous. and
carried with them as manifest a testimony of boldness and military capacity, as those of any whatever.

* Æneid. lib. xii. ver. 521.
2 I 2

His honour by the Greeks.

The Greeks have done him the honour, without contradiction, to pronounce him the greatest man of their nation; and to be the first man of Greece is to be the first of the world.

His knowledge,

As to his knowledge and capacity, we have this ancient judgment of him, "That never any man "knew so much, and spake so little as he:"* for he was of the Pythagorean sect: but, when he did speak, "Never any man spake better;" being an excellent and most persuasive orator.

His manners.

But, as to his manners and conscience, he has vastly surpassed all men that ever undertook the management of affairs; for in this one thing which ought chiefly to be considered, which alone truly denotes us for what we are, and which alone I counterbalance with all the rest put together, he comes not short of any philosopher whatever, not even of Socrates himself. Innocence, in this man, is a quality, peculiar, sovereign, constant, uniform, and incorruptible; compared to which, it appears, in Alexander, subaltern, uncertain, variable, effeminate, and accidental.

His consummate and uniform virtue.

Antiquity has judged, that, in thoroughly sifting all the other great captains, there is found, in every one, some peculiar quality which renders him illustrious. In this man only there is a full and equal virtue and sufficiency throughout, that leaves nothing to be wished for in him, in all offices of human life, whether in private or public employments, either of peace or war, in order for living and dying with grandeur and glory. I do not know of any man whose fortune and talents I so much honour and love.

His obstinacy in poverty.

It is true, that I look up his obstinate poverty, as it is set out by his best friends, a little too scrupulous and nice. And this is the only action, though high

* Plutarch, of Socrates's familiar spirit, cap. 23.

in itself, and well worthy of admiration, that I find so unpleasant as not to desire to imitate, to the degree it was in him.

Scipio Æmilianus, would any attribute to him as brave and magnificent an end, and as profound and universal a knowledge of the sciences, is the only person fit to be put into the other scale of the balance: oh! what a mortification has time given us, to deprive us of the sight of two of the most noble lives, which, by the common consent of all the world, one of the greatest of the Greeks, and the other of the Romans, were in all Plutarch! What a subject! What a workman! *Scipio Æmilianus the only one to be compared with him.*

For a man that was no saint, but, as we say, a gallant man, of civil and ordinary manners, and of a moderate eminence, the richest life that I know, and full of the most valuable and desirable qualities, all things considered, is, in my opinion, that of Alcibiades. *The figure which Alcibiades made.*

But as to Epaminondas, I will here, as an instance of excessive goodness, add some of his opinions. He declared, " That the greatest satisfaction he ever " had in his whole life, was the pleasure he gave his " father and mother by his victory at Leuctra;"* wherein his complaisance is great, preferring their pleasure before his own, so just, and so full of so glorious an action: he did not think it lawful to kill any man for no crime, even though it were to restore the liberty of his country:† which made him so cool in the enterprise of his companion Pelopidas for the relief of Thebes. He was also of opinion, " That " men in battle ought to avoid attacking a friend " that was on the contrary side, and to spare him."‡ And his humanity, even towards his enemies themselves, having rendered him suspected to the Bœo- *Humanity, &c. of Epaminondas.*

---

* Plutarch, in the Life of Coriolanus, cap. 2. And in his treatise, to prove, that there can be no merry life, according to Epicurus.

† Plutarch, of Socrates's Dæmon, cap. 4.

‡ Idem, ibid. cap. 17.

tians; for that, after he had miraculously forced the Lacedæmonians to open to him the pass, which they had undertaken to defend at the entrance of the Morea, near Corinth, he contented himself with having charged through them, without pursuing them to the utmost; for this he had his commission of general taken from him, which was very honourable on such an account, and for the shame it was to them, upon necessity, afterwards to restore him to his command, and to own how much their safety and honour depended upon him: victory, like a shadow, attending him wherever he went: and, indeed, the prosperity of his country, as being from him derived, died with him.*

CHAPTER XXVIII.

Of the Resemblance of Children to their Fathers.

IN compounding this farrago of so many different pieces, I never set pen to paper, but when I have too much idle time, and never any where but at home; so that it is the work of several pauses and intervals, as occasions keep me sometimes many months abroad. As to the rest, I never correct my first by any second conceptions; I perhaps may alter a word or so, but it is only to vary the phrase, and not to cancel my meaning: I have a mind to represent the progress of my humours, that every piece, as it comes from the brain, may be seen: I could wish I had begun sooner, and taken notice of the course of my mutations. A servant of mine, that I employed to transcribe for me, thought he had got a prize by stealing several pieces, which best pleased his fancy; but it is my comfort, that he will be no

* Co:n. Nepos, in the Life of Epaminondas.

greater a gainer, than I shall be a loser by the theft.

I am grown older, by seven or eight years, since I began; neither has it been without some new acquisition: I have, in that time, been acquainted with the cholic, and a long course of years hardly wears off without some such inconvenience. I could have been glad, that, of other infirmities age has to present long-lived men, it had chosen some one that would have been more welcome to me, for it could not possibly have laid upon me a disease, for which, even from my infancy, I have had a greater horror; and it is, in truth, of all the accidents of old-age, the very distemper of which I have ever been most afraid. I have often thought with myself, that I went on too far, and that, in so long a voyage, I should infallibly, at last, meet with some scurvy shock; I perceived, and oft enough declared, that it was time to knock off; that life was to be cut to the quick, according to the surgeons' rule in the amputation of a limb; and that nature usually made him pay very dear interest, who did not, in due time, restore the principal. Yet I was so far from being then ready, that in eighteen months time, or thereabouts, I have been in this uneasy condition, I have inured myself to it, I have compounded with this cholic, and have found therein to comfort myself, and to hope; so much are men enslaved to their miserable being, that there is no condition so wretched that they will not accept, for preserving it, according to that of Mecænas :

Debilem facito manu,
Debilem pede, coxâ,
Lubricos quate dentes :
*Vita dum superest, bene est.**

Maim both my hands and feet, break legs and thighs,
Knock out my teeth, and bore out both my eyes ;
Let me but live, all's well enough, he cries.

* Senec. epist. 101.

And Tamerlane, with a foolish humanity, palliated the fantastic cruelty he exercised upon lepers, when he put all he could hear of to death, by pretending to deliver them from a painful life: for there was not one of them who would not rather have undergone a triple leprosy, than be deprived of their being. Antisthenes, the Stoic;[*] being very sick, and crying out, " Who will deliver me from these evils?" Diogenes, who was come to visit him, " This," said he, presenting him a knife, " presently, if thou " wilt:" " I do not say, from my life," he replied, " but from my disease."[†]   The sufferings that only attack the mind, I am not so sensible of as most other men, and that partly out of judgment : for the world looks upon several things as dreadful, or to be avoided at the expense of life, that are almost indifferent to me; partly through a stupid and insensible complexion I have in accidents which do not hit me point-blank.; and that insensibility I look upon as one of the best parts of my natural constitution ; but essential and corporeal sufferings I am very sensible of. Yet having, long since, foreseen them, though with a sight weak and delicate, and softened with the long and happy health and quiet that God has been pleased to give me the greatest part of my time, I had, in my imagination, fancied them so insupportable, that, in truth, I was more afraid than I have since found I had cause; by which I am still more fortified in this belief, that most of the faculties of the soul, as we employ them, more disturb the repose of life, than any way promote it.

The stone-cholic the most painful of all diseases.

I am in conflict with the worst, the most sudden, the most painful, the most mortal, and the most incurable of all diseases : I have already had five or six very long and painful fits, and yet I either flatter

* Or rather, the Cynic, of which sect he was the head, though, in the main, there is no great difference between the two sects, as to their doctrine.
† Diog. Laertius, in the Life of Antisthenes, lib. v. sect. 18, 19.

myself, or there is even in this state, what is very well to be endured by a man who has his soul free from the fear of death, and from the menaces, conclusions, and consequences, which we are alarmed with by physic. But the effect of the pain itself is not so very acute and intolerable as to drive a solid man into fury and despair. I have, at least, this advantage by my cholic; that what I could not hitherto wholly prevail with myself to resolve upon, as to reconciling and acquainting myself with death, it will perfect; for, the more it presses upon and importunes me, I shall be so much the less afraid to die. I have already gone so far as only to love life for life's sake, but my pain will also dissolve this correspondence; and God grant that, in the end, should the sharpness of it prove greater than I shall be able to bear, it may not throw me into the other not less vicious extreme, to desire and wish to die;

*Summum nec metuas diem, nec optes.**
Neither to wish nor fear to die.

They are two passions to be feared, but the one has its remedy much nearer at hand than the other. As to the rest, I have always found the precept, which so strictly enjoins a constant good countenance, and a serene comportment in the sufferance of pain, to be merely ceremonial. Why should philosophy, which only has respect to life and its effects, trouble itself about these external appearances? Let it leave that care to stage-players, and masters of rhetoric, so much practised in our gestures. Let it, in God's name, allow this vocal frailty, if it be neither cordial nor stomachic, to the disease; and permit the ordinary ways of expressing grief by sighs, sobs, palpitations, and turning pale, that nature has put out of our power to hinder: and provided the courage be undaunted, and the expression not

Complaint may freely be indulged in the agony of pain.

* Mart. lib. x. epig. 47, ver. ult.

sounding of despair, let it be satisfied. What matters it though we wring our hands, if we do not wring our thoughts? philosophy forms us for ourselves, not for others; to be, not to seem. Let it be satisfied with governing our understandings, which it has taken the care of instructing; that, in the fury of the cholic, it may maintain the soul in a condition to examine itself, and to follow its accustomed way, contending with, and supporting, not meanly crouching under, the pain; moved and heated by the struggle, not utterly dejected, but capable of conversation, and other amusements, to a certain degree. In accidents so extreme, it is cruelty to require of us a frame so very composed. It is no great matter what faces we make, if we find any ease by it: if the body find itself relieved by complaining, well and good: if agitation eases it, " Let it tum-" ble and toss at pleasure ;" if it finds the disease evaporate, as some physicians hold, that it helps women in delivery by crying out extremely, or if it amuses its torment, " Let it roar aloud :" let us not command the voice to sally, but permit it. Epicurus not only forgives his wise man for crying out in torments, but advises him to it : *Pugiles etiam quum feriunt adversarium, in jactandis cæstibus ingemiscunt, quia profundenda voce omne corpus intenditur, venitque plaga vehementior :* [*] " When men fight " with clubs, they groan in laying on, because all " the strength of the body is exerted with the voice, " and the blow is laid on with greater force." We have enough to do to deal with the disease, without troubling ourselves with these superfluous rules.

Montaigne kept his temper in the height of his pain. I say this in excuse of those whom we ordinarily see impatient in the assaults and shocks of this infirmity; for as to myself, I have passed it over, hitherto, with a little better countenance, and contented myself with grunting, without roaring out. Not, however, that I put any great task upon my-

* Cic. Tusc. lib. ii. cap. 23.

self to maintain this exterior decency, for I make little account of such an advantage : I allow herein as much as the pain requires, but either my pains are not so excessive, or I have more than ordinary resolution to support them. I complain, and fret, in a very sharp fit, but not to such a degree of despair, as he who with

Ejulatu, questu, gemitu, fremitibus
Resonando multum flebiles voces refert.*
Howling, roaring, and a thousand groans
Express'd his torment in most dismal tones.

I sound myself in the worst of my fits, and have always found, that I was in a capacity to speak, think, and give as rational an answer as at any other time, but not with such steadiness, being troubled and interrupted by the pain. When I am looked upon, by my visitors, to be almost spent, and that they therefore forbear to talk, I often try my own strength, and broach some discourse myself, on subjects the most remote I can contrive from my present condition : I can do any thing by a sudden effort, but not hold long. What pity it is I have not the faculty of that dreamer in Cicero, " Who, dreaming he was " lying with a wench, found he had discharged his " stone in the sheets !" My pains do strangely take off my appetite that way. In the intervals from this excessive torment, when my ureters languish without gnawing, I presently recover my wonted state, forasmuch as my soul takes no other alarm but what is sensible and corporeal, which I certainly owe to the care I have had of preparing myself, by reason, against such accidents :

———— *Laborum*
Nulla mihi nova nunc facies inopinaque surgit,
Omnia præcepi, atque animo mecum ante peregi.†
No face of pain, or labour, now can rise,
Which by its novelty can me surprise ;

* Cic. Tusc. lib. ii. cap. 14.   † Æneid. lib. vi. ver. 103. &c.

I've been accustom'd all things to explore,
Familiar with misfortunes long before.

I am a little roughly handled for a learner, and with
a sudden and sharp alteration, being fallen, in an
instant, from a very easy and happy condition of life,
into the most uneasy and painful that can be imagined. For, besides that it is a disease very much
to be feared in itself, it begins with me after a more
sharp and severe manner than it used to do. My
fits come so thick upon me, that I am scarce ever in
health; and yet I have hitherto kept my mind in
such a frame, that, provided I can continue it, I
find myself in a much better condition of life than a
thousand others, who have no fever, nor other
disease but what they create to themselves for want
of reasoning.

A resem-
blance that
passes to
children,
from grand-
fathers and
great
grand-
fathers, as
well as fa-
thers. There is a certain sort of crafty humility that
springs from presumption; as this, for example, that
we confess our ignorance in many things, and are so
courteous as to acknowledge, that there are, in the
works of nature, some qualities and conditions im-
perceptible by us, and of which our understanding
cannot discover the means and causes. By this honest declaration we hope that people shall also believe us, in those that we say we do understand.
We need not trouble ourselves to seek miracles and
strange difficulties; methinks there are wonders so
incomprehensible amongst the things that we ordinarily see, as surpass all miracles. What a wonderful thing it is that the drop of seed from which we
are produced, should carry in itself the impression
not only of the bodily form, but even of the thoughts
and inclinations of our fathers? Where can the drop
of fluid matter contain that infinite number of
forms? And how do they carry on these resemblances with so precipitant and irregular a progress,
that the grandson shall be like his great grandfather,
the nephew like his uncle? In the family of Lepidus
at Rome, " There were three, not successively, but

" by intervals, that were born with one and the
" same eye covered with a web."* At Thebes,
" There was a race that carried, from their mothers'
" womb, the mark of the spear of a lance," and
who was not born so, was looked upon as illegitimate.† And Aristotle says, " That, in a certain
" nation, where the women were in common, they
" assigned the children to their fathers by their re-
" semblance."

It is probable, that I derive this infirmity from my
father, for he died wonderfully tormented with a
great stone in his bladder; he was never sensible
of his disease till the sixty-seventh year of his age, but
enjoyed a happy state of health, little subject to infirmities; and, having lived seven years in this
disease, died a very painful death. I was born
above twenty-five years before this distemper seized
him, and was his third child in order of birth : where
could his tendency to this malady lurk all that while?
He himself being so free from the infirmity at my
birth, how could that small part of his substance, of
which I was composed, carry away so great an impression of its share? And how was it so concealed,
that, till forty-five years after, I did not begin to be
sensible of it? Being the only one, to this hour,
amongst so many brothers and sisters, and all of one
mother, that was ever troubled with it. He that
can satisfy me in this point, I will believe him in as
many other miracles as he pleases; provided that,
as the manner is, he does not give me a doctrine
much more intricate and fantastic than the thing itself, for current pay.

*The au-
thor's fa-
ther afflict-
ed with the
stone.*

Let the physicians a little excuse the liberty I
take; for by this same infusion and fatal insinuation
it is, that I have conceived a hatred and contempt

*His con-
tempt of
physic.*

---

* Plin. lib. vii. of his Nat. Hist. chap. 12.
† Plutarch, in his Treatise of the Persons whose punishment is
delayed by God, chap. 19 of Amyot's translation; but he does not
say, that those of this race, who had not this mark, as some had
not, were deemed illegitimate.

of their doctrine. The antipathy I have against their art is hereditary to me. My father lived seventy-four years, my grandfather sixty-nine, my great grandfather almost fourscore years, without ever tasting any sort of physic; and, with them, whatever was not ordinary diet, was instead of a drug. Physic is grounded upon experience and examples, so is my opinion; and is not this an express and very advantageous experience? I do not know that they can find me, in all their records, three that were born, bred, and died under the same roof, who have lived so long by their own conduct. It must here, of necessity, be confessed, " That, if reason be not, fortune at " least is on my side," and with physicians fortune goes a great deal further than reason; let them not take me now at this disadvantage; let them not threaten me in the demolished condition I now am, for that were foul play; and, to say truth, I have got so much the better of them by these domestic examples, that they should rest satisfied. Human things are not usually so constant; it has been two hundred years, save eighteen, that this trial has lasted in our family, for the first of them was born in the year 1402. It is now indeed very good reason, that this experience should begin to fail us: let them not therefore reproach me with the infirmities under which I now suffer; is it not enough, for my part, that I have lived forty-seven years in perfect health? Though it should be the end of my career, it is of the longer sort.

The same contempt of it by his ancestors. My ancestors had an aversion to physic by some secret and natural instinct, for the very sight of a potion was loathsome to my father. The Seigneur de Gaviac, my uncle by the father's side, a churchman, and a valetudinarian from his birth, and yet one who made that crazy life to hold out to sixty-seven years, being once fallen into a violent fever, it was ordered, by the physicians, he should be plainly told, " That if he would not make use of " help," for so they call that which is very often a

hindrance, " he would infallibly be a dead man."
The good man, though terrified with this dreadful
sentence, yet replied, " I am then a dead man."—
But God, soon after, proved the prognostic false.
The youngest of the brothers, which were four, and
by many years the youngest, the Sieur de Bussaget,
was the only man of the family that made use of
medicine, by reason, I suppose, of the commerce
he had with the other arts, for he was a counsellor
in the court of parliament, and it succeeded so ill
with him, that, being in outward appearance of the
strongest constitution, he yet died before any of the
rest, the Sieur St. Michel only excepted.

It is possible I may have derived this natural antipathy to physic from them; but, had there been
no other consideration in the case, I would have endeavoured to have overcome it; for all conditions
that spring in us without reason are vicious, and is
a kind of disease that we are to wrestle with. It
may be I had naturally this propensity, but I have
supported and fortified it by arguments and reasons, which have established in me the opinion I
have of it; for I also hate the consideration of refusing physic for the nauseous taste. I would hardly
be of their humour, who find health worth purchas-
ing by all the most painful cauteries and incisions
that can be applied; and, according to Epicurus, I
conceive, " That the pleasures are to be avoided, if
" greater pains be the consequence; and pains to be
" coveted, that will terminate in greater pleasures."
Health is a precious thing, and the only one, in truth,
which merits that a man should lay out, not only his
time, sweat, labour, and goods, but also his life itself to obtain it, forasmuch as, without it, life is a burden, to us. Pleasure, learning, wisdom and virtue,
without it, wither and vanish; and to the most laboured and solid discourses, that philosophy would
imprint in us to the contrary, we need no more but
oppose the idea of Plato, being struck with an epi-
lepsy or apoplexy; and, in this supposition, to defy
him to call the rich faculties of his soul to his assist-

His reason
for making
so very
light of
physic.

ance. All means that conduce to health I can neither think painful nor dear; but I have some other appearances that make me strangely suspect all this merchandise. I do not deny but there may be some art in it, and that there are not, amongst so many works of nature, some things proper for the preservation of health, that is most certain; I very well know that there are some simples that moisten and others that dry; I experimentally know that radishes are windy and senna-leaves laxative; and several other such experiences I have, which I am as sure of as I am that mutton nourishes and wine warms me. Solon was wont to say, " That eating was, " like other drugs, physic against 'the disease of " hunger." I do not disapprove the use we make of things the earth produces, nor doubt, in the least, of the power and fertility of nature, and disapprove not the application of what she affords to our necessities: I very well see that pikes and swallows thrive by its laws; but I mistrust the inventions of our wit, knowledge, and art; to countenance which, we have abandoned nature and her rules, and keep no bounds nor moderation. As we call the modification of the first laws that fall into our hands justice, and their practice and dispensation often very foolish and very unjust: and as those who scoff at, and accuse it, do not mean, nevertheless, to wrong that noble virtue, but only condemn the abuse and profanation of that sacred title; so, in physic, I very much honour that glorious name, and the end for which it is studied, with what it promises to the service of mankind; but its prescriptions I neither honour nor esteem.

Experience not very favourable to medicine.

In the first place, experience makes me dread it; for, amongst all of my acquaintance, I see no race of people so soon sick, and so long before they are well, as those who are slaves to physic. Their very health is altered and corrupted by the regimen they follow. Physicians are not content to deal only with the sick, but they change health into sickness, for fear men should at any time escape their authority.

Do they not, from a continual and perfect health, infer an argument of some great sickness to ensue? I have been sick often enough, and have, without their aid, found my maladies as easy to be supported (though I have made trial of almost all sorts) and as short as those of any other, without swallowing their nauseous doses. The health I have is full and free, without other rule or discipline than my own custom and pleasure; every place serves me well enough to stay in, for I need no other conveniences when I am sick than what I must have when I am well; I never am uneasy that I have no physician, no apothecary, nor any other assistance, which I see most men are more afflicted at than they are with their disease! Do the physicians themselves, by the felicity and duration of their own lives, convince us of the apparent effect of their skill?

There is not a nation in the world that has not been many ages without physic; the first ages, that is to say, the best and most happy, knew no such thing; and the tenth part of the world knows nothing of it to this day. Several nations are ignorant of it, where men live more healthful and longer than we do here, and even amongst us the common people live happily without it. The Romans were six hundred years before they received it;[*] and, after having made a trial of it, banished it from their city at the instance of Cato the censor, who made it appear how easy it was to live without it, having himself lived fourscore and five years,[†]

[*] Montaigne might very well assure us, upon the authority of Pliny, lib. xxix. cap. 1, That the Romans did not admit of physic till six hundred years after the foundation of Rome; and that, after they had made trial of the art, they condemned and banished the physicians from their city; but as to his addition, that they were expelled at the instance of Cato the censor, Pliny is so far from authorising it, that he expressly says, the Romans did not banish the physicians from their city till long after the death of Cato. Several modern writers have fallen into the same error, as Montaigne, as may be seen in Bayle's Dictionary, under the article PORCIUS, in the Note H.

[†] Idem, ibid.

and kept his wife alive to an extreme old age, not
without physic, but without a physician; for every
thing that we find healthful to life may be called
physic. He kept his family in health, as Plutarch
says, if I mistake not, with hare's milk; as Pliny
reports,* that the Arcadians cured all manner of
diseases with that of a cow;† and Herodotus says,‡
" The Lybians generally enjoy a rare health, by a
" custom they have, after their children are arrived
" to four years of age, to burn and cauterise the
" veins of their head and temples, by which means
" they cut off all defluxions of rheums for their
" whole lives."|| The country people of our pro-
vince use nothing, in all sorts of diseases, but the
strongest wine they can get, mixed with a great
deal of saffron and spice, and all with the same success.

Whether the usefulness of medicinal purges is warranted upon good grounds. To say the truth, of all this diversity and confusion of prescriptions, what other end and effect is
there, after all, but to purge the belly? which a
thousand ordinary simples will do as well; and I do
not know whether such evacuations be so much to
our advantage as they pretend, and whether nature
requires not a settlement of her excrementitious
parts, to a certain proportion, as wine does of its
lees, to preserve it. You oft see healthy men taken
with vomiting and fluxes of the belly from unknown
causes, and make a great evacuation of excrements,
without any preceding need, or any following benefit, but rather with hurt and damage to their constitution. It is from the great Plato I lately learned,
" That of three sorts of motions which are natural
" to us, purging is the last and worst; and that no

* In the Life of Cato the Censor, chap. 12.
† Nat. Hist. lib. xxv. cap. 8.
‡ Lib. iv. p. 323.
|| Montaigne should have said, by which means they propose to cut
off such defluxions, &c. for though Herodotus says, they do it with
this view, yet he does not presume to say, that, for this cause, they
enjoy such perfect health. " It is true," says he, " the Lybians are
" more healthy than any people that I know, but that this is the
" cause of it, I cannot affirm positively."

" man, unless he be a fool; ought to take any thing
" to that purpose, but in extreme necessity."*—
Men disturb and irritate the disease by contrary oppositions; it must be the way of living that must
gently weaken and bring it to its period; the violent contest between the drug and the disease is
ever to our loss, since the combat is within ourselves, and that the drug is an assistant not to be
trusted, being, by its own nature, an enemy to our
health, and has no access to our constitution, without making a disturbance. Let it alone a little;
the order of nature that provides for fleas and
moles, provides also for men, if they will have the
patience, which fleas and moles have, to leave it to
itself; we may bawl out, as the earman does to his
horses, till we are hoarse, and the cure be never
the nearer. It is a proud and pitiless order; our
fears, our despair, disgust and stop it from, instead
of inviting it to our relief; it owes its course to the
disease as well as to health, and will not suffer itself
to be corrupted in favour of the one, to the prejudice of the other's right, for it would then fall into
disorder. Let us, in God's name, follow it; it leads
those that follow, and those who will not follow, it
drags along both their fury and physic together;
order a purge for your brain, it will there be better
employed than upon your stomach.

One asking a Lacedæmonian, " What had made
" him live so long?" He made answer, " The ig-
" norance of physic." And the emperor Adrian
continually exclaimed, as he was dying, " That the
" crowd of physicians had killed him."† An ill
wrestler turned physician: " Courage," says Diogenes to him, " thou hast done well, for now thou

[margin note:] Whether physicians do more good or harm, and how they excuse the ill success of their prescriptions.

* In Timæo, p. 551.
† Xiphilinus in Epitome Dionis Vitâ Adriani, and Bayle's Dictionary, in the article HADRIAN. The same complaint was made
before Hadrian, as I learn from Pliny, who has copied an epitaph,
wherein a person deceased complaining, " Turba se medicorum pe-
riisse." Nat. Hist. lib. xxix. cap. 1.

2 K 2

" wilt throw those who have formerly thrown
" thee."* But physicians have this advantage, ac-
córding to Nicocles, " That the sun gives light to
" their success, and the earth covers their miscar-
" riages ;"† and, besides, they have a very advantageous way of making use of all sorts of events ;
for what fortune, nature, or any other causes (of
which the number is infinite) produce of good and
healthful in us, it is the privilege of physic to attribute to itself. All the happy successes that happen
to the patient, who is under its regimen, must be
derived from thence ; the occasions that have cured
me, and that cure a thousand others who do not apply to them, physicians arrogate to themselves :· as
to ill accidents, they either absolutely disówn them,
in laying the fault upon the patient, by such frivolous reasons as they can never be to seek for ; as,
" He lay with his arms out of bed ; or, he was dis-
" turbed with the rattling of a coach :"

> ———— *Rhedarum transitus arcto*
> *Vicorum inflexu :*‡————
>
> He heard the wheels, and horses' trampling feet,
> In the strait turning of a narrow street.

Or, " Somebody had set open the window ; or, he
" had lain on his left side ; or had had some uneasy
" thought in his head :" in short, a word, a dream,
or a look, seem to them excuse sufficient for this
miscarriage ; or, if they so please, they even make
use of their growing worse, and do their business
by a way which can never fail them ; which is, by
buzzing us in the ears, when the disease is inflamed
by their medicaments, that it had been much worse
but for their remedies. He who, for an ordinary
cold, they have thrown into a double tertian ague,

* Diog. Laert. in the Life of Diogenes the Cynic, lib. vi.
sect. 60.
   † Chap. 146 of the Collection of the Monks Antonius and
Maximus.
   ‡ Juv. sat. iii. ver. 236.

had, but for them, been in a continued fever. They do not care what mischief they do, since it turns to their own profit. In earnest, they have reason to require a very favourable belief from their patients; and indeed it need be a hearty and very easy one, to swallow things so hard to be believed. Plato said very well,* " That physicians were the " only men that might lie without control, since our " health depends upon the vanity and falsity of " their promises."

Æsop,† a most excellent author, and of whom few men discover all the graces, pleasantly represents to us the tyrannical authority physicians usurp over poor creatures, weakened and dejected by sickness and fear; for he tells us, " That a sick per- " son, being asked by his physician, what operation " he found of the medicines he had given him ?" " I have sweat very much," says the sick man: " That is good," says the physician : another time, having asked him, " How he felt himself after his " physic;" " I have been very cold, and have had a " great shivering upon me," said he : " That is " good," replied the physician : after the third dose, he asked him again, " How he did ?" " Why, " I find myself swelled and puffed up," said he, " as if I had the dropsy :" " Better still," said the physician : one of his servants coming presently after to inquire " How he felt himself?" " Truly, " friend," said he, " with being too well I am " about to die."

There was a more just law in Egypt, by which A law of the physician, for the three first days, was to take the Egyptian, charge of his patient at the patient's own peril and whereby fortune; but those three days being passed, it was the physito be at his own. For why should their patron to be an-Æsculapius be struck with thunder for restoring for the Hypolitus from death to life :

---

* De Repub. lib. iii.
† Fab. xliii.

succeſs of
their pre-
scriptions,

Nam pater omnipotens aliquem indignatus ab umbris
Mortalem infernis ad lumina surgere vitæ,
Ipse repertorem medicinæ talis et artis
Fulmine Phœbigenam Stygias detrusit at undas.[*]

For Jupiter, offended at the sight
Of one who had been dead, restor'd to light;
Struck with his thunder to the Styx in ire,
The man who dar'd to heavenly pow'r aspire.

and his followers be pardoned, who send so many
men from life to death? A physician, boasting to
Nicocles,[†] "That his art was of great authority:"
" It is so, indeed," said Nicocles, " that can, with
" impunity, kill so many people."

Mystery
very neces-
sary for
physic.

As to what remains, had I been of their counsel,
I would have rendered my discipline more sacred
and mysterious; they had begun well, but they
have not ended so. It was a good beginning to
make gods and dæmons the authors of their science,
and to have used a peculiar way of speaking and writing, though philosophy concludes it folly to persuade a man to his own good by an unintelligible
way; *Ut si quis medicus imperet ut sumat terrige-*
nam, herbigradam, domiportam, sanguine caſſam:[‡]
" As if a physician should order his patient to take
" snails."[§]

Why the
patient
should con-
fide in his
physician.

It was a good rule in their art, and that accompanies all other vain, fantastic, and supernatural arts,
" That the patients' belief should prepossess them
" with good hope and assurance of the effect of
" their operation." A rule they hold to such a degree as to maintain, that the most inexpert and ignorant physician is more proper for a patient that

---

[*] Æneid. lib. vii. ver. 769, &c.
[†] In p. 652, chap. 146, of the Collection of the Monks, just men-
tioned, printed at the end of Stobæus, Barbeyrac thinks, that this
Nicocles, who here banters a certain quack, is the famous king of
Salamina, to whom Socrates addressed one of his orations.
[‡] Cic. de Divin. lib. ii.
[§] Describing it by the epithets of an animal trailing with its slime
over the herbage, without blood or bones, and carrying its house
upon its back.

has confidence in him, than the most learned and experienced whom he is not acquainted with,

Nay, even the choice of most of their drugs is, in some sort, mysterious and divine. The left foot of a tortoise, the urine of a lizard, the dung of an elephant, the liver of a mole, blood drawn from under the wing of a white pigeon; and for us who have the stone (so scornfully they use us in our miseries) the excrement of rats beaten to powder, and such-like fooleries, as rather carry a face of magical enchantment, than of any solid science. I omit the odd number of their pills, the appointment of certain days and feasts of the year, the superstition of gathering their simples at certain hours; and that austere wise look, and grim gesture, which Pliny himself so much derides. *Fraud used in the choice and application of drugs.*

But they have, as I said, failed, in that they have not added, to this fine beginning, the making their meetings and consultations more religious and secret, where no profane person ought to have been admitted, no more than to the secret ceremonies of Æsculapius: for, by reason of this, it falls out, that their resolution, the weakness of their arguments, divination, and foundations,[*] the sharpness of their disputes, full of hatred, jealousy, and self-interest, coming to be discovered by every one, a man must be very blind, not to discern that he runs a very great hazard in their hands. Who ever saw one physician approve of another's prescription, without taking something away, or adding something to it? By which they sufficiently betray their art, and make it manifest to us, that they therein more consider their own reputation, and consequently their profit, than their patient's interest. He was a much wiser man of their tribe, who, of old, gave it for a rule, " That only one physician should undertake a sick " person;" for, if he do nothing to purpose, one single man's fault can bring no great scandal upon *The physicians blamed for having renounced the mysterious in their practice.*

* Plin. Nat. Hist. lib. xxix. cap. 1.

the profession; and, on the contrary, the glory will be great, if he happen to have good success: whereas, when they are many, they, at every turn, bring a disrepute upon their calling, forasmuch as they oftener do hurt than good. They ought to be satisfied with the perpetual disagreement which is found in the opinions of the principal masters, and ancient authors of this science, which is only known to men well read, without discovering to the vulgar the controversies and various judgments which they nourish and continue amongst themselves.

The opposite sentiments of physicians, as to the cause of diseases, a proof of the uncertainty of their science.

Shall we have one example of the ancient controversy in physic? Hierophilus places the original cause of diseases in the humours; Erasistratus, in the blood of the arteries; Asclepiades, in the invisible atoms gliding in our pores; Alcmæon, in the exuberancy, or defect of our bodily strength; Diocles,* in the inequality of the elements of which the body is composed, and in the quality of the air we suck in; Strato, in the abundance, crudity, and corruption of the nourishment we take; and Hippocrates lodges it in the spirits, There is a certain friend of theirs, whom they know better than I, who declares, upon this subject, " That the " most important science in practice, amongst us, " viz. that which is intrusted with our health and " preservation, is, by ill-luck, the most uncertain, " the most perplexed, and the most changeable."† There is no great danger in mistaking the height of the sun, or in the fraction of some astronomical computation: but here, where our whole being is concerned, it is no wisdom to abandon ourselves to the mercy of the agitation of so many contrary winds.

Physic, when, and by whom brought into credit.

Before the Peloponnesian war, there was no great talk of this science: Hippocrates brought it into repute; and whatever he established, Chrysippus overthrew: after that, Erasistratus, Aristotle's grand-

---

* Celsus, in his preface to lib. i.   † Plin. Nat. Hist. lib. xxix. cap. 1,

son, overthrew what Chrysippus had wrote of it:* after these, the Empirics started up, who took a quite contrary method to the ancients, in the management of this art: when the credit of these began a little to decay, Herophilus set another sort of practice on foot, which Asclepiades, in turn, stood up against, and overthrew: the opinion, first of Themison, and then of Musa, and after that, those of Vexius Valens, a physician famous through the intelligence he had with Messalina, came in vogue: the empire of physic, in Nero's time, fell to Thessalus, who abolished and condemned all that had been held of it till his time: this man's doctrine was refuted by Crinas of Marseilles, who accounted for all medicinal operations by the ephemerides and motions of the stars; and reduced eating, sleeping, and drinking, to hours that were most pleasing to Mercury and the Moon. His authority was soon after supplanted by Charinus, a physician of the same city of Marseilles; a man that not only controverted all the ancient practice of physic, but moreover the use of hot public baths, that had been, for so many ages before, in common use: he made men bathe in cold water, even in winter, and plunged his sick patients in the natural waters of brooks. No Roman, till Pliny's time, had ever vouchsafed to practise physic; that office was only performed by Greeks and foreigners, as it is now amongst us French, by those that chop Latin: "For," as a very great physician says, "we do not easily receive the medicine we "understand, no more than we do the drugs we "ourselves gather." If the nations from whence we fetch our guaiacum, sarsaparilla, and China wood, have any physicians, how great a value must we imagine, by the same recommendation of strangeness, rarity, and dear purchase, do they set upon our cabbage and parsley? For, who would dare to contemn

* Plin. Nat. Hist. lib. xxix. cap. 1.

things so far fotched, at the hazard of so tedious and
dangerous a voyage?

Since these ancient alterations in physic, there
have been infinite others down to our own times,
and, for the most part, such as have been entire and
universal; as those, for example, produced, in our
own time, by Paracelsus, Fioravanti, and Argente-
rius; for they, as I am told, not only alter one receipt, but the whole contexture and system of the
body of physic, accusing all others of ignorance and
imposition that have practised before them: at this
rate, in what a condition the poor patient must be,
I leave you to judge.

That sup-
posing phy-
sic to do no
good, it is
not certain
that it does
no harm.
A moor
bathed and
purged to
clear his
complex-
ion.

If we were even assured, that, when they are
mistaken, that mistake of theirs does us no harm,
though it does no good, it were a reasonable bargain
to run the venture of our being made better, without the danger of being worse. Æsop* tells a story,
" That one who had bought a Morisco slave, believ-
" ing that his black complexion was accidental in
" him, and occasioned by the ill-usage of his former
" master, caused him to enter into a course of phy-
" sic, and with great care to be often bathed and
" drenched: it happened, that the Moor was no-
" thing amended in his tawny complexion, but he
" wholly lost his former health." How oft do we
see physicians impute the death of their patients to
one another? I remember, that, some years ago,
there was an epidemical disease, very dangerous, and
for the most part mortal, that raged in the towns
about us: the storm being over, which had sweeped
away an infinite number of men, one of the most famous physicians of all the country published a book
upon that subject, wherein, upon better thoughts,
he confesses, " That the letting of blood in that dis-
" ease was a principal cause of much damage."
Moreover, their authors hold, " That there is no

* Fab. lxxv.

" physic which has not something hurtful in it." And
if even those that are of service to us, do, in some
measure, offend us, what must those do which are
totally misapplied ? For my own part, though there
were nothing else in the case, I am of opinion, that
" To those that loath the taste of physic, it must
" needs be a dangerous and prejudicial endeavour to
" force it down at so incommodious a time, and
" with so much aversion ; and believe, that it mar-
" vellously disturbs the sick person, at a time when
" he has so much need of repose."

Besides this, if we consider the causes to which Physicians
they usually impute our diseases, they are so light very sub-
and nice, that I thence conclude " A very little er- takes; and
" ror in the dispensation of their drugs may do a their perni-
" great deal of mischief." Now, if the mistake of a sequences.
physician be so dangerous, we are in a scurvy condition, for it is almost impossible but he must often
fall into those mistakes : he had need of too many
parts, considerations, and circumstances, rightly to
adjust his design : he must know the sick person's
complexion, his temperature, his humours, inclinations, actions, nay, his very thoughts and imaginations : he must be assured of the external circumstances, of the nature of the place, the quality of the
air and season, the situation of the planets and their
influences : he must know, in the disease, the causes,
prognostics, affections, and critical days ; in the
drugs, the weight, the power of working, the country, the form, the age, and the dispensation ; and
he must know how rightly to proportion and mix
them together ; wherein, if there be the least error;
if, amongst so many springs, there be but any
one that draws wrong, it is enough to destroy us :
God knows with how great difficulty most of these
things are to be understood. As, for example,
" How shall a physician find out the true sign of the
" disease, every disease being capable of an infinite
" number of indications ?" How many doubts and
debates have they amongst themselves upon the in-

terpretation of urines? Otherwise, from whence should the continual debates we see amongst them about the knowledge of the disease proceed? How would we excuse the error, they so oft fall into, of taking one thing for another? In the diseases I have had, were there never so little difficulty in the case, I never found three of one opinion: which I instance, because I love to introduce examples, wherein I myself am concerned.

· A gentleman at Paris was, by order of the physicians, lately cut for the stone in the bladder, where was found no more stone than in the palm of his hand; and a bishop, who was my very good friend, having been earnestly pressed, by the major part of the physicians in town, whom he consulted, to suffer himself to be cut in the same place; to which also, upon their words, I added my interest to persuade him: when he was dead, and opened, it appeared that he had no stone but in the kidneys. They are least excusable for any error in this disease, by reason that it is, in some sort, palpable; and it is by that, that I conclude surgery to be much more certain, by reason that it sees and feels what it does, and so goes less upon conjecture; whereas the physicians have no *speculum matricis*, by which to discover our brains, lungs, and liver.

The promises of the physicians generally incredible. The very promises of physic are not to be credited: for, being to provide against diverse and contrary accidents, that often afflict us at one and the same time, and that have almost a necessary relation, as the heat of the liver, and the coldness of the stomach, they will needs persuade us, that, of their ingredients, one will warm the stomach, and the other cool the liver; one has its commission to go directly to the kidneys, nay, even to the bladder, without scattering its operations by the way, but retaining its power and virtue through all the stops, in so long a course, even to the place to the service of which it is designed, by its own occult property: one will dry the brain, and another will moisten the lungs.

All these things being mixed in one potion, is it not
a kind of madness to imagine, or to hope, that these
different virtues should separate themselves from one
another in this mixture and confusion, to perform so
many various errands? I should very much fear, that
they would either lose or change their labels, and
take up one another's quarters: and who can imagine but that, in this liquid confusion, these faculties must corrupt, confound, and spoil one another?
And is not the danger still more, " When the mak-
" ing up of this medicine is intrusted to another, to
" whose honour and mercy we again abandon our
" lives?"

As we have doublet and breeches makers, distinct
trades, to clothe us, and are so much the better
fitted, while each of them meddles only with his
own pattern, and has less to trouble his head with,
than a tailor who undertakes all; and as, in matter
of diet, great persons, for their convenience and to
the end they may be better served, have distinct
offices, of boilers and roasters, which one cook, who
would undertake the whole service, could not so well
perform; so should we be treated in our cures. The Every sick
Egyptians had reason to reject this general profes- person had
his parti-
sion of a physician, and to divide it to several pecu- cular phy-
liar diseases, allotting to every part of the body a sician
among the
particular operator: for this part was more properly, Egyptians.
and with less confusion, provided for, because it especially regarded this alone: ours are not aware,
" That he who provides for all, provides for no-
" thing;" and that the " entire government of this
" microcosm" is more than they are able to undertake. Whilst they were afraid of " Stopping a loose-
" ness, lest they should put him into a fever," they
killed me a friend that was worth more than the
whole pack of them put together. They counterpoise their own divinations with the present evils;
and, because they will not " Cure the brain to the
" prejudice of the stomach, they offend both with
" their mutinous and tumultuary drugs."

Weakness and uncertainty of the reasons on which the art of physic is grounded.

As to the variety and the weakness of the reasons of this art, it is more manifest than in any other art. " Aperitive medicines are proper for a man " subject to the stone, by reason that, opening and " dilating the passages, they help forward the slimy " matter, whereof gravel and the stone are engen- " dered, and convey that downward which begins " to harden and gather in the kidney. Aperitive " things are dangerous for a man subject to the " stone, by reason that, opening and dilating the " passages, they help forward, towards the reins, " the matter that has a tendency to breed the stone, " which, by their own propension that way, being " apt to seize it, it is not to be imagined but that a " great deal of what has been so conveyed thither " must remain behind. Moreover, if the medicine " happen to meet with any thing a little too gross " to be carried through all those narrow passages it " must pass, in order to be expelled, that obstruc- " tion, whatever it is, being stirred by these aperi- " tive things, and thrown into those narrow pas- " sages, coming to stop them, will occasion a most " certain and most painful death." They have the like consistency in the like advices they give us for the regimen of life. " It is good to make water " often, for we experimentally see, that, in letting it " lie long in the bladder, we give it time to let fall " the sediment which will concrete into a stone. It " is not good to make water often, for the heavy " excrements it carries along with it will not be " voided without violence," as we see by experience, that a torrent which runs with force, washes the ground it rolls over much cleaner than the course of a slow and languid stream. Likewise " It is good " to have often to do with women, for that opens " the passages, and helps to evacuate sand: it is " also very ill to have often to do with women, be- " cause it heats, tires, and weakens the reins. It " is good to bathe frequently in hot waters, foras- " much as that relaxes and mollifies the place,

" where the sand and gravel lurks: and it is also
" ill, by reason that this application of external heat
" helps the reins to bake, harden, and petrify the
" matter therein disposed. For those who are at
" the bath, it is most healthful to eat little at night,
" to the end that the waters they are to drink the
" next morning may have a better operation upon
" an empty stomach; on the contrary, it is better
" to eat little at dinner, that it hinder not the ope-
" ration of the waters, which is not yet perfect;
" and not to oppress the stomach so soon after the
" other labour, but leave the office of digestion to the
" night, which will much better perform it than the
" day, when the body and mind are in perpetual mo-
" tion and action." Thus do they juggle and cant,
in all their disputes, at our expense, and cannot give
me one proposition, against which I cannot erect a
contrary of equal force. Let them then no longer
exclaim against those, who, in this confusion, suffer
themselves to be gently guided by their own appetite, and the advice of nature, and commit themselves
to the common fortune.

I have seen, in my travels, almost all the famous
baths of Christendom, and, for some years past,
have begun to make use of them myself; for I look
upon bathing as generally wholesome, and believe,
that we suffer no slight inconveniences in our health,
by having left off the custom; that was generally observed, in former times, almost by all nations, and
is yet in many, of bathing every day; and I cannot imagine but that we are much the worse by having our limbs crusted, and our pores stopped with
dirt and filth. As to the drinking of the waters, fortune has, in the first place, rendered them not at all
unacceptable to my taste; and, secondly, they are
natural and simple, and, at least, carry no danger
with them, if they do no good: of which, the inf-
nite crowd of people, of all sorts of constitutions,
that repair thither, I take to be a sufficient warrant: and although I have not there observed any
extraordinary and miraculous effects, but, on the

contrary, having more curiously than ordinary
inquired into it, I have found all the reports of
such operations, that have been spread abroad in
those places, ill grounded and false, and those that
believe them (as people are willing to be gulled
in what they desire) deceived in them; yet I
have seldom known any that have been made
worse by those waters, and a man cannot honestly
deny but that they beget a better appetite, help digestion, and do, in some sort, revive us, if we do
not go to them in too weak a condition, which I
would dissuade every one from doing. They have
not the virtue to raise men from desperate and inve-
terate diseases, but they may help in some light in-
disposition, or prevent some threatening alteration.
Whoever does not bring along with him so much
cheerfulness as to enjoy the pleasure of the company
he will there meet, and of the walks and exercises, to
which the beauty of the places, in which those waters are commonly situate, invites us, doubtless loses
the best and surest part of their effect. For this
reason I have hitherto chosen to go to those of the
most pleasant situation, where there was the most
conveniency of lodging, provision, and company;
as the baths of Banieres in France, those of Plom-
bieres on the frontiers of Germany and Lorrain,
those of Baden in Switzerland, those of Lacca in
Tuscany, and especially those of Della-Villa, which
I have the most frequented, and at several seasons.

Every nation has particular opinions, touching
their use, and different rules and methods in using
them, and all of them, according to what I have
seen, almost of like effect. Drinking of them is not
at all received in Germany; they bathe for all diseases, and will lie dabbling in the water almost from
sun to sun. In Italy, when they drink nine days,
they bathe at least thirty, and commonly drink the
water mixed with drugs to make it work the better.
We are here ordered to walk to digest it; they are
there kept in bed, after taking it, till it be worked
off, their stomachs and feet being continually chafed

*Every na-
tion makes
a particu-
lar use of
baths.*

with hot cloaths : and as the Germans generally use cupping and scarification in the bath ; so the Italians have their *doccie*, which are certain channels of this hot water brought through pipes ; and with them bathe an hour in the morning, and as much in the afternoon, for a month together, either the head, stomach, or any other part where the pain lies. There are infinite other different customs in every country, or, rather, they have no manner of resemblance to one another. By which you may see, that this little part of physic, to which alone I have submitted, though the least depending upon art of all others, has yet a great share of the confusion and uncertainty, every where else manifest in this profession.

The poets say whatever they please with greater emphasis and grace ; witness these two epigrams :

> *Alcon hesterno signum Jovis attigit. Ille,*
> *Quamvis marmoreus, vim patitur medici :*
> *Ecce hodie jussus transferri ex æde vetusta,*
> *Effertur, quamvis sit deus, atque lapis.* *

Alcon did yesterday Jove's statue touch,
Which, although marble, suffer'd by it much ;
For though it is a god, and made of stone,
From its old seat 'tis now, by order, gone.

And the other,

> *Lotus nobiscum est hilaris, cœnavit et idem,*
> *Inventus mane est mortuus Andragoras,*
> *Tam subitæ mortis causam Faustine requiris ?*
> *In somnis medicum viderat Hermocratem.* †

Bath'd, supp'd, in glee, Andragoras went to bed
Last night, but in the morning was found dead ;
Would'st know, Faustinus, what was his disease?
He dreaming saw the quack, Hermocrates.

Upon this I will relate two stories : the baron of Caupene in Chalosse, and I, have between us the advowson of a benefice of great extent, at the foot of our mountains, called Lahontan. It is with the inhabitants of this angle, as it is said of those of the

Two pleasant stories against the practice of lawyers and physicians.

---

* Ausod. epig. 74.   † Mart. lib. vi. epig. 53.

vale of Angrougne: " They lived a peculiar sort of
" life, had particular fashions, clothes, and man-
" ners," and were ruled and governed by certain
particular laws and usages, received from father to
son, to which they submitted, without other constraint than the reverence due to custom.   This little state had continued from all antiquity in so happy a condition, that no neighbouring judge was
ever put to the trouble of inquiring into their quarrels, no advocate ever retained to give them counsel,
nor stranger ever called in to compose their differences; nor was ever any of them seen so reduced as
to go a begging.   They avoided all alliances and
traffic with the rest of mankind, that they might not
corrupt the purity of their own government ; till,
as they say, " One of them, in the memory of their
" fathers, having a mind spurred on with a noble
" ambition, contrived, in order to bring his name
" into credit and reputation, to make one of his sons
" something more than ordinary, and, having put
" him to learn to write, made him, at last, a brave
" scrivener for the village : this fellow, being grown
" up, began to disdain their ancient customs, and
" to buz into the people's ears the pomp of the
" other parts of the nation : the first prank he play-
" ed was, to advise a friend of his, whom somebody
" had offended by sawing off the horns of one of his
" she-goats, to make his complaint of it to the
" king's judges thereabouts, and so he went on in
" this practice, till he spoiled all."
    In the progress of this corruption, they say, there
happened another, of worse consequence, by means
of a physician, who fell in love with one of their
daughters, had a mind to marry her, and to live
amongst them.   " This man first of all began to
" teach them the names of fevers, rheums, and
" imposthumes, the seat of the heart, liver, and
" intestines, a science, till then, utterly unknown
" to them ; and, instead of garlic, with which
" they were wont to cure all manner of diseases,

11

" how painful or extreme soever, he taught them;
" though it were but for a cough, or any little cold;
" to taste strange mixtures, and began to make a
" trade, not only of their healths, but of their lives.
" They swear that, till then, they never perceived
" the evening air to be offensive to the head, nor
" that to drink, when they were hot, was hurtful;
" nor that the winds of autumn were more unwhole-
": some than those of the spring; that since this use
" of physic, they find themselves oppressed with a
" legion of unusual diseases, and that they perceive
" a general decay in their wonted vigour, and their
" lives are cut shorter by the half." This is the
first of my stories.

The other is, that, before I was afflicted with the Another
stone, hearing that the blood of a he-goat was, with story which
many, in very great esteem, and looked upon as a no less con-
celestial manna, rained down upon these latter ages cerns phy-
for the safety and preservation of the lives of men, sic.
and having heard it spoken of, by men of understanding, as an admirable drug, and of infallible
operation, I, who have ever thought myself subject
to all the accidents that can befal other men, had a
mind, in my perfect health, to furnish myself with
this admirable medicine, and therefore gave order to
have a goat fed at home according to the receipt:
for he must be taken up in the hottest months of
summer, and must only have aperitive herbs given
to eat, and white wine to drink. I went home, by
chance, the very day he was to be killed; and one
came and told me, that the cook had found two or
three great balls in his paunch, that rattled against
one another amongst what he had eaten: I was
curious to have all his entrails brought before me,
where, having caused the skin that enclosed them to
be cut, there tumbled out three great lumps, as
light as sponges, so that they appeared to be hollow;
but, as to the rest, hard and firm without, and
spotted all over with various colours: one was
perfectly round, and of the bigness of a little ball;

the other two something less, of an imperfect roundness, as seeming not to be arrived at their full
growth. I find, by inquiry of people accustomed to
open these animals, that it is a rare and unusual
accident. It is likely these are stones of the same
nature with ours, and, if so, it must needs be a very
vain hope, in those who have the stone, to extract
their cure from the blood of a beast, which was itself
in a way to die of the same disease : for to say, that
the blood does not participate of this contagion, and
does not alter its wonted virtue, it is rather to be
believed, that nothing is engendered in a body but
by the concurrence and communication of all the
parts. The whole mass works together, though one
part contributes more to the work than another,
according to the diversity of operations. Whether
it is very likely, that there was some petrifying quality in all the parts of this goat. It was not so
much for the fear of the future, and for myself, that
I was curious of this experiment, but because it falls
out in mine, as it does in many other families, that
the women store up such small wares for the service
of the common people, using the same receipt in
fifty several diseases, and such a receipt as they will
not take themselves, and yet triumph in their good
successes.

Physicians
worthy of
esteem,
and why.   As to what remains, I honour physicians, not
according to the rule, from necessity (for to this
passage may be added another of the prophet, re-
proving king Asa for having recourse to a physician),
but for their own sakes, having known many honest
amiable men of that profession. I do not attack
them, but their art ; and do not much blame them
for making their advantage of our folly, for most
men do the same. Many callings, both of greater
and less dignity than theirs, have no other foundation
or support than the abuse of the public. When I
am sick I call them in, if they come by my door,
only to have a little chat, and fee them as others do.
I give them leave to command me to keep myself

warm, because I choose to do it, and to appoint leeks or lettuce for my broth; to order me white wine or claret, and all other things, in like manner, at their own pleasure, which are indifferent to my palate and custom. I know, very well, that I do nothing for them in so doing, because sharpness and odd tastes are accidents of the very essence of physic. Lycurgus ordered wine for the sick Spartans: why? because they abominated the drinking of it when they were well: as a gentleman, a neighbour of mine, takes it for a most wholesome medicine in his fever, because that naturally he mortally hates the taste of it.

Wine prescribed for the sick Spartans.

How many do we see, amongst them, of my humour, who despise taking physic themselves, use a liberal diet, and live a quite contrary sort of life to what they prescribe to others? What is this but flatly to abuse our simplicity? For their own lives and healths are no less dear to them than ours are to us, and they would accommodate their effects to their own rules, if they did not themselves know how false they are.

Many physicians seldom use medicinal drugs themselves.

It is the fear of death, and of pain, an impatience of the disease, and a violent and indiscreet desire of a present cure that so blind us; and it is pure cowardice that makes our belief so pliable and easy; yet most men do not so much believe as they acquiesce and permit, for I hear them find fault, and complain, as well as we: but they resolve at last; " what shall I do then?" As if impatience were, of itself, a better remedy than patience. Is there any one of those who have suffered themselves to be captivated by this miserable subjection, that does not equally surrender himself to all sorts of impostures? who does not give up himself alike to the mercy of whoever has the impudence to promise him a cure? The Babylonians* carried their sick into the public square, the physician was the people, where every

How it happens that men are so resigned to the physicians.

The sick persons of Babylon

* It was a law wisely established, says Herodotus, lib. i. p. 91.

exposed in one that passed by, being in humanity and civility
the market-obliged to inquire of their condition, gave some
place. advice, according to his own experience. We do
little better, there being not a woman so silly, whose
spells and potions we do not make use of; and, according to my humour, if I were to take physic, I
would sooner choose to take theirs than any other,
because, at least, it will do no harm.   What Homer
and Plato said of the Egyptians, that " they were all
physicians," may be said of all people; there is no
one that does not boast of some rare receipt, and
who will not venture it upon his neighbour, if he
will trust him.   I was, the other day, in company
where somebody of the fraternity* told us of a sort
of " pill made up of a hundred and odd ingredients:"
it made us very merry, and was a singular consolation, for what rock could withstand so great a battery?   And yet I hear, by those who made trial of
it, that the least atom of gravel would not stir for it.

Upon what   I cannot take my hand from this paper, before I
the physi- have added a word or two more, concerning the
cians found
their pre- assurance they give us of the certainty of their
tended   drugs, from the experiments they have made.   The
knowledge
of the vir- greatest part, and, I think, above two-thirds of the
tue of their medicinal virtues consist in the quintessence, or oc-
drugs,   cult property of the simples, of which we can have
no other information than the use : for quintessence
is no other than a quality, of which we cannot, by
our reason, find out the cause.   In such proofs,
those, which they pretend to have acquired by the
inspiration of some dæmon, I am content to receive
(for I meddle not with miracles), as also the proofs
which are drawn from things, that, upon some other
account, oft fall into use amongst us; as if in wool,
wherewith we are wont to clothe ourselves, there has
accidently some occult desiccative property been
found out of curing kibed heels; or as if, in the
radish we eat for food, there has been found out

---

* Meaning, that was troubled with the stone.

some aperitive operation. Galen reports, " That a
" man happened to be cured of a leprosy by drink-
" ing wine out of a vessel into which a viper had
" crept by chance." In which example, we find
the means, and a very likely guide to this experience : as we also do in those which physicians pretend to have been directed to by the example of
some beasts : but in most of their other experiments,
wherein they declare to have been conducted by fortune, and to have had no other guide than chance, I
find the progress of this information incredible.
Suppose a man looking round about him upon the
infinite number of things, plants, animals, and metals,
I do not know where he would begin his trial; and
though his first fancy should fix him upon an elk's
horn, wherein there must be a very gentle and easy
belief, he will yet find himself perplexed in his
second operation. There are so many maladies, and
so many circumstances laid before him, that, before
he can arrive at the certainty of the point, to which
the perfection of his experience should arrive, human sense will be nonplussed : and before he can,
amongst this infinity of things, find out what this
horn is; amongst so many diseases, what the epi-
lepsy ; amongst the many constitutions, the melancholic ; the many seasons in winter, the many
nations in the French, the many ages in age, the
many celestial mutations in the conjunction of
Venus and Saturn, and the many parts in man's
body, to a finger : and being, in all this, directed
neither by argument, conjectures, example, nor
divine inspiration, but by the sole motion of fortune, it must be by a fortune perfectly artificial,
regular, and methodical. And, after the cure is
performed, how can he assure himself, that it was
not " Because the disease was arrived at its period,
" or an effect of chance? or the operation of some-
" thing else that he had eaten, drank, or touched
" that day? or by virtue of his grandmother's
" prayers?" And, moreover, had this experiment

been perfect, how many times was it reiterated, and this long bead-roll of fortunes and encounters strung anew from chance to conclude a certain rule? And, when the rule is concluded, by whom I pray you? Of so many millions, there are but three men who take upon them to record their experiments: and must chance needs just meet one of these? What if another, and a hundred others have made contrary experiments? We might, perhaps, have some light in this, were all the judgments and arguments of men known to us. But that three witnesses, three doctors, should lord it over all mankind, is against all reason. It were fit that human nature should have deputed and culled them out, and that they were declared our comptrollers by express letters of attorney.

To Madam De Duras

MADAM,

" THE last time you came to see me, you found
" me at work upon this chapter, and as it may hap-
" pen, that these trifles may one day fall into your
" ladyship's hands, I desire also, that they testify
" how much the author will think himself honoured
" by any favour you shall please to show them.
" You will there find the same air and behaviour
" you have observed in his conversation, and,
" though I might have assumed some better and more
" honourable garb than my own, I would not choose
" it; for I require nothing more of these writings,
" but to present me to your memory, such as I
" naturally am. The same conditions and faculties
" your ladyship has been pleased to receive and
" entertain with much more honour and courtesy than
" they deserve, I will put together (but without
" alteration) in one solid body, that may, perhaps,
" continue for some years, or some days, after I am

" gone; where you may find them again, when your
" ladyship shall please to refresh your memory,
" without putting you to any greater trouble, nei-
" ther are they worth it. I desire you would con-
" tinue the favour of your friendship to me, by the
" same qualities by which it was acquired.

" I am not at all ambitious, that any one should
" love and esteem me more dead than living. The
" humour of Tiberius is ridiculous, but yet com-
" mon, who was more solicitous to extend his re-
" nown to posterity, than to render himself valuable
" and acceptable to men of his own time. If I was
" one of those to whom the world could owe com-
" mendation, I would acquit the one-half to have
" the other in hand, that their praises might come
" quick and crowding about me, more thick than
" long, more full than durable; and let them cease,
" in God's name, with my knowledge, and when the
" sweet sound can no longer ring in my ears. It
" were an idle humour to go about, now that I am
" going to forsake the commerce of men, to offer
" myself to them by a new recommendation.

" I make no account of the goods I could not
" employ in the service of my life: and such as I
" am, and will be elsewhere than in paper. My art
" and industry have been ever directed to set a value
" upon myself; and my studies, to teach me to do,
" and not to write. I have made it my whole busi-
" ness to frame my life. This has been my profession
" and employment. I am less a book-maker than
" any thing else. I have coveted so much under-
" standing for the service of my present and real
" conveniences, and not to lay up a stock for my
" heirs. Whoever has any merit, let him make it
" appear in his ordinary discourses, in his court-
" ships, and his quarrels; in play, in bed, at table,
" in the management of his affairs, in his economy.
" I see some that make good books in ragged
" breeches, who, if they would have been ruled by
" me, should first have mended their breeches,

[margin notes:] Montaigne prefers present esteem to that which is posthumous.

What goods he valued most.

" Ask a Spartan, whether he had rather be a good
" orator, or a good soldier? And, if I was asked
" the same question, I would rather choose to be a
" good cook, had I not one already to serve me.
" Good God! madam, how should I hate the repu-
" tation of being a good writer, and an ass and a
" sot in every thing else: yet I had rather be a fool
" in any thing, than to have made so ill a choice,
" wherein to employ my talent; and I am so far
" from expecting to gain any new reputation by
" these follies, that I shall come off pretty well, if I
" lose nothing by them of that little I had before:
" for, besides that this dead painting will take from
" my natural being, it has no resemblance to my
" better condition, which is also much lapsed from
" my former vigour and cheerfulness, and looks
" faded and withered: I am sunk towards the bot-
" tom of the barrel, which begins to taste of the
" lees.

Why he
has so ral-
lied physic.

" For the rest, madam, I should not have dared
" to make so bold with the mysteries of physic,
" considering the esteem that your ladyship, and so
" many others have of it, had I not had encourage-
" ment from their own authors. I think they have,
" among the ancients, only two Latinists, Pliny and
" Celsus. If these ever fall into your hands, you
" will find that they speak much more rudely of
" their art than I do; I but pinch it, they cut the
" throat of it."

Pliny, amongst other things, twits them with this,
that when they are at the end of the rope, that is,
when they have done the utmost of what they are
able to do, they have a pretty device to save themselves, of recommending their patients, after they
have teased and tormented them with their drugs
and diets to no purpose, some to vows and miracles,
and others to hot baths. " (Be not angry, madam,
" he speaks not of those in our parts, who are under
" the protection of your house, and all Gramontins.)
" They have a third way to save their own credit,

" by ridding their hands of us, and securing them-
" selves from the reproaches we might cast in their
" teeth, of the little amendment we find, when they
" have had us so long in their hands, that they have
" but one more invention left wherewith to amuse
" us ; which is, to send us to the better air of some
" other country. This, madam, is enough ; I hope
" you will give me leave to return to my former
" discourse, from which I have so far digressed, the
" better to divert you."

It was, I think, Pericles,* who being asked, " How
" he did ?" " You may judge," says he, " by
" these," showing some little labels he had tied
about his neck and arms. By this he would infer,
that he must needs be very sick, when he was reduced to a necessity of having recourse to such idle
things, and of suffering himself to be thus equipped.
I do not say, but, some day or other, I may be such
a fool as to commit my life and health to the mercy
and government of physicians. I may fall into such
frenzy : I dare not be responsible for my future constancy : but then, if any one ask me, " How I do ?"
I may also answer as Pericles did, " You may judge
" by this," showing my hand clutched up with six
drachms of opium : it will be a very evident sign of
a violent sickness ; and my judgment will be very
much unhinged. If once fear and impatience get
such an advantage over me, it may very well be concluded, that there is a dreadful fever in my mind. I
have taken the pains to plead this cause, which I do
not very much understand, a little to back and support the natural aversion to drugs, and the practice
of physic, which I have derived from my ancestors.
to the end it may not be a mere stupid and temera-
rious aversion, but have a little more form ; and also,
that they, who shall see me so firm against the exhortations and menaces that will be given me, when my
infirmities are at the worst, may not think it is mere

In what a condition he shall be, if ever he puts him-self into the hands of the phy-sicians.

The desire of glory was his mo-tive of writing against physic.

* Plutarch, in the Life of Pericles, chap. 24.

obstinacy in me; or lest any one be so ill-natured,
as to judge it to be from a view to glory. For it
would be a strange sort of ambition to seek to gain
honour by an action that my gardener or my groom
can perform as well as I. Certainly I have not a
heart so puffed up, and so windy, that I should exchange so solid a pleasure as florid health, and a
good plight, for an airy, spiritual, and imaginary
pleasure. Glory, even that of the four sons of Ay-
mon, is too dear bought by a man of my humour, if
it cost him three smart fits of the stone. Give me
health, in God's name! Such as love our physic,
may also have good, great, and convincing considerations; I do not hate whimsies contrary to my
own. I am so far from being angry to see a difference between mine and other men's judgments, and
so far from rendering myself unsociable with men,
for being of another sense and party than mine,
that, on the contrary (the most general course that
nature has followed being variety, and more in souls
than bodies, forasmuch as they are of a more supple
substance, and more susceptible of forms), I find it
much more rare to see our humours and designs
agree; and there never were in the world two opinions more alike, than two hairs, or two grains;
their most universal quality is diversity.

CHAPTER XXIX.

Of Profit and Honesty.

THERE is no man but at one time or other says
a silly thing; but the worst of it is when he affects it:

Næ ille magno conatu magnas nugas dixerit.[*]

[*] Terence Heauton, act iii. scene 9.

The man in troth with much ado
Has prov'd that one and one make two.

This does not touch me. My nonsense slips from me with as little care as it merits, and it is well it does so. I would quit it on a sudden for the little there is in it of value, and neither buy nor sell it for more than the weight. I speak on paper as I do to the first man I meet; and that this is true observe what follows.

Who would not abhor treachery when Tiberius would not admit of it in a matter of such importance to him?* He had word sent from Germany that, if he thought fit, they would by poison rid him of Ariminius; who was the most powerful enemy the Romans had, he having treated them very basely in the time of Varus, and being the only man that opposed their dominion in those countries." The answer he returned was, that it was the custom of the Romans to be revenged on their enemies by open force, sword in hand; not clandestinely, nor by fraud: wherein he preferred the thing that was honourable to the profitable. He was (you will say) a hector. I believe as much; but that is no great wonder in the gentlemen of his profession. But the acknowledgment of virtue is no less valid by its coming from the lips of him who hates it, forasmuch as truth forces it from him; and if he will not sincerely embrace it, he puts it on at least by way of ornament.

Our structure, both external and internal, is full of imperfection; yet there is nothing in nature but what is of use, not even inutility itself. There is nothing in this universe which has not some proper place in it. Our being is cemented with certain mean qualities; ambition, jealousy, envy, revenge, superstition, despair, have so natural a lodgment in us that the image of them is discerned in the brute

A perfidious action detested by Tiberius.

Human policy so full of imperfection that it needs vice to support it.

* Tacit. Annal. lib. ii. cap. 88.

beásts; nay cruelty itself, a vice so much out of nature; for even in the midst of compassion we feel
within us an unaccountable bitter-sweet titillation of
ill-natured pleasure in seeing another suffer; and
even children are sensible of it:

> Suave mari magno turbantibus æquora ventis
> E terrá magnum alterius spectare laborem.*

> 'Tis sweet from land to see a storm at sea,
> And others sinking whilst ourselves are free.

Whoever would divest man of the seeds of such
qualities would destroy the fundamental conditions
of human life. Likewise in all governments there
are necessary offices, not only abject but vicious.
Vices have their department there, and are employed
as cement to connect us together, like poison that is
administered for the preservation of our health. If
they become excusable, as being necessary for us,
and because the public necessity disguises their real
qualities, we are to resign this part to the strongest
and boldest citizens, who sacrifice their honour and
conscience, as the ancients sacrificed their lives for
the good of their country. We that are weaker
play those parts that are more easy and less hazardous. The public weal requires that a man should
betray, tell lies, and commit murder: let us leave
this commission to men that are more obedient and
more supple.

Malicious justice. I have really been often vexed to see judges by
fraud and false hopes of favour or pardon draw in a
criminal to confess his guilt; and to observe what
recourse they therein have to tricking and impudence. It would be of good service to justice, and
even to Plato himself, who countenances this manner of proceeding, to furnish me with other means
more suitable to my inclination. It is a malicious
kind of justice, and I think it is as much offended

---

* Lucret. lib. ii. ver. 1, 2.

by itself as by others. I said not long since, in
some company, that as I would be very sorry to betray any private man for the service of my prince,
I would be very loth to betray my prince to any
private man. As I have an aversion to cheat another, so I would hate to be deceived myself, and
will not so much as furnish any pretext or occasion
for it.

In the few concerns which I have had to negociate between our princes, in those divisions and sub-
divisions by which we are at this time rent, I have
nicely avoided leading them into any mistakes of
me, and their deceiving others by my mask. The
people of this profession are the most reserved, and
pretend to be the men of the greatest moderation,
and the nearest conformity to the sentiments of
those with whom they have to do. I speak sincerely
what I think, and in my own manner; being a tender negociator, and but a learner, who had rather
fail of success than be wanting to myself. Yet it
has hitherto proved so lucky (for surely it is chiefly
owing to fortune) that few things have passed from
hand to hand with less suspicion, and more favour
and secrecy. I have an open manner, which readily insinuates itself, and gains credit upon the first
acquaintance. Simplicity, and the naked truth, in
what age soever, make their way, and find their account; and moreover the freedom of men who treat
without any interest of their own is neither hateful
nor suspected; and such may very well make use of
the answer of Hyparides to the Athenians, when
they complained of his rough way of speaking,
" Gentlemen, do not regard whether I am free;
" but whether I am so from sincerity, and without
" any advantage from it to my own affairs."[*] My
freedom of speech has also naturally cleared me of
all suspicion of dissimulation by its vehemency

*Montaigne
a very ten-
der conci-
enced nego-
ciator.*

---

* Plutarch, in his Treatise of the Difference between the Flatterer and the Friend, chap. 24.

(leaving nothing unsaid, how pungent and cutting
soever, so that I could not have said worse behind
their backs), and by the full discovery it made of
simplicity and indifference. I aim at no other advantage by my pleading than to plead, and tack no
long arguments or propositions to it. Every plea
plays its own part, hit or miss. For the rest, I am
not swayed by any passion either of love or hatred
to the great men, nor is my will influenced by the
sense of any particular injury or obligation. I honour our kings with an affection that is simply loyal
and respectful, being neither prompted to nor restrained from it, by private interest; and for this
I value myself. Nor does the general and just cause
attract me otherwise than with moderation and cool-
ness. I am not bound by such cogent and penetrating pre-contracts and engagements. Anger and
hatred are not within the sphere of justice, and are
passions of no use but to those who are not to be
kept to their duty by mere reason; *Utatur motu
animi, qui uti ratione non potest:* " He that cannot
" be guided by reason is governed by passion." All
lawful intentions are temperate in themselves, if
otherwise, they become seditious and unlawful.—
This is what makes me walk every where with my
head erect, a frank countenance, and an open heart.
It is a truth, and I fear not to confess it, I could,
were it necessary, hold a candle to St. Michael, and
another to his serpent; after the manner of the old
woman.* I will follow the right side even to the
fire, but will keep out of it if possible. Let Montaigne be overwhelmed in the public ruin, if it must
be so; but if it be not necessary, I would thank my
stars for his safety, and I make use of all the length
of line which my duty allows me for his preservation.

---

* Montaigne means that he would be inclined to make his court
to both the opposite parties, as the old woman did who offered one
wax taper to St. Michael the archangel, and another to the dragon
which is represented fighting with St. Michael. This woman's action has given rise to a sort of proverb.

Was it not Atticus, who being on the just but losing side, preserved himself by his moderation in that universal shipwreck of the world, among so many various changes and revolutions? For a private man as he was, this is more easy; and upon an occasion of the like nature I think men are very excusable for not being ambitious to meddle or make.

For a man to be wavering and trimming, to keep his affection unmoved, and without inclination, in the disturbances of his country, and in a public division, I think it neither decent nor honest, *Ea non media, sed nulla via est, velut eventum expectantium, quo fortunæ consilia sua applicent :* " That is not taking " the middle way, but really no way at all, like " those who wait for the even of things in order to " take their resolution accordingly."[*] This may be allowed with respect to the feuds of our neighbours; and accordingly Gelo the tyrant of Syracuse suspended his resolution in the war of the Barbarians against the Grecians, keeping an embassy at Delphos, with presents, to observe to which side fortune would incline, and to take the critical minute to make the victors his friends.[†] But it would be a sort of treason to proceed after this manner in our own domestic affairs, wherein a man must necessarily be of one side or the other; though for a man to sit still, who has no office nor express command to urge him to action, I think it more excusable (and yet this is no excuse for myself) than to meddle in foreign broils, to which, however, according to our laws, no man is compelled. Yet even those who wholly engage themselves in such broils, may act with such temper and moderation that the storm shall fly over their heads without bursting on them. Had we not reason to expect as much from M. de Morvilliers, the late bishop of Orleans? And among those who behave valiantly at this time, I know some of so much candour and good-nature, that they will

A neutrality in the distractions of one's country is not handsome nor honest.

---

[*] Titus Livy, lib. xxxii. cap. 21.   [†] Herodot. lib. vii. p. 498.

continue steady, whatever may be the change or fate which heaven is preparing for us. I am of opinion, that it properly belongs to kings to quarrel with kings, and laugh at those bullies who out of mere wantonness push themselves into quarrels where the odds are so great. For a man has no particular quarrel with a prince, because he marches against him publicly and courageously, for his own honour, and according to his duty. If he does not love such a personage, he does better, he esteems him. The cause of the laws, and the defence of the ancient government, are always remarkable for this, that such even as for their own private interest disturb the state, excuse if they do not honour its defenders.

Vices disguised under the name of virtues. But we ought not, though it is our daily practice, to call a bitterness and roughness of temper, which spring from private interest and passion, by the name of duty, nor a treacherous and malicious conduct, by the name of courage. They call their propensity to mischief and violence by the name of zeal. It is not the cause by which they are warmed, but their interest. They kindle a war, not because it is just, but because it is war.

The moderation which ought to be observed between those who are at variance. Nothing hinders but men may behave commodiously and loyally too among those who are of the adverse party. Carry yourself, if not with an affection always equal (for it is capable of different degrees), at least moderate, such as may not so engage you to one party that it may challenge all that you are able to do; and content yourself also with a moderate degree of their favour, and to swim in the troubled water without attempting to fish in it.

Double dealers, how far useful. The other way of a man's offering himself to serve both parties is much more conscientious than prudent. Does not he to whom you betray another person, with whom you was on good terms, know that you will do as much by him another time? He holds you for a villain, yet he hears what you have to say, draws intelligence from you, and works his own ends through your treachery; for double-dealing men are useful in what they bring, but care must be taken that they carry away as little as possible.

I say nothing to one party that I may not upon a fit occasion say to the other, with a little alteration of accent; and report nothing but things either indifferent or known, or what is of common consequence. I cannot allow myself for any consideration to tell them a lie. What is trusted with me as a secret, I religiously conceal; but I take as few trusts upon me of that nature as I can: the secrets of princes are a troublesome burden to those who are not interested in them. I am willing that they trust me with little, but that they rely with confidence upon what I tell them. I have always known more than I desired. One open way of speaking introduces another open way of speaking, and draws out discoveries like wine and love. In my opinion Philippides answered king Lysimachus very discreetly, who asking him what share of his estate he should bestow upon him, " What you will," said he, " pro- " vided it be none of your secrets."* I see that every one grumbles and is displeased if the bottom of such affairs as he is concerned in be concealed from him, or that there be any reservation used. For my part I am content to know no more of the matter than what it is intended I should be employed in, nor do I desire that my knowledge should exceed or constrain my promise. If I must serve for an instrument of deceit, let it be at least with a salvo to my conscience. I am not willing to be reputed a servant so affectionate or so loyal as to be thought a fit tool to betray any man. He that is faithless to himself may well be so to his sovereign. But princes do not accept of men by halves, and despise services that are limited and conditional. There is no remedy for it. I tell them frankly how far I can go, and no farther; for a slave I would not be but with reason, and yet I could hardly submit to that condition.

Montaigne's behaviour among those of a different party.

* Plutarch, of Curiosity, chap. iv.

They also are to blame who exact from a free man
the same subjection and obligation to their service as
they do from him whom they have made and bought,
or whose fortune depends particularly and expressly
upon them. The laws have rid me of a great anxiety; they have chosen me a fortune, and given me
a guardian. Every other superiority and obligation
ought to be relative to that appointment, and to be
curtailed. Not that if my affection should incline
me otherwise, I would consent to it immediately.
The will and the desire make a law for themselves,
but actions are to receive theirs from public authority.
All this procedure of mine is somewhat different
from our common forms; it would not be produc-
tive of great effects, nor would it be of long duration. Innocence itself could not in this age either
negociate without dissimulation, or traffick without
lying: and indeed public employments do not at all
suit my taste; what my profession requires I perform
in the most private manner I can. While I was but
young I was deeply engaged in business, and succeeded; but I retired from it in good time. I have
since often avoided meddling in it, rarely accepted,
and never asked it, turning my back to ambition;
and if not like the watermen who advance forward
while they look backward, yet I am not so much
obliged to my resolution as to my good fortune that
I was not embarked in it: for there are ways less
displeasing to my taste, and more suitable to my
ability, by which if she had heretofore called me to
the public service, and my own advancement in the
world's opinion, I know I would in spite of all my
arguments have pursued them. Such as commonly
say in opposition to what I profess, that what I call
freedom, simplicity, and plainness in my manners, is
art and finesse, and rather prudence than goodness,
industry than nature, good sense than good luck, do
me more honour than disgrace, but really they make
my subtlety too refined. Whoever has followed me
close, and pried narrowly into me, I will give him

up the point if he does not confess that there is no rule in their school that could answer to this natural motion, and maintain an appearance of liberty and license so equal and inflexible through so many various and crooked paths, and that all their care and ingenuity could not have carried them through. The path of truth is but one and simple ; but that of private advantage, and of the conveniency of the business which a man has upon his hands, is double, uneven, and casual. I have often seen these counterfeit and artificial liberties taken, but for the most part without success. They are apt to relish of the ass in Æsop's Fables, which, in emulation of the dog, fawningly clapped his two fore-feet upon his master's shoulders, for which his master gave him twice the number of blows with a cudgel, as the dog had caresses for the like sort of complaisance. *Id maximè quemque decet, quod est cujusque suum maximè :* *"* "That is most becoming to every man, which is " most natural to him." I am not willing to deprive deceit of its due rank ; that would be mistaking the world. There are vices which are lawful, as there are many actions either good or excusable, that are in a strict sense illegal.

The justice which in itself is natural and universal, is otherwise and more nobly regulated than that other particular and national justice, which is restrained to the necessity of our state affairs. *Veri juris germanæque justitiæ solidam et expressam effigiem nullam tenemus : umbrá et imaginibus utimur :†* " We retain no solid and express model of true law " and perfect justice ; we have only a shadow and " faint sketch of it ;" insomuch that the sage Dandamys,‡ hearing the lives of Socrates, Pythagoras, and

Universal justice much more perfect than particular and national justice.

---

* Cicero de Offic. lib. i. cap. 31. † Idem, lib. iii. cap. 17.
‡ He was an Indian sage who lived in the time of Alexander. What Montaigne here says of him is reported by Plutarch, who calls him Dandamis, in the Life of Alexander, chap. 20. It is the same in Strabo, lib. xv. where this Indian philosopher is called Mandànis. I have taken all this from M. de la Monnoye.

Diogenes read, esteemed them to be great personages in every other respect but in their too great
subjection to the reverence of the laws, for the authority and support of which true virtue must abate
very much of its original vigour; and many vicious
actions are introduced, not only by their permission,
but also by their persuasion. *Ex senatus-consultis
plebisque scitis scelera exercentur.*[*] " The commis-
" sion of certain crimes is authorised by the decrees
" of the senate and the common people." I follow
the common phrase, which makes a distinction between
things profitable and honest, so as to call some natural actions, which are not only useful but necessary,
dishonest and obscene.

Useful treachery preferred to honesty. But let us proceed in our instances of treachery.
Two pretenders to the kingdom of Thrace fell into a
dispute about their title. The emperor hindered
them from taking arms; but one of them under colour of bringing matters to an amicable issue by an
interview, having invited his competitor to an entertainment at his house, caused him to be secured, and
put to death.[†] Justice required that the Romans
should have satisfaction for this offence, but there
was a difficulty in obtaining it by the common forms.
What therefore they could not do lawfully, without
a war, and without danger, they attempted by
treachery, and what they could not do honestly they
accomplished profitably. For this end one Pomponius Flaccus was pitched upon as a fit instrument.[‡]
This man, by dissembled words and assurances, having drawn the other into his toil, instead of the honour and favour which he had promised, sent him
bound hand and foot to Rome. Here one traitor
betrayed another, contrary to the common custom;
for they are full of mistrust, and it is not easy to
over-reach them in their own art; witness the sad
experience we have lately had of this.

[*] Senec. ep. 95. [†] Tacit. Annal. lib. ii. cap. 65.
[‡] Idem, ibid. cap. 67.

Let who will be Pomponius Flaccus, and there Treachery, how fatal to the man who abandons himself to it. are enough that would ; for my part, both my word and my faith are like all the rest, parts of this common body : the best they can do is to serve the public, and this I take to be presupposed. But as, should one command me to take charge of the palace and the records, or to enter upon the office of conductor of pioneers, I would say, that as to the former, it is what I do not understand, and as to the latter, that I am called to a more honourable employment: so likewise, should any one want me to lie, betray, and forswear myself, for some notable service, much more to assassinate or poison, I would say, if I have robbed or stolen from any one, send me forthwith to the galleys. For it is justifiable for a man of honour to say, as the Lacedæmonians did, when they were just on the point of concluding their agreement after their defeat by Antipater, " You may impose as " heavy and ruinous burdens upon us as you please, " but if you command us to do things that are " shameful and dishonest, you will only lose your " time."* Every one, to be sure, had taken the same oath to himself that the kings of Egypt made their judges swear solemnly; viz. that they would not decree any thing contrary to their consciences, though they themselves should command it.† In such commissions there is an evident mark of ignominy and condemnation: and whoever gives you such a commission does in fact accuse you ; and he gives it you, if you understand it right, for a burden and a punishment. As much as the public affairs are amended by what you do, your own are impaired by it : and the better you behave for the public you act so much the worse for yourself. Nor will it be a new thing, nor perhaps without some colour of

* Plutarch, in his Differences of the Flatterer and the Friend, chap. 21.
† Plutarch, in the remarkable sayings of the ancient kings, &c. towards the beginning.

justice, if the same person ruin you who set you at work.

If treachery ought to be excused in any case, it is only so when employed in chastising and betraying the traitor. There are examples enough of treachery, not only where it was refused, but punished by those in whose favour it had been undertaken. Who knows not the sentence of Fabricius against Pyrrhus's physician?

But we find this also recorded, that a man has given command for an action which he afterwards severely revenged on the person whom he employed in it, rejecting a credit and power so uncontrolled, and disavowing a servitude and obedience so sordid and abandoned. Jaropelc, duke of Russia, tampered with a gentleman of Hungary to betray Boleslaus, king of Poland, by putting him to death, or giving the Russians an opportunity to do him some notable injury. The gentleman acted very craftily in the affair; he devoted himself more than ever to the service of the king, obtained to be of his council, and one of his chief confidents. With these advantages, and choosing the critical opportunity of his sovereign's absence, he betrayed to the Russians the great and rich city of Wisliez, which was entirely plundered and burned, with the total slaughter, not only of its inhabitants, without distinction of sex or age, but of a great number of the neighbouring gentry whom he had convened there for his purpose. Jaropelc being glutted with his revenge, and his wrath being appeased, for which however he had some pretence (for Boleslaus had very much provoked him, by a behaviour too of the like kind), and being gorged with the fruit of this treachery, taking into consideration the deformity of the act in a naked abstracted light, and looking upon it with a calm dispassionate view, conceived such a remorse and disgust, that he caused the eyes of his agent to be plucked out, and his tongue and privy parts to be cut off.

Antigonus persuaded the soldiers called Argyras-
pides to betray his adversary Eumenes their general
into his hands. But after putting him to death, he
himself desired to be the commissioner of the divine
justice for the punishment of so detestable a crime,
and consigned the traitors over to the governor of
the province, with express command by all means to
destroy and bring them to an evil end.* So that of
that great number of men not one ever returned to
Macedonia. The better he had been served by them
the more wicked he judged the service to be, and
the more deserving of punishment.

The slave who betrayed his master P. Sulpicius,
by discovering the place where he lay concealed,
was, according to promise, manumitted from Sylla's
proscription, but by virtue of his edict, though he
was no longer a slave, he was instantly thrown headlong from the Tarpeian rock.†

And our king Clovis, instead, of armour of gold
which he had promised them, caused three of Cana-
cro's servants to be hanged after they had betrayed
their master to him, though had set them upon it.
They were hanged with the purse of their reward
about their necks. After they had satisfied their
second and special engagement, they satisfy the general and first.

Mahomet the second being resolved to rid himself
of his brother out of a jealousy of his power, as is
the custom of the Ottoman race, employed one of
his officers in the execution, who choked him by
pouring water into his throat. When this was done,
Mahomet, to make atonement for the murder, delivered the man who committed it into the hands of
the deceased's mother (for they were only brothers
by the father's side), who in his presence ripped open
the murderer's bosom, and in a fury ran her hands
into his breast, and rifled it for his heart, which she

* Plutarch, in his Life of Eumenes, chap. 9, to the end.
† Valer. Max. lib. vi. cap. 5, in Romanis, sect. 7.

tore out, and threw to the dogs. Even to the vilest of people it is a pleasure, when their end has been served by a criminal action, to patch it up with some mixture of goodness and justice, as by way of compensation and check of conscience. To which may be added, that they look upon the instruments of such horrid crimes, as upon persons that reproach them therewith, and aim by their deaths to cancel the memory and testimony of such practices.

Traitors held accursed by those even who reward them. Now if perhaps you are rewarded, in order not to frustrate the public necessity of this extreme and desperate remedy, he who bestows the reward will notwithstanding, if he be not such a one himself, look upon you as a cursed and execrable fellow; and concludes you to be a greater traitor than he does whom you betray; for he feels the malignity of your courage by your own hands, being employed without reluctance and without objection. He employs you like the most abandoned miscreants in the office of hangman, an office as useful as it is dishonourable. Besides the baseness of such commissioners, there is moreover a prostitution of conscience. Sejanus's daughter being a virgin, and as such not liable to be put to death, according to the form of law at Rome, was first ravished by the hangman, and then strangled.* Thus not only his hand but his soul is a slave to the public convenience.

What Montaigne thinks of those who consent to be the executioners of their own kindred. When Amurath the first, more severely to punish his subjects for having supported the parricide rebellion of his son, ordered that the nearest of kin to them should lend a hand in their execution, I think it was very honourable in any of them who chose rather to be unjustly deemed culpable for another's parricide, than to be obedient to the demand of justice for a parricide of their own. And whereas, at the taking of some little forts, I have seen rascals, who, to save their own lives, have been glad to hang their friends and companions, I have thought them in a

---

* Tacit. Annal. lib. v. cap. 9.

worse condition than those that were hanged. It is
said that Witholde, a prince of Lithuania, introduced a practice, that a criminal who was condemned
to die should dispatch himself with his own hand, for
he thought it strange that a third person, who was
innocent of the crime, should be charged with, and
employed in, homicide.

When some urgent circumstance, and some impe- *In what
tuous and unforseen accident, that very much con- case a
prince is
cerns his government, compels a prince to evade his excusable
engagement, or throws him out of his ordinary duty, for a
breach of
he ought to ascribe this necessity to a scourge of the his word.
divine rod. Vice it is not, for he has given up his
own reason to a more universal and powerful reason ;
but certainly it is a misfortune : so that if any one
should ask me, what remedy ? " None," I would say,
" if he was really racked between these two extremes
(*sed videat ne quæratur latebra perjurio ;* * " But let
" him take care that he does not seek a pretence to
" cover his perjury "), he could not do otherwise ;"
but if he did it without regret, it is a sign his conscience was seared. If there be a person to be found
of so tender a conscience as to think so important a
remedy too good for any cure whatsoever, I shall not
like him at all the worse for it. He could not destroy himself more excusably and decently. We cannot do all we would, so that we are often obliged to
commit the protection of our vessels to the conduct
of heaven as to a sheet-anchor. To what more just
necessity does he reserve himself ? What is less possible for him to do than what he cannot do but at the
expense of his faith and his honour ? Things which
perhaps ought to be dearer to him than his own
safety, and the safety of his people. Though he
should with folded arms call only upon God for his
assistance, will he not have reason to hope that the
divine goodness will not refuse the favour of his extraordinary arm to a hand that is so pure and just ?

* Cic. Offic. lib. iii. cap. 29.

These are dangerous instances, rare and weak exceptions to our natural rules, to which there is a necessity of submitting, but with great moderation and circumspection. No private utility is of such importance as to deserve this effort of our conscience, though the public good well deserves it when it is very apparent and very important.

Timoleon made a proper atonement for his unnatural action by the tears he shed when he recollected that he had killed the tyrant with the hand of a brother: and it stung his conscience that he had been necessitated to purchase the public utility at so great a price as the wounding of his own integrity. Even the senate, which was by his means delivered from slavery, durst not determine positively on an action so considerable, which carried two aspects so important, and so contrary to each other. But the Syracusans having opportunely at that very time sent to the Corinthians to solicit their protection, and to require of them a general fit to re-establish their city in its former dignity, and to clear Sicily of several petty tyrants, by whom it was oppressed, the senate deputed Timoleon for that service, with this artful declaration, " That if he behaved well in " the government of the Syracusans, they would " from that time pronounce by their decree that he " had killed a tyrant; and, on the contrary, if he dis- " covered an avaricious conduct, they would try and " condemn him for fratricide, as having killed his " own brother."* This whimsical conclusion carries along with it some excuse, by reason of the danger of the example, and the importance of so double-faced an action. And they did well to discharge their own judgment of it, or to support it by considerations of a conditional nature. Timoleon's deportment in his voyage rendered his cause still more clear, so worthily and virtuously did he demean himself in all respects. And the good fortune which at-

On what condition the senate of Corinth justified Timoleon when he killed his own brother.

* Diodorus of Sicily, lib. xvi. cap. 19 of Amyot's translation.

tended him in the difficulties he had to overcome in this noble task, seemed to be put in his way by the gods, as favourably combining for his justification. If any man's aim is excusable, this man's is.

But the profit by the increase of the public re-venue, which served the Roman senate for a pretence to the base conclusion I am going to relate, is not sufficient to warrant such injustice. Certain citizens had by the order and consent of the senate re-deemed themselves and their liberty by money, out of the hands of L. Sylla.* The affair coming again upon the carpet, the senate condemned them to be taxable as they were before, and that the money they had disbursed for their redemption should never be repaid them. Civil wars often produce such vile examples, that we punish private men for having taken our words when we were in power: and one and the same magistrate makes another man pay the penalty of his change, though no fault of his. The schoolmaster lashes his scholar for his docility, and the guide beats the blind man whom he leads by the hand. A shocking picture of justice!

The senate of Rome inexcusable for having broke a treaty of its own making.

There are some rules in philosophy that are both false and pusillanimous. The example that is proposed to us for preferring private benefit before the obligation due to faith once given, has not weight enough for the circumstance which they mix with it. Robbers have surprised you, and, after having made you swear to pay them a sum of money, give you your liberty. It is wrong to say that an honest man may be quit of his oath without payment, after he is out of their clutches. The case is quit otherwise. What fear has once prevailed on me to intend, I am obliged to keep the same purpose when I am no longer in fear. And though fear only forced my tongue, and not my will, yet am I bound to stand to my word. For my own part, when my tongue has sometimes rashly outrun

Whether faith that is pledged ought ever to give way to private advantage.

* Cic. de Offic. lib. iii cap. 22.

9

my thought, I have however made a conscience of
disowning it; were we to act otherwise we would
abolish all the right another claims to our promises.
*Quasi vero forti viro vis possit adhiberi :** " As if
" violence could possibly operate upon a great heart."

In what
case a pri-
vate man
is authoris-
ed to break
his pro-
mise.
The only condition in which private interest can
excuse us for the non-performance of a promise is,
when we have promised a thing that is wicked, and
in itself unjust. For the claim of virtue ought to su-
persede the force of any obligation of ours.

How very
delicate
Epaminon-
das was
in the arti-
cle of jus-
tice.
I have formerly placed Epaminondas in the first
class of excellent men, and do not retract it. To
what a pitch did he carry his regard for his private obligation, who never killed a man that he had
overcome, who, for the inestimable benefit of restoring the liberty of his country, made conscience of
killing a tyrant or his accomplices, without the forms
of justice; and who judged him to be a wicked
man, was he ever so good a subject, who, amongst
his enemies, and in battle, spared not his friend and
his host! His was a soul of a rich composition! He
matched good nature and humanity, even the most
delicate, in the school of philosophy, with the rudest
and most violent of all human actions. Was it nature or art that softened a man of his great courage,
high spirit, and obstinate constancy, against pain,
death, and poverty, to such an extreme degree of
good nature and complaisance? Dreadful, with fire
and sword, he over-ran and subdued a nation invincible by all others but himself; and yet, in the midst
of such an expedition, he relaxed when he met his
host and his friend. Verily he was fit to command
in war, who could suffer himself to be checked with
the curb of good nature, in the greatest heat of action, so inflamed and foaming with rage and slaughter. It shows an extraordinary greatness of mind to
mix an idea of justice with such actions; but it was
only possible for such steadiness of mind, as was

* Cic. de Offic. lib. iii. cap. 30.

that of Epaminondas, therein to mix good nature and the facility of the gentlest manners and purest innocence. Whereas one * told the Mammertines that statutes were of no force against men in arms; another† told the tribune of the people, that there was a time for justice, and a time for war; a third,‡ that the noise of arms drowned the voice of the law; this man's ears were always open to hear the calls of civility and courtesy. Did he not borrow from his enemies § the custom of sacrificing to the Muses, when he went to the field of battle, that they might, by their sweetness and gaiety of temper, soften his severity and martial fury? After the example of so great a master, let us not make any sort of doubt that there is something unlawful, even against an enemy; that the common cause ought not to require all things of a man against private interest: *Manente memoria etiam in dissidio publicorum fœderum privati juris:* "The remembrance of private right "subsisting even in the midst of public quarrels."

——— *Et nulla potentia vires*
Præstandi, ne quid peccet amicus, habet.‖

Nor is there any pow'r can authorise
The breach of sacred friendship's solemn ties.

and that an honest man is not at liberty to do every thing for the service of his king, or the common cause, or of the laws. *Non enim patria præstat omnibus officiis—et ipsi conducit pios habere cives in parentes:* ¶ "For the obligation to one's country does not su-"persede every other obligation: and it is of im-"portance to itself to have subjects that have a ve-"neration for their parents." This is an instruction proper for the present time. We need not

* Pompey; see Plutarch's Life of him, ch. 3.
† Cæsar, in Plutarch, ch. 11.
‡ Marius, in his Life by Plutarch, ch. 10.
§ Lacedæmonians.
‖ Ovid de Ponto, lib. i. epist. 7, ver. 37.
¶ Cic. de Offic. lib. iii. cap. 23.

harden our courage with this steel armour: it is
enough that our shoulders are inured to it; it is
enough for us to dip our pens in ink, and not in
blood. If it be magnanimity, and the effect of an
uncommon and singular valour, to contemn friendship, private obligation, a promise, and kindred, for
the public weal, and in obedience to the magistrate;
it is really sufficient to excuse us from it, that this
is a greatness of soul which could have no place in
the magnanimity of Epaminondas.

I abhor the furious exhortations of this other ungovernable soul:*

> *Dum tela micant, non vos pietatis imago*
> *Ulla, nec adversa conspecti fronte parentes*
> *Commoveant, vultus gladior tutate verondos.*

> When swords are drawn, let no remains of love
> To friend or kindred, your compassion move;
> Fear not to wound the venerable face
> Ev'n of your father, if oppos'd in place.

Let us deprive those that are naturally mischievous,
bloody, and treacherous, of this colour of reason;
let us set aside this wild extravagant justice, and
stick to institutions that are more humane. What
great things may not be accomplished by time
and example! In an action of the civil war of Cinna,
one of Pompey's soldiers having inadvertently killed
his brother, who was of the contrary party, killed
himself on the spot, as soon as he knew it, for mere
shame and sorrow.† Some years afterwards, in another civil war of the same people, a soldier, who had
killed his brother, demanded a reward for it from
his officers.‡

The utility of an action is but a sorry plea for the
beauty and honour of it; and it is wrong to infer,
that, because such a thing is useful, it is therefore in-

The utility of an action does not render

---

* Julius Cæsar, who, when in an open war against his country,
with a design to subvert its liberty, cries out, " Dum tela micant,"
&c. Lucan. lib. vii, ver. 320, &c.
† Tacit. Hist. lib. iii. cap. 51.   ‡ Idem, ibid.

cumbent on every one to perform it; and not only it honour-able. a duty, but for his honour :

Omnia non pariter rerum sunt omnibus apta.[*]

All things are no alike for all men fi.

Were we to choose the most necessary and the most useful action of human society, it would be marriage ; yet the saints think celibacy the more honourable state, excluding the most venerable order of men from it, as we set apart those cattle for stallions, which are the least in our estimation.

[*] Propert. lib.

THE END OF VOLUME II.

CPSIA information can be obtained
at www.ICGtesting.com
Printed in the USA
BVOW06*1741040117
472301BV00014B/33/P